Making Sense

As part of Houghton Mifflin's ongoing commitment to the environment,
this text has been printed on recycled paper.

Making Sense

Constructing Knowledge in the Arts and Sciences

Bob Coleman
University of South Alabama

Rebecca Brittenham
Indiana University–South Bend

Scott Campbell
State University of New York at Stony Brook

Stephanie Girard
Spring Hill College

Houghton Mifflin Company Boston New York

Senior Sponsoring Editor: Suzanne Phelps Weir
Senior Development Editor: Martha Bustin
Editorial Assistant: Becky Wong
Project Editor: Carla Thompson
Editorial Assistant: Christian Downey
Production/Design Coordinator: Lisa Jelly Smith
Manufacturing Manager: Florence Cadran
Marketing Manager: Cindy Graff-Cohen
Marketing Assistant: Sandra Krumholz

Cover art: Claire Grace Watson, MST
Cover image: The Phaistos Disk, Crete, c. 1700 B.C.

Acknowledgments appear on pages 659–661, which constitute a continuation of the copyright page.

Printed in the U.S.A.

Library of Congress Control Number: 2001131486

ISBN: 0-395-98630-3

3 4 5 6 7 8 9-QF-06 05 04 03 02

Contents

Preface

Making Sense: Constructing Knowledge in the Arts and Sciences is a collection of thirty-seven essays drawn from across the spectrum of the arts and sciences. Written for general audiences by specialists in their fields, these essays present a variety of perspectives on the central question of how knowledge is communicated across different communities of understanding. *Making Sense* balances essays on topics such as imagination and reality, the construction of personality, and the importance of public debate with histories of science, studies of technology and culture, and biological explanations of social behavior. Analyses of Disney World, comic books, and the Buffalo Bill Museum may be found side by side with discussions of cloning, Hawaiian nationalism, Grant Wood's *American Gothic*, and relations between the races.

The authors included in *Making Sense* are also a mix: we include familiar scholarly names like Gloria Anzaldúa, Clifford Geertz, Sherry Turkle, Thomas Kuhn, and Jane Tompkins; famous popular authors like Walter Mosley, Jeanette Winterson, Ralph Ellison, Annie Dillard, and Jared Diamond; and less well-known but equally accessible writers like Rebecca Solnit, Barbara Mellix, Witold Rybczynski, and Yi-Fu Tuan. Architects, physicists, historians, novelists, and critics, our authors represent a variety of disciplines and professions. We hope that the breadth of these writers' experiences helps students to understand the importance of reading and writing as means of communicating within and between groups.

To provide instructors with maximum flexibility for tailoring the course to the needs of their particular students, we have selected essays of varying lengths, styles, ideas, and approaches. All of these essays, however, demonstrate an awareness of audience, a clarity of purpose, and an engagement with ongoing debate. They make effective use of quotations, they define and apply analytical terms, and above all, they exemplify good writing.

Distinctive Features of *Making Sense*

- **Thesis-driven selections.** The many thesis-driven readings in *Making Sense* present arguments about issues that will engage and stimulate students. These argumentative readings are substantive and intellectually enriching, yet accessible, and they help students to improve their own writing, reading, and critical thinking skills.

- **Cross-disciplinary selections.** The writers in this collection, whatever their "home" discipline, write to readers beyond their discipline's borders in readable, understandable language. Their essays demonstrate the many ways that arguments can be made and supported in order to make sense to particular audiences.
- **Scientific and technological perspectives.** This broad and balanced collection includes essays from the scientific and technological disciplines and from a wide range of disciplines in the humanities. All are readable essays written for a general rather than a specialized audience.
- **Flexible organization.** *Making Sense* is well suited for courses organized by theme, discipline, or argumentative approach. Its readings are arranged alphabetically for maximum flexibility and to emphasize the book's function as a collection of provocative, scholarly essays. Alternative thematic and disciplinary tables of contents are also included in an appendix.
- **Diverse and contemporary readings.** This volume contains a wide range of disciplines, styles, and authors—including Anzaldúa, Berger, Dillard, Ellison, Kaku, Lasch, Geertz, Gould, Mosley, Sontag, Winterson, and many others. The essays were written primarily between the years of 1980 and 2000, with several classic essays from the 1960s and 1970s also included.
- **Substantial art program.** More than fifty photos and pieces of art, including one entire reading in graphic form, support and supplement the reading selections and serve as reference points for discussion and writing.
- **The Introduction.** The Introduction emphasizes the use of rhetoric as a tool for understanding how an author's purpose, persona, and audience contribute to the shaping of his or her argument.
- **"Making Sense Through Writing."** This chapter discusses how to analyze the arguments presented in the readings and how to use that analysis as a basis for generating written responses to the text. It covers the concepts of summary, paraphrase, and analysis, paying particular attention to the sufficiency and relevance of textual evidence.
- **"Making Sense Through Research."** This chapter offers suggestions to students for using the Internet and library reference sources to prepare for discussion of the readings or to develop ideas for writing about the readings. In addition, we include "Questions for Writing a Research Proposal," "Guidelines for Evaluating Internet Sources," and a brief guide to MLA and APA citation styles.

- **"Writing in the Disciplines."** This part features a series of commissioned essays by current faculty in a range of disciplines. These essays address the general requirements for writing for these disciplines and the importance of writing in a range of fields.
- **Engaging questions.** Questions that follow the readings are not of the yes/no, right/wrong variety; instead they are designed to open up discussion, to provoke responses, and to suggest a variety of ways to make sense of each essay. The questions typically build on the answers to previous questions or the results of previous discussion or activity. They are arranged in four categories:
    1. **Getting Started.** These questions are designed to promote discussion and critical thinking about the reading. They may encourage rereading with an eye to identifying key terms, rhetorical strategies, important passages or quotations. Many group activities are suggested in this section.
    2. **Writing.** Building on responses to the Getting Started questions, these questions are meant to help students not only to think about the essay in a new way but also to work out their own positions on the subject. These writing assignments may be framed as a series of questions in order to provide students with a series of alternative ways of thinking about both the text and the assignment.
    3. **Using the Library and the Internet.** These questions invite students to connect their readings to the world outside the text. By conducting research in the library or on the Internet, students can learn to challenge or extend the essay's themes and arguments or to follow up on their own responses.
    4. **Making Connections.** These questions suggest relationships between and among the essays. Using the terms of one essay as a way to read and analyze another can help students to develop an enhanced understanding of the readings or to gain a completely new perspective on an issue. Comparing and contrasting writers' approaches helps students to understand alternative rhetorical strategies. Working with more than one essay empowers students to overcome their hesitation about analyzing the work of an author who may be an expert in his or her field. By focusing on their mastery of particular readings rather than on their expertise on specific issues, these questions enable students to enter the conversation.

- **Headnotes.** Each essay is introduced with a brief headnote providing biographical information about the author and including, where necessary, an explanation of important terms or concepts. The headnotes also include URLs where students can go to learn more about the author or the topic of reading selections. We have tried as much as possible to avoid shaping the student's reading of the text. The essays we have included present a number of options for teaching. The brevity of our notes allows you to prepare students for their reading in keeping with the instructional approach you have chosen or the connections you would like them to see with other essays in an assignment sequence.

Assignment Sequences

Assignment sequencing makes it possible to translate a pedagogical emphasis on revision into practice. Instead of reading one essay, writing a paper on it (and often tossing that paper out once it has been "finished" and graded), and then moving on to completely fresh ground, students responding to sequenced assignments are encouraged to revisit their own earlier papers just as they revisit essays they have already read and worked with.

While teachers may want to create fresh starts at one or two points in the semester, we have found that by and large students produce better work when they are able to incorporate familiar readings and build upon familiar writing processes. In fact, studies of basic writers have shown that students struggling to produce better writing can often be hampered by hypercritical self-editing: Such students often cross out or erase material before they have had the chance to develop an idea, and they throw out drafts of papers before they have a chance to recognize and capitalize on improved skills. Similarly, if students feel they failed to "get" a previous reading, they will often try to bury the failure and move on rather than learning that a return to that same reading through a fresh perspective (sometimes much later in the semester) often provides greater and enriched understanding.

Sequenced assignments allow students to reread and rethink previous essays from new standpoints; they encourage students to rework their own papers from reconsidered, even transformed positions. More than this, sequenced assignments mirror the way that we often appropriate new knowledge—by using the familiar as a way to understand, to make a connection to the unfamiliar. In addition, the new text often helps students to recognize the assumptions that shaped their earlier readings and to learn the power of an alternate interpretive approach.

Each assignment sequence asks students to use one reading as a way to reapproach one or more previous readings, or to use the previous reading(s) to provide an interpretive approach to the new reading. This process of creating connections between texts helps students to understand the interpretive choices involved in reading and writing. It also helps students to break new ground, to find unexpected points of contact between writers, and in that process of negotiation to develop their own committed points of view on an issue. Further, assignments that involve connecting the ideas of two or more writers make particular sense within scholarly communities where essays are rarely limited to an engagement with a single writer, where the conventions of citation, allusion, and footnoting demand that each new conversation make reference to traditions of thought and ongoing conversations about an issue.

Instructor's Manual

A separate Instructor's Manual includes teaching tips and strategies for making the best use of *Making Sense* based on the editors' own experiences in using these essays in composition classrooms at Indiana University at South Bend, the University of South Alabama, Rutgers University, and Montclair State University. The entries provided for each essay include a list of critical vocabulary, suggestions for points of entry and emphasis, a discussion of student responses to the essay, and advice on linking essays in sequences. We also identify selections that work well at the beginning of the semester or the beginning of the sequence.

Making Sense Companion Web Site

The *Making Sense* companion web site provides alternative tables of contents, sample syllabi, sample assignments, research links, Web-based activities, and links to additional visuals that complement essays in *Making Sense* and an e-mail address where you can send us your comments, questions, and ideas.

Acknowledgments

We would like to thank the following reviewers of *Making Sense* for their helpful reading of the manuscript at various stages. Their ideas and suggestions were extremely valuable in the development of this book.

James E. Barcus, Baylor University

Sue Beebe, Southwest Texas State University

Phyllis R. Brown, Santa Clara University

Terry Brown, University of Wisconsin–River Falls

Scherrey Cardwell, Cameron University

Chas S. Clifton, University of Southern Colorado

Cynthia A. Davidson, SUNY at Stony Brook

Colleen M. Dittberner, George Mason University

Ellen Webb Franklin, Lower Columbia College

Charles R. Lewis, Westminster College

Barbara Little Liu, Eastern Connecticut State University

Mike Tierce, Kennesaw State University

Howard Tinberg, Bristol Community College

Our thanks go to Suzanne Phelps Weir, Martha Bustin, Carla Thompson, and the staff of Houghton Mifflin for making this book possible. We also thank good friends and indirect contributors: Jonathan Nashel, Anne Wettersten, Suzanne Diamond, Hildegard Hoeller, Alec Marsh, Cris Hollingsworth, Jim Albrecht, and Claire Berardini. We are particularly grateful to our students and colleagues at Indiana University–South Bend, the University of South Alabama (especially Sue Walker, Jim White, Larry Beason, Jean McIver, Michelle Comstock, Becky McLaughlin, and Tom West), Montclair State University (especially Janet Cutler, Jim Nash, Tom Benediktsson, and Jeff Shalan), Spring Hill College (especially Noreen Carrocci, Michael Kaffer, Martha Patterson, and the students in Publishing—Beth Creighton, Colleen Diez, Caroline Dazet, Mike DeShazo, Corey Mladenka, and Joey Peacher), Princeton University (especially Mary Baum and Kathryn Humphreys), Long Island University (especially Tom Kerr, Harriet Malinowitz, Deborah Mutnick, and Patricia Stephens), and Rutgers University (especially Ron Christ, Barry Qualls, Michael McKeon, Carol Smith, Marianne DeKoven, Bill Galperin, Hugh English, Judy Karwowski, Susan Mayer, Michael Goeller, Kurt Spellmeyer, and Richard Miller). We are especially grateful to Tam Mai, for allowing us to include her student essay; to Mark Van Lummel at Indiana University–South Bend; and to the contributors to "Writing in the Disciplines":

Barbara Scofield, University of Texas at the Permian Basin

Steven Gerencser, Indiana University–South Bend

Ann Grens, Deborah Marr, Andrew Schnabel, Indiana University–South Bend

Kent McClelland, Grinnell College

Heide R. Lomangino, University of South Alabama

Final Note

In compiling and writing *Making Sense*, we recognize that controversies within composition studies, departments of English, divisions of Humanities, and universities as a whole are signs of a fundamental shift in ways of defining what it means to have a college education.

Increasingly, students are vocationally oriented, pursuing not an education but a career. Simultaneously, however, business and industry executives are searching for employees who combine specialized knowledge with excellent writing and oral communication skills, employees who are flexible and able to change as the organization changes. In an effort to respond to these conflicting needs, we have created a composition reader that challenges students not only to think "outside the box," i.e., to examine and investigate ideas rather than simply to absorb and re-present facts, but also to make sense of "the box" for themselves.

B. C.
R. B.
S. C.
S. G.

Illustrations

Part I

Making Sense

Chapter 1

Introduction

HOW OFTEN HAVE YOU HEARD yourself or someone else say "That makes sense!" in response to an idea or explanation? When we say that something "makes sense," we usually mean that it squares with our idea of what is right or truthful. Although we may never have considered the idea or explanation before, if it seems to fit with our experience and our assumptions about how the world works, then it makes sense. We accept this new explanation as a useful addition to our store of knowledge.

As our experience widens, however, we learn that what makes sense to us may not make sense to someone else. Making sense is contextual: it depends, as the anthropologist Clifford Geertz might say, on "local knowledge," on the sharing of ideas, assumptions, and ways of living by a specific group or community. New ideas, as Geertz points out in an essay included in this book, compete with the established ideas of a community; the process of "making sense," then, may cause us to revise what we once thought of as "common sense." As new ways of understanding become accepted by more and more people, these new ideas come to be understood as the new common sense. Making sense, we could say, means grasping ideas and putting them to use in productive and satisfying new ways.

Sherry Turkle gives us a second example of making sense. In "The Triumph of Tinkering," she describes her dissatisfaction with the commonsense idea that the computer is a tool to be used for specific, logical, and directed tasks. She argues that a purely "scientific" approach to computing has given way to a more free-flowing and associative practice that she calls "tinkering." Today's computer users play simulation games, design Web pages, and surf the Internet in a style that has more in common with artists or even cooks than with accountants or scientists. For Turkle, this new idea of imagining the computer to be "less like a hammer and more like a harpsichord" is an idea that makes sense. It's up to us to decide if we think that Turkle's idea works for us as well. *Making Sense: Constructing Knowledge in the Arts and Sciences* asks you to consider a wide range of viewpoints and ideas and to decide if they (or some part of them) make sense to you.

In "I Stand Here Writing," Nancy Sommers describes the complex and exciting way in which the act of writing can draw together and make sense of disparate experiences, new situations, or unfamiliar readings. "Making sense" refers to those moments of connection when readers and writers fit a new concept or a new way of thinking about the world into the facts, experiences, and ways of thinking they already know. Those pieces rarely fit together perfectly as in a jigsaw puzzle; instead, essay writers must create those relationships between ideas and must argue for their applicability to particular examples or experiences. In her essay, Sommers includes a story about her mother sending four-leaf clovers, debates about the Persian Gulf War, and ideas sparked by her reading of Ralph Waldo Emerson. She invites you to share her understanding of how these disparate examples and experiences relate to each other and how they connect to the larger point she is trying to make. As a reader, you take over from there, thinking through Sommers's examples, relating parts of her essay to what you already know and have read, and accepting some of her ideas and linkages and ignoring or rejecting others.

Other people can help you talk through the readings, understand particular concepts or examples, and see relationships that you might have overlooked, but you are the one who will make sense of those possibilities and find ways to reconcile them with the world you know. As an essay writer, too, you are in charge of that process of composing, of drawing together ideas and examples. Through your writing, you are able to convey the arrangement of ideas and examples made possible by your own knowledge, perspective, and understanding. This collection is titled *Making Sense* to focus your attention on the process of forging relationships between readings, between ideas and experiences, and between familiar and unfamiliar views of the world. We hope that the selected readings challenge you to make sense of the ideas, examples, and relationships they propose, and that they inspire you to use the writing process to develop your understanding of them. Finally, we hope that you learn to use writing as a tool for creating relationships of your own and for making sense of the major issues that affect your life.

Writing in the College Setting

Within the education system in the United States, knowledge is often organized into categories, subjects, or disciplines. Each has its own community, its own set of assumptions and standards, and its own way of making sense of the world and our place in it. The further we advance in our education, the more specialized these categories become. For example, in elementary school, we take general science classes. In high school, we may take separate courses in chemistry, biology, and physics. In college, introductory courses in biology are followed by advanced courses in molecular and developmental biology. These increasingly specialized courses produce increasingly specialized audiences.

As biologists and authors Michio Kaku and Richard C. Lewontin demonstrate later in this book, however, it is not true that professional biologists are capable only of making sense to other similarly trained biologists. Both Kaku and Lewontin are concerned with helping individuals who are not biologists to understand the social, ethical, and moral issues arising from new discoveries in the field of genetics. They know that making sense of these discoveries is an ongoing process that depends upon a conversation among many people with many different points of view.

We often think of conversation as a spoken activity such as a phone call or a discussion among friends, but conversation can also refer to any kind of communication between two or more individuals. For example, if you read and respond to comments made by Mary Kingsley (quoted in Julie English Early's essay), in a sense you are having a conversation with a nineteenth-century naturalist! No matter what the source, if you are using it to test and confront your own ideas, you are "conversing." Many such conversations take place through the kind of reading and writing that is characteristic of, although not limited to, the university.

The readings collected in *Making Sense* invite you to become more aware of the various ways in which people such as yourself make sense of the information, debates, research, questions, and philosophies that are a part of the academic conversation. The writers of these essays are careful to locate themselves in that conversation; they cite their reading and they comment on what is presented and how it is presented; they ask, What is worth knowing and how do we know that it is worth knowing? These writers are critical thinkers, and their essays demonstrate ways in which you can become both a better writer and a better critical thinker. Even though they are often specialists with advanced knowledge of a particular field, these writers choose to write for a general audience, hoping that they can find readers like you who will make use of and perhaps challenge the work they have done.

Through the writing you do in your coursework, you will participate in the academic conversation. Instead of merely explaining or absorbing what you read, you will respond to it by presenting your own ideas, reactions, and extensions of the ideas you encounter. There will be passages, and sometimes whole essays, that do not make sense to you, but even these disagreements will help you to expand your knowledge. By discussing these readings with your classmates and friends, you will learn to develop and articulate your own ideas and ways of looking at the world. This book does not ask you to write summaries or answers to simple questions. Instead, we want you to consider writing as an occasion for communicating your ideas to a reader who can use them. We want you to try things out, to experiment with possibilities.

The first step in becoming a better writer is recognizing that there is no single formula for producing a perfect piece of writing. Every time we speak or write we are responding to a particular context, which will determine

1. the purpose for our writing;
2. the persona we will adopt;
3. the audience we will write to; and
4. the kind of argument we will make.

The following questions can help you establish the context of any particular writing you are going to do.

Purpose: Why are you writing? What do you want to accomplish? Do you want to persuade your audience to take a particular action, to understand your interpretation of the readings, or to see a complex issue in a different way? Are you responding to someone else or initiating a conversation? Are you being funny, serious, or ironic? If you are writing in response to an assigned question, you might analyze the assignment to see what sense of purpose it implies. For example, is the assignment asking you to explain a reading or to create a connection between readings? Does it ask you to persuade others to share your perspective? What are the goals of this piece of writing?

Persona: Who are you in this particular language situation? Do you have some knowledge, derived through research, reading, or experience, that helps you to write with authority on the topic? If not, your authority may be derived from the individuality of your perspective; you are the one making sense of a particular reading, creating a unique connection between readings, or showing how one theme links several writers' perspectives. You can learn to take on an authoritative role even before you are certain about your views on the subject. Writing allows you to try out a position. Whenever we communicate, we do so from a particular position that is determined, at least in part, by the role we take on in relation to our audience. In any given day, we may play the roles of student, teacher, employee, friend, relative, team member, or artist. Each of us has many roles available.

Audience: Who are you writing to? It could be an individual you know well or someone you do not know at all; it could be a large group such as the readers of a newspaper or magazine, or it could be a small group of people who you can assume share your views and opinions, such as members of your class. In each of these cases, you will need either to adapt your language and your argument to the expectations of the audience or to understand the consequences of not satisfying those expectations.

Argument: How can you achieve your purpose? Will you present evidence and demonstrate how it can be interpreted? Will you offer examples? Will you appeal to your audience's emotions, intelligence, or perceived self-interests? In what order will you present your ideas to make them most effective, to make them follow logically one from another, and to develop your main points most substantially?

Although purpose, persona, audience, and argument are not the only terms that can be used to define a communication situation, they are the terms used throughout this book. Learning to use these terms in the analysis of your readings will help you to apply them to your own writing in the composition classroom and beyond.

The Process of Making *Making Sense*

The process we used to create *Making Sense* was neither straightforward nor easy. Like any other writing project (especially one involving more than one author), it took time and it was messy. We believe it was also fairly typical of how writing projects evolve. We hope that by describing that process we can give you an inside look at how other writers write, while also explaining our goals and aims in writing this book.

We are experienced composition teachers who have taught basic, standard, and advanced composition courses. Individually, we also have taught technical and business writing, administered writing programs, and worked as professional writers. More importantly, we are all writers who struggle to learn more about the writing process and to add to our range of writing strategies. We have all had the opportunity to use and review a large number of composition readers and grammar handbooks. On the basis of our experience, we agreed that there was a need for a composition reader that both included challenging, well-written, accessible, and scholarly essays of assorted lengths written from a range of perspectives and from within a variety of disciplines, and looked less like a textbook. Creating such a book became our goal.

An important first step was defining our audience. We know that students enrolled in composition courses have a variety of interests as well as a wide range of backgrounds and levels of preparation. Some students consider themselves "good at math," others as "good at English"; some see themselves as performers or poets, others as doctors or engineers or bankers; some are still in the process of discovering what they are good at or what they want to do with their lives. Our students have confided in us their eagerness to "get" something from their coursework, their desire to feel that what they are learning is directly applicable to their work in other classes and in their lives.

We also know that students are not the only audience for a composition reader. Instructors also need to be considered. They too have to read and use the book. We have tried to create a book that is flexible for them and that they can use to complement their own vision of the course. We had to remember that instructors as well as students would be puzzling over and responding to the texts in *Making Sense.*

Having defined our audience, we turned to a consideration of our purpose. What kind of reading, writing, and teaching did we want *Making Sense* to make possible? What did we want you to "get" from this book? These are not simple questions, and we did not arrive at simple answers.

Our answers evolved as the project progressed, but we did begin with the following set of common assumptions and beliefs:

1. Education is an ongoing process of making sense of the world in which we live and of building the world in which we would like to live.
2. Experienced scholars work within a particular set of expectations and conventions that are defined either explicitly or implicitly by the disciplinary community with which they are affiliated. Ideally, these scholars also are able to communicate both across the disciplines and to general as well as specialized audiences. These expectations are based on the presumption of a basic knowledge of the arts and sciences shared by all members of the community.
3. The role of composition courses is to help students develop the general skills in reading and writing that are essential components of that basic knowledge.
4. Students are full members of the scholarly community. The essays they read in their composition classes should be scholarly ones, and they should be good examples of the kinds of writing that students will encounter throughout their college careers.

We returned again and again to these assumptions and goals, expanding and revising them to reflect our developing understanding of the project.

Given these goals and the diverse interests of our audience, we decided to select essays from a variety of disciplines and to use the relationship of the arts and sciences in the academy today as our organizing theme. In keeping with the spirit of the book, we used very broad and elastic definitions of "art" and "science." We think that *every* act of thinking has artful and scientific components and that each discipline—at its best—draws on both art and science. "Art" can mean anything active or creative, any process of experimenting with possibilities. "Science," meanwhile, stands for what is known and what has been described, documented, or established.

The following quotation from Northrop Frye's "The Motive of Metaphor" helped us to arrive at our definitions:

> Science begins with the world we have to live in, accepting its data and trying to explain its laws. From there, it moves towards the imagination: it becomes a mental construct, a model of a possible way of interpreting experience. . . . Art, on the other hand, begins with the world we construct, not with the world we see. It starts with the imagination, and then works towards ordinary experience: that is, it tries to make itself as convincing and recognizable as it can. (p. 220)

Frye sees both art and science as acts of balancing reality (what we already recognize) with imagination (what we can construct or devise). To us, Frye's distinction suggests that although knowledge in the university is organized into specific disciplines, the people working in those disciplines might combine scientific and artistic approaches to varying degrees. In that sense, the boundaries between these disciplines function as convenient fictions that enable us to categorize knowledge, to divide it up into manageable "chunks." We therefore selected essays that not only display expert knowledge but that also look closely at the ways in which that knowledge is expressed. In emphasizing the various fields of knowledge, we underscore the importance of locating and speaking to a particular audience. By addressing the ways in which specialists communicate their ideas, we attend to the shorthands, working models, and assumptions that make communication possible. The cross-disciplinary aspect of *Making Sense* asks students and instructors to use their home bases of knowledge but also to look beyond these boundaries.

Another important selection criterion was quality. These essays demonstrate an awareness of audience, a clarity of purpose, and an engagement with ongoing debate. They make effective use of quotations, they define and apply analytical terms, and above all, they take a stylistic pleasure in effectively communicating knowledge and perspective. In both form and content, then, the essays selected for this volume model the type of writing we all can emulate.

How to Use This Book

The design of this book emphasizes its function as a collection of provocative, scholarly essays rather than as a textbook. Traditional textbook layouts are aimed at conveying information. They try to provide digestible blocks of knowledge to help you absorb and retain content material in an efficient way. This book is less about conveying information or content material and much more about inspiring you to read, explore, and write about the uses of knowledge in the arts and sciences. We want you to make arguments about how information can best be understood and used.

The essays are arranged alphabetically by author. We chose this simple arrangement to make it easy to find an assigned essay. We do not expect you to read the essays in order, or even to read them all. Instead, we invite you to look through the table of contents to see which titles seem appealing. You might flip through the essays themselves, reading a line or two of opening paragraphs to get a feel for the differences in tone and style. We have tried to keep the presentation uncluttered so that you can settle down to a particular reading without being bombarded by extra information telling you how to read or what to think. We would like you to have the opportunity to read and make sense of an essay in your own way.

On the other hand, as readers we are all aware that sometimes it can be hard to find a way into an essay, to get a grip on what the writer is saying, and to think of ways to start writing about it. To help you to read and respond to the essays, we have included a set of questions for each one as well as some background information on each of the authors.

You might read through the questions and the author's background information on your own, before or after you read an essay. You might be asked to think about, discuss, or write about some of the questions as an assignment for your course or to work through some of the questions in groups. None of these questions are of the yes or no, right or wrong variety; they are designed to open up discussion, to provoke responses, and to suggest different possibilities for making sense of the essay. Discussing these essays in small or large groups is possibly the most beneficial way to test your responses to an essay and to improve your comprehension of it. Group work can help you to generate different ways to think and write about the material and to connect it to the world you already know as well as to the world you would like to create.

The questions that follow each essay are grouped under the following headings.

"Getting Started." The questions listed under the heading "Getting Started" are the kinds of questions you might use to begin thinking about an essay: They point you toward some of the key terms, suggest ways to break down the various parts of an essay, focus you on specific examples, and call your attention to some important passages.

"Writing." The questions under the heading "Writing" are all designed as extended writing assignments. They tend to build on the "Getting Started" questions, so your discussion notes and short written responses often will provide you with substantial material for your rough draft response to a "Writing" question. The purpose of "Writing" questions is not only to help you to think about the essay but also to give you some room to work out your own position on the subject. For example, we all might have opinions about environmental issues, but as we read, discuss, and write about Zita Ingham's "Landscape, Drama, and Dissensus," those opinions may gradually develop into more thoughtful and often more complicated reflections on the subject. We all generally have reactions to an essay—from "I like the way this person thinks!" to "I hate this!"—but as we talk and write about the essay, those reactions get synthesized into more persuasive and thoughtful conclusions about its merits. The assignments in the "Writing" section are often phrased as a series of related questions, not because we are trying to pin you down to a particular answer but because we are trying to offer you many different ways to approach the subject.

"Using the Library and the Internet." The questions under the heading "Using the Library and the Internet" suggest ways to do research that can help you to challenge or develop the essay's themes and arguments. Research may also help you to generate a response to the essay.

"Making Connections." The "Making Connections" questions are designed to help you think and write about more than one essay at a time. We have all discovered, as writers and as teachers, that this approach has enormous benefits. Using the terms of one essay as a way to read and analyze another essay can give you an enhanced understanding of both and a completely new perspective on an issue. Comparing and contrasting writers' approaches can throw new light on the way they use evidence or persuasive tactics to make an argument, which in turn can help you to evaluate their work and to develop your own position on the issue. Sometimes writing about a single author can be overwhelming; he or she seems like an expert, and it is hard to know how to challenge that authority or how to get a larger perspective on what is being said. By contrast, reading two or more authors with differing approaches, different arguments about an issue, or even different disciplinary backgrounds (an anthropologist and a historian, for example), gives you a position of relative authority and power. You are the one piecing together and, to some extent, creating the relationship between the essays and between the writers. You are the one making a case for how one reading compares or contrasts with another or reveals something new about it.

However you choose to use this book, we hope that one of the things you "get" from it is a set of strategies for making sense of the structure of higher education and the world it tries to explain.

Chapter 2

Making Sense Through Writing

IT IS NO COINCIDENCE THAT your composition class is likely to be the one class that all students at your school are required to take. Academic success depends on the development of the critical thinking skills associated with strong reading and good writing. In fact, writing is the most common way that people make sense of what they learn in the university.

Much of your time at school is spent either reading other people's writing in course texts or in books and articles that you discover through your research, or writing your own essays, lab reports, and test answers to demonstrate what you are learning. First-semester college students learn quickly that they will be asked to read and write in a variety of contexts. The types of reading and writing required in each context often seem radically different. Your biology lab report about experiments with single-cell organisms will look different from your economics paper on John Maynard Keynes's monetary theories. Likewise, a literature assignment that asks you to write an analysis of diction and punctuation in an Emily Dickinson poem or to analyze representations of race in a Toni Morrison novel will require you to think about and to use language differently than an engineering assignment that asks you to research and write a solution for a hypothetical bridge construction problem. Despite the differences, your biology lab report, your economics paper, your literary analysis, and your engineering plan all have one thing in common: In each case, you use writing to gain a better understanding of knowledge in that discipline and to communicate that understanding to others. Writing helps you to relate what you are learning in the university to the world you already know.

Getting Started—Making Sense of an Assignment

Making sense of an assignment begins with reviewing the teacher's instructions, whether verbal or written. What is he or she asking you to do? You may be asked to present a summary, a brief account of a text's main arguments or ideas. Such assignments give you the opportunity to show that you can identify the key points in your reading. In your composition class, for example, your instructor may ask you to summarize Sir Ronald Aylmer Fisher's ideas on the relationship between smoking and cancer as described by Stephen Jay Gould in "The Smoking Gun of Eugenics." Other assignments in your composition class may require that you move beyond summary to analyze a specific claim a writer makes or to link a key concept from one essay to a key concept in another. For example, your professor may ask you to analyze the strengths and weaknesses of Thomas Kuhn's three-stage theory of scientific discovery as a critical framework for analyzing the significance of Ralph Ellison's anomalous "little man" in his essay, "The Little Man at Chehaw Station." The above examples ask you to *summarize*, *analyze*, and *connect*. Other assignments may ask you to *compare*, *define*, *describe*, or *put into your own words*. Identifying the verbs in an assignment will help you to know where to begin.

Making sense of an assignment also involves rereading the assigned text. Rereading is especially important when the assigned text is a thoughtful and extended exploration of a complex issue. After reading Christopher P. Toumey's "Science in an Old Testament Style" or Gloria Anzaldúa's "Chicana Artists: Exploring *Nepantla, el Lugar de la Frontera*," for instance, you undoubtedly will have questions about what you read. Uncertainty about each writer's main points is not a sign that you have done something wrong as a reader. Instead, you can use your questions or uncertainties about the reading to guide your rereading and to motivate your writing. The purpose of reading is not simply to confirm what we already "know." Reading, thinking, and writing are part of a dynamic process, one in which making sense often involves transformations in what we know. Each time we read a text, it is a different experience. We are not the same reader we were before. The first time we reread a text, we know how it ends or where it leads, and that knowledge helps us to notice and appreciate details and ideas we may have missed in our first reading. With each subsequent reading, we bring new expectations, new ideas, and new contexts for understanding. Good strong reading and writing skills result from taking the time to read, reread, and read again.

Investigating an Issue or Topic

Just as you need to read and reread the essays in *Making Sense*, you also need to write and revise initial written responses to what you have been reading. Writing often helps us to discover what we really think about an issue or topic. Writing can be particularly helpful when you are trying to make sense of what someone else has written. For example, if you have never thought about the complex ethical questions posed by the biomolecular revolution, then responding to Michio Kaku's "Second Thoughts: The Genetics of a Brave New World?" by jotting down questions and ideas in your notebook can help you start to make sense of Kaku's argument. Your notes might include ideas about possible connections to other essays in this anthology or to concepts you are learning or have learned in other classes. Your notes will help you to reread Kaku's essay and make you better able to identify the assumptions underlying his argument. After your second reading, you might write about the assumptions in his concluding sentence: "In a democracy, what is decisive is informed debate by an enlightened electorate." With fewer people voting in national elections today than a generation ago, who makes up an "enlightened electorate"? What constitutes "informed debate" for Kaku? What assumptions does he make about "democracy"? Writing about such questions can be a way of getting started, a way of using writing to help you look more closely at Kaku's argument and to test it against your own knowledge and experience.

Prewriting

Writing about what you read—whether in a journal or on index cards or even on scraps of paper—is one of many prewriting strategies that can help you generate ideas about a topic or interpretations of a particular essay. Other common prewriting strategies include free writing and brainstorming. In free writing, you put your ideas on paper without worrying about grammar, spelling, or organization. The point is to begin thinking through writing without concerning yourself with what the end product will look like. After approximately fifteen minutes of free writing, you should stop and look over what you have written. The thoughts and connections you have begun to work with in the free writing can now become the basis for your rough draft. Brainstorming is another prewriting strategy, one with which you are probably already familiar. In brainstorming, you write down a key word or idea and then make lists of associations, such as examples and details that illustrate the word or idea, or examples and details that go against it. Free writing and brainstorming are helpful methods for generating ideas about a key term or quotation in your reading. For instance, after reading Witold Rybczynski's "Designs for Escape," you might find it useful to free write about the idea of "escape" or to brainstorm about the word "rustic."

Defining Your Audience

The audience you write for affects how and what you write. A paper written for a college course, no matter what grade it received, would require substantial revision before it could be published in a national magazine. A paper written for a history class would emphasize different facts and details than a paper on the same topic written for a political science or literature class. Different audiences have different expectations. Defining those expectations is an important part of the writing process. (For more on the expectations of different disciplinary audiences, see Part IV, a set of essays written by professors in accounting, political science, biology, sociology, and foreign languages.)

Although many of the essays in *Making Sense* deal with subjects that are not typically taught in English departments, we chose them deliberately. These essays are written for a general audience, the kind of audience you may be asked to address in the papers you write for your composition class. As these essays demonstrate, writers targeting a general audience can assume that their readers have some familiarity with the subject being discussed. Sherry Turkle, for example, can expect her readers to know what a computer is and to know the difference between programming and using prepackaged software. Writers for a general audience can also expect their readers to use the descriptions, definitions, and examples included in the text to help them understand unfamiliar words or concepts.

We hope that reading these writers will expose you to the central debates and concerns in departments across the university. Most importantly, however, we hope that you will learn to appreciate and to use the strategies that faculty and students commonly employ to communicate with people who share their field or major, with people in other fields, and with people outside the university.

Making an Argument

In *Making Sense* the term "argument" refers to the purposeful structure that shapes, organizes, and drives an essay. Arguments can take many forms, but at the most basic level, each argument presents and demonstrates a thesis, a claim or debatable proposition that the writer seeks to prove. An argument signals a particular perspective on an issue. Unlike an opinion, however, an argument is based on evidence and examples, and unlike a fact, an argument is not something settled and unchangeable. As a reader, you should be prepared to analyze a writer's argument, to test it against your understanding of the topic and your assessment of the evidence and examples. If the writer's analysis makes sense to you, then think about why you agree. What is persuasive about the way the writer writes? What is persuasive about the way the writer uses evidence? If you do not agree with the writer's overall analysis or if you decide that a part of the argument is not convincing, then think about how you would explain to your classmates what it is that you disagree with or question.

For example, you may be asked to read Sven Birkerts's "The Owl Has Flown" and to analyze Birkerts's argument about the loss of wisdom in our contemporary technological world. Birkerts's essay is an argument because he makes a claim about wisdom that he knows is debatable. To persuade readers that his claim is true, he presents and interprets evidence. Your job is to assess the validity or the persuasiveness of Birkerts's argument. You might begin by defining for yourself Birkerts's main ideas and then testing those ideas against evidence and examples you find in his essay and in other essays you have read. If you decide that Birkerts makes sense, you can then use the evidence and examples you collected to help you develop and prove a thesis that indicates your agreement with Birkerts. If, after reading "The Owl Has Flown" and testing its ideas, you conclude that Birkerts's analysis does not make sense or that parts of his analysis are questionable, you can use your evidence and examples to support an anti-Birkerts argument. Whichever position you take, you can make your argument persuasive by imagining your reader as someone who holds the opposite position and needs to be convinced to change it.

It Is Okay to Change Your Mind

You may decide that Birkerts's argument makes sense, and then write a rough draft that supports his analysis of the fate of wisdom. It is not unusual, however, to question your own understanding in the course of class discussion, more reading, or peer review. Perhaps, in her rough draft, one of your classmates raises a question or presents an argument that you had not thought about. If you are careful about giving your classmate credit for her ideas by citing her as you would any other author, you can use her ideas to help you modify your argument.

Changing your mind about an idea, issue, or argument is not a bad thing. In fact, such changes show your flexibility as a writer. As many of the writers in this book make clear, showing how we test and revise our ideas through conversation with others makes wonderful material for an essay.

What Counts as Evidence?

Evidence, together with your interpretation of it, supports your thesis and persuades the reader that your argument is valid. Different disciplines rely on different types of evidence, as the essays in Part IV, "Writing in the Disciplines," make clear. Quotations, examples from the essays and your own experience, and data collected through research all can be used as evidence. For example, if your instructor asks you to write an analysis of Susan Willis's essay, "Disney World: Public Use/Private State," you could use quotations from Willis's text as specific examples of your general point. Because the meanings of quotations are not necessarily self-evident and because quotations sometimes can be interpreted in several ways, it often makes sense to follow quotations with a specific analysis that shows your reader how you interpret the key words and phrases. Such a detailed analysis of the meanings of individual words and phrases is called "close reading." The purpose of close reading is not to restate the quotation; rather, your close reading gives you a great opportunity to show your readers what is significant about the quotation. For example, you might want to show how a key word or phrase from Willis such as "erasure of spontaneity" connects to another key word or idea in her essay or someone else's. Additionally, your close reading of quotations helps you carefully connect textual evidence with your essay's larger argument or thesis.

It has been our experience that many students are fond of Disney World and are troubled by some of Willis's criticisms of the theme park. To challenge Willis's argument that Disney erases spontaneity and implicitly outlaws play at its park, many students can marshal evidence from their own personal experience, but they often want additional evidence to help corroborate their misgivings about Willis's argument. The following chapter, "Making Sense Through Research," discusses how you can use library and Internet sources to find such evidence.

Revision and the Final Draft

"Revision" means to reexamine or reconsider what you have written—not simply to correct spelling and grammar but to improve the effectiveness of your explanations of ideas and to strengthen your organization of evidence so that your essay persuades your audience.

Some students would like to stop after simply producing one draft of an essay. When you settle for the one-draft approach, you short-change yourself and your audience. Revision allows you to rethink and improve your argument by writing several drafts and getting written feedback from your peers on each draft. This recursive process of revision will help you write well not only in college but also after you graduate.

In your composition classroom, you may read your peers' rough drafts. Sometimes people are shy about letting someone else read what they have written as a rough draft. Such nervousness is understandable, but most students quickly discover that getting feedback from other students really helps in the revision process. If you think of your early drafts as points of entry into an ongoing discussion, you will find that you *want* to hear how others respond to your ideas.

Sometimes students are not sure what kind of advice to give about a peer's rough draft. That uncertainty is also understandable. Remember that no one expects you to be an authority. If something you are reading does not make sense to you, ask the writer to explain it to you, or summarize what you think the main points are and ask if you are correct. If you cannot ask your question directly, write it on the draft so that the writer can think about it during revision. You may have misunderstood something or the writer may not have been clear. Often, we need someone else to help us realize that not all the thoughts in our minds made it to the page. Discussing a rough draft helps both the reader and the writer to understand the argument more fully.

What kinds of advice would best help you to revise your paper? Apply that same advice to the paper you are reading. Make your advice as specific and detailed as you can. Specific advice is much more helpful than general comments such as "looks good," or "add a quotation," or "you need a comma on page three." Examples of specific advice include indicating where and why the writer might add a quotation; explaining why the writer might need to follow a certain quotation with a more developed analysis of the quotation's key word or phrase; or pointing out that an argument in paragraph three seems to contradict a claim in paragraph four. Such specific advice helps your peer because it gives him or her concrete information to think about and to work with.

In addition to giving and receiving helpful advice, there is another benefit to reading and commenting on each other's rough drafts: You get to see how others approached the same writing assignment. What you undoubtedly will notice is that no two drafts are exactly alike. You may have good examples in your draft, but you will discover that others in the class also have good examples or explanations that did not occur to you. By reading others' drafts, you will broaden your own understanding of issues relevant to the assignment. You will see viewpoints that may challenge your own perspective. Different viewpoints are important, because sometimes we discover that they persuade us to rethink our own point of view. Reading a peer's paper can help you enhance your own writing. If you like ideas or examples in someone else's draft, you can incorporate them into your paper simply by giving him or her credit for the ideas or examples. The point is not to "steal" someone else's idea. That would be plagiarism, to use someone else's work as if it were your own. In your final draft, cite the person's name to give him or her credit just as you would cite a source that you found in the library or on the Internet. Bolstering your own argument with someone else's ideas is not a weakness; acknowledging that an example or an idea comes from a peer signals that you are an ethical writer and are willing to look at ideas beyond your own in order to strengthen your writing.

As you move from a rough draft toward a final draft, you should also consider the role that your instructor can play in your revision process. Talk to your instructor early on about your assignments rather than waiting until halfway through the semester to begin a dialogue. Whatever your grade in the class, if you have questions about any written feedback you receive or questions about the essays you are reading, make a point to see your instructor. Students who regularly visit their instructors to talk about their writing and reading are more likely to improve over the course of the term.

The Final Draft

The final draft of your paper is the product of all your hard work. You want it to look good and to make you look good. A reader's first impression is visual. Use clean, high-quality paper, dark ink, and a standard font and type size such as Times New Roman 12 pt. Give your paper a title and number the pages. Check the directions your instructor has given you about format: Include all information he or she has asked for (course name, number, date, and so on) in the place and arrangement that has been designated. Proofread your paper to check for spelling errors, typing mistakes, and missing or incorrect citations. Double-check your grammar and the consistency of your style. Make any corrections and reprint your final document. Following these steps will help you to present a paper that creates a good first impression. A reader who can focus on understanding your ideas without the distraction of grammatical errors or problems of presentation is one more likely to be persuaded by your argument.

Writing is one of the most important tools we have to communicate our ideas. It only makes sense to learn to use it well.

Student Essay

The following essay was written by Tam Mai, a freshman at the University of South Alabama. This assignment asked Tam and her classmates to use Sherry Turkle's ideas of "tinkering" and "hard" and "soft" programming styles from her essay, "The Triumph of Tinkering," to frame an analysis of Susan Willis's argument about conformity in her essay, "Disney World: Public Use/Private State." The assignment required Tam to use Turkle's terminology to help her think more critically about Willis's criticisms of Disney World. Tam did a wonderful job of writing her essay. To prepare, she read Turkle's and Willis's essays more than once so that she could think carefully about their arguments. She wrote a rough draft that several of her peers read in class. They wrote specific revision advice for her. Tam then continued to work diligently to produce a final draft that I think you will enjoy reading. In the margins you will see annotations—commentary about Tam's writing.

Mai 1

Disney World: Utopia?

Tam Mai

Ask any young child where heaven is, and he or she will likely answer Disney World. Making a pilgrimage to this amusement mecca means a chance to meet the cartoon celebrities who seem to have a permanent address there. It means a chance for fun and games all day. Even adults find themselves having a good time when they step on the Space Mountain ride or take a picture with Mickey Mouse. Hence, it seems ungenerous for a professional writer such as Susan Willis to devote a critical essay, "Disney World: Public Use/Private State," to the vindictive bashing of this wonderful place. However, Willis is only using Disney World to get her readers to think about larger issues about conformity and spontaneity in our culture and to think about what these terms mean. While she has a justly dismal outlook on our conformist society, both conformity and spontaneity do serve purposes, fulfill human needs, and are necessary and inevitable parts of our society.

Nice job of complicating the notion that Willis is being "ungenerous"

To better understand Willis's arguments about conformity and spontaneity, it is helpful to consider Sherry Turkle's concept of "hard programming" from "The Triumph of Tinkering." According to Turkle, "hard programming" describes any system or methodology that is structured and rule driven (554). Those in charge of Disney World certainly offer an experience that is hard programmed. They do not gamble with its fantasy-land

Here you smartly turn to Turkle's essay for a critical term, "hard programming," to frame your analysis of Willis's argument

Mai 2

image, but instead have a set of highly structured plans for every event and aspect of the park. Everything, from the rides to the parades to the seemingly spontaneous humor of the tour guides, has been carefully scripted, rehearsed, and scheduled so that all will go smoothly, like parts of a well-oiled machine.

Good connection

Tourists to Disney readily surrender their worldly cares to the enjoyment of the scheduled program and the Disney formula. They ride the rides at the set times, take pictures at the appropriate posts, and buy as much Disney memorabilia as possible, just as intended. They conform to these established routines in order to get the most "amusement" from the Disney World experience; after all, that is what they have paid monstrously high admission and hotel prices for. In fact, every tourist gives up his or her right to spontaneous play and free exploration when purchasing a ticket to the theme park. "Amusement is the negation of play," Willis declares. Why play at Disney when we can do that at home? We come to Disney to be amused!

Here, you should have included a page citation for the quotation

"Conformity" is the key word both from the Disney Corporation's perspective and from the tourists' point of view. For those at Disney offering the experience, it is easy to understand why conformity is encouraged at this amusement haven: conformity maximizes profit. Everything at Disney, from tickets to bottled water, is overpriced. But why, one might ask, would a person want to subject himself or herself to an economic predator disguised as a harmless theme park? Disney provides a

I really like how you ask the question here

Mai 3

much desired escape from the monotony of daily life. From the moment visitors deposit their luggage in their hotels to the moment they wistfully leave Disney, everything is programmed for them. For a few days, they do not have to worry about any business rivalries or life-affecting decisions. It is liberating to be able, for a while, not to have to think, use one's judgment, or care about personal problems. Yet many fail to realize the price of such paradoxical escape. It is ironic to try to escape from the materialistic nature of daily life to the equally profit-driven and rules-governed operations at Disney World.

Wonderful observation

Disney's conformist strategy would not work unless the impulse to conform did not already exist in our minds. If amusement and escape from daily monotony are the goals for some Disney tourists, then for others the trip is perhaps taken out of conformity and because it is "the thing to do." Disney World is not any ordinary theme park—it is an icon of American popular culture. Disney logos are in every corner of the United States, and most people have either gone to Disney World at least once or hope to go some day. The pilgrimage to Disney can also stem from the desire to declare or affirm our social status. As Willis puts it, Disney's wholly themed environments target the "predominantly white, middle-class families" (589).

You do a good job of offering your reader multiple explanations of conformity

Our lack of spontaneity in real life results because we feel we need to be conformists. In the family, the basic unit of society, we are trained from an early age to follow a set of moral, ethical, and legal rules. Most of us consci-

Mai 4

entiously go to school not out of the desire to learn, but out of the need to be like everybody else—that is, to have an education and a career. Eating, working, schooling, and sleeping are part of our daily routine. We usually do not deviate from this habitual schedule because it is comfortable. We wear clothing that is emblematic of our social status and in various ways hope to impress others. We are a culture of conformists. Even people who stray from the norms often quickly find their acts of originality trapped in the wheels of economic conformity, as whatever is the latest new trend soon becomes the norm.

Good point

In real life, this lack of value placed on spontaneity poses a threat, and that is the threat of no progress. Without spontaneity there is no tinkering. Children, Sherry Turkle suggests, learn through physically manipulating objects—tinkering and playing with the objects at their disposal. While rearranging what they know into something completely new, people learn the art of negotiation and compromise; they learn what works and what doesn't work. Similarly a tinkerer in any discipline is an inventor of sorts, playing around with the materials at hand, not knowing what each new combination might bring. A tinkerer arranges, rearranges, all the while feeling his or her way through discovery. For instance, the discovery of penicillin, the wonder drug, is a product of unplanned, spontaneous actions. Such style of "play," which Turkle calls "soft programming," permits room for flexibility. Spontaneity can lead to progress because it allows latitude for new discoveries.

Nice job of returning to Turkle to help explain your interpretation

Mai 5

That is not to say, however, that conformity is bad. We expect, as an organized society, that certain conventions should be followed. Humans have to follow legal conventions or else chaos will result and criminals run amok. Consider serial killer Ted Bundy's criminal acts. His nonconformity did not promote progress or benefit human endeavors in any way. We also expect priests to act with dignity and doctors to behave with compassion. If every child ran wild at Disney World, everybody's enjoyment would be ruined. Thus, this positive aspect of conformity complicates Willis's negative critique of our conformist society. Neither the "soft," flexible, creative, playful, spontaneous approach in our society nor the "hard," rule-driven, conformist approach seems to be better than the other. Both have their places. Our society is increasingly conforming, but it is also increasingly spontaneous, as Sherry Turkle observes in her essay about our growing acceptance of the bricolage, "soft" programming style.

Good point

I really like how you build this argument to challenge part of Willis's argument

Tam—

I really enjoyed reading your essay. You did a wonderful job of using Sherry Turkle's ideas of "hard" and "soft" programming to help you frame your own analysis of Susan Willis's argument about conformity, what Willis calls the "erasure of spontaneity."

Your thesis that "conformity and spontaneity do serve purposes . . ." enables you to complicate, as you say, Willis's "negative critique of our conformist society." Recognizing such a complication results from your careful reflection on both Willis's and Turkle's arguments.

I was also impressed with your observation that many people fail to realize "the price of such paradoxical escape" at Disney. Your point about the irony makes great sense.

Chapter 3

Making Sense Through Research

FOR SOME OF US, THE word "research" conjures up images of laboratories, men and women in white coats, and highly technical equipment. Others may think of students at library tables surrounded by books or people at computer terminals mining data. Although accurate, these images present only a partial picture of how research is done today, and they suggest nothing at all about why research is done. In this text, "research" means using reference or other sources found in the library or on the Internet to learn more about a particular person, place, thing, or idea for the purpose of developing a better understanding of your reading.

By doing some preliminary research on a topic addressed in your reading,

- you gain better access to the reading as a whole because the outside sources and examples you find help you "make sense" of it;
- you develop your own position on issues raised in the reading by testing its major claims against the sources and examples you find; and
- you practice research skills in a manageable, focused area, which prepares you for a more intensive use of these same skills in a full-length research paper.

In short, research is a way of learning. Through it you extend your exploration of a general subject area in a particular direction, develop a specific topic or issue that interests you, or expand your knowledge base on that topic.

Suggestions for Additional Research

The essays in *Making Sense* offer many possibilities for research. You will notice a suggestion for Internet research in the paragraph before each reading and the "Using the Library and the Internet" questions after each reading. Here let us look in more detail at techniques and strategies for pursuing text-based research in the university.

In most libraries, students can access online search tools to find books or articles available on the library shelves, online, or both. Whether your source is hardcopy or electronic, finding it through online searching requires many of the same skills and strategies.

Make your first step in any research project a tour of your college or university library. Just as different libraries subscribe to different magazines and newspapers, they also subscribe to different electronic databases. If a tour is not appropriate, visit the library reference desk or its home page on the university Web site. At most libraries and on many library home pages, you will find important information prepared by your reference librarian on how to use the research tools available. (See Resource 1 for an example.) A reference librarian's job is to help you find the information you need. Do not be afraid or embarrassed to ask one for help.

To learn what different reference resources can do for you, try the following experiment. Choose a search term such as an author's name, the title of a book or article, or a keyword referred to in the reading. Use that search term in a reference database, such as Academic Search Elite, that gives you access to scholarly journals from the social sciences, humanities, general sciences, and education. Then try the same keyword search using a database, such as Lexis/Nexis, that gives you access to a broader collection of magazines, journals, and newspapers. Using the more general database will result in a wider field of examples and case studies related to your topic, but you will have to be more careful about evaluating those sources. Finally, you might try using the same keywords in a search engine such as Alta Vista or Hotbot. You will find that your search results cover a much broader area and will include images and products for sale as well as a list of all the Web sites that may relate to your topic. Exploring some of those Web sites can help you to think about an assigned reading from a fresh perspective and can lead you to a related research topic of your own; however, it will also involve weeding out a great deal of unreliable and unusable information.

Resource 1

Database Searching

Some Advantages of Database Searching

1. The ability to search through several years of published sources at once
2. The ability to search using your own terms ("keyword searching")
3. The ability to combine terms by using "and," "or," or "not" ("Boolean searching")
4. The ability to retrieve precise information quickly

Some Disadvantages of Database Searching

1. A lot of relevant information has not been digitized (put in a computer database).
2. Use an incorrect term or misspell a term, and you miss things that are in the database.

Three Basic Ways to Conduct a Database Search

1. Use a keyword search.
2. Use a keyword search to find subject headings to refine or focus your search.
3. Use a database thesaurus or index to focus your search from the start.

In any database search, find out what subject headings the database uses for your keywords. For example, your keyword is "toddler" but the subject heading used is "child, preschool."

Expanding or Limiting a Database Search

When you want to

- get more information, or
- retrieve as much information as possible, you need to broaden or expand your search.

Ways to expand your search

1. Use broader or related terms.
2. Use a truncation symbol: *.
3. Use the term "or."

When you want to

- limit the amount of information, or
- retrieve very precise information, you must limit or narrow your search.

Ways to limit your search

1. Use narrower terms or subject subheadings.
2. Use the fields that the database provides to narrow your search.
3. Combine terms or set numbers with the term "and."
4. Use the term "not."

Remember, different computer databases

- use different types of searches
- limit or expand in different ways
- provide (or do not provide) an index or thesaurus
- provide (or do not provide) some form of truncation or wildcard symbol
- allow (or do not allow) Boolean searches

In general, however, computers usually will let you expand or limit your search in at least a few ways.

Basic Research Steps for Journal Articles

1. Choose the appropriate databases.
2. Have a list of keywords.
3. Find out how the database classifies your keywords.
4. Limit or expand your search as needed.
5. Evaluate what you find.
6. Use what you find to get other resources.
7. Use only one documentation style.

Source: Mark van Lummel, Indiana University, South Bend.

Experiment with the following suggestions for online searching until you find the one that works best for you.

Search for the author of the assigned reading using his or her full name as your search term. This approach will give you access to other writings by the same author, reviews of the author's books, and related subject areas that you can then use as the keywords for an expanded search for a research paper topic. For example, using "Annie Dillard" as the search term in a scholarly database not only will enable you to learn more about her as a writer, it also will link you to critics' reactions to her work and to topics related to her work, such as "nature writing" or "belief and doubt." Using her name as a keyword in a general search engine such as Alta Vista will open up dozens of entries, including useful items like interviews with Annie Dillard and less reliable items like personal home pages or publicity from booksellers.

Use the key terms from the assigned essay as your search terms. For example, the keywords "scientific literacy" from Emily Martin's article, "Scientific Literacy, What It Is, Why It's Important, and Why Scientists Think We Don't Have It," when used in a scholarly database will give you access to over one hundred related articles. If you make the search more general by expanding the key words to "science and literacy," you will find an even broader pool of results. It helps to try out several of the key terms from an essay.

Use one key term from the assigned reading combined with a topic that interests you. For example, when researching Stephen Jay Gould's "The Smoking Gun of Eugenics," you might enter the search term "eugenics" in a scholarly database. The result will be several hundred articles related to eugenics. However, if you have a particular interest in following up the way eugenics-based arguments have been used to stereotype particular groups of people, the search terms "eugenics and race" will result in about forty articles that are more specifically related to that aspect of the topic.

Collect a number of case studies or examples related to the assigned reading. (Here, using a database such as Lexis/Nexis or a similar research tool that gives you access to newspapers will be helpful.) For example, when reading about Susan Willis's reaction to Disney World, collect articles from popular magazines and newspapers that demonstrate other public reactions to Disney World. Are people gaining emotional satisfaction from these vacation sites that Willis does not acknowledge? Do their testimonies reveal the language of consumption or any of the other prepackaged beliefs that Willis claims Disney World is selling?

You may need to use one or more of these techniques each time you do a search. While it is obvious that some reference databases include information sources that others do not, it is less obvious but equally true that Internet search engines index different information sites. Using the same search terms with a different search engine most likely will yield different results. To learn more about the differences between subject guides and search engines, go to the Tool Kit for the Expert Web Searcher developed and maintained by Pat Ensor for the American Library Association <http://www.lita.org/committe/toptech/toolkit.htm>.

So far we have discussed how to search for information to help you better understand your reading. As we have mentioned in other sections, however, writing about what you read is one of the best ways to make sense of what you read. The same is true with research.

Writing a Research Paper

Writing a research paper combines the writing skills described in Chapter 2 with the research skills described above. The process of writing a research paper requires you to perform the following steps:

1. **Collect additional sources** (readings, data, case studies, and examples) that relate to your chosen subject area.
2. **Develop a topic** by choosing a particular problem or issue in that subject area.
3. **Evaluate** your sources by deciding how reliable they are, whether they are scholarly or popular, and how useful they are for your project.
4. **Read and synthesize** the information contained in the sources you plan to use.
5. **Establish your own position** on that topic or issue in relation to the readings you have chosen.

Although research assignments differ from discipline to discipline and from course to course, following these steps will help you to produce a standard college research paper. Be sure to review your assignment carefully and to check with your instructor if you have any questions about the purpose, persona, audience, or argument required for the paper. Use the questions in Resource 2 ("Questions for a Research Proposal," next page) to develop a research proposal to share with your instructor. Discussing your research strategies and ideas with your instructor can ensure that you begin your research on the right track.

Collecting Sources and Developing a Topic

Instead of picking a research topic out of thin air, develop a topic that relates to the assigned reading you have been doing in *Making Sense.* This gives you two huge advantages. First, you can use the assigned essay to generate key terms for your research, to help focus your topic, and to provide a framework for analyzing your sources in the actual paper. Second, if you have already discussed and written about the assigned essay in class, you can build on some of that earlier work and even revise some of the earlier ideas you had about that reading in relation to your research topic. While your additional research will help you approach the assigned essay from a fresh perspective, the assigned reading will also help you bring a perspective or a set of questions to

Resource 2

Questions for a Research Proposal

To help yourself focus your research, write a one-page proposal that answers the following questions.

1. What subject area interests you?
2. Which of your readings or papers will you use to generate your topic?
3. What narrower topics, issues, or problems could you focus on using that reading or paper?
4. What sources beyond those in *Making Sense* do you hope to find or plan to use?
5. What databases and search engines could you try?
6. What search terms are you planning to try? These might include key terms from the *Making Sense* writer you are using and terms related to your subject area.
7. What additional readings from *Making Sense* might be relevant?
8. What concepts from those readings could you use?
9. What examples from those readings could you use?
10. What examples or case studies are you hoping to find?
11. What key quotes from the readings could you use (include page numbers)?

bear on the new sources. For example, a short paper you wrote using Christopher Lasch's ideas to talk about the need for public debate could lead to a research paper in which you explore current or past presidential debates by collecting and comparing newspaper accounts of the debates. A discussion in class about Warren I. Susman's work might help you to think about whether the reporters who wrote those accounts were more interested in "personality" than in "character." Think about it this way: Scholars in the various disciplines almost *never* approach a brand new topic from scratch; they build on knowledge they already have, reading they have already done, and expertise they have already accumulated in a related topic area. Building your research topic on one or more of the assigned readings and on previous papers gives you the same advantage of being able to use the familiar to make sense of the new sources you collect.

Building on an assigned reading, however, does not stop you from exploring an area of real interest. Say you are interested in baseball. Rather than looking through the essays you have read for specific references to baseball, look for ideas or key terms that you can apply in the subject area of baseball. For example, could Walker Percy's claims about the "symbolic packaging" that prevents us from really experiencing the Grand Canyon hold true for baseball games as well? What effect do baseball cards, announcers, or advertisements have on how we approach the game? Can Patricia J. Williams's essay help you to analyze the role of ethnicity in baseball games or fan loyalties? Could you use Erin McGraw's and Annie Dillard's ideas to talk about learning to "see" the game of baseball through the eyes of the "lover" and the "knowledgeable"? If contemporary music is your real passion, try applying Sven Birkerts's ideas about reading and "deep time" to the process of listening to music, using the lyrics and music reviews you have assembled.

However you begin, the two stages of collecting sources and developing a topic work especially well together. Rather than beginning your research with a perfectly narrowed topic in mind, you can use some early searches in a general topic area to help you define a particular focus. If, for example, you want to follow up on Barbara Mellix's ideas about how we learn to translate our private, family languages into public, academic writing, you might begin searching the index to popular magazines for the terms "standard English," "code switching," or "language and power" (all key terms from Mellix). Among the articles that appear, you might find one on the problems of communication that come up in intercultural businesses, such as the advertisements that do not translate from one culture to another, or the misunderstandings that occur when people from different cultures transact business. If this general topic interests you, you might consider pursuing the slightly narrower topic of the problems of intercultural communication in the computer industry. This topic would still allow you to use Mellix's thoughts about code switching or to bring in some of Sherry Turkle's ideas to show how styles of communication affect our use of technology. You could then collect more sources on communication in the computer industry and on intercultural communication. As you piece several of the sources together, you might see a pattern emerging: Several writers argue that the technology itself will help with communication because it draws so many people together into a global marketplace; others argue that this globalizing effect creates huge communication problems.

As long as you give yourself time, the process of choosing a subject area and collecting sources that help you narrow and focus on a particular topic or issue can be an extremely exciting and creative one. Through the research process, you extend the familiar activities of summarizing, analyzing, and piecing together ideas and examples within one reading; now, you are piecing together ideas and examples from a number of readings, creating relationships between sources that have not been thought of before, and developing the patterns that link them together.

Evaluating Your Sources

Because we are surrounded—sometimes bombarded—with all kinds of information from all kinds of sources, we gradually learn to categorize and sift through the data. We make sense of what we hear in relation to what we already know. When you cite sources for a research paper, you invite your readers to perform a similar evaluative process. To convince your readers that you are presenting trustworthy and valuable ideas, you must show them that those ideas come from reliable sources; and if you include less reliable material, you must let your readers know about the source of that information so that they can make judgments about how much of it to accept. If you are using Michio Kaku to analyze popular reactions to cloning, for example, a series of outlandish articles from *The National Enquirer* "reporting" secret human cloning experiments might offer some useful testimony about extreme public fears and superstitions related to this issue. At the same time, it would be important to identify the unreliable nature of the source and to balance that information by building in some evidence from more reliable medical journals about actual current uses of cloning technology. As you collect research materials, then, it is important to evaluate them for reliability, to determine whether they are popular or scholarly, and to test their usefulness for your particular topic.

How do you determine the reliability of a source, especially one found on the Internet? Keep careful records of how and where you found the source (this is crucial for bibliographic citation format as well). If you know where the information came from, you can deduce a great deal about its reliability: A personal home page or a for-profit business site probably is less reliable than an educational site, for example, but you still need to find out who produces that educational site. If the information is provided by an organization, find out more about that organization and its agenda; if the source has an author, find out more about that person—what are his or her credentials? (See Resource 3 for questions you can use to evaluate information found on the Internet.)

Many college instructors require that the majority of your information come from scholarly sources because they consider them more reliable than popular ones. A scholarly book or journal article has been researched and written in relation to the knowledge already accumulated in that field. Like you, the scholarly author is held responsible for keeping to certain professional standards, for presenting evidence for any claims, for determining the reliability of the sources used, and for citing them carefully so that readers can make their own judgments. By contrast, an article in a popular magazine can be an unresearched account of the writer's experience or a simple declaration of the writer's opinion with little or no evidence to back it up.

Resource 3

Questions to Ask About Information Found on the Internet

1. **Who?**
   Who wrote what I am reading?
   Who maintains the Internet site?
   Who would accept this information as authoritative (my professor, my friends, my mom, etc.)?
2. **What?**
   What kind of organization owns the Internet site: educational (.edu), commercial (.com), nonprofit (.org), governmental (.gov)? Or does an individual own it (personal home page)?
   What exactly am I reading (a research article, an editorial, some gossip, etc.)?
   What information from this Internet source do I include in a bibliographic citation?
3. **Where?**
   Where exactly did I find this information, and can I get back there?
   Where are the credentials of the author or of the people responsible for the Internet site (that is, are they included on the site)?
4. **When?**
   When was the information originally written?
   When was the last time this Internet site was updated?
   When I go back to find this Internet site again, is it there?
5. **Why?**
   Why was the information originally written?
   Why was this specific information put on the Internet (to provide general information, to sell a product, to enlist support, etc.)?
   Why was searching the Internet better than using print sources?
6. **How?**
   How can I cite this information?
   How accurate and up-to-date is the information?
   How well organized and written is the information?
   How can I repeat this search quickly and efficiently if I need this information again?

Source: Mark van Lummel, Indiana University, South Bend.

The best way to decide whether a source is popular or scholarly is to check for footnotes, endnotes, or some other form of bibliographic citation. Scholarly sources must show how their ideas relate to other ideas in the field, so they almost always have some form of bibliographic citation. Popular sources often have few or no citations. Popular sources (from newspapers and magazines, for example) can be useful for gaining general information about a topic, for demonstrating public responses, or for documenting what information about a topic is publicly available. For example, if you are writing a paper using Richard C. Lewontin's ideas about DNA or Emily Martin's examples of how different people understand the immune system, you may want to explore some ways in which the general public hears about these issues. To do this, you might look in such popular sources as *Time* or *Newsweek* or do a search of the major newspapers for these topics. However, if you want to discuss the findings of the medical community on these issues, you might check the scholarly sources, *New England Journal of Medicine* or *American Journal of Public Health.*

Only you can determine the usefulness of a particular source for your topic. As with the issue of reliability, it helps to approach prospective sources with a balance between critical judgment and open-mindedness. At first it may seem that the article you have discovered on the cost of mounting museum exhibits does not exactly connect with the topic you had developed using ideas from Gloria Anzaldúa and Jane Tompkins: a study of the challenges that minority women artists face in presenting their work to mainstream audiences without selling out. A second reading, however, may reveal that the article contains a small but key portion of your argument. For example, you might show that *because* of the high cost of museum and gallery exhibits, women and minority artists, who have less access to funding, also have less access to those spaces to show their work unless they can appeal to mainstream interests. Sometimes a seemingly unusable article can offer one useful example or one useful bit of data. On the other hand, do not let a trail of sources lead you away from your topic or broaden it too much. A key step in the evaluation of sources is asking yourself how you can use *this* information in *this* paper.

Synthesizing Sources and Establishing Your Own Position in Relation to Them

In the course of college writing, you probably have practiced the skills of paraphrase, summary, and analysis. These three terms identify three different levels at which writers engage with a reading: by restating it in their own words (paraphrase); by giving a condensed account of an important point in a reading (summary); and by further exploring the implications of the reading, testing its limitations or usefulness for their own purposes, or demonstrating its larger significance (analysis). Once you have performed these operations with two or more readings by showing the significance of one writer's ideas in relation to the work of another writer, you have begun the process of synthesis.

Synthesis is the operation of piecing together ideas and examples from a number of readings with the aim of producing a meaningful whole. In synthesis, you use the skills you already know (paraphrase, summary, and analysis) to build connections between sources. You create relationships between sources by paying attention to the connections, the overlaps, and the differences that already exist among those sources.

The process of synthesizing sources also helps you to develop your own position or argument in relation to the sources. Once you have developed the connections among sources, you often have developed your thesis statement as well. For example, if your research paper involved an investigation into how the idea of the common good is used in the current debates between the logging industries and "old growth forest" environmentalists, you might collect ideas, examples, case studies, and data from the following sources: from Zita Ingham, the concept of "dissensus" as a means of maintaining community; and from government documents, the policy of protecting public parks from logging. You might use scholarly sources that document the difficulty of regrowing forests, the impact on the logging community in terms of job losses and quality of life, and the use of both legal and illegal tactics by environmentalists trying to stop logging. You might include several newspaper accounts quoting the opinions of loggers and environmentalists on the issue. After synthesizing all these sources, you might conclude that both sides have used inflammatory rhetoric to defend their interests; or, on the basis of the evidence collected, you might end up strongly supporting the loggers' case or the environmentalists'. You might argue that by using the processes of "dissensus" and community-building described in Ingham's article, both sides could negotiate a reasonable compromise; or you might conclude that Ingham's proposal probably would have no power to create a peaceful solution in a situation this complex. The loggers may never have met Ingham, and Ingham has probably never seen the government documents or the other articles you have assembled; you are the one who brought those disparate sources together.

In the process of synthesis, you generate an organizational structure that links sources into a coherent pattern for a meaningful purpose; you create an argument about how those sources connect and what they mean. The argument you make is an interpretation of those sources, but it builds from the evidence and uses the evidence to demonstrate and explore its claims.

Once you have collected your sources, you can synthesize them by:

- comparing and contrasting the positions of several writers in relation to an issue, using the examples and case studies to help you show the overlaps and differences in their positions; or

- testing one of the main theories held by one or two writers on this issue by using their key terms of analysis to explain several of the examples and case studies you have collected; or
- developing your own theory about the issue by showing how a number of readings connect to help us think about that issue in a new or interesting way (that is, by combining key terms from one or two readings with examples and case studies from several sources in a way that reveals something new or interesting about those sources).

However you proceed, the process of synthesis helps you develop an argument and establish your own position in relation to the material you have collected. Establishing your own position requires more than stating your opinion: It means demonstrating how you developed your opinion and tested it through a thoughtful interaction with the readings.

Citing and Documenting Sources

When you are citing sources, you must include two components. The first and most important thing to include is a brief citation for each quotation you use in the body of the paper. The second component is a documentation page placed at the end of your paper that lists full information for all the sources used. In the body of your paper, you give the reader only enough information to find each source in the list at the end of your paper; in the bibliographic list at the end of your paper, you give full information about where your reader can find each source. The rules for presenting this information, the "styles" of citation, vary from discipline to discipline and sometimes from course to course. In this section of the book, we provide some basic information for two of the most commonly used styles of citation and documentation: the Modern Language Association (MLA) style and the American Psychological Association (APA) style. Other styles of citation include the University of Chicago Press style, frequently preferred by history instructors, and the Council of Biology Editors (CBE) style, preferred by some science instructors. Ask your instructor about which system of documentation he or she prefers.

For more information about MLA style, go to <http://www.mla.org/> and click on "MLA Style" and then on "Frequently Asked Questions about MLA Style."

MLA Style

CITING SOURCES IN THE TEXT Whenever you use a quotation, provide in parentheses at the end of the sentence the author's name and the page number on which the quotation appears. Because you are integrating that citation into your sentence, the punctuation mark that ends your sentence should always follow the final parenthesis of the citation.

> *Example 1*
>
> Many individuals in this century would not be interested in having their portraits painted, partly because photography creates a more accurate likeness; in this sense, photography "raised our standards for judging how much an informative likeness should include" (Berger 60).

If you use the author's name in the sentence that introduces the quotation, do not restate it in the parenthetical citation.

> *Example 2*
>
> Berger believes that photography "raised our standards for judging how much an informative likeness should include" and, in doing so, contributed to the decline in portrait painting in this century (60).

By using these citations in the body of your paper you give your readers information about where the quotations come from and who first said them in case they would like to track down the original sources. Your goal is to give clear but concise information about each quotation. Notice in Example 2 that this information *always* comes at the end of your sentence, even if the quote itself falls at the beginning. This holds true unless you are citing works by more than one author and need to incorporate the citation earlier to avoid confusion.

Do not cite the title of a work unless your paper quotes from two different works written by the same author (in which case you would include the title in your sentence or in the final parentheses to avoid confusing your reader). However, as a matter of quotation etiquette, it is customary to fully introduce an essay by title and author the *first* time that the essay is mentioned in a paper.

> *Example 3*
>
> In "The Changing View of Man in the Portrait," John Berger argues that the decline in portrait painting is explained in part by larger historical transformations in "the nature of individual identity" (66).

"WORKS CITED" PAGE In a research paper, it is important to include a "Works Cited" page that gives your readers further information about where to find your sources. The "Works Cited" page should be the last page of your paper, with the accompanying heading giving your last name and the page number, and should give full citations for each source (see sample "Works Cited" on page 42). As you collect sources for the research paper, keep careful track of these four elements:

1. Names (the author or authors, editors of collections, sometimes the group or organization responsible for the source)
2. Titles (titles of the source itself, and of the book, journal, newspaper, or Web site in which it appeared)
3. Dates of publication (including month, volume number, and issue number for articles, the specific day of the month and particular edition for newspapers, and, for Internet sources, both the date of publication and the date you accessed the information)
4. Page numbers for the source and, for Internet sources, the Web addresses and databases involved in finding the source

APA Style

For more information about APA Style, go to <http://www.apa.org/journals/acorner.html> and click on "Frequently Asked Questions" under "Publication Manual (4th ed.)."

For more details about citing electronic sources, go directly to <http://www.apa.org/journals/webref.html>.

CITING SOURCES IN THE TEXT Whenever you use a quotation, provide in parentheses at the end of the sentence the author's name, the date the source was published, and the page number on which the quotation appears. (Note that APA style uses "p." or "pp." before page numbers.) Because you are integrating that citation into your sentence, the punctuation mark that ends your sentence always follows the final parenthesis of the citation.

> ***Example 1***
>
> Many individuals in this century would not be interested in having their portraits painted, partly because photography creates a more accurate likeness; in this sense, photography "raised our standards for judging how much an informative likeness should include" (Berger, 2002, p. 60).

If you use the author's name in the sentence that introduces the quotation, add the date of the source immediately after the name. Because you have already supplied this information, do not restate the author's name or give the date in the parenthetical citation at the end of the sentence.

> ***Example 2***
>
> Berger (2002) believes that photography "raised our standards for judging how much an informative likeness should include" and, in doing so, contributed to the decline in portrait painting in this century (p. 60).

Sample MLA Works Cited page

Works Cited

Berger, John. "The Changing View of Man in the Portrait." *Making Sense: Constructing Knowledge in the Arts and Sciences.* Ed. Bob Coleman, Rebecca Brittenham, Scott Campbell, and Stephanie Girard. Boston: Houghton Mifflin, 2002. 59–68.

Fitzpatrick, John. "Portraiture and the Problem of History." *Art Journal* 49 (1990): 323–43.

Kiernan, Vincent. "Study Finds Errors in Medical Information Available on the Web." *Chronicle of Higher Education* 12 June 1998: A25.

Lorh, Steve. "Now Playing: Babes in Cyberspace." *The New York Times* 3 Apr. 1998, late ed.: C1+.

Martin, Emily, et al. "Scientific Literacy, What It Is, Why It's Important, and Why Scientists Think We Don't Have It: The Case of Immunology and the Immune System." *Making Sense: Constructing Knowledge in the Arts and Sciences.* Ed. Bob Coleman, Rebecca Brittenham, Scott Campbell, and Stephanie Girard. Boston: Houghton Mifflin, 2002. 340–58.

Miller, Rachel. "Why Your Immune System Matters." *South Bend Tribune Online* 13 April 1999, 5 Nov. 2000 <http://www.southbendtribune.com/>.

Richmond, Caroline. "British girl recovering after forced heart transplant." *CMAJ: Canadian Medical Association Journal* 161.6 (21 Sept. 1999): 680. *Ebscohost.* Schurz Library, Indiana University South Bend. 25 Oct. 1999 <http://www.epnet.com/ehost/login.html/>.

By using these citations in the body of your paper you give your readers information about where the quotations come from, when they were published, and who first said them in case they would like to track down the original source. Your goal is to give clear but concise information about each quotation.

If you are citing a general concept rather than a specific quotation, do not cite a page number.

> *Example 3*
>
> Two of the essays (Berger, 2002; Sontag, 2002) demonstrate that photography has significantly changed the way we think about individual identity.

"REFERENCES" PAGE In a research paper, it is important to include a "References" page that gives your readers further information about where to find your sources. This list of references should be the last page of your paper, with the accompanying heading giving your last name and the page number, and should give full citations for each source (see sample "References" on page 44). As you collect sources for the research paper, keep careful track of these four elements:

1. Names (the author or authors, editors of collections, sometimes the group or organization responsible for the source)
2. Titles (titles of the source itself, and of the book, journal, newspaper, or Web site in which it appeared); capitalize only the first word of the title or subtitle
3. Dates of publication (including month, volume number, and issue number for articles, the specific day of the month and particular edition for newspapers, and, for Internet sources, both the date of publication and the date you accessed the information)
4. Page numbers for the source and, for Internet sources, the Web addresses and databases involved in finding the source

Sample APA References page

Running Head 00

References

Berger, J. (2002). The changing view of man in the portrait. In B. Coleman, R. Brittenham, S. Campbell, & S. Girard (Eds.), *Making sense: Constructing knowledge in the arts and sciences* (pp. 59–68). Boston: Houghton Mifflin.

Fitzpatrick, J. (1990). Portraiture and the problem of history. *Art Journal, 49,* 323–43.

Jacobson, J. W., Mulick, J. A., & Schwartz, A. A. (1995). A history of facilitated communication: Science, pseudoscience, and antiscience: Science working group on facilitated communication. *American Psychologist, 50,* 750–765. Retrieved January 25, 1996, from the World Wide Web <http://www.apa.org/journals/jacobson.html>.

Kiernan, V. (1998, June 12). Study finds errors in medical information available on the Web. *Chronicle of Higher Education,* p. A25.

Lohr, Steve. (1998, April 3). Now playing: Babes in cyberspace. *The New York Times,* pp. C1+.

Martin, E., Claeson, B., Richardson, W., Schoch-Spana, M., & Taussig, K. (2002). Scientific literacy, what it is, why it's important, and why scientists think we don't have it: The case of immunology and the immune system. In B. Coleman, R. Brittenham, S. Campbell, & S. Girard (Eds.), *Making sense: Constructing knowledge in the arts and sciences* (pp. 340–58). Boston: Houghton Mifflin.

Schneiderman, R. A. (1997). Librarians can make sense of the Net. *San Antonio Business Journal, 11*(31), pp. 58+. Retrieved January 27, 1999, from EBSCO database (Masterfile) on the World Wide Web <http://www.ebsco.com>.

Part II

Essays

Gloria Anzaldúa

Gloria Anzaldúa (1942–), a Chicana feminist activist and educator, grew up in the borderlands of South Texas. As a young girl, she worked with migrant Chicano field laborers in Arkansas. She turned to reading as an escape from the oppressive sexism of Chicano culture, eventually earning an M.A. in English from the University of Texas in Austin. Through poetry, fiction, children's books, and cultural criticism, Anzaldúa has explored her interests in her own and other cultures. She has won numerous awards for her experimental style of writing. Her book, *Borderlands/La Frontera: The New Mestiza* (1987), weaves Spanish and English poetry, memoir, and historical analysis into an extended exploration of multicultural identity. The following essay was first published in the NACLA Report on the Americas, July/August 1993.

For more information on Chicana life, literature, and art, see <http://www.chicanas.com/>.

Chicana Artists: *Exploring* Nepantla, el Lugar de la Frontera

I stop before the dismembered body of *la diosa de la luna,* Coyolxauhqui, daughter of Coatlicue. The warrior goddess' eyes are closed, she has bells on her cheeks, and her head is in the form of a snail design. She was decapitated by her brother, Huitzilopochtle, the Left-Handed Hummingbird. Her bones jut from their sockets. I stare at the huge round stone of *la diosa.* She seems to be pushing at the restraining orb of the moon. Though I sense a latent whirlwind of energy, I also sense a timeless stillness—one patiently waiting to explode into activity.

Here before my eyes, on the opening day of the "Aztec: The World of Moctezuma" exhibition at the Denver Museum of Natural History, is the culture of *nuestros antepasados indígenas.* I ask myself, What does it mean to me *esta jotita,* this queer Chicana, this *mexicatejana* to enter a museum and look at indigenous objects that were once used by my ancestors? Will I find my historical Indian identity here at this museum among the ancient artifacts and their *mestisaje lineage*?

As I pull out a pad to take notes on the clay, stone, jade, bone, feather, straw, and cloth artifacts, I am disconcerted with the knowledge that I am passively consuming and appropriating an indigenous culture. I arrive at the serpentine base of a reconstructed 16-foot temple where the Aztecs flung down human sacrifices, leaving bloodied steps. Around me I hear the censorious, culturally ignorant words of the Whites who, while horrified by the bloodthirsty Aztecs, gape in vicarious wonder and voraciously consume the exoticized images. Though I too am a gaping consumer, I feel that these artworks are part of my legacy—my appropriation differs from the misappropriation by "outsiders."

I am again struck by how much Chicana artists and writers feel the impact of ancient Mexican art forms, foods, and customs. *Sus símbolos y metáforas todavía viven en la gente chicana/mexicana.* This sense of connection and community compels Chicana writers/artists to delve into, sift through, and rework native imagery. We consistently reflect back these images in revitalized and modernized versions in theater, film, performance art, painting, dance, sculpture, and literature. *La negación sistemática de la cultura mexicana-chicana en los Estados Unidos impide su desarrollo haciéndolo este un acto de colonización.* As a people who have been stripped of our history, language, identity and pride, we attempt again and again to find what we have lost by imaginatively digging into our cultural roots and making art out of our findings.

I recall Yolanda López' *Portrait of the Artist as the Virgin of Guadalupe* (1978), which depicts a Chicana/*mexicana* woman emerging and running from the oval halo of rays that looks to me like thorns, with the mantle of the traditional *virgen* in one hand and a serpent in the other. She wears running shoes, has short hair, and her legs are bare and look powerful—a very dykey-looking woman. *Portrait* represents the cultural rebirth of the Chicana struggling to free herself from oppressive gender roles.[1]

I remember visiting Chicana *tejana* artist Santa Barraza in her Austin studio in the mid 1970s and talking about the merger and appropriation of cultural symbols and techniques by artists in search of their spiritual and cultural roots. As I walked around her studio, I was amazed at the vivid *Virgen de Guadalupe* iconography on her walls and on the drawings strewn on tables and shelves.

La gente chicana tiene tres madres. All three are mediators: *Guadalupe,* the virgin mother who has not abandoned us, *la Chingada (Malinche),* the raped mother whom we have abandoned, and *la Llorona,* the mother who seeks her lost children and is a combination of the other two. *Guadalupe* has been used by the Church to mete out institutionalized oppression: to placate the Indians and *mexicanos* and Chicanos. In part, the true identity of all three has been subverted—*Guadalupe to* make us docile and enduring, *la Chingada* to make us ashamed of our Indian side, and *la Llorona* to make us long-suffering people. This obscuring has encouraged the *virgen/puta* dichotomy. The three *madres* are cultural figures that Chicana writers and artists "reread" in our works.

Now, 16 years later, Barraza is focusing on interpretations of Pre-Columbian codices as a reclamation of cultural and historical mestiza identity. Her "codices" are edged with *milagros* and *ex votos.*[2] Using the folk-art format, Barraza is now painting tin testimonials known as *retablos*. These are traditional popular miracle paintings on metal, a medium introduced to colonial Mexico by the Spaniards. One of her devotional *retablos* is of *la Malinche,* made with *maguey.* (The *maguey* cactus is Barraza's symbol of rebirth.) Like that of many Chicana artists, her work, she says, explores indigenous Mexican "symbols and myths in a historical and contemporary context as a mechanism of resistance to oppression and assimilation."[3]

I wonder about the genesis of *el arte de la frontera.* Border art remembers its roots—sacred and folk art are often still one and the same. I recall the *nichos* (niches or recessed areas) and *retablos* that I had recently seen in several galleries and museums. The *retablos* are placed inside open boxes made of wood, tin, or cardboard. The *cajitas* contain three dimensional figures such as *la virgen,* photos of ancestors, candles, and sprigs of herbs tied together. They are actually tiny installations. I make mine out of cigar boxes or vegetable crates that I find discarded on the street before garbage pickups. The *retablos* range from the strictly traditional to modern, more abstract forms. Santa Barraza, Yolanda López, Marcia Gómez, Carmen Lomas Garza and other Chicana artists connect their art to everyday life, instilling both with political, sacred and aesthetic values. *Haciendo tortillas* becomes a sacred ritual in literary, visual, and performance arts.[4]

Border art, in critiquing old, traditional, and erroneous representations of the Mexico–United States border, attempts to represent the "real world" *de la gente* going about their daily lives. But it renders that world and its people in more than mere surface slices of life. If one looks beyond the tangible, one sees a connection to the spirit world, to the underworld, and to other realities. In the "old world," art was/is functional and sacred as well as aesthetic. When folk and fine art separated, the *metate* (a flat porous volcanic stone with rolling pin used to make corn tortillas) and the *huipil* (a Guatemalan blouse) were put in museums by Western curators of art.[5]

I come to a glass case where the skeleton of a jaguar with a stone in its open mouth nestles on cloth. The stone represents the heart. My thoughts trace the jaguar's spiritual and religious symbolism from its

Olmec origins to present-day jaguar masks worn by people who no longer know that the jaguar was connected to rain, who no longer remember that Tlaloc and the jaguar and the serpent and rain are tightly intertwined.[6] Through the centuries a culture touches and influences another, passing on its metaphors and its gods before it dies. (Metaphors *are* gods.) The new culture adopts, modifies, and enriches these images, and it, in turn, passes them on changed. The process is repeated until the original meanings of images are pushed into the unconscious. What surfaces are images more significant to the prevailing culture and era. The artist on some level, however, still connects to that unconscious reservoir of meaning, connects to that *nepantla* state of transition between time periods, and the border between cultures.

Nepantla is the Nahuatl word for an in-between state, that uncertain terrain one crosses when moving from one place to another, when changing from one class, race, or gender position to another, when traveling from the present identity into a new identity. The Mexican immigrant at the moment of crossing the barbed-wire fence into the hostile "paradise" of *el norte,* the United States, is caught in a state of *nepantla.* Others who find themselves in this bewildering transitional space may be those people caught in the midst of denying their projected/assumed heterosexual identity and coming out, presenting and voicing their lesbian, gay, bi-, or transsexual selves. Crossing class lines—especially from working class to middle classness and privilege—can be just as disorienting. The marginalized, starving Chicana artist who suddenly finds her work exhibited in mainstream museums, or being sold for thousands of dollars in prestigious galleries, as well as the once-neglected writer whose work is on every professor's syllabus for a time inhabit *nepantla.* For women artists, *nepantla* is a constant state; dislocation is the norm. Chicana artists are engaged in "reading" that *nepantla,* that border.

I think of the borderlands as Jorge Luis Borges' *Aleph,* the one spot on earth which contains all other places within it. All people in it, whether natives or immigrants, colored or white, queer or heterosexual, from this side of the border or *del otro lado,* are *personas del lugar,* local people—all of whom relate to the border and to *nepantla* in different ways.

The border is a historical and metaphorical site, *un sitio ocupado,* an occupied borderland where individual artists and collaborating groups transform space, and the two home territories, Mexico and the United States, become one. Border art deals with shifting identities, border crossings, and hybridism. But there are other borders besides the actual Mexico/US *frontera.* Chilean-born artist Juan Davila's *Wuthering Heights* (1990) oil painting depicts Juanito Leguna, a half-caste, mixed breed transvestite. Juanito's body is a simulacrum parading as the phallic mother with hairy chest and hanging tits.[7] Another Latino artist, Rafael Barajas (who signs his work as "El Fisgón"), has a mixed-media piece entitled *Pero eso si . . . soy muy macho* (1989). It shows a Mexican male wearing the proverbial sombrero taking a siesta against the traditional cactus, tequila bottle on the ground, gunbelt hanging from a nopal branch. But the leg sticking out from beneath the sarape-like mantle is wearing a highheeled shoe, pantyhose, and a garter belt. It suggests another kind of border crossing—gender-bending.[8]

According to anthropologist Edward Hall, early in life we become oriented to space in a way that is tied to survival and sanity. When we become disoriented from that sense of space we fall in danger of becoming psychotic.[9] I question this—to be disoriented in space is the "normal" way of being for us mestizas living in the borderlands. It is the sane way of coping with the accelerated pace of this complex, interdependent, and multicultural planet. To be disoriented in space is to be *en nepantla,* to experience bouts of disassociation of identity, identity breakdowns and buildups. The border is in a constant *nepantla* state, and it is an analog of the planet.

This is why the border is a persistent metaphor in *el arte de la frontera,* an art that deals with such themes as identity, border crossings, and hybrid imagery. The Mexico–United States border is a site where many different cultures "touch" each other and the permeable, flexible, and ambiguous shifting grounds lend themselves to hybrid images. The border is the locus of resistance, of rupture, of implosion and explosion, and of putting together the fragments and creating a new assemblage. Border artists *cambian el punto de referencia.* By disrupting the neat separations between cultures, they create a culture mix, *una mestizada* in their artworks. Each artist locates herself in this border "*lugar*" and tears apart then rebuilds the "place" itself. "Imagenes de la Frontera" was the title of the Centro Cultural Tijuana's June 1992 exhibition.[10] Malaquís Montoya's Frontera Series and Irene Pérez' Dos Mundos monoprint are examples of the multisubjectivity, split-subjectivity, and refusal-to-be-split themes of the border artist creating a counter-art.

The *nepantla* state is the natural habitat of women artists, most specifically for the mestiza border artists who partake of the traditions of two or more worlds and who may be binational. They thus create a new artistic space—a border mestizo culture. Beware of *el romance del mestizaje,* I hear myself saying silently. *Puede ser una ficción.* But I and other writers/artists of *la frontera* have invested ourselves in it. *Mestizaje,* not Chicanismo, is the reality of our lives. *Mestizaje* is at the heart of our art. We bleed in *mestizaje,* we eat and sweat and cry in *mestizaje.* But the Chicana is inside the mestiza.

There are many obstacles and dangers in crossing into *nepantla.* Popular culture and the dominant art institutions threaten border artists from the outside with appropriation. "Outsiders" jump on the border artists' bandwagon and work their territory. The present unparalleled economic depression in the arts gutted by government funding cutbacks threatens *los artistas de la frontera.* Sponsoring corporations that judge projects by "family values" criteria force multicultural artists to hang tough and brave out financial and professional instability.

I walk into the Aztec Museum shop and see feathers, paper flowers, and ceramic statues of fertility goddesses selling for ten times what they sell for in Mexico. Border art is becoming trendy in these neocolonial times that encourage art tourism and pop-culture ripoffs. Of course, there is nothing new about colonizing, commercializing, and consuming the art of ethnic people (and of queer writers and artists) except that now it is being misappropriated by pop culture. Diversity is being sold on TV, billboards, fashion runways, department-store windows, and, yes, airport corridors and "regional" stores where you can take home a jar of Tex-Mex *picante* sauce along with Navaho artist R. C. Gorman's "Saguaro" or Robert Arnold's "Chili Dog," and drink a margarita at Rosie's Cantina.

I touch the armadillo pendant hanging from my neck and think, *frontera* artists have to grow protective shells. We enter the silence, go inward, attend to feelings and to that inner *cenote,* the creative reservoir where earth, female, and water energies merge. We surrender to the rhythm and the grace of our artworks. Through our artworks we cross the border into other subjective levels of awareness, shift into different and new terrains of *mestizaje.* Some of us have a highly developed *facultad* and many intuit what lies ahead. Yet the political climate does not allow us to withdraw completely. In fact, border artists are engaged artists. Most of us are politically active in our communities. If disconnected from *la gente,* border artists would wither in isolation. The community feeds our spirits and the responses from our "readers" inspire us to continue struggling with our art and aesthetic interventions that subvert cultural genocide. Border art challenges and subverts the imperialism of the United States, and combats assimilation by either the United States or Mexico, yet it acknowledges its affinities to both cultures.[11]

"Chicana" artist, "border" artist. These are adjectives labeling identities. Labeling creates expectations. White poets don't write "white" in front of their names, nor are they referred to as white by others. Is "border" artist just another label that strips legitimacy from the artist, signaling that she is inferior to the adjectiveless artist, a label designating that she is only capable of handling ethnic, folk, and regional subjects and art forms? Yet the dominant culture consumes, swallows whole the ethnic artist, sucks out her vitality, and then spits out the hollow husk along with its labels (such as Hispanic). The dominant culture shapes the ethnic artist's identity if she does not scream loud enough and fight long enough to name herself. Until we live in a society where all people are more or less equal, we need these labels to resist the pressure to assimilate.

Artistic ideas that have been incubating and developing at their own speed have come into their season—now is the time of border art. Border *arte* is an art that supersedes the pictorial. It depicts both the soul *del artista* and the soul *del pueblo*. It deals with who tells the stories and what stories and histories are told. I call this form of visual narrative *autohistoria*. This form goes beyond the traditional self-portrait or autobiography; in telling the writer/artist's personal story, it also includes the artist's cultural history. The *retablos* I make are not just representations of myself, they are representations of Chicana culture. *El arte de la frontera* is community and academically based—many Chicana artists have M.A.s and Ph.D.s and hold precarious teaching positions on the fringes of universities. They are overworked, overlooked, passed over for tenure, and denied the support they deserve. To make, exhibit, and sell their artwork, and to survive, *los artistas* have had to band together collectively.[12]

I cross the exhibit room. Codices hang on the walls. I stare at the hieroglyphics. The ways of a people, their history and culture put on paper beaten from maguey leaves. Faint traces of red, blue, and black ink left by their artists, writers, and scholars. The past is hanging behind glass. We, the viewers in the present, walk around and around the glassboxed past. I wonder who I used to be, I wonder who I am. The border artist constantly reinvents herself. Through art she is able to reread, reinterpret, re-envision and reconstruct her culture's present as well as its past. This capacity to construct meaning and culture privileges the artist. As cultural icons for her ethnic communities, she is highly visible.

But there are drawbacks to having artistic and cultural power—the relentless pressure to produce, being put in the position of representing her entire *pueblo* and carrying all the ethnic culture's baggage on her *espalda* while trying to survive in a gringo world. Power and the seeking of greater power may create a self-centered ego or a fake public image, one the artist thinks will make her acceptable to her audience. It may encourage self-serving hustling—all artists have to sell themselves in order to get grants, get published, secure exhibit spaces, and get good reviews. But for some, the hustling outdoes the art-making.

The Chicana border writer/artist has finally come to market. The problem now is how to resist corporate culture while asking for and securing its patronage; how to get the dollars without resorting to "mainstreaming" the work. Is the border artist complicit in the appropriation of her art by the dominant art dealers? And if so, does this constitute a self-imposed imperialism? The artist, in making *plata* from the sale of her sculpture, "makes it." Money means power. The access to privilege that comes with the bucks and the recognition can turn the artist on her ear in a *nepantla* spin.

Finally, I find myself before the reconstructed statue of the newly unearthed *el dios murciélago*, the bat god with his big ears, fangs, and protruding tongue representing the vampire bat associated with night, blood sacrifice, and death. I make an instantaneous association of the bat man with the stage of border artists—the dark cave of creativity where they hang upside down, turning the self upside down in order to see from another point of view, one that brings a new state of understanding. Or it may mean transposing the former self onto a new one—the death of the old self and the old ways, breaking down former notions of who you are. Night fear, *susto,* when every button is pushed. The border person constantly moves through that birth canal, *nepantla.* If you stay too long in *nepantla* you are in danger of being blocked, resulting in a breech birth or being stillborn.

I wonder what meaning this bat figure will have for other Chicanas, what artistic symbol they will make of it and what political struggle it will represent. Perhaps the *murciélago* questions the viewer's unconscious collective and personal identity and its ties to her ancestors, *los muertos.* In border art there is always the specter of death in the background. Often *las calaveras* (skeletons and skulls) take a prominent position—and not just on *el día de los muertos* (November 2). *De la tierra nacemos,* from earth we are born, *a la tierra regresaremos,* to earth we shall return, *a dar lo que ella nos dió,* to give back to her what she has given. Yes, I say to myself, the earth eats the dead, *la tierra se come los muertos.*

I walk out of the Aztec exhibit hall. It is September 28, *mi cumpleaños.* I seek out the table with the computer, key in my birthdate and there on the screen is my Aztec birth year and ritual day name: 8 Rabbit, 12 Skull. In that culture I would have been named Matlactli Omome Mizuitzli. I stick my chart under the rotating rubber stamps, press down, pull it out and stare at the imprint of the rabbit (symbol of fear and of running scared) pictograph and then of the skull (night, blood sacrifice, and death). Very appropriate symbols in my life, I mutter. It's so *raza. ¿y qué?*

I ask myself, What direction will *el arte fronterizo* take in the future? The multi-subjectivity and split-subjectivity of the border artist creating various counter arts will continue, but with a parallel movement where a polarized us/them, insiders/outsiders culture clash is not the main struggle, where a refusal to be split will be a given. We are both *nos* (us) and *otras* (others)—*nos/otras.*

My mind reviews image after image. Something about who and what I am and the 200 "artifacts" I have just seen does not feel right. I pull out my "birth chart." Yes, cultural roots are important *but I was not born at Tenochitlán in the ancient past nor in an Aztec village in modern times. I was born and live in that in-between space,* nepantla, *the borderlands.* Hay muchas razas *running in my veins,* mescladas dentro de mi, otras culturas *that my body lives in and out of.* Mi cuerpo vive dentro y fuera de otras culturas *and a white man who constantly whispers inside my skull. For me, being Chicana is not enough. It is only one of my multiple identities. Along with other* border gente, *it is at this site and time,* en este tiempo y lugar *where and when, I create my identity* con mi arte.

1993

Notes

I thank Dianna Williamson and Clarisa Rojas, my literary assistants, for their invaluable and incisive critical comments, and Deidre McFadyen.

1. See Amalia Mesa-Bains, "*El Mundo Femenino:* Chicana Artists of the Movement—A Commentary on Development and Production," in Richard Griswold Del Castillo, Teresa McKenna, and Yvonne Yarbo Bejarano (eds), *CARA, Chicano Art: Resistance and Affirmation* (Los Angeles: Wight Gallery, University of California, 1991).
2. See Luz María and Ellen J. Stekert's untitled art catalog essay in *Santa Barraza,* March 8–April 11, 1992, La Raza/Galería Posada, Sacramento, CA.
3. Quoted in Jennifer Heath's "Women Artists of Color Share World of Struggle," *Sunday Camera,* March 8, 1992, p. 9C.
4. See Carmen Lomas Garza's children's bilingual book, *Family Pictures/Cuadros de familia* (San Francisco: Children's Book Press, 1990), in particular "*Camas para sonar*/Beds for Dreaming."
5. The Maya huipiles are large rectangular blouses which describe the Maya cosmos. They portray the world as a diamond. The four sides of the diamond represent the boundaries of space and time; the smaller diamonds at each corner, the cardinal points. The weaver maps the heavens and underworld.
6. Roberta H. Markman and Peter T. Markman (eds), *Masks of the Spirit: Image and Metaphor in Mesoamerica* (Berkeley: University of California Press, 1989).
7. See Guy Brett, *Transcontinental: An Investigation of Reality* (London: Verso, 1990).
8. See *ex profeso, recuento de afinidades colectiva plástica contemporánea: imágenes: gay-lésbicas-éroticas* put together by Circulo Cultural Gay in Mexico City and exhibited at Museuo Universitario del Chope during Gay Cultural Week, June 14–23, 1989.
9. The exact quote is: "We have an internalization of fixed space learned early in life. One's orientation in space is tied to survival and sanity. To be disoriented in space is to be psychotic." See Edward T. Hall and Mildred Reed Hall, "The Sounds of Silence," in James P. Spradley and David W. McCurdy (eds), *Conformity and Conflict: Readings in Cultural Anthropology* (Boston: Little, Brown, 1987).
10. The exhibition was part of Festival Internacional de la Raza '92. The artworks were produced in the Silkscreen Studios of Self Help Graphics, Los Angeles, and in the studios of Strike Editions in Austin, Texas. Self Help Graphics and the Galería Sin Fronteras, Austin, Texas, organized the exhibitions.
11. Among the alternative galleries and art centers that combat assimilation are the Guadalupe Cultural Arts Center in San Antonio, Mexic-Arte Museum and Sin Fronteras Gallery in Austin, Texas, and the Mission Cultural Center in San Francisco.

12. For a discussion of Chicano posters, almanacs, calendars, and cartoons that join "images and texts to depict community issues as well as historical and cultural themes," and that metaphorically link Chicano struggles for self-determination with the Mexican Revolution, and establish "a cultural and visual continuum across borders," see Tomás Ybarra-Fausto's "Gráfica/Urban Iconography" in *Chicano Expressions: A New View in American Art, April 14–July 31, 1986* (New York: INTAR Latin American Gallery, 1986), pp. 21–4.

GETTING STARTED

1. Mixing English and Spanish words and phrases is a characteristic of Anzaldúa's writing. Select two or three passages from the article in which she mixes languages. How do you respond to this bilingual approach? What effects might Anzaldúa be trying to produce by using this approach?
2. Choose two definitions or examples that help you to explain what Anzaldúa means by *nepantla* or "borderlands," and take some notes explaining each term. In a group, share your findings and list all the meanings that Anzaldúa associates with both words.
3. Individually or in a group, make a list of as many of the positive and productive possibilities of being a border artist as you can find. Then make a list of as many of the threats, dangers, and obstacles faced by border artists as you can find. (Pay particular attention to page 53.) Present your findings to the class.
4. What does Anzaldúa mean on page 50 when she says that "metaphors *are* gods"? Make a list of the places where Anzaldúa uses metaphors in her essay. Rewrite one of the passages without using metaphors. What do these metaphors enable Anzaldúa to accomplish?
5. What is the tone of Anzaldúa's piece? What emotions do you think she expresses? Make a short list of places in the text where you think her language is especially revealing.

WRITING

6. Find at least two passages where Anzaldúa comments on her feelings and thoughts as she views the exhibits in the Denver museum. How does she make sense of her participation as a visitor to the museum? Is her experience unique? Compare it to an experience you have had as a visitor to a museum or an equivalent space. Write a brief essay (1–2 pages) explaining your findings.

7. Toward the end of her essay, Anzaldúa wonders, "What direction will *el arte fronterizo* take in the future?" (p. 54). Write an essay comparing the positive potential of borderland art and artists against the threats, dangers, and obstacles they face. What other positives or negatives to "borderland" art does Anzaldúa not take into consideration? For example, do you share her view of the way art and artifacts are "misappropriated by 'outsiders'"? How is that different from Anzaldúa's "appropriation" of those same artifacts?

8. Summarize Anzaldúa's article using only English words and phrases and without using metaphors. In other words, summarize the article without using two of Anzaldúa's rhetorical strategies: use of Spanish words and metaphor. Write a paper in which you present your summary and compare it to Anzaldúa's essay. How do Anzaldúa's rhetorical strategies, her writing techniques, affect the content of her essay? What do these strategies enable her to convey about herself and her attitude toward her subject and her audience? Would someone reading your summary be surprised by Anzaldúa's essay?

9. Using your ideas from question 5, write a short paper exploring the effects of Anzaldúa's authorial voice. How does she use emotion and strong (even bitter) language to make her point? Does her essay ask for more than just an intellectual response?

USING THE LIBRARY AND THE INTERNET

10. Search a map of the North American continent to identify the geographical "borderland" that Anzaldúa talks about in this essay. List some other potential "borderlands" that you see on the map.

11. Using a popular search engine such as Google, Hotbot, or Alta Vista, search for the terms "border" and"borderlands." From a brief sampling of the Web sites you find, list some of the meanings and issues associated with the concepts. Try the same search terms in a reference database such as Academic Search Elite that includes sources from scholarly journals. List some of the meanings and issues involving "border" and "borderlands" that appear in the articles you find. In a group, compare the differences between the two lists.

MAKING CONNECTIONS

12. In "The Little Man at Chehaw Station," Ralph Ellison is, like Anzaldúa, describing what it means to be "American." Would

these two writers agree with one another on this issue? How might Ellison's "little man" respond to one of Anzaldúa's examples of border art?

13. Like Anzaldúa, Haunani-Kay Trask is interested in the role of language in building culture and identity. How might Anzaldúa respond to Trask's critique of non-Hawaiian historians and her insistence on "authenticity" in her "From a Native Daughter"? Write a paper in which you discuss the role of language in the experiences of marginality that Anzaldúa and Trask describe.

14. In "I Stand Here Writing," Nancy Sommers writes of her difficulty in trying to find a way to write that is true to her life. Can the resulting exploratory essay be considered a "border text"? How well does Anzaldúa's term fit in this case?

JOHN BERGER

John Berger (1926–) is a prolific writer. Although he began his career as an artist and a teacher, he is best known as an art critic. Berger has written over sixteen books of art criticism, including *The Moment of Cubism and Other Essays* (1969), from which "The Changing View of Man in the Portrait" was taken. Berger has also written novels, film scripts, translations, and essays, and has appeared in television series and movies. His varied and wide-ranging interests include the role of art in history and politics and the processes of seeing and thinking that are stimulated by works of art.

For more information on John Berger and his many publications, see <http://www.boondocksnet.com/cb/berger.html>.

The Changing View of Man in the Portrait

It seems to me unlikely that any important portraits will ever be painted again. Portraits, that is to say, in the sense of portraiture as we now understand it. I can imagine multi-medium memento-sets devoted to the character of particular individuals. But these will have nothing to do with the works now in the National Portrait Gallery.

I see no reason to lament the passing of the portrait—the talent once involved in portrait painting can be used in some other way to serve a more urgent, modern function. It is, however, worth while inquiring why the painted portrait has become outdated; it may help us to understand more clearly our historical situation.

The beginning of the decline of the painted portrait coincided roughly speaking with the rise of photography, and so the earliest answer to our question—which was already being asked towards the end of the nineteenth century—was that the photographer had taken the place of the portrait painter. Photography was more accurate, quicker and far cheaper; it offered the opportunity of portraiture to the whole of society: previously such an opportunity had been the privilege of a very small *élite*.

To counter the clear logic of this argument, painters and their patrons invented a number of mysterious, metaphysical qualities with which to prove that what the painted portrait offered was incomparable. Only a man, not a machine (the camera), could interpret the soul of a sitter. An artist dealt with the sitter's destiny: the camera with mere light and shade. An artist judged: a photographer recorded. Etcetera, etcetera.

All this was doubly untrue. First, it denies the interpretative role of the photographer, which is considerable. Secondly, it claims for painted portraits a psychological insight which ninety-nine per cent of them totally lack. If one is considering portraiture as a genre, it is no good thinking of a few extraordinary pictures but rather of the endless portraits of the local nobility and dignitaries in countless provincial museums and town halls. Even the average Renaissance portrait—although suggesting considerable presence—has very little psychological content. We are surprised by ancient Roman or Egyptian portraits, not because of their *insight,* but because they show us very vividly how little the human face has changed. It is a myth that the portrait painter was a revealer of souls. Is there a qualitative difference between the way Velasquez painted a face and the way he painted a bottom? The comparatively few portraits that reveal true psychological penetration (certain Raphaels, Rembrandts, Davids, Goyas) suggest personal, obsessional interests on the part of the artist which simply cannot be accommodated within the *professional* role of the portrait painter. Such pictures have the same kind of intensity as self-portraits. They are in fact works of self-discovery.

Ask yourself the following hypothetical question. Suppose that there is somebody in the second half of the nineteenth century in whom you are interested but of whose face you have never seen a picture. Would you rather find a painting or a photograph of this person? And the question itself posed like that is already highly favourable to painting, since the logical question should be: would you rather find a painting or a whole album of photographs?

Until the invention of photography, the painted (or sculptural) portrait was the only means of recording and presenting the likeness of a person. Photography took over this role from painting and at the same time raised our standards for judging how much an informative likeness should include.

This is not to say that photographs are *in all ways* superior to painted portraits. They are more informative, more psychologically revealing, and in general more accurate. But they are less tensely unified. Unity in a work of art is achieved as a result of the limitations of the medium. Every element has to be transformed in order to have its proper place within these limitations. In photography the transformation is to a considerable extent mechanical. In a painting each transformation is largely the result of a conscious decision by the artist. Thus the unity of a painting is permeated by a far higher degree of intention. The total effect of a painting (as distinct from its truthfulness) is less arbitrary than that of a photograph; its construction is more intensely socialized because it is dependent on a greater number of hu-

FIGURE 1 Rembrandt Harmensz van Rijn, *Old Man with a Gold Chain,* 1631. (1922.4467. E36883. Art Institute of Chicago.)

man decisions. A photographic portrait may be more revealing and more accurate about the likeness and character of the sitter; but it is likely to be less persuasive, less (in the very strict sense of the word) conclusive. For example, if the portraitist's intention is to flatter or idealize, he will be able to do so far more convincingly with a painting than with a photograph.

From this fact we gain an insight into the actual function of portrait painting in its heyday: a function we tend to ignore if we concentrate on the small number of exceptional 'unprofessional' portraits by Raphael, Rembrandt, David, Goya, etcetera. The function of portrait painting was to underwrite and idealize a chosen social role of the sitter. It was not to present him as 'an individual' but, rather, as an individual monarch, bishop, landowner, merchant and so on. Each role had its accepted qualities and its acceptable limit of discrepancy. (A monarch or a pope could be far more idiosyncratic than a mere gentleman or courtier.) The role was emphasized by pose, gesture, clothes and background. The fact that neither the sitter nor the successful professional painter was much involved with the painting of these parts is not to be entirely explained as a matter of saving time: they were thought of and were meant to be read as the accepted attributes of a given social stereotype.

The hack painters never went much beyond the stereotype; the good professionals (Memlinck, Cranach, Titian, Rubens, Van Dyck, Velasquez, Hals, Philippe de Champaigne) painted individual men, but they were nevertheless men whose character and facial expressions were seen and judged in the exclusive light of an ordained social role. The portrait must fit like a hand-made pair of shoes, but the type of shoe was never in question.

The satisfaction of having one's portrait painted was the satisfaction of being personally recognized and *confirmed in one's position:* it had nothing to do with the modern lonely desire to be recognized 'for what one really is'.

If one were going to mark the moment when the decline of portraiture became inevitable, by citing the work of a particular artist, I would choose the two or three extraordinary portraits of lunatics by Géricault, painted in the first period of romantic disillusion and defiance which followed the defeat of Napoleon and the shoddy triumph of the French bourgeoisie.(See, for example, Figure 3 on p. 64.) The paintings were neither morally anecdotal nor symbolic: they were straight portraits, traditionally painted. Yet their sitters had no social role and were presumed to be incapable of fulfilling any. In other pictures Géricault painted severed human heads and limbs as found in the dissecting theatre. His outlook was bitterly critical: to choose to paint dispossessed lunatics was a comment on men of property and power; but it was also an assertion that the essential spirit of man was independent of the role into which society forced him. Géricault found society so negative that, although sane himself, he found the isolation of the mad more meaningful than the social honour accorded to the successful. He was the first and, in a sense, the last profoundly anti-social portraitist. The term contains an impossible contradiction.

After Géricault, professional portraiture degenerated into servile and crass personal flattery, cynically undertaken. It was no longer possible to believe in the value of the social roles chosen or allotted. Sincere artists painted a number of 'intimate' portraits of their friends or models (Corot, Courbet, Degas, Cézanne, Van Gogh), but in these the social role of the sitter is reduced to *that of being painted.* The implied social value is either that of personal friendship (proximity) or that of being seen in such a way (being 'treated') by an original artist. In either case the sitter, somewhat like an arranged still life, becomes

FIGURE 2 Anthony Van Dyck, *Charles I of England,* 1635. (Giraudon/Art Resource, New York.)

subservient to the painter. Finally it is not his personality or his role which impress us but the artist's vision.

Toulouse-Lautrec was the one important latter-day exception to this general tendency. He painted a number of portraits of tarts and cabaret personalities. As we survey them, they survey us. A social reciprocity is established through the painter's mediation. We are presented neither with a disguise—as with official portraiture—nor with mere creatures of the artist's vision. His portraits are the only

FIGURE 3 Théodore Géricault, *Insane*, 1821–1824. (Museum voor Schone Kunsten.)

late nineteenth-century ones which are persuasive and conclusive in the sense that we have defined. They are the only painted portraits in whose social evidence we can believe. They suggest, not the artist's studio, but 'the world of Toulouse-Lautrec': that is to say a specific and complex social milieu. Why was Lautrec such an exception? Because in his eccentric and obverse manner he believed in the social roles of his sitters. He painted the cabaret performers because he admired their performances: he painted the tarts because he recognized the usefulness of their trade.

Increasingly for over a century fewer and fewer people in capitalist society have been able to believe in the social value of the social

FIGURE 4 Gustave Courbet, *Portrait of Jo, the Beautiful Irish Girl,* 1865? (National Museum of Stockholm.)

FIGURE 5 Vincent van Gogh, *Joseph-Etienne Roulin,* 1889. (The Postman, Van Gogh, BF #37 ©. Reproduced with the permission of the Barnes Foundation. All Rights Reserved.)

FIGURE 6 Henri de Toulouse-Lautrec, *Le Clowness assise* (Seated Clowness), Lithograph. Museum of Modern Art, New York. (Giraudon/Art Resource, New York.)

roles offered. This is the second answer to our original question about the decline of the painted portrait.

The second answer suggests, however, that given a more confident and coherent society, portrait painting might revive. And this seems unlikely. To understand why, we must consider the third answer.

The measures, the scale-change of modern life, have changed the nature of individual identity. Confronted with another person today, we are aware, through this person, of forces operating in directions which were unimaginable before the turn of the century, and which have only become clear relatively recently. It is hard to define this change briefly. An analogy may help.

We hear a lot about the crisis of the modern novel. What this involves, fundamentally, is a change in the mode of narration. It is scarcely any longer possible to tell a straight story sequentially unfolding in time. And this is because we are too aware of what is continually traversing the story line laterally. That is to say, instead of being aware of a point as an infinitely small part of a straight line, we are aware of it as an infinitely small part of an infinite number of lines, as the centre of a star of lines. Such awareness is the result of our constantly having to take into account the simultaneity and extension of events and possibilities.

There are many reasons why this should be so: the range of modern means of communication: the scale of modern power: the degree of personal political responsibility that must be accepted for events all over the world: the fact that the world has become indivisible: the unevenness of economic development within that world: the scale of the exploitation. All these play a part. Prophesy now involves a geographical rather than historical projection; it is space not time that hides consequences from us. To prophesy today it is only necessary to know men as they are throughout the whole world in all their inequality. Any contemporary narrative which ignores the urgency of this dimension is incomplete and acquires the over-simplified character of a fable.

Something similar but less direct applies to the painted portrait. We can no longer accept that the identity of a man can be adequately established by preserving and fixing what he looks like from a single viewpoint in one place. (One might argue that the same limitation applies to the still photograph, but as we have seen, we are not led to expect a photograph to be as conclusive as a painting.) Our terms of recognition have changed since the heyday of portrait painting. We may still rely on 'likeness' to identify a person, but no longer to explain or place him. To concentrate upon 'likeness' is to isolate falsely. It is to assume that the outermost surface *contains* the man or object: whereas we are highly conscious of the fact that nothing can contain itself.

There are a few Cubist portraits of about 1911 in which Picasso and Braque were obviously conscious of the same fact, but in these 'portraits' it is impossible to identify the sitter so they cease to be what we call portraits.

It seems that the demands of a modern vision are incompatible with the singularity of static-painted 'likeness'. The incompatibility is connected with a more general crisis concerning the meaning of individuality. Individuality can no longer be contained within the terms

FIGURE 7 Pablo Picasso, *Portrait of Henry Kahnweiler,* 1910. (Gift of Mrs. Gilbert W. Chapman in memory of Charles B. Goodspeed, 1948.561. Art Institute of Chicago. © 2001 Estate of Pablo Picasso/Artists' Rights Society, New York.)

of manifest personality traits. In a world of transition and revolution individuality has become a problem of historical and social relations, such as cannot be revealed by the mere characterizations of an already established social stereotype. Every mode of individuality now relates to the whole world.

1969

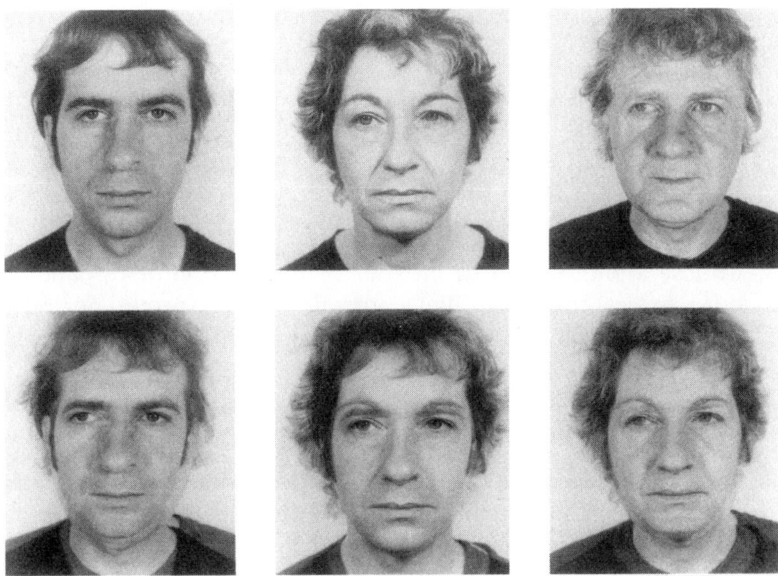

Figure 8 William Wegman, *Family Combinations*, 1972. Six gelatin-silver prints 11 13/16 × 14 1/4 in. each. Collection of Ed Ruscha. (© William Wegman.)

GETTING STARTED

1. List as many painted portraits as you can think of. What features do they have in common? In what ways are painted portraits different from photographs? What advantages do they have over photographs?

2. Is Berger arguing that photographs are better than painted portraits? Find two places where he explains the differences between the two in more detail. Share your findings in a group and prepare a presentation for the class in which you use an example from Berger to explain the distinction he makes between photographs and painted portraits.

3. Look at one of the portraits in the essay. Describe its "message" to you. What do you think the painter is communicating? In a group, compare and contrast the "messages" of the portraits you looked at to the "message" of the William Wegman photograph, *Family Combinations* (above). Present your findings to the class.

4. What does Berger mean by his claim that "the measures, the scale-change of modern life, have changed the nature of individual identity" (p. 66)? In a group, find two examples that help to explain this claim.

WRITING

5. Berger makes much of what he calls the original mission of the portrait painter: "The function of portrait painting was to underwrite and idealize a chosen social role of the sitter" (p. 61). What happens to this idea of portraiture according to Berger? Describe the connection he sees between social roles and portraits.

6. Choose a photograph (from your own collection or from some other source) that seems like a portrait. Is it a respectful portrait? Does it comment on its subject in some way? In two pages, discuss the choices that the photographer made in choosing to render the subject in this way. Use Berger to help you define your sense of what this portrait "says."

7. Why does Berger think it unlikely that "any important portraits will ever be painted again" (p. 59)? Write a short paper in which you discuss the faded significance of the portrait in modem times. If you think Berger overstates his case, explore at least one example that challenges his statement.

USING THE LIBRARY AND THE INTERNET

8. In a book or on the Web, find a painted portrait of an individual and compare it to a photograph of another individual. In what ways do the two images support or challenge Berger's claims? (Hint: On the Internet, try using the name of an artist mentioned by Berger as your search term, using a popular search engine such as AltaVista that allows you to limit your search to images.)

9. Berger uses only male European artists as examples in his piece. Find an example of a portrait painted by a woman or non-European. Does Berger's argument still make sense for this example?

MAKING CONNECTIONS

10. In her essay, "Seeing," Annie Dillard uses the image of the camera to describe the difference between seeing as "analyzing and prying" and seeing as "letting go." Walker Percy seems to think that a sightseer who takes photographs of the Grand Canyon is surrendering his freedom, his sovereignty. Berger seems to have a wholly different sense of what a photograph can do. When is taking photographs a passive activity and when does it involve active engagement? Write an essay in which you establish your

own position on the relationship between photography and individual identity based on a comparison of the positions held by Dillard, Percy, and Berger.

11. Use ideas and examples from Warren I. Susman's " 'Personality' and the Making of Twentieth-Century Culture" or from Christopher Lasch's "The Lost Art of Argument" to test Berger's claim that "the measures, the scale-change of modern life, have changed the nature of individual identity" (p. 66). How has the nature of individual identity changed in the twenty-first century? Which of these writers' explanations of that change seems most powerful and persuasive to you and why?

Sven Birkerts

Sven Birkerts (1951–) is a critic and book reviewer who writes frequently for the *New York Times Book Review,* the *Atlantic Monthly,* and the *New Republic.* Although he has taught creative writing and composition at Harvard University, Bennington College, and Emerson College, Birkerts holds no advanced degrees. His love of books came not from formal training in criticism but from years of working as a bookstore clerk who read during his lunch hour. Birkerts is the author of three books of criticism, including *The Gutenberg Elegies* (1994), from which "The Owl Has Flown" was taken.

To learn more about Birkerts, read a transcript of "Is Cyberspace Destroying Society?", a 1995 online conference in which he participated, available on the *Atlantic Monthly* Web site at <http://www.theatlantic.com/unbound/aandc/trnscrpt/birkerts.htm>.

The Owl Has Flown

Reading has a history. It was not always and everywhere the same. We may think of it as a straightforward process of lifting information from a page; but if we considered it further, we would agree that information must be sifted, sorted, and interpreted. Interpretive schemes belong to cultural configurations, which have varied enormously over time. As our ancestors lived in different mental worlds, they must have read differently, and the history of reading could be as complex as the history of thinking.

—Robert Darnton, *The Kiss of Lamourette*

Reading and thinking are kindred operations, if only because both are actually and historically invisible. Of the two, reading has the stronger claim to invisibility, for thought at least finds a home from time to time in the written sign, whereas the *reception* of the written sign leaves no trace unless in written accounts after the fact. How do people experience the written word, and how have those experiencings, each necessarily unique, changed in larger collective ways down the centuries? The few indications we have only whet the speculative impulse.

We know from historians, for example, that before the seventh century there were few who read silently (writing some centuries before, Saint Augustine professed astonishment that Saint Ambrose read without moving his lips); that in Europe in the late Middle Ages and after, designated readers often entertained or edified groups at social or work-related gatherings. Then there is the fascinating study of Menocchio, the sixteenth-century miller. Historian Carlo Ginzburg anatomizes his intellectual universe by triangulating between Menocchio's few books and the depositions taken at his trial for heresy. In *The Cheese and the Worms,* Ginzburg combines scholarly excavation with shrewd surmise to suggest how this lettered worker assembled a cosmology—one compounded in part from the rich reserves of the dominantly oral culture, and in part from his intense and methodical, if also fanciful, readings of the few texts he owned.

After Menocchio's day, with the proliferation of mechanically produced books and the general democratization of education, reading not only spread rapidly, but changed its basic nature. As Robert Darnton writes in his essay, "The First Steps Toward a History of Reading," summarizing the conclusions of his fellow historian Rolf Engelsing:

> From the Middle Ages until sometime after 1750, according to Engelsing, men read "intensively." They had only a few books—the Bible, an almanac, a devotional work or two—and they read them over and over again, usually aloud and in groups, so that a narrow range of traditional literature became deeply impressed on their consciousness. By 1800 men were reading "extensively." They read all kinds of material, especially periodicals and newspapers, and read it only once, and then raced on to the next item.

That centrifugal tendency has of course escalated right into our present, prompted as much by the expansion of higher education and the demands of social and professional commerce as by the astronomical increase in the quantity of available print. Newspapers, magazines, brochures, advertisements, and labels surround us everywhere—surround us, indeed, to the point of having turned our waking environment into a palimpsest of texts to be read, glanced at, or ignored. It is startling to recall the anecdote about the philosopher Erasmus pausing on a muddy thoroughfare to study a rare scrap of printed paper flickering at his feet.

As we now find ourselves at a cultural watershed—as the fundamental process of transmitting information is shifting from mechanical to circuit-driven, from page to screen—it may be time to ask how modifications in our way of reading may impinge upon our mental life. For how we receive information bears vitally on the ways we experience and interpret reality.

What is most conspicuous as we survey the general trajectory of reading across the centuries is what I think of as the gradual displacement of the vertical by the horizontal—the sacrifice of depth to lateral range, or, in Darnton's terms above, a shift from intensive to extensive reading. When books are rare, hard to obtain, and expensive, the reader must compensate through intensified focus, must like Menocchio read the same passages over and over, memorizing, inscribing the words deeply on the slate of the attention, subjecting them to an interpretive pressure not unlike what students of scripture practice upon their texts. This is ferocious reading—prison or "desert island" reading—and where it does not assume depth, it creates it.

In our culture, access is not a problem, but proliferation is. And the reading act is necessarily different than it was in its earliest days. Awed and intimidated by the availability of texts, faced with the all but impossible task of discriminating among them, the reader tends to move across surfaces, skimming, hastening from one site to the next without allowing the words to resonate inwardly. The inscription is light but it covers vast territories: quantity is elevated over quality. The possibility of maximum focus is undercut by the awareness of the unread texts that await. The result is that we know countless more "bits" of information, both important and trivial, than our ancestors. We know them without a stable sense of context, for where the field is that vast all schemes must be seen as provisional. We depend far less on memory; that faculty has all but atrophied from lack of use.

Interestingly, this shift from vertical to horizontal parallels the overall societal shift from bounded lifetimes spent in single locales to lives lived in geographical dispersal amid streams of data. What one loses by forsaking the village and the magnification resulting from the repetition of the familiar, one may recoup by gaining a more inclusive perspective, a sense of the world picture.

This larger access was once regarded as worldliness—one travelled, knew the life of cities, the ways of diverse people . . . It has now become the birthright of anyone who owns a television set. The modern viewer is a cosmopolitan at one remove, at least potentially. He has a window on the whole world, is positioned, no matter how poor or well-to-do, to receive virtually the same infinite stream of data as every other viewer. There is almost nothing in common between the villager conning his book of scriptures by lantern-light and the contemporary apartment dweller riffling the pages of a newspaper while attending to live televised reports from Bosnia.

How is one to assess the relative benefits and liabilities of these intrinsically different situations? How do we square the pluses and minuses of horizontal and vertical awareness? The villager, who knows every scrap of lore about his environs, is blessedly unaware of cataclysms in distant lands. News of the Lisbon earthquake of 1755 took months to travel across Europe. The media-besotted urbanite, by contrast, never loses his awareness of the tremors in different parts of the world.

We may ask, clumsily, which person is happier, or has a more vital grip on experience? The villager may have possessed his world more pungently, more sensuously; he may have found more sense in things owing both to the limited scope of his concern and the depth of his information—not to mention his basic spiritual assumptions. But I also take seriously Marx's quip about the "idiocy of rural life." Circumscribed conditions and habit suggest greater immersion in circumstance, but also dullness and limitation. The lack of a larger perspective hobbles the mind, leads to suspiciousness and wary conservativism; the clichés about peasants are probably not without foundation. But by the same token, the constant availability of data and macroperspectives has its own diminishing returns. After a while the sense of scale is attenuated and a relativism resembling cognitive and moral paralysis may result. When everything is permitted, Nietzsche said, we have nihilism; likewise, when everything is happening everywhere, it gets harder to care about anything. How do we assign value? Where do we find the fixed context that allows us to create a narrative of sense about our lives? Ideally, I suppose, one would have the best of both worlds—the purposeful fixity of the local, fertilized by the availability of enhancing vistas. A natural ecology of information and context.

We are experiencing in our times a loss of depth—a loss, that is, of the very paradigm of depth. A sense of the deep and natural connectedness of things is a function of vertical consciousness. Its apotheosis is what was once called wisdom. Wisdom: the knowing not of facts but of truths about human nature and the processes of life. But swamped by data, and in thrall to the technologies that manipulate it, we no longer think in these larger and necessarily more imprecise terms. In our lateral age, living in the bureaucracies of information, we don't venture a claim to that kind of understanding. Indeed, we tend to act embarrassed around those once-freighted terms—*truth, meaning, soul, destiny* . . . We suspect the people who use such words of being soft and nostalgic. We prefer the deflating one-liner that reassures us that nothing need be taken that seriously; we inhale the atmospheres of irony.

Except, of course, when our systems break down and we hurry to the therapist's office. Then, trying to construct significant narratives that include and explain us, we reach back into that older lexicon. "'My life doesn't seem to make sense—things don't seem to mean very much." But the therapist's office is a contained place, a parenthetic enclosure away from the general bustle. Very little of what transpires there is put into social circulation. Few people would risk exposing their vulnerable recognitions to the public glare.

The depth awareness, where it exists, is guarded as a secret. If we have truly wise people among us, they avoid the spotlights—it is part of their wisdom to do so. For the fact is that there is no public space available to individuals who profess the vertical awareness. At best there are pop pulpits, public television slots that can accommodate a Joseph Campbell, Betty Friedan, or Rabbi Kushner.

Wisdom, an ideal that originated in the oral epochs—Solomon and Socrates represent wisdom incarnate, and Athena or Minerva were wisdom deified—is predicated on the assumption that one person can somehow grasp a total picture of life and its laws, comprehending the whole and the relation of parts. To *comprehend:* to "hold together." We once presumed that those parts added up, that there was some purpose or explanation to our being here below. If that purpose could not be fully fathomed, if it rested with God or Providence, it could at least be addressed and questioned.

The explosion of data—along with general societal secularization and the collapse of what the theorists call the "master narratives" (Christian, Marxist, Freudian, humanist . . .)—has all but destroyed the premise of understandability. Inundated by perspectives, by lateral vistas of information that stretch endlessly in every direction, we no longer accept the possibility of assembling a complete picture. Instead of carrying on the ancient project of philosophy—attempting to discover the "truth" of things—we direct our energies to managing information. The computer, our high-speed, accessing, storing, and sorting tool, appears as a godsend. It increasingly determines what kind of information we are willing to traffic in; if something cannot be written in code and transmitted, it cannot be important.

The old growth forests of philosophy have been logged and the owl of Minerva has fled. Wisdom can only survive as a cultural ideal where there is a possibility of vertical consciousness. Wisdom has nothing to do with the gathering or organizing of facts—this is basic. Wisdom is a seeing *through* facts, a penetration to the underlying laws and patterns. It relates the immediate to something larger—a context, yes, but also to a big picture that refers to human endeavor *sub specie aeternitatis,* under the aspect of eternity. To see through data, one must have something to see through *to*. One must believe in the possibility of a comprehensible whole. In philosophy this is called the "hermeneutic circle"—one needs the ends to know which means to use, and the means to know which ends are possible. And this assumption of ends is what we have lost. It is one thing to absorb a fact, to situate it alongside other facts in a configuration, and quite another to contemplate that fact at leisure, allowing it to declare its connection with other facts, its thematic destiny, its resonance.

Resonance—there is no wisdom without it. Resonance is a natural phenomenon, the shadow of import alongside the body of fact, and it cannot flourish except in deep time. Where time has been commodified, flattened, turned into yet another thing measured, there is no chance that any piece of information can unfold its potential significance. We are destroying this deep time. Not by design, perhaps, but inadvertently. Where the electronic impulse rules, and where the psyche is conditioned to work with data, the experience of deep time is impossible. No deep time, no resonance; no resonance, no wisdom. The only remaining oases are churches (for those who still worship) and the offices of therapists. There, paying dearly for fifty minutes, the client gropes for a sense of coherence and mattering. The therapist listens, not so much explaining as simply fostering the possibility of resonance. She allows the long pauses and silences—a bold subversion of societal expectations—because only where silence is possible can the vertical engagement take place.

There is one other place of sanctuary. Not a physical place—not church or office—but a metaphysical one. Depth survives, condensed and enfolded, in authentic works of art. In anything that can grant us true aesthetic experience. For this experience is vertical; it transpires in deep time and, in a sense, secures that time for us. Immersed in a ballet performance, planted in front of a painting, we shatter the horizontal plane. Not without some expense of energy, however. The more we live according to the lateral orientation, the greater a blow is required, and the more disorienting is the effect. A rather unfortunate vicious cycle can result, for the harder it is to do the work, the less inclined we are to do it. Paradoxically, the harder the work, the more we need to do it. We cannot be put off by the prospect of fatigue or any incentive-withering sense of obligation.

What is true of art is true of serious reading as well. Fewer and fewer people, it seems, have the leisure or the inclination to undertake it. And true reading is hard. Unless we are practiced, we do not just crack the covers and slip into an alternate world. We do not get swept up as readily as we might be by the big-screen excitements of film. But if we do read perseveringly we make available to ourselves, in a most portable form, an ulterior existence. We hold in our hands a way to cut against the momentum of the times. We can resist the skimming tendency and delve; we can restore, if only for a time, the vanishing assumption of coherence. The beauty of the vertical engagement is that it does not have to argue for itself. It is self-contained, a fulfillment.

1994

GETTING STARTED

1. Working individually or in groups, list several qualities that Birkerts associates with "loss of depth." Then list qualities that Birkerts associates with "wisdom" and "resonance." Report to the class on the differences you see between those two lists.

2. Birkerts uses a series of oppositions such as intensive/extensive, vertical/horizontal, and quantity/quality. How do such oppositions help him organize ideas for his readers? How do such oppositions help him make sense of reading practices over time? Do you see

your own reading practices as being either intensive or extensive, either vertical or horizontal?

3. Find two passages or examples from Birkerts's text that help you to explain what he means by "deep time." Take notes explaining as much as you can about each definition or example. Bring your notes and citations (page numbers for each definition or example) to class.

4. Walk down a street on your campus or in your town or city and take note of all the written language that you see (signs, newspapers, advertisements, logos, and so on). Write a paragraph explaining how you decide which written texts to attend to in your everyday life. How much of the language do you notice, and how much do you ignore? Are these texts meant for you? How do you know? Do you feel that the world around you produces too many texts?

5. Birkerts argues that, because of our reading habits, our memory has "all but atrophied from lack of use" (p. 74). On a sheet of paper, write down the longest quote you can remember from a written or spoken source. After this, write down the longest poem or song lyric you can remember. How does your memory rate? Can you explain why you have remembered what you have?

WRITING

6. What does Birkerts see as the difference between discovering "truth" and "managing information"? Are these two complementary, mutually exclusive, or two sides of the same coin? Write a paper in which you explore these ideas and apply them to your own reading practices.

7. Write an essay in which you use Birkerts's ideas to analyze your Internet experience (in question 9). Your response should consider some of the following questions: To what extent did your reading on the Web demonstrate the "loss of depth," or "lateral" reading, that Birkerts talks about? To what extent did it create a different kind of reading? To what extent did it involve "wisdom" and "resonance" as he defines them? Is it possible to experience "deep time" on the Internet?

USING THE LIBRARY AND THE INTERNET

8. Look up the myth of Minerva in an encyclopedia or on the Internet. Why does Birkerts choose the myth of Minerva and the owl as a metaphor? What does Birkerts's use of the myth tell you about his sense of his audience?

9. Spend thirty minutes surfing the Internet with a pen next to your keyboard. Take notes on the kinds of reading that you do as you surf. Afterwards, write a one-page paper telling the detailed story of your surfing experiences: where you went, what you read, how you read, what you saw, and what you skipped over.

MAKING CONNECTIONS

10. In "The Triumph of Tinkering," Sherry Turkle argues that how we use technology—and how we teach others to use it—determines its value as a positive or negative force in culture. Use Birkerts's concepts of "deep time" and "loss of depth" to analyze the different experiences of the students described in Turkle's essay. Would his analysis differ from Turkle's? Why or why not?

11. Use Birkerts's discussion of vertical and horizontal consciousness to help you analyze Gloria Anzaldúa's "reading" of the Aztec exhibition in the Denver Museum of Natural History. In what ways are Birkerts's discussions of reading and wisdom similar to (or different from) Anzaldúa's experience of attending the exhibition? Why might Anzaldúa object to your use of Birkerts's terminology as a framework to interpret her arguments?

12. Birkerts argues that, amidst our world of surfaces, "depth survives, condensed and enfolded, in authentic works of art" (p. 77). Compare Birkerts's brief comment to Jeanette Winterson's more complete statement about the value of art in "Imagination and Reality." What does art *do* that makes it so important to these two writers?

Wanda M. Corn

Wanda M. Corn (1940–) is the Robert and Ruth Halperin Professor in Art History and a scholar of American art and visual culture at Stanford University. She is particularly interested in the art and artists of the Gilded Age and of the early modern period. Corn has been honored for both her teaching and her scholarship. She has curated numerous museum exhibitions and served as a Commissioner of the National Museum of American Art. Corn is the author of *The Color of Mood: American Tonalism 1880–1910* (1972); *Grant Wood: The Regionalist Vision* (1983); and *The Great American Thing: Modern Art and National Identity, 1915–1935* (1999). In "The Birth of a National Icon: Grant Wood's *American Gothic*," Corn notes that Wood's *American Gothic* is one of the most parodied paintings in American art.

To see some of those parodies, visit <http://www.bcpl.net/~glake/am.html>.

The Birth of a National Icon:
Grant Wood's *American Gothic*

Everyone knows the image: the stern midwestern couple with a pitchfork, standing in front of a trim white farmhouse, their oval heads framing the little building's Gothic window (fig. 9). Though simple, plain, and nameless, the man and woman in *American Gothic* have become as familiar to Americans as the *Mona Lisa*. Their image, mercilessly caricatured and distorted, pervades our culture; greeting card companies use it to wish people well on their anniversaries; political cartoonists change the faces to lampoon the country's First Family; and advertisers, substituting a toothbrush, calculator, or martini glass for the pitchfork, exploit the couple to sell us merchandise.

These parodies may tell us what some Americans think the painting is about, but they say little about what Grant Wood (1891–1942) intended when in 1930 he painted this relatively small (30 × 25 inches) picture. Did Wood want us to laugh at his deadly serious couple? Was he satirizing rural narrow-mindedness, as many critics and historians have claimed? If so, then what motivated this loyal son of Iowa to mock his countrymen? Who, in fact, are the man and woman in the painting and why do they look as though they could have just

FIGURE 9 Grant Wood, *American Gothic,* 1930. Oil on composition board. 30 × 25 inches. (Friends of the American Art Collection, all rights reserved by the Art Institute of Chicago and VAGA, New York, 1930.934.)

stepped out of the late nineteenth century? And, as modern Americans had shown little or no interest in midwestern themes, how did Wood, midway through his career, come to paint *American Gothic* at all?

The literature on the painting is not extensive and offers little help in answering our questions.[1] It makes two principal claims about *American Gothic,* the first being that the painting's most important sources are European. Nearly every historian and critic credits the artist's visit to Munich in the fall of 1928, and his study of the northern Renaissance masterpieces in the Alte Pinakothek, as decisive. There is no doubt that the artist's imagery and style changed around the time of this trip. For the previous fifteen years Wood had been painting loose, quasi-impressionist landscapes. After Munich he inaugurated a new style, one characterized by static compositions, streamlined forms, crisp geometries, and repeating patterns. By Wood's own admission, the Flemish painters were an important stimulus. But historians and critics have tended to glamorize the tale, writing of Wood's Munich visit as if it were a kind of religious conversion experience.

The second claim made about *American Gothic* is that the work is satirical, that Wood is ridiculing or mocking the complacency and conformity of midwestern life. This interpretation seems to have originated in the early 1930s on the East Coast and has been conventional historical wisdom ever since. Reviewing the work in 1930 when it was shown at the Art Institute of Chicago, a critic for the *Boston Herald,* Walter P. Eaton, found the couple "caricatured so slightly that it is doubly cruel, and though we know nothing of the artist and his history, we cannot help believing that as a youth he suffered tortures from these people."[2] In the 1940s H. W Janson came to a similar conclusion: Wood intended *American Gothic* as a "satire on small town life," in the caustic spirit of Sinclair Lewis and H. L. Mencken.[3] In more recent times art historian Matthew Baigell considered the couple savage, exuding "a generalized, barely repressed animosity that borders on venom." The painting, Baigell argued, satirized "people who would live in a pretentious house with medieval ornamentation, as well as the narrow prejudices associated with life in the Bible Belt."[4] In his book-length study of the artist, James Dennis characterized Grant Wood as a "cosmopolitan satirist" and *American Gothic* as a "satiric interpretation of complacent narrow-mindedness."[5]

For the moment, let us set aside the characterization of *American Gothic* as neo-Flemish and satirical and ignore the many parodies of the image so as to see the work afresh. By looking at Grant Wood's midwestern background and his process of creation, we shall find that American sources—not European ones—best explain his famous painting. It will become clear that Iowa architecture, frontier photographs, and midwestern literature and history are much more relevant to an understanding of Wood's painting than are the Flemish masters. Furthermore, a close study of American materials refutes the notion that Wood intended to satirize his couple-with-pitchfork.

The immediate genesis of the painting occurred while Wood was visiting friends in the tiny southern Iowa town of Eldon and came across a little Gothic Revival wooden farmhouse (fig. 10).[6] Not having a word to describe it—the term "Gothic Revival" was not yet current—Wood called it an "American Gothic" house to distinguish it from the French Gothic of European cathedrals.[7] Modest in its size, this house belonged in kind to the hundreds of cottage Gothic homes and farmhouses built throughout Iowa in the latter half of the nineteenth century, when the state was being settled. What caught the artist's eye about this particular example was its simple and emphatic

Figure 10 House in *American Gothic,* built 1881–82. Photograph, 1976. Eldon, Iowa. (Steve Ohrn/Iowa State Historical Society.)

design—its prominent, oversized neo-Gothic window and its vertical board-and-batten siding. The structure immediately suggested to him a long-faced and lean country couple—"American Gothic people to stand in front of a house of this type," as he put it.[8] He made a small oil study of the house, had a friend photograph the structure, and went back to Cedar Rapids, where he persuaded his sister Nan and his dentist, Dr. McKeeby, to become his models.

The couple, Wood tells us, looked like the "kind of people I fancied should live in that house."[9] This is a fact missed by almost all of the painting's interpreters: the painting does not depict up-to-date 1930 Iowans, but rather shows people who could be of the same vintage as the 1881–82 house.[10] To make the couple look archaic, Wood turned to old photographs as sources. He dressed his two models as if they were "tintypes from my old family album," a collection of ancestral photographs which Wood greatly valued and which today is at the Davenport Museum of Art in Iowa.[11] His thirty-year-old sister became transformed from a 1930s woman into a plausible stand-in for one of his nineteenth-century relatives. On his instructions, Nan made an old-fashioned apron trimmed with rickrack taken from an old dress and pulled her marcelled hair back tightly from her face. Wearing the apron with a brooch and a white-collared dress, her appearance now recalled the photographs in Wood's family album. For Dr. McKeeby, the male model in *American Gothic,* Wood found an old-fashioned collarless shirt among his painting rags, to be worn with bibbed overalls and a dark jacket.[12]

Wood adapted not only the dress from late nineteenth-century photographs, but also the poses and demeanor: the stiff upright torsos, the unblinking eyes, and the mute stony faces characteristic of long-exposure studio portraits. In placing the man and woman squarely in front of their house, he borrowed another popular late nineteenth-century convention drawn from the itinerant photographers who posed couples and families in front of their homes (fig. 11). This practice, common in the rural Midwest through World War I, produced untold numbers of photographs, all recording the pride of home as much as a likeness of the inhabitants.

It is common in these photographs to see potted plants decorating the porches and lawns. Indoor plants moved to an outside porch during the spring and summer gave evidence of a woman's horticultural skills and were also a source of pride; in the Midwest it was hard to keep plants alive during the long and bitter winters. When Wood put potted plants on the porch of the house in *American Gothic,* just over the right shoulder of the woman, he was providing her with an appropriate attribute of homemaking and domesticity.

The man's attribute, of course, is the pitchfork. Wood's initial idea was to have the man hold a rake; this was the way he rendered the scene in a preliminary pencil study hastily sketched on the back of an envelope.[13] For reasons of design he discarded the rake for the

FIGURE 11 Solomon D. Butcher, *Mr. Story, 1 mile N.E. of Miller on Wood River, Buffalo County, Nebraska,* 1909. (Photograph courtesy of Nebraska State Historical Society, Solomon D. Butcher Collection.)

pitchfork to emphasize the verticality of the long faces and the slender Gothic window. But it was also because the artist wanted to use a tool clearly associated with farming—not gardening—and with late nineteenth-century farming at that. This offended one Iowa farmer's wife who, viewing the picture in 1930, objected: 'We at least have progressed beyond the three-tined pitchfork stage!"[14]

Whether rake or pitchfork, the idea of the man holding a tool came from old frontier photographs in which men and women, in keeping with an even older painting convention, held objects appropriate to their status and occupation. Men held shovels, rakes, or pitchforks, while women leaned on brooms or chairs. In photography, of course, the long-handled tool was more than an occupational emblem; it helped steady the holder during the long exposure necessitated by slow films and cameras. A classic photograph of this type, dating from the 1880s and showing the man holding a pitchfork and the woman leaning on a chair, is by the Nebraskan itinerant photographer Solomon Butcher (Nebraska State Historical Society). The couple's home is prairie sod rather than American Gothic, but the convention is precisely the one used by Grant Wood, right down to the pioneer woman's potted plants in tin cans on the table by the doorway.

Wood responded to all kinds of old visual sources besides photographs: furniture, china, glass, quilts, popular prints, maps, and atlases. Some of these things were handed down to him as family treasures; other items he bought. He valued objects in keeping with his own aesthetic of simple design and pattern—Victorian oval frames or braided rugs—as well as things that reflected Iowa history. Blue Willow china was important to him because it had been one of the precious luxuries pioneer families had brought with them from the East; he also gave prominent places in his home to the hand-made wooden neo-Gothic clock and sewing box, and the piecrust table that his family had used on the farm.[15]

He borrowed omnivorously from these sources for all of his important paintings. *Fall Plowing* (1931) and other landscapes hark back, in their bird's-eye views and quilted fields, to the primitive prints of farms and villages in a nineteenth-century regional atlas (figs. 12, 13). In 1930, the same year *American Gothic* was painted, Wood made a work that blended a complex range of historical sources. For the Stamats family of Cedar Rapids he painted a five-and-one-half-foot-long overmantel to go above a fireplace, reviving the late eighteenth- and early nineteenth-century taste for large painted landscapes as wall decorations (fig. 14). He took, he said, the elliptical shape of the painting from an old oval china platter; the stylized bulbous trees from his mother's Blue Willow china; and the floral border, as well as the composition of the family strolling in front of its house, from Victorian

FIGURE 12 Grant Wood, *Fall Plowing*, 1931. Oil on canvas, 30 × 30¾ inches. Deere & Co., East Moline, Ill. (© Estate of Grant Wood/Licensed by VAGA, New York, N.Y.)

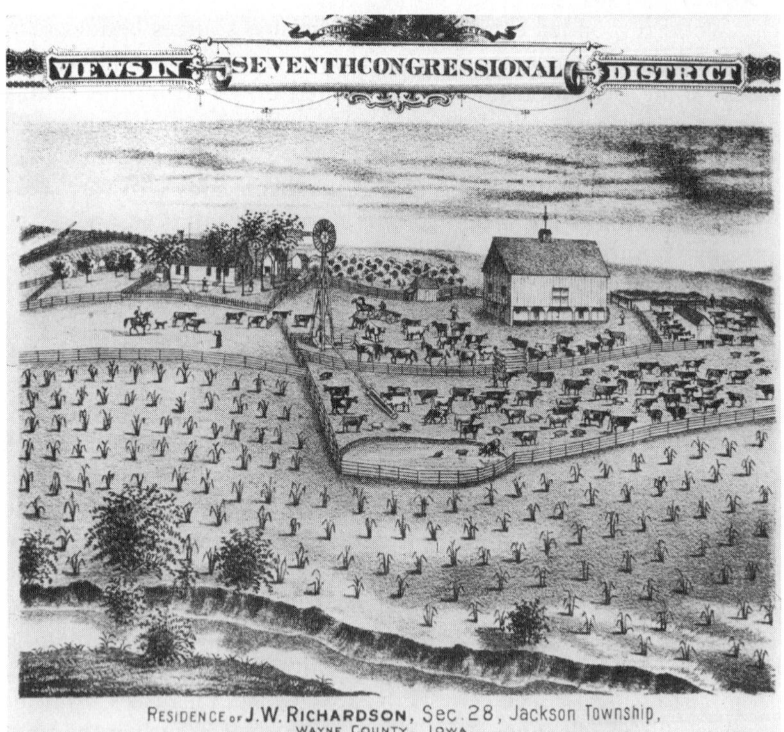

FIGURE 13 "Residence of J. W. Richardson." Lithograph. From *A. T. Andreas' Illustrated Historical Atlas of the State of Iowa* (1875).

FIGURE 14 Grant Wood, *Overmantel Decoration,* Stamats house. Cedar Rapids. 1930. Oil on composition board, 42 × 65 inches. (Cedar Rapids Museum of Art, gift of Isabel R. Stamats in memory of Herbert S. Stamats.)

prints, particularly from ones by Currier and Ives (fig. 15).[16] To add a final touch of historicism, Wood painted the family in nineteenth-century costumes.

Wood's collecting habits and enthusiasm for antiques were part of a nationwide enthusiasm in the late 1910s and the 1920s for old American art and artifacts. This new pride in American things and in national history reflected the country's confidence as it emerged as a world power after World War I. Where Americans had been embarrassed before by their provincial history, now they began to treasure and research their past. Furniture and paintings that had once seemed awkward and second-rate now became charming and quaint—on their way to becoming valuable antiques. Signposts of this antiquarian movement dot the decade: the first exhibitions of nineteenth-century American folk art occurred in 1924; the American Wing opened at the Metropolitan Museum of Art in New York in that same year; in 1926 the nation celebrated its 150th birthday; the restoration of Colonial Williamsburg began in 1927; and in 1929 Henry Ford dedicated the Henry Ford Museum and Greenfield Village in Dearborn, Michigan. It was in the 1920s, as Russell Lynes has observed in his book on American taste, that "wagon wheels became ceiling fixtures, cobbler's benches became coffee tables; black caldrons and kettles hung on irons in fireplaces."[17] "The last touch of absurdity" in the public's embrace of old artifacts, Lewis Mumford caustically observed, was a government bulletin

FIGURE 15 F. F. Palmer, for Currier and Ives, *Life in the Country—Evening,* 1862. Lithograph.

which "suggested that every American house should have at least one 'early American' room."[18]

The passion for early Americana centered on colonial and federal period antiques and architecture. Neocolonial houses, appearing first on the East Coast during the eclectic revivalism of the late nineteenth century, now became popular throughout America, in Iowa and California as well as in New England. Wood painted the overmantel for Mr. and Mrs. Herbert Stamats for just such a house: in that overmantel one can see the 1929 neocolonial structure with its Cedar Rapids family standing in front (see fig. 14). But the fact that Wood painted the overmantel in a neo-Victorian style rather than a neocolonial one is significant, for it suggests that Wood's appreciation of the American past was much broader than that of the period's tastemakers. For most people in the 1920s the arts of Victorian America were ugly, unimaginative, and too reliant upon revival styles.[19] But Wood, self-taught as a connoisseur of Iowa artifacts, came to see that his midwestern heritage was of the nineteenth century, not the eighteenth; Victorian, not colonial. It was for this reason that Wood put a very plain neo-Gothic house behind his couple (see fig. 10). As a close observer, he recognized that Gothic Revival architecture was one of the oldest building styles in the Midwest, and that it provided the same distinctive flavor in his region that saltbox houses gave to New England.

Although Wood seldom talked about his tastes, they fell into patterns. First, as we have already seen, he enjoyed certain pieces of Victoriana such as old photographs, Currier and Ives prints, and oval frames. His strong preference. however, was for objects which had a "folk" look to them, things which were handcrafted or homespun, simple in design, clean in line, or boldly patterned. He liked stenciled country furniture, punched tinware, braided rugs, quilts, and the look of white cupboards with black handwrought iron fixtures.[20] In this he was the midwestern counterpart of those East Coast artists—Charles Sheeler or Hamilton Easter Field, for example—who in the 1910s and 1920s collected American primitives, Pennsylvania German illuminations, and country furniture.[21]

What distinguished Wood's taste from that of eastern artists, however, was his intense interest in items that were not only well designed but reflected the particulars of midwestern history. Sheeler collected Shaker furniture and painted it because he liked its "modern" aesthetic, its functional lines, and its simple geometries. When Wood collected or painted regional artifacts, it was because of their historical significance as well as their aesthetic qualities. In *Fall Plowing* (see fig. 12), he depicted one of the steel plows used by midwestern pioneers to turn the tough prairie sod into farmland. Invented by John Deere around 1840, this kind of plow cut the heavy sod easily and self-scoured itself in the Midwest's moist, sticky soil. It replaced the unsuitable equipment pioneers brought with them from the East. Grant Wood relished the crisp, abstract curves of the steel plow, but at the same time he celebrated its centrality in Iowa's history. In his painting the plow stands alone, without a man to guide it or a horse to pull it, like a sacred relic.[22] A similar conjunction of abstract design and historical association explains Wood's attraction to the farmhouse in *American Gothic*. Even as he greatly admired the formal and repeated verticals of its board-and-batten walls and the mullions of the windows, Wood believed that the structure, in its modest proportions, stark neatness, and unembellished lines, evoked the character of the Midwest. "I know now," Wood said in 1932, "that our cardboardy frame houses on Iowa farms have a distinct American quality and are very paintable. To me their hard edges are especially suggestive of the Middle West civilization."[23]

Wood's interest in clean lines and patterns reflects the modernism of the period. But how, one wonders, did he develop the notion that "hard edges" were distinctively midwestern? Why was he even interested in midwestern buildings, people, and landscapes at a time when every painter considered the middle states an artistic wasteland?

In fact, it was American writers who led Wood to discover and believe in the artistic worth of the Midwest as a subject.[24] When Grant Wood painted *American Gothic* in 1930, writers had been defining the uniqueness of midwestern life for almost half a century. One of the first of these was Hamlin Garland. With *Main-Travelled Roads* (1891), *Prairie Folks* (1892), and *Boy Life on the Prairie* (1899), Garland gained international recognition for his depictions of pioneering and farm life in Iowa, Wisconsin, and the Dakotas, the region he called the "Middle Border."[25] These local-color stories featured vivid descriptions, thick dialects, and idiosyncratic characters and events. Many recounted prairie living as harsh and bleak, giving, Garland said, "a proper proportion of the sweat, flies, heat, dirt and drudgery" of farm life.[26] He was among the first to create a literary notion of the midwesterner as rural, raw, and tough—as "hard-edged."

Even if they hated his harsh views—or the fact that he wrote about the prairie while living in Boston—every subsequent native artist of Garland's "Middle Border," whether painter or writer, would be indebted to him for defining the Midwest as having a distinct regional character. Furthermore, Garland's success conveyed to future generations a clear message: the open land, farm culture, and small towns of the Midwest were not a wasteland but a rich source of artistic material. It is hard to imagine Wood's career—and that of a score of writers—without Garland's example.

In imagery, however, Wood's work depends even more on the next generation of midwestern writers, those of the 1920s, who rejected the highly descriptive prose of Garland and other local colorists to write more crisply and emphatically about what they viewed as archetypical of their region. The most famous of these was Sinclair Lewis, a Minnesotan, whose delineations of the midwestern small town in *Main Street* (1920) and of its booster and materialist mentality in *Babbitt* (1922) became best-sellers. Wood greatly admired these books and publicly credited Lewis for the new "yearning after the arts in the corn-and-beef belt."[27]

Typically, Wood was not very precise regarding what he liked about Lewis's books other than that they were about the Midwest. But one quality surely impressed him: *Main Street* and *Babbitt* were about general character types, not about specific individuals. Carol Kennicott, for example, the central figure in *Main Street,* is a college-educated, idealistic crusader for culture and social reform. Lewis drew her portrait in such a general way that she, along with every other denizen of Gopher Prairie, Minnesota, could be recognized as types found in small towns across the United States. In 1936–37 Wood paid tribute to Lewis by doing the illustrations for a special limited edition of *Main Street.*[28] The names Wood assigned to his nine drawings, all but two of which depict characters in the book, are not of those individuals but of types—The Booster, The Sentimental Yearner, The Practical Idealist.

The man and woman in *American Gothic,* of course, also constitute a type; they are definitely not individualized portraits. But it is an oft-made mistake to compare Wood's couple with the "solid citizen" types featured in Lewis's novels. Sinclair Lewis wrote about modern Americans who lived in towns. traveled in trains and cars, listened to the radio, and went to the movies. While many of them were complacent, conformist, and narrow-minded—traits often attributed to the couple in *American Gothic*—they were not pitchfork-carrying, country types. Grant Wood's folks live in town—you can just catch sight of a church steeple rising over the trees to the left—but it is clear from their dress, their home, and their demeanor that their orientation is rural and behind the times. Their values are Victorian ones, not the modern ones of a Carol Kennicott or a George Babbitt.

It was East Coast critics who first compared Wood's work to that of Sinclair Lewis. Local Iowans knew better; the literary parallels they drew were to contemporary Iowan writers, most particularly Jay Sigmund and Ruth Suckow.[29] Wood, they said, was doing in paint what Sigmund and Suckow for some years had been doing in words: creating significant art out of regional materials. This comparison was apt, for Wood was a great admirer of both writers. Jay Sigmund lived in Cedar Rapids and he and Wood had become close friends a few years before the creation of *American Gothic*. Making his living as an insurance salesman, Sigmund was also an accomplished outdoorsman, a historian of the Wapsipinicon River Valley, and a writer, publishing books of Iowa verse and prose: *Frescoes* in 1922 and *Land O'Maize Folk* in 1924. Sigmund's literary reputation was regional; Ruth Suckow's writing, on the other hand, won her a national following. Her short stories about Iowa were published in H. L. Mencken's *Smart Set* and *American Mercury*, and her novel *The Folks* appeared in 1934 and became a best-seller. Most influential on Wood were probably her first novel, *Country People* (1924), and her collection of short stories, *Iowa Interiors* (1926).[30]

As suggested by titles such as *Land O'Maize Folk* and *Country People*, Sigmund and Suckow wrote about country types, not Sinclair Lewis's *Main Street* types. The farmer, the villager, and the rural family are their protagonists; the couple in *American Gothic* could have stepped out of their pages. The man might well have belonged to what Suckow termed the "retired farmer element" in the town, men who were "narrow cautious, steady and thrifty, suspicious of 'culture' but faithful to the churches."[31] And the woman might have been one of Sigmund's "drab and angular" midwestern spinsters whose moral propriety and excessive duty to family kept her at home caring for a widowed parent.[32] It may come as a surprise that Wood's intention from the outset was to paint an unmarried daughter and her father in *American Gothic*, not a man and wife. In seeking models for the painting, he wanted, he said, to ask an "old maid" to pose but was too embarrassed.[33] So his thirty-year-old married sister agreed to play spinster and to stand next to the sixty-two-year-old dentist playing the father. When the painting was completed and the couple interpreted as man and wife, Wood rarely went to the trouble of explaining otherwise, undoubtedly pleased that it could just as easily be read as a married couple. Indeed, thereafter he himself occasionally referred to the couple as man and wife.[34]

The man and woman in *American Gothic* are "Victorian survivals," more at home in the rural world Grant Wood had known as a child than in the modern Iowa of his adulthood. During the first years of his life, from 1891 to 1901, Wood had lived on a country farm, attended school in a one-room schoolhouse, walked behind the horsedrawn plow, and endured spinster aunts, one of whom, he remembered, pulled her hair back so tightly that he wondered "how she could close her eyes at night."[35] The most exciting event of each childhood year was threshing day, when the big machines and neighboring farmers arrived to help thresh the grain. The threshers' noontime meal was a feast, brimming the little farmhouse over with people, smells, and activity.[36]

Thirty years later, Grant Wood began to paint those scenes. Sitting in his Cedar Rapids studio with a telephone at his elbow and cars going by the window, he painted the spinster in *American Gothic,* the walking plow in *Fall Plowing* (see fig. 12); the one-room schoolhouse on an unpaved road with its hand pump, woodshed, and outhouse in *Arbor Day* (fig. 16); and the noonday harvest meal in *Dinner for Threshers* (Fine Arts Museums of San Francisco). Like *American*

FIGURE 16 Grant Wood, *Arbor Day,* 1932. Oil on masonite panel, 25 × 30 inches. Private collection. (© Estate of Grant Wood/Licensed by VAGA, New York, N.Y.)

Gothic, each of these was on its way to becoming a relic when Wood painted it. By 1930 children rode on motor buses over paved roads to consolidated schools with modern plumbing, tractors plowed the fields, combines made threshing days obsolete, and spinster aunts no longer dominated the family stage as they had in Victorian America.

One wonders, then, about the spirit in which Wood painted. Did he work out of a deep sense of regret about contemporary life, or, as his most recent biographer has suggested, out of a disposition to "withdraw from industrial-urban society"?[37] Neither formulation seems adequate. The facts are that Grant Wood lived contentedly in the modern world and never complained of Cedar Rapids and Iowa City, the two cities in which he lived. He never attempted to farm or to live in the country. His friends were city people like himself. But having experienced a bifurcated life, ten years on a farm followed by thirty in Cedar Rapids, Wood recognized that the insular, rural world into which he had been born was slowly disappearing, that in his own lifetime the telephone, tractor, automobile, radio, and cinema were bringing that era to an end. Here, too, he may have been sensitized by the dominant theme of Ruth Suckow's writing—the gulf between modern, 1920s lifestyles and the nineteenth-century patterns still followed by older rural and country people. Suckow, who always used regional materials to explore broad human issues, made of midwestern generational conflict a vehicle with which to discuss the toll of social change on families. Over and over she wrote of the sadness and incomprehension that result from the horse-and-plow farmer confronting the lifestyles and the values of his car-driving, city-dwelling children.[38]

Wood's response to this confrontation was different. Only occasionally, as in *Victorian Survival,* did he paint it head-on. In Wood's other "ancestor" paintings, as we may term them, he sought to capture the uniqueness of his past and to memorialize his midwestern heritage. Ignoring the technological changes occurring around him, Wood painted his "roots." He wanted to know where his culture had come from, not where it was going. In the same spirit that motivated Americans to collect and restore discarded American folk paintings, or to rehabilitate eighteenth-century colonial villages, Wood painted "bits of American folklore that are too good to lose."[39]

Indeed, the best way to think of this artist is as a kind of folklorist searching out indigenous legends. On two occasions he painted national folktales. In *The Midnight Ride of Paul Revere* of 1931 (Metropolitan Museum of Art), Wood depicted the famous nocturnal gallop warning New Englanders that the British were coming. Later in the decade he painted *Parson Weems' Fable* (1939, Amon Carter Museum, Fort Worth, Texas), a large work retelling the famous tale of the young George Washington cutting down the cherry tree. What challenged Wood most, however, was regional folklore, particularly that of the common farmer, whose culture, Wood believed, formed the bedrock of midwestern life.[40] Farm folklore had never become an integral part of America's national self-image. In the 1920s, indeed, many Americans often thought of the farmer as a "hayseed" or "hick," fortifying the belief that the nation's breadbasket had no history of any interest or consequence. Wood thought otherwise. In *American Gothic* he honored the anonymous midwestern men and women who tamed the prairie, built the towns, and created America's "fertile crescent"—and who, in the process, became insular, set in their ways, and fiercely devoted to home and land. In *Fall Plowing,* Wood celebrated the farmer's harvests, while in *Arbor Day* and *Dinner for Threshers* he transformed annual rituals of rural life into quaint and colorful folktales.

In all of Wood's historical paintings, whether of national or regional themes, the legendary qualities are never bombastic or heroic. Unlike other American regionalists who painted rural life, Wood rarely aggrandized his figures through exaggerated scale, classical idealization, or old master grandiloquence.[41] His paintings tend to be small, his figures closer to puppets or dolls than gods and goddesses. Indeed there is a levity about Wood's work that rescues it from sentimental heroism or strident patriotism. Paul Revere appears to ride a child's hobbyhorse through a storybook landscape constructed of papier mâché and building blocks. In *Dinner for Threshers,* a panel modeled after a religious triptych, the participants look like clothespin dolls in a Victorian dollhouse, not like saints. And the man and woman standing in front of their "cardboardy frame house" in *American Gothic* are so flat and self-contained they could be children's cut-outs.

Sometimes these whimsical, storybook qualities shade into humor, a fact that has confused Wood's critics and led many to think Wood is ridiculing or making fun of his subjects. This is not the case; Wood's use of humor was gentle and good-natured, not mocking or contemptuous. It was a device he used to convey charm and quaintness and to give his works the light-hearted quality of storybook legends. And most important, he found that humor helped create convincing character types. In *American Gothic* we cannot help but smile at the ways Wood emphasized the "hard-edged" midwestern character of his rural couple. He expressed the man's maleness—and rigid personality—in the cold, steely tines of the pitchfork, then playfully mimicked these qualities in the limp seams of his overalls and in the delicate tracery of the Gothic window. To suggest the spinster's unfulfilled womanhood, Wood flattened her bosom and then decorated her apron with a circle-and-dot motif, a form he might well have thought of as a kind of miniature breast hieroglyph. And to underline the controlled and predictable nature of the couple's life, Wood allowed a single strand of wayward hair to escape from the woman's bun and snake mischievously down her neck. It is the only unruly element in an otherwise immaculate conception.

Though he was quiet, slow of speech, and somewhat shy, Grant Wood was one of the finer wits of Cedar Rapids. But until *American Gothic,* his humor surfaced only in conversation, at parties, or in the gag pieces he made for friends and for his studio-apartment.[42] His art was of a different order, serious and reserved. One can argue, in fact, that only when Wood harnessed his gentle wit and made it an integral part of his art did he arrive at a personal and mature style. When he had struggled in 1928 and 1929 in *John B. Turner, Pioneer* (Cedar Rapids Museum of Art) and *Woman with Plants* (fig. 17) to create images of the pioneer, the results were heavy-handed, the types not clearly drawn. For these works Wood chose Iowa settlers as models, people whose faces, he thought, recorded the pioneer experience.

FIGURE 17 Grant Wood. *Woman with Plants,* 1929. Oil on composition board, 20½ × 18 inches. (Cedar Rapids Museum of Art, Art Association Purchase.)

Wood painted John B. Turner as a successful Cedar Rapids businessman, but to indicate his personal history the artist posed him against an 1869 map of the area in Iowa where Turner had settled in the 1880s as a young man.[43] The model for *Woman with Plants,* Hattie Weaver Wood, was the artist's seventy-one-year-old mother—who had been born in Iowa during its early settlement; taught school in a prairie town, and farmed with her husband until his early death in 1901.[44] Experimenting with ideas that would become central to *American Gothic,* Wood dressed his mother as a country woman and had her hold a pioneer woman's attribute, the hardy sansevieria plant popular on the frontier. At either side of her he placed other houseplants, a begonia and a geranium. Though she by now lived with the artist in Cedar Rapids, he depicted her expressionless and still against an emblematic background of farmland, barn, and windmill. In its tightly focused realm and stylized line, *Woman with Plants* reflects the artist's study of the northern Renaissance masters the previous year. It is the most "Flemish" painting Wood ever did. He simulated the translucent qualities of a Flemish work by patiently building up the painted surface with oil glazes. From Flemish portraits he borrowed the close-up, half-figural composition, the body filling the lower frame, the sitter's hand pushed close to the picture plane.

Woman with Plants, however, was still an individualized portrait. It did not come close to the streamlined generic type that the artist finally achieved in *American Gothic.* After this breakthrough Wood never again traveled abroad in search of the old and picturesque or to study the old masters. In midwestern farmlore he had finally discovered his own subject matter. In old American architecture, prints, photographs, and artifacts he had found his sources. And in humor he had found a device to make his paintings light-hearted and accessible, as easy to assimilate as a storybook fable. In the tradition of regionalist writers such as Sinclair Lewis, Wood created a character type both lovable and laughable, one with virtues as well as foibles. "These people had bad points," Wood said of his famous couple, "and I did not paint them under, but to me they were basically good and solid people. I had no intention of holding them up to ridicule."[45]

Wood was also grappling in *American Gothic* with one of the basic tenets of modern painting: the belief that form and content should be one. The imagery and style of his early work had been diffuse and eclectic—trees, barns, cathedrals, old shoes, back alleys—painted sometimes with the thick brush of a Van Gogh, at others with the gentle touch of an impressionist. But as he came to conceive of himself as a painter of midwestern history and legend, of "cardboardy frame houses," *American Gothic* couples, and quilted farmlands, Wood realized he had to create a style consonant with his subject matter. He was groping toward such a synthesis in *John B. Turner, Pioneer* and *Woman with Plants,* but found it only in *American Gothic.* There he used every formal element of the composition to say something about the Midwest and the couple's character. The static composition and immaculate forms expressed the couple's rigid routines and unchanging lives. The repeated verticals and sharp angles emphasized the couple's country hardness, while the blunt palette of white and black, brown and green, echoed their simplicity. To make the couple look entombed, as if relics from another age, the artist bathed the scene in a dry white light, crisply embalming every little detail of the pair and their home. Even the profusion of patterns in *American Gothic* —the dots, circles, stripes, and ovals—Wood saw as a midwestern component of his new style. Decorative patterns abounded in his region, Wood believed, in wire fences, ginghams, rickrack, patchwork quilts, lacy curtains, and cornfields.[46]

In its style, imagery, and sources, then, *American Gothic* grew out of Wood's midwestern experience and earned him the title of "regionalist" painter. To the artist's considerable surprise, the painting won immediate fame, a fame that continues unabated today. It is not hard to understand why. In the best tradition of regionalist art, Wood began with local materials but ultimately transcended time and place. *American Gothic* has matured into a collective self-portrait of Americans in general, not just of rural Victorian survivals. Proof of the point is that even the visually untutored perceive the image as Mr. and Ms. American. So, too, the admen and cartoonists, who find *American Gothic* an infinitely variable mirror in which to portray Americans. In parody, Wood's simple, plain, and nameless couple can be rich or poor, urban or rural, young or old, radical or redneck. The image can be used to comment upon puritanism, the family, the work ethic, individualism, home ownership, and the common man.[47] Rich in associations running deep in myth and experience, *American Gothic* has become a national icon.[48]

1981

Notes

This is a shortened version of an essay that appeared previously in *Art the Ape of Nature: Studies in Honor of H. W. Janson* (New York, 1981), 749–69. Locations are provided for works that were illustrated in the original publication but are not reproduced here.

1. *American Gothic* is treated at some length in Darrell Garwood, *Artist in Iowa: A Life of Grant Wood* (New York, 1944); Matthew Baigell, "Grant Wood Revisited," *Art Journal* 26 (Winter 1966–67): 116–22; Baigell, *The American Scene* (New York, 1974), 109–12; James M. Dennis, *Grant Wood* (New York, 1975).
2. *Boston Herald,* Nov, 14, 1930. For this review and many others see the Nan Wood Graham *Scrapbooks,* Archives of American Art, Smithsonian Institution, Washington, D.C., no. 1216/279–88. *American Gothic* was first exhibited in the 1930 Annual Exhibition of American Painting and

Sculpture at the Art Institute of Chicago, where it won the Harris Bronze Medal and a $300 prize. It has been in the permanent collection of the Art Institute ever since.

3. H. W. Janson, "Benton and Wood, Champions of Regionalism," *Magazine of Art* 39 (May 1946): 199.
4. Baigell, *American Scene,* 110. Baigell basically reiterates the interpretation of *American Gothic* given by Garwood, *Artist in Iowa,* 119–20.
5. Dennis, *Grant Wood,* 120.
6. Wood tells in various lectures and interviews of discovering the Eldon house. See newspaper clippings quoting Wood in the Nan Wood Graham *Scrapbooks,* Archives of American Art.
7. Kenneth Clark's pioneering study *The Gothic Revival: An Essay in the History of Taste* first appeared in 1928, but it was not until after World War II that a historical appreciation flourished for Victorian architecture and decorative arts.
8. Letter to the editor from Grant Wood, printed in "The Sunday Register's Open Forum," *Des Moines Sunday Register,* Dec. 21, 1930.
9. "lowans Get Mad," *Art Digest* 5 (Jan. 1, 1931): 9.
10. See Calder Loth and Julius Trousdale Sadler, Jr., *The Only Proper Style: Gothic Architecture in America* (Boston, 1975), 104, where they give the 1881–82 date for the Eldon house and attribute the building of it to Messrs. Busey and Herald, local carpenters.
11. This comes from a newspaper account of a lecture Wood gave in Los Angeles, reported in an unidentified, undated newspaper in the Cedar Rapids Public Library Clipping File on Grant Wood.
12. Interview with Nan Wood Graham, Oct. 14, 1977. See also Nan Wood Graham, "American Gothic," *Canadian Review of Music and Art* 3 (February–March 1941): 12. Mrs. Graham on several occasions answered my questions about *American Gothic* and about her brother's life and work. I am grateful for her interest in my work.
13. Reproduced in Dennis, *Grant Wood,* 86.
14. Letter from Mrs. Ray R. March of Washta, printed in "The Sunday Register's Open Forum," *Des Moines Sunday Register,* Dec. 14, 1930.
15. Wood's home furnishings, photographs, and books are preserved in the Grant Wood Collection of the Davenport Municipal Art Gallery.
16. Reported to the author by Mrs. Herbert Stamats, in a telephone interview Aug. 19, 1976.
17. Russell Lynes, *The Tastemakers* (New York, 1955), 239.
18. Lewis Mumford, *American Taste,* 1929, excerpted in Loren Baritz, ed., *The Culture of the Twenties* (New York, 1970), 402.
19. See, for example, the perfunctory treatment of Victorian furniture in Walter A. Dyer, *Handbook of Furniture Style* (New York, 1918) and in W. L. Kimerly, *How to Know Period Styles in Furniture,* 7th ed. (Grand Rapids, Mich., 1928).
20. My deductions about Wood's taste are based on a study of his own furnishings, visits to the houses he decorated, and interviews with people who knew him.
21. See this author's "The Return of the Native: The Development of Interest in American Primitive Painting" (M.A. thesis, Institute of Fine Arts, New York University, 1965).

22. There is a display of the steel plow and its role in opening up the prairie at the John Deere and Company headquarters, Moline, Ill.
23. Irma Koen, "The Art of Grant Wood," *Christian Science Monitor,* March 26, 1932.
24. I share here the viewpoint of Matthew Baigell, who argued in "Grant Wood Revisited" that Wood's work "has stronger literary than artistic antecedents." We cite, however, different antecedents and come to different conclusions.
25. Hamlin Garland, *Main-Travelled Roads* (New York, 1891); *Prairie Folks* (New York, 1892); and *Boy Life on the Prairie* (New York, 1899). Two useful sources for midwestern regional literature are Benjamin T. Spencer, "Regionalism in American Literature," in Merrill Jensen, ed., *Regionalism in America* (Madison, Wis., 1951); and Clarence A. Andrews, *A Literary History of Iowa* (Iowa City, 1972).
26. Hamlin Garland, *A Son of the Middle Border* (New York, 1917), 416.
27. In the Paris edition of the *Chicago Tribune,* sometime in July 1926; Nan Wood Graham, *Scrapbooks,* Archives of American Art, no. 1216/271.
28. The Limited Editions Club edition of Sinclair Lewis, *Main Street* (New York, 1937). All nine of Wood's *Main Street* illustrations are reproduced in Dennis, *Grant Wood,* 123–27.
29. See newspaper clippings in the Nan Wood Graham *Scrapbooks,* Archives of American Art, nos. 1216/278, 283, 308. Hazel Brown, in *Grant Wood and Marvin Cone* (Ames, Iowa, 1972), 66, recalls that Wood and friends would sit around and discuss "Frank Lloyd Wright, Ruth Suckow, and Jay Sigmund."
30. Jay G. Sigmund, *Frescoes* (Boston, 1922), and *Land O'Maize Folk* (New York, 1924); Ruth Suckow, *Country People* (New York, 1924), *Iowa Interiors* (New York, 1926), and *The Folks* (New York, 1934).
31. Ruth Suckow, "Iowa," *American Mercury* 9 (September 1926): 45.
32. The phrase "drab and angular" is used by Jay Sigmund to describe a spinster in his short story "First Premium," in *Wapsipinicon Tales* (Cedar Rapids, Iowa, 1927). Also see Sigmund's poems "The Serpent" (*Frescoes,* 40–42), and "Hill Spinster's Sunday" (in Paul Engle, ed., *Jay G. Sigmund* [Muscatine, Iowa, 1939]). Ruth Suckow describes how a very promising young girl ends her life as a lonely spinster in "Best of the Lot," *Smart Set* 69 (November 1922): 5–36.
33. The first public statement claiming that Wood's couple were father and daughter appeared in a letter to the editor by Nan Wood Graham, the model for the picture: see "The Sunday Register's Open Forum," *Des Moines Sunday Register* Dec. 21, 1930. Mrs. Graham gave a fuller account of Wood's original ideas for the painting in "American Gothic," *Canadian Review of Music and* Art 3 (February–March 1941).
34. See, for example, "An Iowa Secret," *Art Digest* 8 (Oct. 1, 1933): 6.
35. Park Rinard, "Return from Bohemia: A Painter's Story," Archives of American Art, no. D24/161–295, 78. Although this biography is always attributed to Grant Wood, it was Park Rinard's master's thesis in the Department of English, University of Iowa, August 1939. Rinard was an extremely close friend and associate of Wood's and wrote the thesis in close consultation with the artist.
36. Rinard, "Return from Bohemia," 45–46, 76f.

37. Dennis, *Grant Wood,* 213.
38. See, for example, Suckow's novel *Country People,* and her short stories "Four Generations" and "Rural Community" in *Iowa Interiors.*
39. Grant Wood, quoted in the *New York Times,* Jan. 3, 1940. Wood was speaking here about his painting *Parson Weems' Fable.* Denying any intent to debunk, Wood claimed to be preserving "colorful bits of our national heritage." James Dennis discounts this statement, arguing that the artist was a debunker and a satirist (*Grant Wood,* 109–29). Dennis is more on target, I think, when he discusses Wood as a mythologizer, as a maker of fantasy and make-believe (87–107).
40. Wood's view that the farmer is "central and dominant" in the Midwest is best expressed in the 1935 essay "The Revolt Against the City," republished in Dennis, *Grant Wood,* 229–35.
41. The major exceptions to this statement are the federally funded murals Wood designed in 1934 for the library of Iowa State University in Ames. In other murals, such as those done for the dining room of the Montrose Hotel in Cedar Rapids, Wood could be just as playful and light-hearted as in his easel paintings.
42. Wood's sense of humor was such a vital part of his personality that everyone who knew him comments on it. Numerous stories of his pranks and jokes can be found in Garwood, *Artist in Iowa,* and Brown, *Grant Wood and Marvin Cone.* See also Park Rinard's essay in *Catalogue of a Loan Exhibition of Drawings and Paintings by Grant Wood* (Chicago, 1935). The Cedar Rapids Museum of Art owns many pieces Wood made for fun—a "mourner's bench" for high school students who were being disciplined, flower pots decorated with flowers made of gears, bottlecaps, and wire; and a door to his studio with a movable indicator telling whether the artist was in, asleep, taking a bath, etc.
43. For information about the Turner family I interviewed John B. Turner II in July and August 1976. His father, David Turner, was Wood's chief patron during the artist's early career; his grandfather was the model in *John B. Turner, Pioneer.* Wood dated this painting twice: "1928" in the lower left *under* the oval frame, and "1930" at the edge of the frame in the lower right. Although historians have considered this work to be post-Munich, I suspect this is wrong. Based on the early date and the style of the piece, Wood probably began the portrait sometime in 1928 and dated it before leaving that fall for Munich, where he stayed until Christmas. In 1930 he made revisions to the painting and dated it anew when he added the oval frame, a shape in keeping with the neo-Victorian features of *American Gothic.*
44. Mrs. Wood's early biography appears in Rinard, "Return from Bohemia," chap. 1.
45. Dorothy Dougherty, "The Right and Wrong of America," *Cedar Rapids Gazette,* Sept. 5, 1942.
46. See Koen, "Art of Grant Wood," and quotations from Grant Wood's lectures and interviews in the clippings in the Nan Wood Graham *Scrapbooks,* Archives of American Art.
47. There are several major collectors of *American Gothic* caricatures. I am grateful to Nan Wood Graham, Edwin Green, and Price E. Slate for having made their large collections available to me. My own collection, begun only in the early 1970s, already numbers hundreds of items.

48. For an extended discussion of the image in American culture, see my "*American Gothic:* The Making of a National Icon," in *Grant Wood: The Regionalist Vision* (New Haven, 1983), 128–42.

GETTING STARTED

1. Working in a group, list the questions that Corn asks in her essay. Choose two of the questions and analyze how she goes about answering them. As a group, discuss what effects Corn creates by asking and answering questions, and present your findings to the class.

2. Corn offers information about a number of American sources that influenced Grant Wood's painting of *American Gothic*. Find her discussion of one of these sources, take some notes on it, and copy down a key quotation. While taking your notes, consider the following: Is the influence historical, literary, or some other kind? In what ways did Grant Wood make use of it? What point is Corn trying to make by using this example? Bring your notes to class.

3. At the beginning of her article, Corn presents the interpretations and perceptions of Grant Wood and *American Gothic* that she is going to argue against. Choose one of those interpretations or perceptions and write a paragraph describing it. Include a key quotation. In class, share paragraphs in groups; each group should then select and present one of the interpretations or perceptions that Corn is arguing against and cite the location in the text where she makes that counterargument.

WRITING

4. Choose one of the examples that Corn cites as a misinterpretation of *American Gothic*. Write a paper in which you compare Corn's argument to the "misinterpretation." How effective is her argument? Which interpretation seems more persuasive to you and why?

USING THE LIBRARY AND THE INTERNET

5. Using a dictionary or a database such as dictionary.com, find definitions and examples that help you to tell the differences between humor, ridicule, and satire. In a group, compare your findings and analyze the difference between the humor that Corn describes in Grant Wood's work and the satire and ridicule that she is arguing against earlier in the essay. Use an example from Corn in presenting your findings to the class.

6. Find a picture or a photograph (on the Internet, at a museum, in an art book, or on a postcard) that you think depicts an icon of America. What makes it "American"? How is it portrayed—realistically, satirically, or humorously? What clues help you determine the artist's intention? (Hint: On the Internet, use a popular search engine such as AltaVista, try a search term such as "American icon" in the "Arts" category, and limit your search to images.)

MAKING CONNECTIONS

7. Using Corn's criteria for defining *American Gothic* as a national icon, write an essay in which you examine the question of how Ralph Ellison's "little man" ("The Little Man at Chehaw Station") might respond to Corn. Would he agree that *American Gothic* is American art? Extend your analysis to the images you discovered in the library or on the Internet. How are these images "American"?

8. Analyze Corn's essay using Clifford Geertz's ideas about the way particular cultures shape "common sense," as outlined in "Common Sense as a Cultural System." In creating her interpretation of *American Gothic,* how is Corn going against commonsense ideas about the painting?

9. In "Bad Eyes," Erin McGraw discusses the problem of seeing selectively (not seeing the faces of friends but clearly seeing weeds and gray hairs), and the idea that seeing is linked to understanding. Write an essay using McGraw's ideas to discuss the ways in which Corn teaches you how to see *American Gothic.* What details does Corn's interpretation help you see for the first time or to see in a new way? Does her interpretation obscure your ability to see the painting in any way?

Scott DeVeaux

Scott DeVeaux is Associate Professor of Music at the University of Virginia, where he specializes in the study of jazz. DeVeaux is also a jazz composer who has written numerous reviews and articles and has edited essay collections on George Gershwin, Thelonious Monk, Miles Davis, Lester Young, and The Grateful Dead. His book, *The Birth of Bebop: A Social and Musical History* (1997), won the American Book Award. DeVeaux presents jazz as both a product of the social forces of race and class in America and an aesthetic development of modernism and popular music. "Progress and the Bean" is a chapter in *The Birth of Bebop.*

To learn more about Coleman Hawkins and jazz before 1930, see the Red Hot Jazz archive at <http://www.redhotjazz.com>.

Progress and the Bean

In spite of all that is written, said and done, this great, big, incontrovertible fact stands out,—the Negro is progressing, and that disproves all the arguments in the world that he is incapable of progress.

James Weldon Johnson

There's no such thing as bop music, but there's such a thing as progress.

Coleman Hawkins

Alto saxophonist Cannonball Adderley remembered it later as a childhood moment that set the direction for his life. His father took him to see the Fletcher Henderson band at the City Auditorium in Tampa, Florida. Featured in the band was the imposing tenor saxophonist Coleman Hawkins. "Man, it was a great day for me," said Adderley. "I think he was the most interesting looking jazz musician I've ever seen in my life. He just looked so authoritative. I kept looking at him. I never did look at Fletcher. I said, 'Well, that's what I want to do when I grow up.' "

Adderley was neither the first nor the last musician to be impressed by Coleman Hawkins. In a field in which charismatic figures were no rarity, Hawkins had a special quality. Hawk, or Bean—as he was affectionately nicknamed—was not a particularly striking or flamboyant man. And yet his quiet dignity and utter confidence in his abilities commanded respect, even awe—at least from musicians, who were in the best position to judge Hawkins's artistic achievement. In a familiar anecdote, a younger musician encountering Hawkins for the first time in the 1960s reportedly told Adderley that the older saxophonist made him nervous: "Man, I told him Hawkins was *supposed* to make him nervous. Hawkins has been making other Sax players nervous for forty years."

Hawkins's place as one of the founders of jazz is secure. He was among the earliest generation of jazz musicians, the men and women who unselfconsciously created a new art form. He is often called the father of the tenor saxophone, the first to discover the expressive potential of an instrument previously thought to have a limited emotional range, and therefore the patriarch of a lineage that extends through John Coltrane, Sonny Rollins, and other moderns to the present.

In the sweep of jazz history, Hawkins is usually classified as a swing musician. This label not only narrows the focus to a particular phase of his career, but also suggests that the artistic attitudes and techniques he acquired during that time served as his compass for the remainder of his life. It also strongly implies that his moment of significance was limited to a specific historical moment: the Swing Era, when his distinctive approach to improvisation was widely accepted as the model for all saxophonists and the standard against which they were measured.

"Body and Soul," recorded in 1939, shortly after his return from a self-imposed five-year exile in Europe, remains Hawkins's best-

FIGURE 18 Coleman Hawkins and Duke Ellington. Photograph. (Down Beat Magazine Archives.)

known record and a landmark in the history of jazz recording, not least for the fact that it was simultaneously a commercial success and admired and studied by musicians. But Hawkins is represented by hundreds of other recordings, from his pre-1934 solos with Fletcher Henderson to the flood of records for various independent labels in the early 1940s. Each combines a confident and assertive manner with a bracing, complex harmonic language that anticipated many of the innovations later associated with bebop, including the so-called flatted fifths. With each recording, his reputation as an innovator grew. "Coleman Hawkins was *the* saxophonist then," remembers pianist Billy Taylor. "Hawk was most highly respected," agrees bassist Milt Hinton. "He seemed to be the most creative man of the era. Everybody just thought he was the top man."

This stature, however, did not long outlive bebop. After 1945 Hawkins's influence declined, and his standing in jazz history automatically became problematic. Even in his last years, as he matched himself against John Coltrane, Thelonious Monk, and Sonny Rollins, he was considered less a full participant in contemporary musical life than an icon—a living legend—of the art.

Hawkins's decline in status is not unexpected. A history of style usually boils down to a history of innovation: novel techniques that stand out against the background of common practice and can be shown, after the fact, to point to the future. Only stylistic "advances" give shape and momentum to such a historical narrative. It follows that the cutting edge must be kept sharp. With jazz, the pace of change has been particularly brisk. Major artists are routinely and unsentimentally shunted from the vanguard to obsolescence before they reach middle age, their later work marginalized or forgotten, their historical role diminished.

Such seems to have been the fate of Coleman Hawkins. In 1944, as he approached his fortieth birthday, his prestige and influence were at their peak. This moment of glory was overshadowed, however, by the onslaught of bebop, and with it, his reputation as innovator vanished. He is now remembered as making only a brief appearance on the periphery of the bop revolution, despite having been very much on the scene. Even the comforting role of paterfamilias to the younger generation has been denied him. The swing tenor saxophonist universally acknowledged to have served as source and inspiration for the emergent idiom is not Hawkins, but Lester Young.

The frequent rhetorical pairing of Coleman Hawkins and Lester Young has the air of a cautionary tale, with Young's rise coming at the expense of Hawkins's decline. The issue is rhythm: specifically, the "logical rhythmic change" that Martin Williams saw as the mainspring of stylistic evolution in jazz. If evolution in jazz is about rhythm, then the "cool" rhythmic language pioneered by Young is a touchstone. As "the most gifted and original improviser between Louis Armstrong and Charlie Parker" (in Williams's reading), Lester

Young is the conduit between the path-breaking innovations of early jazz and the revolution of the 1940s. His improvised solos, full of ironic understatement and witty, unpredictable manipulation of phrase lengths and rhythmic motives, contrasted starkly with the earnest effusions of Hawkins's playing. Young's rhythmic approach anticipated the future, as Hawkins's more ponderous idiom did not. As tenor saxophonist Dexter Gordon, who came of age in the mid-1940s, put it: "Hawk was the master of the horn, a musician who did everything possible with it, the right way. But when Pres [Lester Young] appeared, we all started listening to him alone. Pres had an entirely new sound, one that we seemed to be waiting for."

Some musicians date the passing of the mantle even earlier, to an incident in 1933 in which Hawkins, still a soloist with the Fletcher Henderson band, found himself locked in a marathon after-hours jam session at the Cherry Blossom in Kansas City with Ben Webster, Herschel Evans, and Lester Young. Mary Lou Williams was rousted from her sleep at four in the morning to relieve the exhausted piano players: "Get up, pussycat, Hawkins has got his shirt off and is still blowing." The event, now a staple of jazz folklore, found Hawkins struggling for hours to shake off the competition until finally giving up, tearing off in his Cadillac to make the next job in St. Louis. Mary Lou Williams, herself a historian (she devoted much of her later life to jazz education) had no trouble drawing the moral from this ritual combat: "Yes, Hawkins was king until he met those crazy Kansas City tenor men."

As the critic Jed Rasula has noted, jazz historians are fond of such "primal torch-passing scenes": colorful anecdotes that seem to embody the abstract workings of history. In this case, the story is all the more compelling for being somewhat in advance of events. Hawkins, after all, remained king for a good while longer, his reputation hardly damaged by this obscure encounter in the provinces. But the handful of participant-observers at the Cherry Blossom had seen the future. Through the telling and retelling of the story, later generations have joined them as privileged insiders, better attuned to the true workings of history than the majority of those who lived through it. Hawkins's day had passed almost before it had begun.

Thus, Hawkins's encounters with the bebop revolution have been reduced to mere historical curiosity. Dizzy Gillespie has put it more generously than most: "Hawkins had the great taste in music to understand my generation and to come with us." But the image is still oddly skewed—deliberately so, perhaps, given Gillespie's penchant for self-mocking humor: the young unknowns as the leaders, the forty-year-old "most creative man of the era" as the follower. In early 1944, when Hawkins became increasingly involved with the bop generation, the word *bebop* did not yet exist. Over the course of the year, Hawkins systematically employed musicians from the emerging underground. A recording session under Hawkins's leadership in February of that year featured Gillespie and Max Roach, while his working bands for 1944 included such well-known bebop pioneers as Thelonious Monk, Kenny Clarke, and Oscar Pettiford, as well as others now more obscure: Howard McGhee, "Little Benny" Harris, Vic Coulsen.

For his early encouragement of bebop musicians, Hawkins has been given his due. Unlike others of his generation, whose attitude toward bop ranged from hostility to resentment to bemused indifference, Hawkins championed the music, earning him a degree of loyalty (Thelonious Monk remained a lifelong friend) and respect. The title of a tune from a 1946 recording session, which included J. J. Johnson, Milt Jackson, Fats Navarro, and Max Roach, pays tribute to the relationship between the older saxophonist and his young protégés: "Bean and the Boys."

To make sense of this relationship, one must move beyond the compelling simplifications that dominate jazz history. Music cannot be reduced to a narrative of stylistic development, just as the complexity of a life lived in music cannot be flattened into a set of musical characteristics. This dictum is especially true for bebop, a movement that reflected the totality of the artist's consciousness.

For the bop musicians, Hawkins had a special relevance. As keen-eared aspiring artists, they paid close attention to Hawkins's musical legacy, appropriating some elements while rejecting others. But they also understood these details of craftsmanship as part of a broader picture, inseparable from the qualities of personality and intellect that informed the achievements of an extraordinary elite: black jazz musicians in midcentury America.

Hawkins shared many traits with the Dukes and Counts of that elite: the unshakable confidence of the successfully self-taught man, a tireless professional ambition, and a sense of dignity, tending toward inner reserve, under even the most trying of circumstances. Still, even among his peers, Hawkins stood out. The quality that arrested the attention of the youthful Cannonball Adderley was Hawkins's sense of *purpose*. This quality found its most obvious manifestation in his restless exploration of technical resources, but it cannot be reduced to them. It was both social and musical. The peculiar combination of personal traits and musical abilities that marked Hawkins—steely ambition, a strong intellect, and virtuosity—characterized the bebop revolution as well. He was, as Sonny Rollins has recently put it, one of its most prominent "role models": the prototypical progressive jazz musician.

Jazz and Progress

The word *progressive* makes many people in the late twentieth century uncomfortable. It calls to mind an ideology of continuous and irreversible betterment, one singularly out of sync with contemporary thought and experience.

In particular, it is grating to find notions of progress applied to the arts. To claim progress in the fields of science and technology is one thing. Some may argue whether such "advances" actually improve life, but few disagree that new solutions to old problems have rendered previous efforts obsolete. Old technologies are discarded without a second thought: the slide rule and the typewriter may have equipped one generation, but to the next, they become puzzling curiosities. In the arts, however, such wholesale dismissal of the past seems unthinkable. As museums attest, the old retains its power and actively shapes the sensibilities of the present.

Within the arts, music is a special case. Compared with the tangible objects of the visual arts, music is an inherently evanescent art, more process than product. Music notation, of course, was invented centuries ago as a corrective. Written music embodies musical structure independent of any given performance and makes the category of a "work" possible. But it took time for the reification of music as composition to take effect. The museum-like quality of the "classical" European repertory dates back no earlier than the nineteenth century. Only in the past hundred years has the music of the past, the canon of "timeless" masterpieces, come to dominate the present and undermine any notion of music's evanescence. Before this time, music was created primarily for current value: to be used and discarded. No one gave much thought to what generations beyond the reach of memory might have done, or to what future generations might think.

For jazz, the more modern technology of recording served a function parallel to that of notation. Jazz was a music created, like any other, for immediate consumption. Through recording, particular performances of music were transmuted into durable artifacts capable of outlasting the particular circumstances of their creation. Recordings were not necessarily treated with reverence: like other products of mass-market capitalism, they were meant to be used up. But some survived, in attics and junk shops, to be picked over in later years by eager record collectors.

Jazz history itself grew out of discography, a rational system of classification devised to help collectors sort the "classic" jazz recordings from the ephemera of popular culture. This process led to the wholesale rescue of jazz recordings from planned obsolescence and gradually to the jazz consumers' consciousness of the music as an art form. Today recordings are seen as jazz's museum, housing works of lasting value. It follows that new additions to the museum do not displace the old. The innovations of subsequent decades, whether by Charlie Parker or Ornette Coleman, do not diminish the value placed on contributions by King Oliver or Duke Ellington, but rather furnish another wing in the museum. The process is value neutral: growth, not progress.

It would be a mistake, however, to read this ideology back into the circumstances of the musicians who created the recordings. At the outset of Hawkins's career, jazz was not art music, but dance music. While record collectors shivered in private ecstasy listening to their favorite treasures, others gathered in large public spaces to enjoy dancing to the finest music they could find. Dance music is by nature ephemeral—which does not mean that it is unimportant or inartistic, but simply that it tends not to survive its time. In popular music, continual change is essential, as in sartorial fashion. It is a marker of generational identity, and every generation has the privilege of mocking its predecessor as hopelessly outdated and unhip. For those growing up in the first half of the century, surrounded by the ongoing triumphs of technology, it was virtually irresistible to associate change with progress.

Hawkins broke into the music business in the early 1920s as a callow teenager in rumpled, ill-kept clothes that earned him the nickname "Greasy," but quickly evolved into a dapper sophisticate, keenly sensitive to the imperatives of fashion. To his horror, his involvement with the dance music of the Jazz Age, captured on dozens of recordings with the Henderson band, later became the fetish of jazz collectors and critics. They delighted in playing these recordings in his presence, and the mortified Hawkins acted as if he had just been shown faded photographs of his youthful self in clownishly outmoded attire. The mature Hawkins thought of himself as perpetually young, perpetually in step, and hated admitting to a past. Confronted with evidence of it, he immediately countered with the notion of progress.

That Hawkins was not alone in this regard is evident in the French critic André Hodeir's complaint, from the mid-1950s, that musicians of the swing generation "naively believed their music better than that of their predecessors, just as they would have judged a 1938 automobile faster and more comfortable than a 1925 model." Hawkins, who insisted on owning the latest-model Cadillac, would have appreciated the analogy, but would probably have objected to being characterized as naive. His sense of progress in music was grounded not simply in a chauvinism of the up-to-date, but in an awareness of undeniable improvements in things that could be objectively measured. Musicians played faster, extended the ranges of their instruments, had better control over intonation and timbre (which is not to say that they conformed to European standards, but that any deviations from those standards were *intentional*). They had, on the whole, a sounder grasp of the intellectual components of music: the ability to translate musical notation into sounds and sounds into musical notation, a working knowledge of the syntax of tonal harmony, and a carefully calculated rhythmic assurance that made the dance music of the 1920s seem comparatively awkward and stiff. All of these skills had become the minimum professional equipment for musicians in the 1930s and 1940s, and counted as progress—real, hard-won achievement.

Jazz critics continually held up earlier jazz for admiration, but Hawkins was pained at the thought. "It's like a man thinking back to when he couldn't walk, he had to crawl," he complained after rehearing one of his solos twenty years later. That art, out of all areas of human endeavor, should be singled out and denied the possibility of systematic improvement made him indignant: "That's amazing to me, that so many people in music won't accept progress. It's the only field where advancement meets so much opposition. You take doctors—look what medicine and science have accomplished in the last twenty or thirty years. That's the way it should be in music—that's the way it has to be."

The analogy between science and art that Hawkins suggests seems improbable, but as generations of scholars have discovered, the work of science historian Thomas Kuhn offers some intriguing points of comparison. In science, entire fields are occasionally transformed, or brought into being, by new organizing principles: the discovery of antibiotics in medicine, plate tectonics in geology, quantum mechanics in physics. In *The Structure of Scientific Revolutions,* Kuhn identified such breakthroughs as new "paradigms" and saw in them the basis for understanding revolutionary change in science. Similar breakthroughs have characterized the arts; indeed, the animating purpose of Kuhn's study was to adapt concepts of revolution already widespread in the humanities for use in the sciences. What have come to be known as paradigm shifts in both the humanities and the sciences are the disjunctures dramatized in the telling of history—the sudden irruption of a new sensibility, a fresh way of seeing things, embodied in a particular set of techniques and procedures that becomes the model for all to follow.

Still, as Kuhn emphasizes, the dramatic, paradigm-shattering breakthrough is not characteristic of scientific activity as a whole. What he calls "normal science" is the unglamorous but necessary work that uses the prevailing paradigm to pose problems, and systematically solve them. Progress—the incremental accumulation of knowledge—is made possible only by such unremitting labor. Scientists do not seek revolutionary insights for their own sake (although the achievements of a handful of radical innovators are properly lionized). Most simply extend the existing framework further and assume, for want of any evidence to the contrary, that it will go on indefinitely.

The analogy with jazz seems straightforward and helps in part to explain Coleman Hawkins's preoccupation with progress. One of the most influential truisms of recent historical writing is that jazz was given something like an initial paradigm by "the first great soloist," Louis Armstrong. According to Martin Williams, "jazz musicians spent the late twenties and early thirties absorbing Armstrong's rhythmic ideas, the basis of his swing." Armstrong's performances, especially his recordings from the 1920s, defined the exacting discipline of the improvised solo and provided concrete examples of the rhythmic principle of swing.

For the next two decades, hundreds of musicians applied themselves to the task of absorbing and extending Armstrong's example. The "problems" they sought to "solve" (both words crop up frequently in the secondary literature) differed from a scientist's experiments in that their ultimate goals were aesthetic. But, like a scientist, these musicians systematically applied principles inherent in the original paradigm to novel contexts. Specifically, they learned from Armstrong's example how to construct a solo and how to swing, and they learned to do this within their own musical personalities, on their own instruments, and in the context of changing fashions in dance music. The process can be viewed as intuitive and holistic (learning how to "tell a story"), or intellectual and reducible to such technical problems as range, speed, and articulation. Responsibility for achievement was individual: personal improvement. But, as Coleman Hawkins proudly saw, the net result for the discipline was progress.

Bebop, to continue the analogy, figures as a major paradigm shift. Through the transformative example of Charlie Parker and Dizzy Gillespie, jazz in the 1940s experienced a "reconstitution of the field from new fundamentals." All the familiar symptoms of revolution, the world turned upside down, are there: the youth of the revolutionaries; the startling, unexpected nature of the new insight; the specter of an older generation clinging to the old paradigm, even as hordes of new practitioners rush to embrace the new; and finally, the triumph of the new paradigm and the recasting of the field in its image.

But what is the relationship of the new order to the old? How and why do such revolutions arise? As Kuhn emphasizes, a paradigm is not lightly set aside. It is the foundation of a field, and those who run counter to it risk no longer being recognized as members of the discipline. New paradigms emerge only in moments of great crisis, when the usual ways of doing things prove wholly inadequate. At such times, practitioners are forced, almost against their deepest instincts, to devise radical new ways of constructing their professional world. It is not enough for historians to admire the originality and brilliance of the new paradigm, as if originality and brilliance were sufficient explanation. They must also understand the extraordinary pressures that turned dedicated practitioners into revolutionaries and pushed them to the reckless step of abandoning the old paradigm.

What, then, was the crisis that provoked the bebop revolution? As we have seen, something like a "crisis theory" is already in place in the bebop story. It suggests that by the beginning of the 1940s, jazz musicians found themselves frustrated by the prevailing paradigm. The encouragingly brisk pace of development that had characterized jazz to this point slowed, as if something were impeding musicians from progressing further. Some have imputed the difficulty to musical style per se. "I do not think that one can hear the impeccable swing of a player like Lionel Hampton," wrote Martin Williams, "without sensing that some sort of future crisis was at hand in the music, that . . . a kind of jazz as melodically dull as a set of tone drums might well be in the offing." But this is not a comfortable argument, since it suggests that the musical language itself is somehow at fault. The more usual approach, as I have already noted, is to deflect the blame for the crisis away from the music toward external forces (such as commercialism). Bebop thus emerges as a musical solution to a social problem—or more precisely, a reassertion of the autonomy of music-making in the face of social pressures.

I would frame the argument differently. At the risk of overextending the analogy between art and science, one further aspect of Kuhn's analysis deserves to be mentioned. The revolutions he describes happen not to science in the abstract, but to communities of professional scientists. Insofar as the concept of paradigm "stands for the entire constellation of beliefs, values, techniques, and so on shared by the members of a given community," it is sociological: a "disciplinary matrix" that grounds the putatively autonomous pursuit of science in social realities. To understand fundamental change in science, one must account for its social dimension—not just its institutions (degree programs, journals, scholarly associations), but the cultural values that underlie informal behavior: how information is disseminated, reputations made, and conflicts between competing paradigms resolved.

I would argue that fundamental change in music must similarly be understood as social and cultural as well as musical. The proper analogy for a paradigm in jazz is not musical style, but something like Kuhn's "disciplinary matrix": the sum total of practices, values, and commitments that define jazz as a profession. The romantic myth of the artist working in isolation from (or even in opposition to) the outside world may seem congenial or convenient to jazz critics. But myth it is. All activity in the arts takes place within what the sociologist Howard Becker has called an "art world": "the network of people whose cooperative activity, organized by their joint knowledge of conventional means of doing things, produces the kind of art works that [the] art world is noted for." Only within this context can the decisions of individual jazz musicians to effect dramatic changes not only in musical style, but also in their social role as professional musicians, be properly interpreted.

1997

GETTING STARTED

1. Find three to five places in this essay where DeVeaux uses, defines, or expands on the idea of "progress." Take notes on the way he writes about the concept of "progress" in each example and include page numbers as references. Bring your notes to class.

2. DeVeaux makes a distinction between "growth" and "progress." Reread that section in the essay (pp. 107–108) and find an example that helps you to explain, in your own words, the difference he is exploring.

3. Consider the following claim by DeVeaux in terms of his discussion of Thomas Kuhn and paradigm shifts later in the essay:

   > Music cannot be reduced to a narrative of stylistic development, just as the complexity of a life lived in music cannot be flattened into a set of musical characteristics. This dictum is especially true for bebop, a movement that reflected the totality of the artist's consciousness. (p. 107)

   Take some time to analyze what this means. Which words or phrases seem the most significant to you? Write a brief explanation of the quote by using and defining one or two of these key words or phrases.

4. In a group, explain what DeVeaux is trying to show with the specific example of Coleman Hawkins. What does DeVeaux see as the larger implications of Hawkins's achievement?

WRITING

5. Write an essay exploring the idea of "progress" using DeVeaux's ideas as well as your own experiences and observations. You might begin by sketching out some preliminary ideas in response to the following questions. How does "progress" get defined in this essay? Why do some people argue that there is no "progress" in the field of music, while others, including Hawkins, argue the opposite? What do you think? Use your answers to these questions to help you develop your thesis.

6. Write a short essay interpreting the relations you see between art and progress, on the one hand, and technology and progress, on the other hand. What does DeVeaux's essay illustrate about the relationship between art and technology?

USING THE LIBRARY AND THE INTERNET

7. Use the Internet to find some of the music of the swing and bebop musicians that DeVeaux mentions here: Louis Armstrong, Coleman Hawkins, Charlie Parker, and Dizzy Gillespie. (Hint: Use a search engine such as Google, Hotbot, or AltaVista to look for audio selections.) Describe this music by comparing what you hear with a contemporary piece of music that you like. What are some

of the differences between this older music and the music of today? What are some of the things that seem to have changed over time? Is the word "progress" appropriate in describing those changes? Write a paragraph outlining your discoveries.

8. Using the combined search terms "progress and paradigm," search a reference database such as Academic Search Elite that includes a range of sources from scholarly journals. Skim your findings and print out the titles and abstracts of several articles that seem interesting in relation to DeVeaux.

MAKING CONNECTIONS

9. What do you make of DeVeaux's claim that "fundamental change in music must be understood as social and cultural as well as musical" (p. 112)? In what ways does his claim make sense to you? In what ways does his claim not make sense? Compare these claims to a similar one made by Emily Martin about the importance of understanding science in terms of social and cultural issues as well as facts.

10. Thomas Kuhn's "The Historical Structure of Scientific Discovery," Jared Diamond's "Necessity's Mother," and DeVeaux's essay all challenge in some way the idea that changes take place because a single individual invents or discovers a wholly new way to do things. Write an essay using DeVeaux and one of these other writers to explore this problem. Why do "inventions" get tied to particular individuals? What are some of the advantages and disadvantages of that process?

11. What are the chief differences between the sciences and the arts? Why is a distinction made? How does an essay like "Progress and the Bean" challenge this distinction? Use one other essay in *Making Sense* (perhaps Gloria Anzaldúa, Sven Birkerts, Northrop Frye, Stephen Jay Gould, Thomas Kuhn, or Sherry Turkle) to explore the boundaries between science and the arts.

12. Jazz is an art in which a musician spontaneously tailors his or her ideas to a specific fresh context. How is writing an essay also an act of improvisation? Use Jeanette Winterson's essay, "Imagination and Reality," as an example. What does she do in the course of the essay that confounds "conventional" essay writing practice? Choose one place in her essay that seems improvised, unexpected, or even illogical. What are the features and advantages of writing done in this manner? Write an essay in which you compare her writing to a piece of music.

Jared Diamond

Jared Diamond (1937–) is Professor of Physiology at the UCLA School of Medicine. He may be better known, however, as the author of the Pulitzer Prize–winning book, *Guns, Germs, and Steel: The Fates of Human Societies* (1997), from which "Necessity's Mother" is taken. Diamond's research has taken him to New Guinea more than seventeen times, and it is these trips that triggered his thinking about broad patterns of human history and the different evolutionary courses of people on different continents. In "Necessity's Mother," Diamond asks: If "necessity is the mother of invention," as folklore tells us, then who or what is the mother of necessity? In other words, if invention leads to technological progress, what leads to invention?

To begin exploring this question, visit Inventure Place, the home page of the National Inventors Hall of Fame at <http://www.invent.org>.

Necessity's Mother

On July 3, 1908, archaeologists excavating the ancient Minoan palace at Phaistos, on the island of Crete, chanced upon one of the most remarkable objects in the history of technology. At first glance it seemed unprepossessing: just a small, flat, unpainted, circular disk of hard-baked clay, 6 1/2 inches in diameter. Closer examination showed each side to be covered with writing, resting on a curved line that spiraled clockwise in five coils from the disk's rim to its center. A total of 241 signs or letters was neatly divided by etched vertical lines into groups of several signs, possibly constituting words. The writer must have planned and executed the disk with care, so as to start writing at the rim and fill up all the available space along the spiraling line, yet not run out of space on reaching the center (see fig. 19).

Ever since it was unearthed, the disk has posed a mystery for historians of writing. The number of distinct signs (45) suggests a syllabary rather than an alphabet, but it is still undeciphered, and the forms of the signs are unlike those of any other known writing system. Not another scrap of the strange script has turned up in the 89 years since its discovery. Thus, it remains unknown whether it represents an indigenous Cretan script or a foreign import to Crete.

For historians of technology, the Phaistos disk is even more baffling; its estimated date of 1700 B.C. makes it by far the earliest printed

FIGURE 19 One side of the two-sided Phaistos Disk. (Courtesy Saskia Ltd., © Dr. Ron Wiedenhoeft.)

document in the world. Instead of being etched by hand, as were all texts of Crete's later Linear A and Linear B scripts, the disk's signs were punched into soft clay (subsequently baked hard) by stamps that bore a sign as raised type. The printer evidently had a set of at least 45 stamps, one for each sign appearing on the disk. Making these stamps must have entailed a great deal of work, and they surely weren't manufactured just to do this single document. Whoever used them was presumably doing a lot of writing. With those stamps, their owner could make copies much more quickly and neatly than if he or she had written out each of the script's complicated signs at each appearance.

The Phaistos disk anticipates humanity's next efforts at printing, which similarly used cut type or blocks but applied them to paper with ink, not to clay without ink. However, those next efforts did not appear until 2,500 years later in China and 3,100 years later in medieval Europe. Why was the disk's precocious technology not widely adopted in Crete or elsewhere in the ancient Mediterranean? Why was its printing method invented around 1700 B.C. in Crete and not at some other time in Mesopotamia, Mexico, or any other ancient center of writing? Why did it then take thousands of years to add the ideas of ink and a press and arrive at a printing press? The disk thus constitutes a threatening challenge to historians. If inventions are as idiosyncratic and unpredictable as the disk seems to suggest, then efforts to generalize about the history of technology may be doomed from the outset.

Technology, in the form of weapons and transport, provides the direct means by which certain peoples have expanded their realms and conquered other peoples. That makes it the leading cause of history's broadest pattern. But why were Eurasians, rather than Native Americans or sub-Saharan Africans, the ones to invent firearms, oceangoing ships, and steel equipment? The differences extend to most other significant technological advances, from printing presses to glass and steam engines. Why were all those inventions Eurasian? Why were all New Guineans and Native Australians in A.D. 1800 still using stone tools like ones discarded thousands of years ago in Eurasia and most of Africa, even though some of the world's richest copper and iron deposits are in New Guinea and Australia, respectively? All those facts explain why so many laypeople assume that Eurasians are superior to other peoples in inventiveness and intelligence.

If, on the other hand, no such difference in human neurobiology exists to account for continental differences in technological development, what does account for them? An alternative view rests on the heroic theory of invention. Technological advances seem to come disproportionately from a few very rare geniuses, such as Johannes Gutenberg, James Watt, Thomas Edison, and the Wright brothers. They were Europeans, or descendants of European emigrants to America. So were Archimedes and other rare geniuses of ancient times. Could such geniuses have equally well been born in Tasmania or Namibia? Does the history of technology depend on nothing more than accidents of the birthplaces of a few inventors?

Still another alternative view holds that it is a matter not of individual inventiveness but of the receptivity of whole societies to innovation. Some societies seem hopelessly conservative, inward looking, and hostile to change. That's the impression of many Westerners who have attempted to help Third World peoples and ended up discouraged. The people seem perfectly intelligent as individuals; the problem seems instead to lie with their societies. How else can one explain why the Aborigines of northeastern Australia failed to adopt bows and arrows, which they saw being used by Torres Straits islanders with whom they traded? Might all the societies of an entire continent be unreceptive, thereby explaining technology's slow pace of development there? In this chapter we shall finally come to grips with . . . the question of why technology did evolve at such different rates on different continents.

The starting point for our discussion is the common view expressed in the saying "Necessity is the mother of invention." That is, inventions supposedly arise when a society has an unfulfilled need:

some technology is widely recognized to be unsatisfactory or limiting. Would-be inventors, motivated by the prospect of money or fame, perceive the need and try to meet it. Some inventor finally comes up with a solution superior to the existing, unsatisfactory technology. Society adopts the solution if it is compatible with the society's values and other technologies.

Quite a few inventions do conform to this commonsense view of necessity as invention's mother. In 1942, in the middle of World War II, the U.S. government set up the Manhattan Project with the explicit goal of inventing the technology required to build an atomic bomb before Nazi Germany could do so. That project succeeded in three years, at a cost of $2 billion (equivalent to over $20 billion today). Other instances are Eli Whitney's 1794 invention of his cotton gin to replace laborious hand cleaning of cotton grown in the U.S. South, and James Watt's 1769 invention of his steam engine to solve the problem of pumping water out of British coal mines.

These familiar examples deceive us into assuming that other major inventions were also responses to perceived needs. In fact, many or most inventions were developed by people driven by curiosity or by a love of tinkering, in the absence of any initial demand for the product they had in mind. Once a device had been invented, the inventor then had to find an application for it. Only after it had been in use for a considerable time did consumers come to feel that they "needed" it. Still other devices, invented to serve one purpose, eventually found most of their use for other, unanticipated purposes. It may come as a surprise to learn that these inventions in search of a use include most of the major technological breakthroughs of modern times, ranging from the airplane and automobile, through the internal combustion engine and electric light bulb, to the phonograph and transistor. Thus, invention is often the mother of necessity, rather than vice versa.

A good example is the history of Thomas Edison's phonograph, the most original invention of the greatest inventor of modern times. When Edison built his first phonograph in 1877, he published an article proposing ten uses to which his invention might be put. They included preserving the last words of dying people, recording books for blind people to hear, announcing clock time, and teaching spelling. Reproduction of music was not high on Edison's list of priorities. A few years later Edison told his assistant that his invention had no commercial value. Within another few years he changed his mind and did enter business to sell phonographs—but for use as office dictating machines. When other entrepreneurs created jukeboxes by arranging for a phonograph to play popular music at the drop of a coin, Edison objected to this debasement, which apparently detracted from serious office use of his invention. Only after about 20 years did Edison reluctantly concede that the main use of his phonograph was to record and play music.

The motor vehicle is another invention whose uses seem obvious today. However, it was not invented in response to any demand. When Nikolaus Otto built his first gas engine, in 1866, horses had been supplying people's land transportation needs for nearly 6,000 years, supplemented increasingly by steam-powered railroads for several decades. There was no crisis in the availability of horses, no dissatisfaction with railroads.

Because Otto's engine was weak, heavy, and seven feet tall, it did not recommend itself over horses. Not until 1885 did engines improve to the point that Gottfried Daimler got around to installing one on a bicycle to create the first motorcycle; he waited until 1896 to build the first truck.

In 1905, motor vehicles were still expensive, unreliable toys for the rich. Public contentment with horses and railroads rernained high until World War I, when the military concluded that it really did need trucks. Intensive postwar lobbying by truck manufacturers and armies finally convinced the public of its own needs and enabled trucks to begin to supplant horsedrawn wagons in industrialized countries. Even in the largest American cities, the changeover took 50 years.

Inventors often have to persist at their tinkering for a long time in the absence of public demand, because early models perform too poorly to be useful. The first cameras, typewriters, and television sets were as awful as Otto's seven-foot-tall gas engine. That makes it difficult for an inventor to foresee whether his or her awful prototype might eventually find a use and thus warrant more time and expense to develop it. Each year, the United States issues about 70,000 patents, only a few of which ultimately reach the stage of commercial production. For each great invention that ultimately found a use, there are countless others that did not. Even inventions that meet the need for which they were initially designed may later prove more valuable at meeting unforeseen needs. While James Watt designed his steam engine to pump water from mines, it soon was supplying power to cotton mills, then (with much greater profit) propelling locomotives and boats.

Thus, the commonsense view of invention that served as our starting point reverses the usual roles of invention and need. It also overstates the importance of rare geniuses, such as Watt and Edison. That "heroic theory of invention," as it is termed, is encouraged by patent law, because an applicant for a patent must prove the novelty of the invention submitted. Inventors thereby have a financial incentive to denigrate or ignore previous work. From a patent lawyer's perspective, the ideal invention is one that arises without any precursors, like Athene springing fully formed from the forehead of Zeus.

In reality, even for the most famous and apparently decisive modern inventions, neglected precursors lurked behind the bald claim "X invented Y." For instance, we are regularly told, "James Watt invented the steam engine in 1769," supposedly inspired by watching steam rise from a teakettle's spout. Unfortunately for this splendid fiction, Watt actually got the idea for his particular steam engine while repairing a model of Thomas Newcomen's steam engine, which Newcomen had invented 57 years earlier and of which over a hundred had been manufactured in England by the time of Watt's repair work. Newcomen's engine, in turn, followed the steam engine that the Englishman Thomas Savery patented in 1698, which followed the steam engine that the Frenchman Denis Papin designed (but did not build) around 1680, which in turn had precursors in the ideas of the Dutch scientist Christiaan Huygens and others. All this is not to deny that Watt greatly improved Newcomen's engine (by incorporating a separate steam condenser and a double-acting cylinder), just as Newcomen had greatly improved Savery's.

Similar histories can be related for all modern inventions that are adequately documented. The hero customarily credited with the invention followed previous inventors who had had similar aims and had already produced designs, working models, or (as in the case of the Newcomen steam engine) commercially successful models. Edison's famous "invention" of the incandescent light bulb on the night of October 21, 1879, improved on many other incandescent light bulbs patented by other inventors between 1841 and 1878. Similarly, the Wright brothers' manned powered airplane was preceded by the manned unpowered gliders of Otto Lilienthal and the unmanned powered airplane of Samuel Langley; Samuel Morse's telegraph was preceded by those of Joseph Henry, William Cooke, and Charles Wheatstone; and Eli Whitney's gin for cleaning short-staple (inland) cotton extended gins that had been cleaning long-staple (Sea Island) cotton for thousands of years.

All this is not to deny that Watt, Edison, the Wright brothers, Morse, and Whitney made big improvements and thereby increased or inaugurated commercial success. The form of the invention eventually adopted might have been somewhat different without the recognized inventor's contribution. But the question for our purposes is whether the broad pattern of world history would have been altered significantly if some genius inventor had not been born at a particular place and time. The answer is clear: there has never been any such person. All recognized famous inventors had capable predecessors and successors and made their improvements at a time when society was capable of using their product. As we shall see, the tragedy of the hero who perfected the stamps used for the Phaistos disk was that he or she devised something that the society of the time could not exploit on a large scale.

My examples so far have been drawn from modern technologies, because their histories are well known. My two main conclusions are that technology develops cumulatively, rather than in isolated heroic acts, and that it finds most of its uses after it has been invented, rather than being invented to meet a foreseen need. These conclusions surely apply with much greater force to the undocumented history of ancient technology. When Ice Age hunter-gatherers noticed burned sand and limestone residues in their hearths, it was impossible for them to foresee the long, serendipitous accumulation of discoveries that would lead to the first Roman glass windows (around A.D. 1), by way of the first objects with surface glazes (around 4000 B.C.), the first free-standing glass objects of Egypt and Mesopotamia (around 2500 B.C.), and the first glass vessels (around 1500 B.C.).

We know nothing about how those earliest known surface glazes themselves were developed. Nevertheless, we can infer the methods of prehistoric invention by watching technologically "primitive" people today, such as the New Guineans with whom I work. I already mentioned their knowledge of hundreds of local plant and animal species and each species' edibility, medical value, and other uses. New Guineans told me similarly about dozens of rock types in their environment and each type's hardness, color, behavior when struck or flaked, and uses. All of that knowledge is acquired by observation and by trial and error. I see that process of "invention" going on whenever I take New Guineans to work with me in an area away from their homes. They constantly pick up unfamiliar things in the forest, tinker with them, and occasionally find them useful enough to bring home. I see the same process when I am abandoning a campsite, and local people come to scavenge what is left. They play with my discarded objects and try to figure out whether they might be useful in New Guinea society. Discarded tin cans are easy: they end up reused as containers. Other objects are tested for purposes very different from the one for which they were manufactured. How would that yellow number 2 pencil look as an ornament, inserted through a pierced ear-lobe or nasal septum? Is that piece of broken glass sufficiently sharp and strong to be useful as a knife? Eureka!

The raw substances available to ancient peoples were natural materials such as stone, wood, bone, skins, fiber, clay, sand, limestone, and minerals, all existing in great variety. From those materials, people gradually learned to work particular types of stone, wood, and bone into tools; to convert particular clays into pottery and bricks; to convert certain mixtures of sand, limestone, and other "dirt" into glass; and to work available pure soft metals such as copper and gold, then to extract metals from ores, and finally to work hard metals such as bronze and iron.

A good illustration of the histories of trial and error involved is furnished by the development of gunpowder and gasoline from raw materials. Combustible natural products inevitably make themselves noticed, as when a resinous log explodes in a campfire. By 2000 B.C., Mesopotamians were extracting tons of petroleum by heating rock asphalt. Ancient Greeks discovered the uses of various mixtures of petroleum, pitch, resins, sulfur, and quicklime as incendiary weapons, delivered by catapults, arrows, firebombs, and ships. The expertise at distillation that medieval Islamic alchemists developed to produce alcohols and perfumes also let them distill petroleum into fractions, some of which proved to be even more powerful incendiaries. Delivered in grenades, rockets, and torpedoes, those incendiaries played a key role in Islam's eventual defeat of the Crusaders. By then, the Chinese had observed that a particular mixture of sulfur, charcoal, and saltpeter, which became known as gunpowder, was especially explosive. An Islamic chemical treatise of about A.D. 1100 describes seven gunpowder recipes, while a treatise from A.D. 1280 gives more than 70 recipes that had proved suitable for diverse purposes (one for rockets, another for cannons).

As for postmedieval petroleum distillation, 19th-century chemists found the middle distillate fraction useful as fuel for oil lamps. The chemists discarded the most volatile fraction (gasoline) as an unfortunate waste product—until it was found to be an ideal fuel for internal-combustion engines. Who today remembers that gasoline, the fuel of modern civilization, originated as yet another invention in search of a use?

Once an inventor has discovered a use for a new technology, the next step is to persuade society to adopt it. Merely having a bigger, faster, more powerful device for doing something is no guarantee of ready acceptancc. Innumerable such technologies were either not adopted at all or adopted only after prolonged resistance. Notorious examples include the U.S. Congress's rejection of funds to develop a supersonic transport in 1971, the world's continued rejection of an efficiently designed typewriter keyboard, and Britain's long reluctance to adopt electric lighting. What is it that promotes an invention's acceptance by a society?

Let's begin by comparing the acceptability of different inventions within the same society. It turns out that at least four factors influence acceptance.

The first and most obvious factor is relative economic advantage compared with existing technology. While wheels are very useful in modern industrial societies, that has not been so in some other societies. Ancient Native Mexicans invented wheeled vehicles with axles for use as toys, but not for transport. That seems incredible to us, until we reflect that ancient Mexicans lacked domestic animals to hitch to their wheeled vehicles, which therefore offered no advantage over human porters.

A second consideration is social value and prestige, which can override economic benefit (or lack thereof). Millions of people today buy designer jeans for double the price of equally durable generic jeans—because the social cachet of the designer label counts for more than the extra cost. Similarly, Japan continues to use its horrendously cumbersome kanji writing system in preference to efficient alphabets or Japan's own efficient kana syllabary—because the prestige attached to kanji is so great.

Still another factor is compatibility with vested interests. This book, like probably every other typed document you have ever read, was typed with a QWERTY keyboard, named for the left-most six letters in its upper row. Unbelievable as it may now sound, that keyboard layout was designed in 1873 as a feat of anti-engineering. It employs a whole series of perverse tricks designed to force typists to type as slowly as possible, such as scattering the commonest letters over all keyboard rows and concentrating them on the left side (where right-handed people have to use their weaker hand). The reason behind all of those seemingly counterproductive features is that the typewriters of 1873 jammed if adjacent keys were struck in quick succession, so that manufacturers had to slow down typists. When improvements in typewriters eliminated the problem of jamming, trials in 1932 with an efficiently laid-out keyboard showed that it would let us double our typing speed and reduce our typing effort by 95 percent. But QWERTY keyboards were solidly entrenched by then. The vested interests of hundreds of millions of QWERTY typists, typing teachers, typewriter and computer salespeople, and manufacturers have crushed all moves toward keyboard efficiency for over 60 years.

While the story of the QWERTY keyboard may sound funny, many similar cases have involved much heavier economic consequences. Why does Japan now dominate the world market for transistorized electronic consumer products, to a degree that damages the United States's balance of payments with Japan, even though transistors were invented and patented in the United States? Because Sony bought transistor licensing rights from Western Electric at a time when the American electronics consumer industry was churning out vacuum tube models and reluctant to compete with its own products. Why were British cities still using gas street lighting into the 1920s, long after U.S. and German cities had converted to electric street lighting? Because British municipal governments had invested heavily in gas lighting and placed regulatory obstacles in the way of the competing electric light companies.

The remaining consideration affecting acceptance of new technologies is the ease with which their advantages can be observed. In A.D. 1340, when firearms had not yet reached most of Europe, England's earl of Derby and earl of Salisbury happened to be present in Spain at the battle of Tarifa, where Arabs used cannons against the Spaniards. Impressed by what they saw, the earls introduced cannons to the English army, which adopted them enthusiastically and . . . used them against French soldiers at the battle of Crécy six years later.

Thus, wheels, designer jeans, and QWERTY keyboards illustrate the varied reasons why the same society is not equally receptive to all inventions. Conversely, the same invention's reception also varies greatly among contemporary societies. We are all familiar with the supposed generalization that rural Third World societies are less receptive to innovation than are Westernized industrial societies. Even within the industrialized world, some areas are much more receptive than others. Such differences, if they existed on a continental scale, might explain why technology developed faster on some continents than on others. For instance, if all Aboriginal Australian societies were for some reason uniformly resistant to change, that might account for their continued use of stone tools after metal tools had appeared on every other continent. How do differences in receptivity among societies arise?

A laundry list of at least 14 explanatory factors has been proposed by historians of technology. One is long life expectancy, which in principle should give prospective inventors the years necessary to accumulate technical knowledge, as well as the patience and security to embark on long development programs yielding delayed rewards. Hence the greatly increased life expectancy brought by modern medicine may have contributed to the recently accelerating pace of invention.

The next five factors involve economics or the organization of society: (1) The availability of cheap slave labor in classical times supposedly discouraged innovation then, whereas high wages or labor scarcity now stimulate the search for technological solutions. For example, the prospect of changed immigration policies that would cut off the supply of cheap Mexican seasonal labor to Californian farms was the immediate incentive for the development of a machine-harvestable variety of tomatoes in California. (2) Patents and other property laws, protecting ownership rights of inventors, reward innovation in the modern West, while the lack of such protection discourages it in modern China. (3) Modern industrial societies provide extensive opportunities for technical training, as medieval Islam did and modern Zaire does not. (4) Modern capitalism is, and the ancient Roman economy was not, organized in a way that made it potentially rewarding to invest capital in technological development. (5) The strong individualism of U.S. society allows successful inventors to keep earnings for themselves, whereas strong family ties in New Guinea ensure that someone who begins to earn money will be joined by a dozen relatives expecting to move in and be fed and supported.

Another four suggested explanations are ideological, rather than economic or organizational: (1) Risk-taking behavior, essential for efforts at innovation, is more widespread in some societies than in others. (2) The scientific outlook is a unique feature of post-Renaissance European society that has contributed heavily to its modern technological preeminence. (3) Tolerance of diverse views and of heretics fosters innovation, whereas a strongly traditional outlook (as in China's emphasis on ancient Chinese classics) stifles it. (4) Religions vary greatly in their relation to technological innovation: some branches of Judaism and Christianity are claimed to be especially compatible with it, while some branches of Islam, Hinduism, and Brahmanism may be especially incompatible with it.

All ten of these hypotheses are plausible. But none of them has any necessary association with geography. If patent rights, capitalism, and certain religions do promote technology, what selected for those factors in postmedieval Europe but not in contemporary China or India?

At least the direction in which those ten factors influence technology seems clear. The remaining four proposed factors—war, centralized government, climate, and resource abundance—appear to act inconsistently: sometimes they stimulate technology, sometimes they inhibit it. (1) Throughout history, war has often been a leading stimulant of technological innovation. For instance, the enormous investments made in nuclear weapons during World War II and in airplanes and trucks during World War I launched whole new fields of technology. But wars can also deal devastating setbacks to technological development. (2) Strong centralized government boosted technology in late-19th-century Germany and Japan, and crushed it in China after A.D. 1500. (3) Many northern Europeans assume that technology thrives in a rigorous climate where survival is impossible without technology, and withers in a benign climate where clothing is unnecessary and bananas supposedly fall off the trees. An opposite view is that benign environments leave people free from the constant struggle for existence, free to devote themselves to innovation. (4) There has also been debate over whether technology is stimulated by abundance or by scarcity of environmental resources. Abundant resources might stimulate the development of inventions utilizing those resources, such as water mill technology in rainy northern Europe, with its many rivers—but why didn't water mill technology progress more rapidly in even rainier New Guinea? The destruction of Britain's forests has been suggested as the reason behind its early lead in developing coal technology, but why didn't deforestation have the same effect in China?

This discussion does not exhaust the list of reasons proposed to explain why societies differ in their receptivity to new technology. Worse yet, all of these proximate explanations bypass the question of the ultimate factors behind them. This may seem like a discouraging setback in our attempt to understand the course of history, since technology has undoubtedly been one of history's strongest forces. However, I shall now argue that the diversity of independent factors behind technological innovation actually makes it easier, not harder, to understand history's broad pattern.

For [our] purposes . . . the key question about the laundry list is whether such factors differed systematically from continent to continent and thereby led to continental differences in technological development. Most laypeople and many historians assume, expressly or tacitly, that the answer is yes. For example, it is widely believed that Australian Aborigines as a group shared ideological characteristics contributing to their technological backwardness: they were (or are) supposedly conservative, living in an imagined past Dreamtime of the world's creation, and not focused on practical ways to improve the present. A leading historian of Africa characterized Africans as inward looking and lacking Europeans' drive for expansion.

But all such claims are based on pure speculation. There has never been a study of many societies under similar socioeconomic conditions on each of two continents, demonstrating systematic ideological differences between the two continents' peoples. The usual reasoning is instead circular: because technological differences exist, the existence of corresponding ideological differences is inferred.

In reality, I regularly observe in New Guinea that native societies there differ greatly from each other in their prevalent outlooks. Just like industrialized Europe and America, traditional New Guinea has conservative societies that resist new ways, living side by side with innovative societies that selectively adopt new ways. The result, with the arrival of Western technology, is that the more entrepreneurial societies are now exploiting Western technology to overwhelm their conservative neighbors.

For example, when Europeans first reached the highlands of eastern New Guinea, in the 1930s, they "discovered" dozens of previously uncontacted Stone Age tribes, of which the Chimbu tribe proved especially aggressive in adopting Western technology. When Chimbus saw white settlers planting coffee, they began growing coffee themselves as a cash crop. In 1964 1 met a 50-year-old Chimbu man, unable to read, wearing a traditional grass skirt, and born into a society still using stone tools, who had become rich by growing coffee, used his profits to buy a sawmill for $100,000 cash, and bought a fleet of trucks to transport his coffee and timber to market. In contrast, a neighboring highland people, with whom I worked for eight years, the Daribi, are especially conservative and uninterested in new technology. When the first helicopter landed in the Daribi area, they briefly looked at it and just went back to what they had been doing; the Chimbus would have been bargaining to charter it. As a result, Chimbus are now moving into the Daribi area, taking it over for plantations, and reducing the Daribi to working for them.

On every other continent as well, certain native societies have proved very receptive, adopted foreign ways and technology selectively, and integrated them successfully into their own society. In Nigeria the Ibo people became the local entrepreneurial equivalent of New Guinea's Chimbus. Today the most numerous Native American tribe in the United States is the Navajo, who on European arrival were just one of several hundred tribes. But the Navajo proved especially resilient and able to deal selectively with innovation. They incorporated

Western dyes into their weaving, became silversmiths and ranchers, and now drive trucks while continuing to live in traditional dwellings.

Among the supposedly conservative Aboriginal Australians as well, there are receptive societies along with conservative ones. At the one extreme, the Tasmanians continued to use stone tools superseded tens of thousands of years earlier in Europe and replaced in most of mainland Australia too. At the opposite extreme, some aboriginal fishing groups of southeastern Australia devised elaborate technologies for managing fish populations, including the construction of canals, weirs, and standing traps.

Thus, the development and reception of inventions vary enormously from society to society on the same continent. They also vary over time within the same society. Nowadays, Islamic societies in the Middle East are relatively conservative and not at the forefront of technology. But medieval Islam in the same region was technologically advanced and open to innovation. It achieved far higher literacy rates than contemporary Europe; it assimilated the legacy of classical Greek civilization to such a degree that many classical Greek books are now known to us only through Arabic copies; it invented or elaborated windmills, tidal mills, trigonometry, and lateen sails; it made major advances in metallurgy, mechanical and chemical engineering, and irrigation methods; and it adopted paper and gunpowder from China and transmitted them to Europe. In the Middle Ages the flow of technology was overwhelmingly from Islam to Europe, rather than from Europe to Islam as it is today. Only after around A.D. 1500 did the net direction of flow begin to reverse.

Innovation in China too fluctuated markedly with time. Until around A.D. 1450, China was technologically much more innovative and advanced than Europe, even more so than medieval Islam. The long list of Chinese inventions includes canal lock gates, cast iron, deep drilling, efficient animal harnesses, gunpowder, kites, magnetic compasses, movable type, paper, porcelain, printing (except for the Phaistos disk), sternpost rudders, and wheelbarrows. China then ceased to be innovative for reasons. . . . Conversely, we think of western Europe and its derived North American societies as leading the modern world in technological innovation, but technology was less advanced in western Europe than in any other "civilized" area of the Old World until the late Middle Ages.

Thus, it is untrue that there are continents whose societies have tended to be innovative and continents whose societies have tended to be conservative. On any continent, at any given time, there are innovative societies and also conservative ones. In addition, receptivity to innovation fluctuates in time within the same region.

On reflection, these conclusions are precisely what one would expect if a society's innovativeness is determined by many independent factors. Without a detailed knowledge of all of those factors, innovativeness becomes unpredictable. Hence social scientists continue to debate the specific reasons why receptivity changed in Islam, China, and Europe, and why the Chimbus, Ibos, and Navajo were more receptive to new technology than were their neighbors. To the student of broad historical patterns, though, it makes no difference what the specific reasons were in each of those cases. The myriad factors affecting innovativeness make the historian's task paradoxically easier, by converting societal variation in innovativeness into essentially a random variable. That means that, over a large enough area (such as a whole continent) at any particular time, some proportion of societies is likely to be innovative.

Where do innovations actually come from? For all societies except the few past ones that were completely isolated, much or most new technology is not invented locally but is instead borrowed from other societies. The relative importance of local invention and of borrowing depends mainly on two factors: the ease of invention of the particular technology, and the proximity of the particular society to other societies.

Some inventions arose straightforwardly from a handling of raw materials. Such inventions developed on many independent occasions in world history, at different places and times. One example, which we have already considered at length, is plant domestication, with at least nine independent origins. Another is pottery, which may have arisen from observations of the behavior of clay, a very widespread natural material, when dried or heated. Pottery appeared in Japan around 14,000 years ago, in the Fertile Crescent and China by around 10,000 years ago, and in Amazonia, Africa's Sahel zone, the U.S. Southeast, and Mexico thereafter.

An example of a much more difficult invention is writing, which does not suggest itself by observation of any natural material. [Writing] had only a few independent origins, and the alphabet arose apparently only once in world history. Other difficult inventions include the water wheel, rotary quern, tooth gearing, magnetic compass, windmill, and camera obscura, all of which were invented only once or twice in the Old World and never in the New World.

Such complex inventions were usually acquired by borrowing, because they spread more rapidly than they could be independently invented locally. A clear example is the wheel, which is first attested around 3400 B.C. near the Black Sea, and then turns up within the next few centuries over much of Europe and Asia. All those early Old World wheels are of a peculiar design: a solid wooden circle constructed of three planks fastened together, rather than a rim with spokes. In contrast, the sole wheels of Native American societies (depicted on Mexican ceramic vessels) consisted of a single piece, suggesting a second independent invention of the wheel—as one would expect from other evidence for the isolation of New World from Old World civilizations.

No one thinks that that same peculiar Old World wheel design appeared repeatedly by chance at many separate sites of the Old World within a few centuries of each other, after 7 million years of wheelless human history. Instead, the utility of the wheel surely caused it to diffuse rapidly east and west over the Old World from its sole site of invention. Other examples of complex technologies that diffused east and west in the ancient Old World, from a single West Asian source, include door locks, pulleys, rotary querns, windmills—and the alphabet. A New World example of technological diffusion is metallurgy, which spread from the Andes via Panama to Mesoamerica.

When a widely useful invention does crop up in one society, it then tends to spread in either of two ways. One way is that other societies see or learn of the invention, are receptive to it, and adopt it. The second is that societies lacking the invention find themselves at a disadvantage vis-à-vis the inventing society, and they become overwhelmed and replaced if the disadvantage is sufficiently great. A simple example is the spread of muskets among New Zealand's Maori tribes. One tribe, the Ngapuhi, adopted muskets from European traders around 1818. Over the course of the next 15 years, New Zealand was convulsed by the so-called Musket Wars, as musketless tribes either acquired muskets or were subjugated by tribes already armed with them. The outcome was that musket technology had spread throughout the whole of New Zealand by 1833: all surviving Maori tribes now had muskets.

When societies do adopt a new technology from the society that invented it, the diffusion may occur in many different contexts. They include peaceful trade (as in the spread of transistors from the United States to Japan in 1954), espionage (the smuggling of silkworms from Southeast Asia to the Mideast in A.D. 552), emigration (the spread of French glass and clothing manufacturing techniques over Europe by the 200,000 Huguenots expelled from France in 1685), and war. A crucial case of the last was the transfer of Chinese papermaking techniques to Islam, made possible when an Arab army defeated a Chinese army at the battle of Talas River in Central Asia in A.D. 751, found some papermakers among the prisoners of war, and brought them to Samarkand to set up paper manufacture.

[C]ultural diffusion can involve either detailed "blueprints" or just vague ideas stimulating a reinvention of details. . . . The preceding paragraph gave examples of blueprint copying, whereas the transfer of Chinese porcelain technology to Europe provides an instance of long-drawn-out idea diffusion. Porcelain, a fine-grained translucent pottery, was invented in China around the 7th century A.D. When it began to reach Europe by the Silk Road in the 14th century (with no information about how it was manufactured), it was much admired, and many unsuccessful attempts were made to imitate it. Not until 1707 did the German alchemist Johann Böttger, after lengthy experiments with processes and with mixing various minerals and clays together, hit upon the solution and establish the now famous Meissen porcelain works. More or less independent later experiments in France and England led to Sèvres, Wedgwood, and Spode porcelains. Thus, European potters had to reinvent Chinese manufacturing methods for themselves, but they were stimulated to do so by having models of the desired product before them.

Depending on their geographic location, societies differ in how readily they can receive technology by diffusion from other societies. The most isolated people on Earth in recent history were the Aboriginal Tasmanians, living without oceangoing watercraft on an island 100 miles from Australia, itself the most isolated continent. The Tasmanians had no contact with other societies for 10,000 years and acquired no new technology other than what they invented themselves. Australians and New Guineans, separated from the Asian mainland by the Indonesian island chain, received only a trickle of inventions from Asia. The societies most accessible to receiving inventions by diffusion were those embedded in the major continents. In these societies technology developed most rapidly, because they accumulated not only their own inventions but also those of other societies. For example, medieval Islam, centrally located in Eurasia, acquired inventions from India and China and inherited ancient Greek learning.

The importance of diffusion, and of geographic location in making it possible, is strikingly illustrated by some otherwise incomprehensible cases of societies that abandoned powerful technologies. We tend to assume that useful technologies, once acquired, inevitably persist until superseded by better ones. In reality, technologies must be not only acquired but also maintained, and that too depends on many unpredictable factors. Any society goes through social movements or fads, in which economically useless things become valued or useful things devalued temporarily. Nowadays, when almost all societies on Earth are connected to each other, we cannot imagine a fad's going so far that an important technology would actually be discarded. A society that temporarily turned against a powerful technology would continue to see it being used by neighboring societies and would have the opportunity to reacquire it by diffusion (or would be conquered by neighbors if it failed to do so). But such fads can persist in isolated societies.

A famous example involves Japan's abandonment of guns. Firearms reached Japan in A.D. 1543, when two Portuguese adventurers armed with harquebuses (primitive guns) arrived on a Chinese cargo ship. The Japanese were so impressed by the new weapon that they commenced indigenous gun production, greatly improved gun technology, and by A.D. 1600 owned more and better guns than any other country in the world.

But there were also factors working against the acceptance of firearms in Japan. The country had a numerous warrior class, the samurai, for whom swords rated as class symbols and works of art (and as means for subjugating the lower classes). Japanese warfare had previously involved single combats between samurai swordsmen, who stood in the open, made ritual speeches, and then took pride in fighting gracefully. Such behavior became lethal in the presence of peasant soldiers ungracefully blasting away with guns. In addition, guns were a foreign invention and grew to be despised, as did other things foreign in Japan after 1600. The samurai-controlled government began by restricting gun production to a few cities, then introduced a requirement of a government license for producing a gun, then issued licenses only for guns produced for the government, and finally reduced government orders for guns, until Japan was almost without functional guns again.

Contemporary European rulers also included some who despised guns and tried to restrict their availability. But such measures never got far in Europe, where any country that temporarily swore off firearms would be promptly overrun by gun-toting neighboring countries. Only because Japan was a populous, isolated island could it get away with its rejection of the powerful new military technology. Its safety in isolation came to an end in 1853, when the visit of Commodore Perry's U.S. fleet bristling with cannons convinced Japan of its need to resume gun manufacture.

That rejection and China's abandonment of oceangoing ships (as well as of mechanical clocks and water-driven spinning machines) are well-known historical instances of technological reversals in isolated or semi-isolated societies. Other such reversals occurred in prehistoric times. The extreme case is that of Aboriginal Tasmanians, who abandoned even bone tools and fishing to become the society with the simplest technology in the modern world . . . Aboriginal Australians may have adopted and then abandoned bows and arrows. Torres Islanders abandoned canoes, while Gaua Islanders abandoned and then readopted them. Pottery was abandoned throughout Polynesia. Most Polynesians and many Melanesians abandoned the use of bows and arrows in war. Polar Eskimos lost the bow and arrow and the kayak, while Dorset Eskimos lost the bow and arrow, bow drill, and dogs.

These examples, at first so bizarre to us, illustrate well the roles of geography and of diffusion in the history of technology. Without diffusion, fewer technologies are acquired, and more existing technologies are lost.

Because technology begets more technology, the importance of an invention's diffusion potentially exceeds the importance of the original invention. Technology's history exemplifies what is termed an autocatalytic process: that is, one that speeds up at a rate that increases with time, because the process catalyzes itself. The explosion of technology since the Industrial Revolution impresses us today, but the medieval explosion was equally impressive compared with that of the Bronze Age, which in turn dwarfed that of the Upper Paleolithic.

One reason why technology tends to catalyze itself is that advances depend upon previous mastery of simpler problems. For example, Stone Age farmers did not proceed directly to extracting and working iron, which requires high-temperature furnaces. Instead, iron ore metallurgy grew out of thousands of years of human experience with natural outcrops of pure metals soft enough to be hammered into shape without heat (copper and gold). It also grew out of thousands of years of development of simple furnaces to make pottery, and then to extract copper ores and work copper alloys (bronzes) that do not require as high temperatures as does iron. In both the Fertile Crescent and China, iron objects became common only after about 2,000 years of experience of bronze metallurgy. New World societies had just begun making bronze artifacts and had not yet started making iron ones at the time when the arrival of Europeans truncated the New World's independent trajectory.

The other main reason for autocatalysis is that new technologies and materials make it possible to generate still other new technologies by recombination. For instance, why did printing spread explosively in medieval Europe after Gutenberg printed his Bible in A.D. 1455, but not after that unknown printer printed the Phaistos disk in 1700 B.C.? The explanation is partly that medieval European printers were able to combine six technological advances, most of which were unavailable to the maker of the Phaistos disk. Of those advances—in paper, movable type, metallurgy, presses, inks, and scripts—paper and the idea of movable type reached Europe from China. Gutenberg's development of typecasting from metal dies, to overcome the potentially fatal problem of nonuniform type size, depended on many metallurgical developments: steel for letter punches, brass or bronze alloys (later replaced by steel) for dies, lead for molds, and a tin-zinc-lead alloy for type. Gutenberg's press was derived from screw presses in use for making wine and olive oil, while his ink was an oil-based improvement on existing inks. The alphabetic scripts that medieval Europe inherited from three millennia of alphabet development lent themselves to printing with movable type, because only a few dozen letter forms had to be cast, as opposed to the thousands of signs required for Chinese writing.

In all six respects, the maker of the Phaistos disk had access to much less powerful technologies to combine into a printing system than did Gutenberg. The disk's writing medium was clay, which is much bulkier and heavier than paper. The metallurgical skills, inks, and presses of 1700 B.C. Crete were more primitive than those of A.D. 1455 Germany, so the disk had to be punched by hand rather than by cast movable type locked into a metal frame, inked, and pressed. The disk's script was a syllabary with more signs, of more complex form, than the Roman alphabet used by Gutenberg. As a result, the Phaistos disk's printing technology was much clumsier, and offered fewer advantages over writing by hand, than Gutenberg's printing press. In addition to all those technological drawbacks, the Phaistos disk was printed at a time when knowledge of writing was confined to a few palace or temple scribes. Hence there was little demand for the disk maker's beautiful product, and little incentive to invest in making the dozens of hand punches required. In contrast, the potential mass market for printing in medieval Europe induced numerous investors to lend money to Gutenberg.

Human technology developed from the first stone tools, in use by two and a half million years ago, to the 1996 laser printer that replaced my already outdated 1992 laser printer and that was used to print this book's manuscript. The rate of development was undetectably slow at the beginning, when hundreds of thousands of years passed with no discernible change in our stone tools and with no surviving evidence for artifacts made of other materials. Today, technology advances so rapidly that it is reported in the daily newspaper.

In this long history of accelerating development, one can single out two especially significant jumps. The first, occurring between 100,000 and 50,000 years ago, probably was made possible by genetic changes in our bodies: namely, by evolution of the modern anatomy permitting modern speech or modern brain function, or both. That jump led to bone tools, single-purpose stone tools, and compound tools. The second jump resulted from our adoption of a sedentary lifestyle, which happened at different times in different parts of the world, as early as 13,000 years ago in some areas and not even today in others. For the most part, that adoption was linked to our adoption of food production, which required us to remain close to our crops, orchards, and stored food surpluses.

Sedentary living was decisive for the history of technology, because it enabled people to accumulate non portable possessions. Nomadic hunter-gatherers are limited to technology that can be carried. If you move often and lack vehicles or draft animals, you confine your possessions to babies, weapons, and a bare minimum of other absolute necessities small enough to carry. You can't be burdened with pottery and printing presses as you shift camp. That practical difficulty probably explains the tantalizingly early appearance of some technologies, followed by a long delay in their further development. For example, the earliest attested precursors of ceramics are fired clay figurines made in the area of modern Czechoslovakia 27,000 years ago, long before the oldest known fired clay vessels (from Japan 14,000 years ago). The same area of Czechoslovakia at the same time has yielded the earliest evidence for weaving, otherwise not attested until the oldest known basket appears around 13,000 years ago and the oldest known woven cloth around 9,000 years ago. Despite these very early first steps, neither pottery nor weaving took off until people became sedentary and thereby escaped the problem of transporting pots and looms.

Besides permitting sedentary living and hence the accumulation of possessions, food production was decisive in the history of technology for another reason. It became possible, for the first time in human evolution, to develop economically specialized societies consisting of non-food-producing specialists fed by food-producing peasants. But [we know] . . . that food production arose at different times in different continents . . . [and that] local technology depends, for both its origin and its maintenance, not only on local invention but also on the diffusion of technology from elsewhere. That consideration tended to cause technology to develop most rapidly on continents with few geographic and ecological barriers to diffusion, either within that continent or on other continents. Finally, each society on a continent represents one more opportunity to invent and adopt a technology, because societies vary greatly in their innovativeness for many separate reasons. Hence, all other things being equal, technology develops fastest in large productive regions with large human populations, many potential inventors, and many competing societies.

Let us now summarize how variations in these three factors—time of onset of food production, barriers to diffusion, and human population size—led straightforwardly to the observed intercontinental differences in the development of technology. Eurasia (effectively including North Africa) is the world's largest landmass, encompassing the largest number of competing societies. It was also the landmass with the two centers where food production began the earliest: the Fertile Crescent and China. Its east–west major axis permitted many inventions adopted in one part of Eurasia to spread relatively rapidly to societies at similar latitudes and climates elsewhere in Eurasia. Its breadth along its minor axis (north–south) contrasts with the Americas' narrowness at the Isthmus of Panama. It lacks the severe ecological barriers transecting the major axes of the Americas and Africa. Thus, geographic and ecological barriers to diffusion of technology were less severe in Eurasia than in other continents. Thanks to all these factors, Eurasia was the continent on which technology started its post-Pleistocene acceleration earliest and resulted in the greatest local accumulation of technologies.

North and South America are conventionally regarded as separate continents, but they have been connected for several million years, pose similar historical problems, and may be considered together for comparison with Eurasia. The Americas form the world's second-largest landmass, significantly smaller than Eurasia. However, they're fragmented by geography and by ecology: the Isthmus of Panama, only 40 miles, wide, virtually transects the Americas geographically, as do the isthmus's Darien rain forests and the northern Mexican desert ecologically. The latter desert separated advanced human societies of Mesoamerica from those of North America, while the isthmus separated advanced societies of Mesoamerica from those of the Andes and Amazonia. In addition, the main axis of the Americas is north–south, forcing most diffusion to go against a gradient of latitude (and climate) rather than to operate within the same latitude. For example, wheels were invented in Mesoamerica, and llamas were domesticated in the central Andes by 3000 B.C., but 5,000 years later the Americas' sole beast of burden and sole wheels had still not encountered each other, even though the distance separating Mesoamerica's Maya societies from the northern border of the Inca Empire (1,200 miles) was far less than the 6,000 miles separating wheel- and horse-sharing France and China. Those factors seem to me to account for the Americas' technological lag behind Eurasia.

Sub-Saharan Africa is the world's third largest landmass, considerably smaller than the Americas. Throughout most of human history it was far more accessible to Eurasia than were the Americas, but the Saharan desert is still a major ecological barrier separating sub-Saharan Africa from Eurasia plus North Africa. Africa's north~south axis posed a further obstacle to the diffusion of technology, both between Eurasia and sub-Saharan Africa and within the sub-Saharan region itself. As an illustration of the latter obstacle, pottery and iron metallurgy arose in or reached sub-Saharan Africa's Sahel zone (north of the equator) at least as early as they reached western Europe. However, pottery did not reach the southern tip of Africa until around A.D. 1, and metallurgy had not yet diffused overland to the southern tip by the time that it arrived there from Europe on ships.

Finally, Australia is the smallest continent. The very low rainfall and productivity of most of Australia makes it effectively even smaller as regards its capacity to support human populations. It is also the most isolated continent. In addition, food production never arose indigenously in Australia. Those factors combined to leave Australia the sole continent still without metal artifacts in modern times.

Table [1] translates these factors into numbers, by comparing the continents with respect to their areas and their modern human populations. The continents' populations 10,000 years ago, just before the rise of food production, are not known but surely stood in the same sequence, since many of the areas producing the most food today would also have been productive areas for hunter-gatherers 10,000 years ago.

TABLE [I] **Human Populations of the Continents**

Continent	*1990 Population*	*Area (square miles)*
Eurasia and North Africa	4,120,000,000	24,200,000
(Eurasia)	(4,000,000,000)	(21,500,000)
(North Africa)	(120,000,000)	(2,700,000)
North America and South America	736,000,000	16,400,000
Sub-Saharan Africa	535,000,000	9,100,000
Australia	18,000,000	3,000,000

The differences in population are glaring: Eurasia's (including North Africa's) is nearly 6 times that of the Americas, nearly 8 times that of Africa, and 230 times that of Australia. Larger populations mean more inventors and more by itself goes a long way toward competing societies. Table [1] by itself goes a long way toward explaining the origins of guns and steel in Eurasia.

All these effects that continental differences in area, population, ease of diffusion, and onset of food production exerted on the rise of technology became exaggerated, because technology catalyzes itself. Eurasia's considerable initial advantage thereby was translated into a huge lead as of A.D. 1492—for reasons of Eurasia's distinctive geography rather than of distinctive human intellect. The New Guineans whom I know include potential Edisons. But they directed their ingenuity toward technological problems appropriate to their situations: the problems of surviving without any imported items in the New Guinea jungle, rather than the problem of inventing phonographs.

1997

GETTING STARTED

1. Use a dictionary, an encyclopedia, or the Internet to answer the following questions. What is the difference between a "syllabary" and an "alphabet"? Why does the Phaistos disk pose mysteries for historians of technology?

2. Work with members of a group to answer the following questions. What is the "heroic theory of invention" (p. 117)? Does Diamond agree or disagree with this theory? Why?

3. Work with members of a group to identify the four factors Diamond discusses that influence the acceptance of inventions. What are some other possible factors that Diamond does not identify?

4. Find and list examples in the essay where Diamond presents at least two interpretations of a theory or an invention. Why does Diamond present more than one explanation?

WRITING

5. Write one to two paragraphs that summarize Diamond's explanation of how innovations arise.

6. Write a one-paragraph summary of Diamond's discussion of "the roles of geography and of diffusion in the history of technology" (p. 131).

7. Write a letter to a friend explaining what Diamond means by "an autocatalytic process" (p. 131). In your letter, include one of Diamond's examples and one example that you think of yourself.

USING THE LIBRARY AND THE INTERNET

8. Diamond says that people in medieval Islamic societies "invented or elaborated windmills, tidal mills, trigonometry, and lateen sails" (p. 127). Use your reference library or the Internet to find out more information about inventions and innovations that come from medieval Islamic societies. Write at least three paragraphs that summarize your findings. Be sure to create a "Works Cited" page that lists your sources.

9. Using a reference database such as MAS Full Text Ultra that includes general interest and current-events magazines, try the combined search term "invention and technology." Scan your search results and print out the titles and abstracts of several articles that seem interesting in relation to Diamond.

MAKING CONNECTIONS

10. Write an essay that compares Diamond's arguments about the "commonsense view of necessity as invention's mother" (p. 118) with Clifford Geertz's interpretation of common sense in "Common Sense as a Cultural System." In what ways can Diamond's discussion of technology and innovation be understood as a cultural system?

11. According to Diamond, "many or most inventions were developed by people driven by curiosity or by a love of tinkering, in the absence of any initial demand for the product they had in

mind" (p. 118). Write an essay that uses Diamond's ideas about how we develop and use technology to analyze Sherry Turkle's discussion of "bricolage" in "The Triumph of Tinkering."

12. Although their subjects are different, Richard C. Lewontin's "Science as Social Action," Susan Sontag's "In Plato's Cave," and Diamond's essay all raise questions about how we can best make sense of innovations. Write an essay comparing and contrasting Diamond's main argument to the arguments of one or more of these writers. What are the writers' respective goals? How does the context or subject matter affect the writers' conclusions? Which analysis seems the most persuasive to you and why?

Annie Dillard

Annie Dillard (1945–) wrote poetry for fifteen years before she discovered the poetic possibilities of nonfiction prose. Since that time, she has written several collections of essays, a novel, and a memoir of her childhood. She has taught at numerous universities and writers' workshops and served in 1982 as a member of the U.S. Cultural Delegation to China. "Seeing" is the second chapter of *Pilgrim at Tinker Creek* (1974), Dillard's first and best-known book of nonfiction. *Pilgrim,* winner of the Pulitzer Prize for nonfiction in 1975, is a record of Dillard's conversations with what she read and what she saw in one year spent living on the banks of Tinker Creek in Virginia's Roanoke Valley.

To learn more about nature writing, visit the home page of the Association for the Study of Literature and the Environment at <http://www.asle.umn.edu.>

Seeing

When I was six or seven years old, growing up in Pittsburgh, I used to take a precious penny of my own and hide it for someone else to find. It was a curious compulsion; sadly, I've never been seized by it since. For some reason I always "hid" the penny along the same stretch of sidewalk up the street. I would cradle it at the roots of a sycamore, say, or in a hole left by a chipped-off piece of sidewalk. Then I would take a piece of chalk, and, starting at either end of the block, draw huge arrows leading up to the penny from both directions. After I learned to write I labeled the arrows: SURPRISE AHEAD or MONEY THIS WAY. I was greatly excited, during all this arrow-drawing, at the thought of the first lucky passer-by who would receive in this way, regardless of merit, a free gift from the universe. But I never lurked about. I would go straight home and not give the matter another thought, until, some months later, I would be gripped again by the impulse to hide another penny.

It is still the first week in January, and I've got great plans. I've been thinking about seeing. There are lots of things to see, unwrapped gifts and free surprises. The world is fairly studded and strewn with pennies cast broadside from a generous hand. But—and this is the point—who gets excited by a mere penny? If you follow one arrow, if you crouch motionless on a bank to watch a tremulous ripple thrill on the water and are rewarded by the sight of a muskrat kit paddling from its den, will you count that sight a chip of copper only, and go your rueful way? It is dire poverty indeed when a man is so malnourished and fatigued that he won't stoop to pick up a penny. But if you cultivate a healthy poverty and simplicity, so that finding a penny will literally make your day, then, since the world is in fact planted in pennies, you have with your poverty bought a lifetime of days. It is that simple. What you see is what you get.

I used to be able to see flying insects in the air. I'd look ahead and see, not the row of hemlocks across the road, but the air in front of it. My eyes would focus along that column of air, picking out flying insects. But I lost interest, I guess, for I dropped the habit. Now I can see birds. Probably some people can look at the grass at their feet and discover all the crawling creatures. I would like to know grasses and sedges—and care. Then my least journey into the world would be a field trip, a series of happy recognitions. Thoreau, in an expansive mood, exulted, "What a rich book might be made about buds, including, perhaps, sprouts!" It would be nice to think so. I cherish mental images I have of three perfectly happy people. One collects stones. Another—an Englishman, say —watches clouds. The third lives on a coast and collects drops of seawater which he examines microscopically and mounts. But I don't see what the specialist sees, and so I cut myself off, not only from the total picture, but from the various forms of happiness.

Unfortunately, nature is very much a now-you-see-it, now-you-don't affair. A fish flashes, then dissolves in the water before my eyes like so much salt. Deer apparently ascend bodily into heaven; the brightest oriole fades into leaves. These disappearances stun me into stillness and concentration; they say of nature that it conceals with a grand nonchalance, and they say of vision that it is a deliberate gift, the revelation of a dancer who for my eyes only flings away her seven veils. For nature does reveal as well as conceal: now-you-don't-see-it, now-you-do. For a week last September migrating red-winged blackbirds were feeding heavily down by the creek at the back of the house. One day I went out to investigate the racket; I walked up to a tree, an Osage orange, and a hundred birds flew away. They simply materialized out of the tree. I saw a tree, then a whisk of color, then a tree again. I walked closer and another hundred blackbirds took flight. Not a branch, not a twig budged: the birds were apparently weightless as well as invisible. Or, it was as if the leaves of the Osage orange had been freed from a spell in the form of red-winged blackbirds; they flew from the tree, caught my eye in the sky, and vanished. When I looked again at the tree the leaves had reassembled as if nothing had happened. Finally I walked directly to the trunk of the tree and a final hundred, the real diehards, appeared, spread, and vanished. How could so many hide in the tree without my seeing them? The Osage orange, unruffled, looked just as it had looked from the house,

FIGURE 20 Ansel Adams, *Roots. Foster Gardens, Honolulu, Hawaii,* 1948. 7½ × 6 3/16 in. Collection of Marjorie and Leonard Vernon, Los Angeles. (© Ansel Adams Publishing Rights Trust/CORBIS.)

when three hundred redwinged blackbirds cried from its crown. I looked downstream where they flew, and they were gone. Searching, I couldn't spot one. I wandered downstream to force them to play their hand, but they'd crossed the creek and scattered. One show to a customer. These appearances catch at my throat; they are the free gifts, the bright coppers at the roots of trees.

It's all a matter of keeping my eyes open. Nature is like one of those line drawings of a tree that are puzzles for children: Can you find hidden in the leaves a duck, a house, a boy, a bucket, a zebra, and a boot? Specialists can find the most incredibly well-hidden things. A book I read when I was young recommended an easy way to find caterpillars to rear: you simply find some fresh caterpillar droppings, look up, and there's your caterpillar. More recently an author advised me to set my mind at ease about those piles of cut stems on the ground in grassy fields. Field mice make them; they cut the grass down by degrees to reach the seeds at the head. It seems that when the grass is tightly packed, as in a field of ripe grain, the blade won't topple at a single cut through the stem; instead, the cut stem simply drops vertically, held in the crush of grain. The mouse severs the bottom again and again, the stem keeps dropping an inch at a time, and finally the head is low enough for the mouse to reach the seeds. Meanwhile, the mouse is positively littering the field with its little piles of cut stems into which, presumably, the author of the book is constantly stumbling.

If I can't see these minutiae, I still try to keep my eyes open. I'm always on the lookout for antlion traps in sandy soil, monarch pupae near milkweed, skipper larvae in locust leaves. These things are utterly common, and I've not seen one. I bang on hollow trees near water, but so far no flying squirrels have appeared. In flat country I watch every sunset in hopes of seeing the green ray. The green ray is a seldom-seen streak of light that rises from the sun like a spurting fountain at the moment of sunset; it throbs into the sky for two seconds and disappears. One more reason to keep my eyes open. A photography professor at the University of Florida just happened to see a bird die in midflight; it jerked, died, dropped, and smashed on the ground. I squint at the wind because I read Steward Edward White: "I have always maintained that if you looked closely enough you could *see* the wind—the dim, hardly-made-out, fine debris fleeing high in the air." White was an excellent observer, and devoted an entire chapter of *The Mountains* to the subject of seeing deer: "As soon as you can forget the naturally obvious and construct an artificial obvious, then you too will see deer."

But the artificial obvious is hard to see. My eyes account for less than one percent of the weight of my head; I'm bony and dense; I see what I expect. I once spent a full three minutes looking at a bullfrog that was so unexpectedly large I couldn't see it even though a dozen enthusiastic campers were shouting directions. Finally I asked, "What color am I looking for?" and a fellow said, "Green." When at last I picked out the frog, I saw what painters are up against: the thing wasn't green at all, but the color of wet hickory bark.

The lover can see, and the knowledgeable. I visited an aunt and uncle at a quarter-horse ranch in Cody, Wyoming. I couldn't do much of anything useful, but I could, I thought, draw. So, as we all sat around the kitchen table after supper, I produced a sheet of paper and drew a horse. "That's one lame horse," my aunt volunteered. The rest of the family joined in: "Only place to saddle that one is his neck"; "Looks like we better shoot the poor thing, on account of those terrible growths." Meekly, I slid the pencil and paper down the table. Everyone in that family, including my three young cousins, could draw a horse. Beautifully. When the paper came back it looked as though five shining, real quarter horses had been corraled by mistake with a papier-mâché moose; the real horses seemed to gaze at the monster with a steady, puzzled air. I stay away from horses now, but I can do a creditable goldfish. The point is that I just don't know what the lover knows; I just can't see the artificial obvious that those in the know construct. The herpetologist asks the native, "Are there snakes in that ravine?" "Nosir." And the herpetologist comes home with, yessir, three bags full. Are there butterflies on that mountain? Are the bluets in bloom, are there arrowheads here, or fossil shells in the shale?

Peeping through my keyhole I see within the range of only about thirty percent of the light that comes from the sun; the rest is infrared and some little ultraviolet, perfectly apparent to many animals, but invisible to me. A nightmare network of ganglia, charged and firing without my knowledge, cuts and splices what I do see, editing it for my brain. Donald E. Carr points out that the sense impressions of one-celled animals are not edited for the brain: "This is philosophically interesting in a rather mournful way, since it means that only the simplest animals perceive the universe as it is."

A fog that won't burn away drifts and flows across my field of vision. When you see fog move against a backdrop of deep pines, you don't see the fog itself, but streaks of clearness floating across the air in dark shreds. So I see only tatters of clearness through a pervading obscurity. I can't distinguish the fog from the overcast sky; I can't be sure if the light is direct or reflected. Everywhere darkness and the presence of the unseen appalls. We estimate now that only one atom dances alone in every cubic meter of intergalactic space. I blink and squint. What planet or power yanks Halley's Comet out of orbit? We haven't seen that force yet; it's a question of distance, density, and the pallor of reflected light. We rock, cradled in the swaddling band of darkness. Even the simple darkness of night whispers suggestions to the mind. Last summer, in August, I stayed at the creek too late.

Where Tinker Creek flows under the sycamore log bridge to the tear-shaped island, it is slow and shallow, fringed thinly in cattail marsh. At this spot an astonishing bloom of life supports vast breeding populations of insects, fish, reptiles, birds, and mammals. On windless summer evenings I stalk along the creek bank or straddle the sycamore log in absolute stillness, watching for muskrats. The night I stayed too late I was hunched on the log staring spellbound at spreading, reflected stains of lilac on the water. A cloud in the sky suddenly lighted as if turned on by a switch; its reflection just as suddenly materialized on the water upstream, flat and floating, so that I couldn't see the creek bottom, or life in the water under the cloud. Downstream, away from the cloud on the water, water turtles smooth as beans were gliding down with the current in a series of easy, weightless push-offs, as men bound on the moon. I didn't know whether to trace the progress of one turtle I was sure of, risking sticking my face in one of the bridge's spider webs made invisible by the gathering dark, or take a chance on seeing the carp, or scan the mudbank in hope of seeing a muskrat, or follow the last of the swallows who caught at my heart and trailed it after them like streamers as they appeared from directly below, under the log, flying upstream with their tails forked, so fast.

But shadows spread, and deepened, and stayed. After thousands of years we're still strangers to darkness, fearful aliens in an enemy camp with our arms crossed over our chests. I stirred. A land turtle on the bank, startled, hissed the air from its lungs and withdrew into its shell. An uneasy pink here, an unfathomable blue there, gave great suggestion of lurking beings. Things were going on. I couldn't see whether that sere rustle I heard was a distant rattlesnake, slit-eyed, or a nearby sparrow kicking in the dry flood debris slung at the foot of a willow. Tremendous action roiled the water everywhere I looked, big action, inexplicable. A tremor welled up beside a gaping muskrat burrow in the bank and I caught my breath, but no muskrat appeared. The ripples continued to fan upstream with a steady, powerful thrust. Night was knitting over my face an eyeless mask, and I still sat transfixed. A distant airplane, a delta wing out of nightmare, made a gliding shadow on the creek's bottom that looked like a stingray cruising upstream. At once a black fin slit the pink cloud on the water, shearing it in two. The two halves merged together and seemed to dissolve before my eyes. Darkness pooled in the cleft of the creek and rose, as water collects in a well. Untamed, dreaming lights flickered over the sky. I saw hints of hulking underwater shadows, two pale splashes out of the water, and round ripples rolling close together from a blackened center.

At last I stared upstream where only the deepest violet remained of the cloud, a cloud so high its underbelly still glowed feeble color reflected from a hidden sky lighted in turn by a sun halfway to China. And out of that violet, a sudden enormous black body arced over the water. I saw only a cylindrical sleekness. Head and tail, if there was a head and tail, were both submerged in cloud. I saw only one ebony fling, a headlong dive to darkness; then the waters closed, and the lights went out.

I walked home in a shivering daze, up hill and down. Later I lay openmouthed in bed, my arms flung wide at my sides to steady the whirling darkness. At this latitude I'm spinning 836 miles an hour round the earth's axis; I often fancy I feel my sweeping fall as a breakneck arc like the dive of dolphins, and the hollow rushing of wind raises hair on my neck and the side of my face. In orbit around the sun I'm moving 64,800 miles an hour. The solar system as a whole, like a merry-go-round unhinged, spins, bobs, and blinks at the speed of 43,200 miles an hour along a course set east of Hercules. Someone has piped, and we are dancing a tarantella until the sweat pours. I open my eyes and I see dark, muscled forms curl out of water, with flapping gills and flattened eyes. I close my eyes and I see stars, deep stars giving way to deeper stars, deeper stars bowing to deepest stars at the crown of an infinite cone.

"Still," wrote van Gogh in a letter, "a great deal of light falls on everything." If we are blinded by darkness, we are also blinded by light. When too much light falls on everything, a special terror results. Peter Freuchen describes the notorious kayak sickness to which Greenland Eskimos are prone. "The Greenland fjords are peculiar for the spells of completely quiet weather, when there is not enough wind to blow out a match and the water is like a sheet of glass. The kayak hunter must sit in his boat without stirring a finger so as not to scare the shy seals away. . . . The sun, low in the sky, sends a glare into his eyes, and the landscape around moves into the realm of the unreal. The reflex from the mirror-like water hypnotizes him, he seems to be unable to move, and all of a sudden it is as if he were floating in a bottomless void, sinking, sinking, and sinking. . . . Horror-stricken, he tries to stir, to cry out, but he cannot, he is completely paralyzed, he just falls and falls." Some hunters are especially cursed with this panic, and bring ruin and sometimes starvation to their families.

Sometimes here in Virginia at sunset low clouds on the southern or northern horizon are completely invisible in the lighted sky. I only know one is there because I can see its reflection in still water. The first time I discovered this mystery I looked from cloud to no-cloud in bewilderment, checking my bearings over and over, thinking maybe the ark of the covenant was just passing by south of Dead Man Mountain. Only much later did I read the explanation: polarized light from the sky is very much weakened by reflection, but the light in clouds isn't polarized. So invisible clouds pass among visible clouds, till all slide over the mountains; so a greater light extinguishes a lesser as though it didn't exist.

In the great meteor shower of August, the Perseid, I wail all day for the shooting stars I miss. They're out there showering down, committing hara-kiri in a flame of fatal attraction, and hissing perhaps at last into the ocean. But at dawn what looks like a blue dome clamps down over me like a lid on a pot. The stars and planets could smash and I'd never know. Only a piece of ashen moon occasionally climbs up or down the inside of the dome, and our local star without surcease explodes on our heads. We have really only that one light, one source for all power, and yet we must turn away from it by universal decree. Nobody here on the planet seems aware of this strange, powerful taboo, that we all walk about carefully averting our faces, this way and that, lest our eyes be blasted forever.

Darkness appalls and light dazzles; the scrap of visible light that doesn't hurt my eyes hurts my brain. What I see sets me swaying. Size and distance and the sudden swelling of meanings confuse me, bowl me over. I straddle the sycamore log bridge over Tinker Creek in the summer. I look at the lighted creek bottom: snail tracks tunnel the mud in quavering curves. A crayfish jerks, but by the time I absorb what has happened, he's gone in a billowing smokescreen of silt. I look at the water: minnows and shiners. If I'm thinking minnows, a carp will fill my brain till I scream. I look at the water's surface: skaters, bubbles, and leaves sliding down. Suddenly, my own face, reflected, startles me witless. Those snails have been tracking my face! Finally, with a shuddering wrench of the will, I see clouds, cirrus clouds. I'm dizzy, I fall in. This looking business is risky.

Once I stood on a humped rock on nearby Purgatory Mountain, watching through binoculars the great autumn hawk migration below, until I discovered that I was in danger of joining the hawks on a vertical migration of my own. I was used to binoculars, but not, apparently, to balancing on humped rocks while looking through them. I staggered. Everything advanced and receded by turns; the world was full of unexplained foreshortenings and depths. A distant huge tan object, a hawk the size of an elephant, turned out to be the browned bough of a nearby loblolly pine. I followed a sharp-shinned hawk against a featureless sky, rotating my head unawares as it flew, and when I lowered the glass a glimpse of my own looming shoulder sent me staggering. What prevents the men on Palomar from falling, voiceless and blinded, from their tiny, vaulted chairs?

I reel in confusion; I don't understand what I see. With the naked eye I can see two million light-years to the Andromeda galaxy. Often I slop some creek water in a jar and when I get home I dump it in a white china bowl. After the silt settles I return and see tracings of minute snails on the bottom, a planarian or two winding round the rim of water, roundworms shimmying frantically, and finally, when my eyes have adjusted to these dimensions, amoebae. At first the amoebae look like muscae volitantes, those curled moving spots you seem to see in your eyes when you stare at a distant wall. Then I see the amoebae as drops of water congealed, bluish, translucent, like chips of sky in the bowl. At length I choose one individual and give myself over to its idea of an evening. I see it dribble a grainy foot before it on its wet, unfathomable way. Do its unedited sense impressions include the fierce focus of my eyes? Shall I take it outside and show it Andromeda, and blow its little endoplasm? I stir the water with a finger, in case it's running out of oxygen. Maybe I should get a tropical aquarium with motorized bubblers and lights, and keep this one for a pet. Yes, it would tell its fissioned descendants, the universe is two feet by five, and if you listen closely you can hear the buzzing music of the spheres.

Oh, it's mysterious lamplit evenings, here in the galaxy, one after the other. It's one of those nights when I wander from window to window, looking for a sign. But I can't see. Terror and a beauty insoluble are a ribband of blue woven into the fringes of garments of things both great and small. No culture explains, no bivouac offers real haven or rest. But it could be that we are not seeing something. Galileo thought comets were an optical illusion. This is fertile ground: since we are certain that they're not, we can look at what our scientists have been saying with fresh hope. What if there are *really* gleaming, castellated cities hung upside-down over the desert sand? What limpid lakes and cool date palms have our caravans always passed untried? Until, one by one, by the blindest of leaps, we light on the road to these places, we must stumble in darkness and hunger. I turn from the window. I'm blind as a bat, sensing only from every direction the echo of my own thin cries.

I chanced on a wonderful book by Marius von Senden, called *Space and Sight*. When Western surgeons discovered how to perform safe cataract operations, they ranged across Europe and America operating on dozens of men and women of all ages who had been blinded by cataracts since birth. Von Senden collected accounts of such cases; the histories are fascinating. Many doctors had tested their patients' sense perceptions and ideas of space both before and after the operations. The vast majority of patients, of both sexes and all ages, had, in von Senden's opinion, no idea of space whatsoever. Form, distance, and size were so many meaningless syllables. A patient "had no idea of depth, confusing it with roundness." Before the operation a doctor would give a blind patient a cube and a sphere; the patient would tongue it or feel it with his hands, and name it correctly. After the operation the doctor would show the same objects to the patient without letting him touch them; now he had no clue whatsoever what he was seeing. One patient called lemonade "square" because it pricked on his tongue as a square shape pricked on the touch of his hands. Of another postoperative patient, the doctor writes, "I have found in her no notion of size, for example, not even within the narrow limits which she might have encompassed with the aid of touch. Thus when I asked her to show me how big her mother was, she did not stretch out her hands, but set her two index-fingers a few inches apart." Other doctors reported their patients' own statements to similar effect. "The room he was in . . . he knew to be but part of the house, yet he could not conceive that the whole house could look bigger"; "Those who are blind from birth . . . have no real conception of height or distance. A house that is a mile away is thought of as nearby, but requiring the taking of a lot of steps. . . . The elevator that whizzes him up and down gives no more sense of vertical distance than does the train of horizontal."

For the newly sighted, vision is pure sensation unencumbered by meaning: "The girl went through the experience that we all go through and forget, the moment we are born. She saw, but it did not mean anything but a lot of different kinds of brightness." Again, "I asked the patient what he could see; he answered that he saw an extensive field of light, in which everything appeared dull, confused, and in motion. He could not distinguish objects." Another patient saw "nothing but a confusion of forms and colours." When a newly sighted girl saw photographs and paintings, she asked, " 'Why do they put those dark marks all over them?' 'Those aren't dark marks,' her mother explained, 'those are shadows. That is one of the ways the eye knows that things have shape. If it were not for shadows many things would look flat.' 'Well, that's how things do look,' Joan answered. 'Everything looks flat with dark patches.' "

But it is the patients' concepts of space that are most revealing. One patient, according to his doctor, "practiced his vision in a strange fashion; thus he takes off one of his boots, throws it some way off in front of him, and then attempts to gauge the distance at which it lies; he takes a few steps towards the boot and tries to grasp it; on failing to reach it, he moves on a step or two and gropes for the boot until he finally gets hold of it." "But even at this stage, after three weeks' experience of seeing," von Senden goes on, " 'space,' as he conceives it, ends with visual space, i.e., with colour-patches that happen to bound his view. He does not yet have the notion that a larger object (a chair) can mask a smaller one (a dog), or that the latter can still be present even though it is not directly seen."

In general the newly sighted see the world as a dazzle of color-patches. They are pleased by the sensation of color, and learn quickly to name the colors, but the rest of seeing is tormentingly difficult. Soon after his operation a patient "generally bumps into one of these colour-patches and observes them to be substantial, since they resist him as tactual objects do. In walking about it also strikes him—or can if he pays attention—that he is continually passing in between the colours he sees, that he can go past a visual object, that a part of it then steadily disappears from view; and that in spite of this, however he twists and turns—whether entering the room from the door, for example, or returning back to it—he always has a visual space in front of him. Thus he gradually comes to realize that there is also a space behind him, which he does not see."

The mental effort involved in these reasonings proves overwhelming for many patients. It oppresses them to realize, if they ever do at all, the tremendous size of the world, which they had previously conceived of as something touchingly manageable. It oppresses them to realize that they have been visible to people all along, perhaps unattractively so, without their knowledge or consent. A disheartening number of them refuse to use their new vision, continuing to go over objects with their tongues, and lapsing into apathy and despair. "The child can see, but will not make use of his sight. Only when pressed can he with difficulty be brought to look at objects in his neighbourhood; but more than a foot away it is impossible to bestir him to the necessary effort." Of a twenty-one-year-old girl, the doctor relates, "Her unfortunate father, who had hoped for so much from this operation, wrote that his daughter carefully shuts her eyes whenever she wishes to go about the house, especially when she comes to a staircase, and that she is never happier or more at ease than when, by closing her eyelids, she relapses into her former state of total blindness." A fifteen-year-old boy, who was also in love with a girl at the asylum for the blind, finally blurted out, "No, really, I can't stand it any more; I want to be sent back to the asylum again. If things aren't altered, I'll tear my eyes out."

Some do learn to see, especially the young ones. But it changes their lives. One doctor comments on "the rapid and complete loss of that striking and wonderful serenity which is characteristic only of those who have never yet seen." A blind man who learns to see is ashamed of his old habits. He dresses up, grooms himself, and tries to make a good impression. While he was blind he was indifferent to objects unless they were edible; now, "a sifting of values sets in . . . his thoughts and wishes are mightily stirred and some few of the patients are thereby led into dissimulation, envy, theft and fraud."

On the other hand, many newly sighted people speak well of the world, and teach us how dull is our own vision. To one patient, a human hand, unrecognized, is "something bright and then holes." Shown a bunch of grapes, a boy calls out, "It is dark, blue and shiny. . . . It isn't smooth, it has bumps and hollows." A little girl visits a garden. "She is greatly astonished, and can scarcely be persuaded to answer, stands speechless in front of the tree, which she only names on taking hold of it, and then as 'the tree with the lights in it.' " Some delight in their sight and give themselves over to the visual world. Of a patient just after her bandages were removed, her doctor writes, "The first things to attract her attention were her own hands; she looked at them very closely, moved them repeatedly to and fro, bent and stretched the fingers, and seemed greatly astonished at the sight." One girl was eager to tell her blind friend that "men do not really look like trees at all," and astounded to discover that her every visitor had an utterly different face. Finally, a twenty-two-year-old girl was dazzled by the world's brightness and kept her eyes shut for two weeks. When at the end of that time she opened her eyes again, she did not recognize any objects, but, "the more she now directed her gaze upon everything about her, the more it could be seen how an expression of gratification and astonishment overspread her features; she repeatedly exclaimed: 'Oh God! How beautiful!'"

I saw color-patches for weeks after I read this wonderful book. It was summer; the peaches were ripe in the valley orchards. When I woke in the morning, color-patches wrapped round my eyes, intricately, leaving not one unfilled spot. All day long I walked among shifting color-patches that parted before me like the Red Sea and closed again in silence, transfigured, whenever I looked back. Some patches swelled and loomed, while others vanished utterly, and dark marks flitted at random over the whole dazzling sweep. But I couldn't sustain the illusion of flatness. I've been around for too long. Form is condemned to an eternal danse macabre with meaning: I couldn't unpeach the peaches. Nor can I remember ever having seen without understanding; the color-patches of infancy are lost. My brain then must have been smooth as any balloon. I'm told I reached for the moon; many babies do. But the color-patches of infancy swelled as meaning filled them; they arrayed themselves in solemn ranks down distances which unrolled and stretched before me like a plain. The moon rocketed away. I live now in a world of shadows that shape and distance color, a world where space makes a kind of terrible sense. What gnosticism is this, and what physics? The fluttering patch I saw in my nursery window— silver and green and shape-shifting blue—is gone; a row of Lombardy poplars takes its place, mute, across the distant lawn. That humming oblong creature pale as light that stole along the walls of my room at night, stretching exhilaratingly around the corners, is gone, too, gone the night I ate of the bittersweet fruit, put two and two together and puckered forever my brain. Martin Buber tells this tale: "Rabbi Mendel once boasted to his teacher Rabbi Elimelekh that evenings he saw the angel who rolls away the light before the darkness, and mornings the angel who rolls away the darkness before the light. 'Yes,' said Rabbi Elimelekh, 'in my youth I saw that too. Later on you don't see these things any more.' "

Why didn't someone hand those newly sighted people paints and brushes from the start, when they still didn't know what anything was? Then maybe we all could see color-patches too, the world unraveled from reason, Eden before Adam gave names. The scales would drop from my eyes; I'd see trees like men walking; I'd run down the road against all orders, hallooing and leaping.

Seeing is of course very much a matter of verbalization. Unless I call my attention to what passes before my eyes I simply won't see it. It is, as Ruskin says, "not merely unnoticed, but in the full, clear sense of the word, unseen." My eyes alone can't solve analogy tests using figures, the ones which show, with increasing elaborations, a big square, then a small square in a big square, then a big triangle, and expect me to find a small triangle in a big triangle. I have to say the words, describe what I'm seeing. If Tinker Mountain erupted, I'd be likely to notice. But if I want to notice the lesser cataclysms of valley life, I have to maintain in my head a running description of the present. It's not that I'm observant; it's just that I talk too much. Otherwise, especially in a strange place, I'll never know what's happening. Like a blind man at the ball game, I need a radio.

When I see this way I analyze and pry. I hurl over logs and roll away stones; I study the bank a square foot at a time, probing and tilting my head. Some days when a mist covers the mountains, when the muskrats won't show and the microscope's mirror shatters, I want to climb up the blank blue dome as a man would storm the inside of a circus tent, wildly, dangling, and with a steel knife claw a rent in the top, peep, and, if I must, fall.

But there is another kind of seeing that involves a letting go. When I see this way I sway transfixed and emptied. The difference between the two ways of seeing is the difference between walking with and without a camera. When I walk with a camera, I walk from shot to shot, reading the light on a calibrated meter. When I walk without a camera, my own shutter opens, and the moment's light prints on my own silver gut. When I see this second way I am above all an unscrupulous observer.

It was sunny one evening last summer at Tinker Creek; the sun was low in the sky, upstream. I was sitting on the sycamore log bridge with the sunset at my back, watching the shiners the size of minnows who were feeding over the muddy sand in skittery schools. Again and again, one fish, then another turned for a split second across the current and flash! the sun shot out from its silver side. I couldn't watch for it. It was always just happening somewhere else, and it drew my vision just as it disappeared: flash, like a sudden dazzle of the thinnest blade, a sparking over a dun and olive ground at chance intervals from every direction. Then I noticed white specks, some sort of pale petals, small, floating from under my feet on the creek's surface, very slow and steady. So I blurred my eyes and gazed towards the brim of my hat and saw a new world. I saw the pale white circles roll up, roll up, like the world's turning, mute and perfect, and I saw the linear flashes, gleaming silver, like stars being born at random down a rolling scroll of time. Something broke and something opened. I filled up like a new wineskin. I breathed an air like light; I saw a light like water. I was the lip of a fountain the creek filled forever; I was ether, the leaf in the zephyr; I was flesh-flake, feather, bone.

When I see this way I see truly. As Thoreau says, I return to my senses. I am the man who watches the baseball game in silence in an empty stadium. I see the game purely; I'm abstracted and dazed. When it's all over and the white-suited players lope off the green field to their shadowed dugouts, I leap to my feet; I cheer and cheer.

But I can't go out and try to see this way. I'll fail, I'll go mad. All I can do is try to gag the commentator, to hush the noise of useless interior babble that keeps me from seeing just as surely as a newspaper dangled before my eyes. The effort is really a discipline requiring a lifetime of dedicated struggle; it marks the literature of saints and monks of every order East and West, under every rule and no rule, discalced and shod. The world's spiritual geniuses seem to discover universally that the mind's muddy river, this ceaseless flow of trivia and trash, cannot be dammed, and that trying to dam it is a waste of effort that might lead to madness. Instead you must allow the muddy river to flow unheeded in the dim channels of consciousness; you raise your sights; you look along it, mildly, acknowledging its presence without interest and gazing beyond it into the realm of the real where subjects and objects act and rest purely, without utterance. "Launch into the deep," says Jacques Ellul, "and you shall see."

The secret of seeing is, then, the pearl of great price. If I thought he could teach me to find it and keep it forever I would stagger barefoot across a hundred deserts after any lunatic at all. But although the pearl may be found, it may not be sought. The literature of illumination reveals this above all: although it comes to those who wait for it, it is always, even to the most practiced and adept, a gift and a total surprise. I return from one walk knowing where the killdeer nests in the field by the creek and the hour the laurel blooms. I return from the same walk a day later scarcely knowing my own name. Litanies hum in my ears; my tongue flaps in my mouth Ailinon, alleluia! I cannot cause light; the most I can do is try to put myself in the path of its beam. It is possible, in deep space, to sail on solar wind. Light, be it particle or wave, has force: you rig a giant sail and go. The secret of seeing is to sail on solar wind. Hone and spread your spirit till you yourself are a sail, whetted, translucent, broadside to the merest puff.

When her doctor took her bandages off and led her into the garden, the girl who was no longer blind saw "the tree with the lights in it." It was for this tree I searched through the peach orchards of summer, in the forests of fall and down winter and spring for years. Then one day I was walking along Tinker Creek thinking of nothing at all and I saw the tree with the lights in it. I saw the backyard cedar where the mourning doves roost charged and transfigured, each cell buzzing with flame. I stood on the grass with the lights in it, grass that was wholly fire, utterly focused and utterly dreamed. It was less like seeing than like being for the first time seen, knocked breathless by a powerful glance. The flood of fire abated, but I'm still spending the power. Gradually the lights went out in the cedar, the colors died, the cells unflamed and disappeared. I was still ringing. I had been my whole life a bell, and never knew it until at that moment I was lifted and struck. I have since only very rarely seen the tree with the lights in it. The vision comes and goes, mostly goes, but I live for it, for the moment when the mountains open and a new light roars in spate through the crack, and the mountains slam.

1974

FIGURE 21 Todd Walker, *A photograph of a leaf is not the leaf. It may not even be a photograph.* 1971. Photo-silkscreen, 22$\frac{3}{8}$ × 15$\frac{1}{2}$ in. Collection of the artist. (© Todd Walker. Courtesy of the Todd Walker Foundation.)

GETTING STARTED

1. Find examples in Dillard's essay that help you to explain the difference between seeing as "analyzing and prying" and seeing as "letting go." Share your findings in a group and then list all the examples in her essay that would fit primarily into the first category and all those that would fit primarily into the second category.

2. Practice some of the observational techniques that Dillard models in this essay. Write a paragraph in which you mimic or even parody her techniques for focusing the reader's attention on a particular object or phenomenon.

3. Analyze one place in which Dillard quotes another writer. What does her interpretation of the quotation teach you about that writer? What does Dillard seem to learn from that writer? What point is she trying to make in using that quotation?

WRITING

4. Write a short paper in which you use examples from Dillard and from your own observations and experience to explain some of the different ways of seeing that she discusses in this essay: seeing by constructing an "artificial obvious," seeing as "a matter of verbalization," seeing as "analyzing and prying" and seeing as "letting go." Does Dillard seem to find some of these ways of seeing more valuable than others? Does she believe that some are riskier than others? Which do you find most valuable or most risky?

5. Write a short account of something you have seen, mimicking Dillard's style in your description. Feel free to exaggerate or parody some of her techniques to make your account sound like Dillard's.

6. Summarize the first two and last two paragraphs of this essay. Then write a paragraph or two explaining why Dillard chose to begin and end her essay in these ways. Why did she choose these two particular stories? What larger theme, thesis, or argument is she conveying? What are some of the differences in the way she presents that thesis at the end of the essay as compared to the beginning? What does she learn or what ideas does she develop in between?

USING THE LIBRARY AND THE INTERNET

7. Using a reference database such as Academic Search Elite, which includes sources from scholarly journals, and MAS Full Text Ultra, which includes general interest and current-events magazines, try search terms such as "nature writing" or "seeing and nature" to find examples of other writers observing the natural world. What differences do you notice between Dillard's tone, word choice, and descriptions and those of the other writers you find? Identify several differences and bring examples to class.

MAKING CONNECTIONS

8. Although Dillard is talking about seeing and Erin McGraw is talking about the loss of sight, are there points of connection between these two essays? For example, does Dillard's distinction between seeing as "analyzing and prying" and seeing as "letting go" apply to McGraw's examples as well? Write an essay in which you compare and contrast their ways of seeing in relation to your own experiences with sight.

9. Write an essay in which you use terms from Walker Percy's "The Loss of the Creature" to analyze Dillard's examples. Does she help to dispel the "symbolic packaging" that might prevent us from experiencing the natural world or does she contribute to that packaging? Does she aid in the "loss of the creature" or in its recovery? Use specific examples from Dillard to explore the connection.

10. Use Dillard's terms to analyze Jane Tompkins's way of seeing in "At the Buffalo Bill Museum, June, 1988." In what places is Tompkins "analyzing and prying" and in what places is she "letting go"? Which approach would she value the most? Is Tompkins's relationship to her subject matter analogous to Dillard's relationship to nature? What are some of the similarities and differences?

Julie English Early

Julie English Early (1945–) is a Professor of English at the University of Alabama, Huntsville. "The Spectacle of Science and Self: Mary Kingsley" was taken from *Natural Eloquence: Women Reinscribe Science* (1997), a collection of essays edited by Barbara T. Gates and Ann B. Shteir that explores the often overlooked scientific contributions of women in the nineteenth and twentieth centuries. In this essay, Early concentrates on the idiosyncratic style of British writer Mary Kingsley, showing how Kingsley's rhetoric sheds light on the received ideas of scientific presentation in the late nineteenth century.

For more information on Mary Kingsley and other explorers, see "Into the Unknown," a special millennium edition *of The New York Times Magazine* online at <http://www.nytimes.com/library/magazine/millennium/m3/index.html>.

The Spectacle of Science and Self

Mary Kingsley

Mary Kingsley somewhat regularly skirmished with her publisher, Macmillan, during the preparation *of Travels in West Africa* (1897). Macmillan was confused by its narrative voice, and unsure of its serious or comedic intent; he thought readers would even be uncertain of its author's gender. Kingsley protested, "It does not matter to the General Public what I am as long as I tell them the truth" (Macmillan Letters, 18 December 1894). Kingsley's optimism about the General Public, what she knowingly called the G.P., was realized: a little more than a year later, her book "took the world by storm" (Smith and Ward 349). Yet the confidence she expressed was also disingenuous; the generosity of the G.P. would have to be cultivated.

In the year before publishing *Travels in West Africa,* Kingsley consciously produced and managed a public presence on the lecture platform and in the periodical press that established her not only as a naturalist, an ethnographer, and an observer of West African affairs, but as a distinctly unusual one. Long before her book appeared, Mary Kingsley was an event: a vastly entertaining, sometimes puzzling, and often controversial self-performer—who also laid claim to serious science. This incongruous and compelling public presence guaranteed that *TWA* would be reviewed in publications across the broadest spec-

FIGURE 22 Mary Henrietta Kingsley (1862–1900). Studio Portrait c. 1897 by A. E. Hull, London. (By courtesy of the National Portrait Gallery, London.)

trum: from *Punch* to the Royal Geographical Society's *Geographical Journal*, from the *Illustrated London News* to the *Edinburgh Review.* But if Kingsley's unusual public presence guaranteed attention to her work, it also foregrounded her pointed disorientation of conventional expectations in which the image of the proper scientist stood for the value of the science presented. In her person and in her work, Kingsley stood for reconfigurations that could potentially forestall calcification of disciplines mistakenly confident that their "inherent" objectivity and remote, respectable demeanor were signs of substance. Her methodological and textual self-consciousness pointed to theoretical and political concerns that anthropology would only slowly come to address.

In creating her public presence, Kingsley was astute about herself, her material, and the politics of the sciences at the end of the century. Wisely understanding opportunities for the unconventional contributor to the still loosely formed disciplines of the human sciences, she brought her anthropological fieldwork rather than the work of the naturalist directly to the public. Kingsley limited discussion of collecting and classifying natural specimens to direct exchanges with the British Museum, which, however, provided her with approval in an adjacent discipline. *TWA*, for example, includes plates of the "new" fishes named for her, and, as two of the text's five appendices, the museum reports on her finds. When she received them, she wrote Macmillan with details of the value of her collection, adding, "these things ought to shed a sort of glow of respectability over me" (16 February 1896).

Credentialed only by an impressive intellect, extensive independent study, and firsthand experience, Kingsley lacked an institutional imprimatur and recognized the value of that "sort of glow." The museum's approval secured her a place in the respectable world of species and genera, but as a borrowed glow, also gave her a position from which to challenge a tradition of gentlemanly good science. A clearly defined model of achievement in which the clubbish worth of the individual was collapsed with the value of "his" work shaped, for example, the Royal Geographical Society—a capacious institutional umbrella for all travel-related study. At mid-century, when RGS president Sir Roderick Murchison added public lectures by notable nonmembers, some found the measure too liberally enthusiastic: "[his] popular methods in the reception of the lion of the hour . . . were distasteful to some of the great men of science. . . . There was some uneasiness even amongst his friends" (Mill 80).

At the end of the century, even with pressures on professional societies to adjust their perspectives,[1] Kingsley had good reason to use whatever informal certification she could obtain.[2] Her disadvantages in the face of the gentleman's respectable model were nearly all-encompassing. She was a woman; she had not been formally educated; and, despite the Kingsley name, she did not fully embrace the preferred demeanor of class and/or the professions. As she wrote Macmillan, "I am afraid you have taken up with a complicated criminal" (16 February 1896). Excluded from formal channels of learning, Kingsley, like many women, was a gifted autodidact who educated herself from her father's library, a quixotic collection that may have reflected the individuality of its owner but could prove a treacherous guide for his self-tutored daughter. She recounted that as a young woman

> I happened on a gentleman who knew modern chemistry and tried my information on him. He said he had not heard anything so ridiculous for years, and recommended I should be placed in

> a museum as a compendium for exploded chemical theories, which hurt my feelings very much and I cried bitterly at not being taught things.[3]

Nonetheless, Kingsley had greater experience of her father's library than she had of her father, who existed principally in entertaining letters sent sporadically from his travels around the world. Kingsley's daily influences were not the famous Kingsley relatives, but her mother, a cockney cook whom George Kingsley had married four days before Mary's birth, and the Baileys, her mother's working-class family. At home, Kingsley gained a vocabulary and a cadence to her speech that stood her in good stead with Liverpool's West African traders; but when she moved in other circles, she would choose to control (or not to control) certain tendencies. One newspaper review of a lecture complained of her fashionable gesture of dropping *g*'s, a criticism that amused her "when I am trying so hard to hold on to the 'h's'" (unidentified letter quoted in Frank 24). Her conversational informality was equally an issue. During the preparation of *TWA*, Macmillan's editorial consultant, Henry Guillemard, had consistently attempted to "professionalize" her language and to cut her stories short. She had just as consistently resisted. In the preface, Kingsley parodies the style she has refused, demonstrates her own agility in moving among styles, and takes full responsibility for her choice: "It is I who have declined to ascend to a higher level of lucidity and correctness of diction than I am fitted for" (viii).

In the flux of social and professional redefinitions of the '90s, Kingsley did not attempt to disguise her disadvantages, but instead plainly saw their potential for disturbing existing hierarchies. She wrote to her friend Lady Macdonald:

> I am really beginning to think that . . . the person who writes a book and gets his FRGS [Fellow of the Royal Geographical Society] etc, is a peculiar sort of animal only capable of seeing a certain set of things and always seeing them the same way, and you and me are not of this species somehow. What are we to call ourselves? (undated letter quoted in Gwynn 131)

Kingsley, another "species" who neither would see only "'a certain set of things," nor always "[see] them the same way," built upon the traditional collapse of the person and the work to redefine its implications and possibilities. Whether the "lion of the hour" or, as she put it, "the sea-monster of the season," Kingsley called attention to herself as much as to her material, even multiplying and exaggerating the marginalities she could represent to elude a too swift classification in any one of them.[4]

Just as she would caution against the arrogance of too readily reading the cultures of West Africa, so did she subvert any easy readability of Mary Kingsley. A rather slight figure in her mid-thirties, she appeared on the lecture platform in somber black silks several decades out of fashion. Introducing herself at one gathering, she suggested, "I expect I remind you of your maiden aunt—long since deceased."[5] The archaic chapter headings to *TWA,* too, speak in the voice of another age: Chapter IV, "Which the general reader may omit as the voyager gives herein no details of Old Calabar or of other things of general interest, but discourses diffusely on the local geography and the story of the man who wasted coal" (73). Parodic, pointedly anachronistic, even dandyish, the device recalls a time when the dandy was the "natural" province of the leisured aristocrat, but is now one of the many modes that the woman and her text may, at will, dress up in. Any presuppositions suggested by her "quaint but modest appearance" (*Advertiser and Exchange Gazette* (Hull), 13 November 1897, quoted in Frank 246) and archaic respectability were confounded by her "unladylike" views: Kingsley, for example, supported the liquor traffic, deplored the activities of missionaries, preferred the company of the "palm-oil ruffians," the West Coast traders, and named as her favorite West African tribe, the cannibal Fan. With grim flippancy, Kingsley portrayed herself as an anachronism—a survivor of West Africa, the White Man's Grave; a woman with experiences in pursuit of scientific study as thrilling as those of Mungo Park and Richard Burton in pursuit of geographic knowledge and conquest; and a woman, seeming oddly out of time and place, with the riveting drama, wit, and timing of a masterful (and generally masculine) raconteur.

Kingsley's hyperbolic and flippant humor served as the readiest characteristic for her critics to fasten onto, offering them the opportunity for what appeared even willful misunderstanding. She wrote Macmillan following a lecture early in her public appearances: "The Scotch seem to have on the whole understood me perfectly, not so some distinguished English friends who are now attacking me for speaking flippantly on cannibalism" (16 February 1896). Kingsley's discursive storytelling was, in fact, tightly controlled, relying on impeccable timing, making its points by indirection, surprise, exaggeration, and often irony—a narrative style that fully controls its persona, its material, and its audience. At the beginning of their correspondence, Kingsley wrote Professor and Mrs. E. B. Tylor: "I very humbly beg to plead that statements I make seemingly light-heartedly have really had put into them weeks, sometimes months, of very hard work. . . . It is my apology and I know many things I am going to publish require an apology" (1 October 1896).[6] Her style on the platform and later in her books—what reviewers frequently called "racy"[7]—brought thousands to her dramatic lantern slide lectures; audiences of 1,800 to 2,000 were not unusual.[8] Audiences of the 1890s with a culturally induced appetite for spectacle were little concerned with what to make of her, but instead found her gratifyingly informative and entertaining.

Unlike the General Public, scientific and professional observers were troubled by their inability to explain a woman who cavalierly ruptured the connection between sober science and the demeanor of the scientist. Even Tylor's obituary memoir, while it praises her work, betrays his faint puzzlement over how to account for it:

> Some of Mary Kingsley's readers may have been led astray by her light chaffy style into calling her superficial. . . . During the few years I had the privilege of her friendship, I came to appreciate her power of getting to the back of the negro mind. In her own peculiar way she will hardly be replaced. (Green 7)[9]

Incongruent not only with the demeanor of the proper scientist, Kingsley's self-presentation, "her own peculiar way," prompted an array of defensive memoirs that sought to construct a "normative" woman behind the screen of her talent for farce, disconcertingly deadpan tales, and uncomfortably pointed wit. Alice Green, for example, stressed domestic skills: "She was a skilled nurse, a good cook, a fine needlewoman, an accomplished housewife" (3). Dennis Kemp's memoir for the *London Quarterly Review* stressed devotion to her younger brother, Charley ("a most beautiful love-story might be told" [143–44]); their relations were, in fact, strained. As she had asked, "What are we to call ourselves?"

Decidedly captivating and decidedly odd, Kingsley was clearly adept at performing herself, but also at performing science. Kingsley's critics perhaps registered only imperfectly that the self-performance that brought her a popular audience was intrinsic to her critique of disciplinarity. On the lecture platform and in the narrative voice of her writing, the dual texts of self and science are virtually inseparable. Above all, Kingsley's work reflects a belief not only in the fundamental narrativity of science, but in its constructed nature and voice.[10] Demanding that her audiences attend to the person in the work, Kingsley entangles the stories of self and science to draw attention to a process of learning rather than remote pronouncements of science's definitive conclusions. Focusing on the all too human elements of the human sciences, she effectively avoids a charge of watered-down science in which oversimplifications are offered to satisfy an untutored audience, and instead represents the greater complexities of the practices of science. Through her presence, "her own peculiar way," Kingsley insisted that central to that practice, for good or ill, is its practitioner, a truth too often obscured in Olympian male discourse.

Kingsley's practice suggested that one could not begin to see the ways in which the observer is implicated until the European self, too, could be an object of scrutiny, itself destabilized and denaturalized. Her self-performance refuses the potentially possessive, all-comprehending eye of her audience just as her representations of West Africa disturb the possessive and certain gaze of imperial male narratives—either those of conquest or those indirectly serving conquest through science.[11] She closes the preface to *TWA* with a rather startling warning—and charge—to her readers: "Your superior culture-instincts may militate against your enjoying West Africa" (ix), she told them. Kingsley literally made a spectacle of herself in order to intervene in assumptions of her discipline. In self-performance, she denaturalized the proper woman and the proper scientist to focus on barriers to interpretation formed by an observer's too well-defined self with "superior-culture instincts"—an emphasis that had led Tylor to speculate that the quality of her work may have been enabled by a mysterious "genius and sympathy with the barbarian mind" (Green 7).

In this, Tylor, of course, reflects racial developmental theories grounding nineteenth-century ethnography and anthropology. Entwined with a self-justifying imperialist mission, disciplines concerned with cultural difference placed multifaceted difference on a linear scale ascending to Western European social organization and values. Kingsley too would announce herself "a Darwinian to the core," while also subscribing to a polygenist view of racial and sexual differences as one of kind not evolutionary degree.[12] While she would publicly rank different orders (the white man, the white woman, then all Africans), paradoxically the racism of essential difference also enabled her to insist on taking the West African on his or her own terms, and to rationalize her preference for a culture deemed savage. Tylor's view of her affinity with "the barbarian mind" reiterated her self-characterization in a letter of introduction to the Tylors: "I seem to have a mind so nearly akin to that of the savage that I can enter into his thoughts and fathom them" (1 October 1896). In this identification Kingsley appropriated, not possessive racial superiority, but nineteenth-century developmental theories that placed women and children closer than the white male to what was deemed the (particularly) black savage state.[13] The identification effectively "naturalized" the congeniality that West African social and spiritual systems held for her, and that Tylor had identified as "sympathy" and a "power of getting to the back of the negro mind." Tylor, however, also saw, incongruous to this schema, Kingsley's "genius," an unsettling acknowledgment producing the uncomfortable wonder threading through his praise of her work. Kingsley's work was certainly framed by a racist superstructure; once inside the frame, however, her interest focused on discerning the coherence and integrity of a cultural system. Kingsley defined her work, the study of fetish, rather simply as "the governing but underlying ideas of a man's [*sic*] life" (*TWA* 68). Her large view, theoretically as applicable to British "truths" as to any other culture's, became enacted in the spectacle of herself as British Woman, a produced cultural construction, no more natural than any other. Even more unsettling to careful readers such as Tylor, West African fetish ultimately appeared to Kingsley in many ways more coherent and congenial than Victorian Britain's fetish.[14]

On the lecture platform, Kingsley made both the observer and the observed "artifacts" worthy of study, and through her discursive tales foregrounded the interaction between them. Her work, particularly on the lecture circuit, would answer the question posed in an 1895 address by the retiring president of the American Association for the Advancement of Science, "The Aims of Anthropology": "But you will naturally ask, To what end this accumulating and collecting, this filling of museums with the art products of savages and the ghastly contents of charnel houses? Why write down their stupid stories and make notes of their obscene rites?" (Brinton 63). Certainly, paramount for Kingsley was the effort to disorient prevailing notions of "savage" and "ghastly," "stupid" and "obscene," and to question the methodological structure implied by "accumulating and collecting." Kingsley offered, not a catalog neatly labeled, but a multivoiced narrative of mutual misperceptions and perceptions, alternate scales of value, and, always, a sense of the provisional and partial nature of any "truths." She reoriented her audience to different angles of vision by including countless anecdotal sidesteps that center on exchanges between West Africans who are exceedingly smart about the Europeans they deal with and Europeans who remain remarkably stupid about their relations with West Africans.[15] In pointed contrast to theorists who assumed "the native" could not understand the origin or significance of customs and practices, Kingsley suggested a more realistic (and amusingly deflating) alternative: when seeking explanations, "[t]he usual answer is, 'It was the custom of our fathers,' but that always and only means, 'We don't intend to tell'" (*TWA* 477). In a practical application, Kingsley suggests challenges to a hierarchy of power in terms her audience can understand. England, "that nation of shopkeepers," for example, will find West Africans formidable in the Victorians' own terms: "[In Africa], young and old, men and women, regard trade as the great affair of life, [and] take to it as soon as they can toddle" (*TWA* 56). In Kingsley's view, on the matter of trade West Africans can hold their own, and it is up to the Englishman to prove that he is "an intelligent trader who knows the price of things" ("Lecture on West Africa" 267).

The European not only fails to see the West African apart from preconceptions, but also fails to see himself in the transaction. The two closely connected failures are brought together in Kingsley's insistence on learning to see the unfamiliar and on learning to see the familiar as unfamiliar—whether this is seeing "a racy maiden aunt" as scientist on the lecture platform, or seeing the presence of both the narrator and West Africans in her texts. Without remade vision, the scientist could be (or the audience could be gulled by) someone like "a German gentleman once who evolved a camel out of his inner consciousness. It was a wonderful thing; still, you know, it was not a good camel, only a thing which people personally unacquainted with camels could believe in" (*TWA* 10). Kingsley contrasts the vision produced by an "inner consciousness" with the gradual and receptive process of learning to see the forest: "As you get used to it, what seemed at first an inextricable tangle ceases to be so. . . . a whole world grows up out of the gloom before your eyes" (*TWA* 101); "The proudest day in my life was the day on which an old Fan hunter said to me—'Ah! you see'" (102). In Kingsley's lexicon, only relearned vision can ground, morally or intellectually, comprehension of the practices of West Africans: "At first you see nothing but a confused stupidity and crime; but when you get to see—well! . . . you see things worth seeing" (103). Kingsley, herself "a complicated criminal," as she had told Macmillan, and the West African, thought to embody "stupidity and crime," are indeed not what they seem, "but when you get to see—well!"

Kingsley's awareness of the complexities of vision and comprehension that must precede scientific interpretation strikes at the heart of the claim for mastery over another culture that was underwritten by professional suppositions of uninflected objectivity. Not surprisingly, reviews of her work during her lifetime are less interested than the obituary memoirs in puzzling over apparent incongruities between the style of the woman and the quality of her work and are more concerned with damping a disruptive, even alarming presence. Her most judicious critics find themselves unable to dismiss her work as unsound, but have instead to rely on distinguishing the higher and lower values of theory and praxis. One of *TWA*'s most significant reviews, Alfred Lyall's *Edinburgh Review* essay, places Kingsley in relation to F. B. Jevons and F. Max Müller. As a collector of materials, she is distinct from (and inferior to) the "philosophic savant" (Jevons and Müller) who "remains at home to receive what is brought to him . . . to classify, collate, and form his scientific inductions" (213). Kingsley was nonetheless pleased that the *Edinburgh Review* found her a force to contend with and was equanimous about Lyall's condescending (and gender-based) distinction, for much of her work, as the reviewer for *Folk-Lore* recognized, was a critique of armchair theorists:

> Miss Kingsley's repeated cautions to the anthropological student as to the reception and interpretation of evidence, the patience, the ingenuity, the tenacity of purpose, the open-mindedness required, and her warnings, none too emphatic, that no master-key will open all locks, are of a kind that ingenious theorists too often forget. ("Travels in West Africa" 163)

Kingsley, in fact, was an able—and cautious—theoretician who readily targeted the weaknesses of Frazer's "master-key," *The Golden Bough*, in her correspondence with Tylor,[16] and she well knew, as a later review of *West African Studies* pointed out, that in *TWA* "her observations [on the relation of witchcraft to religion] . . . have brought her athwart the theory of Sir Alfred Lyall and Professor Jevons" (Hartland 448).

Lyall uses both Kingsley's style and her method of organization to disqualify her work from the realm of higher science, hazarding that "she may peradventure have become unconsciously possessed by a jocose and humoristic fiend, whom in this Christian land she would do well to cast out" (214–15).[17] In his attempt to undo the threat of Kingsley's eclectic self-performance, Lyall reconstructs her as domestic worker, a scrubwoman to science, and makes the markers to a hierarchy of value clear: "From this curious and valuable description of primitive beliefs and customs in their natural state of entangled confusion we turn to the philosophic and well-ordered survey of their origin, interconnexion, and underlying psychology that is presented to us by Mr. Jevons" (224). Her work is both "curious and valuable," but Lyall cannot acknowledge the valuable disciplinary implications of its curiosity. In preferring an adaptation of the orderly classifications of natural science, he reflects an unwillingness to recognize, first, that one culture has indeed encountered rather than simply studied another, and second, that the encounter inevitably will be complex and untidy. On the lecture platform, Kingsley had the resources of her own physicality, her animated mannerisms, her incongruent appearance, and her discursive asides in the voice of the "'jocose and humoristic fiend" to disorient the linking of authority and appropriateness. In person, Kingsley could use these resources to complicate schematic classifications as she liked. By framing her first book as a travel narrative, she established continuity between public performance and text through a genre that seemed most accommodating to her performative practice. Yet, in negotiations with Macmillan's editor, she found she would have to fight to include in her books the wealth of information that Lyall mistook for a "natural state of entangled confusion." As her letters indicate, her narrative "confusion" was carefully considered, and reflected a virtue in African storytelling: "Very few African stories bear on one subject alone, and they hardly ever stick to a point" (*TWA* 436). Kingsley contrasted her own work and writing with science's traditional, male model:

> These white men who make a theory first and then go hunting travellers' tales for facts to support the same may say what they please of the pleasure of the process. Give me the pleasure of getting a mass of facts and watching them. It is just like seeing a crystal build itself up. But it *is* slower I own. (To Alice Stopford Green, 27 March 1897, quoted in Birkett 173)

Her later book, *West African Studies,* includes a central portion of analysis reflecting her theorizing, the crystal that had grown, but she also insisted on retaining narrativity to show the crystal growing. She wrote Macmillan,

> The new book, though it will seem flippant enough and to spare when it is done, is heavy work for me. I am holding onto the main idea, round which it is written, by the scruff of its neck—but the selection of the facts that will bring that idea clearly out to the minds of people who do not know is hard work. (4 October 1897)

She reported one reader's response when she was preparing its opening section:

> She always tells me . . . that I *ought not* to go on like that. Take myself seriously, etc. I really *am* always serious and 'duller than a great thaw' compared with the things I speak of, and I feel you really cannot understand W.A. unless you understand the steamboat. . . . this laughable stuff is in the thing—just as much as fetish is, etc.; and when Lyall and Mrs. G. and Guillemard and Strong and so on come along and expect me to stand on my head, all my innate vulgarity breaks out. (undated letter quoted in Gwynn 55)

Indiscriminate inclusiveness is here marked as a sign of class difference that separates her from the "white men who make a theory first and then go hunting . . . facts." Further, Kingsley's insistence that the steamboat "is in the thing" registers her acuity about adaptations of indigenous cultures to British imperialism. An outsider by class and gender, Kingsley uses her "innate vulgarity" to invert the delicacy of the "practices too disgusting to mention" school of ethnography. In this version the sense of delicacy or indelicacy shifts from the observed to the observer, and from science to the politicized self embedded in the science.[18]

Kingsley's agentless construction of a self in which "vulgarity breaks out" is a consistent and characteristic mode often borrowed by critics who see her as unable to control the "naturally" unconventional and her career as the fortuitous, if surprising, effect of that inability. Yet her success was clearly anything but natural. Kingsley carefully managed her career even before her December 1895 arrival from her second major trip to West Africa. She had proposed a book to Macmillan a full year before her return; a notation on her 18 December 1894 letter indicates "Miss Kingsley accepts 1/2 profits on her book of travels. Dec. 1894." In Liverpool, a Reuters news service reporter interviewed her: his story, a somewhat sensational summary of her "exploits" in pursuit of fish and fetish with a sprinkling of her highly quotable remarks, appeared as a news/feature in important British and American dailies. Subsequently, the *Spectator* took issue with some of those remarks, then printed her rejoinder, other readers' responses, and so on.[19] This initial "conversation" in the periodical press is an early measure of the ways in which she will be misunderstood: Townsend, the *Spectator* writer, errs in taking her comments to support his racist views, while in another *Spectator* piece responding to her corrections, she is chastised for appearing to defend cannibalism ("Negro Capacity"). The first month of her presence in the press established the ways in which she would stay in the public eye as she engendered and managed controversy. In the following weeks, she continued to elaborate and defend her views, thus adding the voice of the judicious (if controversial) interpreter of important scientific information to her status as a public event.[20]

Against her editor's advice, Kingsley's initial editorial column debates quickly gave way to consistent publishing in journals for an informed readership (she published twenty-seven articles in less than five years) and an exhausting lecture schedule. Guillemard was concerned that overexposure would cause the public to tire of her and that her unconventionality would damage her claims to serious science. She wrote Macmillan: "Dr. Guillemard has gone for me like a tiger for publishing articles. I am sorry if you similarly object to my having done so but my commercial instinct tells me that if I had not done so I should by now be forgotten by the fickle public" (6 July 1896). With her articles in periodicals like the *Liverpool Geographical Society* and the *Scottish Geographical Magazine,* "the fickle public" included the scientific community as well as the informed readership of *Cornhill* and the *National Review.* Kingsley saw no incompatibility of her "commercial instinct" with scholarly substance. At the same time that she was courting the G.P., she was writing Macmillan to urge *TWA*'s presentation as a scholarly work. "Personally I should like the book to be about the size and general get up of your Westermarck on Human Marriage" (1 May 1896).

Macmillan acquiesced in the book's "get up"; Guillemard's concerns about controlling Kingsley's public presence appeared, according to his lights, coherent with the stature of the work she intended. Indeed, the size and format of the published work were somewhat forbidding; its 743 pages, including five appendices and an index, belied its pose as a travel narrative, and its uncut pages—and stiff price of 21s.—announced a serious work. Nonetheless, the range of publications that reviewed *TWA* indicated that, after a year of Kingsley's omnipresence in periodicals and on the lecture circuit, its audience had become nearly everyone; published on 21 January 1897, it was in its fifth edition by June, and an abridged version appeared by the end of the year (Frank 230). *Punch* complained of its length, and other reviewers remarked on the onerous task of cutting so many pages; but, even if the book were more reviewed and talked about than read, the breadth of response validated Kingsley's commercial instincts. By the time that St. Loe Strachey reviewed her second book, *West African Studies,* for the *Spectator,* he could preface a passage from it with the unlikelihood, "In case anybody does not know how Miss Kingsley writes . . ." (169).[21] In many wholly respectable quarters, Kingsley had successfully forced a reconsideration of the appropriate demeanor of science and the scientist. That this was an issue—and an issue that she won—is reflected in the numbers of reviews that felt compelled to authenticate her: "Miss Kingsley is a true scientist," the *Church Quarterly* avowed ("West African Problems"); the *Folk-Lore* reviewer insisted she showed "the true scientific spirit" (Hartland); *Nature* found "much material of the greatest scientific importance" ("West African Fetish"); the *Dial* identified "a thoroughly scientific temper" (Stanley); and even the RGS's *Geographical Journal* grudgingly deemed her work "to possess permanent value" (Heawood).

Understandably, Kingsley found nothing threatening in the notion of popularizing science, if that meant bringing its processes under scrutiny, for she understood popularization as communicating the joys of process and the complex, provisional nature of discovery. Just as important, she represented the necessary but often serendipitous violations of methodology that conveyed the capacious vision and open mind required for good science. The qualities needed to practice science were also the qualities that Kingsley demanded of an audience that would watch a woman work. Kingsley's own experience could model an audience's response: "One by one I took my old ideas derived from books and thoughts based on imperfect knowledge and weighed them against the real life around me, and found them either worthless or wanting" (*TWA* 6). As a self-educated scholar, Kingsley applied a discerning critical judgment and demanded that audiences similarly evaluate authority independent of institutional credentials and "professional" demeanor. Despite her respect for the work of E. B. Tylor, "this greatest of Ethnologists" (*TWA* 435), Kingsley read and evaluated his work with great care. After hearing a paper that he had presented, she wrote to ask for a copy: "I want to read it and reread it for I am not smart on my intellectual legs, and like Mark Twain's horse frequently desire to lean up against a wall and think" (25 May 1898).

Kingsley's concern with reaching both the general and the scientific public reflected her understanding that science offered opportunities to challenge not only the demeanor of authority, but the methodology of authority; that those opportunities were themselves market-driven; and that they were not limited to the practice of science. In Kingsley's view, the General Public was an entity that could be named, marshaled, and empowered to resist an increasingly arcane and remote posture of professionalization across a broad spectrum.[22] Kingsley used herself as a prime "artifact" to communicate a conviction that the human sciences could be a space of meeting for marginalized voices, and that the empowered marginal voice could have significance extending considerably beyond a critique of the practice of science. Her debates on cultural and religious practices in West Africa, and on British economic, political, and administrative policies, argued for interconnections of knowledge forming a larger project of reconfiguring cultural and gendered commitments. Kingsley's practice openly challenged the pure and isolate construction of scientific inquiry, and the imperial politics those constructions supported. Regrettably, the breadth of her interests has retrospectively been parceled out—largely to historical studies, area studies, genre studies, and feminist studies often focusing on Englishwomen in relation to the nineteenth-century British racism of empire. Splintering her interests, isolating what appear to be clear statements (yet necessarily choosing them from among disarmingly contradictory pieces of text) to bring together a satisfactorily coherent "whole," has not made Kingsley any less elusive today than she was to her contemporaries. "I foresee a liability to become diffuse," she said as the anecdotes in *TWA* multiplied. Readings of Kingsley's work that ignore that diffusion miss the destabilizing metadiscursive critique that her career embodies.

Kingsley was always concerned to make her information matter: by reconfiguring the processes of science, by revising the common view of West Africa, and by showing the fundamental importance of scientific understanding to the practical workings of the British Empire. As a "conscience of imperialism"[23] Kingsley repeatedly argued in her lectures and in fiery periodical exchanges that scientific understanding of the coherence of West African practices and beliefs must be brought to bear on devising political and economic policies that would impose the least institutional apparatus and that would least interfere with West Africans. Correcting the missionaries' moralistic perception of one practice, she explained its practical significance, commenting to Tylor, "What a charming world that black world is—always so proper and so reasonable away down inside" (16 April 1898). Kingsley refused the categorization and hierarchical charting of practices that would override contextualization and instead pointed to a plurality of culture with insistence particularly upon the coherence of cultures of often disarming difference. Intelligent and respectful policy acknowledging in difference—and beyond difference—a world "so proper and so reasonable away down inside" would come about only under pressure from an informed public, a public with the tools for critically resisting the certainties of the authoritative voice.

Kingsley's management of her career—her impulse to take it to the public—owed much to her partisanship for free trade in West Africa, and to her hopes about the place of science within the common purview. However, just as her economic policies for West Africa swam against the tide of increased governmental administration, so too did her desire to make specialized knowledge accessible swim against the tide of increasingly determined institutional professionalization. Her career was overwhelmingly productive and successful, but, diminishing its potential to make a significant difference, unfortunately brief. Kingsley was in the public eye only a little over four years. She died in South Africa in June of 1900. Entering a discipline at a time when its methodologies were not yet "closed," Kingsley made substantial demands on its self-consciousness by forcing attention to the narrativity of science, and to the positioning of its narrator. With only a few short years of her public presence, however, the self-consciousness of the human sciences that she insisted upon was regrettably tabled for some time to come.

1997

Mary H. Kingsley (1862–1900): Major Works:

Travels in West Africa, Congo Français, Corisco and Cameroons (1897)

West African Studies (1899)

Life in West Africa (1899)

The Story of West Africa (1900)

Notes on Sport and Travel (1900) [By George Henry Kingsley, with a memoir by his daughter Mary H. Kingsley]

Notes

My thanks to Sheila Sullivan for comments on drafts of this essay, to Martha Vicinus for guiding my thinking about the 1890s, to the University of Chicago and the NEH for financial support of research, and to the University of Alabama in Huntsville's Humanities Center for supporting travel to conferences.

1. In 1892–93, the RGS Council selected twenty-two "well-qualified ladies" for membership. The intensely debated policy was overturned; women were not again elected until 1913. Lord Curzon wrote to "contest *in toto* the general capability of women to contribute to scientific geographical knowledge" (*Times,* 31 May 1893). Gender also introduced class issues with "derogatory references to school teachers and governesses," (Birkett 219). See Middleton 11–16; Birkett 211–30.
2. Kingsley asked E. B. Tylor to sponsor her in the anthropological institute ("I am for a West Coaster fairly respectable & will not steal the other members' umbrellas or hats if I am allowed to join and pay my fee" [25 May 1898]). For the most part, Kingsley objected to women in professional societies, and found informal networks preferable. She wrote Alice Green: "Set yourself to gain personal power. . . . [T]he reins of power . . . are lying on the horse's neck; quietly get them into your hands and drive" (14 March 1900, quoted in Birkett 233).
3. Kingsley included this incident in an autobiographical essay ("In the Days of My Youth"). Other personal detail appears in her two-hundred-page preface to her father's *Notes on Sport and Travel* (1900). Both pieces stress the Kingsley connection, but Katherine Frank gives a more candid view of an unhappy childhood of isolation and social exclusion by the Kingsleys.
4. Kingsley first appeared in print (5 December 1895) angrily to rebut the *Daily Telegraph*'s New Woman label in their story of her arrival at Liverpool (3 December 1895).

5. A member of the audience recalled her appearance as "a bit of stagecraft designed to heighten her achievements" (E. Muriel Joy to Dorothy Middleton, 22 June 1966, quoted in Frank 258).
6. Highly regarding his work, Kingsley called Tylor her "great ju-ju" and initiated correspondence on returning to England.
7. The *Nation* termed it "racy . . . unconventional" ("Travels in West Africa"), although later cautioned that "the author . . . [falls] into colloquy, even into vulgarity, and almost profanity" ("West African Studies"); the *Bookman* noted "racy . . . even slangy English" (Dods); *The Illustrated London News* identified "a romping style" ("Notes on Books"); *Punch* saw "humour that bubbles over in all places" ("Our Booking-Office").
8. Frank summarizes some of her engagements (214–22, 234–40, 245–47, 252-58). Within eight weeks of her return to England, she wrote Macmillan detailing a punishing schedule: "I am going to Scotland for the reading of my paper at the RSGS then onto Glasgow . . . on the 12th I am to be in Liverpool for their Geographical and the Chamber of Commerce here have asked me for a paper. Professor Mahaffey . . . has also asked me to Dublin" (31 January 1896). By 1897 she had hired an agent (Frank 215).
9. The first article of the first issue of the African Society's journal (the society was founded in Kingsley's memory) was a tribute with reminiscences from friends and colleagues.
10. For foundational work, see Geertz; Clifford and Marcus. The latter considers the textuality of ethnography, but excludes a feminist perspective because, Clifford explains, "[feminist ethnography] has not produced either unconventional forms of writing or a developed reflection on ethnographic textuality as such" (21). In *Imperial Eyes* (1992), Mary Louise Pratt considers gendered positioning of narratives in relation to imperialist ideology. For specific discussion of gender and disciplinarity, see Moore.
11. The possessive, masculine view that feminizes the landscape has been widely commented on, e.g., Kolodny; Griffin. Ungendered cultural views appear in Said; Sternberger. Pratt's *Imperial Eyes* specifically considers the "eye" of scientific travel writing.
12. See Stocking's superb intellectual history for detailed analysis of currents of thought and their competing positions in the nineteenth-century development of the discipline.
13. In their survey of nineteenth-century intellectual currents concerning women, Helsinger et al. conclude, "[t]his equation of woman and black is one of the most important features of the Woman Question" (2:91). For detail of the anthropological debate on woman's place in the hierarchy, see Stocking 187–237.
14. Examining fully the complexities of Kingsley's work in relation to race exceeds the scope of this essay. Kingsley publicly committed to political and scientific agendas of imperialism and the hierarchies of social Darwinism that embed racism. Readers who have found such precise lines inadequate to the representations and strategies of her texts have, however, tended to shape defensive arguments. In light of Kingsley's decentering strategies, approaches to her work that categorize it as racist, nonracist, or the apologetic "not-so-racist" may close down valuable inquiry into the incoherencies of acquiescence and resistance in the conflicted position of British women enabled by imperialism. This essay

elaborates Kingsley's self-performance as one aspect of that incoherence: the specific nature of her gendered intervention in the professional discourse "denaturalized" the hierarchies underwriting nineteenth-century ethnography and imperialism at the same time that she committed to both.

15. In this essay, I use the broad term "West Africans" to discuss Kingsley's general perspective. Her books carefully specify indigenous peoples and cultures of the region.
16. Kingsley prefaced a ten-page letter to Tylor detailing Frazer's errors on animism and totemism, "My cap frills are vibrating with vexation" (9 April 1898). In *TWA,* she is dismissive: "I was particularly confident that from Mr. Frazer's book, *The Golden Bough,* I had got a semi-universal key to the underlying idea of native custom and belief. But I soon found this was very far from being the case" (435).
17. Virtually all reviewers commented on style before considering her positions. Many delighted in it, but others shared Lyall's distaste, expressing it with less avuncular preciosity. *Nature*'s angry reviewer felt that "hyperbole is frequently carried too far. . . . Serious students who, when they ask for facts, do not care to be offered a cryptic joke" ("Miss Kingsley's Travels"). The reviewer for *Science* allowed that "an easy flippancy of manner . . . carries you on, . . . [although] the writer is 'on very thin ice'. . . . The off-hand way in which some rather serious problems are treated is hardly fair" (Libbey).
18. Kingsley "vulgarized" herself in text by foregrounding breaches of conventional delicacy and an exaggerated horror of them. These incidents frequently involve mishaps with sex- and gender-marked clothing when she is with Europeans. Readings of these episodes as signs of a self-effacing and anxiety-ridden gender conservatism seem to miss the point.
19. Slightly different versions appear in the *Daily Telegraph* (3 Dec. 1895), the *New York Times* (2 December 1895), and the London *Times* ("Miss Kingsley's Travels," 2 December 1895). Her comments on "the nature of the West African" quickly elicited a *Spectator* article that misunderstood her (Townsend, 7 December 1895); she responded in the letters column (28 December 1895); the same issue ran an article responding to her letter ("Negro Capacity"). The *New York Times* then commented on the entire exchange ("African Character Studied," 10 January 1896). The *Illustrated London News* ("Lady Traveler," 4 January 1896) profiled this new public figure (with photographs that she supplied). The RGS's *Geographical Journal* introduced her material: "Miss Kingsley has kindly sent, at short notice, the following notes on her recent journeys in West Africa" ("Miss Kingsley's Travels").
20. Less than three weeks after her return, Guillemard wrote, "I am quite a distinguished person here because I am a friend of Miss Kingsley. I enliven the dinner table with anecdotes about you. . . . Your book should run—I estimate—to about the 68th thousand, like Mrs. Henry Wood's *East Lynne* or Zola's *The Debacle*" (Macmillan Letters, 20 December 1895).
21. In the first week, 1,200 copies of *West African Studies* were sold (Frank 261).
22. Kingsley was acutely aware of ironies in distinguishing the professional from general public: "These literary and scientific institutions amuse me

much. They . . . inform you they don't want science. . . . [but] 'something bright and amusing and magic lantern slides'" (to E. Sidney Harland, 25 March 1897, quoted in Birkett 203). Adapting to audiences from Oxbridge societies to Boys' Institutes in city slums, she profited from question-and-answer sessions to craft in text an implied dialogue considerably removed from the magisterial pronouncements that Lyall favored.

23. Kingsley's political activity was substantial. Historian Kenneth Dike Nworah argues that the self-named "Third Party" opposed the racist school that "advertised the inferiority and incapacity" of the West African, and the damaging philanthropic and missionary interests that would denationalize West Africa by eroding its traditional systems. The "Liverpool Sect" "was mainly apotheosized in the ideals of Mary Kingsley, John Holt, and E. D. Morel." In Nworah's view, the "small but perceptible sect . . . identified itself with the development of a true colonial conscience in Britain" (349–50). Although earlier free trade had meant the slave trade, Kingsley had faith in the process of knowledge (to which she contributed). Her advocacy reflected a utopian view of trade in which the skills of West Africans would ground an equality of interest with Europe and obviate the need for any "benevolent" control that would imbalance relations.

Works Cited

"African Character Studied." *New York Times,* 10 January 1896, 2.

Birkett, Dea. *Spinsters Abroad; Victorian Lady Explorers.* Oxford and New York: Basil Blackwell, 1989.

Brantlinger, Patrick. *Rule of Darkness; British Literature and Imperialism, 1830–1914.* Ithaca: Cornell UP, 1988.

Brinton, Daniel G. "The Aims of Anthropology." *Popular Science Monthly* 48 (November 1895): 59–72.

Bullen, Frank T. "Some Memories of Mary Kingsley." *Mainly about People,* 16 June 1900, 570.

Clifford, James, and George E. Marcus, eds. *Writing Culture: The Poetics and Politics of Ethnography.* Berkeley: U of California P, 1986.

Dods, Marcus. "West African Studies." *Bookman* 15 (March 1899): 179–80.

Fling, J. E. "Mary Kingsley—A Reassessment." *Journal of African History* 4, no.1 (1963): 105–26.

Frank, Katherine. *A Voyager Out: The Life of Mary Kingsley.* Boston: Houghton Mifflin, 1986.

Geertz, Clifford. *Works and Lives: The Anthropologist as Author.* Stanford: Stanford UP, 1988.

Green, Alice Stopford. "Mary Kingsley." *Journal of the African Society* 1 (1901): 1–16.

Griffin, Susan. *Woman and Nature.* New York: Harper & Row, 1978.

Gwynn, Stephen. *The Life of Mary Kingsley.* London: Macmillan, 1932.

Harland, E. Sidney. "West African Studies." *Folk-Lore* 10 (1899): 447–50.

Heawood, Edward. "Some New Books on Africa." *Geographical Journal* 13 (April 1899): 412–22.

Helsinger, Elizabeth K., Robin Lauterbach Sheets, and William Veeder. *The Woman Question: Society and Literature in Britain and America, 1837–1883.* 3 vols. New York: Garland, 1983.

Kemp, Dennis. "The Late Miss M.H. Kingsley." *London Quarterly Review* 94 (1900): 137–52.
Kingsley, George. *Notes on Sport and Travel, with a Memoir by His Daughter, Mary H. Kingsley.* London: Macmillan, 1900.
Kingsley, Mary H. "In the Days of My Youth; Chapter of Autobiography." *Mainly about People,* 20 May 1899, 468–69.
Kingsley, Mary H. "A Lecture on West Africa." *Cheltenham Ladies' College Magazine* 38 (Autumn 1898): 264–80.
Kingsley, Mary H. Letters to George Macmillan. Macmillan Papers. Correspondence. Manuscript Collection. British Library, London.
Kingsley, Mary H. Letters to Professor and Mrs. E. B. Tylor. Photocopies from originals in the possession of D. J. Holt. Manuscript Collection. Rhodes House Library, Oxford.
Kingsley, Mary H. "The Negro Future." *Spectator* 75 (28 December 1895): 930–31.
Kingsley, Mary H. *Travels in West Africa, Congo Français, Corisco and Cameroons.* London: Macmillan, 1897.
Kingsley, Mary H. *West African Studies.* London: Macmillan, 1899.
Kolodny, Annette. *The Lay of the Land: Metaphor as Experience and History in American Life and Letters.* Chapel Hill: U of North Carolina P, 1975.
"Lady Traveller in West Africa, A." *Illustrated London News* 108 (4 January 1896): 19.
Libbey, William. "Scientific Literature: Travels in West Africa." *Science,* n.s. 6, no. 139 (27 August 1897): 325–26.
Lyall, Alfred. "Origins and Interpretations of Primitive Religions." *Edinburgh Review* 186 (July 1897): 213–44.
Markham, Clements R. *The Fifty Years' Work of the Royal Geographical Society.* London: John Murray, 1881.
Middleton, Dorothy. *Victorian Lady Travellers.* Chicago: Academy Chicago, 1982.
Mill, Hugh Robert. *The Record of the Royal Geographical Society, 1830–1930.* London: Royal Geographical Society, 1930.
Mills, Sara. *Discourses of Difference: An Analysis of Women's Travel Writing and Colonialism.* London: Routledge, 1991.
"Miss Kingsley's Travels." *Times,* 2 December 1895, 6.
"Miss Kingsley's Travels in West Africa." *Geographical Journal* 7 (1896): 95–96.
"Miss Kingsley's Travels in West Africa." *Nature* 55 (4 March 1897): 416–17.
"Miss Mary Kingsley." *Times,* 6 June 1900, 8.
Moore, Henrietta L. *Feminism and Anthropology.* Minneapolis: U of Minnesota P, 1988.
"Negro Capacity—A Suggestion." *Spectator* 75 (28 December 1895): 927–28.
"Notes on Books." *Illustrated London News* 110 (6 February 1897): 185.
Nworah, Kenneth Dike. "The Liverpool 'Sect' and British West African Policy, 1895–1915." *Journal of the Society of African Affairs* 70 (July 1971): 222–35.
"Our Booking-Office." *Punch* 112 (20 February 1897): 88.

Pakenham, Thomas. *The Scramble for Africa: White Man's Conquest of the Dark Continent from 1876 to 1912.* New York: Avon Books, 1991.
Pratt, Mary Louise. *Imperial Eyes: Travel Writing and Transculturation.* London and New York: Routledge, 1992.
Robinson, Ronald, and John Gallagher with Alice Denny. *Africa and the Victorians.* New York: St. Martin's, 1961.
Said, Edward W. *Orientalism.* New York: Vintage Books, 1979.
Showalter, Elaine. *Sexual Anarchy: Gender and Culture at the Fin-de-Siècle.* New York: Viking Penguin, 1990.
Smith, Lucy Toulmin, and Mrs. Humphrey [*sic*] Ward. *Folk-Lore* 11 (1900):348–50.
Stanley, Hiram M. "An English Woman in West Africa." *Dial* 22 (16 March 1897): 183–84.
Sternberger, Dolf. *Panorama of the Nineteenth Century.* Translated by Joachim Neugroschel, with an introduction by Erich Heller. New York: Urizen Books, 1977.
Stevenson, Catherine. "Female Anger and African Politics: The Case of Two Victorian 'Lady Travellers.'" *Turn-of-the-Century Women* 2 (Summer 1985): 7–17.
Stevenson, Catherine. *Victorian Women Travel Writers in Africa.* Boston: G. K. Hall, 1982.
Stocking, George W., Jr. *Victorian Anthropology.* New York: Free P, 1987.
Strachey, J. St. Loe. "Miss Mary Kingsley." *Spectator* 84 (16 June 1900): 836.
Strachey, J. St. Loe. "West African Studies." *Spectator* 82 (4 February 1899): 169–71.
Townsend, Meredith. "The Negro Future." *Spectator* 75 (7 December 1895): 815–17.
"Travels in West Africa." *Folk-Lore* 8 (1897): 162–65.
"Travels in West Africa." *Nation* 64 (1 April 1897): 249.
Walker, Bruce. "Travels in West Africa." *Athenaeum,* no. 3615 (6 February 1897): 173–76.
"West African Fetish." *Nature* 60 (13 July 1899): 243–44.
"West African Problems." *Church Quarterly* 49 (October 1899): 98–115.
"West African Studies." *Nation* 68 (23 March 1899): 228–29.

GETTING STARTED

1. Choose an example from the essay that shows how Mary Kingsley challenged the accepted images of "the scientist" of her day. Write a paragraph summarizing the example you have chosen, identifying what people's expectations of scientists at the time were and discussing how Kingsley differed from, challenged, or opposed them.

2. As a group or individual project, divide a sheet into two columns. In one column, list all the potential disadvantages that Kingsley had to overcome in order to be accepted by the general public as a

scientist. In the other column, list what she did to overcome each disadvantage or even to turn it into an advantage. What does the list tell you about how and why Kingsley went against the accepted expectations and practices of scientific protocols? What are the advantages of resisting "respectability" as she did?

WRITING

3. Write a paper analyzing the strategies that Kingsley used in the effort to present herself as a scientist to the general public. To what extent did she deliberately challenge contemporary expectations of scientists? To what extent did she simply seek acceptance for herself and her methods? Use specific quotations and examples from the essay to support and explain your response.
4. Write a "travel narrative" of a recent trip you took. (The "trip" can be anything from a simple drive to the grocery store to a vacation in Europe.) Direct your narrative to an imaginary (or real) pen pal or friend who is unfamiliar with the culture, place, and people you describe. Use as many of Kingsley's techniques as possible to engage your reader's interest: Mix personal narrative with anthropological or "scientific" details; show your own perspective interacting with the perspective of the "people" you are studying; or use your gender, class, appearance, or interests to your best advantage in presenting yourself as a "scientist" of human life.

USING THE LIBRARY AND THE INTERNET

5. Use a reference database such as Health Source Plus that includes scientific publications and try a keyword search using "fish," "beetle," or a topic that would have interested Kingsley. From your list of results, choose one article that seems to be intended for the general public and one that seems intended for a more specialized scientific community. What are some of the clues that help you make that distinction? Bring your two articles and your notes on the differences to class.

MAKING CONNECTIONS

6. Write an essay comparing and contrasting Kingsley's methods of popularizing science to those of Stephen Jay Gould, Michio Kaku, or Sherry Turkle. To what extent do Gould, Kaku, or Turkle adopt Kingsley's use of "racy" topics, her mixing of personal narrative with scientific data, or her interest in seeing "things worth see-

ing"? Do Gould, Kaku, or Turkle ever seem to "make a theory first and then go hunting travellers' tales for facts to support the same" (p. 165)?

7. Write an essay using Annie Dillard's ideas about "seeing" to analyze Kingsley's methods as described by Early. Does Kingsley primarily approach seeing as "analyzing and prying" or as "letting go" (p. 151)? What would Dillard think about Kingsley's "insistence on learning to see the unfamiliar and on learning to see the familiar as unfamiliar" (p. 163)? Feel free to draw on your own knowledge and experience of learning to see the unfamiliar in writing this essay, but work with specific quotations and examples from Dillard and Kingsley to make your points as well.

Ralph Ellison

Ralph Ellison (1914–1994) was a novelist and critic who began his career in 1938 as a writer and researcher for the Federal Writers' Project in New York City. His experiences as a young black man from Oklahoma encountering the politics and prejudices of the supposedly "free" North were the foundation for his best-known work, the 1952 novel *Invisible Man*. Similarly, Ellison's study of music at the Tuskegee Institute in Alabama informs "The Little Man at Chehaw Station," the first essay in his collection *Going to the Territory* (1986).

To learn more about Ralph Ellison, surf his webliography at <http://www. centerx. gseis.ucla.edu/weblio/ellison.html>.

The Little Man at Chehaw Station

It was at Tuskegee Institute during the mid-1930s that I was made aware of the little man behind the stove. At the time I was a trumpeter majoring in music, and had aspirations of becoming a classical composer. As such, shortly before the little man came to my attention, I had outraged the faculty members who judged my monthly student's recital by substituting a certain skill of lips and fingers for the intelligent and artistic structuring of emotion that was demanded in performing the music assigned to me. Afterward, still dressed in my hired tuxedo, my ears burning from the harsh negatives of their criticism, I had sought solace in the basement studio of Hazel Harrison, a highly respected concert pianist and teacher. Miss Harrison had been one of Ferruccio Busoni's prize pupils, had lived (until the rise of Hitler had driven her back to a U.S.A. that was not yet ready to recognize her talents) in Busoni's home in Berlin, and was a friend of such masters as Egon Petri, Percy Grainger and Sergei Prokofiev. It was not the first time that I had appealed to Miss Harrison's generosity of spirit, but today her reaction to my rather adolescent complaint was less than sympathetic.

"But, baby," she said, "in this country you must always prepare yourself to play your very best wherever you are, and on all occasions."

"But everybody tells you that," I said.

"Yes," she said, "but there's more to it than you're usually told. Of course you've always been taught to *do* your best, *look* your best, *be* your best. You've been told such things all your life. But now you're becoming a musician, an artist, and when it comes to performing the classics in this country, there's something more involved." Watching me closely, she paused. "Are you ready to listen?"

"Yes, ma'am."

"All right," she said, you must *always* play your best, even if it's only in the waiting room at Chehaw Station, because in this country there'll always be a little man hidden behind the stove."

"A *what?*"

She nodded. "That's right," she said. "There'll always be the little man whom you don't expect, and he'll know the *music,* and the *tradition,* and the standards of *musicianship* required for whatever you set out to perform!"

Speechless, I stared at her. After the working-over I'd just received from the faculty, I was in no mood for joking. But no, Miss Harrison's face was quite serious. So what did she mean? Chehaw Station was a lonely whistle-stop where swift north- or southbound trains paused with haughty impatience to drop off or take on passengers; the point where, on homecoming weekends, special coaches crowded with festive visitors were cut loose, coupled to a waiting switch engine, and hauled to Tuskegee's railroad siding. I knew it well, and as I stood beside Miss Harrison's piano, visualizing the station, I told myself, *She has* got *to be kidding!*

For in my view, the atmosphere of Chehaw's claustrophobic little waiting room was enough to discourage even a blind street musician from picking out blues on his guitar, no matter how tedious his wait for a train. Biased toward disaster by bruised feelings, my imagination pictured the vibrations set in motion by the winding of a trumpet within that drab, utilitarian structure: first shattering, then bringing its walls "a-tumbling down"—like Jericho's at the sounding of Joshua's priest-blown ram horns.

True, Tuskegee possessed a rich musical tradition, both classical and folk, and many music lovers and musicians lived or moved through its environs, but—and my regard for Miss Harrison notwithstanding—Chehaw Station was the last place in the area where I would expect to encounter a connoisseur lying in wait to pounce upon some rash, unsuspecting musician. Sure, a connoisseur might hear the haunting, blues-echoing, train-whistle rhapsodies blared by fast express trains as they thundered past, but the classics? Not a chance!

So as Miss Harrison watched to see the effect of her words, I said with a shrug, "Yes, ma'am."

She smiled, her prominent eyes a-twinkle. "I hope so," she said. "But if you don't just now, you will by the time you become an artist. So remember the little man behind the stove."

With that, seating herself at her piano, she began thumbing through a sheaf of scores, a signal that our discussion was ended.

So, I thought, *you ask for sympathy and you get a riddle.* I would have felt better if she had said, "Sorry, baby, I know how you feel, but after all, I was *there,* I *heard* you, and you treated your audience as though you were some kind of confidence man with a horn. So forget it, because I will not violate my own standards by condoning sterile musicianship." Some such reply, by reaffirming the "sacred principles" of art to which we were both committed, would have done much to supply the emotional catharsis for which I was appealing. By refusing, she forced me to accept full responsibility and thus learn from my offense. The condition of artistic communication is, as the saying goes, hard but fair.

But although disappointed and puzzled by Miss Harrison's sibylline response, I respected her artistry and experience too highly to dismiss it. Besides, something about her warning of a cultivated taste that asserted its authority out of obscurity sounded faintly familiar. Hadn't I once worked for an eccentric millionaire who prowled the halls and ballrooms of his fine hotel looking like a derelict who had wandered in off the street? Yes! And woe unto the busboy or waiter, hallman or maid—or anyone else—caught debasing the standards of that old man's house. For then, lashing out with the abruptness of reality shattering the contrived façade of a practical joke, the apparent beggar revealed himself as an extremely irate and exacting host of taste.

Thus, as I leaned into the curve of Miss Harrison's Steinway and listened to an interpretation of a Liszt rhapsody (during which she carried on an enthusiastic, stylistic analysis of passages that Busoni himself had marked for expressional subtlety), the little man of Chehaw Station fixed himself in my memory. And so vividly that today he not only continues to engage my mind, but often materializes when I least expect him.

As, for instance, when I'm brooding over some problem of literary criticism—like, say, the rhetoric of American fiction. Indeed, the little stove warmer has come to symbolize nothing less than the enigma of aesthetic communication in American democracy. I especially associate him with the metamorphic character of the general American audience, and with the unrecognized and unassimilated elements of its taste. For me he represents that unknown quality which renders the American audience far more than a receptive instrument that may be dominated through a skillful exercise of the sheerly "rhetorical" elements—the flash and filigree—of the artist's craft. While that audience is eager to be transported, astounded, thrilled, it counters the artist's manipulation of forms with an attitude of antagonistic cooperation, acting, for better or worse, as both collaborator and judge. Like a strange orchestra upon which a guest conductor would impose his artistic vision, it must be exhorted, persuaded, even wooed, as the price of its applause. It must be appealed to on the basis of what it assumes to be truth as a means of inducting it into new dimensions of artistic truth. By playing artfully upon the audience's sense of experience and form, the artist seeks to shape its emotions and perceptions to his vision, while it, in turn, simultaneously cooperates and resists, says yes and says no in an it-takes-two-to-tango binary response to his effort. As representative of the American audience writ small, the little man draws upon the uncodified *Americanness* of his experience, whether of life or of art, as he engages in a silent dialogue with the artist's exposition of forms, offering or rejecting the work of art on the basis of what he feels to be its affirmation or distortion of American experience.

Perhaps if they were fully aware of his incongruous existence, the little man's neighbors would reject him as a source of confusion, a threat to social order, and a reminder of the unfinished details of this powerful nation. But out of a stubborn individualism born of his democratic origins, he insists upon the cultural necessity of his role, and argues that if he didn't exist, he would have to be invented. If he were not already manifest in the flesh, he would still exist and function as an idea and ideal because—like such character traits as individualism, restlessness, self-reliance, love of the new, and so on—he is a linguistic product of the American scene and language, and a manifestation of the idealistic action of the American word as it goads its users toward a perfection of our revolutionary ideals.

For the artist, a lightning rod attracting unexpected insights and a warning against stale preconceptions, the man behind Chehaw's stove also serves as a metaphor for those individuals we sometimes meet whose refinement of sensibility is inadequately explained by family background, formal education or social status. These individuals seem to have been sensitized by some obscure force that issues undetected from the chromatic scale of American social hierarchy: a force that throws off strange, ultrasonic ultrasemi-semitones that create within those attuned to its vibrations a mysterious enrichment of personality. In this, heredity doubtless plays an important role, but whatever that role may be, it would appear that culturally and environmentally such individuals are products of errant but sympathetic vibrations set up by the tension between America's social mobility, its universal education, and its relative freedom of cultural information. Characterized by a much broader "random accessibility" than class and economic restrictions would appear to allow, this cultural information includes many of the finest products of the arts and intellect—products that are so abundantly available in the form of books, graphics, recordings, and pictorial reproductions as to escape sustained attempts at critical evaluation. Just how these characteristics operate in concert involves the mysterious interaction between environment and personality, instinct and culture. But the frequency and wide dispersal of individuals who reveal the effects of this mysterious configuration of forces endows each American audience, whether of musician, poet, or plastic artist, with a special mystery of its own.

I say "mystery," but perhaps the phenomenon is simply a product of our neglect of serious cultural introspection, our failure to conceive of our fractured, vernacular-weighted culture as an intricate whole. And since there is no reliable sociology of the dispersal of ideas, styles, or tastes in this turbulent American society, it is possible that, personal origins aside, the cultural circumstances here described offer the intellectually adventurous individual what might be termed a broad "social mobility of intellect and taste"—plus an incalculable scale of possibilities for self-creation. While the force that seems to have sensitized those who share the little man of Chehaw Station's unaccountable knowingness—call it a climate of free-floating sensibility—appears to be a random effect generated by a society in which certain assertions of personality, formerly the prerogative of high social rank, have become the privilege of the anonymous and the lowly.

If this be true, the matter of the artist's ability to identify the mixed background and general character of his audience can be more problematical than might be assumed. In the field of literature it presents a problem of rhetoric, a question of how to fashion strategies of communication that will bridge the many divisions of background and taste which any representative American audience embodies. To the extent that American literature is both an art of discovery and an artistic agency for creating a consciousness of cultural identity, it is of such crucial importance as to demand of the artist not only an eclectic resourcefulness of skill, but an act of democratic faith. In this light, the American artist will do his best not only because of his dedication to his form and craft, but because he realizes that despite an inevitable unevenness of composition, the chances are that any American audience will conceal at least *one* individual whose knowledge and taste will complement or surpass his own. This (to paraphrase Miss Harrison) is because even the most homogeneous audiences are culturally mixed and embody, in their relative anonymity, the mystery of American cultural identity.

This identity—tentative, controversial, constantly changing—is confusing to artist and audience alike. To the audience, because it is itself of mixed background, and seldom fully conscious of the cultural (or even political) implications of its own wide democratic range. To the artist, because in the broadest thrust of his effort he directs his finest effects to an abstract (and thus ideal) refinement of sensibility which, because it is not the exclusive property of a highly visible elite, is difficult to pinpoint. As one who operates within the historical frame of his given art, the artist may direct himself to those who are conscious of the most advanced state of his art: his artistic peers. But if his work has social impact, which is one gauge of its success as symbolic communication, it will reach into unpredictable areas. Many of us, by the way, read our first Hemingway, Fitzgerald, Mann in barbershops, and heard our first opera on phonographs. Thus, the ideal level of sensibility to which the American artist would address himself tends to transcend the lines of class, religion, region, and race—floating, as it were, free in the crowd. There, like the memory registers of certain computer systems, it is simultaneously accessible at any point in American society. Such are the circumstances that render the little man at Chehaw Station not only possible but inevitable.

But who, then, *is* this little man of Miss Harrison's riddle? From behind what unlikely mask does he render his judgments? And by what magic of art can his most receptive attention, his grudging admiration, be excited? No idle questions these; like Shakespeare's Hamlet, the little man has his pride and complexity. He values his personal uniqueness, cherishes his privacy, and clings to that tricky democratic anonymity which makes locating him an unending challenge. Hamlet masked himself with madness; the little man plays mute. Drawn to the brightness of bright lights, he cloaks himself in invisibility—perhaps because in the shadow of his anonymity he can be both the vernacular cat who looks at (and listens to) the tradition-bound or fad-struck king *and* the little boy who sees clearly the artist-emperor's pretentious nakedness. García Lorca writes of a singer who presented an audience of *cante hondo* lovers with a voice and restraint of passion better suited to a recital of *bel canto.* "Hurray," responded a deadpan Spanish cousin of the ghost of Chehaw Station, "for the school of Paris!"

Which is to say that having been randomly exposed to diverse artistic conventions, the little man has learned to detect the true transcendent ambience created by successful art from chic shinola. "Form should fit function," says he, "and style theme. Just as punishment should fit crime—which it seldom does nowadays—or as a well-made shoe the foot." Something of an autodidact, he has his own hierarchal ranking of human values, both native American and universal. And along with these, his own range of pieties—filial, sacred, racial—which constitute, in effect, the rhetorical "stops" through which his sensibilities are made responsive to artistic structurings of symbolic form.

Connoisseur, critic, trickster, the little man is also a day-coach, cabin-class traveler, but the timing of his arrivals and departures is uncertain. Sometimes he's there, sometimes he's here. Being quintessentially American, he enjoys the joke, the confounding of hierarchal expectations fostered by his mask: that cultural incongruity through which he, like Brer Rabbit, is able to convert even the most decorous of audiences into his own brier patch and temper the chilliest of classics to his own vernacular taste. Hence, as a practitioner of art, a form of symbolic communication that depends upon a calculated refinement of statement and affect, the American artist must also know the special qualities of that second instrument: his native audience; an audience upon which—arousing, frustrating, and fulfilling its expectations to the conventionalized contours of symbolic action—he is called upon to play as a pianist upon a piano. But here a special, most American problem arises. Thanks to the presence of the little man, this second instrument can be most unstable in its tuning, and downright ornery in its responses. In approaching it, the artist may, if he will, play fast and loose with modes and traditions, techniques and styles, but only at his peril does he treat an American audience as though it were as easily manipulated as a jukebox.

Reject the little man in the name of purity or as one who aspires beyond his social station or cultural capacity—fine! But it is worth remembering that one of the implicitly creative functions of art in the U.S.A. (and certainly of narrative art) is the defining and correlating of diverse American experiences by bringing previously unknown patterns, details and emotions into view along with those that are generally recognized. Here one of the highest awards of art is the achievement of that electrifying and creative collaboration between the work of art and its audience that occurs when, through the unifying force of its vision and its power to give meaningful focus to apparently unrelated emotions and experiences, art becomes simultaneously definitive of specific and universal truths.

In this country, the artist is free to choose, but cannot limit, his audience. He may ignore the unknown or unplaced sector of the public, but the mystifications of snobbery are of no avail against the little man's art hunger. Having arrived at his interest in art through familiar but uncharted channels, he disdains its use either as a form of social climbing or of social exclusion. Democratically innocent of hierarchal striving, he takes his classics as he takes his tall tales or jazz: without frills. But while self-effacing, he is nevertheless given to a democratic touchiness, and is suspicious of all easy assumptions of superiority based upon appearances. When fretted by an obtuse artistic hand, he can be quite irritable, and what frets him utterly is any attitude that offends his quite human pieties by ignorance or disregard for his existence.

And yet the little man feels no urge to impose censorship upon the artist. Possessing an American-vernacular receptivity to change, a healthy delight in creative attempts at formalizing irreverence, and a Yankee trader's respect for the experimental, he is repelled by works of art that would strip human experience, especially American experience, of its wonder and stubborn complexity. Not that he demands that his own shadowy image be dragged into each and every artistic effort; that would make a shambles of art's necessary illusion by violating the social reality in which he finds his being. It is enough that the artist (above all, the novelist, dramatist, poet) forge images of American experience that resonate symbolically with his own ubiquitous presence. In *The Great Gatsby,* Nick Carraway tells us, by way of outlining his background's influence upon his moral judgments, that his family fortune was started by an Irish uncle who immigrated during the Civil War, paid a substitute to fight in his stead, and went on to become wealthy from war profiteering. Enough said! This takes hardly a paragraph, but the themes of history, wealth and immigration are struck like so many notes on a chime. Assuming his Afro-American identity, costume and mask, the little man behind the stove would make the subtle symbolic connections among Gatsby's ill-fated social climbing, the wealthy wastrels whose manners and morals are the focus of the action, the tragic ironies echoing so faintly from the Civil War (that seedbed of so many Northern fortunes), and his own social condition; among the principles of democracy that form the ground upon which the novel's drama of manners and social hierarchy is enacted, and the cost to Gatsby of confusing the promises of democracy with the terms governing their attainment. In so doing, the little underground-outsider would incorporate the inside-outsider Gatz-Gatsby's experience into his own, and his own into Gatsby's—a transposition that Gatsby would probably have abhorred but one that might have saved his life.

Or again, the little man, by imposing collaboratively his own vision of American experience upon that of the author, would extend the novel's truth to levels below the threshold of that frustrating and illusory social mobility which forms the core of Gatsby's anguish. Responding out of a knowledge of the manner in which the mystique of wealth is intertwined with the American mysteries of class and color, he would aid the author in achieving the more complex vision of American experience that was implicit in his material. As a citizen, the little man endures with a certain grace the social restrictions that limit his own social mobility, but *as a reader* he demands that the relationship between his own condition and that of those more highly placed be recognized. He senses that American experience is of a whole, and he wants the interconnections revealed. This not out of a penchant for protest, nor out of petulant vanity, but because he sees his own condition as an inseparable part of a larger truth in which the high and the lowly, the known and the unrecognized, the comic and the tragic are woven into the American skein. Having been attuned at Chehaw Station to the clangor of diverse bell sounds, he asks not for *whom* the bell tolls, only that it be struck artfully and with that fullness of resonance which warns all men of man's fate. At his best he does not ask for scapegoats, but for the hero as witness. How ironic it was that in the world of *The Great Gatsby* the witness who could have identified the driver of the death car that led to Gatsby's murder was a black man whose ability to communicate (and communication implies moral judgment) was of no more consequence to the action than that of an ox that might have observed Icarus's sad plunge into the sea. (This, by the way, is not intended as a criticism of Fitzgerald, but only to suggest some of the problems and possibilities of artistic communication in the U.S.A.) In this light, the little man is a cautionary figure who challenges the artist to reach out for new heights of expressiveness. If we ignore his possible presence, violence might well be done to that ideal of cultivated democratic sensibility which was the goal of the likes of Emerson and Whitman, and for which the man at Chehaw Station is a metaphor. Respect his presence and even the most avant-garde art may become an agency for raising the general level of artistic taste. The work of art is, after all, an act of faith in our ability to communicate symbolically.

But why would Hazel Harrison associate her humble metaphor for the diffusion of democratic sensibility with a mere whistle-stop? Today I would guess that it was because Chehaw Station functioned as a point of arrival and departure for people representing a wide diversity of tastes and styles of living. Philanthropists, businessmen, sharecroppers, students and artistic types passed through its doors. But the same, in a more exalted fashion, is true of Carnegie Hall and the Metropolitan Museum; all three structures are meeting places for motley mixtures of people. So while it might require a Melvillean imagination to reduce American society to the dimensions of either concert hall or railroad station, their common feature as gathering places, as juncture points for random assemblies of sensibilities, reminds us again that in this particular country even the most homogeneous gatherings of people are mixed and pluralistic. Perhaps the mystery of American cultural identity contained in such motley mixtures arises out of our persistent attempts to reduce our cultural diversity to an easily recognizable unity.

On the other hand, Americans tend to focus on the diverse parts of their culture (with which they can more easily identify), rather than on its complex and pluralistic wholeness. But perhaps they identify with the parts because the whole is greater, if not of a different quality, than its parts. This difference, that new and problematic quality—call it our "Americanness"—creates out of its incongruity an uneasiness within us, because it is a constant reminder that American democracy is not only a political collectivity of individuals, but culturally a collectivity of styles, tastes and traditions.

In this lies the source of many of our problems, especially those centering upon American identity. In relationship to the cultural whole, we are, all of us—white or black, native-born or immigrant—members of minority groups. Beset by feelings of isolation because of the fluid, pluralistic turbulence of the democratic process, we cling desperately to our own familiar fragment of the democratic rock, and from such fragments we confront our fellow Americans in that combat of civility, piety and tradition which is the drama of American social hierarchy. Holding desperately to our familiar turf, we engage in that ceaseless contention whose uneasily accepted but unrejectable purpose is the projection of an ever more encompassing and acceptable definition of our corporate identity as Americans. Usually this contest (our improvised moral equivalent for armed warfare) proceeds as a war of words, a clash of styles, or as rites of symbolic sacrifice in which cabalistic code words are used to designate victims consumed with an Aztec voracity for scapegoats. Indeed, so frequently does this conflict erupt into physical violence that one sometimes wonders if there is any other viable possibility for co-existing in so abstract and futuristic a nation as this.

The rock, the terrain upon which we struggle, is itself abstract, a terrain of ideas that, although man-made, exerts the compelling force of the ideal, of the sublime: ideas that draw their power from the Declaration of Independence, the Constitution, and the Bill of Rights. We stand, as we say, united in the name of these sacred principles. But indeed it is in the name of these same principles that we ceaselessly contend, affirming our ideals even as we do them violence.

For while we are but human and thus given to the fears and temptations of the flesh, we are dedicated to principles that are abstract, ideal, spiritual: principles that were conceived linguistically and committed to paper during that contention over political ideals and economic interests which was released and given focus during the period of our revolutionary break with traditional forms of society, principles that were enshrined—again linguistically—in the documents of state upon which this nation was founded. Actuated by passionate feats of revolutionary will which released that dynamic power for moralizing both man and nature, instinct and society, which is a property of linguistic forms of symbolic action, these principles—democracy, equality, individual freedom and universal justice—now move us as articles of faith. Holding them sacred, we act (or *fail* to act) in their names. And in the freewheeling fashion of words that are summoned up to name the ideal, they prod us ceaselessly toward the refinement and perfection of those formulations of policy and configurations of social forms of which they are the signs and symbols. As we strive to conduct social action in accordance with the ideals they evoke, they in turn insist upon being made flesh. Inspiriting our minds and bodies, they dance around in our bones, spurring us to make them ever more manifest in the structures and processes of ourselves and our society. As a nation, we exist in the communication of our principles, and we argue over their application and interpretation as over the rights of property or the exercise and sharing of authority. As elsewhere, they influence our expositions in the area of artistic form and are involved in our search for a system of aesthetics capable of projecting our corporate, pluralistic identity. They interrogate us endlessly as to who and what we are; they demand that we keep the democratic faith.

Words that evoke our principles are, according to Kenneth Burke, charismatic terms for transcendent order, for perfection. Being forms of symbolic action, they tend, through their nature as language, to sweep us in tow as they move by a process of linguistic negation toward the ideal. As a form of *symbolic* action, they operate by negating nature as a given and amoral condition, creating endless series of man-made or man-imagined positives. By so doing, they nudge us toward that state of human rectitude for which, ideally, we strive. In this way, Burke contends, man uses language to moralize both nature and himself. Thus, in this nation the word democracy possesses the aura of what Burke calls a "god-term," and all that we are and do exists in the magnitude of its intricate symbolism. It is the rock upon which we toil, and we thrive or wane in the communication of those symbols and processes set in motion in its name.

In our national beginnings, all redolent with Edenic promises, was the word *democratic,* and since we vowed in a war rite of blood and sacrifice to keep its commandments, we act in the name of a word made sacred. Yes, but since we are, as Burke holds, language-using, language-misusing animals—beings who are by nature vulnerable to both the negative *and* the positive promptings of language as symbolic action—we Americans are given to eating, regurgitating, and, alas, re-eating even our most sacred words. It is as though they contain a substance that is crucial to our national existence but that, except in minute and infrequently ingested doses, we find extremely indigestible. Some would call this national habit of word-eating an exercise in the art of the impossible; others attribute it to the limitations imposed by the human condition. Still others would describe it as springing from the pathology of social hierarchy, a reaction to certain built-in conditions of our democracy that are capable of amelioration but impossible to cure. Whatever the case may be, it would seem that for many our cultural diversity is as indigestible as the concept of democracy in which it is grounded. For one thing, principles in action are enactments of ideals grounded in a vision of perfection that transcends the limitations of death and dying. By arousing in the believer a sense of the disrelation between the ideal and the actual, between the perfect word and the errant flesh, they partake of mystery. Here the most agonizing mystery sponsored by the democratic ideal is that of our unity-in-diversity, our oneness-in-manyness. Pragmatically we cooperate and communicate across this mystery, but the problem of identity that it poses often goads us to symbolic acts of disaffiliation. So we seek psychic security from within our inherited divisions of the corporate

American culture while gazing out upon our fellows with a mixed attitude of fear, suspicion and yearning. We repress an underlying anxiety aroused by the awareness that we are representative not only of one but of several overlapping and constantly shifting social categories, and we stress our affiliation with that segment of the corporate culture which has emerged out of our parents' past—racial, cultural, religious—and which we assume, on the basis of such magical talismans as our mother's milk or father's beard, that we "know." Grounding our sense of identity in such primary and affect-charged symbols, we seek to avoid the mysteries and pathologies of the democratic process. But that process was designed to overcome the dominance of tradition by promoting an open society in which the individual could achieve his potential unhindered by his ties to the past. Here, theoretically, social categories are open, and the individual is not only considered capable of transforming himself, but is encouraged to do so. However, in undertaking such transformations he opts for that psychic uncertainty which is a condition of his achieving his potential, a state he yearns to avoid. So despite any self-assurance he might achieve in dealing with his familiars, he is nevertheless (and by the nature of his indefinite relationship to the fluid social hierarchy) a lonely individual who must find his own way within a crowd of other lonely individuals. Here the security offered by his familiar symbols of identity is equivocal. And an overdependence upon them as points of orientation leads him to become bemused, gazing backward at a swiftly receding—if not quasi-mythical—past, while stumbling headlong into a pre-described but unknown future.

So perhaps we shy from confronting our cultural wholeness because it offers no easily recognizable points of rest, no facile certainties as to who, what or where (culturally or historically) we are. Instead, the whole is always in cacophonic motion. Constantly changing its mode, it appears as a vortex of discordant ways of living and tastes, values and traditions, a whirlpool of odds and ends in which the past courses in uneasy juxtaposition with those bright, futuristic principles and promises to which we, as a nation, are politically committed. In our vaguely perceived here and now, even the sounds and symbols spun off by the clashing of group against group appear not only alarmingly off-key, but threatening to our inherited eyes, ears, and appetites. Thus in our intergroup familiarity there is a brooding strangeness, and in our underlying sense of alienation a poignant, although distrusted, sense of fraternity. Deep down, the American condition is a state of unease.

During the nineteenth century an attempt was made to impose a loose conceptual order upon the chaos of American society by viewing it as a melting pot. Today that metaphor is noisily rejected, vehemently disavowed. In fact, it has come under attack in the name of the newly fashionable code word "ethnicity," reminding us that in this country code words are linguistic agencies for the designation of sacrificial victims, and are circulated to sanction the abandonment of policies and the degrading of ideas. So today, before the glaring inequities, unfulfilled promises and rich possibilities of democracy, we hear heady evocations of European, African and Asian backgrounds accompanied by chants proclaiming the inviolability of ancestral blood. Today blood magic and blood thinking, never really dormant in American society, are rampant among us, often leading to brutal racial assaults in areas where these seldom occurred before. And while this goes on, the challenge of arriving at an adequate definition of American cultural identity goes unanswered. (What, by the way, is one to make of a white youngster who, with a transistor radio screaming a Stevie Wonder tune glued to his ear, shouts racial epithets at black youngsters trying to swim at a public beach—and this in the name of the ethnic sanctity of what has been declared a neighborhood turf?)

The proponents of ethnicity—ill concealing an underlying anxiety and given a bizarre bebopish stridency by the obviously American vernacular inspiration of the costumes and rituals ragged out to dramatize their claims to ethnic (and genetic) insularity—have helped give our streets and campuses a rowdy, All Fool's Day carnival atmosphere. In many ways, then, the call for a new social order based upon the glorification of ancestral blood and ethnic background acts as a call to cultural and aesthetic chaos. Yet while this latest farcical phase in the drama of American social hierarchy unfolds, the irrepressible movement of American culture toward the integration of its diverse elements continues, confounding the circumlocutions of its staunchest opponents.

In this regard I am reminded of a light-skinned, blue-eyed, Afro-American-featured individual who could have been taken for anything from a sun-tinged white Anglo-Saxon, an Egyptian, or a mixed-breed American Indian to a strayed member of certain tribes of Jews. This young man appeared one sunny Sunday afternoon on New York's Riverside Drive near 151st Street, where he disrupted the visual peace of the promenading throng by racing up in a shiny new blue Volkswagen Beetle decked out with a gleaming Rolls Royce radiator. As the flow of strollers came to an abrupt halt, this man of parts emerged from his carriage with something of that magical cornucopian combustion by which a dozen circus clowns are exploded from an even more miniaturized automobile. Looming as tall as a professional basketball center, he unfolded himself and stretched to his full imposing height.

Clad in handsome black riding boots and fawn-colored riding breeches of English tailoring, he took the curb wielding, with an ultra-pukka-sahib haughtiness, a leather riding crop. A dashy dashiki (as bright and as many-colored as the coat that initiated poor Joseph's troubles in biblical times) flowed from his broad shoulders down to the arrogant, military flare of his breeches-tops, while six feet six inches or so above his heels, a black homburg hat tilted at a jaunty angle floated majestically on the crest of his huge Afro-coiffed head.

As though all this were not enough to amaze, delight, or discombobulate his observers—or precipitate an international incident involving charges of a crass invasion of stylistic boundaries—this apparition proceeded to unlimber an expensive Japanese single-lens reflex camera, position it atop the ornamental masonry balustrade which girds Riverside Park in that area, and activate its self-timer. Then, with a ballet leap across the walk, he assumed a position beside his car. There he rested his elbow upon its top, smiled, and gave himself sharp movie director's commands as to desired poses, then began taking a series of self-portraits. This done, he placed the camera upon the hood of his Volkswagen and took another series of self-shots in which, manipulating a lengthy ebony cigarette holder, he posed himself in various fanciful attitudes against the not-too-distant background of the George Washington Bridge. All in all, he made a scene to haunt one's midnight dreams and one's noon repose.

Now, I can only speculate about what was going on in the elegant gentleman's mind, who he was, or what visual statement he intended to communicate. I only know that his carefully stylized movements (especially his "pimp-limp" walk) marked him as a native of the U.S.A., a home-boy bent upon projecting and recording with native verve something of his complex sense of cultural identity. Clearly he had his own style, but if—as has been repeatedly argued—the style is the man, who on earth was this fellow? Viewed from a rigid ethnocultural perspective, neither his features nor his car nor his dress was of a whole. Yet he conducted himself with an obvious pride of person and of property, inviting all and sundry to admire and wonder in response to himself as his own sign and symbol, his own work of art. He had gotten himself, as the Harlem saying goes, "together," and whatever sheerly ethnic identity was communicated by his costume depended upon the observer's ability to see order in an apparent cultural chaos. The man himself was hidden somewhere within, his complex identity concealed by his aesthetic gesturing. And his essence lay not in the somewhat comic clashing of styles, but in the mixture, the improvised form, the willful juxtaposition of modes.

Perhaps to the jaundiced eyes of an adversary of the melting-pot concept, the man would have appeared to be a militant black nationalist bent upon dramatizing his feelings of alienation—and he may have been. But most surely he was not an African or an Englishman. His Volks-Rolls-Royce might well have been loaded with Marxist tracts and Molotov cocktails, but his clashing of styles nevertheless sounded an integrative, vernacular note, an American compulsion to improvise upon the given. His garments were, literally and figuratively, of many colors and cultures, his racial identity interwoven of many strands. Whatever his politics, sources of income, hierarchal status and such, he revealed his essential "Americanness" in his free-wheeling assault upon traditional forms of the Western aesthetic. Whatever the identity he presumed to project, he was exercising an American freedom and was a product of the melting pot and the conscious or unconscious comedy it brews. Culturally he was an American joker. If his Afro and dashiki symbolized protest, his boots, camera, Volkswagen and homburg imposed certain qualifications upon that protest. In doing so, they played irreverently upon the symbolism of status, property and authority, and suggested new possibilities of perfection. More than expressing protest, these symbols ask the old, abiding American questions: Who am I? What about me?

Still, ignoring such questions (as they would ignore the little man of Chehaw Station), the opponents of the melting-pot concept utter their disavowals with an old-fashioned, camp-meeting fervor—solemnly, and with an air of divine revelation. Most amazingly, these attacks upon the melting pot are led by the descendants of peasants or slaves or inhabitants of European ghettos, people whose status as spokesmen is a product of that very melting of hierarchal barriers they now deny. With such an attitude, it is fortunate that they, too, are caught up in the society's built-in, democracy-prodded movement toward a perfection of self-definition. Hence such disavowals, despite their negative posture, have their positive content. And to the extent that they are negatives uttered in an attempt to create certain attitudes and conditions that their exponents conceive as positives, these disavowals are, in part, affirmations of the diverse and unique pasts out of which have emerged the many groups that this nation comprises. As such they might well contribute to a clarification of our pluralistic cultural identity, and are thus a step in the direction of creating a much-needed cultural introspection.

As of now, however, I see the denial of that goal of cultural integration for which the melting pot was an accented metaphor as the current form of an abiding American self-distrust. I see it as an effort to dismiss the mystery of American identity (our unity-within-diversity) with a gesture of democracy-weary resignation, as an attempt to dispel by sociological word-magic the turbulence of the present, and as a self-satisfied vote against that hope which is so crucial to our cultural and political fulfillment. For if such disavowals be viable, what about the little man behind the stove?

Ironically, the attacks on the melting-pot idea issue from those who have "made it." Having been reborn into a higher hierarchal status, they now view those who have *not* made it as threats to their newly achieved status, and therefore would change both the rules and the game plan. Thus they demonstrate anew the built-in opportunism of their characteristically American shortness of memory. But lest we ourselves forget, the melting-pot concept was never so simplistic or abstract as current arguments would have it. Americans of an earlier day, despite their booster extravagances, recognized the difference between the ideal and the practical, even as they clung desperately to, and sought to default upon, the responsibilities that went with achieving their democratic ideal. Their outlook was pragmatic, their way with culture vernacular, an eclectic mixing of modes. Having rejected the hierarchal ordering of traditional societies, they improvised their culture as they did their politics and institutions—touch and go, by ear and by eye—fitting new form to new function, new function to old form. Deep down they sensed that in the process of nation-building their *culture,* like their institutions, was always more "American" (that futuristic concept) than they could perceive—or even fully accept—it to be. Even the slaves, although thrust below the threshold of social hierarchy, were given a prominent place in our national iconography; their music, poetic imagery and choreography were grudgingly recognized as seminal sources of American art. In the process of creating (and re-creating or diverting) themselves, the melting-pot Americans brazenly violated their ideals. They kept slaves or battened on the products of slave labor. They exploited and abused those who arrived later than themselves, kinsmen and aliens alike. While paying lip service to their vaunted forms of justice, they betrayed, brutalized and scapegoated one another in the name of the Constitution, the Bill of Rights, and the Ten Commandments. But because of their fidelity to their parents' customs and their respect for the pieties of their traditions, if not for those of their fellows, none of the groups that made up the total culture ever really desired to lose its sense of its unique past, not even when that past lay clouded in slavery.

Instead, they wished to use the techniques, ways of life, and values developed within their respective backgrounds as sources of morale in that continuing process of antagonistic cooperation, and of adjusting the past to the present in the interest of the future, which was so necessary in building what they imagined as a more humane society. Indeed, during their most candid, self-accepting moments they saw themselves as living embodiments of the ancestral past, people who had seized the democracy-sponsored opportunity to have a second chance. As such, they saw themselves as the best guarantee that whatever was most desirable and salvageable from that past would be retained and brought to flower, free of hierarchal hindrances. The little man behind the stove would know from his own condition that the melting-pot concept was a conceit, but his forced awareness of American cultural pluralism would assure him that it was by no means the product of a con game contrived by the powerful. Here not even the powerful were so perceptive.

So our current disavowals are not only misdirected; they are productive of more social disorder, more crises of cultural and personal identity than they could possibly resolve. It is here, on the level of culture, that the diverse elements of our various backgrounds, our heterogeneous pasts, have indeed come together, "melted" and undergone metamorphosis. It is here, if we would but recognize it, that elements of the many available tastes, traditions, ways of life, and values that make up the total culture have been ceaselessly appropriated and made their own—consciously, unselfconsciously, or imperialistically—by groups and individuals to whose own backgrounds and traditions they are historically alien. Indeed, it was through this process of cultural appropriation (and misappropriation) that Englishmen, Europeans, Africans, and Asians *became* Americans.

The Pilgrims began by appropriating the agricultural, military, and meteorological lore of the Indians, including much of their terminology. The Africans, thrown together from numerous ravaged tribes, took up the English language and the biblical legends of the ancient Hebrews and were "Americanizing" themselves long before the American Revolution. They also had imposed upon them a goodly portion of European chromosomes, and thereby "inherited" both an immunity to certain European diseases and a complexity of bloodlines and physical characteristics that have much to do with the white American's reluctance to differentiate between race and culture, African and American, and are a major source of our general confusion over American identity. One of the many questions posed by the man on Riverside Drive is how one so "white" could be simply "black" without being impossibly simpleminded. Especially when his skin and facial bone structure ask, "Where went the blood of yesteryear?" There is no point in answering the question as did Villon, because the man's face was as Anglo and his hairstyle as Afro as his car's radiator and body were English and German.

Everyone played the appropriation game. The whites took over any elements of Afro-American culture that seemed useful: the imagery of folklore, ways of speaking, endurance of what appeared to be hopeless hardship, and singing and dancing—including the combination of Afro-American art forms that produced the first musical theater of national appeal: the minstrel show. And in improvising their rather tawdry and opportunistic version of a national mythology, the moviemakers—Christian and Jewish, Northerners and Southerners—ransacked and distorted for their own purposes the backgrounds and images of everyone, including the American Indians.

So, melting-pot disclaimers notwithstanding, Americans seem to have sensed intuitively that the possibility of enriching the individual self by such pragmatic and opportunitistic appropriations has constituted one of the most precious of their many freedoms. Having opted for the new, and being unable to create it out of thin air or from words inscribed on documents of state, they did what came naturally: they pressured the elements of the past and present into new amalgams. In lieu of a usable cultural tradition, there were always the cultural improvisations of the Afro-Americans, the immigrants, or design-gifted religious groups like the Shakers—all so close to eye and ear, hand and imagination. Considering that the newness achieved by Americans has often been a matter of adapting to function and a matter of naming, of designation, we are reminded of how greatly the "Americanness" of American culture has been a matter of Adamic wordplay—of trying, in the interest of a futuristic dream, to impose unity upon an experience that changes too rapidly for linguistic or political exactitude. In this effort we are often less interested in what we are than in projecting what we will be. But in our freewheeling appropriations of culture we appear to act on the assumption that as members of a "nation of nations," we are, by definition and by the processes of democratic cultural integration, the inheritors, creators and creations of a culture of cultures.

So perhaps the complex actuality of our cultural pluralism is perplexing because the diverse interacting elements that surround us, traditional and vernacular, not only elude accepted formulations, but take on a character that is something other than their various parts. Our old familiar pasts become, in juxtaposition with elements appropriated from other backgrounds, incongruously transformed, exerting an energy (or synergy) of a different order than that generated by their separate parts—and this with incalculable results. Nor should we forget the role played by objects and technology in the integration of our cultural styles, and in the regional and political unification of the nation. If we put the blues, bluegrass music, English folk songs, et cetera, together with Afro-American rhythms and gospel shouts, we have, God help us, first rock and now "funk," that most odoriferous of musical(?) styles. Still, such mixtures of cultural elements are capable of igniting exciting transformations of culture. Even more mysteriously (and here, perhaps, we have a further source of the little man of Chehaw Station's rich sensibility), they provide for exciting and most unexpected metamorphoses within the self-creating personality.

Frankly, many of the foregoing speculations have been arrived at over the years since I left Tuskegee. If I had been more mature or perceptive back when I first heard of the little man behind the stove, an object that lay atop Miss Harrison's piano would have been most enlightening. It was a signed Prokofiev manuscript that had been presented to her by the composer. Except for the signature, it looked like countless other manuscripts. Yet I suspect that to anyone who possessed a conventional notion of cultural and hierarchal order, its presence in such a setting would have been as incongruous as a Gutenberg

Bible on the altar of a black sharecropper's church or a dashiki worn with a homburg hat. Still, there it was, an artifact of contemporary music, a folio whose signs and symbols resonated in that setting with the intricate harmonies of friendship, admiration and shared ideals through which it had found its way from Berlin to Tuskegee. Once there, and the arrangement of society beyond the campus notwithstanding, it spoke eloquently of the unstructured possibilities of culture in this pluralistic democracy. Yet despite its meticulous artistic form, in certain conventional minds its presence could arouse intimations of the irrational—of cultural, if not social, chaos.

Given the logic of a society ordered along racial lines, Miss Harrison's studio (or even the library) was simply off limits for such an artifact, certainly in its original form. But there it was, lying in wait to play havoc with conventional ideas of order, lending a wry reality to Malraux's observation that art is an assault upon logic. Through its presence, the manuscript had become an agency of cultural transformation and synthesis. By charging Miss Harrison's basement studio with the spirit of living personages, ideals and purposes from afar, it had transformed that modest room from a mere spot on a segregated Negro campus into an advanced outpost on the frontiers of contemporary music, thus adding an unexpected, if undetected, dimension to Alabama's cultural atmosphere. In my innocence I viewed the manuscript as a property of Miss Harrison's, a sign of her connection with gifted artists across the ocean. It spoke to me of possibility. But that it also endowed the scene—place, studio, campus—with a complex cultural ambiguity escaped my conscious mind. Though aware of certain details of the total scene, I was unattuned to the context in which they sounded, the cultural unity-within-diversity that the combination of details made manifest. Perhaps we are able to see only that which we are prepared to see, and in our culture the cost of insight is an uncertainty that threatens our already unstable sense of order and requires a constant questioning of accepted assumptions.

Had I questioned Miss Harrison as to how the racial identity of her little Chehaw man squared with the culture she credited to him, she might well have replied:

"Look, baby, the society beyond this campus is constantly trying to confuse you about the relationship between culture and race. Well, if you ask me, artistic talent might have something to do with race, but you do *not* inherit culture and artistic skill through your genes. No, sir. These come as a result of personal conquest, of the individual's applying himself to that art, that music—whether jazz, classical, or folk—which helps him to realize and complete himself. And that's true *wherever* the music or art of his choice originates."

Or in the words of André Malraux (whom I was to discover a year or two later), she might have told me that music is important as an artistic form of symbolic action "because its function is to let men escape from their human condition, not by means of an evasion, but through a possession, [for] art is a way of possessing destiny." And that therefore, even at racially segregated Tuskegee (as witnessed by, among countless other details, the library and Miss Harrison's Prokofiev manuscript), one's "cultural heritage is the totality, not of works that men must respect [or that are used to enhance the mystifications that support an elite], but those that can help them live." Entering into a dialogue with Malraux, she might have added on a more specifically American note: "Yes, and most important, you must remember that in this country things are always all shook up, so that people are constantly moving around and rubbing off on one another culturally. Nor should you forget that here all things—institutions, individuals and roles—offer more than the function assigned them, because beyond their intended function they provide forms of education and criticism. They challenge, they ask questions, they offer suggestive answers to those who would pause and probe their mystery. Most of all, remember that it is not only the images of art or the sound of music that pass through walls to give pleasure and inspiration; it is in the very *spirit* of art to be defiant of categories and obstacles. They are, as transcendent forms of symbolic expression, agencies of human freedom."

Three years later, having abandoned my hope of becoming a musician, I had just about forgotten Miss Harrison's mythical little man behind the stove. Then, in faraway New York, concrete evidence of his actual existence arose and blasted me like the heat from an internally combusted ton of coal.

As a member of the Federal Writers' Project, I was spending a clammy late-fall afternoon of freedom circulating a petition in support of some now long-forgotten social issue that I regarded as indispensable to the public good. I found myself inside a tenement building in San Juan Hill, a Negro district that disappeared with the coming of Lincoln Center. Starting on the top floor of the building, I had collected an acceptable number of signatures, and having descended from the ground floor to the basement level, was moving along the dimly lit hallway toward a door through which I could hear loud voices. They were male Afro-American voices, raised in violent argument. The language was profane, the style of speech a Southern idiomatic vernacular such as was spoken by formally uneducated Afro-American workingmen. Reaching the door, I paused, sounding out the lay of the land before knocking to present my petition.

But my delay led to indecision. Not, however, because of the loud, unmistakable anger sounding within; being myself a slum dweller, I knew that voices in slums are often raised in anger, but that the *rhetoric* of anger, itself cathartic, is not necessarily a prelude to physical violence. Rather, it is frequently a form of symbolic action, a verbal equivalent of fisticuffs. No, I hesitated because I realized that behind the door a mystery was unfolding. A mystery so incongruous, outrageous, and surreal that it struck me as a threat to my sense of rational order. It was as though a bizarre practical joke had been staged and its perpetrators were waiting for me, its designated but unknowing scapegoat, to arrive: a joke designed to assault my knowledge of American culture and its hierarchal dispersal. At the very least, it appeared that my pride in my knowledge of my own people was under attack.

For the angry voices behind the door were proclaiming an intimate familiarity with a subject of which, by all the logic of their linguistically projected social status, they should have been oblivious. The subject of their contention confounded all my assumptions regarding the correlation between educational levels, class, race and the possession of conscious culture. Impossible as it seemed, these foul-mouthed black workingmen were locked in verbal combat over which of two celebrated Metropolitan Opera divas was the superior soprano!

I myself attended the opera only when I could raise the funds, and I knew full well that opera-going was far from the usual cultural pursuit of men identified with the linguistic style of such voices. Yet, confounding such facile logic, they were voicing (and loudly) a familiarity with the Met far greater than my own. In their graphic, irreverent, and vehement criticism they were describing not only the two sopranos' acting abilities, but were ridiculing the gestures with which each gave animation to her roles, and they shouted strong opinions as to the ranges of the divas' vocal equipment. Thus, with such a distortion of perspective being imposed upon me, I was challenged either to solve the mystery of their knowledge by entering into their midst or to leave the building with my sense of logic reduced forever to a level of college-trained absurdity.

So challenged, I knocked. I knocked out of curiosity, I knocked out of outrage. I knocked in fear and trembling. I knocked in anticipation of whatever insights—malicious or transcendent, I no longer cared which—I would discover beyond the door.

For a moment there was an abrupt and portentous silence; then came the sound of chair legs thumping dully upon the floor, followed by further silence. I knocked again, loudly, with an authority fired by an impatient and anxious urgency.

Again silence, until a gravel voice boomed an annoyed "Come in!"

Opening the door with an unsteady hand, I looked inside, and was even less prepared for the scene that met my eyes than for the content of their loudmouthed contention.

In a small, rank-smelling, lamp-lit room, four huge black men sat sprawled around a circular dining-room table, looking toward me with undisguised hostility. The sooty-chimneyed lamp glowed in the center of the bare oak table, casting its yellow light upon four water tumblers and a half-empty pint of whiskey. As the men straightened in their chairs I became aware of a fireplace with a coal fire glowing in its grate, and leaning against the ornate marble facing of its mantelpiece, I saw four enormous coal scoops.

"All right," one of the men said, rising to his feet. "What the hell can we do for *you?*"

"And we ain't buying nothing, buddy," one of the seated men added, his palm slapping the table.

Closing the door, I moved forward, holding my petition like a flag of truce before me, noting that the men wore faded blue overalls and jumper jackets, and becoming aware that while all were of dark complexion, their blackness was accentuated in the dim lamplight by the dust and grime of their profession.

"Come on, man, speak up," the man who had arisen said. "We ain't got all day."

"I'm sorry to interrupt," I said, "but I thought you might be interested in supporting my petition," and began hurriedly to explain.

"Say," one of the men said, "you look like one of them relief investigators. You're not out to jive us, are you?"

"Oh, no, sir," I said. "I happen to work on the Writers' Project . . ."

The standing man leaned toward me. "You on the Writers' Project?" he said, looking me up and down.

"That's right," I said. "I'm a writer."

"Now is that right?" he said. "How long you been writing?"

I hesitated. "About a year," I said.

He grinned, looking at the others. "Y'all hear that? Ol' Homeboy here has done up and jumped on the *gravy* train! Now that's pretty good. Pretty damn good! So what did you do before that?" he said.

"I studied music," I said, "at Tuskegee."

"Hey, now!" the standing man said. "They got a damn good choir down there. Y'all remember back when they opened Radio City? They had that fellow William L. Dawson for a director. Son, let's see that paper."

Relieved, I handed him the petition, watching him stretch it between his hardened hands. After a moment of soundlessly mouthing the words of its appeal, he gave me a skeptical look and turned to the others.

"What the hell," he said, "signing this piece of paper won't do no good, but since Home here's a musician, it won't do us no harm to help him out. Let's go along with him."

Fishing a blunt-pointed pencil from the bib of his overalls, he wrote his name and passed the petition to his friends, who followed suit.

This took some time, and as I watched the petition move from hand to hand, I could barely contain myself or control my need to unravel the mystery that had now become far more important than just getting their signatures on my petition.

"There you go," the last one said, extending the petition toward me. "Having our names on there don't mean a thing, but you got em."

"Thank you," I said. "Thank you very much."

They watched me with amused eyes, expecting me to leave, but, clearing my throat nervously, I stood in my tracks, too intrigued to leave and suddenly too embarrassed to ask my question.

"So what are you waiting for?" one of them said. "You got what you came for. What else do you want?"

And then I blurted it out. "I'd like to ask you just one question," I said.

"Like what?" the standing one said.

"Like where on earth did you gentlemen learn so much about grand opera?"

For a moment he stared at me with parted lips; then, pounding the mantelpiece with his palm, he collapsed with a roar of laughter. As the laughter of the others erupted like a string of giant firecrackers, I looked on with growing feelings of embarrassment and insult, trying to grasp the handle of what appeared to be an unfriendly joke. Finally, wiping coal-dust-stained tears from his cheeks, he interrupted his laughter long enough to initiate me into the mystery.

"Hell, son," he laughed, "we learn it down at the Met, that's where . . ."

"You learned it *where*?"

"At the Metropolitan Opera, just like I told you. Strip us fellows down and give us some costumes and we make about the finest damn bunch of Egyptians you ever seen. Hell, we been down there wearing leopard skins and carrying spears or waving things like palm leafs and ostrich-tail fans for *years*!"

Now, purged by the revelation, and with Hazel Harrison's voice echoing in my ears, it was my turn to roar with laughter. With a shock of recognition I joined them in appreciation of the hilarious American joke that centered on the incongruities of race, economic status and culture. My sense of order restored, my appreciation of the arcane ways of American cultural possibility was vastly extended. The men were products of both past *and* present; were both coal heavers *and* Met extras; were both workingmen *and* opera buffs. Seen in the clear, pluralistic, melting-pot light of American cultural possibility, there was no contradiction. The joke, the apparent contradiction, sprang from my attempting to see them by the light of social concepts that cast less illumination than an inert lump of coal. I was delighted, because during a moment when I least expected to encounter the little man behind the stove (Miss Harrison's vernacular music critic, as it were), I had stumbled upon four such men. Not behind the stove, it is true, but even more wondrously, they had materialized at an even more unexpected location: at the depth of the American social hierarchy and, of all possible hiding places, behind a coal pile. Where there's a melting pot there's smoke, and where there's smoke it is not simply optimistic to expect fire, it's imperative to watch for the phoenix's vernacular, but transcendent, rising.

1986

GETTING STARTED

1. Who is the "little man at Chehaw Station"? Write a paragraph describing him and discussing his significance.

2. In a group, find two examples that show Ellison's attitude toward the melting pot concept of democracy. Prepare a presentation for the class in which you explain the melting pot concept and present Ellison's attitude toward it using the evidence you have found.

3. Who is Ellison's audience? What is he trying to tell his audience about the rhetorical concept of audience? As a member of Ellison's audience, are you a version of the "little man"?

4. In a group, examine the anecdote about the Volkswagen and consider how this example relates to Ellison's larger argument. Compare and contrast the point Ellison is making in this example to the anecdotes he uses to begin and end the essay. Present your findings to the class.

WRITING

5. Examine Ellison's use of the melting pot metaphor. What are the problems with this metaphor? What are its strengths? Write a paper of 3–4 pages in which you analyze this metaphor and its ability to describe the American population. You also might consider discussing another metaphor that you have read about or heard of that you think provides a more accurate description, or consider inventing a metaphor of your own.

6. Write a short paper describing your own version of the "little man at Chehaw station." What metaphor or story best conveys your ideas about audience or your vision of the American audience? How do your ideas compare and contrast to Ellison's?

USING THE LIBRARY AND THE INTERNET

7. Use the Internet or your library's reference section to learn more about Prokofiev. What does Ellison's use of this example tell us about how he imagines his audience? How much does he expect us to know? What impression do you get of Ellison from this and other examples in the essay?

8. Using Academic Search Elite or a similar reference database that includes a range of scholarly journal articles, try several searches using "melting pot," "American culture," and "multicultural" as search terms. Scan your results list to find differing attitudes toward the melting pot concept and to find other metaphors that people use to describe American culture. Print out your best findings and bring them to class.

MAKING CONNECTIONS

9. Compare and contrast Ellison's ideas about how democracy works to those of Christopher Lasch in "The Lost Art of Argument." To what extent would Lasch agree that public debate is fundamental to a democracy? Would he share Ellison's reaction to the melting pot metaphor?

10. Write a short paper using ideas and examples from Patricia J. Williams's "The Ethnic Scarring of American Whiteness" to further explain and evaluate Ellison's discussion of the role of ethnicity in American culture. To what extent would Williams support or find problems with Ellison's analysis?

11. Write a paper analyzing the ways in which Richard C. Lewontin's ideas about the relationship of the organism to the environment in "Science as Social Action" apply to Ellison's ideas about the relationship of the individual to society. For example, does the concept of "reductionism" from Lewontin apply to examples from Ellison? How would Lewontin respond to Ellison's imagined speech by Miss Harrison about not inheriting "culture and artistic skill through your genes" (p. 196)?

Stuart Ewen

Stuart Ewen is Chair of the Department of Film and Media at Hunter College. He is also a professor in the Ph.D. Programs in History and in Sociology at the City University of New York Graduate Center. Ewen is the author of *Captains of Consciousness: Advertising and the Social Roots of the Consumer Culture* (1976), *All Consuming Images: The Politics of Style in Contemporary Culture* (1988), *Channels of Desire: Mass Images and the Shaping of American Consciousness* (coauthored with Elizabeth Ewen) (1992), and *PR!: The Social History of Spin* (1996). *All Consuming Images,* from which "The Marriage Between Art and Commerce" was excerpted, served as the source for an award-winning Public Broadcasting System series, "The Public Mind." In addition to lecturing on art and design at museums and universities around the country, Ewen has taken his social and political criticism to the street. Using the name Archie Bishop, Ewen has produced political protest art and street installations for the past thirty years.

To learn more about Stuart Ewen and his critique of consumer capitalism, read an online transcript of his interview with ABC News at <http://www.abcnews.go.com/sections/us/DailyNews/chat_ewen.html>.

The Marriage Between Art and Commerce

Integrated Visions

In the United States, and throughout much of industrialized Europe, the years between 1890 and the 1920s saw qualitative changes in the organization of industries and in methods of production. Industrial corporations grew into giant enterprises, implementing an increasingly mechanized system of mass production.

In the midst of these changes, culture itself was undergoing a fateful transition. If *culture* can be understood as the accumulated stock of understandings and practices by which a given people live and maintain themselves in a given society, the industrialization of daily life may be said to have, in large measure, displaced the customary fabric of culture. Increasingly, resources of survival were being produced by modern systems of mass manufacture. As this mode of production demanded broadened national or international markets, corporations made expanded use of advertising, among other merchandising techniques. Advertising not only sought to inform people about the availability and appeal of industrially produced goods, it also contributed to a restructured perception of the resources and alternatives that were available to people in their everyday lives.

Partly as a response to unprecedented marketing needs; partly to establish a uniform and easily recognizable corporate identity; partly in response to avant-garde tendencies in the arts, giant industrial corporations began to develop multipurpose styling divisions in the first decades of the twentieth century. A pioneer in this development was Walter Rathenau, head of Allgemeine Elektricitäts-Gesellschaft (AEG), the huge German electric company that had been founded (as Deutsche Edison Gesellschaft) by his father, Emil, in 1883.

By 1907 AEG had become one of Europe's great industrial corporations. It "had a capital value exceeding 100 million marks and employed some 70,000 people. Its sales catalogs listed hundreds of different products."[1] Rathenau, according to his friend Franz Blei, was a man possessed and disturbed by the chaotic social world that had emerged alongside the apparatus of corporate industrialism. Rathenau held the passionate conviction that spiritual content and form could be given to the chaotic and inert body of trade and industry.[2]

For Rathenau, it was necessary to invent a new definition and application of style, one not rooted in the past, but derived from "the techniques of mass production and . . . the widespread dissemination of industrial products." What made Rathenau unique was his implementation of this idea within the bureaucratic structure of a modern corporation. Believing that a new style, all industrial aesthetic, could be a "means of alleviating the devastation that industrialization had wrought on such basic areas as labor, production, housing, and human relations," Rathenau commissioned Peter Behrens, an architect and designer, to create a uniform corporate *look* for the AEG. Behrens's assignment was "to redesign the company's buildings, products, and publicity material," from a huge "turbine hall down to tiny publicity seals."[3] Between 1907 and 1914, Behrens created what he called an "artistic context," designed to encompass all elements of the corporation. This was the beginning of the consciously promulgated "corporate image," a uniform reminder that in a world of the ephemeral, the corporation is a constant.

In the nineteenth century, an indiscriminate reverence for the grandiosities of the past had given rise to a shoddy imagistic chaos. By the early twentieth century, the industrial exigencies of coordination, standardization, and control were beginning to find aesthetic expression, part of a move toward more coherent corporate design strategies. Behrens's work at AEG created the prototype for industrial design departments to come. He understood that design could not be limited to a particular building or commodity. In order for design to project a new "spiritual content," it was necessary to erect an imagistic panorama: a new symbolic totality, constituted by an interconnected, cross-referenced, visible world.

This integrated vision was remarkably inclusive in its application. Behrens designed lamps, table fans, humidifiers, motors, dental drills, light switches, clocks, electric kettles, electric heaters, and numerous other products. His designs also shaped the factories in which these products were manufactured, the exhibition pavilions in which they were displayed, and the advertisements by which they were promoted. In each case, Behrens's designs were infused with the look of the "modern." Clean lines and a strictly regulated geometry replaced the encrusted ornamentation that had marked many industrial products to that time. Where ornament did appear, it was spare and understated, its links with the past for the most part severed.

Consumer Engineering

In the United States, during the years that Behrens worked at AEG, the instrumental use of style as a business device was also gaining adherents and practitioners. Speaking to the Chicago Commercial Club in 1907, Daniel H. Burnham, the architect and chief designer of the Columbian Exposition, asserted an intimate and important link between style and profitability. "Beauty," he advised his audience, "has always paid better than any other commodity, and always will."[4] By 1915, the marriage between business planning and aesthetics had already shaped the visible aspect of commerce.

One of the most ubiquitous examples of this development was advertising. Writing in 1914, Walter Lippmann commented upon the flowering of advertising as a sign that businessmen were attempting to "take charge of consumption as well as production." Inextricably linked to the development of consciously styled products, advertising projected images of these products, and of the "happy" consumers who purchased them, across the horizons of everyday life. A seductive, imagistic panorama had been installed above the American landscape:

> The eastern sky [is] ablaze with chewing gum, the northern with toothbrushes and underwear, the western with whiskey, and the southern with petticoats, the whole heavens . . . [are] brilliant with monstrously flirtatious women, . . . When you glance at magazines . . . [a] rivulet of text trickles through the meadows of automobiles, baking powders, corsets and kodaks.[5]

Business was coming to embrace advertising as the "ignition system of the economy, the dynamo of mass dissatisfaction and the

FIGURE 23 The influence of consumer engineering can be seen in this 1936 radio, designed by Walter Dorwin Teague. (The Minneapolis Institute of Arts.)

creator of illusions in a most materialistic world."[6] Advertising was becoming established as what C. Wright Mills once called "the prime means of acclaim."[7]

From the 1920s onward, advertising agencies broadened their field of action, organizing multifaceted merchandising campaigns for clients. A central figure in the development of this coordinated image-management was Earnest Elmo Calkins, of the Calkins & Holden advertising agency. Calkins intuited that the success of merchandising depended on the ability to construct an unbroken, imagistic corridor between the product being sold and the consciousness (and unconsciousness) of the consumer. Following this logic, Calkins created an agency that linked a diverse but interrelated range of "creative services," including product design, packaging, aesthetic counseling, and, of course, advertising. Calkins assembled an extraordinarily talented and innovative staff, including Egmont Arens, a leading product and package designer, and Walter Dorwin Teague, who, along with a few others, would become one of the most influential industrial designers from the 1930s on. While at Calkins & Holden, between 1929 and 1933, Arens coined the phrase "consumer engineering" to describe what was entailed in a complex, coordinated merchandising effort.

Central to consumer engineering was the notion that style, or, as Calkins called it, "beauty," was the "new business tool," whose intelligent use could generate sales and profits. Following in a path laid by

Walter Rathenau and Peter Behrens at AEG, Calkins delineated many of his ideas in "Beauty The New Business Tool," published in *The Atlantic Monthly* in 1927. In the article, Calkins offered a historical account of the systematic integration of business and aesthetics. In the early days of industrialism, he noted, the use of beauty was piecemeal, or disregarded as an economic factor. Where goods were decorative they lacked "integrity"; they celebrated the values of another time, while ignoring the signals of the machine age. Calkins himself was enamored with modern art—"the new art," he called it—and he believed that even more than realism, this art contained enormous powers of "suggestion." Advertising artists, influenced by these modern artistic developments, pioneered in the transformation and aestheticization of business. The youthful advertising industry, Calkins argued, "seized upon the power of the artist to say things which could not be said in words, and thus a large group of men trained in artistic standards was brought to work in close conjunction with factories producing goods." This mixture left its mark across the wide tableau of American commercial life.

> This first step toward making the advertising attractive was to make the goods attractive. It was frequently necessary to introduce the article sold into the advertisement, or at least its package, and most products and packages were so ugly or so commonplace *they spoiled the picture; and thus began that steady, unremitting pressure on the manufacturer to make his goods or packages worthy of being placed in an artistic setting.* Bales and boxes and cans and wrappers and labels and trademarks were revised and redesigned.[8]

The first merchandise to be affected by these make-overs were fashion goods and cosmetics. Then, General Motors (GM) began to implement general design strategies in the production of automobiles, leading to the development of the GM "Styling Section," under the directorship of Harley Earl. General Electric coordinated the design of their image and products as well. Phonographs and radios, two important fixtures in the new way of life that was emerging, were also seductively styled. Moving beyond product design and labeling, advertising now entered the realm of retail environments:

> These better designed goods and packages demanded a better environment in which to be sold, and thus we have a revolution in the furnishing of shops and stores. The old-fashioned store was a stereotype—a long, narrow room with two windows and a door in front and in back, counters down the full length on both sides. . . . Today, the store has given way to the shop* . . . The

---

*The term *store* connotes a place where goods are simply stored; the arrival of the term *shop* implies an increased focus on the act of consumption.

> shop front, the tinting of the walls, the furniture, the arrangement of goods—everything has been transformed. . . . Everything is done to create a setting for the new style of goods. You see this in every industry.[9]

Continuing his rhapsody on a totally administered environment, Calkins discussed the innovative uses of color and light in the creation of a sensuous commercial atmosphere. Behind all of these stylistic metamorphoses lay the bottom line: *sales.* "Beauty is introduced into material objects," he explained, "to enhance them in the eyes of the purchaser. The appeal of efficiency alone is nearly ended. Beauty is the natural and logical next step. It is in the air."[10]

Ultimately, Calkins's approach was not one of combining efficiency and aesthetics. A product's efficiency, its durability, was, for Calkins, a stumbling block to sales. Beauty, according to Calkins, would allow for the undermining of the efficiency factor, stimulating compulsive consumption. He wrote that "this new influence on articles of barter and sale is largely used to make people dissatisfied with what they have of the old order, still good and useful and efficient, but lacking in the newest touch. In the expressive slang of the day . . . [these goods] 'date.'"[11]

By the end of the 1920s, the stylization of the marketplace was in full swing. It had influenced goods, packages, retail establishments, advertisements. It had also affected the orientation of the popular mass media. Previously, style had been a concern in publications geared toward a primarily wealthy audience; the 1920s witnessed the flowering of style in magazines aimed at a mass market. Robert S. Lynd, the sociologist, noted that the "increased emphasis on style was encouraged by advertising and editorial content in periodicals and newspapers" of the 1920s. He continued,

> The *Ladies' Home Journal,* for example, after devoting but 16% of its non-fiction editorial content to fashion in 1918 and 1920, raised this to 28% in 1921 and to 30 in 1922–23, while popular magazines have increasingly taken over high style artists formerly used only by exclusive style journals such as *Vogue* and *Harper's Bazaar.*[12]

The play of surfaces was becoming a deliberate and decisive component of consumer merchandising, and a more general obsession of the consumer culture. Seventy years before Calkins's "Beauty The New Business Tool" appeared in *The Atlantic,* Oliver Wendell Holmes had predicted that the ephemeral surface would soon overwhelm the objective world in the pages of the same magazine. Holmes's vision had been prophetic. Vast new industries were now engaged in the process and business of generating evanescent meanings. This turn of events was not unnoticed by Egon Friedell, writing in Vienna in 1931. "There are no realities anymore," he lamented.

"There is only apparatus. . . . *Neither are there goods any more, but only advertisements:* the most valuable article is the one most effectively lauded, the one that the most capital has gone to advertise. We call all this," he added, "Americanism."[13]

Image and Desire

In service of the emerging apparatus of representation, many corporations simultaneously employed a social scientific apparatus; for monitoring and analyzing mass psychology; for studying—among other things—the impact of images on the mind of the consumer. "Understanding the consumer's mind," wrote ad man Harry Dexter Kitson in 1923, comes down to the question of appealing to and enhancing desire. To do this, he proposed, it is necessary to create a context in which "pictures are painted before the consumer's imagination representing the pleasurable aspects of possession of the commodity."[14]

Such strategic thinking, however, went beyond making rational appeals to the consumer's desire for pleasure. Styling, it was increasingly argued, must speak to the unconscious, to those primal urges and sensations that are repressed in the everyday confines of civilization. Like art, psychoanalysis was being evaluated as a "new business tool." Roy Sheldon, who along with Egmont Arens wrote the definitive guide *Consumer Engineering* (1932), spoke of the "astonishing fruits" being borne by the work of Freud, Jung, Alfred Adler, Pavlov, and others. These pioneers in the areas of psychoanalysis and behavioral psychology, they asserted, were providing business with tools that could be used to its "active advantage."

An example of this approach is seen in Sheldon and Arens's instrumental discussion of the *sense of touch* which, along with smell, was the least acknowledged and most repressed of the senses in modern Western civilization. Taking cues from Freud's ruminations on "civilization and its discontents," they outlined a technique for product merchandising:

> If it is true that the exigencies of civilization have driven it [the sense of touch] below the surface, it persists in the unconscious mind as a powerful motivating force. Every day the average person makes hundreds of judgements in which the sense of touch casts the deciding vote, whether or not it rises into the consciousness. . . . undercover decisions [are] made by this sense. Such simple judgements as the acceptance or rejection of a towel, washrag, hairbrush, underwear, stockings, hinge upon how these things feel in the hands; their acceptance or rejection is motivated by the unconscious.[15]

Given this reality, they maintained, the study of human sensory systems and the integration of this study with merchandising practice was essential. Designs should be executed with an appeal to tactile senses. On some level, Sheldon and Arens saw style as a symbolic return of the repressed, offering consumers a subliminal promise of polymorphous gratification. Rather than verbal appeals in advertising, they were proposing a depth-psychological strategy, one that would promote "the exploitation of the 'sublimated sense' in the field of product design":

> Manufacturing an object that delights this [tactile] sense is something that you do but don't talk about. Almost everything which is bought is handled. After the eye, the hand is the first censor to pass on acceptance, and if the hand's judgement is unfavorable, the most attractive object will not gain the popularity it deserves. On the other hand, merchandise designed to be pleasing to the hand wins an approval that may never register in the mind, but which will determine additional purchases. . . . *Make it snuggle in the palm.*[16]

By the 1930s, such approaches to emotion, desire, and the unconscious had become part of the jargon of the style industries. Harold Van Doren, a major industrial designer of the period, noted that "design is fundamentally the art of using lines, forms, tones, colors and textures to arouse an emotional reaction in the beholder."[17] The very meaning of aesthetics was changing. Once the study of beauty and its universal appeal, it was becoming, within the style industries, a study of art insofar as it could provoke and promote consumer response. At a time when the idea of "art for art's sake" was taking hold as a dominant faith among art critics, *art for control's sake* was becoming the dominant practice in the marketplace.

Jean Abel, of the Pasadena Architects School of Arts, wrote of the ideas of "simplification and control" as the paramount concepts governing "modern design." To Abel, designs should be accessible to as many people as possible and should be executed—deliberately—with specific responses in mind. To do this, designers needed to understand that design "speaks a scientific language, with universal laws and principles, governing elements." An effective use of this semiological "language," Abel insisted, could help artists and their employers achieve the "conscious control of ideas":

> The design of today is dynamic. In diagonal lines it moves with the speed and precision of the airplane. In geometric forms, it presents the cold calculating power of the adding machine. In color, it suffocates, chills, shocks or soothes through choices and combinations of hues, values and intensities. It invents strange realms, insane with distortion; or creates new worlds, ideal with release into new spaces, *hence the need of control.*[18]

Not all designers employed such a scientific (psychological or semiotic) approach; many worked more intuitively. From the 1930s onward, however, major figures in industrial design had internalized such instrumental thinking into their work. For Harold Van Doren, the role of the industrial designer was "to interpret the function of useful things in terms of appeal to the eye; to endow them with beauty of form and color; above all to create in the consumer the desire to possess."[19] For J. Gordon Lippincott, another designer, "the appearance of a product" had become "an integral feature in its success or failure" as "the industrial designer . . . seeks to imbue the consumer with the desire of ownership."[20] Raymond Loewy put it more concisely. Industrial design was "the shaping of everyday life with the marketplace in mind."[21]

In the commercial world of style, the fundamental assumption underlying the "shaping of everyday life" is that life must visibly change, every day. Roland Barthes called this phenomenon *neomania*, a madness for perpetual novelty where "the new" has become defined strictly as a "purchased value," something to buy.[22] What will appear next is not always predictable. That *something new* will appear is entirely predictable. "Style obsolescence," reported a major industrial design firm in 1960, "is the *sine qua non* of product success."[23]

In the 1930s, with the consumer economy in serious straits, styling and "style obsolescence" came to the forefront as methods designed to stimulate markets, and to keep them stimulated. Roy Sheldon and Egmont Arens counseled that "styles wear out faster than gears," and encouraged industry to utilize style to motivate purchases.[24] Earnest Calkins concurred, and suggested that even durable goods must be reconceptualized and sold as if they were nondurables:

> Goods fall into two classes, those we use, such as motor-cars or safety razors, and those we use *up*, such as toothpaste or soda biscuit. Consumer engineering must see to it that we use *up* the kind of goods we now merely use. Would any change in the goods or habits of people speed up their consumption? Can they be displaced by newer models: Can artificial obsolescence be created? Consumer engineering does not end until we can consume all we can make.[25]

Such thinking was catalyzed by the collapse of markets during the Depression, and it has persevered as the basic logic of consumer capitalism ever since. Though the long-term ecological implications of this trajectory may be disastrous, from a strictly merchandising point of view, it is *the air we breathe*. Style and changes in style, once part of a privileged competition among merchant princes, have become routine ingredients in almost everybody's lives, from the clothes we wear to our daily gruel. With the institutionalization of "style obsolescence," the perpetual challenge to offer *something new* became a cornerstone of business planning. While corporations, and political institutions, and people of wealth and power employ and project images of stability for themselves, daily life—for most other Americans—carries a visual message of unpredictability and impermanence.

Another of Oliver Wendell Holmes's predictions has come to pass. In 1859 Holmes had written that "every conceivable object" would soon "scale off its surface for us." Like animals in a trophy hunt, all manners of "Nature and Art" would be hunted down "for their skins," with the carcasses left to rot. To a large extent, this describes the practices of the style industries today. In their continual search for ever-evolving novelty, all manners of human expression and creativity are mined for their surfaces: their *look,* their *touch,* their *sound,* their *scent.* This booty is then attached to the logic of the marketplace: mass produced and merchandised. Visions of a preindustrial, more "natural" form of life are appropriated by the corporate food industry. Graffiti artists from the Bronx provide "the look" for Macy's new fall line. The "anti-style" of the punk subculture inspires the layout for a Warner Communications annual report. All faces are seen; few are heard from.

Whatever the "skin," or its vernacular origin, its meaning is most often compromised or lost once it enters the style market. The meaning that *will* remain constant, that *will* be expressed across the shifting tableau of style—regardless of the skins it appropriates—is the continual message of consumption. Art historians speak of *styles*—Gothic, Romanesque, neoclassical, and so on—as coherent embodiments of the epochs that produced them. The facades of style in contemporary culture, however, are ever-changing, often incoherent. It is this volatility that embodies the period we inhabit. Style is something to be *used up.* Part of its significance is that it will lose significance.

1988

Notes

1. Tilmann Buddensieg and Henning Rogge, *Industriekultur: Peter Behrens and the AEG,* trans. I. B. White (1984), p. x.
2. Ibid., p. 2.
3. Ibid., pp. x, 2.
4. Paul S. Boyer, *Urban Masses and Moral Order in America, 1820–1920* (1978), p. 264.
5. Walter Lippmann, *Drift and Mastery* (1914), pp. 52–53.
6. George Mowry, ed., *The Twenties: Fords, Flappers and Fantasies* (1963), p. 15. See also Stuart Ewen, *Captains of Consciousness* (1976), for a fuller discussion of the rise of modern advertising.
7. C. Wright Mills, *The Power Elite* (1956), p. 84.
8. Earnest Elmo Calkins, "Beauty The New Business Tool," *The Atlantic Monthly* 140 (August 1927), pp. 147–48, emphasis added.

9. Ibid., p. 149.
10. Ibid., p. 151.
11. Ibid., p. 152.
12. Robert S. Lynd, "The People as Consumers," in Report of the President's Research Committee on Social Trends, *Recent Social Trends in the United States* (1933), p. 878.
13. Egon Friedell, *A Cultural History of the Modern Age: The Crisis of the European Soul from the Black Death to the World War,* 3 vols. (1954), 3: 475–76.
14. Harry Dexter Kitson, "Understanding the Consumer's Mind," *The Annals* 110 (November 1923), pp. 131–38.
15. Roy Sheldon and Egmont Arens, *Consumer Engineering* (1932), p. 97.
16. Ibid., pp. 100–101, emphasis added.
17. Harold Van Doren, *Industrial Design* (1940), pp. 121–22.
18. Jean Abel, "An Explanation of Modern Art," *California Arts and Architecture* 37 (June 1930), pp. 34–35.
19. Van Doren, *Industrial Design,* p. xviii.
20. J. Gordon Lippincott, *Design for Business* (1947), p. 19.
21. Raymond Loewy, *Industrial Design* (1979), p. 8.
22. Roland Barthes, *The Fashion System* (1983), p. 300.
23. J. Gordon Lippincott and Walter Margulies, "We Couldn't Have Done It in Wichita," *Industrial Design* 7 (October 1960), p. 103.
24. Sheldon and Arens, *Consumer Engineering,* pp. 61, 63.
25. Ibid., pp. 13–14.

GETTING STARTED

1. How does Ewen define culture? List the places in the essay where Ewen defines or talks about culture. Then, list your ideas about what culture is. Bring both lists to class.

2. What does the word "style" make you think of? How are we accustomed to using it in conversation? What does it mean to say that someone "has style"? In a group, share your associations with the term. Then find an example in which Ewen discusses issues of style and compare his use of the term to yours. Present your findings to the class.

3. Bring an advertisement to class. In a group, discuss the different ways in which the advertiser is relying on our expectations and understandings of "style."

WRITING

4. Ewen quotes Egon Friedell, who defines "Americanism" (p. 209). Write a journal entry that examines what Friedell and Ewen mean by "Americanism." Write a second journal entry that applies the

quotation to another aspect of American life such as politics, education, or family life. Is it true, for instance, that the "most valuable" politician is the one who has the most money to spend on advertising?

5. Write a paper in which you use Ewen's ideas about style to analyze an advertisement. What qualities does the ad want you to associate with the product? How does the paradox of style—that "part of its significance is that it will lose significance" (p. 212)—apply?

USING THE LIBRARY AND THE INTERNET

6. Use an Internet directory such as Yahoo! or About to examine a corporate Web site that includes advertising. What is the company's corporate image? Is the Web site selling you a product, a service, or the company itself? Who is likely to visit the Web site and why?

7. According to Ewen, who is Peter Behrens, and why is he important? For the next class, find out what you can on the Internet about Behrens. Then write a journal entry that discusses the relationship you see between Ewen's interest in Behrens's work and Ewen's concern with modern ideas about product advertising and obsolescence.

MAKING CONNECTIONS

8. Write a paper using terms and ideas from Zita Ingham's "Landscape, Drama, and Dissensus: The Rhetorical Education of Red Lodge, Montana" to test Ewen's claims about the function of advertising. Find a print advertisement that interests you and use Zita Ingham's terms—emotional appeal, logical appeal, and ethical appeal—to analyze the rhetoric of the ad. How does your analysis connect to Ewen's argument? What is the particular style of the ad? What associations do the advertisers want you to have with the product or service? Beyond the literal product being sold, what other concepts or messages is the ad selling?

9. Write an essay using Ewen's ideas about style and product marketing to analyze Witold Rybczynski's "Designs for Escape." Is the concept of "rusticity" in architecture a function of style? Would Rybczynski agree with Ewen about the relationship between image and desire, novelty and style obsolescence?

10. Write an essay exploring the meaning of contemporary American identity using ideas and examples from Ewen and from Ralph Ellison's "The Little Man at Chehaw Station." How do Ellison's

arguments about the "mystery of American cultural identity" compare to Ewen's ideas about "Americanism" and his vision of how our culture functions?

11. Compare and contrast Ewen's account of the history and development of the advertising industry with Susan Sontag's account of the history and development of photography. What are some of the effects of these two developments on the way we think about the world? Are there ways in which Sontag's vision of photography's effect on our culture challenges or points to the limitations of Ewen's vision?

Northrop Frye

Northrop Frye (1912–1991) was one of the most influential and prolific literary critics of the second half of the twentieth century. Frye's many works, including his best-known book, *Anatomy of Criticism* (1957), sought to establish a rigorous system for categorizing and analyzing literary works. A Professor of English at the University of Toronto, Frye lectured at universities around the world and wrote educational radio and television programs for the Canadian Broadcasting Company. "The Motive for Metaphor" is the first chapter of his book, *Educated Imagination* (1964).

For photographs and additional information on Northrop Frye, visit The Northrop Frye Center at the University of Toronto online at <http://vicu.utoronto.ca/fryecentre/>.

The Motive for Metaphor

For the past twenty-five years I have been teaching and studying English literature in a university. As in any other job, certain questions stick in one's mind, not because people keep asking them, but because they're the questions inspired by the very fact of being in such a place. What good is the study of literature? Does it help us to think more clearly, or feel more sensitively, or live a better life than we could without it? What is the function of the teacher and scholar, or of the person who calls himself, as I do, a literary critic? What difference does the study of literature make in our social or political or religious attitude? In my early days I thought very little about such questions, not because I had any of the answers, but because I assumed that anybody who asked them was naive. I think now that the simplest questions are not only the hardest to answer, but the most important to ask, so I'm going to raise them and try to suggest what my present answers are. I say try to suggest, because there are only more or less inadequate answers to such questions—there aren't any right answers. The kind of problem that literature raises is not the kind that you ever "solve." Whether my answers are any good or not, they represent a fair amount of thinking about the questions. As I can't see my audience, I have to choose my rhetorical style in the dark, and I'm taking the classroom style, because an audience of students is the one I feel easiest with.

There are two things in particular that I want to discuss with you. In school, and in university, there's a subject called "English" in

English-speaking countries. English means, in the first place, the mother tongue. As that, it's the most practical subject in the world: you can't understand anything or take any part in your society without it. Wherever illiteracy is a problem, it's as fundamental a problem as getting enough to eat or a place to sleep. The native language takes precedence over every other subject of study: nothing else can compare with it in its usefulness. But then you find that every mother tongue, in any developed or civilized society, turns into something called literature. If you keep on studying "English," you find yourself trying to read Shakespeare and Milton. Literature, we're told, is one of the arts, along with painting and music, and, after you've looked up all the hard words and the Classical allusions and learned what words like imagery and diction are supposed to mean, what you use in understanding it, or so you're told, is your imagination. Here you don't seem to be in quite the same practical and useful area: Shakespeare and Milton, whatever their merits, are not the kind of thing you must know to hold any place in society at all. A person who knows nothing about literature may be an ignoramus, but many people don't mind being that. Every child realizes that literature is taking him in a different direction from the immediately useful, and a good many children complain loudly about this. Two questions I want to deal with, then, are, first: what is the relation of English as the mother tongue to English as a literature? Second: What is the social value of the study of literature, and what is the place of the imagination that literature addresses itself to, in the learning process?

Let's start with the different ways there are of dealing with the world we're living in. Suppose you're shipwrecked on an uninhabited island in the South Seas. The first thing you do is to take a long look at the world around you, a world of sky and sea and earth and stars and trees and hills. You see this world as objective, as something set over against you and not yourself or related to you in any way. And you notice two things about this objective world. In the first place, it doesn't have any conversation. It's full of animals and plants and insects going on with their own business, but there's nothing that responds to you: it has no morals and no intelligence, or at least none that you can grasp. It may have a shape and a meaning, but it doesn't seem to be a human shape or a human meaning. Even if there's enough to eat and no dangerous animals, you feel lonely and frightened and unwanted in such a world.

In the second place, you find that looking at the world, as something set over against you, splits your mind in two. You have an intellect that feels curious about it and wants to study it, and you have feelings or emotions that see it as beautiful or austere or terrible. You know that both these attitudes have some reality, at least for you. If the ship you were wrecked in was a Western ship, you'd probably feel that your intellect tells you more about what's really there in the outer world, and that your emotions tell you more about what's going on inside you. If your background were Oriental, you'd be more likely to reverse this and say that the beauty or terror was what was really there, and that your instinct to count and classify and measure and pull to pieces was what was inside your mind. But whether your point of view is Western or Eastern, intellect and emotion never get together in your mind as long as you're simply looking at the world. They alternate, and keep you divided between them.

The language you use on this level of the mind is the language of consciousness or awareness. It's largely a language of nouns and adjectives. You have to have names for things, and you need qualities like "wet" or "green" or "beautiful" to describe how things seem to you. This is the speculative or contemplative position of the mind, the position in which the arts and sciences begin, although they don't stay there very long. The sciences begin by accepting the facts and the evidence about an outside world without trying to alter them. Science proceeds by accurate measurement and description, and follows the demands of the reason rather than the emotions. What it deals with is there, whether we like it or not. The emotions are unreasonable: for them it's what they like and don't like that comes first. We'd be naturally inclined to think that the arts follow the path of emotion, in contrast to the sciences. Up to a point they do, but there's a complicating factor.

That complicating factor is the contrast between "I like this" and "I don't like this." In this Robinson Crusoe life I've assigned you, you may have moods of complete peacefulness and joy, moods when you accept your island and everything around you. You wouldn't have such moods very often, and when you had them, they'd be moods of identification, when you felt that the island was a part of you and you a part of it. That is not the feeling of consciousness or awareness, where you feel split off from everything that's not your perceiving self. Your habitual state of mind is the feeling of separation which goes with being conscious, and the feeling "this is not a part of me" soon becomes "this is not what I want." Notice the word "want": we'll be coming back to it.

So you soon realize that there's a difference between the world you're living in and the world you want to live in. The world you want to live in is a human world, not an objective one: it's not an environment but a home; it's not the world you see but the world you build out of what you see. You go to work to build a shelter or plant a garden, and as soon as you start to work you've moved into a different level of human life. You're not separating only yourself from nature now, but constructing a human world and separating it from the rest of the world. Your intellect and emotions are now both engaged in the same activity, so there's no longer any real distinction between them. As soon as you plant a garden or a crop, you develop the conception of a "weed," the plant you don't want in there. But you can't say that "weed" is either an intellectual or an emotional conception, because it's both at once. Further, you go to work because you feel you have to, and because you want something at the end of the work. That means that the important categories of your life are no longer the subject and the object, the watcher and the things being watched: the important categories are what you have to do and what you want to do—in other words, necessity and freedom.

One person by himself is not a complete human being, so I'll provide you with another shipwrecked refugee of the opposite sex and an eventual family. Now you're a member of a human society. This human society after a while will transform the island into something with a human shape. What that human shape is, is revealed in the shape of the work you do: the buildings, such as they are, the paths through the woods, the planted crops fenced off against whatever animals want to eat them. These things, these rudiments of city, highway, garden, and farm, are the human form of nature, or the form of human nature, whichever you like. This is the area of the applied arts and sciences, and it appears in our society as engineering and agriculture and medicine and architecture. In this area we can never say clearly where the art stops and the science begins, or vice versa.

The language you use on this level is the language of practical sense, a language of verbs or words of action and movement. The practical world, however, is a world where actions speak louder than words. In some way it's a higher level of existence than the speculative level, because it's doing something about the world instead of just looking at it, but in itself it's a much more primitive level. It's the process of adapting to the environment, or rather of transforming the environment in the interests of one species, that goes on among animals and plants as well as human beings. The animals have a good many of our practical skills: some insects make pretty fair architects, and beavers know quite a lot about engineering. In this island, probably, and certainly if you were alone, you'd have about the ranking of a second-rate animal. What makes our practical life really human is a third level of the mind, a level where consciousness and practical skill come together.

This third level is a vision or model in your mind of what you want to construct. There's that word "want" again. The actions of man are prompted by desire, and some of these desires are needs, like food and warmth and shelter. One of these needs is sexual, the desire to reproduce and bring more human beings into existence. But there's also a desire to bring a social human form into existence: the form of cities and gardens and farms that we call civilization. Many animals and insects have this social form too, but man knows that he has it:

he can compare what he does with what he can imagine being done. So we begin to see where the imagination belongs in the scheme of human affairs. It's the power of constructing possible models of human experience. In the world of the imagination, anything goes that's imaginatively possible, but nothing really happens. If it did happen, it would move out of the world of imagination into the world of action.

We have three levels of the mind now, and a language for each of them, which in English-speaking societies means an English for each of them. There's the level of consciousness and awareness, where the most important thing is the difference between me and everything else. The English of this level is the English of ordinary conversation, which is mostly monologue, as you'll soon realize if you do a bit of eavesdropping, or listening to yourself. We can call it the language of self-expression. Then there's the level of social participation, the working or technological language of teachers and preachers and politicians and advertisers and lawyers and journalists and scientists. We've already called this the language of practical sense. Then there's the level of imagination, which produces the literary language of poems and plays and novels. They're not really different languages, of course, but three different reasons for using words.

On this basis, perhaps, we can distinguish the arts from the sciences. Science begins with the world we have to live in, accepting its data and trying to explain its laws. From there, it moves towards the imagination: it becomes a mental construct, a model of a possible way of interpreting experience. The further it goes in this direction, the more it tends to speak the language of mathematics, which is really one of the languages of the imagination, along with literature and music. Art, on the other hand, begins with the world we construct, not with the world we see. It starts with the imagination, and then works towards ordinary experience: that is, it tries to make itself as convincing and recognizable as it can. You can see why we tend to think of the sciences as intellectual and the arts as emotional: one starts with the world as it is, the other with the world we want to have. Up to a point it is true that science gives an intellectual view of reality, and that the arts try to make the emotions as precise and disciplined as sciences do the intellect. But of course it's nonsense to think of the scientist as a cold unemotional reasoner and the artist as somebody who's in a perpetual emotional tizzy. You can't distinguish the arts from the sciences by the mental processes the people in them use: they both operate on a mixture of hunch and common sense. A highly developed science and a highly developed art are very close together, psychologically and otherwise.

Still, the fact that they start from opposite ends, even if they do meet in the middle, makes for one important difference between them. Science learns more and more about the world as it goes on: it evolves and improves. A physicist today knows more physics than

Newton did, even if he's not as great a scientist. But literature begins with the possible model of experience, and what it produces is the literary model we call the classic. Literature doesn't evolve or improve or progress. We may have dramatists in the future who will write plays as good as *King Lear,* though they'll be very different ones, but drama as a whole will never get better than *King Lear. King Lear* is it, as far as drama is concerned; so is *Oedipus Rex,* written two thousand years earlier than that, and both will be models of dramatic writing as long as the human race endures. Social conditions may improve: most of us would rather live in [the] nineteenth-century United States than in thirteenth-century Italy, and for most of us Whitman's celebration of democracy makes a lot more sense than Dante's Inferno. But it doesn't follow that Whitman is a better poet than Dante: literature won't line up with that kind of improvement.

So we find that everything that does improve, including science, leaves the literary artist out in the cold. Writers don't seem to benefit much by the advance of science, although they thrive on superstitions of all kinds. And you certainly wouldn't turn to contemporary poets for guidance or leadership in the twentieth-century world. You'd hardly go to Ezra Pound, with his fascism and social credit and Confucianism and anti-semitism. Or to Yeats, with his spiritualism and fairies and astrology. Or to D. H. Lawrence, who'll tell you that it's a good thing for servants to be flogged because that restores the precious current of blood-reciprocity between servant and master. Or to T. S. Eliot, who'll tell you that to have a flourishing culture we should educate an Elite, keep most people living in the same spot, and never disestablish the Church of England. The novelists seem to be a little closer to the world they're living in, but not much. When Communists talk about the decadence of bourgeois culture, this is the kind of thing they always bring up. Their own writers don't seem to be any better, though; just duller. So the real question is a bigger one. Is it possible that literature, especially poetry, is something that a scientific civilization like ours will eventually outgrow? Man has always wanted to fly, and thousands of years ago he was making sculptures of winged bulls and telling stories about people who flew so high on artificial wings that the sun melted them off. In an Indian play fifteen hundred years old, *Sakuntala,* there's a god who flies around in a chariot that to a modern reader sounds very much like a private aeroplane. Interesting that the writer had so much imagination, but do we need such stories now that we have private aeroplanes?

This is not a new question: it was raised a hundred and fifty years ago by Thomas Love Peacock, who was a poet and novelist himself, and a very brilliant one. He wrote an essay called *Four Ages of Poetry,* with his tongue of course in his cheek, in which he said that poetry was the mental rattle that awakened the imagination of mankind in its infancy, but that now, in an age of science and technology, the poet has outlived his social function. "A poet in our times," said Peacock, "is a semi-barbarian in a civilized community. He lives in the days that are past. His ideas, thoughts, feelings, associations, are all with barbarous manners, obsolete customs, and exploded superstitions. The march of his intellect is like that of a crab, backwards." Peacock's essay annoyed his friend Shelley, who wrote another essay called *A Defence of Poetry* to refute it. Shelley's essay is a wonderful piece of writing, but it's not likely to convince anyone who needs convincing. I shall be spending a good deal of my time on this question of the relevance of literature in the world of today, and I can only indicate the general lines my answer will take. There are two points I can make now, one simple, the other more difficult.

The simple point is that literature belongs to the world man constructs, not to the world he sees; to his home, not his environment. Literature's world is a concrete human world of immediate experience. The poet uses images and objects and sensations much more than he uses abstract ideas; the novelist is concerned with telling stories, not with working out arguments. The world of literature is human in shape, a world where the sun rises in the east and sets in the west over the edge of a flat earth in three dimensions, where the primary realities are not atoms or electrons but bodies, and the primary forces not energy or gravitation but love and death and passion and joy. It's not surprising if writers are often rather simple people, not always what we think of as intellectuals, and certainly not always any freer of silliness or perversity than anyone else. What concerns us is what they produce, not what they are, and poetry, according to Milton, who ought to have known, is "more simple, sensuous and passionate" than philosophy or science.

The more difficult point takes us back to what we said when we were on that South Sea island. Our emotional reaction to the world varies from "I like this" to "I don't like this." The first, we said, was a state of identity, a feeling that everything around us was part of us, and the second is the ordinary state of consciousness, or separation, where art and science begin. Art begins as soon as "I don't like this" turns into "this is not the way I could imagine it." We notice in passing that the creative and the neurotic minds have a lot in common. They're both dissatisfied with what they see; they both believe that something else ought to be there, and they try to pretend it is there or to make it be there. The differences are more important, but we're not ready for them yet.

At the level of ordinary consciousness the individual man is the centre of everything, surrounded on all sides by what he isn't. At the level of practical sense, or civilization, there's a human circumference, a little cultivated world with a human shape, fenced off from the jungle and inside the sea and the sky. But in the imagination anything goes that can be imagined, and the limit of the imagination is a totally human world. Here we recapture, in full consciousness, that original lost sense of identity with our surroundings, where there is nothing outside the mind of man, or something identical with the mind of man. Religions present us with visions of eternal and infinite heavens or paradises which have the form of the cities and gardens of human civilization, like the Jerusalem and Eden of the Bible, completely separated from the state of frustration and misery that bulks so large in ordinary life. We're not concerned with these visions as religion, but they indicate what the limits of the imagination are. They indicate too that in the human world the imagination has no limits, if you follow me. We said that the desire to fly produced the aeroplane. But people don't get into planes because they want to fly; they get into planes because they want to get somewhere else faster. What's produced the aeroplane is not so much a desire to fly as a rebellion against the tyranny of time and space. And that's a process that can never stop, no matter how high our Titovs[1] and Glenns[2] may go.

For each of these six talks I've taken a title from some work of literature, and my title for this one is "The Motive for Metaphor," from a poem of Wallace Stevens. Here's the poem:

> You like it under the trees in autumn,
> Because everything is half dead.
> The wind moves like a cripple among the leaves
> And repeats words without meaning.
>
> In the same way, you were happy in spring,
> With the half colors of quarter-things,
> The slightly brighter sky, the melting clouds,
> The single bird, the obscure moon—
>
> The obscure moon lighting an obscure world
> Of things that would never be quite expressed,
> Where you yourself were never quite yourself
> And did not want nor have to be,
>
> Desiring the exhilarations of changes:
> The motive for metaphor, shrinking from
> The weight of primary noon,
> The A B C of being.
>
> The ruddy temper, the hammer
> Of red and blue, the hard sound—
> Steel against intimation—the sharp flash,
> The vital, arrogant, fatal, dominant X.

---

1. Sherman Titov, Russian astronaut and first man to make a multi-orbital flight (August 1961).

2. John H. Glenn, astronaut and first American to make an orbital flight (February 1962).

What Stevens calls the weight of primary noon, the A B C of being, and the dominant X is the objective world, the world set over against us. Outside literature, the main motive for writing is to describe this world. But literature itself uses language in a way which associates our minds with it. As soon as you use associative language, you begin using figures of speech. If you say this talk is dry and dull, you're using figures associating it with bread and breadknives. There are two main kinds of association, analogy and identity, two things that are like each other and two things that are each other. You can say with Burns, "My love's like a red, red rose," or you can say with Shakespeare:

> Thou that art now the world's fresh ornament
> And only herald to the gaudy spring.

One produces the figure of speech called the simile; the other produces the figure called metaphor.

In descriptive writing you have to be careful of associative language. You'll find that analogy, or likeness to something else, is very tricky to handle in description, because the differences are as important as the resemblances. As for metaphor, where you're really saying "this *is* that," you're turning your back on logic and reason completely because logically two things can never be the same thing and still remain two things. The poet, however, uses these two crude, primitive, archaic forms of thought in the most uninhibited way, because his job is not to describe nature, but to show you a world completely absorbed and possessed by the human mind. So he produces what Baudelaire called a "suggestive magic including at the same time object and subject, the world outside the artist and the artist himself." The motive for metaphor, according to Wallace Stevens, is a desire to associate, and finally to identify, the human mind with what goes on outside it, because the only genuine joy you can have is in those rare moments when you feel that although we may know in part, as Paul says, we are also a part of what we know.

1964

GETTING STARTED

1. In a group, map out and summarize the three levels of consciousness that Frye describes. What are the three levels of language associated with each?

2. What is the relationship between art and science? Draw or diagram it. Be ready to explain your drawing to the class.

3. Write a journal entry about reading Frye's essay. Is he more of an artist or a scientist? Does he appeal more to reason or to emotion? Give an example or two from his essay as evidence for your points.

4. In a group, develop an interpretation of Wallace Stevens's poem that says something more than what Frye says about it or that complicates or questions Frye's interpretation.

WRITING

5. Why does Frye provide us with a Robinson Crusoe scenario—"suppose you're shipwrecked"? How does the image of the island operate in his essay? What does the imaginative experiment provide that mere facts or objective data do not?

6. Imagine that, due to budget cuts, schools were eliminating the study of either literature or science. Write a letter to the editor of your school or local newspaper discussing which should be kept and why.

USING THE LIBRARY AND THE INTERNET

7. Using a database such as Academic Search Elite that includes a wide range of scholarly sources, try the search term "metaphor and science." Scan the resulting articles and print out several examples of scientific metaphors. In a group, discuss how your findings support, challenge, or go beyond some of Frye's ideas.

MAKING CONNECTIONS

8. Frye argues that "literature doesn't evolve or improve or progress" (p. 221). What, then, does it do? Why can't it be treated like a science? Compare your answer to the relative ideas of progress in science and music introduced in Scott DeVeaux's "Progress and the Bean."

9. Write an essay comparing and contrasting Frye's approach to art and science with Jeanette Winterson's ideas about art in "Imagination and Reality." What is your sense of Winterson's attitude towards science? To what extent does she seem to support or challenge Frye's claim that "writers don't seem to benefit much by the advance of science, although they thrive on superstitions of all kinds" (p. 221)? To what extent does Frye seem to agree with Winterson's statements that "art is visionary" and that "the arts fare much better alongside religion than alongside either capitalism or communism" (p. 595)?

10. Write an essay using Frye's argument about metaphor to frame your own argument about Stephen Jay Gould's use of and analysis

of metaphors in "The Smoking Gun of Eugenics." Could someone argue that Gould is both a scientist and an artist?

11. Use Frye's discussion of metaphor to help you develop an interpretation of Ralph Ellison's "motive of metaphor" in "The Little Man of Chehaw Station." Why does Ellison invoke the metaphor of the "little man?" What does the metaphor help Ellison accomplish? If you do not find the metaphor helpful, then discuss why you think it is problematic.

Clifford Geertz

Clifford Geertz (1926–) is the Harold F. Linder Professor of Social Science at the Institute for Advanced Study in Princeton, New Jersey. Geertz trained as an anthropologist and did extensive fieldwork in Indonesia and Morocco. He is best known for exploring new ways of understanding and interpreting culture. In *The Interpretation of Cultures* (1973), he wrote, "Believing . . . that man is an animal suspended in webs of significance he himself has spun, I take culture to be those webs and the analysis of it to be therefore not an experimental science in search of law but an interpretive one in search of meaning." "Common Sense as a Cultural System" is excerpted from a chapter in his book *Local Knowledge: Further Essays in Interpretive Anthropology* (1983).

To learn more about cultural anthropology, explore the Minnesota State University Emuseum at <http://emuseum.mnsu.edu/cultural/index.html>.

Common Sense as a Cultural System

I

There are a number of reasons why treating common sense as a relatively organized body of considered thought, rather than just what anyone clothed and in his right mind knows, should lead on to some useful conclusions; but perhaps the most important is that it is an inherent characteristic of common-sense thought precisely to deny this and to affirm that its tenets are immediate deliverances of experience, not deliberated reflections upon it. Knowing that rain wets and that one ought to come in out of it, or that fire burns and one ought not to play with it (to stick to our own culture for the moment) are conflated into comprising one large realm of the given and undeniable, a catalog of in–the–grain–of–nature realities so peremptory as to force themselves upon any mind sufficiently unclouded to receive them. Yet this is clearly not so. No one, or no one functioning very well, doubts that rain wets; but there may be some people around who question the proposition that one ought to come in out of it, holding that it is good for one's character to brave the elements—hatlessness is next to godliness. And the attractions of playing with fire often, with some people usually, override the full recognition of the pain that will result. Religion rests its case on revelation, science on method, ideology on moral passion; but common sense rests its on the assertion that it is not a case at all, just life in a nutshell. The world is its authority.

The analysis of common sense, as opposed to the exercise of it, must then begin by redrawing this erased distinction between the mere matter-of-fact apprehension of reality—or whatever it is you want to call what we apprehend merely and matter-of-factly—and down-to-earth, colloquial wisdom, judgments or assessments of it. When we say someone shows common sense we mean to suggest more than that he is just using his eyes and ears, but is, as we say, keeping them open, using them judiciously, intelligently, perceptively, reflectively, or trying to, and that he is capable of coping with everyday problems in an everyday way with some effectiveness. And when we say he lacks common sense we mean not that he is retarded, that he fails to grasp the fact that rain wets or fire burns, but that he bungles the everyday problems life throws up for him: he leaves his house on a cloudy day without an umbrella; his life is a series of scorchings he should have had the wit not merely to avoid but not to have stirred the flames for in the first place. The opposite of someone who is able to apprehend the sheer actualities of experience is, as I have suggested, a defective; the opposite of someone who is able to come to sensible conclusions on the basis of them is a fool. And this last has less to do with intellect, narrowly defined, than we generally imagine. As Saul Bellow, thinking of certain sorts of government advisors and certain sorts of radical writers, has remarked, the world is full of high-IQ morons.

This analytical dissolution of the unspoken premise from which common sense draws its authority—that it presents reality neat—is not intended to undermine that authority but to relocate it. If common sense is as much an interpretation of the immediacies of experience, a gloss on them, as are myth, painting, epistemology, or whatever, then it is, like them, historically constructed and, like them, subjected to historically defined standards of judgment. It can be questioned, disputed, affirmed, developed, formalized, contemplated, even taught, and it can vary dramatically from one people to the next. It is, in short, a cultural system, though not usually a very tightly integrated one, and it rests on the same basis that any other such system rests; the conviction by those whose possession it is of its value and validity. Here, as elsewhere, things are what you make of them.

The importance of all this for philosophy is, of course, that common sense, or some kindred conception, has become a central category, almost *the* central category, in a wide range of modern philosophical systems. It has always been an important category in such systems from the Platonic Socrates (where its function was to demonstrate its own inadequacy) forward. Both the Cartesian and Lockean traditions depended, in their different ways—indeed, their culturally different ways—upon doctrines about what was and what was not self-evident, if not exactly to the vernacular mind at least to the unencumbered one. But in this century the notion of (as it tends to be put) "untutored" common sense—what the plain man thinks when sheltered from the vain sophistications of schoolmen—has, with so much else disappearing into science and poetry, grown into almost the thematic subject of philosophy. The focus on ordinary language in Wittgenstein, Austin, Ryle; the development of the so-called phenomenology of everyday life by Husserl, Schutz, Merleau-Ponty; the glorification of personal, in-the-midst-of-life decision in continental existentialism; the taking of garden-variety problem solving as the paradigm of reason in American pragmatism—all reflect this tendency to look toward the structure of down-to-earth, humdrum, *brave type* thought for clues to the deeper mysteries of existence. G. E. Moore, proving the reality of the external world by holding up one hand and saying here is a physical object and then holding up the other and saying here is another, is, doctrinal details aside, the epitomizing image of a very large part of recent philosophy in the West.

Yet though it has thus emerged as a focus of so much intense attention, common sense remains more an assumed phenomenon than an analyzed one. Husserl, and following him Schutz, have dealt with the conceptual foundations of "everyday" experience, how we construe the world we biographically inhabit, but without much recognition of the distinction between that and what Dr. Johnson was doing when he kicked the stone to confute Berkeley, or Sherlock Holmes was doing when he reflected on the silent dog in the night; and Ryle has at least remarked in passing that one does not "exhibit common sense or the lack of it in using a knife and fork. [One does] in dealing with a plausible beggar or a mechanical breakdown when [one has] not got the proper tools." But generally, the notion of common sense has been rather commonsensical: what anyone with common sense knows.

Anthropology can be of use here in much the same way as it is generally: providing out-of-the-way cases, it sets nearby ones in an altered context. If we look at the views of people who draw conclusions different from our own by the mere living of their lives, learn different lessons in the school of hard knocks, we will rather quickly become aware that common sense is both a more problematical and a more profound affair than it seems from the perspective of a Parisian café or an Oxford Common Room. As one of the oldest suburbs of human culture—not very regular, not very uniform, but yet moving beyond the maze of little streets and squares toward some less casual shape—it displays in a particularly overt way the impulse upon which such developments are built: the desire to render the world distinct.

II

Consider, from this perspective rather than the one from which it is usually considered (the nature and function of magic), Evans-Pritchard's famous discussion of Azande witchcraft. He is, as he explicitly says but no one seems much to have noticed, concerned with common-sense thought—Zande common-sense thought—as the general background against which the notion of witchcraft is developed. It is the flouting of Zande notions of natural causation, what in the mere experience of the world leads to what, that suggests the operation of some other sort of causation—Evans-Pritchard calls it "mystical"—which an in fact rather materialistic concept of witchcraft (it involves a blackish substance located in an individual's belly, and so on) sums up.

Take a Zande boy, he says, who has stubbed his foot on a tree stump and developed an infection. The boy says it's witchcraft. Nonsense, says Evans-Pritchard, out of his own common-sense tradition: you were merely bloody careless; you should have looked where you were going. I did look where I was going; you have to with so many stumps about, says the boy—*and if I hadn't been witched I would have seen it.* Furthermore, all cuts do not take days to heal, but on the contrary, close quickly, for that is the nature of cuts. But this one festered, thus witchcraft must be involved.

Or take a Zande potter, a very skilled one, who, when now and again one of his pots cracks in the making, cries "witchcraft!" Nonsense! says Evans-Pritchard, who, like all good ethnographers, seems never to learn: of course sometimes pots crack in the making; it's the way of the world. But, says the potter, I chose the clay carefully, I took pains to remove all the pebbles and dirt, I built up the clay slowly and with care, and I abstained from sexual intercourse the night before. And *still* it broke. What else can it be but witchcraft? And yet another time, when he was ill—feeling unfit as he puts it—Evans-Pritchard wondered aloud to some Zandes whether it may have been that he had eaten too many bananas, and they said, nonsense! bananas don't cause illness; it must have been witchcraft.

Thus, however "mystical" the content of Zande witchcraft beliefs may or may not be (and I have already suggested they seem so to me only in the sense that I do not myself hold them), they are actually employed by the Zande in a way anything but mysterious—as an elaboration and defense of the truth claims of colloquial reason. Behind all these reflections upon stubbed toes, botched pots, and sour stomachs lies a tissue of common-sense notions the Zande apparently regard as being true on their face: that minor cuts heal rapidly, that stones render baked clay liable to cracking; that abstention from sexual intercourse is prerequisite to success in pot making; that in walking about Zandeland it is unwise to daydream, for the place is full of stumps. And it is as part of this tissue of common-sense assumptions, not of some primitive metaphysics, that the concept of witchcraft takes on its meaning and has its force. For all the talk about its flying about in the night like a firefly, witchcraft does not celebrate an unseen order, it certifies a seen one.

It is when ordinary expectations fail to hold, when the Zande man-in-the-field is confronted with anomalies or contradictions, that the cry of witchcraft goes up. It is, in this respect at least, a kind of dummy variable in the system of common-sense thought. Rather than transcending that thought, it reinforces it by adding to it an all-purpose idea which acts to reassure the Zande that their fund of commonplaces is, momentary appearances to the contrary notwithstanding, dependable and adequate. Thus, if a man contracts leprosy it is attributed to witchcraft only if there is no incest in the family, for "everyone knows" that incest causes leprosy. Adultery, too, causes misfortune. A man may be killed in war or hunting as a result of his wife's infidelities. Before going to war or out to hunt, a man, as is only sensible, will often demand that his wife divulge the names of her lovers. If she says, truthfully, that she has none and he dies anyway, then it must have been witchcraft—unless, of course, he has done something else obviously foolish. Similarly, ignorance, stupidity, or incompetence, culturally defined, are quite sufficient causes of failure in Zande eyes. If, in examining his cracked pot, the potter does in fact find a stone, he stops muttering about witchcraft and starts muttering about his own negligence–instead, that is, of merely assuming that witchcraft was responsible for the stone's being there. And when an inexperienced potter's pot cracks it is put down, as seems only reasonable, to his inexperience, not to some ontological kink in reality.

In this context, at least, the cry of witchcraft functions for the Azande as the cry of *Insha Allah* functions for some Muslims or crossing oneself functions for some Christians, less to lead into more troubling questions—religious, philosophical, scientific, moral—about how the world is put together and what life comes to, than to block such questions from view; to seal up the common-sense view of the world—"everything is what it is and not another thing," as Joseph Butler put it—against the doubts its inevitable insufficiencies inevitably stimulate.

"From generation to generation," Evans-Pritchard writes, "Azande regulate their economic activities according to a transmitted body of knowledge, in their building and crafts no less than their agricultural and hunting pursuits. They have a sound working knowledge of nature in so far as it concerns their welfare. . . . It is true that their knowledge is empirical and incomplete and that it is not transmitted by any systematic teaching but is handed over from one generation to another slowly and casually during childhood and early manhood. Yet it suffices for their everyday tasks and seasonal pursuits." It is this conviction of the plain man that he is on top of things, and not only economic things, that makes action possible for him at all, and which—here through invoking witchcraft to blunt failures, with us by appealing to a long tradition of cracker-barrel philosophizing to commemorate successes—must therefore be protected at all costs. It has, of course, often been remarked that the maintenance of religious faith is a problematic matter in any society; and, theories of the supposed spontaneity of primitives' religious impulses aside, that is, I think, true. But it is at least as true, and very much less remarked, that maintaining faith in the reliability of the axioms and arguments of common sense is no less problematical. Dr. Johnson's famous device for silencing common-sense doubts—"and that's an end on the matter!"—is, when you get right down to it, not that much less desperate than Tertullian's for halting it of religious doubts—"*credo quia impossible*"—and "witchcraft!" is no worse than either of them. Men plug the dikes of their most needed beliefs with whatever mud they can find.

All this comes out rather more dramatically when, instead of confining oneself to a single culture looked at generally one views several at once with respect to a single-problem focus. An excellent example of such an approach can be found in an article in the *American Anthropologist* of a few years back by Robert Edgerton on what is now called intersexuality, but is perhaps more commonly known as hermaphroditism.

Surely if there is one thing that everyone takes to be part of the way in which the world is arranged it is that human beings are divided without remainder into two biological sexes. Of course, it is recognized everywhere that some people—homosexuals, transvestites, and so on—may not behave in terms of the role expectations ascribed to them on the basis of their biological sex, and more recently some people in our society have gone so far as to suggest that roles thus differentiated should not be assigned at all. But whether one wants to shout "*vive la différence!*" or "*à bas la différence!,*" the sheer existence of *la différence* is not subject to much discussion. The view of that legendary little girl—that people come in two kinds, plain and fancy—may have been lamentably unliberated; but that she noticed something anatomically real seems apparent enough.

Yet, as a matter of fact, she may not have inspected a large enough sample. Gender in human beings is not a purely dichotomous variable. It is not an evenly continuous one either, of course, or our love life would be even more complicated than it already is. But a fair number of human beings are markedly intersexual, a number of them to the point where both sorts of external genitalia appear, or where developed breasts occur in an individual with male genitalia, and so on. This raises certain problems for biological science, problems with respect to which a good deal of headway is right now being made. But it raises, also, certain problems for common sense, for the network of practical and moral conceptions woven about those supposedly most rooted of root realities: maleness and femaleness. Intersexuality is more than an empirical surprise; it is a cultural challenge.

It is a challenge that is met in diverse ways. The Romans, Edgerton reports, regarded intersexed infants as supernaturally cursed and put them to death. The Greeks, as was their habit, took a more relaxed view and, though they regarded such persons as peculiar, put it all down as just one of those things—after all, Hermaphroditus, the son of Hermes and Aphrodite who became united in one body with a nymph, provided precedent enough—and let them live out their lives without undue stigma. Edgerton's paper indeed pivots around a fascinating contrast among three quite variant responses to the phenomenon of intersexuality—that of the Americans, the Navaho, and the Pokot (the last a Kenyan tribe)—in terms of the common-sense views these people hold concerning human gender and its general place in nature. As he says, different people may react differently when confronted with individuals whose bodies are sexually anomalous, but they can hardly ignore them. If received ideas of "the normal and the natural" are to be kept intact, something must be said about these rather spectacular disaccordances with them.

Americans regard intersexuality with what can only be called horror. Individuals, Edgerton says, can be moved to nausea by the mere sight of intersexed genitalia or even by a discussion of the condition. "As a moral and legal enigma," he continues, "it knows few peers. Can such a person marry? Is military service relevant? How is the sex on a birth certificate to be made out? Can it properly be changed? Is it psychologically advisable, or even possible, for someone raised as a girl, suddenly to become a boy? . . . How can an intersexed person behave in school shower rooms, in public bathrooms, in dating activities?" Clearly, common sense is at the end of its tether.

The reaction is to encourage, usually with great passion and sometimes with rather more than that, the intersexual to adopt either a male or female role. Many intersexuals do thus "pass" for the whole of their lives as "normal" men or women, something that involves a good deal of careful artifice. Others either seek or are forced into surgery to "correct," cosmetically anyway, the condition and become "legitimate" males or females. Outside of freak shows, we permit only one solution to the dilemma of intersexuality, a solution the person with the condition is obliged to adopt to soothe the sensibilities of the rest of us. "All concerned," Edgerton writes, "from parents to physicians are enjoined to discover which of the two natural sexes the intersexed person most appropriately is and then to help the ambiguous, incongruous, and upsetting 'it' to become at least a partially acceptable 'him' or 'her.' In short, if the facts don't measure up to your expectations, change the facts, or, if that's not feasible, disguise them."

So much for savages. Turning to the Navaho, among whom W. W. Hill made a systematic study of hermaphroditism as early as 1935, the picture is quite different. For them, too, of course, intersexuality is abnormal, but rather than evoking horror and disgust it evokes wonder and awe. The intersexual is considered to have been divinely blessed and to convey that blessing to others. Intersexuals are not only respected, they are practically revered. "They know everything," one of Hill's informants said, "they can do the work of both a man and a woman. I think when all the [intersexuals] are gone, that it will be the end of the Navaho." "If there were no [intersexuals]," another informant said, "the country would change. They are responsible for all the wealth in the country. If there were no more left, the horses, sheep, and Navaho would all go. They are leaders, just like President Roosevelt." Yet another said, "An [intersexual] around the hogan will bring good luck and riches. It does a great deal for the country if you have an [intersexual] around." And so on.

Navaho common sense thus places the anomaly of intersexuality—for, as I say, it seems no less an anomaly to them than it does to us, because it *is* no less an anomaly—in a quite different light than does ours. Interpreting it to be not a horror but a blessing leads on to notions that seem as peculiar to us as that adultery causes hunting accidents or incest leprosy, but that seem to the Navaho only what anyone with his head screwed on straight cannot help but think. For example, that rubbing the genitals of intersexed animals (which are also highly valued) on the tails of female sheep and goats and on the noses of male sheep and goats causes the flocks to prosper and more milk to be produced. Or, that intersexed persons should be made the heads of their families and given complete control over all the family property, because then that too will grow. Change a few interpretations of a few curious facts and you change, here anyway, a whole cast of mind. Not size-up-and-solve, but marvel-and-respect.

Finally, the East African tribe, the Pokot, adopt yet a third view. Like the Americans, they do not regard intersexuals highly; but, like the Navaho, they are not at all revolted or horrified by them. They regard them, quite matter of factly, as simple errors. They are, in what is apparently a popular African image, like a botched pot. "God made a mistake," they say, rather than, "the gods have produced a wondrous gift," or "we are faced with an unclassifiable monster."

Pokot regard the intersexed person as useless—"it" cannot reproduce or extend the patriline as can a proper man nor can it bring in bride-price as can a proper woman. Nor can "it" indulge in what the Pokot say "is the most pleasant thing of all," sex. Frequently, intersexed children are killed, in the offhand way one discards an ill-made pot (so, too, are microcephalics, infants without appendages, and so on; so, too, grossly deformed animals), but often they are allowed, in an equally offhand way, to live. The lives they live are miserable enough, but they are not pariahs—merely neglected, lonely, treated with indifference as though they were mere objects, and ill-made ones at that. Economically they tend to be better off than the average Pokot because they have neither the ordinary kinship drains on their wealth nor the distractions of family life to hinder their accumulation of it. They have, in this apparently typical segmentary lineage and bride-wealth sort of system, no place. Who needs them?

One of Edgerton's cases admits to great unhappiness. "I only sleep, eat, and work. What else can I do? God made a mistake." And another: "God made me this way. There was nothing I could do. All the others [are] able to live as Pokot. I [am] no real Pokot." In a society where common sense stamps even a normally equipped childless man as a forlorn figure and a childless woman is said to be "not even a person," an intersexual's life is the ultimate image of futility. He is "useless" in a society that values the "useful," as, in its cattle-wives-and-children way, it conceives it, very highly.

In short, given the given, not everything else follows. Common sense is not what the mind cleared of cant spontaneously apprehends; it is what the mind filled with presuppositions—that sex is a disorganizing force, that sex is a regenerative gift, that sex is a practical pleasure—concludes. God may have made the intersexuals, but man has made the rest.

III

But there is more to it than this. What man has made is an authoritative story. Like *Lear*, the New Testament, or quantum mechanics, common sense consists in an account of things which claims to strike at their heart. Indeed, it is something of a natural rival to such more sophisticated stories when they are present, and when they are not to the phantasmagoric narratives of dream and myth. As a frame for thought, and a species of it, common sense is as totalizing as any other: no religion is more dogmatic, no science more ambitious, no philosophy more general. Its tonalities are different, and so are the arguments to which it appeals, but like them—and like art and like ideology—it pretends to reach past illusion to truth, to, as we say, things as they are. "Whenever a philosopher says something is 'really real,' " to quote again that great modern celebrant of common sense, G. E. Moore, "you can be really sure that what he says is 'really real' isn't real, really." When a Moore, a Dr. Johnson, a Zande potter, or a Pokot hermaphrodite say something is real, they damn well mean it.

And what is more, you damn well know it. It is precisely in its "tonalities"—the temper its observations convey, the turn of mind its conclusions reflect—that the differentiate of common sense are properly to be sought. The concept as such, as a fixed and labeled category, an explicitly bounded semantic domain, is, of course, not universal, but, like religion, art, and the rest, part of our own more or less common-sense way of distinguishing the genres of cultural expression. And, as we have seen, its actual content, as with religion, art, and the rest, varies too radically from one place and time to the next for there to be much hope of finding a defining constancy within it, an ur-story always told. It is only in isolating what might be called its stylistic features, the marks of attitude that give it its peculiar stamp, that common sense (or indeed any of its sister genres) can be transculturally characterized. Like the voice of piety, the voice of sanity sounds pretty much the same whatever it says; what simple wisdom has everywhere in common is the maddening air of simple wisdom with which it is uttered.

Just how to formulate such stylistic features, marks of attitude, tonal shadings—whatever you want to call them—is something of a problem, because there is no ready vocabulary in which to do so. Short of simply inventing new terms, which, as the point is to characterize the familiar not to describe the unknown, would be self-defeating here, one can only stretch old ones in the way a mathematician does when he says a proof is deep, a critic does when he says a painting is chaste, or a wine connoisseur does when he says a Bordeaux is assertive. The terms I want to use in this way with respect to common sense, each with a "-ness" added on to substantivise it, are: natural, practical, thin, immethodical, accessible. "Naturalness," "practicalness," "thinness," "immethodicalness," and "accessibleness" are the somewhat unstandard properties I want to attribute to common sense generally, as an everywhere-found cultural form.

The first of these quasi-qualities, naturalness, is perhaps the most fundamental. Common sense represents matters—that is, certain matters and not others—as being what they are in the simple nature of the case. An air of "of-courseness," a sense of "it figures" is cast over things—again, some selected, underscored things. They are depicted as inherent in the situation, intrinsic aspects of reality, the way things go. This is true even with respect to an anomaly like intersexuality. What divides the American attitude from the other two is not that people with bisexual organs seem that much more peculiar to us, but that the peculiarity seems unnatural, a contradiction in the settled terms of existence. Navaho and Pokot take, in their different ways, the view that intersexuals are a product, if a somewhat unusual product, of the normal course of things— gifted prodigies, botched pots—where the Americans, to the degree their view is being properly portrayed, apparently regard femaleness and maleness as exhausting the natural categories in which persons can conceivably come: what falls between is a darkness, an offense against reason.

But naturalness as a characteristic of the sorts of stories about the real we call common sense can be more plainly seen in less sensational examples. Among the Australian aborigines, to choose one more or less at random, a whole host of features of the physical landscape are considered as resulting from the activities of totemic ancestors—

mostly kangaroos, emus, witchety grubs, and the like—performed in that time-out-of-time usually glossed in English as "the dreaming." As Nancy Munn has pointed out, this transformation of ancestral persons into natural features is conceived to have occurred in at least three ways: by actual metamorphosis, the body of the ancestor changing into some material object; by imprinting, the ancestor leaving the impression of his body or of some tool he uses; and by what she calls externalization, the ancestor taking some object out of his body and discarding it. Thus, a rocky hill or even a stone may be seen as a crystalized ancestor (he did not die, the informants say, he ceased moving about and "became the country"); a waterhole, or even a whole campsite, may be seen as the impress left by the buttocks of an ancestor who in his wanderings sat down to rest there; and various other sorts of material objects—string crosses and oval boards—are considered to have been drawn by some primordial kangaroo or snake out of his belly and "left behind" as he moved on. The details of all this (and they are enormously complicated) aside, the external world as the aborigines confront it is neither a blank reality nor some complicated sort of metaphysical object, but the natural outcome of trans-natural events.

What this particular example, here so elliptically given, demonstrates is that the naturalness, which as a modal property characterizes common sense, does not rest, or at least does not necessarily rest, on what we would call philosophical naturalism—the view that there are no things in heaven and earth undreamt of by the temporal mind. Indeed, for the aborigines, as for the Navaho, the naturalness of the everyday world is a direct expression, a resultant, of a realm of being to which a quite different complex of quasi-qualities—"grandeur," "seriousness," "mystery," and "otherness"—is attributed. The fact that the natural phenomena of their physical world are the remains of actions of inviolable kangaroos or thaumaturgical snakes does not make those phenomena any less natural in aboriginal eyes. The fact that a particular creek was formed because Possum happened to drag his tail along the ground right there makes it no less a creek. It makes it, of course, something more, or at least something other, than a creek is to us; but water runs downhill in both of them.

The point is general. The development of modern science has had a profound effect—though perhaps not so profound as sometimes imagined—upon Western common-sense views. Whether, as I rather doubt, the plain man has become a genuine Copernican or not (to me, the sun still rises and shines upon the earth), he has surely been brought round, and quite recently, to a version of the germ theory of disease. The merest television commercial demonstrates that. But, as the merest television commercial also demonstrates, it is as a bit of common sense, not as an articulated scientific theory, that he believes it. He may have moved beyond "feed a cold and starve a fever," but only to "brush your teeth twice a day and see your dentist twice a year." A similar argument could be made for art—there was no fog in London until Whistler painted it, and so on. The naturalness commonsense conceptions give to . . . well, whatever they give it to—drinking from fast-running creeks in preference to slow-running ones, staying out of crowds in the influenza season . . . may be dependent on other sorts of quite unordinary stories about the way things are. (Or, of course, may not: "Man is born to trouble as the sparks fly upward" depends for its persuasiveness on one's merely having lived long enough to discover how terribly accurate it is.)

The second characteristic, "practicalness," is perhaps more obvious to the naked eye than the others on my list, for what we most often mean when we say an individual, an action, or a project displays a want of common sense is that they are impractical. The individual is in for some rude awakenings, the action is conducing toward its own defeat, the project won't float. But, simply because it seems so more readily apparent, it is also more susceptible to misconstruction. For it is not "practicalness" in the narrowly pragmatical sense of the useful but in the broader, folk-philosophical sense of sagacity that is involved. To tell someone, "be sensible," is less to tell him to cling to the utilitarian than to tell him, as we say, to wise up: to be prudent, levelheaded, keep his eye on the ball, not buy any wooden nickels, stay away from slow horses and fast women, let the dead bury the dead.

There has been, in fact, something of a debate—part of the larger discussion concerning the cultural inventories of "simpler" peoples, I mentioned earlier—as to whether "primitives" have any interest in matters of empirical fact which do not bear, and rather directly bear, on their immediate material interests. This is the view—that is, that they do not—to which Malinowski largely held and which Evans-Pritchard, in a passage I deliberately elided earlier, affirms concerning the Zande. "They have a sound working knowledge of nature insofar as it concerns their welfare. Beyond this point it has for them no scientific interest or sentimental appeal." Against this, other anthropologists, of whom Lévi-Strauss is if not the first anyway the most emphatic, have argued that "primitives," "savages," or whatever have elaborated, and even systematized, bodies of empirical knowledge which have no very clear practical import for them. Some Philippine tribes distinguish over six hundred types of named plants, most of these plants being unused, unusable, and in fact but rarely encountered. American Indians of the northeastern United States and Canada have an elaborate taxonomy of reptiles they neither eat nor otherwise have very much traffic with. Some Southwestern Indians—Pueblans—have names for every one of the types of coniferous tree in their region, most of which barely differ from one another and certainly in no way of material concern to the Indians. Southeast Asian

Pygmies can distinguish the leaf-eating habits of more than fifteen species of bats. Against Evans-Pritchard's primitive utilitarian sort of view—know what it profits you to know and leave the rest to witchcraft—one has Lévi-Strauss's primitive intellectual one—know everything your mind provokes you to know and range it into categories. "It may be objected," he writes, "that science of this kind [that is, botanical classification, herpetological observation, and so forth] can scarcely be of much practical effect. The answer to this is that its main purpose is not a practical one. It meets intellectual requirements rather than or instead of satisfying [material] needs."

There is little doubt that the consensus in the field now supports the Lévi-Strauss sort of view rather than the Evans-Pritchard sort—"primitives" are interested in all kinds of things of use neither to their schemes nor to their stomachs. But that is hardly all there is to the matter. For they are not classifying all those plants, distinguishing all those snakes, or sorting out all those bats out of some overwhelming cognitive passion rising out of innate structures at the bottom of the mind either. In an environment populated with conifers, or snakes, or leaf-eating bats it is practical to know a good deal about conifers, snakes, or leaf-eating bats, whether or not what one knows is in any strict sense materially useful, because it is of such knowledge that "practicalness" is there composed. Like its "naturalness," the "practicalness" of common sense is a quality it bestows upon things, not one that things bestow upon it. If, to us, studying a racing form seems a practical activity and chasing butterflies does not, that is not because the one is useful and the other is not; it is because the one is considered an effort, however feckless, to know what's what and the other, however charming, is not.

The third of the quasi-qualities common sense attributes to reality, "thinness," is, like modesty in cheese, rather hard to formulate in more explicit terms. "Simpleness," or even "literalness," might serve as well or better, for what is involved is the tendency for common-sense views of this matter or that to represent them as being precisely what they seem to be, neither more nor less. The Butler line I quoted earlier—"every thing is what it is and not another thing"—expresses this quality perfectly. The world is what the wide-awake, uncomplicated person takes it to be. Sobriety, not subtlety, realism, not imagination, are the keys to wisdom; the really important facts of life lie scattered openly along its surface, not cunningly secreted in its depths. There is no need, indeed it is a fatal mistake, to deny, as poets, intellectuals, priests, and other professional complicators of the world so often do, the obviousness of the obvious. Truth is as plain, as the Dutch proverb has it, as a pikestaff over water.

Again, like Moore's oversubtle philosophers discoursing musefully on the real, anthropologists often spin notional complexities they then report as cultural facts through a failure to realize that much of what their informants are saying is, however strange it may sound to educated ears, meant literally. Some of the most crucial properties of the world are not regarded as concealed beneath a mask of deceptive appearances, things inferred from pale suggestions or riddled out of equivocal signs. They are conceived to be just there, where stones, hands, scoundrels, and erotic triangles are, invisible only to the clever. It takes a while (or, anyway, it took me a while) to absorb the fact that when the whole family of a Javanese boy tells me that the reason he has fallen out of a tree and broken his leg is that the spirit of his deceased grandfather pushed him out because some ritual duty toward the grandfather has been inadvertently overlooked, that, so far as they are concerned, is the beginning, the middle, and the end of the matter: it is precisely what they think has occurred, it is all that they think has occurred, and they are puzzled only at my puzzlement at their lack of puzzlement. And when, after listening to a long, complicated business from an old, illiterate, no-nonsense Javanese peasant woman—a classic type if ever there was one—about the role of "the snake of the day" in determining the wisdom of embarking on a journey, holding a feast, or contracting a marriage (the story was actually mostly loving accounts of the terrible things that happened—carriages overturning, tumors appearing, fortunes dissolving—when that role was ignored), I asked what this snake of the day looked like and was met with, "Don't be an idiot; you can't see Tuesday, can you?," I began to realize that patentness, too, is in the eye of the beholder. "The world divides into facts" may have its defects as a philosophical slogan or a scientific creed; as an epitomization of the "thinness"—"simpleness," "literalness"—that common sense stamps onto experience it is graphically exact.

As for "immethodicalness," another not too well named quality common-sense thought represents the world as possessing, it caters at once to the pleasures of inconsistency which are so very real to any but the most scholastical of men ("A foolish consistency is the hobgoblin of little minds," as Emerson said; "I contradict myself, so I contradict myself. I contain multitudes," as Whitman did); and also to the equal pleasures, felt by any but the most obsessional of men, of the intractable diversity of experience ("The world is full of a number of things"; "Life is one damn thing after another"; "If you think you understand the situation, that only proves you are misinformed"). Common-sense wisdom is shamelessly and unapologetically ad hoc. It comes in epigrams, proverbs, *obiter dicta,* jokes, anecdotes, *contes morals*—a clatter of gnomic utterances—not in formal doctrines, axiomized theories, or architectonic dogmas. Silone says somewhere that southern Italian peasants pass their lives exchanging proverbs with one another like so many precious gifts. Elsewhere the forms may be polished witicisms à la

Wilde, didactic verses à la Pope, or animal fables à la La Fontaine; among the classical Chinese they seem to have been embalmed quotations. Whatever they are, it is not their interconsistency that recommends them but indeed virtually the opposite: "Look before you leap," but "He who hesitates is lost"; "A stitch in time saves nine," but "Seize the day." It is, indeed, in the sententious saying, in one sense, the paradigmatic form of vernacular wisdom—that the immethodicalness of common sense comes out most vividly. In witness of which, consider the following bundle of Ba-Ila proverbs I excerpt from Paul Radin (who excerpted them in turn from Smith and Dale):

> Get grown up and then you will know the things of the earth.
>
> Annoy your doctors and sicknesses will come laughing.
>
> The prodigal cow threw away her own tail.
>
> It is the prudent hyena that lives long.
>
> The god that speaks up gets the meat.
>
> You may cleanse yourself but it is not to say that you cease to be a slave.
>
> When a chief's wife steals she puts the blame on the slaves.
>
> Build rather with a witch than with a false-tongued person, for he destroys the community.
>
> Better help a fighting man than a hungry man, for he has no gratitude.

And so on. It is this sort of potpourri of disparate notions—again not necessarily or even usually expressed proverbially—which not only characterizes systems of common sense generally but which in fact recommends them as capable of grasping the vast multifariousness of life in the world. The Ba-Ila even have a proverb expressing this: "Wisdom comes out of an ant heap."

The final quasi-quality—final here, surely not so in actuality—"accessibleness," more or less follows as a logical consequence once the others are acknowledged. Accessibleness is simply the assumption, in fact the insistence, that any person with faculties reasonably intact can grasp common-sense conclusions, and indeed, once they are unequivocally enough stated, will not only grasp but embrace them. Of course, some people—usually the old, sometimes the afflicted, occasionally the merely orotund—tend to be regarded as rather wiser in an "I've been through the mill" sort of way than others, while children, frequently enough women, and, depending upon the society, various sorts of underclasses are regarded as less wise, in an "they are emotional creatures" sort of way, than others. But, for all that, there are really no acknowledged specialists in common sense. Everyone thinks he's an expert. Being common, common sense is open to all, the general property of at least, as we would put it, all solid citizens.

Indeed, its tone is even anti-expert, if not anti-intellectual: we reject, and so, as far as I can see, do other peoples, any explicit claim to special powers in this regard. There is no esoteric knowledge, no special technique or peculiar giftedness, and little or no specialized training—only what we rather redundantly call experience and rather mysteriously call maturity—involved. Common sense, to put it another way, represents the world as a familiar world, one everyone can, and should, recognize, and within which everyone stands, or should, on his own feet. To live in the suburbs called physics, or Islam, or law, or music, or socialism, one must meet certain particular requirements, and the houses are not all of the same imposingness. To live in the semi-suburb called common sense, where all the houses are *sans façon*, one need only be, as the old phrase has it, sound of mind and practical of conscience, however those worthy virtues be defined in the particular city of thought and language whose citizen one is. . . .

1983

GETTING STARTED

1. Before reading the essay, develop your own definition of "common sense." Start by thinking of someone you know who exhibits common sense. List the qualities and character traits you associate with that person. Then, do the same for someone you know who seems to lack common sense. Write a paragraph that compares the two lists.

2. Make separate lists of words and of names in the essay that are unfamiliar to you. Do you think that Geertz assumes his readers will know these words and names? How would you describe the primary audience for this essay?

3. Geertz's essay presents examples from various cultures (for example, Navaho, Zande, Pokot). Choose the one that interests you the most and write a paragraph that summarizes Geertz's discussion of the culture. In your summary, quote a key sentence or two from the essay and explain why you chose it. How does it help you to understand the culture you have selected?

4. Working in a group, list the contradictions in commonsense thought that Geertz identifies and discusses. For example, Geertz notes that common sense teaches us both "Look before you leap"

and "He who hesitates is lost" (p. 241). What other contradictory commonsense notions can your group identify?

5. In a group, discuss Geertz's use of the words "natural, practical, thin, immethodical, [and] accessible" (p. 236) to characterize common sense. Think about how the opposites of these words could be used to define a lack of common sense. Choose one example that Geertz gives and prepare a group presentation for the class on how that example helps you to understand common sense.

WRITING

6. Quote a key passage from the essay that gives you a good sense of what Geertz means by "common sense." Write a brief paper in which you discuss what words, examples, or images attracted you to this particular quotation. Use an example from Geertz and one from your own experience to help explain the quotation and why you chose it.
7. Put the following quotation into your own words: "The analysis of common sense, as opposed to the exercise of it, must . . . begin by redrawing this erased distinction between the mere matter-of-fact apprehension of reality . . . and down-to-earth, colloquial wisdom, judgments or assessments of it" (p. 228). Follow this paraphrase with a written analysis of the process you used to create it. What was difficult to paraphrase? What was easy?
8. Write at least three paragraphs discussing the connections you see between Geertz's discussion of Zande witchcraft and his discussion of Navaho attitudes toward intersexuality. What point is he making with these examples?

USING THE LIBRARY AND THE INTERNET

9. Use an encyclopedia and a popular Internet search engine such as AltaVista or Hotbot to learn more about where the Zande live and about their culture. Note some of the differences between the information you found in the encyclopedia and that found on the Internet. Share your findings in a group and prepare a class presentation showing how that information contributes to your understanding of Geertz's examples in this essay.
10. Using a reference database such as Academic Search Elite that includes a range of scholarly sources, try the combined search term "common sense and culture." Scan the results and choose two

articles that relate to Geertz's ideas in interesting ways. Print out the articles or abstracts and bring them to class.

MAKING CONNECTIONS

11. Write an essay that examines intersections between "common sense" as defined by Geertz and "wisdom" as defined by Sven Birkerts in "The Owl Has Flown." Why might one argue that common sense is the same as wisdom? Could one also argue that they are entirely different?

12. Use Geertz's main ideas about common sense to write an essay that analyzes Thomas Kuhn's discussion of anomaly and scientific discovery in "The Historical Structure of Scientific Discovery."

13. Compare Geertz's claim that "common sense is not what the mind cleared of cant spontaneously apprehends; it is what the mind filled with presuppositions . . . concludes" (p. 235) with Walker Percy's discussion of "symbolic packages" in "The Loss of the Creature." What connections do you see? Is Percy's "symbolic package" related in any way to Geertz's "common sense"?

Stephen Jay Gould

Stephen Jay Gould (1941–) is the Alexander Agassiz Professor of Zoology and Professor of Geology at Harvard University and Curator of Invertebrate Paleontology in the Harvard Museum of Comparative Zoology. He also teaches in the Department of the History of Science at Harvard and holds the Vincent Astor Visiting Research Professor of Biology at New York University. Gould is widely recognized as a scientist who makes science accessible to the public by connecting it to literature, sports, history, and popular culture. He is the author of eleven books and has appeared in documentaries and on television. "The Smoking Gun of Eugenics" is a chapter from his book, *Dinosaur in a Haystack: Reflections in Natural History* (1995).

To learn more about the use and misuse of science and statistics, explore the Web site of The Chance Program at Dartmouth University at <http://www.dartmouth.edu/~chance>.

The Smoking Gun of Eugenics

Do Baptist preachers cause public drunkenness? I raise this unlikely inquiry because an old and famous tabulation clearly shows a strong positive correlation between the number of preachers and the frequency of arrests for inebriation during the second half of the nineteenth century in America.

You don't need a Ph.D. in logic to spot the fallacy in my first sentence. Correlation is not causality. The undeniable association of preachers and drunks might mean that hellfire inspires imbibing; but the same correlation could also (and more reasonably) suggest the opposite causal hypothesis that a rise in public drinking promotes the hiring of more preachers. But yet another possibility—almost surely correct in this particular case—holds that preaching and drinking may have no causal relationship, while their simultaneous increase only records a common link to a third, truly determining factor. The steady rise of the American population during the late nineteenth century promoted an increase in thousands of phenomena linked to total numbers, but otherwise unrelated—arrests for drinking and hiring of clergy among them. This tale has long served as the standard textbook example for illustrating the difference between correlation and causality.

But good principles can also be used to buttress bad arguments. I have often stated . . . that only great thinkers are allowed to fail greatly—meaning that such errors, although large in scope and import, are invariably rich and instructive rather than petty and merely embarrassing. This essay treats the two greatest errors of the twentieth century's patron saint in my profession of evolutionary biology.

Most general readers may not know the name of Sir Ronald Aylmer Fisher (1890–1962), for he wrote nothing for nonprofessional consumption, and the highly mathematical character of his technical work debars access to many full-time naturalists as well. But no scientist is more important as a founder of modern evolutionary theory, particularly for his successful integration of Mendelian genetics with Darwinian natural selection. Fisher's 1930 book, *The Genetical Theory of Natural Selection,* is the keystone for the architecture of modern Darwinism. Fisher built with mathematics, and most biologists will say (though I would disagree in important respects) that the field he founded—population genetics—is the centerpiece of evolutionary theory. Fisher was also one of the world's most distinguished statisticians; he invented a technique called the "analysis of variance"—now about as central to statistics as the alphabet is to orthography. In short, Fisher is the Babe Ruth of statistics and evolutionary theory.

But the Babe also struck out a lot, and Fisher made some major-league errors. Most of my colleagues know about the two key mistakes that I will analyze in this essay, but these errors just aren't discussed in polite, professional company. One is dismissed as an inconsequential foible of Fisher's old age, while the other tends to be bypassed in silence, though it occupies more than one third of Fisher's most important 1930 book.

During the last half-dozen years of his life, Fisher spent considerable time and several publications trying to debunk the idea that smoking can cause lung cancer. Sir Ronald, who enjoyed his pipe, did not deny that a real correlation between smoking and lung cancer had been found. But, following the textbook paradigm of preachers and drunkards, he disputed the claim that causation ran directly from smoke to cancer. He presented the two other logical possibilities, just as the texts always do for Baptists and boozers. First, cancer might cause smoking rather than vice versa. This inherently implausible version seems hard to defend, even as an abstract argument for the sake of conjecture, but Fisher found a way.

As a smoker, Fisher extolled the soothing effects of tobacco. He also recognized that cancers take years to develop and that future sufferers live for several years in a "pre-cancerous state." He supposed that lungs might be chemically irritated during this pre-cancerous phase, and that people so afflicted might be led to increased smoking for psychological relief from an unrecognized physical ailment. A bit strained, but not illogical. Fisher wrote in 1958:

> Is it possible, then, that lung cancer—that is to say, the pre-cancerous condition which must exist and is known to exist for years in those who are going to show overt lung cancer—is one of the causes of smoking cigarettes? I don't think it can be excluded . . . The pre-cancerous condition is one involving a certain amount of slight chronic inflammation . . .
>
> A slight cause of irritation—a slight disappointment, an unexpected delay, some sort of mild rebuff, a frustration—is commonly accompanied by pulling out a cigarette, and getting a little compensation for life's minor ills in that way. And so anyone suffering from chronic inflammation in part of the body (something that does not give rise to conscious pain) is not unlikely to be associated with smoking more frequently, or smoking rather than not smoking . . . To take the poor chap's cigarettes away from him would be rather like taking away his white stick from a blind man.

But Fisher recognized that the second alternative for the correlation of smoking and lung cancer—the association of both, independently, with a truly causal third factor—held much greater plausibility and promise. And Fisher had no doubt about the most likely common factor—genetic predisposition. He wrote: "For my part, I think it is more likely that a common cause supplies the explanation . . . The obvious common cause to think of is the genotype." In other words, genes that make people more susceptible to lung cancer might also lead to behaviors and personalities that encourage smoking. Again, the argument is undeniably logical; genes may have multiple effects, both physical and behavioral. To choose an obvious example, several forms of mental retardation have no causal relationship with correlated physical features. Short stature does not produce retardation (or vice versa) in people with Down's syndrome.

With the hindsight of an additional twenty-five years, we may say conclusively that Fisher was wrong, and tragically so. Smoking is a direct and potent cause of lung cancer—the reason, therefore, for hundreds of thousands of premature deaths in America each year. Yet I cannot fault Fisher on the logic of his argument: correlation is not causality, and the bare fact of correlation does permit the three causal scenarios that Fisher detailed. If Fisher had presented his objections to the indictment of smoking only as a cautionary claim in the absence of conclusive data, then we could not blame him today. (One cannot always be right in our complex world; no dishonor attends an incorrect choice among plausible outcomes drawn from a properly constructed argument.) But in Fisher's case, we have reason to question his motives and his objectivity—and some judgment for his incorrect conclusion may therefore be exacted.

Fisher did present his case with the conventional rhetoric of science. He claimed to be both objective in his weighing of evidence and agnostic about the outcome. He maintained that he raised the issue only in a proper scientific spirit of caution and love of truth. Fisher made three explicit arguments for special and scrupulous care in treating such a socially charged issue, a potential matter of life and death.

1. Millions of people enjoy smoking. We dare not poison the source of their pleasure without conclusive evidence. Fisher pleaded for the psychic health of ordinary smokers in the elitist language of an Oxbridge don (Fisher was the Balfour Professor of Genetics at Cambridge and, at the end of his career, president of Gonville and Caius College):

> After all, a large number of the smokers of the world are not very clever, perhaps not very strong-minded. The habit is an insidious one, difficult to break, and consequently in many, many cases there would be implanted what a psychologist might recognize as a grave conflict . . . Before one interferes with the peace of mind and habits of others, it seems to me that the scientific evidence—the exact weight of the evidence free from emotion—should be rather carefully examined.

Writing more forcefully in a letter to the *British Medical Journal* (July 6, 1957), Fisher compared the claims of anti-smoking forces with the classic case of hysteria-mongering: "Surely the 'yellow peril' of modern times is not the mild and soothing weed but the organized creation of states of frantic alarm."

2. If we make a strident claim for smoking as a cause of cancer, and if we then turn out to be wrong, the entire enterprise of statistics will be discredited. In a further letter to the *British Medical Journal* (August 3, 1957), Fisher pleaded for caution as a protection for science:

> Statistics has gained a place of modest usefulness in medical research. It can deserve and retain this only by complete impartiality . . . I do not relish the prospect of this science being now discredited by a catastrophic and conspicuous howler.

3. Situations of uncertainty require more research above all. Premature conclusions stifle further investigation. In yet another letter, this time to *Nature,* Britain's leading journal for professional scientists, Fisher wrote (August 30,1958): "Considerable propaganda is now being developed to convince the public that cigarette smoking is dangerous." In his letter of August 1957, Fisher had already specified the perils of such a campaign: "Excessive confidence that the solution

has already been found is the main obstacle in the way of more penetrating research."

Fisher's last point about further research backfired strongly upon him—an ironic illustration of its power and truth. Fisher supported his suspicion that smoking does not cause cancer with two poorly documented sets of data—a curious claim that people who inhale develop fewer cancers, for the same amount of smoking, than those who do not inhale; and a puzzling contention that lung cancer had increased faster in men than in women, whereas smoking had risen more rapidly in women.

The data on inhaling came from a very poorly constructed questionnaire. Most respondents may not even have known the meaning of the word "inhale," and may have checked "no" in simple confusion. Later information shows a strongly positive correlation of cancer with inhaling, when all other factors are held constant. As for men and women, Fisher made a sound argument, but the data were wrong. The ever-accelerating incidence of lung cancer in women now ranks among the strongest points of evidence for a causal connection.

The basis for judging Fisher negatively in this sorry incident emerges neither from the logic of his argument (which was sound, despite his false conclusion, based on inadequate data), nor from his proper words of caution, but from a clear inference that he did not live by his own stated strictures. Evidently, Fisher did not approach the issue of smoking and cancer with the open mind that he championed as so necessary for any good science. He maintained an obvious preference for denying that smoking causes cancer—even though he states, again and again, that the raw data of an admitted correlation offers no preference for any of the three potential interpretations. Two aspects of his writing give the game away. First, his language. Consider the small sample quoted above. His words call for argument "free from emotion," and for "complete impartiality." Yet he labels the claim that smoking might cause cancer as "propaganda," probably a "catastrophic and conspicuous howler," and a "frantic alarm" acting as the " 'yellow peril' of modern times."

Second, his treatment [was] of limited data then available. Fisher accepted, virtually without question or criticism, the inadequate but exculpatory data, previously cited, on inhaling and incidence in men vs. women—even though both sets would soon be discredited. Fisher then showcased some even more dubious data supposedly consonant with his favored view that both cancer and smoking arise independently from a common genetic predisposition. Two studies compared the smoking behaviors of identical and fraternal twin pairs. Smoking preferences (either yea or nay) were more often shared by identical than by fraternal twins. Since identicals form from one egg and therefore share the same genetic program, while fraternals develop from two eggs and are no closer genetically than any ordinary pair of siblings, Fisher concluded that the greater similarity of identicals must indicate a strong genetic basis for smoking preferences.

But this inference is both potentially wrong and largely irrelevant to Fisher's argument. First of all, the greater smoking similarity of identicals could, at most, indicate a genetic predisposition for attitudes toward the weed; such data say nothing at all about genetic bases for cancer, or about correlation of the two potential predispositions. Moreover, Fisher's data do not even prove his basic assertion of genetic predisposition for smoking. Fisher's explanation does represent one potential interpretation of the data, but another clearly exists, and he hardly considers this alternative. Identical twins look alike and are frequently raised to emphasize their eerie similarity; they are often dressed alike, learn to act as surrogates one for the other, etc. Perhaps this greater similarity in rearing leads to a stronger likelihood for identical smoking habits.

In any case, Fisher should have considered all these possibilities if he had truly pursued this issue with an open mind. We must conclude, rather, that he entered the fray with a clear preference, even a mission—the debunking of smoking as a cause and a championing of joint genetic predisposition as an alternative explanation. We must therefore probe deeper and ask why Fisher had such a clear preference. Two factors stand out, one immediate and practical, the other long-standing and theoretical.

The immediate reason is easy to state and hard to gainsay: In 1956, Fisher became paid scientific consultant for the Tobacco Manufacturers' Standing Committee. Fisher took great umbrage at any implication that his objectivity might be compromised thereby, arguing that he wouldn't sell his soul for the pittance they paid him. Higher powers must judge the tangled commitments wrought by such employment; I will only observe that we generally, and with good reason, require institutional impartiality as a prerequisite for genuine objectivity of mind.

The long-standing reason is more interesting intellectually, and permits us to work back toward Fisher's first great error, thereby revealing an important continuity in his life and career. Fisher was a strong, lifelong supporter of eugenics, the proposition that human life and culture could be bettered if we implemented strategies for genetic improvement by selective breeding—either encouraging childbearing by those judged genetically more fit (positive eugenics), or preventing procreation by the supposedly unfit (negative eugenics). I must emphasize at the start that I do not single out Fisher for any special opprobrium on this score. The great majority of geneticists advocated some form of eugenics, at least until Hitler showed so graphically how a ruthless program of negative eugenics might operate. . . . Moreover, Fisher's idiosyncratic version was, as we shall see, relatively benign politically, and largely in the positive mode. Eugenics commanded a big and motley group of supporters, including fascists to be sure, but also idealistic socialists and committed democrats. . . .

Fisher's strong and lifelong preference for genetic explanations of behavior, the foundation of his eugenical sympathies, surely predisposed him to the argument that both smoking and cancer might be linked to genetic variation among people. The same preference for genetic explanations inspired his much more extensive and encompassing first great error—his general theory of racial decline (and possible eugenic salvation), as presented in his magnum opus of 1930, *The Genetical Theory of Natural Selection.*

Just as most of my colleagues ignore Fisher's late and embarrassing work on smoking, they also pay little or no attention to the eugenical chapters of our profession's Bible. Evolutionists may not know much about Fisher's campaign to exonerate the tobacco industry, but how can they bypass several chapters of a crucial volume present in every professional's library? One leading book on the history of population genetics says this and no more about Fisher's eugenical chapters: "In the concluding five chapters he extended his genetical ideas to human populations."

We don't like to admit flaws in our saints. Perhaps my colleagues are embarrassed that a truly great work, the abstract and theoretical foundation of our field, should include a practical view of society that most of us find both fatally flawed and politically unacceptable. Perhaps we tend to view the eugenical chapters as an unfortunate and discardable appendage to a great work of very different character. But such dismissal cannot be defended. The eugenical chapters are no ending frill; they represent more than one third of the book. Moreover, Fisher explicitly insists that these chapters both follow directly from his general theory and cannot be separated from his more abstract conclusions. He states that he only gathered these chapters together for convenience and might, instead, have scattered the eugenical material throughout the book. Fisher writes, "The deductions respecting man are strictly inseparable from the more general chapters."

A single, if complex, argument runs through the five eugenical chapters: advanced civilizations destroy themselves by "the social promotion of the relatively infertile"—that is, people who rise into the ruling classes (the "better people" so necessary to successful government) tend, alas, to have fewer children for reasons of relative genetic infertility, not mere (and reversible) social choice. The upper classes therefore deplete themselves and society eventually weakens and crumbles. If this assertion seems implausible *a priori*, then follow Fisher's rationale through six steps. Again, as with smoking, the argument is impeccably logical (in the narrow, technical sense of following from premises), but entirely wrong, almost nonsensical, based on the fallacy of these key premises.

1. All great civilizations cycle from initial prosperity to eventual decline and fall. Though conquest may eventually befall a depleted race, the cause of decline is internal and intrinsic. The major reason for ultimate failure must lie with a predictable weakening of the elite classes. Can this decline be stemmed and stability with greatness imparted? Fisher writes: "The fact of the decline of past civilizations is the most patent in history . . . The immediate cause of decay must be the degeneration or depletion of the ruling classes."

2. Fisher now notes, but misinterprets, the long-known and well-documented relationship between family size and social status in modern Western nations. Poorer families have more children, while the elite are relatively infertile because the upper classes marry later, have fewer children after marriage, and contain a higher percentage of permanent bachelors or spinsters. This relative infertility of the upper classes leads to their depletion and eventually, thereby, to a decline of civilization by failure of the most able to replenish themselves. Fisher writes: "The birth rate is much higher in the poorer than in the more prosperous classes, and this difference has been increasing in recent generations."

Interestingly, and on this basis, Fisher rejects the two most common alternative explanations for racial decay advanced by eugenicists of his time. He denies, first, that the upper classes alone are being vitiated by dangerous inbreeding. The decline in fertility is gradual and pervasive through the social hierarchy, not confined to the ruling elite. Fisher writes: "The deficiency in procreation is not especially characteristic of titled families or of the higher intellects, but is a graded quality extending by a regular declivity from the top to the bottom of the social scale."

Second, Fisher also rejected the common argument with the most unfortunate moral and political consequences—that superior civilizations decay by racial mixture with inferior groups. Fisher's rejection arises directly from his general evolutionary views—and this link supplies the best proof that Fisher's eugenical chapters are integrally connected with his general evolutionary theory, and that the two parts of his book cannot be separated, with the theory exalted and the eugenics ignored in embarrassment. The book's centerpiece is a proposition now known as "Fisher's fundamental theorem of natural selection": "The rate of increase in fitness of any organism at any time is equal to its genetic variance in fitness at that time." Or, roughly, the rate of evolution by natural selection is directly proportional to the amount of usable genetic variation maintained in a population. Or, even more roughly, genetic variation is a good thing if you want to accelerate the rate of evolution. Therefore, since eugenic betterment requires effective evolution, anything that boosts the amount of usable variation should be strongly desirable. In Fisher's view, racial mixing represents a powerful way to increase variation, and Fisher had to acknowledge the potential benefits. (Fisher, following a common prejudice of his time, did not deny the general superiority of some races. Thus, race mixture might lower the average quality of a people. Nonetheless, the *range* of variation would increase, even while the mean declined, and natural selection could produce improvement by favoring rare individuals on the extended upper end.)

3. One might think that the elite have fewer children for purely social reasons (greater access to contraception, postponement of childbearing for work or education, more access to types of leisure enjoyed better without large families); but in fact the cause of the correlation is largely genetic and the elite are less fertile for constitutional reasons.

This statement provides the centerpiece for Fisher's eugenics. He argues that the low fertility of modern elites is a pernicious and recent development, not a permanent state of all societies. In "primitive" social organizations, rulers generally have *more* children. (Fisher discreetly bypasses the major reason for this former positive correlation—concubinage and multiple marriage by males in power—largely, I suspect, because he rejects such practices morally but wishes to think well of elites in any age!) Fisher writes: "The normal destiny of accumulated wealth was to provide for a numerous posterity."

But "advanced" civilization has reversed this old and biologically healthy correlation. The elite now have fewer children, primarily for reasons of relative genetic infertility. How did the tragic reversal occur? This sorry situation could only have arisen, Fisher argues, if tendencies for social promotion of the less fertile predictably arise in "advanced" civilizations, thus flooding the upper classes with the source of their eventual depletion in numbers. But how could such a tendency originate?

4. People who rise from the lower to the upper classes (in a democracy permitting such mobility) do so by virtue of genetic superiority and the advantages thus conferred via intelligence and business acumen. But, unfortunately, these people also tend to be less fertile. Fisher's argument precisely follows the form of his later claim for smoking. High ability does not cause infertility, nor does infertility produce brilliance. Rather, the correlation of high ability and infertility originates because both traits are independently linked to a pernicious circumstance that only arises in "advanced" civilizations. A man has to possess strong, genetically based ability in order to rise at all. (Fisher, following the pervasive sexism of his time, does formulate this argument explicitly for males.) But if a man comes from a large family (and therefore inherits a propensity for high fertility), his chances for rising are diminished because his family will be poorer (more mouths to feed, all other things being equal) and he will have less access to education. But a man with the same high ability, if he

comes from a small family (with heritable low fertility), has a better chance to rise. By this noncausal correlation of ability and infertility, the chief reason for declining civilization emerges: the social promotion of the relatively infertile.

This situation breeds tragedy all around. The lower classes decline by loss of their most able members; the upper classes sink by infertility of these upwardly mobile people. Society goes down the tubes. Fisher, at least, tried to do his personal bit to stem the tide by raising a bevy of kids.

5. Fisher now faced a problem in the logic of his argument. If the upper classes are so infertile, shouldn't rising immigrants from lower levels help to replenish the dearth even if these newcomers are less fertile than their compatriots remaining at the bottom? Fisher, following a curious argument first advanced by Francis Galton, argued that men who rise by ability tend to marry particularly infertile upper class women, thus diluting their own capacity for childbearing. Such men, knowing their advantages (and clever enough for exploitation), tend to marry heiresses should the opportunity arise (for these men so desperately need a financial leg-up in order to use their considerable abilities). Now an heiress tends to be particularly infertile because she is so often the only daughter in a family that had no male children. Fisher laments: "This puts in the same class the children of comparatively infertile parents and the men of ability, and their intermarriage has the result of uniting sterility and ability."

When you dissect this preciously absurd argument for its hidden assumptions, sexist and otherwise, you get some sense of Fisher's own background and social biases—and you realize how illusory must be the notion of absolute impartiality, and obedience only to the logic of argument and the dictates of empirical data. Only men rise from lower classes. Infertility is the burden and fault of women. In other words, men advance and women then pull the whole family line down.

6. Fisher summarized the baneful effect of this genetically based inverse correlation between childbearing and social status:

> Whenever, then, the socially lower occupations are the more fertile, we must face a paradox that the biologically successful members of our society are to be found principally among its social failures, and equally that classes of persons who are prosperous and socially successful are, on the whole, the biological failures, the unfit of the struggle for existence, doomed more or less speedily, according to their social distinction, to be eradicated from the human stock.

If the social promotion of infertility is the cause of this destructive inverse correlation, then our only hope for reversal and salvation lies in legislated policies aimed at social *promotion* of the *more fertile*. Fisher advocated some form of payments and bonuses for childbearing, so that lower-class people of both ability *and* fertility would be able to rise—as I said at the outset, a relatively benign form of eugenics.

I need hardly detail the numerous false assumptions that derail Fisher's complex argument. I only note that they represent exactly the same mistake—uncritical acceptance of genetic conjectures—that invalidated his later case for smoking. Why should we assume that people who rise socially do so, in large part, by genetic endowment? And even if this argument is valid, why assume that the well-known negative correlation of childbearing and social status results from differential *genetic* fertility—especially when so many excellent and obvious nongenetic explanations cry out for attention (though Fisher mentions them only in quick derision)—including, as mentioned before, longer years of schooling and delayed marriage, and greater access to contraception and abortion. The first genetic conjecture (a biological basis for social promotion) seems less implausible, though quite unproven; but the second conjecture (a genetic basis for fewer children in the upper classes) seems wildly improbable, even bordering on the absurd. Yet Fisher's case absolutely requires that both genetic conjectures be valid—for if we rise genetically but then have fewer children only for social reasons, then his argument falls apart, for no "social promotion of infertility" would exist.

We may take a kindly view of Fisher's eugenics and say that his genetic conjectures did no harm, for, try as he might in press and before parliament, Fisher's recommendations made no practical headway. But false genetic hypotheses of human behaviors and statuses are politically potent. They represent an ultimate weapon for social conservatives who wish to "blame the victim" for any correctable social ill or inequity. Are workplaces toxic? Screen workers and fire those with genetic predispositions to react badly. Is adequate access available to members of minority races? Argue that these people are inferior by nature and therefore already occupy an appropriate number of slots. The genetic fallacy is generic—and applicable almost anywhere for the all too common and lamentable social aim of preserving an unfair status quo.

We may excuse Fisher's eugenics as relatively harmless, but we cannot be so sanguine about his conceptually similar campaign against a causal link between cancer and smoking. Joan Fisher Box wrote a fine biography of her father, marred only be an understandably hagiographical approach. She depicts Fisher's smoking campaign as rousing good fun for her father, a kind of harmless little game enjoyed by a gadfly against powerful interests. But her last paragraph is chilling, unintentionally so, I suspect:

> In 1958 Fisher was brought into discussion of the evidence in the United States in connection with legal suits expected to be brought to trial against tobacco manufacturers for personal damage caused

> by their products. Early in 1960 he visited the United States at the invitation of a legal firm representing an American tobacco company, whose case was brought to trial in April that year. Other suits were either not brought or were unsuccessful, and the legal pressure on tobacco companies was relieved for a time.

And that, friends, translates into many, many deaths—as pressure to quit and to restrict advertising diminished. Fisher may have been only the tiniest cog in a great machine rolled out by the tobacco industry, but he did contribute. Charles Lamb once wrote a humorous couplet:

> For thy sake, Tobacco I
> Would do anything but die.

Bad and biased arguments can have serious, even deadly, consequences.

1995

GETTING STARTED

1. Analyze the title and first two paragraphs of the essay. On the basis of that introduction, what would you guess that this essay is about? What expectations does Gould set up? What can you deduce about his tone and approach, the argument he is planning to make, or the debate he is planning to enter? At what point in the essay does he return to the material in these first two paragraphs?

2 "Fisher was wrong, and tragically so," according to Gould (p. 247). Summarize the main points Gould makes to support this claim. Describe the two errors Sir Ronald Aylmer Fisher is cited for and explore the ways in which these two errors are connected.

3. Why does Gould pay such attention to the difference between a logical argument and a correct one? Use an example from the essay to explain the difference. In a group, create an example of a logical but incorrect argument.

4. What does Gould mean by "correlation without causation"? Use one example from the essay and one example from your own knowledge or experience to explain the concept. Share your examples in groups. What patterns emerge? Can you think of any significant assumptions in our present-day world that are spoken of as causative but might be only correlative?

5. Gould refers to Fisher's important text as "our profession's Bible" (p. 251), and admits that, as scientists, "we don't like to admit flaws in our saints" (p. 251). Why does Gould use religious metaphors?

In what ways is science like religion? List as many qualities associated with science and with religion as you can think of. What are the overlaps and differences?

WRITING

6. Gould ends the essay by saying, "Bad and biased arguments can have serious, even deadly, consequences." Is he most concerned in this essay with bad arguments or with bad science? In what cases do the two overlap? Write a response to these questions using examples from the essay, from your own experience or knowledge, and from your library or Internet research for question 8 or 9.

7. Write an essay exploring the places where science and religion have different arenas of interest, methods, even audiences, and where those arenas overlap. Use Gould's examples and your own to show some of the differences and overlaps.

USING THE LIBRARY AND THE INTERNET

8. Use the library or a reference database such as Lexis/Nexis that includes a variety of newspapers to find an article describing a new scientific discovery or new data. Then look for information on the same topic in a scholarly, scientific database such as the General Science Index or Comp Medline. Scan your findings, choose a representative article from each search, and note the differences. What level of knowledge does each article assume on the part of its readers? Can you detect any logical flaws, false assumptions, or problems of scientific objectivity in either of the articles you have found?

9. Using Academic Search Elite or another reference database that includes a range of scholarly sources, look up "eugenics." Scan the resulting articles, and choose one or two that seem to connect in interesting ways to Gould's work. Print out the articles or their abstracts, and bring them to class.

MAKING CONNECTIONS

10. Write an essay using concepts from Christopher P. Toumey's "Science in an Old Testament Style" to analyze Gould's argument. To what extent is Fisher's work disproving the links between smoking and cancer an example of "conjuring science"? Explore examples from both essays, as well as from Internet

research, magazine or newspaper articles, or television programs, to show how scientific materials are sometimes used to promote ideas that run counter to scientific ideals or objectives. To what extent might the objectives of scientists and "conjurers" such as advertisers overlap? Do scientists "conjure science" as much as nonscientists do?

11. Write an essay comparing and contrasting Gould's methods for presenting himself to a general audience with Mary Kingsley's methods described in Julie English Early's "The Spectacle of Science and Self." To what extent does each challenge the norms of scientific writing for the time? How does each writer establish his or her authority as a scientist?

12. Use ideas from Gould to analyze Michio Kaku's discussion of the potential uses of DNA in "Second Thoughts: The Genetics of a Brave New World?." Would Gould find logical flaws in some of the arguments that Kaku cites? What criteria does each author use to distinguish good science from bad science? What are some of the possible consequences of bad science? To what extent do bad science and bad arguments overlap?

Zita Ingham

Zita Ingham is Professor of English at Southwestern Oregon Community College, Curry County. She received her doctorate in Rhetoric and Composition from the University of Arizona and her bachelor's degree in Bacteriology from the University of California, Berkeley. "Landscape, Drama, and Dissensus: The Rhetorical Education of Red Lodge, Montana" is excerpted from the essay collection edited by Carl G. Herndl and Stuart C. Brown, *Green Culture: Environmental Rhetoric in Contemporary America* (1996).

To learn more about Red Lodge, read about its history at <http://www.jps.net/gplains/festival/rl_page/rl_hist.htm>.

Landscape, Drama, and Dissensus

The Rhetorical Education of Red Lodge, Montana

Some Better Way to Live

On the night of Friday, 19 June 1992, more than 120 people milled around in the main hall of the Roberts Senior Citizens Center in Red Lodge, Montana. An old Western drama was about to be enacted, with all the usual players: ranchers, townspeople, miners. The central player in the Western drama has always been the land—the land as water, timber, ore, grazing rights, creatures—and the subject of this drama is, as always, land use. Who has, and who will have, the right to do what with the land in and around Red Lodge? The conflict persists, down through the decades—"who runs this town?"—although more sophisticated ways of asking that question have evolved. If indeed the town will build an airport, what part of the landscape would become the runway, the parking area, the flyway? Who owns Rock Creek, the stream that runs through town? Who has the right to walk along it? Who controls—who determines and who benefits from—the zoning and taxing of the supremely developable ranch land surrounding the town? Who decides what constitutes "ownership" and "control" of the land and its resources?

The boundaries between the western dramas of novels and films, and the historical dramas of the West—range wars, Indian wars, all the larger and smaller conflicts over land use—have long been blurred; the qualities of each illuminate the other. In writing about the Western drama, as seen in movies such as *Shane* and *High Noon,* Jane Tompkins and, earlier, Peter Homans investigate this "moral dynamic." For Tompkins, as she argues in *West of Everything: The Inner Life of Westerns,* this dynamic culminates in a "moment of moral ecstasy. The hero is *so right* (that is, so wronged) that he can kill with impunity. . . . The feeling of supreme righteousness in this instant is delicious and hardly to be distinguished from murderousness" (229). She argues that what's most important about this moment—the shoot-out as the moment of righteous violence on which the mythic stories of the West turn—is our ability to reflect on it. This "moment of righteous ecstasy, . . . the moment of murderousness. . . . [is] a moment when there's still time to stop, there's still time to reflect, there's still time to recall what happened in *High Noon,* there's still time to say, 'I don't care who's right or who's wrong. There has to be some better way for people to live' " (233). For Homans, "the key to the Western" is "[t]his process whereby desire is at once indulged and veiled. . . . What is required is that temptation be indulged while providing the appearance of having been resisted" (89). As the transparency of this dynamic of Western films and novels becomes more popularly evident, some communities in the West have begun attempts at living some better way.

This better way, at least for the community of Red Lodge, begins as a traditional Western, as what Homans describes as a "puritan morality tale in which the savior-hero redeems the community from the temptations of the devil" (89). In Red Lodge a group of concerned residents formed the Beartooth Front Community Forum and invited Luther Propst to conduct a series of community dialogue workshops. Propst is executive director of the Sonoran Institute, a nonprofit conservation organization based in Tucson, Arizona, that promotes the Successful Communities Dialogue program as a way to help resolve community disputes. The stage was set: a limited and unstable economic base made land use a charged issue, tensions arose from increasing population and impending development, and polarized factions in the community verbally fought each other. Enter the redemptive stranger, come to put things right and then vanish, leaving behind a more peaceful and productive, not to mention grateful, community.

But this is not the old West. Discussion, argument, legal actions, and decrees replace shoot-outs. Finding a better way to live and to manage environmental issues such as land use rests on language, on the use of language to discover, initiate, persuade, understand, anger, conciliate: on rhetoric. In June 1992, citizens in Red Lodge met to begin a process that has changed the economic, environmental, and sociocultural identity of the town and will continue to do so. Crucial to those changes has been the rhetorical education of many of its residents. Through public forums, workshops, committee meetings, committee reports to the communities, and news stories, residents of Red Lodge began to discuss and argue in public. Where once, for instance, townspeople grumbled about what the owners of large ranches might do when the financial rewards of development exceeded those of ranching, they now meet to develop plans. There is broad-based citizen participation in zoning and environmental impact studies and in grant writing to foster local economic development.

Because these situations—all rhetorical, all dependent on how people are persuaded by the use of language—now exist, residents are learning to articulate what they believe about the community, its past, present, and future, and their actions depend on what they articulate. The Beartooth Front forum meeting on that Friday night and the next day in June 1992 initiated a rhetorical education of active citizens—training and practice in how and what to argue with each other. This essay describes some features of the initial steps of this rhetorical education.

The Rhetoric of Community

Whether we adopt Aristotle's definition of rhetoric as the discovery of "the available means of persuasion" (24), or J. Frederick Crews's notion of rhetoric as "the placement of ideas" (6), or the definition of rhetoric as the possibilities of language to deform as well as formulate the truth of events, places, people, ideas, rhetoric is situated and can be analyzed only in the context of literal and figurative location. A speaker or writer—a rhetor—always occupies a particular ideological, cultural, geographical place from which to speak or write. The rhetor's rhetorical stance, as delineated by Wayne Booth, depends on the contexts of "the available arguments about the subject itself, the interests and peculiarities of the audience, and the voice, the implied character of the speaker" (141). Members of audiences, in turn, listen, read, and respond from their own places. As the messages fly back and forth in communities like Red Lodge, or even as they hang in the air without visible, immediate responses, communication changes the speakers and listeners, the writers and readers themselves, and this exchange can transform both the community and its environment. As M. Jimmie Killingsworth notes, "In addition to changing language and changing minds, the enterprise of rhetoric suggests that speakers and writers have the power to transform the site of discourse, the community itself" (110). In the case of Red Lodge, as in many other locations of environmental disputes, the rhetorical enterprise alters not only the rhetorical landscape, but the physical landscape as well.

The Scene

Red Lodge, Montana (population 2,000), lies at the foot of the Beartooth mountain range, northeast of Yellowstone National Park, and like other Montana towns in the Yellowstone area, Red Lodge is changing rapidly. The area encompassed by the Greater Yellowstone ecosystem—which includes parts of Montana, Idaho, and Wyoming and all of the communities in and around Yellowstone and Grand Teton National Parks and the surrounding national forests—faces particular pressure to resolve issues associated with rapid population growth. The 1990 census shows that if the twenty adjacent counties in this area were considered as one state, it would be the fastest-growing state in the country. Between 1991 and 1992, subdivision activity in Carbon County, where Red Lodge is located, increased 44 percent, most occurring along the Beartooth Front. This figure does not include parcels twenty acres or larger, which are currently exempt from evaluation. Carbon County ranks first in Montana Greater Yellowstone ecosystem counties in land development on a per capita basis ("Successful Communities" 5).

Because of economic and demographic pressures, Red Lodge and towns like it are forced to resolve issues (even if by ignoring them) that will determine qualities of the population and of the environment in the future. To do that, and to insure that the resolutions consider the well-being of as many residents as possible, the citizens of Red Lodge need to learn how to argue better, how to speak and write to each other and to others about these issues. The first requirement for the "rhetorical health" of a community is that opportunities exist for all voices to be heard. Seeking consensus, in the context of a community beginning to grapple with issues of growth, is not perhaps as useful as the thorough exploration of "dissensus." Rhetorical theorist John Trimbur suggests that the goal of consensus in a community may not be as useful as was once thought. Depending on its political context, dissensus can replace consensus as "a powerful instrument . . . to generate differences, . . . and to transform the relations of power that determine who may speak and what counts as a meaningful statement" ("Consensus and Difference" 602). Before communities can approach the resolution of issues, Trimbur suggests,

> we will need to rehabilitate the notion of consensus by redefining it in relation to a rhetoric of dissensus. We will need, that is, to look at collaborative learning not merely as a process of consensus-making but, more importantly, as a process of identifying differences and locating these differences in relation to each other. (610)

Trimbur is speaking about the "community" of a writing classroom, but his insight into consensus and dissensus applies to other, larger communities; as we all know, consensus is notoriously difficult in environmental disputes. In order to resolve their disputes and protect their environment, communities like Red Lodge need to engage in the collaborative learning that characterizes Trimbur's rhetorical education. A community of residents who hold differing opinions about, for instance, whether or not to build an airport for their town must learn to articulate their differences and to explore their different values and how these would shape their environment.

The danger of beginning to talk to each other is always the same: the pressure for consensus, the ultimate requirement of consent, is always uncomfortable. If the nature of events or the community demands consensus, the situation can, paradoxically, dissolve, the rhetorical enterprise break down, and the various factions withdraw, taking with them the chance to resolve the issue. Everyone is aware of this risk; it often constitutes the basis of factional power. Everyone in Red Lodge knows, for example, that drawing larger businesses requires an airport, that airports destroy huge amounts of wildlife habitat, and that, eventually, some residents will have to concede something. That kind of anticipation of concessions inhibits the rhetorical process from the beginning. For Trimbur, as for the organizers of the Beartooth Front Community Forum, "The revised notion of consensus I am proposing here depends paradoxically on its deferral, not its realization" ("Consensus and Difference" 614). This essay describes the way this community and the Sonoran Institute use the strategy of deferred consensus.

The Script

The process of planning a future for Red Lodge was deliberate and initiated by local citizens but catalyzed by outsiders. The rhetorical education of Red Lodge began with the activism of an ad hoc group of citizens, but was guided by a Successful Communities Dialogue workshop developed by the Sonoran Institute. The Sonoran Institute, a nonprofit conservation organization based in Tucson, Arizona, was created in 1990 with technical and financial assistance from the World Wildlife Fund. The institute's mission is to work "nationwide to preserve the integrity of protected natural areas and adjacent communities by cooperatively resolving potential conflicts between conservation and meeting the needs and aspirations of adjacent communities and landowners. The Institute also works to insure that development occurring adjacent to protected areas adheres to the highest level of environmental compatibility and sensitivity" (*Annual Report 1991–1992* i). The institute first began with projects to protect Saguaro National Monument outside Tucson, but now has extended its work throughout the West and into Mexico. The institute is guided by a board of directors that includes conservation and business leaders, and "works with diverse groups (including natural resource managers, landowners, conservation leaders, and local officials) to create and implement tangible projects which link sustainable development and protection of natural resources" (*Annual Report 1991–1992* i). One such project, with the goal of initiating activities at the local level, is the Successful Communities Dialogue workshops. Such workshops (which began in 1988 as a pilot program of the Conservation Foundation, now incorporated in the World Wildlife Fund) have been held in various communities throughout the Greater Yellowstone area. These workshops use something like Killingsworth's idea of the enterprise of rhetoric to resolve environmental disputes and, ultimately, preserve natural resources. The emphasis on deferred consensus is key to the initial stages of community dialogue.

Propst and the Beartooth Front Community Forum organizers argue that community members must develop a consciousness of rhetorical stance, of how citizens stand in relation to each other, given their view points. Community members must become more conscious and more deliberate in their uses of language so that they can know what they want to argue for in relation to Red Lodge and how to go about manifesting and settling those arguments. Increasingly, serious environmental disputes are resolved by outside mediators through a process that leaves existing community relations mostly untouched. In contrast, the rhetorical education promoted in Red Lodge helps communities develop and articulate working relationships themselves. Outside mediators help parties reach agreement relative to a specific conflict, with a process and outcome that may be voluntary or may be legally determined. But in the case of community dialogue, building and remaining a community is the goal, rather than more or less specific consensus. In the literature of environmental mediation, where building community is more likely to be seen as the "socialization of opponents" (Lake 62), leaving antagonisms and misunderstandings intact, less than ideal valuations of "community" are evident. In his investigation of the dynamics of mediation, Scott Mernitz uses social and psychological research into the nature of community conflict to argue for the positive social effects of mediation:

> conflict tends to act in group-binding and group-preserving capacity. Conflict maintains, rather than disrupts, the well-balanced society by facilitating communication and defining relationships and group structures, so as to clarify for a participant his position and status relative to others. . . . conflict and the ensuing settlement establish and maintain the balance of power, so that a legitimate distribution of resources is achieved. Parties perceive themselves *in equilibrium*—a condition that is the desired end of most conflict situations. (51)

In this view, mediation—the search for a resolution of conflict that has escalated into litigation—seems successful when a balance of power is reached. In contrast, community dialogue has as its goal not equilibrium, but connection.

A crucial difference between the approach of community dialogue and that of mediation is in the timing of intervention in the community's history and in assumptions about the rhetorical effectiveness of community members and factions. The Sonoran Institute tries to intervene early in the process because it believes individuals can develop the rhetorical skills and set up the rhetorical situations that prevent litigious conflicts. Mediators, on the other hand, generally intervene only at the eleventh hour and use their knowledge of rhetorical skills and situations to facilitate agreements, not to facilitate the education of community members in ways to reach agreements on their own. Thus, the Sonoran Institute's idea of rhetorical dialogue about the environment ties the health of the environment to the rhetorical health of the community. If environmental health can be defined as the flourishing of diverse species, then rhetorical health denotes the flourishing of diverse voices.

The rhetorical education of Red Lodge began with this workshop in June 1992. The objectives of the two-day forum, conducted by Luther Propst, were "(1) to bring together diverse citizens, organizations, and government agencies to identify local values and assets, develop a vision for the future of the community and identify practical and tangible steps for realizing this vision; and (2) to provide a forum and process for informed communications and consensus-building that transcend the limits of single-value advocacy and special interest politics" ("Successful Communities" 3). These objectives are fundamentally rhetorical in nature: bringing members of the community into dialogue with each other, articulating a vision of the community's future and steps toward the manifestation of that vision (which only exists in language), and providing outlets and strategies for "informed communication." In essence, the workshop was a place, a situation, to display the value of skill in rhetoric, and to argue that changes in the community and its natural environment depend first on the kinds of rhetorical choices citizens make.

Advance Notice

The crucial step in this process of rhetorical education was to provide a forum for discussion. The rhetoric surrounding the invitation to discuss the town's future is an example of how rhetorical education begins with the demonstration and modeling of strategies, attitudes, rhetorical stances. In studying events at Red Lodge, Kenneth Burke's rhetorical concept of "identification" is useful, because the impetus for the entire process of planning the community's future depends on the reinforcement of Red Lodge *as* a community. The crucial strategy is an attitude of social cohesion: the adoption, by individuals, of a common identity from which to act together. In Burke's words,

> "Identification" at its simplest is also a deliberative device, as when the politician seeks to identify himself with his audience. . . . But identification can also be an end, as when people earnestly yearn to identify themselves with some group or other. Here they are not necessarily being acted upon by a conscious external agent, but may be acting upon themselves to this end. ("Rhetoric—Old and New" 203)

The persuasive aim of the forum was to enable residents to envision themselves as a community—"acting upon themselves" by identifying with each other, by establishing stances in relationship to each other. In the context of the discussion at Red Lodge, the "external agent," the Sonoran Institute, uses the desire to facilitate identification between individuals within the community as a persuasive strategy—as a way of increasing its credibility in the community and as a way of demonstrating the power of such a strategy, such an attitude. All of the forum activities—the presentations by community members and by outside "experts," the recounting of regional and individual histories, the small and large group discussions—are strategies to increase group identification among community members.

Identification began with flyers posted around town in early June announcing that the Beartooth Front Community Forum (the group "dedicated to forging cooperative solutions to the challenges of tomorrow," as noted on the flyer) would be sponsoring a community dialogue, a Friday evening and all-day Saturday event to which "You're Invited! Share your thoughts about growth and economic development, preservation, and other important matters affecting you and your family." The sponsoring group, although anonymous, makes an appeal to its audience based on its credibility as constructed on the flyer: the group is "dedicated," earnest in recognizing and valiant in meeting the "challenges of tomorrow," and fair, not elitest but "cooperative." The flyer's authors also display the virtuous aim of including as many residents as possible in the invitation; the forum was advertised as "FREE," and "Lunch will be provided on Saturday. Babysitting is available if needed." Citizens were not only invited to lunch, but also to "Please lend a hand!" to participate in "forging cooperative solutions to the challenges of tomorrow." The initial anonymity of the group prevented its being dismissed because of objections to certain members, and no doubt such an appeal would draw the skeptical—those wondering who these people were and what they were planning—as well as those who wished to become proponents for change. Anonymity also prevented the forum from being perceived as a closed group. Cooperation and inclusion are further emphasized by the question posed in the largest type on the flyer, "WHAT KIND OF FUTURE WOULD YOU CHOOSE FOR RED LODGE AND THE BEARTOOTH FRONT?" The flyer invites identification with the community at large by suggesting that every community member can have a voice in planning. Over 120 residents attended the opening session of the workshop, more than 5 percent of the population of the town.

The Lights Dim: Opening Shots

The Friday evening session of the workshop began with an invocation by Kent Young, a Red Lodge attorney, to remember that these meetings were not about "what we *don't* want the community to be, but what we *want* the community to be." The question at the core of the long-standing Western dilemma—"who runs this town?"—is revised, cast positively, if a bit more vaguely: "What do you want Red Lodge to be?" The answer being formulated here assumes that individuals who make up the community will have the opportunity and ability to decide and to act on achieving those goals. For the moment—for as long as possible—the naiveté of these assumptions is suspended, as the organizers and other residents tacitly agree to participate.

The program begins with a visually rich, unabashedly emotional appeal to an idealistic sense of community in general, and an ideal sense of Red Lodge in particular. The audience watches a slide montage, by local photographer Merv Coleman, entitled "Red Lodge, A Place for All Seasons": fields of flowers, quaint downtown views, rodeo scenes, children playing in the snow, dancers at the town festival, all set to John Denver's sentimental and familiar "Season Suite" ("Oh, I love the life around me"). The audience oohs and aahs at the scenes, whispering to each other the names of particular places and people as they appear. Afterward, the moderator acknowledges the show as "meant to bring a tear to your eye." The strength of persuasion that rests on just such an arousal of the audience's emotions was articulated by Aristotle, who argued the importance of this appeal of *pathos*:

> Particularly in political oratory . . . it adds much to an orator's influence that his own character should look right and that he should be thought to entertain the right feelings towards his hearers; and also that his hearers themselves should be in just the right frame of mind. . . . The Emotions are all those feelings that so change men as to affect their judgements. (91)

A sentimental view of Red Lodge appeals emotionally, but the program organizers cannot allow the audience to feel it is being manipulated, because that would undercut the program's *ethos,* its credibility. *Ethos* rests on the appeal of a speaker's character who "should be thought to entertain the right feelings towards his hearers." The argument for community connections rests on the perceptions that the program organizers have moral authority, that they are committed to what's best for the community but not domineering in their methods.

The *pathos,* the emotional appeal of the arguments, is established, as is the *ethos*—the credibility, good will, and intelligence—of the program organizers. The work that remains is to get down to the subject at hand: Red Lodge, as it exists now and as it is envisioned. The program completes the triumvirate of Aristotle's modes of persuasion by moving on to *logos,* rational appeals. The appeals to logic—the most basic being the various reasons why Red Lodge, as an entire community, needs to plan for its future—begin with a series of speakers, of whom Luther Propst will be the last. The speakers are public figures and experts, specialists in the issues that affect the community. The rhetorical intention of this part of the program is to ground the discussions in evidence from authorities, to encourage participation, and to set the context—one of reasoned discussion—for tomorrow's workshop. The desired rhetorical effect is a commitment to action.

John Prinkki, a Carbon County commissioner, notes fundamental changes in the area: growth in Red Lodge and the paradoxical decline in the tax base. Because of the lack of oil revenue in recent years, the tax base has dropped from $30 million to $17 million. He asserts the county's commitment to working with businesses, and reiterates what residents often say: "We are looking for better than service industry jobs; we need a diverse business community." He ends by citing two instances of lack of city/county planning that have created problems: the inability of the county to maintain existing roads while building new, outlying roads, and a development, the Country Club Estates, that continues to draw heavily on tax money because of a lack of controls on the developer. Prinkki aligns himself with his listeners by asserting that their concerns are his. He argues that Red Lodge has severe economic problems, some of which could be averted by better planning and by controls on development.

Other speakers include Barbara Campbell, head of a private community development consulting firm and author of the 1989 Carbon County Economic Development Plan, who speaks on the three greatest needs of the area: adequate infrastructure (roads, sewage), affordable housing, and jobs. The most polemical, and also the most knowledgeable, of the speakers, she warns that "big developers *will* come, and they can easily take away any chance you have for self-direction."

The participation of speakers such as Prinkki and Campbell, who are the most knowledgeable about the economic issues of the county, insures that the dialogue proceeds from a foundation of authority, of facts. Both authorities argue for planning, but implicit in these arguments is the notion that the environment is at risk because of economic development. It is assumed, by the speakers, the program organizers, and the audience, that challenges to the environmental health of the community will result from the growth of its economy.

Whether or not this assumption is valid, it underlies the entire workshop. Campbell's final remark, that developers are set to pounce on Red Lodge, is especially motivating, because anyone in the audience can reel off the names of small western communities that did not muster the resources and vision to remain "livable" as they grew. What these speakers most strongly argue for, based on the logic of their knowledge and experience, is immediate action.

The Hero: Where's the Shoot-out?

Luther Propst begins his presentation by establishing his own ethical appeal: as a former Washington lawyer, who worked there for the World Wildlife Fund, he tells a self-denigrating and actually funny lawyer joke, about the obsolescence of lab rats, who are being replaced by Washington lawyers because these occur in greater numbers and because "there are some things even rats won't do." In beginning his logical appeal, he cites demographic trends in particular counties in the Greater Yellowstone area, thereby assuring the audience that he's an expert, even though he's an outsider—perhaps an expert in ways only an outsider can be. He has a slide show of his own, displaying results of lack of planning for conservation from around the country. The scenes are familiar to anyone who has traveled even a little: conversion of farmland to suburbs, loss of regional architectural character and degradation of historical features because of commercial development, obliteration of landscape features, human conflict with wildlife. He contrasts these with views of instances of effective planning: clustered housing, retention of local architecture in commercial development, protection of views and wildlife habitat. He emphasizes the goal of these workshops: that residents of Red Lodge can set an agenda for action, whatever that agenda and action may be, but only if they act quickly and as a community. The urgency to act has been established by Prinkki and Campbell as well; Propst underscores it, and takes the further steps of suggesting concrete possibilities.

Propst argues that the real power to effect conservation and preservation is always at the local level. He briefly delineates factors that "successful communities" have drawn on to best enact this power, including special physical aspects of the community, shared community vision, and proactive policies. Most important to successful communities is the willingness to look beyond ecological and economic factors to the quality of the lives of all community members and to work beyond laying down regulations, which, in Propst's words, "are too blunt a tool with which to fashion a livable community." Propst cites the need for "hometown heroes"—local individuals who can channel energy into constructive rather than divisive agendas, who cultivate responsible, local developers, and who remain active to ensure plans are implemented and developments monitored.

In describing the factors of such communities, Propst constructs an ideal that Red Lodge can aspire to, while maintaining that this ideal has been successfully approximated in other places. To return to Burke's concept of identification, which "includes the realm of transcendence" ("Rhetoric—Old and New" 203), "The machinery of language is so made that things are necessarily placed in terms of a range broader than the terms for those things themselves" (*Language as Symbolic Action* 200). At the heart of the strategies used by Propst and the organizers of the forum are those that draw on transcending the view of Red Lodge as it is today, on Richard Weaver's ideal function of rhetoric, which, "at its truest seeks to perfect men by showing them better versions of themselves" (16). And better versions of their communities.

Propst ends with a series of rhetorical devices. He enhances his ethos, the credibility of his character, and disarms anticonservation arguments by citing research that shows that the economic vitality of a community is intimately connected to the quality of life of all inhabitants—that scenery does indeed provide jobs. He underscores his authority by elaborating on problems in nearby communities, such as those faced in relation to the proposed Targhee Ski Resort expansion in Driggs, Idaho, where, Propst suggests, residents have not yet identified common interests and goals. He casts the workshop experience itself positively, differentiating it from contentious public hearing processes, and suggests that nearby communities that face seemingly insurmountable problems have attempted too late the process the forum demonstrates, providing further motivation for the residents of Red Lodge to begin work now.

These presentations have moved from community members and to authoritative outsiders, from emotional appeals to appeals based on the credibility and authority of the speakers. The local presenters rely more on identification with the audience based on devotion to their hometown and its inhabitants, while the outside authorities use quantifiable information about the economic situation, or about cases of similar situations and outcomes in other communities. The combined rhetorical thrust, the major argument for action, rests on the premise that Red Lodge suffers from a variety of economic woes that will increase as environmental degradation increases, given present economic and demographic trends. The desired rhetorical outcome is the motivation of citizens to discuss and reach consensus on an agenda for action, although not yet to reach consensus on particular actions.

By forestalling consensus on particular decisions and actions the community should take, forum organizers hoped to solidify individual commitments to the community and to action on its behalf. Propst argues that the community can begin to create its agenda when it begins to identify where there is consensus, where there is not, and where there are degrees of consensus. To return to Trimbur's critique of "community" in the literature of rhetoric and social theory, "the ideal of community participates in . . . a metaphysics that denies difference" ("Ideal of the Community" 1). Although, as Trimbur believes, "the desire for mutual understanding and reciprocity underlying the ideal of community is similar to the desire for identification that underlies racial and ethnic chauvinism"—a community is defined by what it excludes—Propst aims for a wider definition of community in Red Lodge. Propst suggests that residence and action, not degree of conformation to viewpoints, determine membership in the community, and that the idea of community in Red Lodge admits differences, and in fact those differences are to be studied. The danger for the community is not lack of consensus on an issue, but divisiveness that prevents any possibility of action. While the Sonoran Institute is a proponent of environmental conservation and historical preservation, not interested in mediating neutral solutions, in this forum Propst's purposes are to increase awareness of options for resolving issues, not to push particular resolutions.

Audience as Actors

Saturday's forum begins with stories. Two residents speak; a local rancher in his sixties gives a brief history of ranching in Carbon County, and a young housewife and nurse recounts her personal history in Red Lodge. Both cover the changes in the area, recent and not so recent, and cite shared histories in support of the communal effort required today and in the future. Albert Ellis tells of one Montana pioneer who, when asked on his ninetieth birthday if he'd seen a lot of changes in his lifetime, answered, "You bet I have, sonny, and I voted against every one of them." In recounting the changes that have affected ranching, Ellis reminds us that, however stubborn Montanans are, change will come, and citizens need to direct it. Kim Shelley relies on a personal, emotional appeal to make her point: how her family were forced for economic reasons to move away for part of her childhood, and now she's grateful to be back. She reminds the audience of the biggest snowstorm last winter, and how cars parked in the streets were buried: "We all wondered, why do we live here? But that's why—because of nature." She shares her worries about having to leave again, forever, if the hospital, presently in a financially precarious position, should have to close, and reminds us that despite what she loves about living in a small town, a higher population would mean saving the hospital. She ends with a plea for concerted effort: "I know I just can't not try to give something back to this town." The audience, most of whom are at least acquainted with Ellis and Shelley, identify with the historical and personal narratives that range across time, gender, age, and profession and which constitute an acknowledgment of the foundation of the community (or an idealized view of that foundation): hard times, the identity of the region based on the difficulties encountered here, that identity in opposition to what lies beyond it, changes past, changes to come. Taken together, the two narratives set a rhetorical stage, a context in which discussion of community values will take place in a different light. Ellis and Shelley have modeled their stories, their rhetorical stances as community members, and now the other residents take up this same task in smaller groups.

All the other narratives come spilling out as audience members introduce themselves to each other in these smaller, randomly formed groups of nine or ten. For example, one group is facilitated by Keith Zimmer, owner of a T-shirt business on Red Lodge's main street, and includes a rancher's wife, housewives, a teacher, a city roads worker, the owner of a secretarial business, a ski resort worker. Their talk about positive aspects of living in Red Lodge provides common ground for the rest of the discussion. This common ground elicits Burkean identification and demonstrates the usefulness of story *as* argument, as Walter R. Fisher points out in *Human Communication as Narration:* "The world as we know it is a set of stories that must be chosen among in order for us to live life in a process of continual re-creation" (5). What these stories argue for, explicitly and implicitly, is action to preserve qualities of Red Lodge. In this group, Nancy Krekeler's story, for instance, is about how she left a lucrative job in Washington, D.C. years ago to join the working class of Red Lodge: "Tourists thought we all were twins, when they'd see us in the morning helping them onto the skilift and in the evening waiting on them at dinner. . . . Everyone gives up something to be here, whether you've always lived here or you're from somewhere else." Bob Holm, a city roads worker, recounts how he used to make his living working construction in other parts of the country, how his kids were really raised by his wife alone. These stories, and indeed all the stories and conversation that day, argue for particular visions of Red Lodge, past and future.

Even in the first round of discussion, the group is tempted to jump ahead to the town's problems, past defining "what we love about Red Lodge." Within five minutes, Bob Holm is wondering aloud if the town could ever pass a resort tax to pay for infrastructure development; Ruth Uebar says she thinks some development is good, that the golf course fits in with the atmosphere of the town, and then Mike Beye complains that the streets leading out of the golf course development look like "7-11 territory; is a strip mail next?" Zimmer calls them back to the task at hand, and the group devises a list of the town's positive attributes: its western flavor, natural environment, physical safety, political diversity, spirit of giving and openness, and its access to wilderness, health care, and skiing. People in the group state that what they like most is always meeting friends all over town, at the post office and stores, and "being able to hold a conversation with a 'wrong number' on the phone." Members of the group all agree that they don't want outside developers "to be able to do *anything*." After an hour, the small groups break up to form the large group (about ninety people in all), and the facilitators of each group report their group members' lists of attributes. The next two rounds of discussion proceed similarly.

In this way every participant at the meeting is guaranteed a voice, and at this point no hierarchy of problems or solutions is established, so all concerns can be expressed. In these discussions, individuals express concern over degradation of the environment as easily as concern over lack of economic opportunity, and these concerns are not seen as conflicting. Participants are tempted to voice their personal concerns and solutions, but because each group must report its results for the question being put to it, discussion irrelevant to the task is held in check.

In the third round of dialogue, the groups identify specific steps to meet threats and achieve goals. The group agrees on the needs to organize, to use the public forums—the newspaper, meetings like this, town government meetings—to insure better communication among the townspeople, to gather information about property restrictions and zoning, to establish committees to research and initiate action on particular issues. Imagining the individuals likely to be on these committees, the group begins to wonder, what's to stop committee members from acting out of special interests or not acting at all? Propst joins the group and points out that the first objective is to establish committees that will continue the dialogue, not solve problems or take positions on issues yet, and that diversity of committee membership is crucial to success. The priorities are community dialogue and recognition of dissensus. The rhetorical processes that may eventually facilitate consensus on particular issues—the processes, strategies, attitudes that individuals and committees use to persuade other people to align themselves with particular views and actions—depend on both the sense of community (the feeling that the people of the town are connected to each other in ways that benefit them) and the sense of diversity (that both individuals and the larger group will accommodate "other" viewpoints and actions).

Intermission: Implications

That a "rhetorical education" of Red Lodge began with this forum is seen by the continued dialogue in the public discourse of the town; the success of this education is seen in the activities and achievements of citizen groups originating at the June 1992 forum. In the months following the first forum, criticism of the workshop and meetings circulated, and response to rumors provided a forum for organizers and participants to further their work. In August 1992, these comments from the organizers appeared in a letter to the editor of the *Montana Free Press:*

> We'd also like to take this opportunity to state again that the Beartooth Front Community Forum is a non-political community-based organization. We have no agenda and are not supported by any interest groups. While we hope to inspire people to express their opinions, the Forum as a body does not take stands. Our sole goal is to involve as many people as possible in discussions about planning for our community's future. (Beartooth Front Community Forum Steering Committee 3)

In November, the contradictory rumors that the Beartooth Front Community Forum is a front for developers and that its purpose is to halt all development were countered in another letter from the steering committee, appearing in the same newspaper, explaining that

> The Community Forum is not an "it"—a political organization with positions or an agenda. The Community Forum is a process, a *vehicle,* through which any and all residents of the area can try to have a voice in the future of their home. ("Thanks From the Forum Front" 4).

In the March 1993 "Beartooth Front Community Forum Progress Report," the authors conclude with an emotional appeal that valorizes the sense of a community made up of individuals who hold different viewpoints:

> Those involved in the Forum (as well as those on the sidelines) have been impressed with the scope and energy of their fellow volunteers. Many expected the community would not find such consensus; others expected that projects would not get off the ground so quickly; still others that enthusiasm would wane. Those expectations have been dashed magnificently. . . . the journey—the process—has been as exciting as its results. We have come together, in our disparate beliefs and needs and ambitions, to affirm our love for this area. We have come together to dream about its future, and share those dreams. We have seen how similar the dreams are, how within the realm of possibility. And in that process we have come together as that wondrous and often elusive entity, a community. (Beartooth Front Community Forum 7)

The forum participants tie the ideal of community to the ideal of every voice being heard, replacing, momentarily, the typical view of consensus, in which all community members agree to viewpoints and courses of action. They see consensus, as Trimbur does, as not necessarily "an acculturative practice that reproduces business as usual" but "as an oppositional one that challenges the prevailing conditions of production" ("Consensus and Difference" 614).

These kinds of sophisticated rhetorical moves continue: more letters to the editor, two more well-attended public forums with significant numbers of new participants, increased interest in local government as measured by attendance at town meetings. Committees formed at the end of the first forum, on 23 June 1992, have, by the persuasive strategies in their grant writing, received grants totaling over $300,000 to initiate a planning process for the town and its surrounding one-mile area, to establish water quality testing of the town's creek, to study the creation of a local development corporation, and to construct a site near the town for viewing local elk herds. The community of Red Lodge, through effective rhetorical work that realizes an agenda driven by both economic and environmental health, is forging some better way to live.

Red Lodge, 1995: The Sequel

Lest this movie seem saddled with an unrealistically happy ending, the results visible three years after the first Successful Communities Dialogue workshop continue to point to tangible successes. A specific, broad-based planning process has been established, led by the Beartooth Front Alliance, which enjoys the support of a wide range of citizens, including the chamber of commerce, a group of quilters who raise funds, and a group of ranchers. The Alliance is currently completing a planning initiative—funded by $20,000 from the city council—that has developed from several meetings, each attended by about a hundred people, over the last six months. Smaller but very important projects have developed as well: volunteer water quality monitors continue to gather data on the Rock Creek drainage, and the town now has a Boys and Girls Club that serves two hundred children, with an average of sixty children participating every weekday afternoon.

The Alliance has narrowed its focus to the town of Red Lodge for the present, although they continue to solicit rural participants especially, sometimes by inviting ranchers and cowboys to speak at the meetings. While the town has not implemented all the ideas that came out of the first meetings, successful planning efforts and other projects contribute to a heightened sense of shared community and viable opportunities in the town. These would not have developed without the community's deliberate and inclusive rhetorical activities, facilitated by the Beartooth Front Alliance and the Successful Communities workshops.

1996

Works Cited

Aristotle. *The Rhetoric and the Poetics of Aristotle.* Trans. W. Rhys Roberts and Ingram Bywater. New York: Modern Library, 1984.

Beartooth Front Community Forum. "Progress Report." March 1992.

Beartooth Front Community Forum Steering Committee. Letter to the editor. *Montana Free Press*, August 1992, 3.

Beartooth Front Community Forum Steering Committee. "Thanks from the Forum Front." *Montana Free Press,* November 1992.

Booth, Wayne C. "The Rhetorical Stance." *College Composition and Communication* 14 (1963): 139–145.

Burke, Kenneth. *Language as Symbolic Action: Essays on Life, Literature, and Method.* Berkeley: U of California P, 1966.

Burke, Kenneth. "Rhetoric—Old and New." *Journal of General Education* 5 (April 1951): 203.

Crews, Frederick, and Ann Jesse Van Sant. *The Random House Handbook.* 4th ed. New York: Random House, 1984.

Ferguson, Gary. "Guest Opinion: Beartooth Front Forum Advocates Public Involvement in Planning Issues." *Montana Free Press,* November 1992, 6.

Fisher, Walter. *Human Communication as Narration: Toward a Philosophy of Reason, Value, and Action.* Columbia: U of South Carolina P, 1987.

Homans, Peter. "The Western: The Legend and the Cardboard Hero." *Look,* 13 March 1962, 82–89.

Killingsworth, M. Jimmie. "Discourse Communities—Local and Global." *Rhetoric Review* 11 (1992): 110–122.

Lake, Laura. " Characterizing Environmental Mediation." *Environmental Mediation: The Search for Consensus.* Boulder, CO: Westview P, 1980.

Mernitz, Scott. *Mediation of Environmental Disputes: A Sourcebook.* New York: Praeger, 1980.

Propst, Luther, and Trudy Halvorson. "Successful Communities in Greater Yellowstone; Revised Draft, May 13, 1993." Tucson: Sonoran Institute, 1993.

"The Sonoran Institute Annual Report, 1991–1992." Tucson: Sonoran Institute, 1992.

"Successful Communities Dialogue." Tucson: Sonoran Institute, 1992.

Tompkins, Jane. *West of Everything: The Inner Life of Westerns.* New York: Oxford UP, 1992.

Trimbur, John. "Consensus and Difference in Collaborative Learning." *College English* 51 (1989): 601–616.

Trimbur, John. "The Ideal of the Community and the Politics of Difference." *Social Theory and Practice* 12 (Spring 1986): 110–121.

Weaver, Richard. *Ethics of Rhetoric.* Chicago: Henry W. Regnery, 1953.

GETTING STARTED

1. In a group, discuss the genre of the Western and list its elements. Name some recent examples of Westerns. Next, discuss what Ingham sees as specifically "Western" about Red Lodge's problems and its proposed solutions. Use particular examples from Ingham's essay to help explain your interpretation.

2. Look up the word "rhetoric" in your dictionary. Then, in your journal, discuss what Ingham means by "rhetorical education." How does the dictionary definition compare with your sense of what Ingham means by the term? How does rhetoric contribute to solving the problems of Red Lodge?

3. Find two passages in Ingham's essay where she discusses the concepts of "consensus" and "dissensus." Write a paragraph explaining what Ingham means by the terms and exploring the positive and negative aspects of each.

WRITING

4 Write a short paper comparing and contrasting the give-and-take methods used by the different constituencies in Red Lodge with a situation you have witnessed or know about in which a group had to reach a potentially contentious decision. What rhetorical methods were used in each case, and what was learned from those methods? What level of rhetorical education took place in each case?

5. What does Ingham mean by ethical appeals (ethos), emotional appeals (pathos), and logical appeals (logos)? Write a letter to a local editor, governmental representative, or community group in which you make use of one or more of these forms of appeal on behalf of a cause you care about. In a group, analyze the letters to decide which forms of appeal are being implemented by each writer, which approaches seem the most convincing, and why.

6. Bring in flyers for campus or local events, direct mail from charities, newspaper editorials or articles, or ads from local or national political campaigns. Analyze the rhetoric. How do your examples construct their audience? What are they "selling"? What type of appeals (ethos, pathos, logos) do they use? Write a paper discussing your findings. Be sure to attach a copy of the flyer, letter, or other document that your paper refers to.

USING THE LIBRARY AND THE INTERNET

7. In a database that includes a range of scholarly sources, such as Academic Search Elite, use the search terms "environment and argument" or "environment and debate" to find another example of an environmental issue that has created community dissension. What movie genre might you use to describe the community debate around this issue: action, horror, science fiction? Bring the article and your notes to class.

MAKING CONNECTIONS

8. Write an essay in which you build a definition of "rhetoric" using quotations and examples from Ingham's essay, and use it to identify problems involving rhetoric in Witold Rybczynski's "Designs

for Escape," Haunani-Kay Trask's "From a Native Daughter," or Patricia J. Williams's "The Ethnic Scarring of American Whiteness." In each case, what are the problems involving language, and what solutions might a "rhetorical education" provide?

9. Use Ingham's discussion of rhetorical methods, (such as ethos, logos, pathos, and identification) to write an essay analyzing the ways in which advertisers market their products as described in Stuart Ewen's "The Marriage Between Art and Commerce." For example, how do Ewen's examples of the connections between image and desire function as rhetorical education?

10. How is Stephen Jay Gould's discussion of Sir Ronald Aylmer Fisher in "The Smoking Gun of Eugenics" a version of "rhetorical education"? Write an essay exploring how Gould uses rhetorical appeals (ethos, logos, pathos, and identification) as he tries to shake up the received consensus about Fisher in the scientific community. Does Gould make use of rhetorical strategies other than the ones that Ingham describes?

Michio Kaku

Michio Kaku (1947–) is Henry Semat Professor of Theoretical Physics at the City College and the Graduate Center of the City University of New York. In addition to teaching and lecturing at universities around the world, Kaku hosts a weekly hour-long radio program on science. He has also appeared on television news shows and in several documentaries. Of his nine books, the last two, *Hyperspace: A Scientific Odyssey Through Parallel Universes, Time Warps, and the Tenth Dimension* (1995) and *Visions: How Science Will Revolutionize the Twenty-first Century* (1997), were written for popular audiences and became international bestsellers. "Second Thoughts: The Genetics of a Brave New World?" is a chapter from *Visions.*

To learn more about Michio Kaku or to ask him a question, go to <http://www.mkaku.org/>.

Second Thoughts

The Genetics of a Brave New World?

There are some things about which we must simply say you can't do.

—James Watson

Any attempt to shape the world and modify human personality in order to create a self-chosen pattern of life involves many unknown consequences. Human destiny is bound to remain a gamble, because at some unpredictable time and in some unforeseeable manner nature will strike back.

—René Dubos, *Mirage of Health,* 1959

The very reductionism to the molecular level that is fueling the medical revolution also poses the greatest moral challenge we face. We need to decide to what extent we want to design our descendants.

—Arthur Caplan, University of Pennsylvania Center for Bioethics

THE DNA REVOLUTION gives us at least two startling divergent visions of the future. One vision, promoted by the biotech industry, is that of health and prosperity: gene therapy will eliminate hereditary diseases and possibly cure cancer, bioengineering will create new drugs to vanquish infectious diseases, and gene splicing will create new animals and plants which will feed the world's exploding population.

However, a much darker vision of the future was painted by Aldous Huxley in his unsettling yet prophetic book *Brave New World,* written in 1932, with the world still reeling from the unremitting savagery unleashed by World War I and from the grinding poverty of the Great Depression.

The novel is set six hundred years in the future, when a similar series of disastrous wars have convinced the world's leaders to impose a radical new order. Recoiling from the chaos of the past, they decide to impose a Utopia based on happiness and stability, rather than concepts that have proven to be inherently unstable and messy, such as democracy, freedom, and justice. To be unhappy is against the law of the land. And the key to this state-mandated paradise is biotechnology.

Babies are mass-produced in huge embryo factories and are cloned to produce a caste system of Alpha, Beta, Gamma, Delta, and Epsilon human beings. By restricting the oxygen given to the embryos, scientists can cause selective brain damage and clone an army of obedient workers. The most brain-damaged are the Epsilon morons, subhumans who are carefully brainwashed into happily doing all the menial labor in society. The highest caste are the Alphas, who are, by contrast, carefully groomed and educated to become the ruling elite. Happiness is guaranteed by incessant, numbing brainwashing and unlimited access to mind-dulling drugs and sex.

The world was scandalized by Huxley's outrageous novel, and many attempts were made to censor it. Ironically, events have outpaced even Huxley's fertile imagination. In the 1950s he wrote: "I projected it six hundred years into the future. Today, it seems quite possible that the horror may be upon us within a single century."[1] But even a century may seem too long; already, many of his technological predictions are within grasp.

Huxley's predictions were certainly prophetic. He wrote in a time when the laws of embryonic development were largely unknown. Less than forty years later, however, Louise Brown, the first "test tube baby," was born. By the 1980s, parents had a wide selection of commercially available birthing options: embryos can be frozen and then thawed out years later, infertile couples could employ surrogate mothers to bear their children, and even grandmothers could give birth to their own grandchildren (by having the fertilized egg taken from their grown daughter implanted into their uterus). And with the coming of the biomolecular revolution, many of his other predictions may also be within reach—human cloning, selective breeding, and so on.

Therefore the question must be asked: which future will we choose?

In this chapter, I will look at how the biomolecular revolution will impact on society, for better or for worse. Few will dispute the tremendous accomplishments and potential of the biomolecular revolution. However, even the creators of the revolution have expressed reservations about the moral and ethical direction of this revolution if its excesses are not checked. In a democracy, only informed debate by an educated citizenry can make the mature decisions about a technology so powerful that we can dream of controlling life itself.

Nuclear Energy vs. Genetic Revolution

The awesome scientific knowledge that will be unveiled early in the next century must be tempered by the enormous ethical, social, and political questions that it raises. One framework in which to discuss the implications of the biomolecular revolution is to compare it with the nuclear revolution.

Biomolecular scientists are determined to avoid the kind of blunders committed in atomic energy research, which was originally conducted in total secrecy under the cloak of "national security." Because there was little democratic discussion of the implications of atomic energy, the United States is now faced with seventeen leaking nuclear weapons dumps, which may cost upward of $500 billion to clean up. The human price is incalculable; unethical radiation experiments were conducted on 20,000 unsuspecting human subjects since the 1940s, including injecting plutonium into the veins of innocent patients, releasing radioactive materials over populated areas, and exposing pregnant women.

Mindful of this parallel, the originators of the Human Genome Project set aside 3 percent of the budget for what they called the Ethical, Legal, and Social Implications Branch (ELSI) of the Human Genome Project. It is the first time in history that a crash government project has ever devoted even a fraction of its resources to larger societal questions.

One danger that both supporters and critics of the technology fear is the equivalent of a Three Mile Island—i.e., a catastrophic accident due largely to human error, design flaws, or inadequate testing that could endanger the lives of millions and give the entire industry a black eye.

But there is an important difference between the atomic and biomolecular revolutions. It is possible, to some degree, to control the proliferation of nuclear weapons because of the tens of billions of dollars in resources necessary to develop a large nuclear infrastructure, complete with enrichment facilities, reactors, and top nuclear scientists. One cannot simply start up a nuclear program in one's basement. For example, the flow of enriched uranium and plutonium is restricted via stringent security measures, which has been one of the principal reasons only a handful of nations possess nuclear weapons today.[2] The genie cannot be put back into the bottle, but we can limit the number of genies set loose on the world.

The nature of bioengineering is radically different. With only a modest $10,000 investment, one can conduct biotech experiments in one's living room and begin to manipulate the genome of plants and animals. With a few million, one can create a fledgling biotech industry. The low initial investment, high return, and potential for feeding its people are some reasons why a poor nation such as Cuba has decided to jump into biotechnology.

But this also means that biotechnology is impossible to contain. One cannot restrict the flow of DNA; it's everywhere. Because the technology can never be entirely banned, it is important to discuss and decide which of the various technologies should be allowed to flourish and which ones should be restricted, either via governmental fiat or by social and political pressure.

You Can't Recall a Crop

Jane Rissler of the Union of Concerned Scientists worries that the lack of proper oversight may release a seemingly harmless gene into our food supply which may cause life-threatening allergies to the unwary customer. (Banana genes, for example, have been inserted into tomatoes; such tomatoes could be unwittingly eaten by children with severe allergies to bananas.) Rebecca Goldburg, senior scientist at the Environmental Defense Fund, points out that there are 5 million people with food allergies ranging from mild to life-threatening. Goldburg recounts the recent case of a soybean that was engineered to contain a gene from the Brazil nut. Subsequent testing by the company showed that it was allergenic and could have caused life-threatening shock if the product had been prematurely released to the public.[3]

Critics also worry that the FDA is approving new foods for the supermarket without adequate testing, while the Department of Agriculture allows companies to do field testing without permits. "I think they've taken a good idea and taken it too far," concludes Rebecca Goldburg.[4]

Under pressure from powerful agribusiness interests to cut red tape, the Department of Agriculture streamlined the process of field testing these plants. From 1987 to 1995, 500 field test permits covering forty new species were granted by the Agriculture Department (including barley, carrots, chicory, soybeans, peanuts, broccoli, cranberry, various berries, and watermelons) with minimal oversight.[5]

What worries Goldburg is that the same corporations that are pushing pesticides are now pushing genetically altered plants that are more resistant to pesticides. This, she thinks, smacks of self-interest. The net result will be that farmers buy more pesticides, thinking that their crops can handle the increased load, which means more pesticides in our foods, and potentially the creation of a new generation of pesticide-resistant bugs. This could spark a new "arms race" between insects and bioengineered products, creating a host of "super-bugs" that are resistant to potent levels of pesticides and also leaving more pesticides in our food.

But the primary fear is that entirely new plants never seen before in nature may escape into the wild once the floodgates are opened, where they may displace native plants and take over whole ecosystems, with unforeseen results.

"If the plants are raised outdoors and the new genes get into the wild gene pool, it could have a potentially destabilizing effect on the ecological system," says Jeremy Rifkin of the Foundation for Economic Trends, one of the leading critics of the biotech revolution.

The worry over transgenic crops is summarized by the phrase: "bioengineered crops can't be recalled." Many critics point out the unforeseen consequences of alien species being introduced, deliberately or accidentally, into new environments, as has happened with zebra mussels, Dutch elm disease, kudzu, and chestnut blight.[6] The delicate ecological balance can be severely affected by a new species.

A case in point is the African bee (*Apis mellifera adansonii scrutellata,* sometimes referred to as the "killer bee" by the press), which was deliberately imported into Brazil in 1957 to replace the European honeybee (*Apis mellifera*), which did not adjust well to the daylight cycle of the country's equatorial climate.[7] When scores of queen bees escaped, this highly aggressive species spread out of control and wreaked havoc with the bee industry. Unlike the gentler European bee, the African bee is easily aroused and attacks and swarms by the thousands. It has already killed 1,000 people and caused millions of dollars in losses.

Today, the African bee is the dominant bee species over 20 million square kilometers of the Western Hemisphere, including all of South and Central America. The bees reached Texas in 1990, Arizona in 1993, and are expected to colonize most of the American Southwest until they are stopped by the colder climate of the North around the year 2000.

This is a telling example of how humans have upset a natural ecosystem by unwittingly introducing a new life form which is aggressive enough to displace the milder, domestic one.

Instead of pesticides, Rissler advocates an alternative vision of the future, something called "sustainable agriculture," which involves using natural enemies of certain insects to control their population, which can be done without pesticides. By balancing the ecology of insects in a field, one may be able to keep certain insect populations within limits by importing its natural enemies.

"Who Owns the Genome?"

Critics point out that the secret of life is being unraveled by companies with the freewheeling morality which prevailed in the Wild West. *Science* even devoted its cover to the issue with the title "Who Owns the Genome?"

Daniel Cohen, of the Center for the Study of Human Polymorphisms in Paris, has compared the patenting process to "trying to patent the stars. . . . By patenting something without knowing the use of it, you inhibit industry. That could be a catastrophe."[8]

In 1996, Jeremy Rifkin led a coalition to protest the patenting of the tumor suppressor breast cancer gene *BRCA1*. Myriad Genetics of Salt Lake City, whose scientists isolated the gene in 1994, patented it and began marketing commercially available genetic tests. The coalition argued that patenting the gene would jeopardize women's privacy, especially if the information wound up in the hands of insurance companies. It also argued that patenting genes constricts scientific competition, drives up prices, and allows private industry to reap profits from publicly funded research.[9]

But Collins believes that this thorny problem will gradually disappear with time. "When the Human Genome Project is done, all the sequences are going to be publicly available; no one is going to be able to patent the sequence anymore. At that point, the patenting (if there is patenting, and I think there will be) will be on uses of the sequence, showing that this particular region can be used to make a product that benefits people. And that will probably be for the best."[10]

Genes and Privacy

"Should you have a legal right to demand someone accused of rape to give a DNA sample?" asks James Watson. "Should you, if you're running for President, have to say what your DNA constitution is?"[11] What might have happened if J. Edgar Hoover, the pugnacious and ruthless director of the FBI, had the genetic profiles of politicians in his drawer? Watson wonders. For many decades, J. Edgar Hoover bullied politicians because he had their sexual peccadilloes and drinking habits on file. How much more pressure might he have applied if he knew the complete genetic history of Washington's sometimes wayward politicians?

What is to prevent someone from swiping strands of hair from a presidential candidate and having them genetically analyzed? John Kennedy, for example, may never have been elected President had it been known that he had a serious medical problem with his adrenal glands, which became known only after his death. Recent studies of preserved DNA samples taken in 1967 from former Vice President Hubert Humphrey showed they possessed a cancerous *p-53* mutation associated with bladder cancer (Humphrey died of cancer in 1976). With modern techniques, he could have been diagnosed as being predisposed to cancer before the 1968 presidential elections, possibly eliminating him from the race. David Sidransky of Johns

Hopkins, who led this study, says, it "could have changed the course of political history."[12]

A related question concerns mandatory testing. Already, DNA data banks in this country are being formed by testing prisoners. But should the government be allowed to force people to be tested against their will? Arthur Caplan of the Center for Bioethics believes that thirty years from now, health costs in the United States will be so exorbitant that some in the government may be tempted to call for mandatory testing for genetic diseases and simply refuse to pay the health costs for a baby whose genetic disease was preventable if it had been tested.[13]

Caplan believes that within fifteen years the debate over whether or not to have your future baby genetically tested will become even more raucous than the abortion debate today. Are you irresponsible if you have children without genetic testing? And if so, should the government pay for such genetic irresponsibility? Eventually, he believes, people who have children without genetic testing may be treated as pariahs.

Next, what happens if our genome is leaked out publicly, to our employers, our insurance company, our fiancé, especially for those who harbor potentially deleterious genes? Since time immemorial, societies have committed some form of genetic discrimination. People with obvious deformities or diseases were taunted, labeled witches (as in Huntington's disease), systematically isolated from society, or even killed. What is new, however, is that today it will be possible to screen individuals for a genetic disease even if the disease never appears. Someone who may never suffer from a particular genetic disease may be denied insurance or a job if the person has a high probability of developing a genetic disease.

Nancy Wexler, head of the Ethical, Legal, and Social Implications Branch (ELSI) of the Human Genome Project, says, "Genetic information itself is not going to hurt the public. What could hurt the public is existing social structures, policies, and prejudices against which information can ricochet. We need genetic information right now in order to make better choices so we can live better lives. We need the improved treatments that will eventually be developed using genetic information. So I think the answer is certainly not to slow down the advancing science, but to try, somehow, to make the social system more accommodating to the new knowledge."

According to the now defunct Office of Technology Assessment, the former investigative arm of the U.S. Congress, 164,000 applications for medical insurance are being turned down for medical reasons. The OTA report stated: "Applicants for insurance plans are already being asked to provide information to prospective insurers related to genetic conditions like sickle cell anemia. Some experts fear that individual policies will become increasingly difficult to acquire as more genetic screening tests become available."[14]

A recent study done by Harvard and Stanford universities identified 200 cases in which people were denied insurance, fired from their jobs, or prevented from adopting children because of their genes.

Four bills have been introduced in Congress and twenty bills in various state legislatures to prohibit genetic discrimination. Fourteen states have so far passed laws against it. President Clinton in 1996 signed a bill that prohibits insurance companies from discriminating on the basis of a "preexisting condition."

Genetic discrimination could also affect your marriage prospects. Since everyone has some genetic disease in their genome, this could play havoc with dating rituals. Already, there are dating services exclusively for singles who have tested negative for AIDS. In the future, there may be dating services for people who have tested negative for potentially fatal diseases, like cancer.

But Collins thinks some of these fears of "genetic wallflowers" are exaggerated. "Those concerns are somewhat lessened when you realize that we are all walking around with four or five genes that are pretty badly screwed up, and maybe another twenty or thirty that are moderately defective. So if you're going to wait around for the perfect genetic specimen to walk in, to be your mate, you're going to be single for the rest of your life. It's not going to happen. And you're not going to be able to offer them a perfect genetic specimen either. So we are all flawed. That's the way it is."[15]

Are Genes Us?

One area that could cause considerable misunderstanding is the link between genes and human behavior. Although human behavior is influenced by genes in complex ways, to say that we have a gene for this or that behavior goes too far. Caplan thinks that for the next thirty to forty years this link between genes and behavior will be a "ticking time bomb." While he believes that math ability, personality types, mental illness (depression and schizophrenia), homosexuality, alcoholism, and obesity all have genetic roots, he cautions, "It would be silly to just equate our behavior with genes. It's obvious that even in the same family twins don't turn out to have precisely the same behavior."[16] Genes are only one ingredient in the mix.

Christopher Wills of the University of California at San Diego says, "Simply determining the sequence of all this DNA will not mean we have learned everything there is to know about human beings, any more than looking up the sequence of notes in a Beethoven sonata gives us the capacity to play it. In the future, the true virtuosos of the genome will be those who can put this information to work, and who can appreciate the subtle interactions of genes with each other and with the environment."[17]

Mistakes have already been made. In 1996, the announcement that the gene *D4DR* controls "novelty seeking" in humans made the front page of the *New York Times*. But an exhaustive study of 331 people failed to show any such link.[18]

A more controversial claim which has not held up under scrutiny is the genetic link to violence. The initial controversy was sparked in 1965 by a study which reportedly found that out of 197 patients in a high-security mental hospital in Scotland, 3.5 percent had an unusual XYY chromosome. XYY males were widely stereotyped as being violent and subnormal.[19] The press dubbed the Y chromosome the "criminal chromosome."[20] (Actually, later studies showed that males with XYY chromosomes are known to be more widespread than previously thought, and 96 percent of them lead perfectly normal lives. The most common traits among XYY males seem to be tallness, higher IQ than normal, and slight slurring of speech.)

There is a lesson for the future. By 2020, when personalized DNA sequencing is widely available, there will be many claims to have isolated the "violence gene." By then, it will be a simple matter to correlate prison populations with any number of genes. Genes will certainly be discovered which will, superficially at least, appear to be associated with violent individuals. For example, genes will be found which influence the production of male hormones like testosterone, which some believe may increase aggression under certain circumstances. However, to claim that the "violence gene" has been discovered might be a gross error. Although these genes may in fact be found in a tiny fraction of violent individuals, the vast majority of violent individuals may be linked to totally unrelated factors (e.g., poverty or racism).

This controversy erupted again in 1992, when preparations were made for a major government-funded conference on violence and genetics. African-American critics charged that the conference was unbalanced, giving the impression that genetics was a driving feature of violence, rather than one among a host of contributing factors. Said psychiatrist Peter Breggin, "If you think back, the genetic policy argument used to be that blacks were docile—in one generation they are now genetically violent. This is not science. This is the use of psychiatry and science in the interest of racist social policy."[21]

One controversy about the genetic roots of behavior which will continue for many decades into the future concerns one of the touchiest issues in modern society, race and IQ. In general, most molecular biologists avoid simplistic comments about genes being the sole source of human behavior. However, there is a tendency of others, especially those with a hidden political agenda, to use the results of genetic research to support their often exaggerated claims.

The whole question of DNA, genetics, and race burst upon the national scene in 1995 with the publication of *The Bell Curve* by Richard Hernstein and Charles Murray. It soon ignited a national controversy and opened deep wounds.

Some facts are indisputable. African-Americans consistently score about 10 percent lower than white Americans on the IQ exam. And Asian-Americans consistently score a bit higher than Caucasians. But does that mean that Asian-Americans are a bit smarter than Caucasians, who are in turn 10 percent smarter than African-Americans?

From an evolutionary point of view, it seems unlikely that race and intelligence are strongly linked. The various races of the earth began to diverge about 100,000 years ago in waves of migration from Africa, long after humans had evolved their large brains, which took millions of years of evolution. So the races of the world are a relatively new phenomenon, whereas human intelligence is much more ancient. (DNA analysis, furthermore, clearly shows that the greatest genetic variations exist not between races, but within the races. So the genetic distance between Richard Hernstein and Nelson Mandela, for example, may be much smaller in principle, than the genetic difference between Hernstein and Murray.)

Caplan, echoing the comments of many other scientists, believes that intelligence is actually multidimensional, involving many facets that are totally neglected by IQ exams. He concludes: "*The Bell Curve* was pretty dopey. Psychiatrists and geneticists know that intelligence is a very complex trait made up of many different things. We all know people who can compute well but can't interact socially with anyone, or people who are very good at finding their way around a neighborhood and others who cannot seem to locate the door in their house. Many different things contribute to intelligence. *The Bell Curve* didn't reflect any of this."[22]

One lesson for the future is this: Commentators have noted that the issue of race and IQ usually surfaces during times of economic hardship. Inevitably, because of the business cycle, there will be many periods in the twenty-first century when the economy descends into recession. Demagogues looking for scapegoats will find a receptive ear among the millions who are thrown out of work. In American history, racial theories of intelligence usually receive widespread publicity during times of economic crisis, when people feel threatened by new waves of immigrants. In 1923, for example, Carl Brigham published *A Study of American Intelligence,* using IQ tests to prove that Alpine and Mediterranean "races" were inferior to the Nordic "race" and that Africans were inferior to both. This fueled the movement to exclude people from Southern and Eastern Europe, especially Italians and Jews. One congressman said, "The primary reason for the restriction of the alien stream . . . is the necessity for purifying and keeping pure the blood of America."[23] President Calvin Coolidge, who signed the Immigration Act enforcing quotas on certain nationalities, was on record as stating, "Biological laws show . . . that Nordics deteriorate when mixed with other races."[24]

After 2020: Manipulating Our Germ Line?

Beyond 2020 new ethical questions are likely to be raised. Gene therapy . . . relies on manipulating the genes of somatic cells. Thus the new genes cannot be passed on to succeeding generations. The new genes die when the patient eventually dies. But germ-line therapy would change the genome of our sex cells, so the new gene can be passed on permanently to our offspring. As with transgenic mice, using microinjection of human embryos to permanently change the genetic heritage of the patient could, for example, eliminate cystic fibrosis from a family forever.

Although the idea of eliminating genetic diseases from one's germ line is appealing, there is also enormous potential to misuse germ-line therapy. By and large, the scientific community is against the idea of germ-line therapy. In 1988, the European Research Council stated flatly, "Germ-line gene therapy should not be contemplated."[25] There are, however, some disagreements among scientists.[26]

Would parents opt for germ-line gene therapy, if it were available, to choose the height, sex, strength, eye, and hair color of their children?

"Are you kidding? Yes!" claims Arthur Caplan.[27] There is ample evidence that some families, given the chance, would readily pay to have this done. Parents already try to shape their children in hundreds of ways, such as giving them lessons in piano, languages, sports, etc. "I think there is no doubt that many parents will want to use genetic information to design their kids," Caplan says.[28]

But is this a good thing? The question is: what should be the role of doctors? Are they servants who are expected to simply carry out the wishes of the consumer? Or do we want them to be ministers and guardians of morality, deciding what forms of treatment are unethical? Caplan predicts that it's going to be "one whopping moral debate."[29]

Yet banning such therapy could create a thriving black market in germ-line therapy, especially in Third World countries. Even a simple test such as determining the sex of the unborn infant is causing a major demographic earthquake.

"The use of this technology for sex selection insults the reasons I went into genetics in the first place. Sex is not a disease but a trait!" declares Francis Collins.[30]

Will parents, for example, primarily ask for children who are male, tall, strong, and handsome? The answer, unfortunately, in many countries and in many families, is yes. The laws of evolution dictate that animals will try to give every possible genetic advantage to their unborn children. And humans are no different. Consciously or unconsciously, we want our children to have a head start on life.

To poor families in the Third World, the idea of tinkering with their unborn children seems one way out of poverty. Even before gene modification becomes a reality in the next century, the introduction of a simple device like the sonogram is creating a major demographic shift in China and India, with grave implications for the next generation.

In large portions of the developing world, peasant families place an inordinate emphasis on male children. Not only do male children carry on the name and enjoy numerous feudal privileges, but families with females are required to prepare an expensive dowry at the time of marriage, which is a drain on a poverty-stricken family's finances. According to Monica Das Gupta of Harvard University, from 1981 to 1991 a million girls in India were lost to selective abortions when sonograms were introduced. Four million other girls simply "disappeared" during their first four to six years of life. In other words, 3.6 percent of the female population for that age bracket disappeared.[31]

China's one-child-per-family policy, which has finally brought its population explosion under control, had the unintended side effect of fostering female infanticide. Informal estimates of the young female population in rural areas have shown that up to 10 million female children are "missing." On the southern coast of China, the normal sex ratio, which is 100 females to every 103 male babies born, became skewed in 1995 to 100 females for every 115.4 males. [32]

If the introduction of the simple sonogram could unleash this demographic nightmare, think of the social upheaval that could result from the ability to genetically control our progeny. To give a mild example, in the case of the genetically engineered human growth hormone (HGH)—which only children who suffer from HGH deficiency or chronic kidney failure can qualify for—a recent study found that 60 percent of the children receiving HGH did not qualify. Apparently, anxious parents, concerned about the height of their children, have been pressuring doctors to administer HGH, even at costs of up to $16,000 a year for treatments.[33]

Inevitably, science in the twenty-first century will require the passing of certain laws to prohibit rampant meddling with the human genome, and certainly the human germ line. Some argue that pernicious genetic defects which have caused excruciating pain and suffering for generations should be eliminated from our germ line forever. Others argue the Law of Unintended Side Effects—that by playing God we will inadvertently cause even more suffering later. The question that will dominate ethical battles in the next century is precisely where this fine line should be drawn. Many scientists believe genetic manipulation of our germ line for strictly cosmetic reasons should be banned, as this is a frivolous (and potentially dangerous) application of a powerful technology. However, if it can be proven that grotesque diseases like Huntington's serve no practical purpose, then an equally powerful case can be made to eliminate them forever from one's germ line.

There may be no definitive answer to where to draw the line, as public perceptions and scientific advances change over the decades. However, since random chemical errors, cosmic rays, chemical pollution, poor diet, and other environmental insults continually create new mutations in our genome, it is a question that will be with us for centuries to come.

To Clone a Human

Some predictions from Huxley's *Brave New World* remain firmly in the distant future. At present, it is impossible to bring a fertilized egg to full term in a test tube. Thus, Huxley's prediction that birthing might be replaced by huge embryo factories is far beyond today's technology. Reproducing the delicate, complex chemical environment found in a womb necessary to nurture a human fetus for nine months will probably remain technically out of reach for several decades.

The cloning of humans, however, is now distinctly within the realm of possibility. The astonishing announcement by lan Wilmut of the successful cloning of an adult sheep has opened up enormous ethical and social questions. Many biologists now believe that only technical and legal barriers prevent the cloning of humans.

The ramifications of human cloning are considerable, ranging from the silly and the humane to the fantastic:

- Prominent athletes from different sports and even different decades may be cloned to create a lucrative "dream team."
- Wealthy individuals and aging monarchs without children might bequeath their fortunes and thrones to their clones.
- Parents might want to clone a child who died from a fatal disease or accident.
- Cells may be stolen from famous or glamorous figures and then sold to people who want these individuals for children.
- Graves of famous people may be raided to obtain DNA samples capable of being cloned.
- Dictators may create armies of cloned soldiers or slaves with great physical strength but limited mental capacity, or human hybrids resembling the nightmares from *The Island of Dr. Moreau.*

Other possibilities, such as cloning individuals to perform the undesirable menial tasks necessary for society, as in *Brave New World,* are not such farfetched concepts, given the fact that industrialized societies already import cheap immigrant labor to perform these duties.

Some have even speculated about a mythical society based entirely on clones, in which males would be superfluous. Parthenogenesis, whereby a female produces offspring without a male, could become the dominant mode of human reproduction. (In the long term, such a society would probably be unstable, since one of the evolutionary purposes of sex is to ensure genetic diversity, which is essential to survival in a constantly changing environment.)

There will certainly be a demand for this technology, legal or not. If some parents yearn for a "chip off the old block," then why settle for anything less than an exact copy? Some see clones as fulfilling a deep-seated wish for immortality. After all, the search for immortality probably led the Pharaohs of Egypt to build the pyramids and dying kings to build opulent tombs. Cloning offers a kind of immortality that would be infinitely cheaper.

Cloning also raises a host of other unresolved questions. Theologians have debated whether a human clone has a "soul." If humans can be cloned without limit, then what determines their individuality and essence? Ethicists have asked whether it is morally right to force our own genetic desires onto our offspring, who have no say in the matter. Moralists have been disturbed at the thought of the hundreds of embryos that may be sacrificed in order to produce a single successful clone. Lawyers have asked what are the legal rights of clones—can they assume the legal rights, privileges, and debts of their predecessor? If clones are produced in order to "harvest" their organs, what happens if they refuse to be sacrificed?

Certain things are clear. There is no guarantee that cloning well-known figures will produce equally great offspring. In the movie *The Boys from Brazil,* for example, neo-Nazis cloned young versions of Hitler to resurrect the Third Reich. However, many historians have argued that it was the economic collapse of the German middle classes in the 1930s that set the stage for fascism and gave rise to Hitler. A social or political movement is rarely created by one man alone. Cloning Hitler may do no more than produce a second-rate artist. Similarly, cloning an Einstein does not guarantee that a great physicist will be born, since Einstein lived in a time when physics was in deep crisis; many of the great problems in physics today have already been solved. Great individuals are probably as much the product of great turmoil and opportunity as the product of favorable genes.

It may be that human cloning will be banned in most countries. Even before Wilmut's announcement, the United Kingdom passed the Human Embryo Act prohibiting experimentation on human embryos. President Bill Clinton previously restricted federal funding for human embryo research. In 1997, a federal panel appointed by President Clinton recommended legislation to restrict both public and private research for at least three years.

Ironically, barring some unforeseen technical problem, it is likely that human cloning will soon become a fact of life. Laws banning cloning will simply push cloning research into private, foreign, and underground laboratories, which will be able to continue this line of research because start-up costs are so low and the economic incentives so attractive.

Because of the laws of the marketplace, some predict a small but bustling underground economy based on cloning. "I don't see how you can stop these things. We are at the mercy of these technological developments. Once they're here, it's hard to turn back," says bioethicist Daniel Callahan of the Hastings Center in Briarcliff Manor.[34]

In the future, it is likely that a small fraction of society will, in fact, be clones, given the demand for cloning. For the most part, society may eventually learn to accept the presence of small numbers of clones, in the same way that society has already accepted the presence of test tube babies from surrogate mothers and other unorthodox birthing options.

For all the controversy generated by cloning, the ultimate social impact from these clones could ultimately be negligible. People will learn that the few clones that exist will probably not pose a threat to society. After all, we already live in a world with twins; the more insidious possibility is that cloning may revive the eugenics movement.

The Eugenics Movement

We sometimes forget that the eugenics movement in the United States has a long and unsavory history with deep roots in our culture.

The movement's founder and chief propagandist was Francis Galton, a cousin of Charles Darwin. Inspired by Darwin's work, Galton spent several decades studying the ancestral trees of eminent writers, scientists, philosophers, artists, and statesmen and became convinced that their great abilities were passed down from generation to generation. (Coming from a wealthy family, Galton was apparently blind to environmental influences. He could not admit that perhaps poor people rarely produced great statesmen because they spent most of their time trying to survive.)

Galton concluded that it would be desirable "to produce a highly gifted race of men by judicious marriages during several consecutive generations." In 1883, he coined the word "eugenics" from the Greek to mean "endowed by heredity with noble qualities."[35] Attempts were even made to breed the perfect race. In 1886, Elizabeth Nietzsche, the sister of the philosopher, selected a group of pure-blooded individuals and set sail for Paraguay to create Nueva Germania (New Germany). According to geneticist Steve Jones: "'Today the people of Nueva Germania are poor, inbred, and diseased. Their Utopia has failed."[36]

One of Galton's disciples was Charles Davenport, a professor at the University of Chicago. He used his influence to launch a major institution at Cold Spring Harbor on Long Island to collect a massive database on family hereditary histories. His popular book *Heredity in Relation to Eugenics* helped to inspire the eugenics movement in the United States. In the book, not only did he call for selective breeding to enhance the intellectual qualities found among artists, musicians, scientists, etc., but he also said it may be necessary to use forcible methods to eliminate undesirables with unwanted characteristics. "Society must protect itself," he wrote. "As it claims the right to deprive the murderer of his life so also may it annihilate the hideous serpent of hopelessly vicious protoplasm."[37]

In 1927, this was given legal stature when the U.S. Supreme Court upheld the constitutionality of sterilization in the case of *Buck v. Bell,* involving a Virginia sterilization statute. Justice Oliver Wendell Holmes wrote: "It is better for all the world, if instead of waiting to execute degenerate offspring for crime, or to let them starve for their imbecility, society can prevent those who are manifestly unfit for continuing their kind. The principle that sustains compulsory vaccination is broad enough to cover cutting the Fallopian tubes."[38]

By 1930, twenty-four states had passed laws allowing for the sterilization of a wide variety of "undesirables," which included criminals, epileptics, the insane, and the retarded. By 1941, 36,000 people were sterilized in the United States.

The Nazis openly expressed a deep gratitude to the eugenics movement in the United States, which provided an inspiration for their own ideas. Eugenics was incorporated as an integral part of the Nazi ideology, based on breeding the Aryan "master race." Eventually, millions would he rounded up, thrown into camps, or gassed, victims of the abstract, theoretical ideas proposed by the eugenicists.

Many of these ideas still percolate in the United States. In the 1980s, Nobel Prize-winning physicist William Shockley, co-inventor of the transistor, called for Nobel Laureates to contribute to a sperm bank. Any eligible female could then perform her duty to humanity and improve the human race by being inseminated from this sperm bank of "geniuses."

One long-term danger for the far future is that those who are the wealthiest will be able to afford to improve their germ line, while others will not, leaving the rest of society behind, eventually creating a new biological caste system. Gregory Kavka, a philosopher at the University of California at Irvine, says, "Any such move toward genetic enhancement has the potential of reestablishing social inequality, though along new lines. Old aristocracies of birth, color, or gender may dissipate, only to be replaced by a new genetic aristocracy, or 'genetocracy.' "[39]

The deep fracture lines of society could become chasms if only the wealthy have access to choosing their germ line (eventually creating a nightmarish, two-tiered society like the one portrayed by H. G. Wells in *The Time Machine,* when the Morlocks toiled with their machines in underground caverns while the childlike Eloi pranced and frolicked aboveground).[40]

In the future, society must be wary of those who would use the benefits of the genetics revolution to further their own social agenda.

Biological Warfare

But perhaps the greatest fear concerning biotechnology is the deliberate misuse of this technology, especially for warfare.

Unfortunately, biological warfare has a long and ugly history. When conquest or national survival is at stake, nations often resort to the most destructive weapons at their disposal, including biological ones.

One of the earliest recorded uses of biological warfare was in 600 B.C., when Solon from Athens contaminated the water supply of the city of Kirrah with the poisonous hellebore plant. During the fourteenth century the Tartars catapulted the bodies of dead plague victims over the walls of the Crimean town of Kaffa in order to ignite an epidemic. And in the eighteenth century both British soldiers and U.S. government agents traded smallpox-infected blankets to Native Americans, which accelerated their extermination.[41]

During World War I, 100,000 tons of poison gases (chlorine, phosgene, and mustard gas) were used to kill 100,000 soldiers and incapacitate 1.3 million more.[42]

During World War II, the Nazis gassed millions of Jews, Russians, Gypsies, and other "undesirables," and Japanese conducted hideous germ warfare experiments on prisoners of war (even Britain and the United States had plans, never put into effect, to use anthrax as a weapon, either stored in 200-kilogram bombs or employed as a poison to infect enemy livestock).[43]

In March 1995, a fanatical Buddhist cult in Japan unleashed the nerve gas sarin in the Tokyo subway system, killing twelve and injuring 5,500. The only thing that prevented tens of thousands from dying was the fact that the mixture was impure. (Like other nerve agents, sarin, developed by the Germans in the 1930s, blocks the chemical acetylcholinesterase, which is necessary for the transmission of nerve impulses.) There is evidence that this same cult actively tried to obtain samples of the Ebola virus as well.

But perhaps the greatest fear is that an accidental release of an incurable virus from one of the biological warfare centers (such as Fort Detrick outside Washington, D.C.) may threaten the very existence of the human race. A mutated, airborne Ebola or HIV virus could infect most of the planet within a matter of weeks or months.

Some scientists' greatest fears were voiced by Karl Johnson of the CDC when he said, "I worry about all this research on virulence. It's only a matter of months—years, at most—before people nail down the genes for virulence and airborne transmission in influenza, Ebola, Lassa, you name it. And then any crackpot with a few thousand dollars' worth of equipment and a college biology education under his belt could manufacture bugs that would make Ebola look like a walk around the park."[44]

Such a doomsday scenario cannot be ignored. D. A. Henderson, who helped to lead the campaign against smallpox, has observed: "Where would we be today if HIV were to become an airborne pathogen? And what is there to say that a comparable infection might not do so in the future?"[45]

A warring nation could also use biotechnology to create a disease to destroy an enemy's crops, thereby unleashing famine. "It can easily be done. This is not science fiction," says A. N. Mukhopadyay, dean of agriculture for the G. S. Pant University in India.[46]

Barbara Rosenberg of the Federation of American Scientists, comments: "None of the equipment is so high-tech that it could not be homemade by any nation intent on developing BW [biological warfare] capacity. No nation is immune to the dangers."[47]

At the annual meeting of the American Society of Tropical Medicine and Hygiene in Honolulu in 1989, scientists staged an extraordinary but purely hypothetical war games exercise involving germ warfare. In that exercise, a civil war and mass chaos erupts in central Africa. An airborne Ebola virus suddenly emerges out of the squalor of a refugee camp. Within days, it begins to spread outside the camp, eventually reaching the airports and spreading to Europe and America. Within ten days, it reaches Washington, D.C., New York, Honolulu, Geneva, Frankfurt, Manila, Bangkok. Within a month, a global pandemic is unleashed, triggering worldwide panic.[48]

Recalling that chilling exercise, Karl Johnson said, "You may say 'ridiculous,' but I don't think we can disregard that possibility. It was, and still is, a potential," he says.[49]

Perhaps one of the most frightening forms of germ warfare to contemplate is what are called "ethnic weapons"—i.e., genetically altered germs which attack specific ethnic groups or races. Ethnic weapons were first proposed publicly in 1970 in *Military Review* magazine, which noted that certain Asian people cannot digest milk.[50] The article used this example to demonstrate that certain races are vulnerable to certain chemicals.

Recently declassified documents reveal that back in 1951 the U.S. Navy conducted top secret tests to determine how vulnerable it was to an enemy attack which selectively affected primarily African-American defense workers by using *Coccidioides immitis,* which causes San Joaquin Valley fever, which kills ten times more African-Americans than Caucasians.[51]

Charles Piller, author of *Gene Wars,* notes that San Joaquin Valley fever, a systemic fungal disease, was developed by the United States as a potential biological weapon back in the 1940s. Military planners once considered mutating the organism so that it would attack one specific ethnic group.[52]

Legislating the Genome

Francis Collins says, "I am not such a Pollyanna as to imagine that information this powerful cannot in some future instance be used in the wrong way. . . . If you believe that one of the strongest mandates of humankind is to pursue ways to alleviate human suffering, you really can't be against this research. But it's knowledge. It's not good or evil. It's just knowledge."[53]

But knowledge is power, and power is inherently a political and social question. To help clarify the essential issues at stake with the genetics of the future, the ELSI has come out with simple guidelines for dealing with some of these thorny ethical issues. What they advocate is this:

Fairness for all—no genetic discrimination
The right to privacy—prevent disclosure
The delivery of health care—services made available to all
The need for education—raising public consciousness

These guidelines identify some of the essential issues and give cogent responses to them. However, how to implement these guidelines is still in question. Ultimately, many of these ethical questions may be solved by a combination of social pressure, legislation, and treaties between nations.

There is no viable way to completely stop the progress of science — but we must find a way to carefully control the excesses of technology. Certain aspects of genetics research may need to be banned entirely. But the best overall policy is to air the risks and potentials of genetics research in public, and democratically pass laws which will shape the direction of the technology toward alleviating sickness and pain.

Caplan thinks that some of the simpler questions can be resolved by peer pressure. For example, today many women in their late thirties or older voluntarily ask that an amniocentesis be performed, which can determine if the fetus is suffering from Down's syndrome. In the future, as testing for more genetic diseases is perfected, women may voluntarily agree to be tested during their pregnancy.

Other issues, however, will require outright legislation. Already, for example, several bills in Congress are being considered to ban insurance companies from discriminating on the basis of one's genetic makeup.

Similarly, society may have to pass legislation to decide which germ-line therapies will be banned. For example, is being short a disease? Many scientists working on gene therapy are horrified that the fruits of their work may be used for purely cosmetic reasons. They argue persuasively that germ-line therapy for cosmetic reasons should be banned, but germ-line therapy might be allowed for certain classes of debilitating genetic diseases.

Ultimately, the question of germ warfare will have to be decided by treaty. The Biological Weapons Convention of 1972, signed by the United States, the former Soviet Union, and scores of other countries, was a milestone in trying to ban or restrict germ warfare. Unfortunately, it was signed before the coming of recombinant DNA technology; hence there are many potential flaws. First, it banned the use of biological weapons for "hostile purposes or armed conflict." However, in the age of recombinant DNA, there is precious little difference between the offensive and defensive use of deadly germs. Second, it outlawed the "development" of germ weapons, but allowed for "research" on them. Unfortunately, this means that it is legal to do "research" on large quantities of deadly germs with the intent to use them in a future war. In the biotech business, there is no great distinction between researching a biological weapon and developing it.

Given that there is no easy dividing line between defensive and offensive uses of germ warfare, ultimately the entire field of biological weapons might have to be banned. In 1995, in a report by the Office of Technology Assessment, seventeen countries were said to be working on biological weapons.[54]

Ultimately there must be tight international restrictions on this kind of weapons technology, including on-site inspections, dismantling known biological weapons facilities, monitoring the flow of certain chemicals and life forms, etc. It will not be easy, but such guarantees are necessary to prevent dangerous life forms from emerging from renegade laboratories.

Banning these weapons of war may be generally accepted once nations realize that biological weapons are unstable, unpredictable, and unreliable in actual warfare.

Ultimately, society must make democratic decisions on whether or not to restrict certain kinds of technology. Unlike nuclear technology, the debate about the risks and benefits of biotechnology is in its early stages, giving society time in which to decide which forms of the technology should be allowed to flourish and which ones should be restricted. In a democracy, what is decisive is informed debate by an enlightened electorate.

1997

Notes

1. Aldous Huxley, *Brave New World,* Harper, New York, 1946, p. xvii.
2. The avowed nuclear powers are the United States, Great Britain, France, Russia, and China, although the nuclear status of the various parts of the former Soviet Union are still being negotiated. The South African government admitted to creating seven atomic bombs, which it has since dismantled. Israel is reputed to have about two hundred atomic bombs.

India exploded an atomic bomb in the 1970s. Pakistan is believed to have nuclear weapons. The status of North Korea is not clear.

3. Interview with Rebecca Goldburg.
4. *New York Times,* Aug. 27, 1995, p. 30.
5. Interview with Rebecca Goldburg.
6. Ibid.
7. Ibid.
8. Thomas F. Lee, *Gene Future,* Plenum Press, New York, 1993, p. 301.
9. *Discover,* Jan. 1997, p. 78.
10. Interview with Francis Collins.
11. Lois Wingerson, *Mapping Our Genes,* Penguin Books, New York, 1990, p. 297.
12. *Newsweek,* Dec. 23, 1996, p. 47.
13. Interview with Arthur Caplan.
14. Jeff Lyon and Peter Gorner, *Altered Fates,* W. W. Norton, New York, 1995, p. 484.
15. Interview with Francis Collins.
16. Interview with Arthur Caplan, July 21, 1996.
17. Christopher Wills, *Exons, Introns, and Talking Genes,* Basic Books, New York, 1991, p. 10.
18. *Washington Post,* Nov. 4, 1996, p. A2.
19. Usually, males have XY, and females have XX chromosomes.
20. Wingerson, *Mapping Our Genes,* p. 95.
21. *Washington Post,* Jan. 29, 1995, p. C4.
22. Interview with Arthur Caplan.
23. Enzo Russo and David Cove, *Genetic Engineering,* W. H. Freeman, New York, 1991, p. 170.
24. Thomas F. Lee, *The Human Genome Project,* Plenum Press, New York, 1991, p. 276.
25. Lee, *Gene Future,* p. 160.
26. At the Council for International Organizations of Medical Sciences, meeting in Japan in 1990, the participants took a different position: "Although germ-cell gene therapy is not contemplated at present, continued discussion of germ-cell gene therapy is nonetheless important. The option of germ-cell therapy must not be prematurely foreclosed. It may someday offer clinical benefits attainable in no other way." (Ibid., p. 161.)
27. Interview with Arthur Caplan
28. Ibid.
29. Ibid.
30. Interview with Francis Collins.
31. *Washington Post,* May 11, 1996, p. A1.
32. *New York Times,* June 7, 1996, p. A11.
33. *Science News,* Sept. 7, 1996, p. 154.
34. *Time,* March 10, 1997, p. 72.
35. Lee, *The Human Genome Project,* p. 275.
36. Steve Jones, *The Language of Genes,* Anchor Books, New York, 1993, p. 224.
37. Ibid., p. 224.
38. Ibid., p. 150.
39. Cranor, *Are Genes Us?,* p. 170.

40. The irony in all of this is that the Morlocks have their ultimate revenge. They eat the Eloi.
41. Suzuki, *Genetics,* p. 197.
42. Ibid.
43. Ibid.
44. Ibid.
45. Ibid.
46. Ibid.
47. Ibid.
48. Ibid., pp. 93–94.
49. Ibid.
50. Charles Piller and Keith R. Yamamoto, *Gene Wars,* William Morrow, New York, 1988, p. 99.
51. These secret tests were conducted at the military's Mechanicsburg, Pennsylvania, supply depot. The document says, "Within this system there are employed large numbers of laborers, including many Negroes, whose incapacitation would seriously affect the operation of the supply system. Since Negroes are more susceptible to *Coccidioides* than are whites, this fungus was simulated by using *Asperfillus fumigatus.*" (Ibid.)
52. Interview with Charles Piller; Piller and Yamamoto, *Gene Wars,* p. 100.
53. Interview with Francis Collins.
54. *Scientific American,* Dec. 1996, p. 62.

GETTING STARTED

1. In the first section of the essay, Kaku offers two different visions of the future that scientific and technological changes might create, one positive and one negative. As you read, create two columns in which you list the main examples of each vision. In groups, compare the examples in each column and add positive or negative predictions you have heard, imagined, read, or seen depicted on television or in movies. Which column tends to have more extreme fictional examples? What are some of your group's reactions to each column (for example, amusement, anxiety, disbelief)?

2. Choose one issue that Kaku discusses in the essay: bioengineered foods, mandatory DNA or genetic testing, links between genes and behavior, manipulating germ lines, cloning, eugenics, or biological warfare. Summarize the important aspects of the issue. What does an "enlightened electorate" need to know about this issue? What point is Kaku making by discussing this issue?

WRITING

3. Near the beginning of his essay, Kaku states his faith in the workings of democracy: "In a democracy, only informed debate by an educated citizenry can make the mature decisions about a technology

so powerful that we can dream of controlling life itself" (p. 281). Write a short paper using one or more specific examples from Kaku to test this claim. Who controls the debate on this issue? Who has access to the pertinent information? Can an informed and educated citizen have an impact on this issue? What hope does Kaku offer us that democracy has the power to handle these issues?

4. Write your own science fiction account of a future in which one major technological change mentioned by Kaku has come to pass. Use your fictional narrative to show some of the imagined implications of that change on people's lives.

5. Kaku calls on us to have a national debate on the issues he raises. As a way of starting such a debate, choose one of the issues in biotechnology that he identifies. Write a one-page argument in favor of and a one-page argument against some potential use of that technology. Which argument is more persuasive and why?

USING THE LIBRARY AND THE INTERNET

6. Use Lexis/Nexis, Newspaper Source, or a similar database that includes newspaper articles to find out what has happened with the Human Genome Project since Kaku published this chapter in 1997. In a group, pool your findings and list the major developments. What has the project accomplished to date, and how does that news impact the point Kaku is trying to make with this example?

7. Using a popular search engine such as Google, search using the keyword "doomsday" and sample several of the resulting Web sites. Try another search on Google using the combined term "science and technology and future" and do a comparative sampling. Choose one representative sample Web site from each search and list the similarities and differences in the way the two Web sites portray the future. In a group, compare your findings and note the places where the Web sites from either search overlap with Kaku's vision of technology's role in our future.

MAKING CONNECTIONS

8. Who controls science and its products or practices? Write a paper using Kaku's ideas with those from Stephen Jay Gould's "The Smoking Gun of Eugenics," Richard C. Lewontin's "Science as Social Action," or Christopher P. Toumey's "Science in an Old Testament Style." Analyze how scientific knowledge is controlled and used in a democracy. How well informed can the general public be about the goals and findings of science? To what extent

should scientists protect the public by withholding potential breakthroughs until their implications are fully studied? In what other ways should the public be protected or given more control over the products and practices of science?

9. Kaku's ideas about democratic debate remain rather undefined. Use ideas from Zita Ingham's "Landscape, Drama, and Dissensus: The Rhetorical Education of Red Lodge, Montana," or from Christopher Lasch's "The Lost Art of Argument" to imagine an effective means for encouraging the kind of debate that Kaku thinks we need. Write a short paper using ideas from Ingham or Lasch to explore the possibility of a democratic debate around one of the issues Kaku discusses. (You may choose to write this paper as an editorial encouraging your readers to enter into such a debate.)

10. To what extent do Jared Diamond's ideas in "Necessity's Mother" apply to the technology that Kaku describes? Write an essay in which you test some of Diamond's claims about how and why technologies are invented against the case studies of evolving technology described by Kaku. In each case, what is the safest and best role for the nonscientific community to play in that evolution?

THOMAS KUHN

Thomas Kuhn (1922–1996) was a Professor of Philosophy and the History of Science at the Massachusetts Institute of Technology from 1979 to 1991. Kuhn wrote "The Historical Structure of Scientific Discovery" while a graduate student in theoretical physics at Harvard University. Soon after receiving his doctorate in physics, Kuhn left the laboratory to pursue his interest in the structure of change in scientific thought. Kuhn is considered one of the founders of the history of science, and his concept of the paradigm shift is considered one of the most influential ideas in twentieth-century intellectual history.

To learn more about Thomas Kuhn, see the *Harvard Science Review* online at <http://hcs.harvard.edu/~hsr/hsr/winter97/kuhn.html>.

The Historical Structure of Scientific Discovery

My object in this article is to isolate and illuminate one small part of what I take to be a continuing historiographic revolution in the study of science. The structure of scientific discovery is my particular topic, and I can best approach it by pointing out that the subject itself may well seem extraordinarily odd. Both scientists and, until quite recently, historians have ordinarily viewed discovery as the sort of event which, though it may have preconditions and surely has consequences, is itself without internal structure. Rather than being seen as a complex development extended both in space and time, discovering something has usually seemed to be a unitary event, one which, like seeing something, happens to an individual at a specific time and place.

This view of the nature of discovery has, I suspect, deep roots in the nature of the scientific community. One of the few historical elements recurrent in the textbooks from which the prospective scientist learns his field is the attribution of particular natural phenomena to the historical personages who first discovered them. As a result of this and other aspects of their training, discovery becomes for many scientists an important goal. To make a discovery is to achieve one of the closest approximations to a property right that the scientific career affords. Professional prestige is often closely associated with these acquisitions.[1] Small wonder, then, that acrimonious disputes about priority and independence in discovery have often marred the normally placid tenor of scientific communication. Even less wonder that many historians of science have seen the individual discovery as an appropriate unit with which to measure scientific progress and have devoted much time and skill to determining what man made which discovery at what point in time. If the study of discovery has a surprise to offer, it is only that, despite the immense energy and ingenuity expended upon it, neither polemic nor painstaking scholarship has often succeeded in pinpointing the time and place at which a given discovery could properly be said to have "been made."

That failure, both of argument and of research, suggests the thesis that I now wish to develop. Many scientific discoveries, particularly the most interesting and important, are not the sort of event about which the questions "Where?" and, more particularly, "When?" can appropriately be asked. Even if all conceivable data were at hand, those questions would not regularly possess answers. That we are persistently driven to ask them nonetheless is symptomatic of a fundamental inappropriateness in our image of discovery. That inappropriateness is here my main concern, but I approach it by considering first the historical problem presented by the attempt to date and to place a major class of fundamental discoveries.

The troublesome class consists of those discoveries—including oxygen, the electric current, X rays, and the electron—which could not be predicted from accepted theory in advance and which therefore caught the assembled profession by surprise. That kind of discovery will shortly be my exclusive concern, but it will help first to note that there is another sort and one which presents very few of the same problems. Into this second class of discoveries fall the neutrino, radio waves, and the elements which filled empty places in the periodic table. The existence of all these objects had been predicted from theory before they were discovered, and the men who made the discoveries therefore knew from the start what to look for. That foreknowledge did not make their task less demanding or less interesting, but it did provide criteria which told them when their goal had been reached.[2] As a result, there have been few priority debates over discoveries of this second sort, and only a paucity of data can prevent the historian from ascribing them to a particular time and place. Those facts help to isolate the difficulties we encounter as we return to the troublesome discoveries of the first class. In the cases that most concern us here there are no benchmarks to inform either the scientist or the historian when the job of discovery has been done.

As an illustration of this fundamental problem and its consequences, consider first the discovery of oxygen. Because it has repeatedly been studied, often with exemplary care and skill, that discovery is unlikely to offer any purely factual surprises. Therefore it is particularly well suited to clarify points of principle.[3] At least three scientists—Carl Scheele, Joseph Priestley, and Antoine Lavoisier—have a legitimate claim to this discovery, and polemicists have occasionally entered the same claim for Pierre Bayen.[4] Scheele's work, though it was almost certainly completed before the relevant researches of Priestley and Lavoisier, was not made public until their work was well known.[5] Therefore it had no apparent causal role, and I shall simplify my story by omitting it.[6] Instead, I pick up the main route to the discovery of oxygen with the work of Bayen, who, sometime before March 1774, discovered that red precipitate of mercury (HgO) could, by heating, be made to yield a gas. That aeriform product Bayen identified as fixed air (CO_2), a substance made familiar to most pneumatic chemists by the earlier work of Joseph Black.[7] A variety of other substances were known to yield the same gas.

At the beginning of August 1774, a few months after Bayen's work had appeared, Joseph Priestley, repeated the experiment, though probably independently. Priestley, however, observed that the gaseous product would support combustion and therefore changed the identification. For him the gas obtained on heating red precipitate was nitrous air (N_2O), a substance that he had himself discovered more than two years before.[8] Later in the same month Priestley made a trip to Paris and there informed Lavoisier of the new reaction. The latter repeated the experiment once more, both in November 1775 and in February 1774. But, because he used tests somewhat more elaborate than Priestley's, Lavoisier again changed the identification. For him, as of May 1775, the gas released by red precipitate was neither fixed air nor nitrous air. Instead, it was "[atmospheric] air itself entire without alteration . . . even to the point that . . . it comes out more pure."[9] Meanwhile, however, Priestley had also been at work, and, before the beginning of March 1775, he, too, had concluded that the gas must be "common air." Until this point all of the men who had produced a gas from red precipitate of mercury had identified it with some previously known species.[10]

The remainder of this story of discovery is briefly told. During March 1775 Priestley discovered that his gas was in several respects very much "better" than common air, and he therefore reidentified the gas once more, this time calling it "dephlogisticated air," that is, atmospheric air deprived of its normal complement of phlogiston.° This conclusion Priestley published in the *Philosophical Transactions,* and it was apparently that publication which led Lavoisier to reexamine his own results.[11] The reexamination began during February 1776 and within a year had led Lavoisier to the conclusion that the gas was actually a separable component of the atmospheric air which both he and Priestley had previously thought of as homogeneous. With this point

---

Phlogiston Was once believed to be the element that caused combustion and that was given off by anything burning.

reached, with the gas recognized as an irreducibly distinct species, we may conclude that the discovery of oxygen had been completed.

But to return to my initial question, when shall we say that oxygen was discovered and what criteria shall we use in answering that question? If discovering oxygen is simply holding an impure sample in one's hands, then the gas had been "discovered" in antiquity by the first man who ever bottled atmospheric air. Undoubtedly, for an experimental criterion, we must at least require a relatively pure sample like that obtained by Priestley in August 1774. But during 1774 Priestley was unaware that he had discovered anything except a new way to produce a relatively familiar species. Throughout that year his "discovery" is scarcely distinguishable from the one made earlier by Bayen, and neither case is quite distinct from that of the Reverend Stephen Hales, who had obtained the same gas more than forty years before.[12] Apparently to discover something one must also be aware of the discovery and know as well what it is that one has discovered.

But, that being the case, how much must one know? Had Priestley come close enough when he identified the gas as nitrous air? If not, was either he or Lavoisier significantly closer when he changed the identification to common air? And what are we to say about Priestley's next identification, the one made in March 1775? Dephlogisticated air is still not oxygen or even, for the phlogistic chemist, a quite unexpected sort of gas. Rather it is a particularly pure atmospheric air. Presumably, then, we wait for Lavoisier's work in 1776 and 1777, work which led him not merely to isolate the gas but to see what it was. Yet even that decision can be questioned, for in 1777 and to the end of his life Lavoisier insisted that oxygen was an atomic "principle of acidity" and that oxygen *gas* was formed only when that "principle" united with caloric, the matter of heat.[13] Shall we therefore say that oxygen had not yet been discovered in 1777? Some may be tempted to do so. But the principle of acidity was not banished from chemistry until after 1810 and caloric lingered on until the 1860s. Oxygen had, however, become a standard chemical substance long before either of those dates. Furthermore, what is perhaps the key point, it would probably have gained that status on the basis of Priestley's work alone without benefit of Lavoisier's still partial reinterpretation.

I conclude that we need a new vocabulary and new concepts for analyzing events like the discovery of oxygen. Though undoubtedly correct, the sentence "Oxygen was discovered" misleads by suggesting that discovering something is a single simple act unequivocally attributable, if only we knew enough, to an individual and an instant in time. When the discovery is unexpected, however, the latter attribution is always impossible and the former often is as well. Ignoring Scheele, we can, for example, safely say that oxygen had not been discovered before 1774; probably we would also insist that it had been discovered by 1777 or shortly thereafter. But within those limits any attempt to date the discovery or to attribute it to an individual must inevitably be arbitrary. Furthermore, it must be arbitrary just because discovering a new sort of phenomenon is necessarily a complex process which involves recognizing both *that* something is and *what* it is. Observation and conceptualization, fact and the assimilation of fact to theory, are inseparably linked in the discovery of scientific novelty. Inevitably, that process extends over time and may often involve a number of people. Only for discoveries in my second category—those whose nature is known in advance—can discovering *that* and discovering *what* occur together and in an instant.

Two last, simpler, and far briefer examples will simultaneously show how typical the case of oxygen is and also prepare the way for a somewhat more precise conclusion. On the night of 13 March 1781, the astronomer William Herschel made the following entry in his journal: "In the quartile near Zeta Tauri . . . is a curious either nebulous star or perhaps a comet."[14] That entry is generally said to record the discovery of the planet Uranus, but it cannot quite have done that. Between 1690 and Herschel's observation in 1781 the same object had been seen and recorded at least seventeen times by men who took it to be a star. Herschel differed from them only in supposing that, because in his telescope it appeared especially large, it might actually be a *comet*! Two additional observations on 17 and 19 March confirmed that suspicion by showing that the object he had observed moved among the stars. As a result, astronomers throughout Europe were informed of the discovery, and the mathematicians among them began to compute the new comet's orbit. Only several months later, after all those attempts had repeatedly failed to square with observation, did the astronomer Lexell suggest that the object observed by Herschel might be a planet. And only when additional computations, using a planet's rather than a comet's orbit, proved reconcilable with observation was that suggestion generally accepted. At what point during 1781 do we want to say that the planet Uranus was discovered? And are we entirely and unequivocally clear that it was Herschel rather than Lexell who discovered it?

Or consider still more briefly the story of the discovery of X rays, a story which opens on the day in 1895 when the physicist Roentgen interrupted a well-precedented investigation of cathode rays because he noticed that a barium platinocyanide screen far from his shielded apparatus glowed when the discharge was in process.[15] Additional investigations—they required seven hectic weeks during which Roentgen rarely left the laboratory—indicated that the cause of the glow traveled in straight lines from the cathode ray tube, that the radiation cast shadows, that it could not be deflected by a magnet, and much else besides. Before announcing his discovery Roentgen had convinced himself that his effect was not due to cathode rays themselves but to a new form of radiation with at least some similarity to light. Once again the question suggests itself: When shall we say that X rays were actually discovered? Not, in any case, at the first instant, when all that had been noted was a glowing screen. At least one other investigator had seen that glow and, to his subsequent chagrin, discovered nothing at all. Nor, it is almost as clear, can the moment of discovery be pushed back to a point during the last week of investigation. By that time Roentgen was exploring the properties of the new radiation he had *already* discovered. We may have to settle for the remark that X rays emerged in Würzburg between 8 November and 28 December 1895.

The characteristics shared by these examples are, I think, common to all the episodes by which unanticipated novelties become subjects for scientific attention. I therefore conclude these brief remarks by discussing three such common characteristics, one which may help to provide a framework for the further study of the extended episodes we customarily call "discoveries."

In the first place, notice that all three of our discoveries—oxygen, Uranus, and X rays—began with the experimental or observational isolation of an anomaly, that is, with nature's failure to conform entirely to expectation. Notice, further, that the process by which that anomaly was educed displays simultaneously the apparently incompatible characteristics of the inevitable and the accidental. In the case of X rays, the anomalous glow which provided Roentgen's first clue was clearly the result of an accidental disposition of his apparatus. But by 1895 cathode rays were a normal subject for research all over Europe; that research quite regularly juxtaposed cathode-rays tubes with sensitive screens and films; as a result, Roentgen's accident was almost certain to occur elsewhere, as in fact it had. Those remarks, however, should make Roentgen's case look very much like those of Herschel and Priestley. Herschel first observed his oversized and thus anomalous star in the course of a prolonged survey of the northern heavens. That survey was, except for the magnification provided by Herschel's instruments, precisely of the sort that had repeatedly been carried through before and that had occasionally resulted in prior observations of Uranus. And Priestley, too—when he isolated the gas that behaved almost but not quite like nitrous air and then almost but not quite like common air—was seeing something unintended and wrong in the outcome of a sort of experiment for which there was much European precedent and which had more than once before led to the production of the new gas.

These features suggest the existence of two normal requisites for the beginning of an episode of discovery. The first, which throughout this paper I have largely taken for granted, is the individual skill, wit, or genius to recognize that something has gone wrong in ways that may prove consequential. Not any and every scientist would have noted that no unrecorded star should be so large, that the screen ought not to have glowed, that nitrous air should not have supported life. But that requisite presupposes another which is less frequently taken for granted. Whatever the level of genius available to observe them, anomalies do not emerge from the normal course of scientific research until both instruments and concepts have developed sufficiently to make their emergence likely and to make the anomaly which results recognizable as a violation of expectation.[16] To say that an unexpected discovery begins only when something goes wrong is to say that it begins only when scientists know well both how their instruments and how nature should behave. What distinguished Priestley, who saw an anomaly, from Hales, who did not, is largely the considerable articulation of pneumatic techniques and expectations that had come into being during the four decades which separate their two isolations of oxygen.[17] The very number of claimants indicates that after 1770 the discovery could not have been postponed for long.

The role of anomaly is the first of the characteristics shared by our three examples. A second can be considered more briefly, for it has provided the main theme for the body of my text. Though awareness of anomaly marks the beginning of a discovery, it marks only the beginning. What necessarily follows, if anything at all is to be discovered, is a more or less extended period during which the individual and often many members of his group struggle to make the anomaly lawlike. Invariably that period demands additional observation or experimentation as well as repeated cogitation. While it continues, scientists repeatedly revise their expectations, usually their instrumental standards, and sometimes their most fundamental theories as well. In this sense discoveries have a proper internal history as well as prehistory and a posthistory. Furthermore, within the rather vaguely delimited interval of internal history, there is no single moment or day which the historian, however complete his data, can identify as the point at which the discovery was made. Often, when several individuals are involved, it is even impossible unequivocally to identify any one of them as the discoverer.

Finally, turning to the third of these selected common characteristics, note briefly what happens as the period of discovery draws to a close. A full discussion of that question would require additional evidence and a separate paper, for I have had little to say about the aftermath of discovery in the body of my text. Nevertheless, the topic must not be entirely neglected, for it is in part a corollary of what has already been said.

Discoveries are often described as mere additions or increments to the growing stockpile of scientific knowledge, and that description has helped make the unit discovery seem a significant measure of progress. I suggest, however, that it is fully appropriate only to those discoveries which, like the elements that filled missing places in the periodic table, were anticipated and sought in advance and which therefore demanded no adjustment, adaptation, and assimilation from the profession. Though the sorts of discoveries we have here been examining are undoubtedly additions to scientific knowledge, they are also something more. In a sense that I can now develop only in part, they also react back upon what has previously been known, providing a new view of some previously familiar objects and simultaneously changing the way in which even some traditional parts of science are practiced. Those in whose area of special competence the new phenomenon falls often see both the world and their work differently as they emerge from the extended struggle with anomaly which constitutes the discovery of that phenomenon.

William Herschel, for example, when he increased by one the time-honored number of planetary bodies, taught astronomers to see new things when they looked at the familiar heavens even with instruments more traditional than his own. That change in the vision of astronomers must be a principal reason why, in the half century after the discovery of Uranus, twenty additional circumsolar bodies were added to the traditional seven.[18] A similar transformation is even clearer in the aftermath of Roentgen's work. In the first place, established techniques for cathode-ray research had to be changed, for scientists found they had failed to control a relevant variable. Those changes included both the redesign of old apparatus and revised ways of asking old questions. In addition, those scientists most concerned experienced the same transformation of vision that we have just noted in the aftermath of the discovery of Uranus. X rays were the first new sort of radiation discovered since infrared and ultraviolet at the beginning of the century. But within less than a decade after Roentgen's work, four more were disclosed by the new scientific sensitivity (for example, to fogged photographic plates) and by some of the new instrumental techniques that had resulted from Roentgen's work and its assimilation.[19]

Very often these transformations in the established techniques of scientific practice prove even more important than the incremental knowledge provided by the discovery itself. That could at least be argued in the cases of Uranus and of X rays; in the case of my third example, oxygen, it is categorically clear. Like the work of Herschel and Roentgen, that of Priestley and Lavoisier taught scientists to view old situations in new ways. Therefore, as we might anticipate, oxygen was not the only new chemical species to be identified in the aftermath of their work. But, in the case of oxygen, the readjustments demanded by assimilation were so profound that they played an integral and essential role—though they were not by themselves the cause—in the gigantic upheaval of chemical theory and practice which has since been known as the chemical revolution. I do not suggest that every unanticipated discovery has consequences for science so deep and so far-reaching as those which followed the discovery of oxygen. But I do suggest that every such discovery demands, from those most concerned, the sorts of readjustment that, when they are more obvious, we equate with scientific revolution. It is, I believe, just because they demand readjustments like these that the process of discovery is necessarily and inevitably one that shows structure and that therefore extends in time.

1962

Notes

1. For a brilliant discussion of these points, see R. K. Merton, "Priorities in Scientific Discovery: A Chapter in the Sociology of Science," *American Sociological Review* 22 (1957): 635. Also very relevant, though it did not appear until this article had been prepared, is F. Reif, "The Competitive World of the Pure Scientist," *Science* 134 (1961): 1957.
2. Not all discoveries fall so neatly as the preceding into one or the other of my two classes. For example, Anderson's work on the positron was done in complete ignorance of Dirac's theory from which the new particle's existence had already been very nearly predicted. On the other hand, the immediately succeeding work by Blackett and Occhialini made full use of Dirac's theory and therefore exploited experiment more fully and constructed a more forceful case for the positron's existence than Anderson had been able to do. On this subject see N. R. Hanson, "Discovering the Positron," *British Journal for the Philosophy of Science* 12 (1961): 194; 12 (1962): 299. Hanson suggests several of the points developed here. I am much indebted to Professor Hanson for a preprint of this material.
3. I have adapted a less familiar example from the same viewpoint in "The Caloric Theory of Adiabatic Compression," *Isis* 49 (1958): 132. A closely similar analysis of the emergence of a new theory is included in the early pages of my essay "Energy Conservation as an Example of Simultaneous Discovery," in *Critical Problems in the History of Science*, ed. M. Clagett (Madison: University of Wisconsin Press, 1959), pp. 321–56. . . . Reference to these papers may add depth and detail to the following discussion.
4. The still classic discussion of the discovery of oxygen is A. N. Meldrum, *The Eighteenth Century Revolution in Science: The First Phase* (Calcutta, 1930), chap. 5. A more convenient and generally quite reliable discussion is included in J. B. Conant, *The Overthrow of the Phlogiston Theory: The Chemical Revolution of 1775–1789,* Harvard Case Histories in Experimental Science, case 2 (Cambridge: Harvard University Press, 1950). A recent and indispensable review which includes an account of the development of the priority controversy, is M. Daumas, *Lavoisier, théoricien et expérimentateur* (Paris, 1955), chaps. 2 and 3. H. Guerlac has added much significant detail to our knowledge of the early relations between Priestley and Lavoisier in his "Joseph Priestley's First Papers on Gases and Their Reception in France," *Journal of the History of Medicine* 12 (1957): 1 and in his very recent monograph, *Lavoisier: The Crucial Year* (Ithaca: Cornell University Press, 1961). For Scheele see J. R. Partington, A *Short History of Chemistry,* 2d ed. (London, 1951), pp. 104–109.
5. For the dating of Scheele's work, see A. E. Nordenskjöld, *Carl Wilhelm Scheele, Nachgelassene Briefe und Aufzeichnungen* (Stockholm, 1892).
6. U. Bocklund ("A Lost Letter from Scheele to Lavoisier," *Lychnos,* 1957–58, pp. 39–62) argues that Scheele communicated his discovery of oxygen to Lavoisier in a letter of 30 Sept. 1774. Certainly the letter is

important, and it clearly demonstrates that Scheele was ahead of both Priestley and Lavoisier at the time it was written. But I think the letter is not quite so candid as Bocklund supposes, and I fail to see how Lavoisier could have drawn the discovery of oxygen from it. Scheele describes a procedure for reconstituting common air, not for producing a new gas, and that, as we shall see, is almost the same information that Lavoisier received from Priestley at about the same time. In any case, there is no evidence that Lavoisier performed the sort of experiment that Scheele suggested.

7. P. Bayen, "Essai d'expériences chymiques, faites sur quelques précipités de mercure, dans la vue de découvrir leur nature, Seconde partie," *Observations sur la physique* 3 (1774): 280–295, particularly pp. 289–291.
8. J. B. Conant, *The Overthrow of the Phlogiston Theory,* pp. 34–40.
9. Ibid., p. 23. A useful translation of the full text is available in Conant.
10. For simplicity I use the term *red precipitate* throughout. Actually, Bayen used the precipitate; Priestley used both the precipitate and the oxide produced by direct calcination of mercury; and Lavoisier used only the latter. The difference is not without importance, for it was not unequivocally clear to chemists that the two substances were identical.
11. There has been some doubt about Priestley's having influenced Lavoisier's thinking at this point, but, when the latter returned to experimenting with the gas in February 1776, he recorded in his notebooks that he had obtained "l'air dephlogistique de M. Priestley" (M. Daumas, *Lavoisier,* p. 36).
12. J. R. Partington, *A Short History of Chemistry,* p. 91.
13. For the traditional elements in Lavoisier's interpretations of chemical reactions, see H. Metzger, *La philosophie de la matière chez Lavoisier* (Paris, 1935), and Daumas, *Lavoisier,* chap. 7.
14. P. Doig, *A Concise History of Astronomy* (London: Chapman, 1990), pp. 115–116.
15. L. W. Taylor, *Physics, the Pioneer Science* (Boston: Houghton Mifflin Co., 1941), p. 790.
16. Though the point cannot be argued here, the conditions which make the emergence of anomaly likely and those which make anomaly recognizable are to a very great extent the same. That fact may help us understand the extraordinarily large amount of simultaneous discovery in the sciences.
17. A useful sketch of the development of pneumatic chemistry is included in Partington, *A Short History of Chemistry,* chap. 6.
18. R. Wolf, *Geschichte der Astronomie* (Munich, 1877), pp. 513–515, 683–693. The prephotographic discoveries of the asteroids is often seen as an effect of the invention of Bode's law. But that law cannot be the full explanation and may not even have played a large part. Piazzi's discovery of Ceres, in 1801, was made in ignorance of the current speculation about a missing planet in the "hole" between Mars and Jupiter. Instead, like Herschel, Piazzi was engaged on a star survey. More important, Bode's law was old by 1800 (ibid., p. 683), but only one man before that date seems to have thought it worthwhile to look for another planet. Finally, Bode's law, by itself, could only suggest the utility of looking for additional planets; it did not tell astronomers where to look. Clearly, however, the drive to look for additional planets dates from Herschel's work on Uranus.

19. For α-, β-, and γ-radiation, discovery of which dates from 1896, see Taylor, *Physics,* pp. 800–804. For the fourth new form of radiation, N rays, see D. J. S. Price, *Science Since Babylon,* (New Haven: Yale University Press, 1961), pp. 84–89. That N rays were ultimately the source of a scientific scandal does not make them less revealing of the scientific community's state of mind.

GETTING STARTED

1. In a group, summarize Kuhn's three-stage model of discovery. What is "anomaly," and where and how does it fit in Kuhn's model?
2. What does Kuhn mean when he says that scientists "struggle to make the anomaly lawlike" (p. 309)? Find an example in Kuhn that helps you to explain the quotation and write a paragraph summarizing your findings.
3. In a group, track the organization of Kuhn's essay by looking at the first sentence of each paragraph. List the main organizational moves he makes. What kinds of transitional words and phrases, such as "as an illustration of this," or "I conclude that," does he use to help you follow his train of thought?
4. Choose one of the examples of discovery that Kuhn uses—X rays, the planet Uranus, or oxygen—and analyze how that example connects to Kuhn's larger argument or thesis about discovery and scientific progress. In a group, compare your findings and decide which examples are most helpful in explaining Kuhn's main thesis and why. As you prepare to present your findings to the class, choose a quotation that helps you to identify Kuhn's main thesis.

WRITING

5. Write a short paper using one or more examples from Kuhn to explore his ideas about scientific discovery. Why does Kuhn believe that it is so hard to pinpoint the moment of scientific discovery? What do your examples show about the difficulties of attributing a "who" or a "when" to a given situation?

USING THE LIBRARY AND THE INTERNET

6. Find information about the discovery of the planet Uranus (including pictures) on the Internet or in an encyclopedia. How does your research compare with Kuhn's explanation of its discovery? Next, find information about Neptune. What does your research

reveal about Neptune's discovery? How is the process like or unlike the process that Kuhn describes?

7. Using a reference database such as Academic Search Elite that includes a range of scholarly sources, try combining the search term "paradigm" with a general scientific topic such as "oxygen." Then try a search in the same database using "paradigm" with a general nonscientific topic such as "education" or "criminal," or "justice." Take notes from several of the articles you find showing how the term "paradigm" is used in these differing contexts.

MAKING CONNECTIONS

8. Write a paper using Kuhn's ideas about scientific discovery to analyze one or more examples from Kaku's "Second Thoughts: The Genetics of a Brave New World?". In what ways do the discoveries Kaku describes present "who" and "when" problems similar to those discussed by Kuhn? To what extent can they be described as anomalies? Do Kaku's examples offer an understanding of scientific discovery that is different from Kuhn's?

9. Write a paper using Kuhn's essay and Scott DeVeaux's "Progress and the Bean" to discuss the idea of progress. In what ways does DeVeaux's argument benefit from Kuhn's ideas about progress and discovery? To what extent are Kuhn's ideas about scientific progress useful in DeVeaux's field of music? To what extent are they applicable to other fields as well?

10. In "Imagination and Reality," Jeanette Winterson describes the way that artists use imagination to "see outside of [a] dead vision" (p. 598). Write an essay comparing and contrasting that process with the process of scientific discovery that Kuhn describes. What are some of the overlaps and differences in the roles of the artist and the scientist?

11. Rebecca Solnit's "Aerobic Sisyphus and the Suburbanized Psyche," Susan Sontag's "In Plato's Cave," and Warren I. Susman's "'Personality' and the Making of Twentieth-Century Culture" each describe a fundamental shift in human thought and behavior. Choose one or more of these essays and write a paper in which you use the history traced by the other writers to explain and to complicate Kuhn's ideas about progress.

Christopher Lasch

Christopher Lasch (1932–1994) was professor of history at the University of Rochester. He was also a cultural critic well known for his biting social and political commentary. In particular, he protested against consumer capitalism's effects on American culture and against the growing power of bureaucratic elites. "The Lost Art of Argument" is taken from *The Revolt of the Elites and the Betrayal of Democracy* (1995), a book completed just prior to his death.

> **To learn more about Lasch and others who share his political ideas, see the home page of The Preservation Institute, an organization "dedicated to developing a new politics that recognizes the limits of technology," at <http://www.preservenet.com/>.**

The Lost Art of Argument

For many years now we have been regaled with the promise of the information age. The social effects of the communications revolution, we are told, will include an insatiable demand for trained personnel, an upgrading of the skills required for employment, and an enlightened public capable of following the issues of the day and of making informed judgments about civic affairs. Instead we find college graduates working at jobs for which they are vastly overqualified. The demand for menial labor outstrips the demand for skilled specialists. The postindustrial economy, it appears, promotes an interchangeability of personnel, a rapid movement from one type of work to another, and a growing concentration of the labor force in technically backward, labor-intensive, nonunion sectors of the economy. Recent experience does not bear out the expectation that technological innovations, improvements in communications in particular, will create an abundance of skilled jobs, eliminate disagreeable jobs, and make life easy for everyone. Their most important effect, on the contrary, is to widen the gap between the knowledge class and the rest of the population, between those who find themselves at home in the new global economy and who "relish the thought that the information flows to them can become bigger" all the time (in the words of Arno Penzias of AT&T Bell Laboratories) and those who, having little use for cellular phones, fax machines, or on-line information services, still live in what Penzias contemptuously refers to as the Age of Paper Work.

As for the claim that the information revolution would raise the level of public intelligence, it is no secret that the public knows less about public affairs than it used to know. Millions of Americans cannot begin to tell you what is in the Bill of Rights, what Congress does, what the Constitution says about the powers of the presidency, how the party system emerged or how it operates. A sizable majority, according to a recent survey, believe that Israel is an Arab nation. Instead of blaming the schools for this disheartening ignorance of public affairs, as is the custom, we should look elsewhere for a fuller explanation, bearing in mind that people readily acquire such knowledge as they can put to good use. Since the public no longer participates in debates on national issues, it has no reason to inform itself about civic affairs. It is the decay of public debate, not the school system (bad as it is), that makes the public ill informed, notwithstanding the wonders of the age of information. When debate becomes a lost art, information, even though it may be readily available, makes no impression.

What democracy requires is vigorous public debate, not information. Of course, it needs information too, but the kind of information it needs can be generated only by debate. We do not know what we need to know until we ask the right questions, and we can identify the right questions only by subjecting our own ideas about the world to the test of public controversy. Information, usually seen as the precondition of debate, is better understood as its by-product. When we get into arguments that focus and fully engage our attention, we become avid seekers of relevant information. Otherwise we take in information passively—if we take it in at all.

Political debate began to decline around the turn of the century, curiously enough at a time when the press was becoming more "responsible," more professional, more conscious of its civic obligations. In the early nineteenth century the press was fiercely partisan. Until the middle of the century papers were often financed by political parties. Even when they became more independent of parties, they did not embrace the ideal of objectivity or neutrality. In 1841 Horace Greeley launched his *New York Tribune* with the announcement that it would be a "journal removed alike from servile partisanship on the one hand and from gagged, mincing neutrality on the other." Strong-minded editors like Greeley, James Gordon Bennett, E. L. Godkin, and Samuel Bowles objected to the way in which the demands of party loyalty infringed upon editorial independence, making the editor merely a mouthpiece for a party or faction, but they did not attempt to conceal their own views or to impose a strict separation of news and editorial content. Their papers were journals of opinion in which the reader expected to find a definite point of view, together with unrelenting criticism of opposing points of view.

It is no accident that journalism of this kind flourished during the period from 1830 to 1900, when popular participation in politics was at its height. Of the eligible voters, 80 percent typically went to the polls in presidential elections. After 1900 the percentage declined sharply (to 65 percent in 1904 and 59 percent in 1912), and it has continued to decline more or less steadily throughout the twentieth century. Torchlight parades, mass rallies, and gladiatorial contents of oratory made nineteenth-century politics an object of consuming popular interest, in which journalism served as an extension of the town meeting. The nineteenth-century press created a public forum in which issues were hotly debated. Newspapers not only reported political controversies but participated in them, drawing in their readers as well. Print culture rested on the remnants of an oral tradition. Print was not yet the exclusive medium of communication, nor had it severed its connection with spoken language. The printed language was still shaped by the rhythms and requirements of the spoken word, in particular by the conventions of verbal argumentation. Print served to create a larger forum for the spoken word, not yet to displace or reshape it.

The Lincoln-Douglas debates exemplified the oral tradition at its best. By current standards, Lincoln and Douglas broke every rule of political discourse. They subjected their audiences (which were as large as fifteen thousand on one occasion) to a painstaking analysis of complex issues. They spoke with considerably more candor, in a pungent, colloquial, sometimes racy style, than politicians think prudent today. They took clear positions from which it was difficult to retreat. They conducted themselves as if political leadership carried with it an obligation to clarify issues instead of merely getting elected.

The contrast between these justly famous debates and present-day presidential debates, in which the media define the issues and draw up the ground rules, is unmistakable and highly unflattering to ourselves. Journalistic interrogation of political candidates—which is what debate has come to—tends to magnify the importance of journalists and to diminish that of the candidates. Journalists ask questions—prosaic, predictable questions for the most part—and press the candidates for prompt, specific answers, reserving the right to interrupt and to cut the candidates short whenever they appear to stray from the prescribed topic. To prepare for this ordeal, candidates rely on their advisers to stuff them full of facts and figures, quotable slogans, and anything else that will convey the impression of wide-ranging, unflappable competence. Faced not only with a battery of journalists ready to pounce on the slightest misstep but with the cold, relentless scrutiny of the camera, politicians know that everything depends on the management of visual impressions. They must radiate confidence and decisiveness and never appear to be at a loss for words. The nature of the occasion requires them to exaggerate the reach and effectiveness of public policy, to give the impression that the right programs and the right leadership can meet every challenge.

The format requires all candidates to look the same: confident, untroubled, and therefore unreal. But, it also imposes on them the obligation to explain what makes them different from the others. Once the question has to be asked, it answers itself. Indeed, the question is inherently belittling and degrading, a good example of TV's effect of lowering the object of estimation, of looking through every disguise, deflating every pretension. Bluntly stated with the necessary undertone of all-pervasive skepticism that is inescapably part of the language of TV, the question turns out to be highly rhetorical. What makes *you* so special? Nothing.

This is the quintessential question raised by TV, because it is in the medium's nature to teach us, with relentless insistence, that no one is special, contrary claims notwithstanding. At this point in our history the best qualification for high office may well be a refusal to cooperate with the media's program of self-aggrandizement. A candidate with the courage to abstain from "debates" organized by the media would automatically distinguish himself from the others and command a good deal of public respect. Candidates should insist on directly debating each other instead of responding to questions put to them by commentators and pundits. Their passivity and subservience lower them in the eyes of the voters. They need to recover their self-respect by challenging the media's status as arbiters of public discussion. A refusal to play by the media's rules would make people aware of the vast, illegitimate influence the mass media have come to exercise in American politics. It would also provide the one index of character that voters could recognize and applaud.

What happened to the tradition exemplified by the Lincoln-Douglas debates? The scandals of the Gilded Age gave party politics a bad name. They confirm the misgivings entertained by the "best men" ever since the rise of Jacksonian democracy. By the 1870s and 1880s a bad opinion of politics had come to be widely shared by the educated classes. Genteel reformers—"mugwumps" to their enemies—demanded a professionalization of politics, designed to free the civil service from party control and to replace political appointees with trained experts. Even those who rejected the invitation to declare their independence from the party system, like Theodore Roosevelt (whose refusal to desert the Republican party infuriated the "independents"), shared the enthusiasm for civil service reform. The "best men" ought to challenge the spoilsmen on their own turf, according to Roosevelt, instead of retreating to the sidelines of political life.

The drive to clean up politics gained momentum in the progressive era. Under the leadership of Roosevelt, Woodrow Wilson, Robert La Follette, and William Jennings Bryan, the progressives preached "efficiency," "good government," "bipartisanship," and the "scientific management" of public affairs and declared war on "bossism." They attacked the seniority system in Congress, limited the powers of the Speaker of the House, replaced mayors with city managers, and delegated important governmental functions to appointive commissions staffed with trained administrators. Recognizing that political machines were welfare agencies of a rudimentary type, which dispensed jobs and other benefits to their constituents and thereby won their loyalty, the progressives set out to create a welfare state as a way of competing with the machines. They launched comprehensive investigations of crime, vice, poverty, and other "social problems." They took the position that government was a science, not an art. They forged links between government and the university so as to assure a steady supply of experts and expert knowledge. But they had little use for public debate. Most political questions were too complex, in their view, to be submitted to popular judgment. They liked to contrast the scientific expert with the orator, the latter a useless windbag whose rantings only confused the public mind.

Professionalism in politics meant professionalism in journalism. The connection between them was spelled out by Walter Lippmann in a notable series of books: *Liberty and the News* (1920), *Public Opinion* (1922), and *The Phantom Public* (1925). These provided a founding charter for modern journalism, the most elaborate rationale for a journalism guided by the new ideal of professional objectivity. Lippmann held up standards by which the press is still judged—usually with the result that it is found wanting.

What concerns us here, however, is not whether the press has lived up to Lippmann's standards but how he arrived at those standards in the first place. In 1920 Lippmann and Charles Merz published a long essay in the *New Republic* examining press coverage of the Russian Revolution. This study, now forgotten, showed that American papers gave their readers an account of the Revolution distorted by anti-Bolshevik prejudices, wishful thinking, and sheer ignorance. *Liberty and the News* was also prompted by the collapse of journalistic objectivity during the war, when the newspapers had appointed themselves "defenders of the faith." The result, according to Lippmann, was a "breakdown of the means of public knowledge." The difficulty went beyond war or revolution, the "supreme destroyers of realistic thinking." The traffic in sex, violence, and "human interest"—staples of modern mass journalism—raised grave questions about the future of democracy. "All that the sharpest critics of democracy have alleged is true if there is no steady supply of trustworthy and relevant news."

In *Public Opinion* and *The Phantom Public,* Lippmann answered the critics, in effect, by redefining democracy. Democracy did not require that the people literally govern themselves. The public's stake in government was strictly procedural. The public interest did not extend to the substance of decision making: "The public is interested in law, not in the laws; in the method of law, not in the substance." Questions of substance should be decided by knowledgeable administrators whose access to reliable information immunized them against the emotional "symbols" and "stereotypes" that dominated public debate. The public was incompetent to govern itself and did not even care to do so, in Lippmann's view. But as long as rules of fair play were enforced, the public would be content to leave government to experts—provided, of course, that the experts delivered the goods, the ever-increasing abundance of comforts and conveniences so closely identified with the American way of life.

Lippmann acknowledged the conflict between his recommendations and the received theory of democracy, according to which citizens ought to participate in discussions of public policy and to have a hand, if only indirectly, in decision making. Democratic theory, he argued, had roots in social conditions that no longer obtained. It presupposed an "omnicompetent citizen," a "jack of all trades" who could be found only in a "simple self-contained community." In the "wide and unpredictable environment" of the modern world, the old ideal of citizenship was obsolete. A complex industrial society required a government carried on by officials who would necessarily be guided—since any form of direct democracy was now impossible—either by public opinion or by expert knowledge. Public opinion was unreliable because it could be united only by an appeal to slogans and "symbolic pictures." Lippmann's distrust of public opinion rested on the epistemological distinction between truth and mere opinion. Truth, as he conceived it, grew out of disinterested scientific inquiry; everything else was ideology. The scope of public debate accordingly had to be severely restricted. At best public debate was a disagreeable necessity—not the very essence of democracy but its "primary defect," which arose only because "exact knowledge," unfortunately, was in limited supply. Ideally public debate would not take place at all; decisions would be based on scientific "standards of measurement" alone. Science cut through "entangling stereotypes and slogans," the "threads of memory and emotion" that kept the "responsible administrator" tied up in knots.

The role of the press, as Lippmann saw it, was to circulate information, not to encourage argument. The relationship between information and argument was antagonistic, not complementary. He did not take the position that reliable information was a necessary precondition of argument; on the contrary, his point was that information precluded argument, made argument unnecessary. Arguments were what took place in the absence of reliable information. Lippmann had forgotten what he learned (or should have learned) from William James and John Dewey: that our search for reliable information is itself guided by the questions that arise during arguments about a given course of action. It is only by subjecting our preferences and projects to the test of debate that we come to understand what we know and what we still need to learn. Until we have to defend our opinions in public, they remain opinions in Lippmann's pejorative sense—half-formed convictions based on random impressions and unexamined assumptions. It is the act of articulating and defending our views that lifts them out of the category of "opinions," gives them shape and definition, and makes it possible for others to recognize them as a description of their own experience as well. In short, we come to know our own minds only by explaining ourselves to others.

The attempt to bring others around to our own point of view carries the risk, of course, that we may adopt their point of view instead. We have to enter imaginatively into our opponents' arguments, if only for the purpose of refuting them, and we may end up being persuaded by those we sought to persuade. Argument is risky and unpredictable, therefore educational. Most of us tend to think of it (as Lippmann thought of it) as a clash of rival dogmas, a shouting match in which neither side gives any ground. But arguments are not won by shouting down opponents. They are won by changing opponents' minds—something that can happen only if we give opposing arguments a respectful hearing and still persuade their advocates that there is something wrong with those arguments. In the course of this activity we may well decide that there is something wrong with our own.

If we insist on argument as the essence of education, we will defend democracy not as the most efficient but as the most educational form of government, one that extends the circle of debate as widely as possible and thus forces all citizens to articulate their views, to put their views at risk, and to cultivate the virtues of eloquence, clarity of thought and expression, and sound judgment. As Lippmann noted, small communities are the classic locus of democracy—not because they are "self-contained," however, but simply because they allow everyone to take part in public debates. Instead of dismissing direct democracy as irrelevant to modern conditions, we need to re-create it on a large scale. From this point of view the press serves as the equivalent of the town meeting.

This is what Dewey argued, in effect—though not, unfortunately, very clearly—in *The Public and Its Problems* (1927), a book written in reply to Lippmann's disparaging studies of public opinion. Lippmann's distinction between truth and information rested on a "spectator theory of knowledge," as James W. Carey explains in his *Communication as Culture*. As Lippmann understood these matters, knowledge is what we get when an observer, preferably a scientifically trained observer, provides us with a copy of reality that we can all recognize. Dewey, on the other hand, knew that even scientists argue among themselves. "Systematic inquiry," he contended, was only the beginning of knowledge, not its final form. The knowledge needed by any community—whether it was a community of scientific inquirers or a political community—emerged only from "dialogue" and "direct give and take."

It is significant, as Carey points out, that Dewey's analysis of communication stressed the ear rather than the eye. "Conversation," Dewey wrote, "has a vital import lacking in the fixed and frozen words of written speech. . . . The connections of the ear with vital and outgoing thought and emotion are immensely closer and more varied than those of the eye. Vision is a spectator; hearing is a participator."

The press extends the scope of debate by supplementing the spoken word with the written word. If the press needs to apologize for anything, it is not that the written word is a poor substitute for the pure language of mathematics. What matters, in this connection, is that the written word is a poor substitute for the spoken word. It is an acceptable substitute, however, as long as written speech takes spoken speech and not mathematics as its model. According to Lippmann, the press was unreliable because it could never give us accurate representations of reality, only "symbolic pictures" and stereotypes. Dewey's analysis implied a more penetrating line of criticism. As Carey puts it, "The press, by seeing its role as that of informing the public, abandons its role as an agency for carrying on the conversation of our culture." Having embraced Lippmann's ideal of objectivity, the press no longer serves to cultivate "certain vital habits" in the community: "the ability to follow an argument, grasp the point of view of another, expand the boundaries of understanding, debate the alternative purposes that might be pursued."

The rise of the advertising and public relations industries, side by side, helps to explain why the press abdicated its most important function—enlarging the public forum—at the same time that it became more "responsible." A responsible press, as opposed to a partisan or opinionated one, attracted the kind of readers advertisers were eager to reach: well-heeled readers, most of whom probably thought of themselves as independent voters. These readers wanted to be assured that they were reading all the news that was fit to print, not an editor's idiosyncratic and no doubt biased view of things. Responsibility came to be equated with the avoidance of controversy because advertisers were willing to pay for it. Some advertisers were also willing to pay for sensationalism, though on the whole they preferred a respectable readership to sheer numbers. What they clearly did not prefer was "opinion"—not because they were impressed with Lippmann's philosophical arguments but because opinionated reporting did not guarantee the right audience. No doubt they also hoped that an aura of objectivity, the hallmark of responsible journalism, would also rub off on the advertisements that surrounded increasingly slender columns of print.

In a curious historical twist, advertising, publicity, and other forms of commercial persuasion themselves came to be disguised as information. Advertising and publicity substituted for open debate. "Hidden persuaders" (as Vance Packard called them) replaced the old-time editors, essayists, and orators who made no secret of their partisanship. Information and publicity became increasingly indistinguishable. Most of the "news" in our newspapers—40 percent, according to the conservative estimate of Professor Scott Cutlip of the University of Georgia—consists of items churned out by press agencies and public relations bureaus and then regurgitated intact by the "objective" organs of journalism. We have grown accustomed to the idea that most of the space in newspapers, so called, is devoted to advertising—at least two-thirds in most newspapers. But if we consider public relations as another form of advertising, which is hardly farfetched since private, commercially inspired enterprises fuel both, we now have to get used to the idea that much of the "news" consists of advertising too.

The decline of the partisan press and the rise of a new type of journalism professing rigorous standards of objectivity do not assure a steady supply of usable information. Unless information is generated by sustained public debate, most of it will be irrelevant at best, misleading and manipulative at worst. Increasingly information is generated by those who wish to promote something or someone—a product, a cause, a political candidate or officeholder—without arguing their case on its merits or explicitly advertising it as self-interested material either. Much of the press, in its eagerness to inform the public, has become a conduit for the equivalent of junk mail. Like the post office—another institution that once served to extend the sphere of face-to-face discussion and to create "committees of correspondence"—it now delivers an abundance of useless, indigestible information that nobody wants, most of which ends up as unread waste. The most important effect of this obsession with information, aside from the destruction of trees for paper and the mounting burden of "waste management," is to undermine the authority of the word. When words are used merely as instruments of publicity or propaganda, they lose their power to persuade. Soon they cease to mean anything at all. People lose the capacity to use language precisely and expressively or even to distinguish one word from another. The spoken word models itself on the written word instead of the other way around, and ordinary speech begins to sound like the clotted jargon we see in print. Ordinary speech begins to sound like "information"—a disaster from which the English language may never recover.

1995

GETTING STARTED

1. As you read, develop a definition of what Lasch means when he talks about the "decay in public debate." What does the phrase suggest? What does Lasch believe are some of the consequences of that decay? What historical reasons does he give for that decay?

2. Summarize Lasch's discussion of the history of print journalism's relationship to public debate. Work in groups to create a chronology showing the role of the press in the nineteenth century and how it changed in subsequent periods.

3. Various ideas of "democracy" are presented throughout this essay, not only by Lasch himself, but also by Walter Lippmann, John Dewey, and others. List as many different uses of the concept of "democracy" as you can find in Lasch's essay, share them in groups, and discuss the differences that emerge.

4. Analyze an argument from a front-page newspaper story or a network news story. Do Lasch's descriptions of modern-day journalism seem justified? Why or why not? To what extent are you simply presented with objective information and to what extent are you presented with a debate?

WRITING

5. Lasch seems critical of the "aura of objectivity" that became part of the professionalization of the modern press. How can he argue that public debate actually declined with the rise of an "objective," "neutral," and more professional press? Use examples from his essay, as well as from newspapers, the Internet, and television sources, to write a paper that explains and tests his claims. From your research and observation, are Lasch's arguments about the modern-day press accurate? Do professionalization and the goal of neutrality damage public debate? Do you see any echoes in today's press of the nineteenth-century role of journalism that Lasch praises?

6. Lasch argues that there has been a decline in the kind of public debate that is the key to a working democracy. Test Lasch's argument by considering the press coverage of a current political issue. Choose a newspaper article as the basis for your analysis. Does the article have an "aura of objectivity," does it present information, or does it openly argue an opinion? Does it present a "painstaking analysis of complex issues" (p. 317)? Does it show more than one side to the issue or help you to understand the controversy? Does it offer evidence of a public debate or a way in which public debate

might reshape this political issue? Which of the historical factors that Lasch brings up would best explain the way the article is written? Even if you end up disagreeing with Lasch, you must demonstrate an understanding of his examples and his point of view.

USING THE LIBRARY AND THE INTERNET

7. Lasch does not mention the newest information medium—the Internet. Choose a recent news issue and find an account of it published in a well-known newspaper. Then, using an Internet directory such as About or Yahoo!, find two Web sites that relate to that same issue. Finally, look for that issue (or a similar one) being addressed on a television or radio talk show. What are the differences in the way the information is presented? How much information is given? How reliable does the information seem? How objective does the source seem? What degree of public debate is indicated (does the source present quotes from people with contradictory views on the subject, for example)?

8. Using your library's reference collection or a database such as JStor that includes historical journals, look up the Lincoln-Douglas debates discussed by Lasch (p. 317). Take some notes comparing and contrasting their methods of debate to a current political debate or to a set of current campaign advertisements or brochures. Bring your notes to class.

MAKING CONNECTIONS

9. Compare and contrast Lasch's and Sven Birkerts's views on how our reading practices create and define the world we live in. How might different practices of reading (and public debate) lead to (positive or negative) changes? Discuss to what extent these two authors seem to be merely resistant to advances in information technology and to what extent you find their cautions justifiable. Use examples from the essays and from your own knowledge and experiences to answer these questions.

10. Use Lasch's ideas about argument and the role of public debate to analyze examples from Gloria Anzaldúa's "Chicana Artists: Exploring *Nepantla, el Lugar de la Frontera*" or Zita Ingham's "Landscape, Drama, Dissensus: The Rhetorical Education of Red Lodge, Montana." Could any of the rhetorical strategies used by Anzaldúa or by the Red Lodge community be used productively in larger American political debates, or is their use limited to small communities? Explain why.

RICHARD C. LEWONTIN

Richard C. Lewontin (1929–) is the Alexander Agassiz Research Professor at the Museum of Comparative Zoology at Harvard University. Lewontin is a controversial evolutionary biologist whose work seeks to relate biology to human affairs. His books include *The Genetic Basis of Evolutionary Change* (1974), *Not in Our Genes: Biology, Ideology, and Human Nature* (coauthored with Steven Rose and Leon J. Kamin) (1984), *Human Diversity* (1982), and *The Triple Helix: Gene, Organism, and Environment* (2000). "Science as Social Action" is from *Biology as Ideology: The Doctrine of DNA* (1991). Lewontin is concerned about the misuse of science in the formation of public policy.

To learn more about this issue, see The Science & Environmental Policy Project Web site at <http://www.sepp.org/>.

Science as Social Action

The previous pages have all been concerned with a particular ideological bias of modern biology. That bias is that everything that we are, our sickness and health, our poverty and wealth, and the very structure of the society we live in are ultimately encoded in our DNA. We are, in Richard Dawkins's metaphor, lumbering robots created by our DNA, body and mind. But the view that we are totally at the mercy of internal forces present within ourselves from birth is part of a deep ideological commitment that goes under the name of *reductionism.* By reductionism we mean the belief that the world is broken up into tiny bits and pieces, each of which has its own properties and which combine together to make larger things. The individual makes society, for example, and society is nothing but the manifestation of the properties of individual human beings. Individual internal properties are the causes and the properties of the social whole are the effects of those causes. This individualistic view of the biological world is simply a reflection of the ideologies of the bourgeois revolutions of the eighteenth century that placed the individual at the center of everything.

Such a view about causes and effects and the autonomy of individual bits and pieces not only results in a belief that internal forces beyond our control govern what we are as individuals. It also posits an external world with its own bits and pieces, its own laws, which we as individuals confront but do not influence. Just as the genes are totally inside of us, so the environment is totally outside of us, and we as actors are at the mercy of both these internal and external worlds. This gives rise to the false dichotomy of nature and nurture. Against those who say that our ability to solve problems, our intelligence, is determined by our genes, there exists a contrary party that claims that our intelligence is determined by our environment. And so the struggle goes on between those who believe in the primacy of nature and those who believe in the primacy of nurture.

The separation between nature and nurture, between the organism and the environment, goes back to Charles Darwin, who finally brought biology into the modern mechanistic world view. Before Darwin, it was the general view that what was outside and what was inside were part of the same whole system and one could influence the other. The most famous theory of evolution before Darwin was that of Jean Baptiste Lamarck, who believed in the inheritance of acquired characteristics. Changes occurred in the environment that caused changes in the body or behavior of organisms, and it was believed that the changes induced by the environment would enter into the hereditary structure of the organisms and would be passed on to the next generation. In this view, nothing separates what is outside from what is inside because external alterations would enter into the organism and be perpetuated in future generations.

Darwin completely rejected this world view and replaced it with one in which organisms and environment were totally separated. The external world had its own laws, its own mechanisms of operation. Organisms confronted these and experienced them and either successfully adapted to them or failed. The rule of life, according to Darwin, is "adapt or die." Those organisms whose properties enabled them to cope with the problems set by the external world would survive and leave offspring, and the others would fail to do so. The species would change, not because the environment directly caused physical and body changes in organisms, but because those organisms smart enough to be able to handle the problems thrown at them by nature would leave more offspring, who would resemble them. The deep point of Darwinism was the separation between the forces of the environment that create the problems and the internal forces of the organism that throw up solutions to problems more or less at random, the correct solutions being preserved. The external and internal forces of the world behave independently. The only connection between them is a passive one. The organisms who happen to be lucky enough to find a match between what is going on inside themselves and what is going on outside themselves survive.

Darwin's view was essential to our successful unraveling of evolution. Lamarck was simply wrong about the way the environment influences heredity, and Darwin's alienation of the organism from the environment was an essential first step in a correct description of the way the forces of nature act on each other. The problem is that it was only a *first* step, and we have become frozen there. Modern biology has become completely committed to the view that organisms are nothing but the battle grounds between the outside forces and the inside forces. Organisms are the passive consequences of external and internal activities beyond their control. This view has important political reverberations. It implies that the world is outside our control, that we must take it as we find it and do the best we can to make our way through the mine field of life using whatever equipment our genes have provided to us to get to the other side in one piece.

What is so extraordinary about the view of an external environment set for us by nature, and essentially unchangeable except in the sense that we might ruin it and destroy the delicate balance that nature has created in our absence, is that it is completely in contradiction to what we know about organisms and environment. When we free ourselves of the ideological bias of atomism and reductionism and look squarely at the actual relations between organisms and the world around them, we find a much richer set of relations, relations that have very different consequences for social and political action than are usually supposed, for example, by the environmental movement.

First, there is no "environment" in some independent and abstract sense. Just as there is no organism without an environment, there is no environment without an organism. Organisms do not experience environments. They create them. They construct their own environments out of the bits and pieces of the physical and biological world and they do so by their own activities. Are the stones and the grass in my garden part of the environment of a bird? The grass is certainly part of the environment of a phoebe that gathers dry grass to make a nest. But the stone around which the grass is growing means nothing to the phoebe. On the other hand, the stone is part of the environment of a thrush that may come along with a garden snail and break the shell of the snail against the stone. Neither the grass nor the stone are part of the environment of a woodpecker that is living in a hole in a tree. That is, bits and pieces of the world outside of these organisms are made relevant to them by their own life activities. If grass is used to make a nest, then grass is part of the environment. If stones are used to break snails on, then stones are part of the environment.

There is an infinity of ways in which parts of the world can be assembled to make an environment, and we can know what the environment of an organism is only by consulting the organism. Not only do we consult the organism, but when we describe the environment we describe it in terms of the organism's behavior and life activities. If you are in any doubt of this, you might try asking a professional ecologist to describe the environment of some bird. He or she will say something like the following. "Well, the bird builds its nest three feet off the ground in hardwoods. It eats insects part of the year but then may switch to seeds and nuts when insects are no longer available. It flies south in the winter and comes back north in the summer, and when it is foraging for its food it tends to stay in the higher branches and at their outer tips," and so on. Every word uttered by the ecologist in describing the environment of a bird will be a description of the life activities of the bird. That process of description reflects the fact that the ecologist has learned what the environment of the bird is by watching birds.

A practical demonstration of the difficulty of describing an environment without having seen an organism that determined and defined it is the case of the Mars Lander. When the United States decided to send a landing module to Mars, biologists wanted to know if there was any life there. So the problem was to design a machine to detect life on Mars. There were several interesting suggestions. One was to send a kind of microscope with a long sticky tongue that would unroll on the planet's surface and then roll back up and put whatever dust it found under the microscope. If there was anything that looked like a living organism, we would see it in the images sent back to Earth. One might call this the morphological definition of life. If it looks right and it wiggles, then it is alive.

What appears to be a more sophisticated approach was taken. Instead of asking whether things on Mars look alive, it was decided to ask whether they have the metabolism of living things. So the Mars Lander contained what was essentially a long hose attached to a vacuum cleaner inside of which was a container of radioactive growth medium. When the Lander got to Mars, it would suck up some dust into the medium and if there were any living organisms in the dust, they would break down the medium as bacteria do on Earth, radioactive carbon dioxide would be produced, and a detector in the machine would signal the presence of this gas. And that is exactly what happened. When the Mars Lander sucked up the dust, radioactive carbon dioxide was produced in a pattern that had everyone convinced that there was life on Mars fermenting the medium. But then suddenly the process shut down and there was no further fermentation. This was not what living organisms were supposed to do, and the consequence was scientific confusion. After a debate among those concerned with the experiment, it was decided that there was no life on Mars. Instead, it was postulated that there was a kind of chemical reaction on finely divided clay particles catalyzed by the particles, which were not ordinarily seen on Earth. Later, this reaction was successfully mimicked in the laboratory, so everybody has now agreed that they decided correctly and that there is no life on Mars.

The problem with this experiment arises precisely from the fact that organisms define their own environment. How can we know whether there is life on Mars? We present Martian life with an environment and see whether it can live in it. But how can we know what the environment of Martian life is unless we have seen Martian organisms? All that the experiment of the Mars Lander showed was that there is no Earth-like bacterial life on Mars. We may know the temperature, the gas content of the atmosphere, the humidity, and something about the soil on Mars, but we do not know what a Martian environment is like because the environment does not consist of temperature, gas, moisture, and soil. It consists of an organized set of relationships among bits and pieces of the world, which organization has been created by living Martian organisms themselves.

We must replace the adaptationist view of life with a constructionist one. It is not that organisms find environments and either adapt themselves to the environments or die. They actually *construct* their environment out of bits and pieces. In this sense, the environment of organisms is coded in their DNA and we find ourselves in a kind of reverse Lamarckian position. Whereas Lamarck supposed that changes in the external world would cause changes in the internal structures, we see that the reverse is true. An organism's genes, to the extent that they influence what that organism does in its behavior, physiology, and morphology, are at the same time helping to construct an environment. So, if genes change in evolution, the environment of the organism will change too.

Consider the immediate environment of a human being. If one takes motion pictures of a person, using schlieren optics that detect differences in the refractive index of the air, one can see that a layer of warm, moist air completely surrounds each one of us and is slowly rising from our legs and bodies and going off the top of our heads. In fact, every living organism including trees has this boundary layer of warm air that is created by the organism's metabolism. The result is that we are encapsulated in a little atmosphere created by our own metabolic activities. One consequence is what is called the wind-chill factor. The reason that it gets much colder when the wind blows across us is because the wind is blowing away the boundary layer and our skins are then exposed to a different set of temperatures and humidities. Consider a mosquito feeding on the surface of the human body. That mosquito is completely immersed in the boundary layer that we have constructed. It is living in a warm, moist world. Yet one of the most common evolutionary changes for all organisms is a change in size, and over and over again organisms have evolved to be larger. If the mosquito species begins to evolve to a larger size, it may in fact find itself with its back in the "stratosphere" and only up to its knees in the warm, moist boundary layer while it is feeding. The consequence will be that the mosquito's evolution has put it into an entirely different world. Moreover, as human beings early in their evolution lost hair and the distribution of sweat glands over their bodies changed, the thickness of the boundary layer changed and so changed the micro-world that they carry with them, making it rather less hospitable for fleas, mosquitoes, and other parasites that live on hairy animals. The first rule of the real relation between organisms and environment is that environments do not exist in the absence of organisms but are constructed by them out of bits and pieces of the external world.

The second rule is that the environment of organisms is constantly being remade during the life of those living beings. When plants send down roots, they change the physical nature of the soil, breaking it up and aerating it. They exude organic molecules, humic acids, that change the soil's chemical nature as well. They make it possible for various beneficial fungi to live together with them and penetrate their root systems. They change the height of the water table by removing water. They alter the humidity in their immediate neighborhood, and the upper leaves of a plant change the amount of light that is available to the lower leaves. When the Canadian Department of Agriculture takes weather records for agricultural purposes, they do not set up a weather station in an open field or on the roof of a building. They take measurements of temperature and humidity at various levels above the ground in a field of growing plants because the plants are constantly changing the physical conditions that are relevant to agriculture. Moles burrow in the soil. Earthworms through their castings completely change the local topology. Beavers have had at least as important an effect on the landscape in North America as humans did until the beginning of the last century. Every breath you take removes oxygen and adds carbon dioxide to the world. Mort Sahl once said, "Remember, no matter how cruel and nasty and evil you may be, every time you take a breath you make a flower happy."

Every living organism is in a constant process of changing the world in which it lives by taking up materials and putting out others. Every act of consumption is also an act of production. And every act of production is an act of consumption. When we consume food, we produce not only gases but solid waste products that are in turn the material for consumption of some other organism.

A consequence of the universality of environmental change induced by the life activity of organisms is that every organism is both producing and destroying the conditions of its existence. There is a great deal of talk about how we as human beings are destroying the environment. But we are not unique in the fact that our life processes are recreating the world in a way that is in part hostile to the continuation of our own lives. Every bacterium uses up food material and excretes waste products that are toxic to it. Organisms ruin the world not only for their own lives but for their children as well.

The entire vegetational landscape of New England is a consequence of that process. The primeval forest in New England consisted of a mixture of hardwoods, pines and hemlocks. As agriculture spread at the end of the eighteenth and through the nineteenth century, all these forests were cut down and replaced by farms. Then, just before and after the Civil War, there were wholesale migrations out of the rocky soils of New England, where one could barely plant a crop, to the deep and productive soils of the Middle West. As a result, farms were abandoned and plants started to infiltrate these old fields. The first thing that came in was a variety of weeds and herbs. These were replaced later by white pines. White pines can form an almost pure stand in an old field and many such pure white pine stands could be seen in New England earlier in this century. However, they do not last. The pines make a dense shade that is inhospitable to the growth of their own seedlings, and so they cannot replace each other. As the pines die or if, as in New England, they are cut wholesale, what comes in are hardwoods, whose seedlings have been waiting around for a little opening. The white pines disappear forever with the exception of an occasional old tree, and a composition similar to the prehistoric virgin forest appears. This old-field white pine to hardwood succession is a consequence of the conditions of light and soil being changed by the pine trees in such a way that their own offspring cannot succeed them. The generation gap is not simply a human phenomenon.

So, we must put away the notion that out there is a constant and fixed world that human beings alone are disturbing and destroying. We are certainly changing it, as all organisms do, and we certainly have a power that other organisms do not have, both to change the world extremely rapidly and, by willful activity, to change the world in various ways that we may think beneficial. Nevertheless, we cannot live without changing the environment. That is the second law of the relationship between organism and environment.

Third, organisms determine the statistical nature of the environment at least as far as it has an influence on themselves. Organisms are capable of averaging over time and buffering out the fluctuations in physical factors. An important example is the way animals and plants store sunlight. Even though the conditions for growth and good nutrition do not exist all year around in a temperate zone, it is not only farmers who make hay while the sun shines. Potatoes are the storage organs of potato plants and acorns form the storage for oak trees. Other organisms, in turn, use these storage devices for their own storage. Squirrels store away acorns for use in the winter and human beings store away potatoes. As human beings, we have even a further level of averaging: money. Money is the way in which, through futures contracts, fluctuations in the availability of natural products are ironed out for the market, and savings banks are where we put money for a rainy day. So organisms do not, in fact, perceive at a physiological level much of the fluctuation that goes on in the external world.

Conversely, organisms have techniques of reacting to the rates of change of the external world rather than the actual levels of resources. Water fleas are sometimes sexual and sometimes asexual.

They change from nonsexual reproduction to sexual reproduction when a drastic change occurs in the environment, say, the change in the amount of oxygen in the water in which they live or a change in its temperature or a change in food availability. They do not alter from nonsexual to sexual when the temperature is high or when it is low but when it changes rapidly in either direction. They are detectors of change pure and simple. Our visual system is also a sensitive detector of change. Our central nervous system, by complex processing of images, enables us to see differences in intensity of light across edges in a way that is superior to what physical and electronic devices can do. We accomplish this by magnifying differences across small distances. Thus, we have greater visual acuity than optical scanning machinery. The third rule of organism and environment, then, is that fluctuations in the world matter only as organisms transform them.

Finally, organisms actually change the basic physical nature of signals that come to them from the external world. As the temperature in a room rises, my liver detects that change, not as a rise in temperature, but as a change in the concentration of sugar in my blood and the concentration of certain hormones. What begins as a change in the rate of a vibration of air molecules—a change in temperature—becomes converted inside the body into a change in the concentration of certain chemical substances. The nature of that conversion is a consequence of the action of genes, which have a strong influence on anatomy and physiology. When I am out in the desert doing my field work and I hear and see a rattlesnake, those rarefactions of the air that impinge on my eardrums and those photons of light that come into my eye are changed by my central nervous system into a chemical signal and suddenly my adrenaline starts to flow. But these vibrations and photons would be changed to a very different chemical signal in the body of another snake that is receiving exactly the same sights and sounds, especially if it were a snake of the opposite sex. This difference in transformation of one signal into another is coded in the difference between human genes and the genes of a snake. The last rule of the relation between organism and environment is that the very physical nature of the environment as it is relevant to organisms is determined by the organisms themselves.

It may be objected that such an interactive picture of organism and environment is all very well but it ignores some obvious aspects of the external world over which organisms have no control. A human being may have *discovered* the law of gravitation, but he certainly did not *pass* it. You cannot fight gravity. But that, in fact, is not true. A bacterium living in liquid does not feel gravity because it is so small and its buoyant properties free it from what is essentially a very weak force. But the size of a bacterium is a consequence of its genes, and so it is the genetic difference between us and bacteria that determines whether the force of gravitation is relevant to us.

On the other hand, bacteria feel a universal physical force that we do not, the force of Brownian motion. Precisely because bacteria are so small, they are battered from one side to the other by the motion of molecules in the liquid in which they are suspended. We, fortunately, are not constantly reeling from one side of the room to the other under the influence of that bombardment because we are so large. All forces of nature depend for their influence on size, distance, and time duration. How large an organism is, how rapidly it alters its state and position, how far it is from other organisms of different sizes and kinds are all deeply influenced by the organism's genes. So, in a very important sense, the physical forces of the world, insofar as they are relevant to living beings, are encoded in those beings' genes. Just as we cannot talk about living organisms as just products of their genes but must recognize that the genes interact with the environment in producing the organism in its development and activity, so reciprocally we cannot make the mistake of saying that organisms confront an autonomous external world. The environment influences organisms only through interaction with their genes. The internal and the external are inextricably bound up with each other.

The facts of the relationship between organism and environment have important consequences for current political and social movements. There is a widespread perception that in many ways the world is becoming a rather less pleasant and more threatening place to live in, and there is a good possibility that it may grow catastrophically unpleasant in the not too distant future. It may get a lot warmer. A good deal more ultraviolet light may strike us than now does. The world does not smell very good. There are all sorts of noxious substances that are the agents of illness and even death, and we recognize all these changes as the consequence of human activity. It is entirely correct that human beings should want to make a world in which they can live happy, healthful, and reasonably long lives. But we cannot do that under the banner of "Save the Environment," because this slogan assumes that there is *an* environment that has been created by nature and that we in our foolishness are destroying. It assumes, too, that there is such a thing as the balance of nature, that everything is in a balance and harmony that is being destroyed only by the foolishness and greed of human beings.

There is nothing in our knowledge of the world to suggest there is any particular balance or harmony. The physical and biological worlds since the beginning of the earth have been in a constant state of flux and change, much of which has been far more drastic than anyone can now conceive. Indeed, much of what we conceive of as the environment has been the creation of living organisms. The atmosphere that we all breathe and that we hope we can continue to breathe is about 18 percent oxygen and a fraction of a percent of carbon dioxide. But that atmosphere was not on earth before living organisms. Most of the oxygen was bound up in chemicals. Oxygen is a very unstable compound and does not exist stably in free form. There was, however, a high concentration of free carbon dioxide. The carbon dioxide was removed from the atmosphere and deposited in limestone and chalk by the action of algae and bacteria during the early history of the earth and in oil and coal by plants somewhat later. The oxygen, which was not present at all, was put into the atmosphere by the activity of plants, and then animals evolved in a world made for them by the earlier organisms. Only 60,000 years ago, Canada was completely under ice, as was the middle of the United States. *The* environment has never existed and there has never been balance or harmony. Fully 99.999 percent of all species that have ever existed are already extinct, and in the end all will become extinct. Indeed, life is about half over. Our estimates are that the first living organisms appeared on earth in the order of 3 to 4 billion years ago, and we know from stellar evolution that our sun will expand and burn up the earth in another 3 to 4 billion years, putting an end to everything.

So any rational environmental movement must abandon the romantic and totally unfounded ideological commitment to a harmonious and balanced world in which the environment is preserved and turn its attention to the real question, which is, how do people want to live and how are they to arrange that they live that way? Human beings do have a unique property not shared by other organisms. It is not the destructive property but the property that they can plan the changes that will occur in the world. They cannot stop the world from changing, but they may be able with appropriate social organization to divert those changes in a more beneficial direction, and so, perhaps, even postpone their own extinction for a few hundred thousand years.

Is it within the biological capability of human beings to reorganize their futures? This question brings us back to the issue of human nature and its biological determination. If sociobiologists are right, then human beings have limitations coded in their genes that make them individually entrepreneurial, selfish, aggressive, xenophobic, family oriented, driven toward dominance, self-interested in a way that precludes any real possibility for a radical reorganization of society. You cannot fight human nature. On the other hand, if Kropotkin was right that human beings are biologically impelled toward cooperation and have been artificially held away from it historically, then such a reorganization might be possible. So it would seem that we would need to know the truth about individual human biological limitations. After all, we cannot transcend the limitations that are part of our biological nature. Perhaps we really had better sequence the entire human DNA because that is a first step, although an insufficient one, to learn what human limitations may be. In his book *Sociobiology,* Professor Wilson says,

> If the decision is taken to mold cultures to fit the requirements of the ecological steady state, some behaviors can be altered experientially without emotional damage or loss in creativity. Others cannot . . . We do not know how many of the most valued qualities are linked genetically to the more obsolete destructive ones. Cooperativeness towards group mates might be coupled with aggressivity towards strangers, creativeness with the desire to own and dominate. If the planned society, the creation of which seems inevitable in the coming century, were deliberately to steer its members past those stresses and conflicts that once gave the destructive phenotypes their Darwinian edge, the other phenotypes might dwindle with them. In this, the ultimate genetic sense, social control would rob man of his humanity.[1]

It appears, then, that we need to know the genetic linkages between the various aspects of an individual's behavior, because if we do not, we may ruin the world altogether in our blundering attempts to make it better.

The demand for biological information and the implied assumption that society needs to be guided, in the end, by a technocratic elite who understand genetics totally confounds the properties and limitations of individuals with the properties and limitations of the social institutions that they create. It is the ultimate political manifestation of the belief that individual autonomous units determine the properties of the collectivities in which they assemble.

But when we look around at society, we see that the opposite is true. If we have to characterize social organization and its consequences, it is that social organization does not reflect the limitations of individual biological beings but is their *negation*. No individual human being can fly by flapping his or her arms and legs. That is indeed a biological limitation having to do with our size and the size of our appendages. Nor could human beings fly if a very large number of them assembled in one place and all flapped their arms and legs simultaneously. Yet I did fly to Toronto last year, and the ability to fly was a consequence of social action. Airplanes and airports are products of educational institutions, scientific discoveries, the organization of money, the production of petroleum and its refining, metallurgy, the training of pilots, the actions of government in creating air traffic control systems, all of which are social products. These social products have come together to make it possible for us as individuals to fly.

It is important to note that although flight is a social product, it is not society that flies. Society cannot fly. Individuals fly. But they fly as a consequence of social organization.

---

1. E. O. Wilson, *Sociobiology*, 575.

Sherlock Holmes once explained to Dr. Watson that he did not know whether the sun went around the earth or the earth went around the sun because it made no difference whatsoever to his affairs. He analogized the mind to a kind of attic in which one could put just a certain amount of lumber, and every new fact added had to displace an old one. There is indeed a limit to what any human being can remember if by "remember" we mean the number of things that one can pull out of one's head. No historian of health and disease can remember all the bills of mortality, all the demographic statistics since the nineteenth century. Yet historians do remember those facts because they can look them up in books, and books are a social product, as are the libraries that hold them. So social activity makes it possible for us to remember what no human being could remember as an isolated entity.

Individual biological limitations understood from viewing individuals as isolated entities in a vacuum are not individual limitations for individuals embedded in society. It is not that the whole is more than the sum of its parts. It is that the properties of the parts cannot be understood except in their context in the whole. Parts do not have individual properties in some isolated sense, but only in the context in which they are found. The theory of human nature that searches for that nature in the products of genes in individuals and the limitations of individuals caused by those genes, or in the properties of an external world that are fixed and that cannot be altered except in a destructive way, misses the whole point.

It is indeed the case that human social and political organization is a reflection of our biological being, for, after all, we are material biological objects developing under the influence of the interaction of our genes with the external world. It is certainly not the case that our biology is irrelevant to social organization. The question is, what part of our biology is relevant? If one were to choose a simple biological property of human beings that was of supreme importance, it would be our size. The fact that we are somewhere between five and six feet tall has made all of human life possible as we know it. Gulliver's Lilliputians, who were said to be six inches tall, could not, in fact, have had the civilization that he ascribed to them because six-inch-tall human beings, no matter how they were shaped and formed, could not have created the rudiments of a technological civilization. For example, they could not have smelted iron. They could not have mined minerals, because a six-inch-tall being could not get sufficient kinetic energy from swinging a tiny pickax to break rocks. That is why when babies fall they do not hurt themselves. Nor could the Lilliputians have controlled fire, because the tiny twigs that they could bring to a fire would burn up instantly. Nor is it likely that they could have thought about mining or have been able to speak, because their brains would be physically too small. It probably takes a central nervous system of a certain size to have enough connections and enough complexity of topology for speech. Ants may be terribly strong and terribly clever for their size, but their size alone guarantees that they will never write books about people.

The most important fact about human genes is that they help to make us as big as we are and to have a central nervous system with as many connections as it has. However, there are not enough genes to determine the detailed shape and structure of that nervous system nor of the consciousness that is an aspect of that structure. Yet it is consciousness that creates our environment, its history and the direction of its future. This then provides us with a correct understanding of the relation between our genes and the shape of our lives.

Our DNA is a powerful influence on our anatomies and physiologies. In particular, it makes possible the complex brain that characterizes human beings. But having made that brain possible, the genes have made possible human nature, a social nature whose limitations and possible shapes we do not know except insofar as we know what human consciousness has already made possible. In Simone de Beauvoir's clever but deep apothegm, a human being is *"l'être dont l'être est de n'être pas,"* the being whose essence is in not having an essence.

History far transcends any narrow limitations that are claimed for either the power of genes or the power of the environment to circumscribe us. Like the House of Lords that destroyed its own power to limit the political development of Britain in the successive Reform Acts to which it assented, so the genes, in making possible the development of human consciousness, have surrendered their power both to determine the individual and its environment. They have been replaced by an entirely new level of causation, that of social interaction with its own laws and its own nature that can be understood and explored only through that unique form of experience, social action.

1991

GETTING STARTED

1. What is the nature/nurture split? In a group, describe the split and list the ways in which thinkers like Darwin and Lamarck have influenced our perception of the split. What is Lewontin's attitude toward the split?

2. Describe Lewontin's problems with the environmental movement. Do you think that his criticisms have merit? Why or why not?

3. What is "social action" as Lewontin describes it? Think of at least two other forms of "social action." What do they have in common with science?

4. In a group, identify Lewontin's main argument in this essay and write a sentence or two describing it.

WRITING

5. Write two paragraphs summarizing why Darwin's "discovery" led to "important political reverberations." What did Darwin do that so rankles Lewontin?

6. Lewontin argues that "modern biology has become completely committed to the view that organisms are nothing but the battle grounds between the outside forces and the inside forces" (p. 328). Write a short paper using one or two examples from Lewontin's essay to explain this statement and to identify where he stands on this issue.

USING THE LIBRARY AND THE INTERNET

7. Using an Internet directory, such as About or Yahoo!, locate several Web sites that concern the environment. Choose sites from a broad spectrum of political viewpoints, and look especially at the Web sites' slogans and rallying cries. What assumptions about the relationship between organisms and the environment are made on these Web sites compared to the relationship Lewontin describes? Bring some examples and your notes to class.

MAKING CONNECTIONS

8. Why is science "social action" for Lewontin? Write an essay exploring the meaning of "science as social action" in Lewontin's essay. Include an analysis of the extent to which science is also presented as "social action" in Mary Kingsley's work (Julie English Early, "The Spectacle of Science and Self: Mary Kingsley") or in examples from Emily Martin et al.'s "Scientific Literacy, What It Is, Why It's Important, and Why Scientists Think We Don't Have It."

9. Lewontin asks, "Is it within the biological capability of human beings to reorganize their futures?" (p. 335) Explore the debate around this question using Lewontin and one or both of the following essays: Erin McGraw's "Bad Eyes" or Barbara Mellix's "From Outside, In."

EMILY MARTIN, BJORN CLAESON,
WENDY RICHARDSON, MONICA SCHOCH-SPANA,
AND KAREN-SUE TAUSSIG

Emily Martin (1944–) is a Professor of Anthropology at Princeton University. Martin's research focuses on science and medicine as forms of knowledge about the body and the world. Her teaching includes courses on the anthropology of health, the practice of ethnography, and the study of U.S. society and culture. She is the author of four books, including her most recent, *Flexible Bodies: Tracking Immunity in American Culture from the Days of Polio to the Age of AIDS* (1994). Martin was previously a professor at Johns Hopkins University where her coauthors were among her graduate students. "Scientific Literacy, What It Is, Why It's Important, and Why Scientists Think We Don't Have It" is from *Naked Science: Anthropological Inquiry into Boundaries, Power, and Knowledge,* a collection of essays edited by Laura Nader.

To learn more about the state of scientific literacy in this country and around the globe, visit the Web site of the International Center for the Advancement of Scientific Literacy at <http://www.icasl.org/>.

Scientific Literacy, What It Is, Why It's Important, and Why Scientists Think We Don't Have It

The Case of Immunology and the Immune System

"Science matters," we have been told in a recent spate of publications. In *Science Matters: Achieving Scientific Literacy,* "science literacy" is defined as "the knowledge you need to understand public issues . . . to put new [scientific] advances into a context that will allow you to take part in the national debate about them" (1991a:xii). Unproblematic as this definition might seem at first glance, the authors contend that by any measure, "Americans as a whole simply have not been exposed to science sufficiently or in a way that communicates the knowledge they need to have to cope with the life they will have to lead in the twenty-first century" (xv). This dire (and, we would like to argue, unfair) diagnosis becomes more understandable when one confronts the extremely narrow and technocratic content of the knowledge contained in *Science Matters* and most other books about science literacy. For example, in media publications spun off from *Science Matters,* readers are given a "pop quiz" that tests scientific literacy, a quiz that the great majority of Americans at all educational levels would fail (Hazen and Trefil 1991b). One question from the quiz is

The blueprint for every form of life is contained in

a. The National Institutes of Health near Washington, D.C.

b. DNA molecules

c. Proteins and carbohydrates

d. Viruses

For Hazen and Trefil, the correct answer, measuring a person's ability to understand public issues and function responsibly as citizens, is *b.* But in a broader, and more socially and culturally informed, definition of science literacy, one might wish people to debate the postulated role of DNA as the blueprint for every form of life. Following the lead of Ruth Hubbard and Eliza Wald in *Exploding the Gene Myth,* for example, one might hope that people would appreciate how little about every life form is actually determined by the gene. Following the lead of Bruno Latour, one might want people to understand how much the establishment of science "facts" owe[s] to the funds and credibility given particular researches by institutions like the one mentioned in answer *a,* the National Institutes of Health near Washington, DC (Latour 1987).

Even though some publications on science literacy contain reference to social and cultural issues, these issues are usually posed as afterthoughts, or at least as reflections to ponder after the real science is mastered. For example, in *Benchmarks for Science Literacy,* the summary section on "health technology" for high-school students lists six paragraphs of facts about the genetics, immunology, and epidemiology of health. Not until the seventh paragraph do we read that "biotechnology has contributed to health improvement in many ways, but its cost and application have led to a variety of controversial social and ethical issues" (American Association for the Advancement of Science 1993:207).

In our social anthropological research we are uncovering another picture of what science literacy might consist of by asking nonscientists, at all educational levels and from a variety of ethnic and socioeconomic settings, to tell us in their own terms what they know about health and their bodies, in particular about immunity and the immune system.[1] In this paper we will introduce some examples of this knowledge and argue that the definition of scientific "literacy" needs to be broadened to include the existential, metaphysical, moral, political, and social knowledge that is already embedded in people's talk about the immune system and the actions they take to protect it. Below we introduce four stories we were told about the immune system by people in four quite different contexts. We will argue that the people in these stories are engaged in producing what Clifford Geertz has called "local knowledge"; that is, "the artisan task of seeing broad principles in parochial facts" (1983:168) and "stories about events cast in imagery about principles" (215).

Story 1. Professor Keller, a scientist and a professor of microbiology at a large northeastern university, is teaching an undergraduate class on the biology of cancer and AIDS. He seeks to alleviate his students' sense of helplessness in the face of both social expectations and health-endangering illnesses by encouraging students to look within themselves to guide their lives and to find the resources to maintain their health.[2] The class, which he teaches every semester to about five hundred people, is known by students as "the best class on campus."

Professor Keller brings to the class a critical awareness of the limits of Western medical science. In particular, he stresses its lack of understanding of the powers inherent in the human body. He raises questions about the causes of cancer and other illnesses and suggests the possibility that Western medicine cannot answer these questions. He tells stories about miraculous recoveries from illnesses and invites to the class ordinary men and women who have performed feats of self-healing deemed impossible by the medical establishment, thus suggesting everything we do not know about healing. And he criticizes the medical establishment for being "completely interested in keeping all alternatives off the books."

The purpose of the class, then, is to teach students "other ways of thinking" about the body, self, health, illness, and death and to "empower" students by giving them a sense of their internal capacity for control over their lives, a capacity that is ignored or denied by medical science. To this end he uses "biology as . . . a common language"; he "talks the language that [the students] are ready to hear" and "interweaves it with stuff that they are not ready to hear, but that they will accept because it is interwoven."

The description of the immune system is part of this common language. As students scribble furiously in their notebooks, Professor Keller tells them about the amazing world within their own bodies: the "dumb" macrophages who "eat foreign objects, stick them out of their own body," and "present" them to "smarter" cells; the "advanced" T-helper cells, "the quarterbacks of the immune system," who "send signals from one part of the immune system to another"; the B cells "who can recognize any foreign shape"; and the suppressor T cells "who are in charge of keeping the immune system within bounds."

Professor Keller stretches students' imaginations by using this depiction of the world of the immune system as a "metaphor for the real power we have" inside us. He tells students that they are powerful, "so much more powerful than [they] even imagine." According to Professor Keller:

> If you believe you've got this, then . . . you start believing you're powerful. . . . I tell this group, "you have this stuff. Your B lymphocytes are incredible. . . . And it's us, and we're really strong." I think they're saying, "Oh." And you almost stand up a little taller and you walk around and say "I'm powerful." . . . It's almost like the scientific version of thinking about an angel or a protector or something that they probably did in the middle ages.

The amazing world of the immune system is not separated from us; rather, "it is us." To know about it gives us a sense of a powerful self.

Mike took Professor Keller's class two years ago. Now, in his final year of college, he ponders the possibilities that lie ahead. According to Mike:

> I think a lot of people, at that age [their twenties], they want to do something with social justice and they really want to get involved. I think it bothers a lot of people, just with the environment, education, and health care, everything. And they don't know if they should go into being a social worker. . . . [There's] kind of a pull between that end of the spectrum and the other end of living a realistic, not a realistic life, but I mean you have to make a lot of sacrifices . . . if you go that route.

Professor Keller's class "gave you the feeling," he says, that "you're in control" of your life:

> Even before this class, I promised never to do something I really didn't want to do, and if I didn't want to do it, I'd go on to something else. And so in taking this class I think it just reinforced that, to really go with a gut feeling, go with what you're happy with, go with what you feel good about.

The class empowered Mike to "go into" and believe in himself.

But Mike believes Professor Keller's presentation of the immune system had little impact on him. Mike could see no connection between himself and an immune system that seemed to be existing independently inside his body. As he says:

> [They] show how the immune system fights off disease. I think they make it sound as if it's only the immune system. The immune system and the disease . . . this happens here, and then this, this, then this happens, then this step, and this type of cell invades here, the virus attacks the white cells. . . . I couldn't relate to that, I felt that that couldn't help me, so I didn't take anything from it. I didn't care about it.

The microprocesses of the immune system may be "amazing [and] overwhelming," but, to him, they are distant, and not empowering.

In contrast to Mike, Elizabeth came to Professor Keller's class with a conception of the world as a series of separate, but interconnected layers. According to her:

> Everything's all connected. . . . Inside me is like a whole other universe. . . . I have like micro cells within me, and then I'll go up to the bones and the organs, put together, and then just after that just my automatic systems, just like my breathing and stuff like that, and then comes my self. . . . And like this building that I'm living in is like a monster and I'm part of . . . that person, and then this building is part of this town, which is like another person. . . .

Her immune system may be a "separate community in there," like her other organs, but she is nevertheless able to relate to it and interact with it.

This sense of connection with her immune system creates the possibility for her empowerment. For Elizabeth, the immune system is more than a mechanism of use only in emergencies to "fight diseases." She interacts with it on a "day-to-day" basis. During their twenty years together, she says, she and her immune system have gotten used to each other:

> It's gotten used to my way of living. My lack of sleep, and my bad eating habits, it's sort of grown to accept it, because I'm not sick the entire school year, but I hardly sleep the entire school year, and I don't eat right. If I were to get a new immune system, then I would be sick the entire school year until I had it trained that this is me and this is how I function, so help me out a little bit.

Rather than changing her life to meet the needs of her immune system, she has been able to "train" it to accommodate her life. In the context of her conception of the interconnectedness of the world, and her day-to-day interaction with her immune system, scientific knowledge of the immune system becomes empowering. For her, the immune system is, indeed, the "scientific version of . . . an angel or a protector."

Story 2. Two of our informants, George and Phillip, are a gay white male couple in their early twenties. Coming of age sexually in the first decade of the AIDS epidemic, these two men have known gay circles as places in which conversations about the immune system are commonplace. Interest in a possible lover readily becomes an interest in whether or not he has been tested for HIV and whether or not he will wear a condom. Concern over a friend or acquaintance with AIDS easily becomes worry over his falling T-cell count. While Keller's students may gain a sense of empowerment from his lectures on the immune system, Phillip and George, who have witnessed the loss of a generation of gay men to AIDS and who have heeded the safe-sex campaign among gays, speak more of vulnerability. In their descriptions of the immune system and AIDS, they draw heavily upon an idiom of boundaries. Their talk of boundaries, safety, and risk, used in depicting the body and the threat of HIV, is consonant with their descriptions of danger on a different scale, danger that threatens the neighborhood through crime.

Phillip laments that AIDS and a preoccupation with protecting oneself, that is, wearing a condom, is at odds with love, which is an act of letting down one's barriers. He explains:

> a lot of time, and this happens with straight and gay people . . . the issue of love enters the scenario and sometimes . . . when you love someone [you] don't feel that . . . you should have to protect yourself, and I think that not using protection is a result of that, because [you] feel that you love this person, that this persons loves [you] and because you love each other, you shouldn't have to hide or protect anything about yourself from this person.

The biology of sex and of HIV mandates a barrier, the condom, between two bodies, while the sociality of lovemaking mandates openness between two people.

In his description of how a fetus might contract HIV from a[n] infected mother, Phillip focuses again upon boundaries, this time describing the function of skin as a barrier to disease. "While the baby's inside the mother, that baby is part of the mother. . . . All her body fluids are coming into contact with it . . . even if its blood type is different, the blood is still coming into contact with this baby. . . . It does not have its fully developed skin on it to protect it." Because of a breach in its skin through which the mother's infected blood can pass, the fetus is vulnerable to HIV. Compromised boundaries, openings in the skin, constitute vulnerability to HIV.

His partner, George, also emphasizes that caution toward HIV entails not only vigilance against possible points of entry, but also care toward the fluid medium containing HIV. He draws upon an example from his own life, recounting the time he threw away an exacto knife at his office after a coworker cut himself with it. He defends his act to Phillip, who thinks him somewhat paranoid, by arguing that HIV is highly contagious because of its presence in fluids and because of fluid's special quality of permeating boundaries. It is the "bodily fluids" of others, from outside, he suggests, that one must avoid getting inside oneself. "I mean, you know that this disease is transmitted through fluid, o.k., simple. . . . If I've got an open wound on me, I'm not going to roll around in bed with someone, and like, have all this semen or fluid or whatever have a chance to enter my body, you know." Protesting that he was not paranoid in throwing out the knife, he argues further that he would act within reason if he encountered a person with HIV:

> If I know someone has AIDS . . . I will take precautions. I'm not going to be . . . total[ly], well, "you stay ten feet away from me, and if you sneeze, cover your mouth, don't get any fluid on me." . . . I'm not going to be like that, because that would be kind of ridiculous, but on the same chance, I'm not going to welcome the opportunity by . . . getting horny and sleeping with the person, [or] . . . shar[ing] a needle."

In order to articulate the value of AZT (an antiviral medicine) for someone who has tested positive for HIV, George draws upon a boundary metaphor, describing the medication as at least some protection, however compromised, against the progression of disease. He explains that while this drug may be of only limited help to the person, merely delaying the onset of symptoms of AIDS, that help should not be ignored or criticized:

> AZT is good. . . . You can't fuck with it because it's the only thing we got. . . . You know, it's like you're out in the rain, and you see this awning, and you know, it's got a few leaks in it, but you'll be a hell of a lot dryer from standing under those few leaks than you will if you stand out in this pouring down rain. There's nothing else there, so you got to go for what's there.

In thinking through issues of health and illness, Phillip and George employ notions of barriers and their permeation by bodily fluids. Talk of vulnerability shifts easily, however, from the level of the body to that of the neighborhood. Just as skin is seen to circumscribe the body, protecting a vulnerable interior from exterior threats, so are streets seen to delineate the margins of a neighborhood, marking good areas from bad. When describing their area of the central city, George and Phillip give street names to outline the "safe" portion of the neighborhood. George notes that not only have gentrification efforts on streets south and west of the lines of safety failed but also that "bad" areas are encroaching upon "good" ones. "They tried to build that up, and a lot of yuppies moved in, but for some reason, they just didn't make it. . . . That's really all that's there. . . . I think bad areas are kind of moving in, all the good areas are kind of moving up toward this way."

Phillip invokes an image of a safe, enclosed area, outside of which one faces possible dangers:

> I mean to me, it's almost as though we're a little box. . . . If you go over past Lake Avenue, you start to get into, you know, an area where you might put yourself at risk, you get down towards Packard Street going north, you're starting to put yourself at risk. . . . If you go toward Central Street, that same thing applies, and it just pretty much . . . it's a nice little square, your safe, little, cozy square right here. If you leave it, you're increasing your

> chances of crime, not to overly worry about it often, but I walk around all the time, I mean I'm always aware, I always keep my eyes and my ears open.

Two related themes are apparent. First, boundaries mark off or contain an area of safety. In one's neighborhood, one knows what streets to avoid and at what streets "bad" areas appear to begin. Second, if one knowingly crosses such borders, one must assume the risk of harm. Cross the street and you may be asking for trouble.

The same could be said of "risky" sexual practices and contracting HIV. Indeed, Phillip warns:

> If you're going to have sex, you can play it safe if you want, but just . . . be aware of what you're playing with . . . and condoms aren't 100 percent certain. . . . If it's right for you, go ahead and do it, but just be willing to deal with the consequences. . . . You know, if you're going to go around and act like a slut, and then catch it, don't scream "it's not fair, it's not fair, it's not fair," you know, it's not fair for anyone, but you were well aware of what you were doing at the time.

Others share the concerns of Phillip and George about crime in the neighborhood. They also hold similar cognitive maps of dangerous and safe zones in the area. Residents and business owners, for instance, have organized a citizens' patrol of the neighborhood streets at night to supplement the surveillance provided by the police department. A fatal shotgun blast to the face of a young gay man who was leaving an after-hours nightclub in late spring of 1990 was the event instigating the patrols. In this murder, people saw a number of dangers that the neighborhood unfortunately hosts. Some gays and lesbians considered it another example of the increasing violence directed toward the homosexual community during a time marked by a fear of AIDS. A few considered it the plight of a neighborhood not cohesive enough to exclude such "outsiders" as criminals.

Crucial to the initial stages of the organization of this citizens' group were debates over what area of the neighborhood the patrol would cover. The limited number of participants to schedule for patrols constrained the size of the beat, as did the decision not to place patrols on the "questionable" streets, those being the most peripheral. Patrols were not to walk east of Lake Avenue or west of Central Street. To go beyond these limits was to put oneself in considerable danger, particularly if on foot. Within the perimeter, however, patrols would monitor the streets for crime, calling in the police to investigate and remove, if necessary, suspicious characters from the neighborhood.

Concern over bad areas spilling into good ones and criminal elements circulating within the neighborhood prompted residents to be keenly watchful of activities in their area. Phillip and George are similarly vigilant against the threats that may lie outside their "little, cozy square." Apprehension about the breach of boundaries, however, also marks their appraisal of the threat that HIV poses to the body. Mindful of their safety on the streets and cautious about any contact with "bodily" fluids that may contain HIV, Phillip and George elaborate the social significance of boundaries.

Story 3. Another informant, Bill, also made references to boundaries in his discussion of the immune system, relating "borders" of the body to those of nation-states. Bill is a white man in his thirties. He lives with his wife, originally from Argentina, in a small row house. Theirs was one of the first racially integrated neighborhoods in Baltimore. The residents are both renters and owners and many live openly as gay couples. When asked why he and his wife chose this area of Baltimore, Bill explained,

> I think affordability is part of it, although I think probably mostly sort of progressive community type stuff. . . . Affordability, community, yeah not only views of people but also the fact that people did stuff here, they were active. We wanted to live somewhere where there was a community association we could get involved in stuff if we wanted to, that sort of thing.

Bill's concern with individual rights and autonomy were evident throughout our interview. Significantly, his interest in decentralization was reflected in the way he described his work and also became apparent when he began to talk about the immune system. Bill has a degree in architecture but found that office-oriented work did not appeal to him. In graduate school he took a course on creating low-income housing in developing countries. He found this approach more satisfying. This is how Bill described his interest. "In a developing country context, housing is, is all user. I mean the best [that] the public realm, the government and stuff, can do is maybe push a few laws aside or give somebody a scrap of land, but other than that it's whatever, whatever the user or the squatter or whatever can do for themselves." His research took him to Sri Lanka and Chile.

Working on a housing project for the city of Boston, Bill felt involving the community in decisions was, as he put it, a "more progressive way to deal with this notion of developing houses." He now works as a development consultant for nonprofit organizations, including the family center in his neighborhood. Bill's fascination with questions of local autonomy and centralized power were also plain when we asked what he knew about the immune system. At first he was reserved and responded, "I don't think I think much about the immune system per se. . . . I mean the immune system is all these little white blood cells running around eating up all the bad shit in your body right? That's my understanding of the immune system technically speaking."

As Bill oriented his thoughts around a metaphor of organized systems of authority, however, he became excited and the immune system took on a larger significance. He went on to say,

> I mean there's a natural policing thing that happens in the body right? And, I mean it's an incredible policing thing, when you think about it, or at least it's incredible in my mind, because it's a system-wide authority that works. I don't know of any system-wide authorities that work in our culture, so this is amazing right?

Having compared the immune system to a social system, Bill has given it a culture that can be compared to our own. If the metaphor of the police state makes the immune system comprehensible to Bill, at the same time it also becomes a commentary on political organization. It allows him to relate different states of the body to different political systems. As he exclaimed, "I'm sure there are diseases [in which] the immune system ends up destroying the body. . . . It's more like an Argentina or a Bulgaria kind of immune system."

Through his use of a body-country metaphor Bill reveals his conceptions of both bodies and nations as bounded and independent. When asked how he would describe to a child how the body repairs, or takes care of itself, he answered:

> It would [be] an explanation that would involve having to explain that the body is a self-contained system, that it has its own discipline. . . . I suppose one would want to use a metaphor, you know. . . . Obviously using Argentina or Bulgaria would be an ineffective metaphor. You would have to think of something in the child's world that was a comfortable notion of a closed, self-nurturing system.

As a closed system, the body must protect its boundaries. The body when sick, like a nation at war, is threatened by what Bill describes as, "a foreign organism . . . that is competing for the body's resources in some way or another." Having described the body as a social system, Bill also encountered the moral dilemmas of the social world. What about the individual's rights? What about cultural relativism? In reference to a *Time* magazine cartoon drawing of a virus and a white blood cell fighting, Bill said:

> I was thinking about this notion of good guy versus bad guy. It's really pretty silly because, I mean the virus is just trying to make a living right? It's trying to bring up its family just like the white blood cells are, so there's not really . . . a clear good and bad in it, unless you take somebody's point of view of the larger . . . organism, then you have a point of view. . . . It depends on where you position yourself, where you sit.

By using a social metaphor to describe the body, it becomes a system with logic, an aggregate of players with motivations and intentions. Earlier in the interview Bill explained, "It's easy to talk about policing systems and white blood cells being the good guys and all this kind of good stuff, and then making metaphors around countries, these political things are easy things to talk about and understand for me."

The nation-body metaphors that Bill uses not only enable him to understand the immune system. As Bill suggested earlier, his descriptions of the body also become a commentary on the social world. The words he uses to describe the world of the body also orient his understanding of social interaction and global politics. The role of the politician can move from the global politics of the cold war to the global politics described in the immune system. Looking at a micrograph of bacteria being showered with enzymes, Bill exclaims:

> Oh that's neat! This is great. I mean this is like star wars and I don't mean Reagan's version. This is like a battle, an action shot, right? This thing blowing the other one away. That's great. See, if the people that are so good at making those kind of stupid political arguments, like Reagan, so good at actually convincing people about things like star wars? If he would concentrate that level of creative fabrication [on these] kind of issues, I think this would be a better world to live in.

Later in the interview, discussing the effectiveness of prevention in the control of AIDS, Bill returned to the issue of star wars. We asked, "How effective do you think prevention would be?" Bill responded,

> From what I understand of the disease, again which isn't much, but the way in which it is spread, it sounds like it could probably be very effective. . . . People don't talk much about prevention, I don't even know what something like that might look like. It's interesting though actually. . . . Earlier I was . . . [speaking about] Reagan with his star wars thing. That was a preventative piece and people really sought that out, right? 'Cause it was the notion of things going up and intercepting . . . right? And that actually, I mean that's, those are like, that's like a giant condom network, right, in a sense. So that's actually interesting. So maybe there is some hope, maybe there is a political angle on prevention that is every bit as sellable as curing. I don't know.

In order to communicate his understanding of the immune system and orient his thoughts, Bill has chosen the image of the nation-state. To Bill the topic of the immune system is versatile and allows him to move the discussion from health and illness to issues of global politics and the rights of the individual. Discussion of the immune system becomes a forum to think not only about our bodies and scientific "facts," but about political structures and what positions we must take to understand the rights of others. But these are not just arbitrary subjects held together by a central metaphor, they are also interconnected queries of great relevance to Bill. By speaking about the immune system, Bill was able to convey his views on the interrelations of preventative health, national priorities, and individual rights.

Story 4. Unlike Bill, for whom AIDS is one of many questions about individual rights and national structures, for Mara, AIDS and the problems of immunity are of primary concern. Mara is a thirty-one-year-old white woman who works as a technical writer for an engineering firm, volunteers by writing grant applications for a local performing arts group, and lives with her husband in a quiet Baltimore neighborhood. All four of Mara's college roommates have died from AIDS. In 1989 Mara became the primary care giver for another close friend who was sick with AIDS. She was with him when he died in a hospice the day after her thirtieth birthday. He was over six feet tall and weighed seventy pounds when he died. Mara is an AIDS activist. In describing her experience with AIDS she said that "a lot of gay people are very angry, a lot of straight people too. And especially those of us involved in the arts—to watch our world crumble, and nobody even look at us . . . nobody even give a shit . . . and we're fighting for little bones that they throw us." She told us that AIDS, the body, and health are things that she thinks about every single day of her life.

Mara is, by anybody's standards, scientifically literate. During our interview we showed her an unlabeled micrograph of a white blood cell surrounding an asbestos fiber and asked her what she thinks of when she sees such pictures. Her instant and stunning response was, "Oh, that's an asbestos fiber in a white blood cell."

Mara's familiarity with the language of science seems to come from her experience with AIDS. She is extremely well informed about the disease, how it is transmitted, and different possibilities for treatment. She is able to clearly articulate her understanding of what she thinks happens inside the body of someone with AIDS. She told us that what she imagines happens inside the body of someone with AIDS has "changed" with the course of the disease. She said, "I used to feel like it was a total loss of control, and like it was Sisyphus, that you would push it up the hill just two feet and then it will roll back down over you. I used to feel like it was only chaos. Now I feel like it's still chaos but that we have a handle on it. . . . I know that it is war, absolutely, it's war inside the body." She goes on to tell us:

> I've never seen anything like this . . . seen twenty-six-year-old men not able to make it up the stairs. I have never seen diarrhea so bad that, that, you put a mouth full of water in your mouth and swallow it and you, you are having explosive diarrhea. . . . This is the weirdest and the most bizarre thing I can . . . imagine.

> I mean, every nightmare that I ever would have had of what could happen to the human body has come true, and we're right in it every day.

Mara's concern is about the effects of the disease on society. She believes that AIDS is something society may not be able to withstand. She told us that she feels "like we all have AIDS . . . whether we have the virus or not." When asked to elaborate on her suggestion that everybody has AIDS, Mara said, "I really believe that we all have AIDS. I mean, I don't believe that I carry the virus in my body, and I've proven that to myself by getting tested, but my life has been changed forever by AIDS, and I feel that by the time the crisis is over, if it's ever over, and that I'm not sure about, everyone will be touched by it, directly affected by it."

Mara's answer to a question regarding her view of what the course of the disease will be in the United States and the world also reflects her concern for society. She told us:

> I think we're really in for it. . . . I don't have any hope at all. I used to, but I don't. I think that it's, it's here . . . widespread throughout the general population. . . . We're already seeing it moving heavily into the IV-drug-using populations of color in our urban areas. I think that the next really big hit is going to be teenagers and people in their early twenties. Where you first saw it was in a population that, in general, had access to medical care, had access to knowledge and information about their bodies, and in general works, so the course of their illness is a little different. . . . I think that in the inner cities we're seeing a holocaust, and I don't . . . have any idea how, how it can be slowed down or stopped at this point, unless the government took on a real heavy campaign.

While Mara sees the effects of AIDS moving easily through society, she doesn't think that the virus is very contagious. She describes the disease as "just a virus." She said:

> That's one of the things I say . . . like when people give value judgments about people with AIDS, I mean it's just a virus, the virus . . . happens to be transmitted by people having sex with each other, it's blood borne, so it's . . . specific in its transmission route. But that's all it is . . . just a virus. . . . I think it's very difficult to get it. . . . I mean I think it's impossible to get it unless you engage in unprotected sex, or share needles. . . . I worked with bare hands on bodies of people that were sick. . . . I've been splashed with vomit, I've been splashed with feces, I've been splashed with . . . saliva, tears, sweat, the whole bit, and if anybody was going to get AIDS from having contact, I would have it.

Mara sees her role as an activist as "something that is every day, all day. . . . I feel like I do it every day. But you know, that's what an activist does." She describes her role, telling us:

> I don't talk in a prejudiced way about people with AIDS. Some of it is hands-on, direct care where I'm needed. . . . I also . . . have kind of a special challenge, being a heterosexual female, voices like mine aren't often heard. . . . I can go to a Baptist church and say I'm a married, heterosexual female, I'm thirty-one years old, and here's what I've been through. And they will let me in.

She also sees her role on what she calls a "microlevel" and describes her boss who "told AIDS jokes and made comments" when she first started working with him and now she describes him as "real sensitized to [AIDS], and real supportive and . . . share[s] with me . . . issues of his own, having to do with a brother who died of cancer at twenty." In spite of the horror she finds in the reality of AIDS, she also expresses hope about possibilities for new kinds of collective awareness.

Mara discusses her experiences with death by talking about caring for her friend and being with him when he died. Significantly, although she sees the effects of AIDS as "every nightmare that . . . could happen to the human body" and as a "holocaust," she describes her friend's death as "really an amazing and positive experience." She describes his death, telling us that:

> He could sort of talk. And then he died, but when he died it was really wild because our eyes were really glued to each other. It was like his eyes died. That was it. His heart kept beating for a while, but it was great. It was like catching the baby. . . . I felt different the next day. . . . I have felt different ever since. . . . He was such a strong, intelligent person. . . . He died in a really, in sort of a strong way, strange to say but really true. And so there are times, when that strength and that endurance and that ability, it doesn't seem like it's all gone, and some of it, I felt like I got a big hit of that power from him.

For Mara, death is not only about dying. Her concept of death is imbued with a concept of transcendence and involves ideas about strength and birth.

Logically following from her ideas about death, Mara does not see the body as a boundary. Mara's discussion of her relationships with her friends who have died illustrates her ideas about metaphysical relationships. One of Mara's concerns is about keeping the memory of her friends alive. She feels their presence in her life and makes a point of talking about them. In her discussion of her friend's death she told us that:

> You know . . . I try to keep him, he's the person that I knew the best that died of AIDS, but . . . there are other people too that I . . . try to remember as they go through all . . . this process I always do talk to them . . . those people won't be around to be uncles to my kids. . . . There's a huge crowd of people with whom I hung around in college, and that was real important . . . the whole intellectual development. . . . Everything else was leading up to that time. Those people were very important to me. But they're not there, and I can't pick up the phone and call "Scott" and tell him about the book I just read and I can't pick up the phone and call "Gary" and, you know, ask him a question about my hairstyle. I mean, you know, I can't, I can't do that, and so I feel like we have a responsibility—those of us who have been with these people, in their lives but also through their illness—not only to carry on the stories about them and . . . facts about their [lives]. They don't have children, or people sitting around the fire talking about them. But also the way they died was so unnecessary, and sometimes I really feel like their spirits are really noisy in my ear.

These stories illustrate that science literacy is much more than merely knowing some basic "facts" and simple concepts (Hazen and Trefil 1991a:xix). Individuals use "facts" in very different ways and often make them work with their particular local circumstances as well as express their most overarching views of the world. Bill uses "facts" he has learned about the immune system to construct broader visions about the nature of social and political forms that relate to his political views and actions. Mara weaves "facts" she has learned about the immune system into profoundly moral and metaphysical views of the meaning of life and death. These views enable her to maintain both important relationships in her life and hope of a better society.

Both Bill and Mara relate disease to a state of war, a metaphor that is not uncommon in scientific texts, the popular media, or conversations with our informants. To Mara the horror of war expresses her shock over the effects of AIDS. For Bill, a metaphorical national system of authority in a defended nation-state provides a way to understand immunity as a system.

Using metaphor to conceptualize the body may affect our conceptualization of social situations. Some theorists emphasize the interactive nature of the elements paired in a metaphor, so that when Dante says "Hell is a lake of ice," the hearer extends the association of "hell" to a "lake of ice," thus transforming both elements of the metaphor (Hesse 1961; Black 1962:37). Through the use of a body/war metaphor we may not only be thinking of the body as naturally warlike, but we may also be thinking of the state of war as natural.

While Bill and Mara both make use of a metaphor that associates war with an immutable part of our biological nature (the immune system), at the same time they also suggest that AIDS is not only a biological but a social condition. Bill expressed his belief that a change in national priorities from the arms race to health would make prevention effective in the control of AIDS. To Mara the body/war metaphor not only speaks of a war within the body but of a social war being waged upon bodies. Within the contexts of their larger commentaries, Bill's and Mara's uses of the war/body metaphor signify much more than just ways to understand science.

In these stories people use scientific "facts" to create knowledge about a whole range of topics. For George and Phillip, to talk about the immune system is to talk above all about boundaries. Talk of boundaries appeared in another area of our research, participant-observation in a laboratory pursuing immunological research. In this research setting, the central tenet of contemporary immunology is the ability of the immune system to distinguish self from nonself. As our examples have just shown, when nonscientists talk about the immune system they also talk above all about boundaries. Those between the self and others—spatial, racial, gendered, class, and relational—and how these various boundaries can clash or be superimposed in complex ways. The concept of the boundary between self and nonself is a touchstone for broader social meanings. Since we find such concepts so commonly in interviews, it raises the question of whether the central role of boundaries in current research immunology is not culturally based in its inception.[3]

This position is explicit in Keller's view of his course. He intends much more than "facts" to be conveyed by his scientific account of the immune system. The students respond in kind. Certainly Mike did not take away "facts" about the immune system from his biology course, but rather the idea that in life one should "go into" and believe in one's self.

One might ask if implicit and local knowledge might be integrated into all areas of science, including those covered in overviews such as *Science Matters.* Suppose that the "facts" of science entail a whole worldview that is often left implicit. If it were made explicit, the way would be opened to begin a dialogue with people who might be living with different worldviews. Certainly such a dialogue would fit with Mara's vision of a better society. Quizzes from the experts which we, the public, fail, could give way to conversations about matters in which we are all experts in our own way.

Recognizing that worldviews are inscribed in scientific images would allow scientists to examine the implicit cultural assumptions that are used to explain scientific "facts." What else is being communicated when scientists describe the immune system as a national defense force or a T-cell as a quarterback?

The "facts" of science, important as they are, can never be more than tiny pieces of the maps that people devise to guide them in life. Even if we could all magically be made to "know" the answers to the science pop quiz, the process of our coming to know those "facts" would entail our embedding them in the diverse social, political, moral, and metaphysical meanings with which we construct our daily lives.

We began by asking how scientific literacy might be defined. We have shown that the people we interviewed are highly literate in the enormously complex social, political, moral, and metaphysical aspects of such matters as health or illness. If we were to turn now to a detailed look at Hazen and Trefil's notion of what it would take to be literate about these issues, we might be struck by the narrowly technocratic nature of the knowledge they regard as relevant. We might wonder whether that knowledge would really be sufficient to enable meaningful public discussion of AIDS, for example. This raises the question of whether it is actually scientists, rather than members of the public, that suffer from illiteracy on the range of considerations that need to be brought to bear on these complex human issues.

1996

Notes

This title is a slightly modified version of the title of the introductory chapter of Robert M. Hazen and James Trefil's *Science Matters: Achieving Scientific Literacy* (1991a).

1. An extended account of the fieldwork is contained in Martin (1994). All quotations are from observed situations or interviews.
2. We have used pseudonyms for the names of the people we interviewed as well as street names.
3. See G. E. R. Lloyd's *Revolutions of Wisdom* (1987) for how concepts from daily life were taken up into early science.

GETTING STARTED

1. Examine the title of this essay and the names of the authors. Who are the authors? Who is their intended audience? What does "scientific literacy" mean to you? What does the title lead you to expect from the article? Are your expectations satisfied?

2. In the fourth paragraph, the authors attribute the term "local knowledge" to Clifford Geertz, also an author in this book. Define "local knowledge" in your own words. How do the authors use it to challenge or complicate the idea that scientific literacy is "merely knowing some basic 'facts' and simple concepts" (p. 354)? Working in groups, characterize elements in each of the four stories that could be called local knowledge.

3. Choose one of the four stories as an example of different kinds of scientific literacy. How is one of the people in that story thinking about the immune system? What metaphors does that person use to better understand how the immune system works? How do the details of that person's life affect how he or she understands the immune system?

WRITING

4. Write an essay in which you describe your own view of the immune system and compare it to the four views presented here. What metaphors help you to make sense of the immune system? Do the four case studies in the article help you to frame your own ideas? Has reading this article affected your way of thinking about the immune system? How?

5. How might a scientist respond to the authors' conclusion that scientists and not the public "suffer from illiteracy on the range of considerations that need to be brought to bear on these complex human issues" (p. 356)? Write a paper in which you explore the relationship between facts and local knowledge. What does it mean "to know" something? Is knowledge the same for everyone?

USING THE LIBRARY AND THE INTERNET

6. Find a Web site or a book or magazine that discusses HIV/AIDS in some detail. (Hint: On the Internet, try "The Megasite Project: A Metasite Comparing Health Information Megasites and Search Engines," <http://henry.ugl.lib.umich.edu/megasite/toc.html> for evaluations and links to the best health sites.) Take note of all the metaphorical language you see. (Keep in mind, words like "defenses," "attack," or "shield" are all examples of metaphorical language.) What kinds of stories about the disease does the language suggest? Compare your examples to one of the four stories in this essay.

MAKING CONNECTIONS

7. Examine the descriptions of how scientists work in either Thomas Kuhn's "The Historical Structure of Scientific Discovery" or Richard C. Lewontin's "Science as Social Action." How might either of these writers define "scientific literacy"? Write a paper in which you explore how Kuhn or Lewontin might respond to the argument presented by Martin and her coauthors.

8. In "The Motive for Metaphor," Northrop Frye paraphrases the poet Wallace Stevens: "the motive for metaphor . . . is a desire to associate, and finally to identify, the human mind with what goes on outside it, because the only genuine joy you can have is in those rare moments when you feel that although we may know in part, as Paul says, we are also a part of what we know" (p. 224). How do the metaphors employed by Mike, Elizabeth, and the others whose stories are presented here help them to become a part of what they know? Write a paper in which you analyze the metaphors used in these stories. Do they represent a scientific or an artistic approach to the problem of making sense of the immune system? Is one way of knowing "better" than the other? Why or why not?

9. Martin and her coauthors use Geertz's concept of local knowledge to help develop their argument that the stories and levels of understanding generated by nonscientists are an important part of scientific literacy. Write a paper using some additional concepts from Geertz's "Common Sense as a Cultural System" to further analyze the case studies provided in this essay. How are commonsense understandings of the immune system partly developed by an individual's cultural surroundings? How do Geertz's ideas about common sense connect to his concept of local knowledge as explained in this essay?

Scott McCloud

Scott McCloud (1960–   ) is a comic book writer and artist who now runs <http://www. scottmccloud.com>, a Web site that serves as the launchpad for his online comics experiments. "Setting the Record Straight" is the first chapter of his book, *Understanding Comics* (1993). He has now published a second book, *Reinventing Comics* (2000).

You can read more about Scott McCloud and other contemporary comic book artists in McCloud's monthly column in *The Comic Reader* online at <http://www.thecomicreader.com>.

IN LESS THAN A YEAR, I BECAME TOTALLY OBSESSED WITH COMICS! I DECIDED TO BECOME A COMICS ARTIST IN 10th GRADE AND BEGAN TO PRACTICE, PRACTICE, PRACTICE!

I FELT THAT THERE WAS SOMETHING LURKING IN COMICS... SOMETHING THAT HAD NEVER BEEN DONE.
SOME KIND OF HIDDEN POWER!

BUT WHENEVER I TRIED TO EXPLAIN MY FEELING, I FAILED MISERABLY.
COMIC BOOKS?! HA! HA! HA!
BUT IT-- BUT IT'S-- BUH...

SURE, I REALIZED THAT COMIC BOOKS WERE USUALLY CRUDE, POORLY-DRAWN, SEMILITERATE, CHEAP, DISPOSABLE KIDDIE FARE--

--BUT--
THEY DON'T HAVE TO BE!

THE PROBLEM WAS THAT FOR MOST PEOPLE, THAT WAS WHAT "COMIC BOOK" MEANT!
DON'T GIMME THAT COMIC BOOK TALK, BARNEY!

IF PEOPLE FAILED TO UNDERSTAND COMICS, IT WAS BECAUSE THEY DEFINED WHAT COMICS COULD BE TOO NARROWLY!

A PROPER DEFINITION, IF WE COULD FIND ONE, MIGHT GIVE LIE TO THE STEREOTYPES--
--AND SHOW THAT THE POTENTIAL OF COMICS IS LIMITLESS AND EXCITING!

THIS IS WHERE OUR JOURNEY BEGINS.

THE WORLD OF COMICS IS A HUGE AND VARIED ONE. OUR DEFINITION MUST ENCOMPASS ALL THESE TYPES--
--WHILE NOT BEING SO BROAD AS TO INCLUDE ANYTHING WHICH IS CLEARLY NOT COMICS.
"COMICS" IS THE WORD WORTH DEFINING, AS IT REFERS TO THE MEDIUM ITSELF, NOT A SPECIFIC OBJECT AS "COMIC BOOK" OR "COMIC STRIP" DO.
WE CAN ALL VISUALIZE A COMIC.
GENERIC GUY
BUT WHAT--
--IS--
--COMICS?

MASTER COMICS ARTIST WILL EISNER USES THE TERM SEQUENTIAL ART WHEN DESCRIBING COMICS.
TAKEN INDIVIDUALLY, THE PICTURES BELOW ARE MERELY THAT-- PICTURES.
HOWEVER, WHEN PART OF A SEQUENCE, EVEN A SEQUENCE OF ONLY TWO, THE ART OF THE IMAGE IS TRANSFORMED INTO SOMETHING MORE: THE ART OF COMICS!
NOTICE THAT THIS DEFINITION IS STRICTLY NEUTRAL ON MATTERS OF STYLE, QUALITY OR SUBJECT MATTER.
BANG!
BANG!
EEEK!
MUCH HAS ALREADY BEEN WRITTEN ON THE VARIOUS SCHOOLS OF COMIC ART; ON PARTICULAR ARTISTS, PARTICULAR TITLES, PARTICULAR TRENDS...
BUT TO DEFINE COMICS, WE MUST FIRST DO A LITTLE AESTHETIC SURGERY AND SEPARATE FORM FROM CONTENT!

*EISNER'S OWN *COMICS AND SEQUENTIAL ART* BEING A HAPPY EXCEPTION.

*JUXTAPOSED= ADJACENT, SIDE-BY-SIDE. GREAT ART SCHOOL WORD.

HOWEVER
YOU MIGHT
SAY THAT
BEFORE IT'S
PROJECTED,
FILM IS
JUST A
VERY
VERY
VERY
VERY
SLOW
COMIC!
ANYWAY, THIS SHOULD MAKE IT A BIT MORE SPECIFIC.
JUXTAPOSED SEQUENTIAL VISUAL ART
DOES IT HAVE TO SAY "ART"? DOESN'T THAT IMPLY SOME SORT OF VALUE JUDGMENT?
WELL...
OKAY, HOW ABOUT THIS?
JUXTAPOSED SEQUENTIAL STATIC IMAGES
NOW IT SOUNDS KIND OF ARBITRARY.
OKAY, HOW ABOUT THIS?
JUXTAPOSED STATIC IMAGES IN DELIBERATE SEQUENCE
WHAT ABOUT WORDS?
OH, IT DOESN'T HAVE TO CONTAIN WORDS TO BE COMICS...
JUXTAPOSED STATIC IMAGES IN DELIBERATE SEQUENCE
NO, NO. I MEAN, DOESN'T THAT DEFINITION DESCRIBE WORDS??
HUH?
LETTERS ARE STATIC IMAGES, RIGHT?
JUXTAPOSED STATIC IMAGES IN DELIBERATE SEQUENCE
WHEN THEY'RE ARRANGED IN A DELIBERATE SEQUENCE, PLACED NEXT TO EACH OTHER, WE CALL THEM WORDS!
YOU TELL 'IM, BOB!

adv.
com·ics (kom'iks)**n.** plural in form, used with a singular verb. **1.** Juxtaposed pictorial and other images in deliberate sequence, intended to convey information and/or to produce an aesthetic response in the viewer.
2. Superheroes in bright colorful costumes, fighting dastardly villains who want to conquer the world, in violent sensational pulse-pounding action sequences!! **3.** Cute, cuddly bunnies, mice and roly-poly bears, dancing to and fro. Hippity-Hop, Hippity-Hop. **4.** Corruptor of our Nation's Youth.
com·ing (kum'ing) **adj**

* OR "OCELOT'S CLAW" DEPENDING ON WHOSE BOOK YOU READ. THIS SEQUENCE IS BASED ON A READING BY MEXICAN HISTORIAN AND ARCHAEOLOGIST ALFONSO CASO.

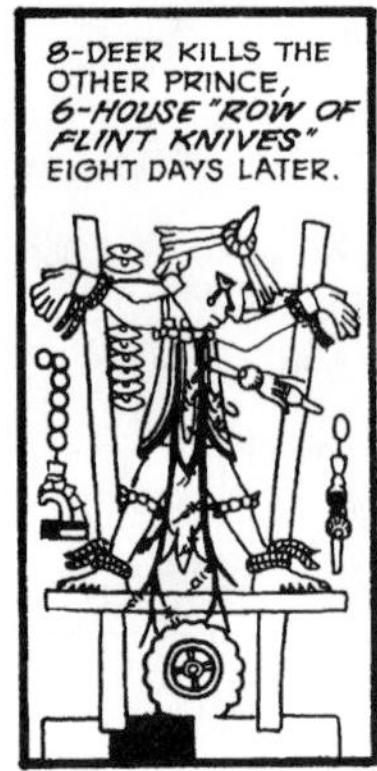

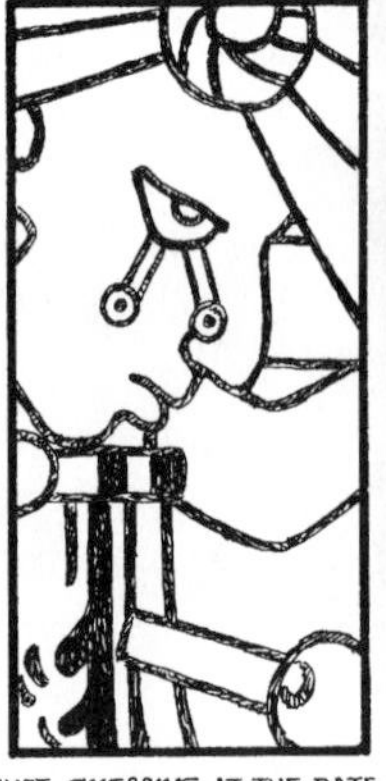

*WE KNOW THE YEAR; I'M JUST GUESSING AT THE DATE REPRESENTED BY "12 MONKEY"

HUNDREDS OF YEARS BEFORE CORTÉS BEGAN COLLECTING COMICS, FRANCE PRODUCED THE STRIKINGLY SIMILAR WORK WE CALL THE BAYEUX TAPESTRY.
THIS 230 FOOT LONG TAPESTRY DETAILS THE NORMAN CONQUEST OF ENGLAND, BEGINNING IN 1066.
TRANSLATION: THE BATTLE RAGES
BISHOP ODIN ENCOURAGES HIS SOLDIERS
FAR FROM DISQUALIFYING THESE AS COMICS, I THINK MODERN COMIC BOOK ARTISTS SHOULD TAKE NOTE OF THE POSSIBILITIES OF SUCH WHOLE PAGE COMPOSITIONS AND HOW FEW ARTISTS HAVE MADE GOOD USE OF THEM SINCE!
PERENNIAL EXCEPTION WILL EISNER.
WHICH ONE IS THE PRINCE?
WHAT, NO HORSES?
FINDING COMICS BEYOND OUR OWN MILLENNIUM IS A BIT TRICKIER.
1000
1100
1200
JUXTAPOSED PICTORIAL AND OTHER IMAGES IN DELIBERATE SEQUENCE ?
AT FIRST GLANCE, EGYPTIAN HIEROGLYPHICS WOULD SEEM TO FIT OUR DEFINITION PERFECTLY.
BUT MUCH DEPENDS ON OUR USE OF THE WORD "PICTORIAL."
I'M USING IT TO INDICATE AT LEAST SOME RESEMBLANCE TO THE SUBJECT. BUT THESE GLYPHS REPRESENT ONLY SOUNDS, NOT UNLIKE OUR ALPHABET.
= "baíu"
= "nek"

READING LEFT TO RIGHT WE SEE THE EVENTS OF THE CONQUEST, IN DELIBERATE CHRONOLOGICAL ORDER UNFOLD BEFORE OUR VERY EYES.
AS WITH THE MEXICAN CODEX, THERE ARE NO PANEL BORDERS PER SE, BUT THERE ARE CLEAR DIVISIONS OF SCENE BY SUBJECT MATTER.
DUKE WILLIAM REMOVES HIS HELMET TO RALLY HIS SOLDIERS
HAROLD'S ARMY IS CUT TO PIECES

THUS, THEIR REAL DESCENDENT IS THE WRITTEN WORD AND NOT COMICS.
"ses tu baiu abta, hennu-nek baiu amenta"
"FOLLOW THEE, THE SOULS OF THE EAST. PRAISE THEE, THE SOULS OF THE WEST."

EGYPTIAN PAINTING IS ANOTHER MATTER. SOME, LIKE THIS, MAY SEEM TO BE CONCERNED WITH SEQUENCE, BUT ARE ACTUALLY SHOWING TWO DIFFERENT LOCATIONS, EVENTS AND CASTS, GROUPED ONLY BY SUBJECT.

I HAD BEEN TRYING TO FIND SEQUENCE IN EGYPTIAN PAINTINGS FOR YEARS WHEN I BEGAN THIS BOOK AND WAS READY TO CALL IT QUITS--
--UNTIL I DISCOVERED THAT THE BOOKS I HAD BEEN USING AS REFERENCE--

--HAD ONLY BEEN SHOWING ME PART OF THE PICTURE!

STARTING AT THE *LOWER LEFT,* WE SEE THREE WORKERS REAPING WHEAT WITH THEIR SICKLES--

--THEN CARRYING IT IN *BASKETS* TO A *THRESHING* LOCATION. (IN THE BACKGROUND TWO GIRLS FIGHT OVER BITS OF WHEAT LEFT BEHIND, AS TWO WORKERS SIT UNDER A TREE, ONE SLEEPING, ONE PLAYING THE *FLUTE!*)

PAINTING TRACED FOR BLACK AND WHITE REPRODUCTION.

* FACE GOUGED OUT BY FUTURE GENERATIONS OF LEADERS

* MAYBE I SHOULDN'T SAY "INVENT". EUROPEANS WERE A BIT LATE IN DISCOVERING PRINTING.

"A HARLOT'S PROGRESS" AND ITS SEQUEL *"A RAKE'S PROGRESS"* PROVED SO POPULAR, NEW *COPYRIGHT LAWS* WERE CREATED TO PROTECT THIS NEW FORM.

UNFORTUNATELY, TÖPFFER HIMSELF FAILED TO GRASP AT FIRST THE FULL POTENTIAL OF HIS INVENTION, SEEING IT AS A MERE *DIVERSION*, A SIMPLE *HOBBY*..

"IF FOR THE FUTURE, HE [TÖPFFER] WOULD CHOOSE A LESS FRIVOLOUS SUBJECT AND RESTRICT HIMSELF A LITTLE, HE WOULD PRODUCE THINGS BEYOND ALL CONCEPTION."

-Goethe

EVEN SO, TÖPFFER'S CONTRIBUTION TO THE *UNDERSTANDING* OF COMICS IS CONSIDERABLE, IF ONLY FOR HIS REALIZATION THAT HE WHO WAS NEITHER ARTIST NOR WRITER--

-- HAD CREATED AND MASTERED A FORM WHICH WAS AT ONCE *BOTH* AND *NEITHER*.

A LANGUAGE ALL ITS OWN.

BRITISH CARICATURE MAGAZINES KEPT THE TRADITIONS ALIVE AND AS THE 20TH CENTURY DREW NEAR, THE COMICS WE CALL COMICS BEGAN TO APPEAR AND EVENTUALLY TO THRIVE IN A STEADY STREAM OF WAKING DREAMS THAT HAS YET TO ABATE.
1870
1880
1890
1900
1910
1920
1930
1940

BUT EVEN IN THIS CENTURY, OUR DEFINITION CAN HELP TO ILLUMINATE THE WORKS OF SOME UNSUNG HEROES.
JUXTAPOSED PICTORIAL AND OTHER IMAGES IN DELIBERATE SEQUENCE

SOME OF THE MOST INSPIRED AND INNOVATIVE COMICS OF OUR CENTURY HAVE NEVER RECEIVED RECOGNITION AS COMICS, NOT SO MUCH IN SPITE OF THEIR SUPERIOR QUALITIES AS BECAUSE OF THEM.
FOR MUCH OF THIS CENTURY, THE WORD "COMICS" HAS HAD SUCH NEGATIVE CONNOTATIONS THAT MANY OF COMICS' MOST DEVOTED PRACTITIONERS HAVE PREFERRED TO BE KNOWN AS "ILLUSTRATORS," "COMMERCIAL ARTISTS" OR, AT BEST, "CARTOONISTS"!
Shel Silverstein
TANTRUM
Jules Feiffer
The Snowman
RAYMOND BRIGGS
MILT GROSS
HEART OF

AND SO, COMICS' LOW SELF-ESTEEM IS SELF-PERPETUATING! THE HISTORICAL PERSPECTIVE NECESSARY TO COUNTERACT COMICS' NEGATIVE IMAGE IS OBSCURED BY THAT NEGATIVITY.

WOODCUT ARTIST LYND WARD IS ONE SUCH MISSING LINK. WARD'S SILENT "WOODCUT NOVELS" ARE POWERFUL MODERN FABLES, NOW PRAISED BY COMICS ARTISTS, BUT SELDOM RECOGNIZED AS COMICS.
FROM WARD'S GOD'S MAN, 1929

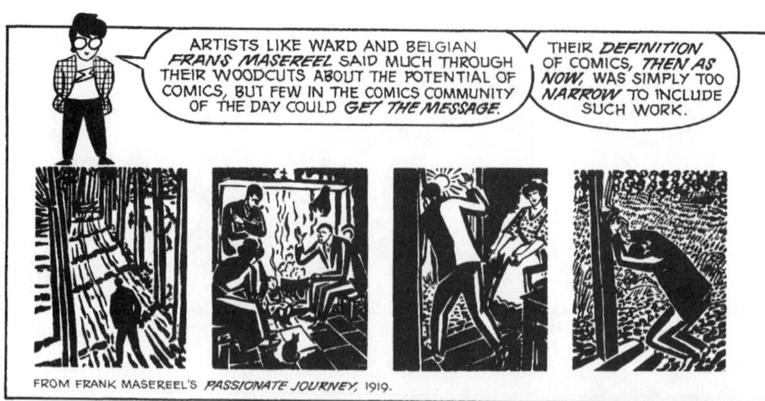

FROM FRANK MASEREEL'S PASSIONATE JOURNEY, 1919.

IF WE DON'T EXCLUDE PHOTOGRAPHY FROM OUR DEFINITION, THEN HALF OF AMERICA HAS BEEN IN COMICS AT ONE TIME OR ANOTHER.
IN SOME COUNTRIES, PHOTO-COMICS ARE, IN FACT, QUITE POPULAR.

MEANWHILE, PICTURES IN SEQUENCE ARE FINALLY BEING RECOGNIZED AS THE EXCELLENT COMMUNICATION TOOL THAT THEY ARE, BUT STILL NOBODY REFERS TO THEM AS COMICS! "DIAGRAMS" SOUNDS MORE DIGNIFIED, I SUPPOSE.
1
2
3
4

FROM STAINED GLASS WINDOWS SHOWING BIBLICAL SCENES IN ORDER TO MONET'S SERIES PAINTINGS, TO YOUR CAR OWNER'S MANUAL, COMICS TURN UP ALL OVER WHEN SEQUENTIAL ART IS EMPLOYED AS A DEFINITION.
THANKS TO MATT FEAZELL FOR THE SUGGESTIONS.

com·ics (kom'iks)n. plural in form, used with a singular verb. 1. Juxtaposed pictorial and other images in deliberate sequence, intended to convey information and/or to produce an aesthetic response in the viewer.
FOR ALL THE DOORS THAT OUR DEFINITION OPENS, THERE IS ONE WHICH IT CLOSES.

SINGLE PANELS LIKE THIS ONE ARE OFTEN LUMPED IN WITH COMICS, YET THERE'S NO SUCH THING AS A SEQUENCE OF ONE!
SUCH SINGLE PANELS MIGHT BE CLASSIFIED AS "COMIC ART" IN THE SENSE THAT THEY DERIVE PART OF THEIR VISUAL VOCABULARY FROM COMICS--
"Mommy, why ain't I Juxtaposed?"

BUT I SAY THEY'RE NO MORE COMICS THAN THIS STILL OF HUMPHREY BOGART IS FILM!
HI, BOGEY.

THEY ARE CARTOONS, AS AM I, AND THERE IS A LONG-STANDING RELATIONSHIP BETWEEN COMICS AND CARTOONS.

--BUT THEY ARE NOT THE SAME THING! ONE IS AN APPROACH TO PICTURE-MAKING-- A STYLE, IF YOU LIKE--WHILE THE OTHER IS A MEDIUM WHICH OFTEN EMPLOYS THAT APPROACH.
HEY!
MORE ON THIS LATER.

THIS SAME SINGLE PANEL MIGHT ALSO BE LABELLED COMICS FOR ITS JUXTAPOSITION OF WORDS AND PICTURES.
"Mommy, why ain't Juxtaposed?"

A GREAT MAJORITY OF MODERN COMICS DO FEATURE WORDS AND PICTURES IN COMBINATION AND IT'S A SUBJECT WORTHY OF STUDY, BUT WHEN USED AS A DEFINITION FOR COMICS, I'VE FOUND IT TO BE A LITTLE TOO RESTRICTIVE FOR MY TASTE.

OF COURSE, IF ANYONE WANTS TO WRITE A BOOK TAKING THE OPPOSITE VIEW, YOU CAN BET I'LL BE THE FIRST IN LINE TO BUY A COPY!

IF COMICS' SPECTACULARLY VARIED PAST IS ANY INDICATION, COMICS' FUTURE WILL BE VIRTUALLY IMPOSSIBLE TO PREDICT USING THE STANDARDS OF THE PRESENT.
BUT OUR DEFINITION CAN OFFER US SOME CLUES.
1980 1990 2000 2010 2020 2030 2040

AND THIS TIME, THE SECRET IS NOT IN WHAT THE DEFINITION SAYS BUT IN WHAT IT DOESN'T SAY!
SEQUENTIAL ART

DADA
BIOGRAPHY
HORROR
ROMANCE
SURREALISM
BLANK VERSE
HISTORICAL FICTION
EPIC POETRY
FOLK TALES
SOCIAL ALLEGORY
SEQUENTIAL ART
EROTICA
MYSTERY
ADAPTATIONS
RELIGIOUS TOPICS
STREAM OF CONSCIOUSNESS
SATIRE
FOR EXAMPLE, OUR DEFINITION SAYS NOTHING ABOUT SUPERHEROES OR FUNNY ANIMALS. NOTHING ABOUT FANTASY/SCIENCE-FICTION OR READER AGE.
NO GENRES ARE LISTED IN OUR DEFINITION, NO TYPES OF SUBJECT MATTER, NO STYLES OF PROSE OR POETRY.

NOTHING IS SAID ABOUT PAPER AND INK. NO PRINTING PROCESS IS MENTIONED. PRINTING ITSELF ISN'T EVEN SPECIFIED! NOTHING IS SAID ABOUT TECHNICAL PENS OR BRISTOL BOARD OR WINDSOR & NEWTON FINEST SABLE SERIES 7 NUMBER TWO BRUSHES!
NO MATERIALS ARE RULED OUT BY OUR DEFINITION. NO TOOLS ARE PROHIBITED.
SEQUENTIAL ART
SPRAY PAINT

THERE IS NO MENTION OF BLACK LINES AND FLAT COLORED INK. NO CALLS FOR EXAGGERATED ANATOMY OR FOR REPRESENTATIONAL ART OF ANY KIND.
NO SCHOOLS OF ART ARE BANISHED BY OUR DEFINITION, NO PHILOSOPHIES, NO MOVEMENTS, NO WAYS OF SEEING ARE OUT OF BOUNDS!
SEQUENTIAL ART

1993

GETTING STARTED

1. Find several different places where McCloud defines comics. List the different definitions and bring them to class.

2. Write a paragraph analyzing one or more of the frames of this comic strip. What does McCloud do with images that makes this essay different from one that is conventionally written? What are some particular ways in which the images add to his meaning?

3. Bring a "sequence of images" to class that seems to support or challenge traditional ideas about comics. Work in groups to test each person's sequence using McCloud's definition.

4. In a group, create an outline of McCloud's essay in which you list his major points. How does he create transitions from one point to the next? What is the comic book equivalent of a paragraph break?

WRITING

5. At the beginning of this essay, McCloud cites the definition of comics as "crude, poorly-drawn, semiliterate, cheap, disposable kiddie fare" (p. 360). Write a two-page paper analyzing the methods he uses to move us beyond that definition. Which of his points do you find persuasive and which do you find unconvincing? Why?

6. Write an essay in which you use McCloud's definition of comics to test a sequence of images that interests you. Is the sequence a comic by his definition? How does the sequence compare to some of the images in McCloud's essay? What future does McCloud predict for comics and how does that measure up to the future you would predict based on the sequence you have analyzed?

USING THE LIBRARY AND THE INTERNET

7. In a reference database such as Academic Search Elite that includes a range of scholarly sources, do a search using the term "comics." Then do a second search on "comics" using a popular search engine such as Alta Vista or Hotbot. What are some of the differences in the results of the two searches? Based on the results of your two searches, what images, terms, and ideas do people seem to associate with comics? Make a list of those associations and bring them to class.

MAKING CONNECTIONS

8. Both McCloud and Annie Dillard are trying to illustrate a new way of seeing their subject matter. Write an essay comparing and contrasting the methods they use to direct our attention to the subject matter in a new way or to help us understand the process of

seeing in a new way. Which methods do you find most successful and why? How would you characterize both writers' purposes overall? What do they most want their essays to accomplish? What arguments are they making?

9. Use ideas and examples from John Berger, Wanda M. Corn, and McCloud to explore how the "artform," the "medium," the ways in which ideas and images are presented—or the "messenger"—can affect the content of those ideas and images—or the "message" (p. 363). Write an essay in which you examine the impact of the medium or the artform on the message or content that gets communicated; use two or more concrete examples.

Erin McGraw

Erin McGraw (1957–) is Associate Professor of English at the University of Cincinnati, where she teaches creative writing and American fiction. McGraw has won awards for her teaching and for her writing. She is the author of two novels, *Bodies at Sea* (1989) and *Lies of the Saints* (1996), and has published short stories and essays. McGraw claims to have become a writer to avoid working in the field of financial management. "Bad Eyes" was first published in the *Gettysburg Review.*

To learn more about blindness, visit the home page of A Blind Net at <http://www.blind.net/blindind.htm>.

Bad Eyes

The subject veers almost uncontrollably toward metaphor, but I mean to take it literally: I have unusually poor vision, minus thirteen hundred diopters and still losing ground, ordinary progressive myopia that never stopped progressing. In me, the process by which light is supposed to focus images at the back of the eye has gone berserk, and the point of focus shifts ever closer to the front, like the projection of a movie falling short of its screen.

My eyeballs aren't round, like marbles or baseballs, but are oblong, like little footballs. This awkward shape puts so much strain on the retinas that a rip has developed in my left one, where the tissue gave out like exhausted cloth. Now my ophthalmologist carefully includes a retina evaluation at annual checks, and I have a list of warning signs that would indicate a significant rupture: sudden, flashing lights; floaters showering into my vision like rain.

Mostly, though, nothing about my vision is so fraught or dramatic. I am shortsighted, is all, mope-eyed, gravel-blind, blind-buck and Davy; a squinter, the sort who taps her companions at plays and baseball games: "What just happened? I missed that." I live in a world where objects collapse into haze. Beyond the narrow realm that my contact lenses permit me to see clearly, I navigate by memory and assumption.

Here are some of the things I can't see, even with my contacts in: a baseball in play, birds in trees, numbers and subtitles on TV, roads at night, constellations, anything by candlelight, street signs, faces of people in cars, faces of people twenty feet away. One of my consistent embarrassments comes from snubbing friends who stood more than a shadow's length from me, friends I didn't even nod to because I couldn't tell who they were. So I've adopted a genial half-smile that I wear when I walk around my neighborhood or down the corridors of the department where I work. I have the reputation of being a very friendly person.

Here are some of the things I can find when I narrow my eyes and look: tiny new weeds in the front garden, fleas scurrying across my dog's belly, gray hairs. My mother, watching me struggle before the bathroom mirror for ten minutes while I spray and brush and bobby-pin to hide the worst of the gray, comments, "I don't know why you bother. You don't have much. No one even sees it."

"I see it every time I look in the mirror."

"Well, you see what you're looking for."

She's told me this all my life. I roll my eyes and keep working the bobby pins.

The glasses I remember best and loved most arrived when I was eight years old. They were my second pair; the first were brown with wings at the corners, the eyeglass equivalent to orthopedic shoes. I was delighted when the doctor announced that they needed to be replaced.

My parents didn't share my delight—only a year had passed since we had gotten that first pair. For six months, unconsciously, I had been moving books closer to my face and inching nearer the TV. Nothing was said about it. I think my parents assumed that I must have been aware of a development so obvious to them, but I was a dreamy, preoccupied child and hadn't noticed that the edges of illustrations in my books were no longer crisp. When I was moved to the front row of my classroom, it never occurred to me to ponder why.

I was pleased to be there, though, and preened in my new glasses. Sleek cat eyes, the white plastic frames featuring jaunty red stripes, they were 1965's cutting edge. I often took them off to admire them. When my correction needed to be stepped up again, I insisted on using the same frames, even though by then I had to keep the glasses on all the time, and could only take pleasure in the candy-cane stripes if I happened to pass a window. In my school pictures for three years running I wore these same glasses. By the third year they were clearly too small for my face, and my eyes practically disappeared behind the thick glass.

Every six months my mother took me to the eye doctor, and nearly every visit meant new, slightly heavier lenses. At first I resented only the hours spent in the waiting room, where I was often the only child, but gradually I began to dread the examination itself, the stinging dilation drops and my frustrating attempts to read the eye chart. While I struggled to focus on letters that seemed to slip and buckle on the far wall, fear bloomed in my stomach.

"T," I would begin rashly, remembering that much from the visit before, but then I strained to make out the next wobbly shape. "U, maybe, or C. It could be O." Not bothering to comment, the doctor tilted back my chair, pulled around one of the clicking, finicky machines, and began the measurements for the next set of lenses. Both he and I ignored my quick, anxious breathing and dry mouth, but when he was finished I burst out of the office as if I were making a jail break.

Back in the world, my panic dropped away, and my worsening vision seemed nothing more than an inconvenience. Perhaps if I had been an outdoorsy kind of child, a girl who noticed leaves or clouds or insect life, I might have grieved the first time I was unable to detect a distant, sly animal. But I wasn't especially fond of the natural world, which was too hot or too cold and full of things that made me itch. The steady loss of detail—my inability first to make out the petals of a flower, and before long to discern the flower at all without glasses to help me—felt unimportant. I jammed on my glasses first thing in the morning, took them off after turning out my light at night, now and then remembered to clean them. Easy enough.

Only occasionally did I get the sense that I was hampered. The sisters at my Catholic school made me take my glasses off before games at recess, a sensible precaution; I was a terrible athlete and could be relied on to stop dead in front of almost any moving object. So I was hit in the face by kickballs, tetherballs, basketballs, and once, memorably, by a softball bat that caught me square on the cheek. The sister blew her whistle and bustled toward me, scolding. Why hadn't I gotten out of the way?

I didn't cry when the bat hit me, although it hurt, but her chiding made my lips start to quiver. I hadn't *seen* it, I protested. All of a sudden something had hit my face; the blow came out of nowhere.

It came out of the batter's box, the sister pointed out. *You shouldn't have been standing so close. You know you can't see well, so you have to be cautious.*

She handed me my glasses and I walked off—sulkily, coddling my sense of injustice—to the nurse's office. The nurse said I'd suffered only a bruise, but I couldn't easily dismiss the incident. Up to that point, no one had told me, *You are at risk, you must take precautions.*

Back at home, I took my glasses off and looked at the house across the street. I recognized its shape and details, but that hardly required vision. I saw the house every day, and could have drawn from memory its long, flat roof and the row of bunkerlike windows.

So I walked up the street, turned onto a cul-de-sac that I didn't know well, and took off my glasses again. Instantly, the turquoise stucco bungalow before me smeared into a vague blue box. I could make out windows, but couldn't tell if the curtains were open or closed; could find the front door but not the mail slot; the wrought-iron handrail but not the steps it accompanied.

A shout erupted and I spun around, shoving my glasses back on to find that the shout had nothing to do with me: a couple of boys were playing catch at the top of the street. Nevertheless, my heart was whapping now, hurting me. I was foolish to stand so publicly, blinking and helpless, right in the middle of the sidewalk. Anyone could have sneaked up, knocked me to the ground, and taken my wallet, if I had had a wallet.

I thought of comic-strip blind beggars on city streets, their canes kicked away, their tin cups stolen. For the first time, my bad eyes took on meaning: they were an invitation to bullies, and the fact that no one had yet taken my glasses and knocked me down was just dumb luck. Pressing my glasses in place, I ran home. This new notion of myself seized my imagination, and I fell asleep for several nights imagining scenarios in which I was unfairly set upon, a lamb before wolves. I saw myself suffering nobly and being remembered reverently.

And then I forgot about my experiment in front of the blue house. I continued to play games without glasses at school, continued to get smacked with kickballs, continued not to be accosted by glasses-snatching bullies. Finally tired of my red-and-white striped glasses, I zipped through half a dozen new pairs, trying out granny glasses in three different shapes, including ones with octagonal lenses that made me look unnervingly like John Lennon.

By the time I was entering junior high, though, I was tired of wearing glasses. More precisely, I was tired of my bespectacled reflection, how glasses made my eyes look tiny and dim, my nose like a tremendous land mass. So I initiated a campaign to get contact lenses, which were just becoming widely available, although not usually for twelve-year-olds. To my astonishment, my cautious, conservative ophthalmologist immediately agreed.

"Contacts help sometimes, with myopia like this," he explained to my skeptical mother. "The theory is that the contact flattens the lens of the eye. It can slow down the disease's progress." I was so elated that I hardly flinched when he called what I had a "disease," a word we usually avoided. And so, a month later, we began a regime that I was in no way ready for.

These were the days when the only contact lenses were made of inflexible plastic, thick by today's standards, hard, immovable foreign bodies that had to be introduced to the protesting eyes at gradual intervals. The first day, the wearer put them in for two hours, then took them out for an hour of recovery, then in again, out, in, out. The second day, three hours.

The optometrist guided my shaking hand, showing me how to slip the lens directly in place. Before I could even look up, I had blinked the contact out; it bounced off the counter beneath us and hit the floor. My mother hissed. The optometrist ordered me not to move; he gently dropped to his knees and patted the linoleum until he found the lens and laboriously cleaned it again.

I blinked the lenses out twice more before he could get them centered on my corneas. Then, tentatively, he stepped back and asked, "How's that?" I was too stunned to answer. For all the talk about wearing schedules and tolerance, no one had told me that contact lenses would *hurt*. Each eye felt as though a hair had been coiled precisely on top of it, and hot, outraged tears poured out. Although the optometrist kept telling me to look up so that he could take measurements, I couldn't keep my eyes from snapping shut. Light was like a blade.

"It always takes a little while," he was telling my mother, "but she'll get used to them. Just take it easy. Don't let her overdo."

No fear of that. I was already frantic to take the lenses back out again, and the remaining hour and forty-five minutes of my first wearing period seemed interminable, an eon of torment. My mother had to lead me back out to the car by the hand; even with the sunglasses the optometrist had given me, I had to close my eyes. Light bouncing off of car windows and storefronts was searing.

For the next month, all I could think about was my eyes. As the optometrist had promised, they began to accommodate to the contacts, but accommodation wasn't comfort. My eyes stung, lightly, all the time. Every blink set the lenses shifting, and that slight movement felt as if it were grinding a ridge into the moist corneal tissue. The irritation made me blink again, shifting the contacts some more.

I spent the summer steeped in resentment. I refused invitations to parties and shopping trips because I had to put my contacts in and take them out, in and out, none of which would have happened if I had had reasonable eyes to begin with. Even after I built up some expertise and didn't have to spend ten minutes tugging the corners of my eyes raw to dislodge the lenses, the contacts kept falling out on their own, vaulting away from my eyes, forcing me to freeze in midstep. With slow, scared care I would sink to my knees and begin patting first my clothes, then the ground around me, feeling for a tiny, mean-spirited disk.

For the first year I spent a lot of time apologizing about lost lenses, ones I rinsed down the drain or cracked, one that the dog snuffled up, and ones that simply shot out of my eyes and disappeared. My parents were understandably unhappy, and I became familiar with the dread that curled through me as soon as I felt one of the lenses begin to shimmy, the indicator that it would soon try for a getaway.

But that dread, at least, was practical. Cresting through me like high tide was the other dread, the one I had forgotten about and put off for years. With the contacts ejecting themselves at malicious whim, I was constantly aware that my next breath might leave me marooned, half-blind, vulnerable. The fact that no one ever treated me with anything but solicitude—often strangers got down on their hands and knees with me—did nothing to soften my fear. I started to walk more slowly, to avoid shag carpeting, to sit with my head tilted slightly back, hoping gravity would keep the contacts in place. Outside, I lingered by the sides of buildings.

By now the myopia was at a full gallop, and the world I saw without any lenses was no longer blurry; it was pure blur. If, for some reason, I had to walk across a room without glasses or contacts, I shuffled like a blind girl, groping for handholds, batting at the air in case something—a lamp, a shelf, some pot hanging from the ceiling—might be ready to strike. Smudged, bulging shapes crowded against me. I imagined fists or rocks or sudden, steep edges, threats from dreams that seemed probable in this shapeless landscape.

At visits to the ophthalmologist, I strained and fought to see the eye chart, memorizing E F O T Z and F X I O S C before the doctor caught on. I paid closer attention to the toneless way he informed my mother that I needed, again, a stronger correction, and felt my throat clench. My mother said, "I thought the contacts were supposed to slow this down."

"They might be doing that," he said. "There's no way of telling. She might be going downhill even faster without them." He bent over to write notes on my chart, which was half an inch thick by now. My eyes were good enough to see that.

I could see other things, too. I could see the expression on my friend's face when I came to spend the night and unpacked all my cumbersome equipment: cleansing solution, wetting solution, saline solution, and the heat-sterilization unit that had to be plugged in for two hours. I could also see her expression after I emerged from the bathroom wearing my glasses. "Let me try them on," she said. I handed them over to let her giggle and bang into walls, and tried not to betray how anxious I was to get them back.

In biology class, I saw my teacher's impatient look when I told her that I couldn't draw the cells clustered on the microscope's slide. "Just close one eye and draw what you see," she said, and so, hopelessly, I did, even though I knew no cell ever had such peculiar zigzags. When I got my lab book back, the teacher had written, "You obviously have trouble seeing enough. Or correctly."

Maybe it was that prim, striving-for-accuracy last phrase that caught me. Or the clinical tone. Whichever, instead of feeling embarrassed or crushed, I was relieved. In a voice that didn't whine or tremble, her note offered me an interesting new self-definition. I grabbed it.

With relief, I gave up trying to make out faces across a football field and stopped straining to read the face of a bell tower clock, tasks I had been using to gauge my vision's deterioration. By this time I was wearing a new, flexible kind of contact lens made out of silicone, far more comfortable and less apt to fall out, so I was confident enough to stroll across parks and thickly carpeted rooms. I started asking the people around me what words were written on the blackboard, what images were flickering by on the TV screen, and people told me. I was a person who had trouble seeing enough, or correctly, so they filled me in on the nuances I would miss on my own.

At a movie, nodding at the screen, my friend whispered, "She keeps noticing the clock. That clock has something to do with the murder." Or, gesturing at the teacher the next day in class: "She's smiling; she's in a good mood. I'll bet she's started smoking again."

I was being given not only facts, but also interpretations. Those who could see sharply gave me shadow as well as object, context in addition to text. Did I resent all of these explanations and asides, pronounced slowly as if for the dimwitted? Not on your life. Friends and family were making things easy for me, and after years of constant unease, I was happy with that.

I drew other people's opinions over me like a blanket. Sight, it seemed, blended right into insight, and to perceive anything was to make a judgment call. Since the people around me had the first kind of sight, I was willing to grant that they had the second. And then the corollary: since I lacked the one, I surely lacked the other.

Anybody with half an eye can see where this story is going: I got lazy. Knowing that many details were going to be lost to me anyway, I stopped trying to see them. I could get the notion of a landscape, but not the trees it contained; I could recognize a skyline, but not the buildings within it. I was all big picture, untroubled by the little stuff.

During my junior year in college, when I was an exchange student in England, I traveled to public gardens and scenic overlooks and took pictures. Only when the pictures were developed did I find out that candy wrappers had clogged the shrubbery, and that across the top slat of the pretty green park bench somebody had carved BOLLOCKS. These weren't microscopic flaws; they were clear to anybody, even myopic me. I had been fully able to see the candy wrappers, but hadn't bothered to. My photo album from that year is a catalogue of England's trash, none of which I looked at until the pictures came back. Then I felt outraged and—this is the kicker—betrayed.

Somewhere, at a juncture I couldn't pinpoint, I had made a tactical shift in how I used my bad eyes. Not only had I given up trying to see the actual, physical world, but I had begun to let myself see a better world, one cut to my taste and measure, a world that, just for starters, didn't contain flyaway Snickers wrappers. And I believed in that world firmly enough to feel cheated when the wrappers got caught on the thorns of barberry bushes.

My inability to see the physical world had infected my mind: I had learned to deceive myself using my mind's eye, just as my real eyes had been deceiving me for years. When I came home from that year abroad, I saw myself as English and annoyed the daylights out of my friends for months by calling the place we lived in a *flat* (although it was in fact a house), by stowing groceries in the car's *boot,* and by pulling beer out of the refrigerator to let it warm up. Had anyone had a mind's camera in those days, they might have pictured me with highway trash wrapped around my ankles and *BOLLOCKS* scrawled on my forehead.

Permitting someone with so shaky a grasp of reality to enter relationships was just asking for trouble. The catalogue of my romances from those years is unrelievedly dreary—boys taking short vacations from their long-term girlfriends, boys who didn't like girls, boys who needed a place to stay and someone to do the cooking. And then the hurt boys, the ones whose long-term girlfriends had left them, who called their therapists twice a day, who were too depressed to go to class. By this point I hardly need add that I saw nothing inappropriate about any of these choices.

When, at twenty-one, I announced my intention to marry a man I knew only slightly and understood less, dismayed family members and friends ringed around me, trying to make me see how inappropriate the choice was, how poorly we were matched, how little pleasure we took, even then, in each other's company. Their attempts hardened my resolve. I looked into the eyes of my intended and saw a soul misunderstood by the world, whose inability to hold a steady job indicated his need for a supportive wife, whose vague visions of success I could share without quite having to get them into focus.

The marriage lasted seven years—longer than it should have. Even when it finally collapsed, its flimsy walls giving way under disappointment, disillusion, and broken promises on both sides, I still couldn't make sense of the ruin, or understand why it had happened. I couldn't *see,* I wailed to a therapist, week after week.

"If you want to see, you have to look," she told me.

"I do look. But I can't see."

"Then you don't know how to look," she said.

Irritated by the smug shrinkishness of her answer, I said, "Okay. Fine. Tell me how to look."

"This isn't some kind of mystical thing. Just pay attention. Your only problem is that you don't pay attention."

As always when I am handed an accurate piece of information about myself, I was stung. Days had to pass before I calmed down and heard the invitation behind the therapist's words, weeks before I was willing to act on them. Not that I knew how to act. All I knew was that a new world was taking shape at my perceptions' furthest horizons, still distant and faint, but visible just barely.

Five years ago my second husband and I bought a house, the first I had ever owned, and with it came property. The house sits on an ordinary suburban lot; we are not talking about Sissinghurst here. Still, space had to be filled up in gardens and around trees, and I learned, generally by error, about bloom time, soil acidity, shade tolerance, and zone hardiness.

Like most chores, gardening teaches me about myself, and I have learned that I am never going to be a prize-winning gardener whose lilies glisten and whose roses scent the air a block away. But I am a tidy gardener: I make time to stake perennials and deadhead the coreopsis; I struggle to preserve clean edges around the beds.

And I am a heroic weeder, a merciless one, driven. I sometimes come into department stores with dirt under my fingernails from digging out knotweed from planting strips in the parking lot. Many gardening tasks are too heavy for me, or require too delicate a touch, but weeding means the staving off of brute chaos, a task I approach with brio.

A year or so after I started gardening, I visited my mother, who has a garden of her own. Stooping to pluck weeds as we talked, I sought out the infant tufts of Bermuda grass that hadn't yet had a chance to sprawl and colonize. "How can you even *see* those tiny things?" my mother asked, and I was so startled that I paused for a moment, still crouched at plant level.

How *can* I even see those tiny things? I can spot an errant sprig of clover from halfway across the yard, but can't make out the face of a good friend five rows down in an auditorium. I can see my gray hairs as if they were outlined in neon, but can't read a football scoreboard on TV. The college co-ed who didn't notice trash and graffiti has become a woman who scours every scene, vigilant in her pursuit of jarring notes, infelicitous details. She has learned to look, and to pay attention. But she still can't see the picture itself, or the happy accidents it might contain.

Bad eyes pick out the bad—it makes sense. Put like that, the condition sounds dire, requiring corrective lenses for the brain or soul. But my myopia is physical before anything else; I am truly unable to make out the face of my friend in that auditorium, however much I might want to see her. A hinge exists between the literal and the metaphorical reality of my crummy vision. I can bear in mind that my vision is untrustworthy, but I can't change it.

All of which brings me back to my high-school biology teacher, God bless her, who diagnosed me more accurately than anyone else. I am a person who has trouble seeing enough, or correctly. Knowing this, I must go forth with useful caution, avoiding quick turns and snap decisions.

And, truly, I do all right. I haven't yet stepped off a cliff or driven into a pedestrian, and my judgments in recent years seem little worse than anyone else's. I just have to look, then look again. I have to remember that I am seeing only part of the picture. I have to remind myself to allow for my margin of error, and then bear in mind that the world is, always, more populous and bright and bountifully landscaped than it appears.

1998

GETTING STARTED

1. Find several examples in which McGraw demonstrates how her failing eyesight affected her identity, how she felt about herself, or how she behaved toward others.
2. In a group, track the stages that McGraw goes through in relation to her loss of sight. How does her personality shift in relation to her changing attitudes about not being able to see?
3. Is this essay only valuable as a story about failing eyesight? Find one or two places where McGraw's story seems to have a larger point or significance. Write a paragraph discussing that significance and exploring what a reader might learn from McGraw's essay.
4. McGraw starts off with the claim that her "subject veers almost uncontrollably toward metaphor" (p. 383). Working in pairs, list as many metaphors or figures of speech as you can find.

WRITING

5. Why is McGraw able to see some things—"an errant sprig of clover from halfway across the yard"—but not able to see other things from a similar distance— "the face of a good friend five rows down in an auditorium" (p. 391)? Use examples from her essay and from your own knowledge and experience to explain this seeming contradiction.
6. Using McGraw's essay as a model, choose some other literal process that you have experienced or noticed (for example, learning something new, planting a garden, writing a paper, finding or losing an important object, and so on). Write a paper in which you analyze the process on the literal level, but also develop its larger significance, using examples and perhaps some figurative language to help show its broader implications.

USING THE LIBRARY AND THE INTERNET

7. Search a reference database that includes magazines and journals, such as MAS Full Text Ultra, Newspaper Source, or Lexis/Nexis, for other accounts of nearsightedness or blindness.

How common are McGraw's reactions, for example, her sense of fear and potential victimization? What is most unusual about her account compared to the others you have uncovered? (Hint: Try a variety of search terms, including "blindness," "blindness and story," "nearsighted," "loss of sight.")

MAKING CONNECTIONS

8. Although Annie Dillard is talking about "seeing" and McGraw is talking about the loss of sight, what points of connection do you find in these two essays? For example, does Dillard's distinction between seeing as "analyzing and prying" and seeing as "letting go" (p. 151) apply to McGraw's examples as well? Write an essay comparing and contrasting their ways of seeing in relation to your own experiences with sight.

9. Write an essay in which you use some of Barbara Mellix's terms and ideas to analyze the processes by which McGraw negotiates the gradual transformation in her identity. How does her understanding of her relationship to "others" change? Does she do any "code-switching"? Does McGraw, like Mellix, use language (or, like Dillard, use "verbalization") to help in her transformation?

10. Emily Martin and her coauthors discuss the process by which different people gain imaginative and scientific insight into the workings of their own bodies and the threat of disease. How does McGraw's account of her nearsightedness compare to the examples that Martin et al. provide? How much "scientific literacy" does McGraw seem to gain? Does she develop her knowledge of the disease in a way that Martin and her coauthors would encourage? Write a paper in which you analyze the degree of scientific literacy that McGraw develops in comparison to the other examples that Martin and her coauthors provide.

Barbara Mellix

Barbara Mellix is the Executive Assistant Dean of the College of Arts and Sciences at the University of Pittsburgh. After completing her undergraduate degree at the University of Pittsburgh, Mellix went on to earn a Masters of Fine Arts degree. In addition to her administrative duties, Mellix teaches writing in the university's English department and writes articles for the alumni magazine. She has won awards for her teaching and writing. "From Outside, In" was originally published in the *Georgia Review*.

> **To learn more about the history of black vernacular English, see the article by James Clyde Sellman at The Africana.com Web site, <http://www.africana.com/tt_262.htm>.**

From Outside, In

Two years ago, when I started writing this paper, trying to bring order out of chaos, my ten-year-old daughter was suffering from an acute attack of boredom. She drifted in and out of the room complaining that she had nothing to do, no one to "be with" because none of her friends were at home. Patiently I explained that I was working on something special and needed peace and quiet, and I suggested that she paint, read, or work with her computer. None of these interested her. Finally, she pulled up a chair to my desk and watched me, now and then heaving long, loud sighs. After two or three minutes (nine or ten sighs), I lost my patience. "Looka here, Allie," I said, "you too old for this kinda carryin' on. I done told you this is important. You wronger than dirt to be in here haggin' me like this and you know it. Now git on outta here and leave me off before I put my foot all the way down."

I was at home, alone with my family, and my daughter understood that this way of speaking was appropriate in that context. She knew, as a matter of fact, that it was almost inevitable; when I get angry at home, I speak some of my finest, most cherished black English. Had I been speaking to my daughter in this manner in certain other environments, she would have been shocked and probably worried that I had taken leave of my sense of propriety.

Like my children, I grew up speaking what I considered two distinctly different languages—black English and standard English (or as I thought of them then, the ordinary everyday speech of "country" coloreds and "proper" English)—and in the process of acquiring these languages, I developed an understanding of when, where, and how to use them. But unlike my children, I grew up in a world that was primarily black. My friends, neighbors, minister, teachers—almost everybody I associated with every day—were black. And we spoke to one another in our own special language: *That sho is a pretty dress you got on. If she don' soon leave me off I'm gon tell her head a mess. I was so mad I could'a pissed a blue nail. He all the time trying to low-rate somebody. Ain't that just about the nastiest thing you ever set ears on?*

Then there were the "others," the "proper" blacks, transplanted relatives and one-time friends who came home from the city for weddings, funerals, and vacations. And the whites. To these we spoke standard English. "Ain't?" my mother would yell at me when I used the term in the presence of "others." "You *know* better than that." And I would hang my head in shame and say the "proper" word.

I remember one summer sitting in my grandmother's house in Greeleyville, South Carolina, when it was full of the chatter of city relatives who were home on vacation. My parents sat quietly, only now and then volunteering a comment or answering a question. My mother's face took on a strained expression when she spoke. I could see that she was being careful to say just the right words in just the right way. Her voice sounded thick, muffled. And when she finished speaking, she would lapse into silence, her proper smile on her face. My father was more articulate, more aggressive. He spoke quickly, his words sharp and clear. But he held his proud head higher, a signal that he, too, was uncomfortable. My sisters and brothers and I stared at our aunts, uncles, and cousins, speaking only when prompted. Even then, we hesitated, formed our sentences in our minds, then spoke softly, shyly.

My parents looked small and anxious during those occasions, and I waited impatiently for our leave-taking when we would mock our relatives the moment we were out of their hearing. "Reeely," we would say to one another, flexing our wrists and rolling our eyes, "how dooo you stan' this heat? Chile, it just too hy*ooo*-mid for words." Our relatives had made us feel "country," and this was our way of regaining pride in ourselves while getting a little revenge in the bargain. The words bubbled in our throats and rolled across our tongues, a balming.

As a child I felt this same doubleness in uptown Greeleyville where the whites lived. "Ain't that a pretty dress you're wearing!" Toby, the town policeman, said to me one day when I was fifteen. "Thank you very much," I replied, my voice barely audible in my own ears. The words felt wrong in my mouth, rigid, foreign. It was not that I had never spoken that phrase before—it was common in black English, too—but I was extremely conscious that this was an occasion for proper English. I had taken out my English and put it on as I did my church clothes, and I felt as if I were wearing my Sunday best in the middle of the week. It did not matter that Toby had not spoken grammatically correct English. He was white and could speak as he wished. I had something to prove. Toby did not.

Speaking standard English to whites was our way of demonstrating that we knew their language and could use it. Speaking it to standard-English-speaking blacks was our way of showing them that we, as well as they, could "put on airs." But when we spoke standard English, we acknowledged (to ourselves and to others—but primarily to ourselves) that our customary way of speaking was inferior. We felt foolish, embarrassed, somehow diminished because we were ashamed to be our real selves. We were reserved, shy in the presence of those who owned and/or spoke *the* language.

My parents never set aside time to drill us in standard English. Their forms of instruction were less formal. When my father was feeling particularly expansive, he would regale us with tales of his exploits in the outside world. In almost flawless English, complete with dialogue and flavored with gestures and embellishment, he told us about his attempt to get a haircut at a white barbershop; his refusal to acknowledge one of the town merchants until the man addressed him as "Mister"; the time he refused to step off the sidewalk uptown to let some whites pass; his airplane trip to New York City (to visit a sick relative) during which the stewardesses and porters—recognizing that he was a "gentleman"—addressed him as "Sir." I did not realize then—nor, I think, did my father—that he was teaching us, among other things, standard English and the relationship between language and power.

My mother's approach was different. Often, when one of us said, "I'm gon wash off my feet," she would say, "And what will you walk on if you wash them off?" Everyone would laugh at the victim of my mother's "proper" mood. But it was different when one of us children was in a proper mood. "You think you are so superior," I said to my oldest sister one day when we were arguing and she was winning. "Superior!" my sister mocked. "You mean I'm acting 'biggidy'?" My sisters and brothers sniggered, then joined in teasing me. Finally, my mother said, "Leave your sister alone. There's nothing wrong with using proper English." There was a half-smile on her face. I had gotten "uppity," had "put on airs" for no good reason. I was at home, alone with the family, and I hadn't been prompted by one of my mother's proper moods. But there was also a proud light in my mother's eyes; her children were learning English very well.

Not until years later, as a college student, did I begin to understand our ambivalence toward English, our scorn of it, our need to master it, to own and be owned by it—an ambivalence that extended to the public-school classroom. In our school, where there were no whites, my teachers taught standard English but used black English to do it. When my grammar school teachers wanted us to write, for example, they usually said something like, "I want y'all to write five sentences that make a statement. Anybody git done before the rest can color." It was probably almost those exact words that led me to write these sentences in 1953 when I was in the second grade:

> The white clouds are pretty.
> There are only 15 people in our room.
> We will go to gym.
> We have a new poster.
> We may go out doors.

Second grade came after "Little First" and "Big First," so by then I knew the implied rules that accompanied all writing assignments. Writing was an occasion for proper English. I was not to write in the way we spoke to one another: The white clouds pretty; There ain't but 15 people in our room; We going to gym; We got a new poster; We can go out in the yard. Rather I was to use the language of "other": clouds *are,* there *are,* we *will,* we *have,* we *may.*

My sentences were short, rigid, perfunctory, like the letters my mother wrote to relatives:

> Dear Papa,
>
> How are you? How is Mattie? Fine I hope. We are fine. We will come to see you Sunday. Cousin Ned will give us a ride.
>
> Love,
> Daughter

The language was not ours. It was something from outside us, something we used for special occasions.

But my coloring on the other side of that second-grade paper is different. I drew three hearts and a sun. The sun has a smiling face that radiates and envelops everything it touches. And although the sun and its world are enclosed in a circle, the colors I used—red, blue, green, purple, orange, yellow, black—indicate that I was less restricted with drawing and coloring than I was with writing standard English. My valentines were not just red. My sun was not just a yellow ball in the sky.

By the time I reached the twelfth grade, speaking and writing standard English had taken on new importance. Each year, about half of the newly graduated seniors of our school moved to large cities—particularly in the North—to live with relatives and find work. Our English teacher constantly corrected our grammar: "Not 'ain't,' but 'isn't.'" We seldom wrote papers, and even those few were usually plot summaries of short stories. When our teacher returned the papers, she usually lectured on the importance of using standard English: "I *am;* you *are;* he, she, or it *is,*" she would say, writing on the chalkboard as she spoke. "How you gon git a job talking about 'I is,' or 'I isn't' or 'I ain't'?"

In Pittsburgh, where I moved after graduation, I watched my aunt and uncle—who had always spoken standard English when in Greeleyville—switch from black English to standard English to a mixture of the two, according to where they were or who they were with. At home and with certain close relatives, friends, and neighbors, they spoke black English. With those less close, they spoke a mixture. In public and with strangers, they generally spoke standard English.

In time, I learned to speak standard English with ease and to switch smoothly from black to standard or a mixture, and back again. But no matter where I was, no matter what the situation or occasion, I continued to write as I had in school:

> Dear Mommie,
>
> How are you? How is everybody else? Fine I hope. I am fine. So are Aunt and Uncle. Tell everyone I said hello. I will write again soon.
>
> Love,
> Barbara

At work, at a health insurance company, I learned to write letters to customers. I studied form letters and letters written by co-workers, memorizing the phrases and the ways in which they were used. I dictated:

> Thank you for your letter of January 5. We have made the changes in your coverage you requested. Your new premium will be $150 every three months. We are pleased to have been of service to you.

In a sense, I was proud of the letters I wrote for the company: they were proof of my ability to survive in the city, the outside world—an indication of my growing mastery of English. But they also indicate writing was still mechanical for me, something that didn't require much thought.

Reading also became a more significant part of my life during those early years in Pittsburgh. I had always liked reading, but now I devoted more and more of my spare time to it. I read romances, mysteries, popular novels. Looking back, I realize that the books I liked best were simple, unambiguous: good versus bad and right versus wrong with right rewarded and wrong punished, mysteries unraveled and all set right in the end. It was how I remembered life in Greeleyville.

Of course I was romanticizing. Life in Greeleyville had not been so very uncomplicated. Back there I had been—first as a child, then as a young woman with limited experience in the outside world—living in a relatively closed-in society. But there were implicit and explicit principles that guided our way of life and shaped our relationships with one another and the people outside—principles that a newcomer would find elusive and baffling. In Pittsburgh, I had matured, become more experienced: I had worked at three different jobs, associated with a wider range of people, married, had children. This new environment with different prescripts for living required that I speak standard English much of the time, and slowly, imperceptibly, I had ceased seeing a sharp distinction between myself and "others." Reading romances and mysteries, characterized by dichotomy, was a way of shying away from change, from the person I was becoming.

But that other part of me—that part which took great pride in my ability to hold a job writing business letters—was increasingly drawn to the new developments in my life and the attending possibilities, opportunities for even greater change. If I could write letters for a nationally known business, could I not also do something better, more challenging, more important? Could I not, perhaps, go to college and become a school teacher? For years, afraid and a little embarrassed, I did no more than imagine this different me, this possible me. But sixteen years after coming north, when my youngest daughter entered kindergarten, I found myself unable—or unwilling—to resist the lure of possibility. I enrolled in my first college course: Basic Writing, at the University of Pittsburgh.

For the first time in my life, I was required to write extensively about myself. Using the most formal English at my command, I wrote these sentences near the beginning of the term:

> One of my duties as a homemaker is simply picking up after others. A day seldom passes that I don't search for a mislaid toy, book, or gym shoe, etc. I change the Ty-D-Bol, fight "ring around the collar," and keep our laundry smelling "April fresh." Occasionally, I settle arguments between my children and suggest things to do when they're bored. Taking telephone messages for my oldest daughter is my newest (and sometimes most aggravating) chore. Hanging the toilet paper roll is my most insignificant.

My concern was to use "appropriate" language, to sound as if I belonged in a college classroom. But I felt separate from the language—as if it did not and could not belong to me. I couldn't think and feel genuinely in that language, couldn't make it express what I thought and felt about being a housewife. A part of me resented, among other things, being judged by such things as the appearance of my family's laundry and toilet bowl, but in that language I could only imagine and write about a conventional housewife.

For the most part, the remainder of the term was a period of adjustment, a time of trying to find my bearings as a student in a college composition class, to learn to shut out my black English whenever I composed, and to prevent it from creeping into my formulations; a time for trying to grasp the language of the classroom and reproduce it in my prose; for trying to talk about myself in that language, reach others through it. Each experience of writing was like standing naked and revealing my imperfection, my "otherness." And each new assignment was another chance to make myself over in language, reshape myself, make myself "better" in my rapidly changing image of a student in a college composition class.

But writing became increasingly unmanageable as the term progressed, and by the end of the semester, my sentences sounded like this:

> My excitement was soon dampened, however, by what seemed like a small voice in the back of my head saying that I should be careful with my long awaited opportunity. I felt frustrated and this seemed to make it difficult to concentrate.

There is a poverty of language in these sentences. By this point, I knew that the clichéd language of my Housewife essay was unacceptable, and I generally recognized trite expressions. At the same time, I hadn't yet mastered the language of the classroom, hadn't yet come to see it as belonging to me. Most notable is the lifelessness of the prose, the apparent absence of a person behind the words. I wanted those sentences—and the rest of the essay—to convey the anguish of yearning to, at once, become something more and yet remain the same. I had the sensation of being split in two, part of me going into a future the other part didn't believe possible. As that person, the student writer at that moment, I was essentially mute. I could not—in the process of composing—use the language of the old me, yet I couldn't imagine myself in the language of "others."

I found this particularly discouraging because at midsemester I had been writing in a much different way. Note the language of this introduction to an essay I had written then, near the middle of the term:

> Pain is a constant companion to the people in "Footwork." Their jobs are physically damaging. Employers are insensitive to their feelings and in many cases add to their problems. The general public wounds them further by treating them with disgrace because of what they do for a living. Although the workers are as diverse as they are similar, there is a definite link between them. They suffer a great deal of abuse.

The voice here is stronger, more confident, appropriating terms like "physically damaging," "wounds them further," "insensitive," "diverse"—terms I couldn't have imagined using when writing about my own experience—and shaping them into sentences like, "Although the workers are as diverse as they are similar, there is a definite link between them." And there is the sense of a personality behind the prose, someone who sympathizes with the workers: "The general public wounds them further by treating them with disgrace because of what they do for a living."

What caused these differences? I was, I believed, explaining other people's thoughts and feelings, and I was free to move about in the language of "others" so long as I was speaking *of* others. I was unaware that I was transforming into my best classroom language my own thoughts and feelings about people whose experiences and ways of speaking were in many ways similar to mine.

The following year, unable to turn back or to let go of what had become something of an obsession with language (and hoping to catch and hold the sense of control that had eluded me in Basic Writing), I enrolled in a research writing course. I spent most of the term learning how to prepare for and write a research paper. I chose sex education as my subject and spent hours in libraries, searching for information, reading, taking notes. Then (not without messiness and often-demoralizing frustration) I organized my information into categories, wrote a thesis statement, and composed my paper—a series of paraphrases and quotations spaced between carefully constructed transitions. The process and results felt artificial, but as I would later come to realize I was passing through a necessary stage. My sentences sounded like this:

> This reserve becomes understandable with examination of who the abusers are. In an overwhelming number of cases, they are people the victims know and trust. Family members, relatives, neighbors and close family friends commit seventy-five percent of all reported sex crimes against children, and parents, parent substitutes and relatives are the offenders in thirty to eighty percent of all reported cases.[12] While assault by strangers does occur, it is less common, and is usually a single episode.[13] But abuse by family members, relatives and acquaintances may continue for an extended period of time. In cases of incest, for example, children are abused repeatedly for an average of eight years.[14] In such cases, "the use of physical force is rarely necessary because of the child's trusting, dependent relationship with the offender. The child's cooperation is often facilitated by the adult's position of dominance, an offer of material goods, a threat of physical violence, or a misrepresentation of moral standards."[15]

The completed paper gave me a sense of profound satisfaction, and I read it often after my professor returned it. I know now that what I was pleased with was the language I used and the professional voice it helped me maintain. "Use better words," my teacher had snapped at me one day after reading the notes I'd begun accumulating from my research, and slowly I began taking on the language of my sources. In my next set of notes, I used the word "vacillating"; my professor applauded. And by the time I composed the final draft, I felt at ease with terms like "overwhelming number of cases," "single episode," and "reserve," and I shaped them into sentences similar to those of my "expert" sources.

If I were writing the paper today, I would of course do some things differently. Rather than opening with an anecdote—as my teacher suggested—I would begin simply with a quotation that caught my interest as I was researching my paper (and which I scribbled, without its source, in the margin of my notebook): "Truth does not do so much good in the world as the semblance of truth does evil." The quotation felt right because it captured what was for me the central idea of my essay—an idea that emerged gradually during the making of my paper—and express it in a way I would like to have said it. The anecdote, a hypothetical situation I invented to conform to the information in the paper, felt forced and insincere because it represented—to a great degree—my teacher's understanding of the essay, *her* idea of what in it was most significant. Improving upon my previous experiences with writing, I was beginning to think and feel in the language I used, to find my own voices in it, to sense that how one speaks influences how one means. But I was not yet secure enough, comfortable enough with the language to trust my intuition.

Now that I know that to seek knowledge, freedom, and autonomy means always to be in the concentrated process of becoming—always to be venturing into new territory, feeling one's way at first, then getting one's balance, negotiating, accommodating, discovering one's self in ways that previously defined "others"—I sometimes get tired. And I ask myself why I keep on participating in this highbrow form of violence, this slamming against perplexity. But there is no real futility in the question, no hint of that part of the old me who stood outside standard English, hugging to herself a disabling mistrust of a language she thought could not represent a person with her history and experience. Rather, the question represents a person who feels the consequence of her education, the weight of her possibilities as a teacher and writer and human being, a voice in society. And I would not change that person, would not give back the good burden that accompanies my growing expertise, my increasing power to shape myself in language and share that self with "others."

"To speak," says Frantz Fanon, "means to be in a position to use a certain syntax, to grasp the morphology of this or that language, but it means above all to assume a culture, to support the weight of a civilization."* To write means to do the same, but in a more profound sense. However, Fanon also says that to achieve mastery means to "get" in a position of power, to "grasp," to "assume." This, I have learned—both as a student and subsequently as a teacher—can involve tremendous emotional and psychological con-

---

***Black Skin, White Masks* (1952; rpt. New York: Grove Press, 1967), pp. 17–18.

flict for those attempting to master academic discourse. Although as a beginning student writer I had a fairly good grasp of ordinary spoken English and was proficient at what Labov calls "code-switching" (and what John Baugh in *Black Street Speech* terms "style shifting"), when I came face to face with the demands of academic writing, I grew increasingly self-conscious, constantly aware of my status as a black and a speaker of one of the many black English vernaculars—a traditional outsider. For the first time, I experienced my sense of doubleness as something menacing, a built-in enemy. Whenever I turned inward for salvation, the balm so available during my childhood, I found instead this new fragmentation which spoke to me in many voices. It was the voice of my desire to prosper, but at the same time it spoke of what I had relinquished and could not regain: a safe way of being, a state of powerlessness which exempted me from responsibility for who I was and might be. And it accused me of betrayal, of turning away from blackness. To recover balance, I had to take on the language of the academy, the language of "others." And to do that, I had to learn to imagine myself a part of the culture of that language, and therefore someone free to manage that language, to take liberties with it. Writing and rewriting, practicing, experimenting, I came to comprehend more fully the generative power of language. I discovered—with the help of some especially sensitive teachers—that through writing one can continually bring new selves into being, each with new responsibilities and difficulties, but also with new possibilities. Remarkable power, indeed. I write and continually give birth to myself.

1987

GETTING STARTED

1. Find several examples in the essay that help to explain Mellix's ideas of "doubleness" or "code-switching." Think of some examples from your own knowledge or experience that involve a kind of "code-switching." Bring a list of examples from the essay and from your own experience to class.

2. In a group, create an outline of Mellix's essay, paying particular attention to the transitions she makes from paragraph to paragraph. What are some of the primary changes that she goes through? What are some of the organizational structures or patterns that she uses in this essay?

3. Analyze the way Mellix quotes and interprets Frantz Fanon (pp. 402–403). What is she learning from Fanon? What is she teaching us about Fanon? What point does she want to make using Fanon?

WRITING

4. Write an essay comparing and contrasting the process by which Mellix became comfortable with academic language and your own experiences in switching from informal to formal languages. What risks are involved in using a new language? What are the rewards and losses?

USING THE LIBRARY AND THE INTERNET

5. Search for the terms "standard English" and "code-switching" in a scholarly database such as Academic Search Elite or one recommended by your reference librarian. From the sources you find, choose five titles and abstracts that seem most deeply or most interestingly related to the issues raised by Mellix. Print the list of titles and abstracts, and bring it to class.

MAKING CONNECTIONS

6. Write an essay analyzing ideas and examples from Walter Mosley's "For Authors, Fragile Ideas Need Loving Every Day" and Nancy Sommers's "I Stand Here Writing" in relation to Mellix's account of her evolving relationship to academic language. Would Mellix agree with Sommers that writing involves "a radical loss of certainty" (p. 463)? Did Sommers or Mosley experience a kind of "doubleness" the way Mellix has? Did their journeys take different directions? What are some of the similarities and dissimilarities in the lessons that each writer learned along the way?

7. Use ideas and examples from Mellix, Gloria Anzaldúa's "Chicana Artists: Exploring *Nepantla, el Lugar de la Frontera*" and Haunani-Kay Trask's "From a Native Daughter," to write an essay in which you analyze the process of "code-switching" between standard English and other languages. What are some of the risks and losses involved for each of these writers? How do they respond differently to the challenges of communicating between different social groups?

WALTER MOSLEY

Walter Mosley (1952–   ) is a writer best known for his hard-boiled detective novels featuring Los Angeles detective Ezekiel "Easy" Rawlins in such books as *Devil in a Blue Dress*. Mosley began his professional life as a computer programmer, but once he started writing, he quit the office and has never looked back. "For Authors, Fragile Ideas Need Loving Every Day" was printed in the "Writers on Writing" column of the *New York Times*.

To learn more about Mosley, visit the Walter Mosley Page at <http://www.wwnorton.com/mosley.htm>.

For Authors, Fragile Ideas Need Loving Every Day

If you want to be a writer, you have to write every day. The consistency, the monotony, the certainty, all vagaries and passions are covered by this daily reoccurrence.

You don't go to a well once but daily. You don't skip a child's breakfast or forget to wake up in the morning. Sleep comes to you each day, and so does the muse.

She comes softly and quietly, behind your left ear or in a corner of the next room. Her words are whispers, her ideas shifting renditions of possibilities that have not been resolved, though they have occurred and reoccurred a thousand times in your mind. She, or it, is a collection of memories not exactly your own.

These reminiscences surface in dreams or out of abstract notions brought on by tastes and excitations, failures and hopes that you experience continually. These ideas have no physical form. They are smoky concepts liable to disappear at the slightest disturbance. An alarm clock or a ringing telephone will dispel a new character; answering the call will erase a chapter from the world.

Our most precious ability, the knack of creation, is also our most fleeting resource. What might be fades in the world of necessity.

How can I create when I have to go to work, cook my dinner, remember what I did wrong to the people who have stopped calling? And even if I do find a moment here and there—a weekend away in the mountains, say—how can I say everything I need to say before the world comes crashing back with all of its sirens and shouts and television shows?

"I know I have a novel in me," I often hear people say. "But how can I get it out?"

The answer is, always is, every day.

The dream of the writer, of any artist, is a fickle and amorphous thing. One evening you're remembering a homeless man, dressed in clothes that smelled like cheese rinds, who you once stood next to on a street corner in New York. Your memory becomes a reverie, and in this daydream you ask him where he's from. With a thick accent he tells you that he was born in Hungary, that he was a freedom fighter, but that now, here in America, his freedom has deteriorated into the poverty of the streets.

You write down a few sentences in your journal and sigh. This exhalation is not exhaustion but anticipation at the prospect of a wonderful tale exposing a notion that you still only partly understand.

A day goes by. Another passes. At the end of the next week you find yourself in the same chair, at the same hour when you wrote about the homeless man previously. You open the journal to see what you'd written. You remember everything perfectly, but the life has somehow drained out of it. The words have no art to them, you no longer remember the smell. The idea seems weak, it has dissipated, like smoke.

This is the first important lesson that the writer must learn. Writing a novel is gathering smoke. It's an excursion into the ether of ideas. There's no time to waste. You must work with that idea as well as you can, jotting down notes and dialogue.

The first day the dream you gathered will linger, but it won't last long. The next day you have to return to tend to your flimsy vapors. You have to brush them, reshape them, breathe into them and gather more.

It doesn't matter what time of day you work, but you have to work every day because creation, like life, is always slipping away from you. You must write every day, but there's no time limit on how long you have to write.

One day you might read over what you've done and think about it. You pick up the pencil or turn on the computer, but no new words come. That's fine. Sometimes you can't go further. Correct a misspelling, reread a perplexing paragraph, and then let it go. You have re-entered the dream of the work, and that's enough to keep the story alive for another 24 hours.

The next day you might write for hours; there's no way to tell. The goal is not a number of words or hours spent writing. All you need to do is to keep your heart and mind open to the work.

Nothing we create is art at first. It's simply a collection of notions that may never be understood. Returning every day thickens the atmosphere. Images appear. Connections are made. But even these clearer notions will fade if you stay away more than a day.

Reality fights against your dreams, it tries to deny creation and change. The world wants you to be someone known, someone with solid ideas, not blowing smoke. Given a day, reality will begin to scatter your notions; given two days, it will drive them off.

The act of writing is a kind of guerrilla warfare; there is no vacation, no leave, no relief. In actuality there is very little chance of victory. You are, you fear, like that homeless man, likely to be defeated by your fondest dreams.

But then the next day comes, and the words are waiting. You pick up where you left off, in the cool and shifting mists of morning.

2000

GETTING STARTED

1. Identify and summarize one of the lessons that Mosley wants to pass along to others who want to become writers. Although Mosley is talking primarily about fiction writing, to what extent can you apply his advice to the processes involved in college writing?
2. Using Mosley's column as an example, take some notes about advice you might give a group of high school students who want to become proficient college writers. Share your advice in a group and then compile the group's list of advice to present to the class.

WRITING

3. Take Mosley's advice by keeping a journal for one week. Write something every day, even if it is only a few sentences about something you observed. At the end of the week, write a one- to two-page paper in which you discuss the merits and drawbacks of Mosley's advice, drawing on quotations from Mosley and from your own journal as evidence for your points.
4. Write a one- to two-page paper modeled on Mosley's column in which you describe your writing process. Then give some advice about the writing process to others.
5. Use the results of your research in response to question 6 to write a one- to two-page paper analyzing the comparisons and contrasts between the two writers. Compare and contrast the two writers' approaches in relationship to your writing. Work with specific quotes and examples from both pieces and examples from your own experience to make your points.

USING THE LIBRARY AND THE INTERNET

6. Look up the *New York Times* "Writers on Writing" series using your library's reference services. (Some libraries have online access to the *New York Times* through the Lexis/Nexis database or its equivalent, while others may use reference volumes and microfilm.) Choose one of the other columns in the series and compare that writer's advice to Mosley's. What differences are there in the two writers' approaches to writing? Which column connects best to your experiences as a writer and why?

7. On the Internet, research what kinds of writing Mosley has published and how critics and reviewers have received his work. (Hint: Searching a reference database such as Academic Search Elite using the author's name will result in a number of reviews.) How do your research findings compare to the answers you would predict based only on Mosley's column? Bring your findings to class.

MAKING CONNECTIONS

8. In "I Stand Here Writing," Nancy Sommers would like to teach her students that "being personal . . . does not mean being autobiographical" (p. 456). Use examples from Sommers and Mosley and from your own knowledge or experience to explain what she might mean. To what extent would Mosley agree with Sommers's other advice to her students or with her idea that "writing is a radical loss of certainty" (p. 451)?

9. In "The Loss of the Creature," Walker Percy describes the way objects, such as the sonnet or the dogfish, can become obscured by "symbolic packages" (p. 417). Is Mosley also creating a symbolic package around the process of writing fiction, or does he help to free the process from that symbolic packaging? Use Mosley's piece to explain and to test Percy's definition of symbolic packages.

10. Use Northrop Frye's discussion of figures of speech in "The Motive for Metaphor" to analyze Mosley's piece. What figurative analogies or associations does Mosley use to describe the act of writing?

WALKER PERCY

Walker Percy (1916–1990) was a novelist and essayist best known for his depictions of life in the New South. Percy was born in Alabama and raised in Mississippi. He began his professional life as a doctor, practicing pathology at Bellevue Hospital in New York City. Through his work, he contracted tuberculosis. The disease eventually left him too weak either to practice or to teach medicine, and so he began his career as a writer. In his novels and essays, Percy pursued an answer to the modern question, why does scientific progress seem to bring us no closer to understanding how to live? "The Loss of the Creature" has been widely anthologized. It was first published in the essay collection, *The Message in the Bottle: How Queer Man Is, How Queer Language Is, and What One Has to Do with the Other* (1975).

To learn more about Percy, visit the Walker Percy Project at <http://www.ibiblio.org/wpercy/>.

The Loss of the Creature

Every explorer names his island Formosa, beautiful. To him it is beautiful because, being first, he has access to it and can see it for what it is. But to no one else is it ever as beautiful—except the rare man who manages to recover it, who knows that it has to be recovered.

García López de Cárdenas discovered the Grand Canyon and was amazed at the sight. It can be imagined: One crosses miles of desert, breaks through the mesquite, and there it is at one's feet. Later the government set the place aside as a national park, hoping to pass along to millions the experience of Cárdenas. Does not one see the same sight from the Bright Angel Lodge that Cárdenas saw?

The assumption is that the Grand Canyon is a remarkably interesting and beautiful place and that if it had a certain value *P* for Cárdenas, the same value *P* may be transmitted to any number of sightseers—just as Banting's discovery of insulin can be transmitted to any number of diabetics. A counterinfluence is at work, however, and it would be nearer the truth to say that if the place is seen by a million sightseers, a single sightseer does not receive value *P* but a millionth part of value *P*.

It is assumed that since the Grand Canyon has the fixed interest value *P*, tours can be organized for any number of people. A man in Boston decides to spend his vacation at the Grand Canyon. He visits his travel bureau, looks at the folder, signs up for a two-week tour. He and his family take the tour, see the Grand Canyon, and return to Boston. May we say that this man has seen the Grand Canyon? Possibly he has. But it is more likely that what he has done is the one sure way not to see the canyon.

Why is it almost impossible to gaze directly at the Grand Canyon under these circumstances and see it for what it is—as one picks up a strange object from one's back yard and gazes directly at it? It is almost impossible because the Grand Canyon, the thing as it is, has been appropriated by the symbolic complex which has already been formed in the sightseer's mind. Seeing the canyon under approved circumstances is seeing the symbolic complex head on. The thing is no longer the thing as it confronted the Spaniard; it is rather that which has already been formulated—by picture postcard, geography book, tourist folders, and the words *Grand Canyon*. As a result of this preformulation, the source of the sightseer's pleasure undergoes a shift. Where the wonder and delight of the Spaniard arose from his penetration of the thing itself, from a progressive discovery of depths, patterns, colors, shadows, etc., now the sightseer measures his satisfaction *by the degree to which the canyon conforms to the preformed complex*. If it does so, if it looks just like the postcard, he is pleased; he might even say, "Why it is every bit as beautiful as a picture postcard!" He feels he has not been cheated. But if it does not conform, if the colors are somber, he will not be able to see it directly; he will only be conscious of the disparity between what it is and what it is supposed to be. He will say later that he was unlucky in not being there at the right time. The highest point, the term of the sightseer's satisfaction, is not the sovereign discovery of the thing before him; it is rather the measuring up of the thing to the criterion of the preformed symbolic complex.

Seeing the canyon is made even more difficult by what the sightseer does when the moment arrives, when sovereign knower confronts the thing to be known. Instead of looking at it, he photographs it. There is no confrontation at all. At the end of forty years of preformulation and with the Grand Canyon yawning at his feet, what does he do? He waives his right of seeing and knowing and records symbols for the next forty years. For him there is no present; there is only the past of what has been formulated and seen and the future of what has been formulated and not seen. The present is surrendered to the past and the future.

The sightseer may be aware that something is wrong. He may simply be bored; or he may be conscious of the difficulty: that the great thing yawning at his feet somehow eludes him. The harder he looks at it, the less he can see. It eludes everybody. The tourist cannot see it; the bellboy at the Bright Angel Lodge cannot see it: for him it is only one side of the space he lives in, like one wall of a room; to the ranger it is a tissue of everyday signs relevant to his own prospects—the blue haze down there means that he will probably get rained on during the donkey ride.

How can the sightseer recover the Grand Canyon? He can recover it in any number of ways, all sharing in common the stratagem of avoiding the approved confrontation of the tour and the Park Service.

It may be recovered by leaving the beaten track. The tourist leaves the tour, camps in the back country. He arises before dawn and approaches the South Rim through a wild terrain where there are no trails and no railed-in lookout points. In other words, he sees the canyon by avoiding all the facilities for seeing the canyon. If the benevolent Park Service hears about this fellow and thinks he has a good idea and places the following notice in the Bright Angel Lodge: *Consult ranger for information on getting off the beaten track*—the end result will only be the closing of another access to the canyon.

It may be recovered by a dialectical movement which brings one back to the beaten track but at a level above it. For example, after a lifetime of avoiding the beaten track and guided tours, a man may deliberately seek out the most beaten track of all, the most commonplace tour imaginable: he may visit the canyon by a Greyhound tour in the company of a party from Terre Haute—just as a man who has lived in New York all his life may visit the Statue of Liberty. (Such dialectical savorings of the familiar as the familiar are, of course, a favorite stratagem of *The New Yorker* magazine.) The thing is recovered from familiarity by means of an exercise in familiarity. Our complex friend stands behind his fellow tourists at the Bright Angel Lodge and sees the canyon through them and their predicament, their picture taking and busy disregard. In a sense, he exploits his fellow tourists; he stands on their shoulders to see the canyon.

Such a man is far more advanced in the dialectic than the sightseer who is trying to get off the beaten track—getting up at dawn and approaching the canyon through the mesquite. This stratagem is, in fact, for our complex man the weariest, most beaten track of all.

It may be recovered as a consequence of a breakdown of the symbolic machinery by which the experts present the experience to the consumer. A family visits the canyon in the usual way. But shortly after their arrival, the park is closed by an outbreak of typhus in the south. They have the canyon to themselves. What do they mean when they tell the home folks of their good luck: "We had the whole place to ourselves"? How does one see the thing better when the others are absent? Is looking like sucking: the more lookers, the less there is to see? They could hardly answer, but by saying this they testify to a state of affairs which is considerably more complex than the simple statement of the schoolbook about the Spaniard and the millions who followed him. It is a state in which there is a complex distribution of sovereignty, of zoning.

It may be recovered in a time of national disaster. The Bright Angel Lodge is converted into a rest home, a function that has nothing to do with the canyon a few yards away. A wounded man is brought in. He regains consciousness; there outside his window is the canyon.

The most extreme case of access by privilege conferred by disaster is the Huxleyan novel of the adventures of the surviving remnant after the great wars of the twentieth century. An expedition from Australia lands in Southern California and heads east. They stumble across the Bright Angel Lodge, now fallen into ruins. The trails are grown over, the guard rails fallen away, the dime telescope at Battleship Point rusted. But there is the canyon, exposed at last. Exposed by what? By the decay of those facilities which were designed to help the sightseer.

This dialectic of sightseeing cannot be taken into account by planners, for the object of the dialectic is nothing other than the subversion of the efforts of the planners.

The dialectic is not known to objective theorists, psychologists, and the like. Yet it is quite well known in the fantasy-consciousness of the popular arts. The devices by which the museum exhibit, the Grand Canyon, the ordinary thing, is recovered have long since been stumbled upon. A movie shows a man visiting the Grand Canyon. But the moviemaker knows something the planner does not know. He knows that one cannot take the sight frontally. The canyon must be approached by the stratagems we have mentioned: the Inside Track, the Familiar Revisited, the Accidental Encounter. Who is the stranger at the Bright Angel Lodge? Is he the ordinary tourist from Terre Haute that he makes himself out to be? He is not. He has another objective in mind, to revenge his wronged brother, counterespionage, etc. By virtue of the fact that he has other fish to fry, he may take a stroll along the rim after supper and then we can see the canyon through him. The movie accomplishes its purpose by concealing it. Overtly the characters (the American family marooned by typhus) and we the onlookers experience pity for the sufferers, and the family experience anxiety for themselves; covertly and in truth they are the happiest of people and we are happy through them, for we have the canyon to ourselves. The movie cashes in on the recovery of sovereignty through disaster. Not only is the canyon now accessible to the remnant; the members of the remnant are now accessible to each other; a whole new ensemble of relations becomes possible—friendship, love, hatred, clandestine sexual adventures. In a movie when a man sits next to a woman on a bus, it is necessary either that the bus break down or that the woman lose her memory. (The question occurs to one: Do you imagine there are sightseers who see sights just as they are supposed to? a family who live in Terre Haute, who decide to take the canyon tour, who go there, see it, enjoy it immensely, and go home content? a family who are entirely innocent of all the barriers, zones, losses of sovereignty I have been talking about? Wouldn't most people be sorry if Battleship Point fell into the canyon, carrying all one's fellow passengers to their death, leaving one alone on the South Rim? I cannot answer this. Perhaps there are such people. Certainly a great many American families would swear they had no such problems, that they came, saw, and went away happy. Yet it is just these families who would be happiest if they had gotten the Inside Track and been among the surviving remnant.)

It is now apparent that as between the many measures which may be taken to overcome the opacity, the boredom, of the direct confrontation of the thing or creature in its citadel of symbolic investiture, some are less authentic than others. That is to say, some stratagems obviously serve other purposes than that of providing access to being—for example, various unconscious motivations which it is not necessary to go into here.

Let us take an example in which the recovery of being is ambiguous, where it may under the same circumstances contain both authentic and unauthentic components. An American couple, we will say, drives down into Mexico. They see the usual sights and have a fair time of it. Yet they are never without the sense of missing something. Although Taxco and Cuernavaca are interesting and picturesque as advertised, they fall short of "it." What do the couple have in mind by "it"? What do they really hope for? What sort of experience could they have in Mexico so that upon their return, they would feel that "it" had happened? We have a clue: Their hope has something to do with their own role as tourists in a foreign country and the way in which they conceive this role. It has something to do with other American tourists. Certainly they feel that they are very far from "it" when, after traveling five thousand miles, they arrive at the plaza in Guanajuato only to find themselves surrounded by a dozen other couples from the Midwest.

Already we may distinguish authentic and unauthentic elements. First, we see the problem the couple faces and we understand their efforts to surmount it. The problem is to find an "unspoiled" place. "Unspoiled" does not mean only that a place is left physically intact; it means also that it is not encrusted by renown and by the familiar (as is Taxco), that it has not been discovered by others. We understand that the couple really want to get at the place and enjoy it. Yet at the same time we wonder if there is not something wrong in their dislike of their compatriots. Does access to the place require the exclusion of others?

Let us see what happens.

The couple decide to drive from Guanajuato to Mexico City. On the way they get lost. After hours on a rocky mountain road, they find themselves in a tiny valley not even marked on the map. There they discover an Indian village. Some sort of religious festival is going on. It is apparently a corn dance in supplication of the rain god.

The couple know at once that this is "it." They are entranced. They spend several days in the village, observing the Indians and being themselves observed with friendly curiosity.

Now may we not say that the sightseers have at last come face to face with an authentic sight, a sight which is charming, quaint, picturesque, unspoiled, and that they see the sight and come away rewarded? Possibly this may occur. Yet it is more likely that what happens is a far cry indeed from an immediate encounter with being, that the experience, while masquerading as such, is in truth a rather desperate impersonation. I use the word *desperate* advisedly to signify an actual loss of hope.

The clue to the spuriousness of their enjoyment of the village and the festival is a certain restiveness in the sightseers themselves. It is given expression by their repeated exclamations that "this is too good to be true," and by their anxiety that it may not prove to be so perfect, and finally by their downright relief at leaving the valley and having the experience in the bag, so to speak—that is, safely embalmed in memory and movie film.

What is the source of their anxiety during the visit? Does it not mean that the couple are looking at the place with a certain standard of performance in mind? Are they like Fabre, who gazed at the world about him with wonder, letting it be what it is; or are they not like the overanxious mother who sees her child as one performing, now doing badly, now doing well? The village is their child and their love for it is an anxious love because they are afraid that at any moment it might fail them.

We have another clue in their subsequent remark to an ethnologist friend. "How we wished you had been there with us! What a perfect goldmine of folkways! Every minute we would say to each other, if only you were here! You must return with us." This surely testifies to a generosity of spirit, a willingness to share their experience with others, not at all like their feelings toward their fellow Iowans on the plaza at Guanajuato!

I am afraid this is not the case at all. It is true that they longed for their ethnologist friend, but it was for an entirely different reason. They wanted him, not to share their experience, but to certify their experience as genuine.

"This is it" and "Now we are really living" do not necessarily refer to the sovereign encounter of the person with the sight that enlivens the mind and gladdens the heart. It means that now at last we are having the acceptable experience. The present experience is always measured by a prototype, the "it" of their dreams. "Now I am really living" means that now I am filling the role of sightseer and the sight is living up to the prototype of sights. This quaint and picturesque village is measured by a Platonic ideal of the Quaint and the Picturesque.

Hence their anxiety during the encounter. For at any minute something could go wrong. A fellow Iowan might emerge from a 'dobe hut; the chief might show them his Sears catalogue. (If the failures are "wrong" enough, as these are, they might still be turned to account as rueful conversation pieces: "There we were expecting the chief to bring us a churinga and he shows up with a Sears catalogue!") They have snatched victory from disaster, but their experience always runs the danger of failure.

They need the ethnologist to certify their experience as genuine. This is borne out by their behavior when the three of them return for the next corn dance. During the dance, the couple do not watch the goings-on; instead they watch the ethnologist! Their highest hope is that their friend should find the dance interesting. And if he should show signs of true absorption, an interest in the goings-on so powerful that he becomes oblivious of his friends—then their cup is full. "Didn't we tell you?" they say at last. What they want from him is not ethnological explanations; all they want is his approval.

What has taken place is a radical loss of sovereignty over that which is as much theirs as it is the ethnologist's. The fault does not lie with the ethnologist. He has no wish to stake a claim to the village; in fact, he desires the opposite: he will bore his friends to death by telling them about the village and the meaning of the folkways. A degree of sovereignty has been surrendered by the couple. It is the nature of the loss, moreover, that they are not aware of the loss, beyond a certain uneasiness. (Even if they read this and admitted it, it would be very difficult for them to bridge the gap in their confrontation of the world. Their consciousness of the corn dance cannot escape their consciousness of their consciousness, so that with the onset of the first direct enjoyment, their higher consciousness pounces and certifies: "Now you are doing it! Now you are really living!" and, in certifying the experience, sets it at nought.)

Their basic placement in the world is such that they recognize a priority of title of the expert over his particular department of being. The whole horizon of being is staked out by "them," the experts. The highest satisfaction of the sightseer (not merely the tourist but any layman seer of sights) is that his sight should be certified as genuine. The worst of this impoverishment is that there is no sense of impoverishment. The surrender of title is so complete that it never even occurs to one to reassert title. A poor man may envy the rich man, but the sightseer does not envy the expert. When a caste system becomes absolute, envy disappears. Yet the caste of layman-expert is not the fault of the expert. It is due altogether to the eager surrender of sovereignty by the layman so that he may take up the role not of the person but of the consumer.

I do not refer only to the special relation of layman to theorist. I refer to the general situation in which sovereignty is surrendered to a class of privileged knowers, whether these be theorists or artists. A reader may surrender sovereignty over that which has been written about, just as a consumer may surrender sovereignty over a thing which has been theorized about. The consumer is content to receive an experience just as it has been presented to him by theorists and planners. The reader may also be content to judge life by whether it has or has not been formulated by those who know and write about life. A young man goes to France. He too has a fair time of it, sees the sights, enjoys the food. On his last day, in fact as he sits in a restaurant in Le Havre waiting for his boat, something happens. A group of French students in the restaurant get into an impassioned argument over a recent play. A riot takes place. Madame la concierge joins in, swinging her mop at the rioters. Our young American is transported. This it "it." And he had almost left France without seeing "it"!

But the young man's delight is ambiguous. On the one hand, it is a pleasure for him to encounter the same Gallic temperament he had heard about from Puccini and Rolland. But on the other hand, the source of his pleasure testifies to a certain alienation. For the young man is actually barred from a direct encounter with anything French excepting only that which has been set forth, authenticated by Puccini and Rolland—those who know. If he had encountered the restaurant scene without reading Hemingway, without knowing that the performance was so typically, charmingly French, he would not have been delighted. He would only have been anxious at seeing things get so out of hand. The source of his delight is the sanction of those who know.

This loss of sovereignty is not a marginal process, as might appear from my example of estranged sightseers. It is a generalized surrender of the horizon to those experts within whose competence a particular segment of the horizon is thought to lie. Kwakiutls are surrendered to Franz Boas; decaying Southern mansions are surrendered to Faulkner and Tennessee Williams. So that, although it is by no means the intention of the expert to expropriate sovereignty—in fact he would not even know what sovereignty meant in this context—the danger of theory and consumption is a seduction and deprivation of the consumer.

In the New Mexican desert, natives occasionally come across strange-looking artifacts which have fallen from the skies and which are stenciled: *Return to U.S. Experimental Project, Alamogordo. Reward.* The finder returns the object and is rewarded. He knows nothing of the nature of the object he has found and does not care to know. The sole role of the native, the highest role he can play, is that of finder and returner of the mysterious equipment.

The same is true of the layman's relation to *natural* objects in a modern technical society. No matter what the object or event is, whether it is a star, a swallow, a Kwakiutl, a "psychological phenomenon," the layman who confronts it does not confront it as a sovereign person, as Crusoe confronts a seashell he finds on the beach. The highest role he can conceive himself as playing is to be able to recognize the title of the object, to return it to the appropriate expert and have it certified as a genuine find. He does not even permit himself to see the thing—as Gerard Hopkins could see a rock or a cloud or a field. If anyone asks him why he doesn't look, he may reply that he didn't take that subject in college (or he hasn't read Faulkner).

This loss of sovereignty extends even to oneself. There is the neurotic who asks nothing more of his doctor than that his symptoms should prove interesting. When all else fails, the poor fellow has nothing to offer but his own neurosis. But even this is sufficient if only the doctor will show interest when he says, "Last night I had a curious sort of dream; perhaps it will be significant to one who knows about such things. It seems I was standing in a sort of alley—" (I have nothing else to offer you but my own unhappiness. Please say that it, at least, measures up, that it is a *proper* sort of unhappiness.)

2

A young Falkland Islander walking along a beach and spying a dead dogfish and going to work on it with his jackknife has, in a fashion wholly unprovided in modern educational theory, a great advantage over the Scarsdale high-school pupil who finds the dogfish on his laboratory desk. Similarly the citizen of Huxley's *Brave New World* who stumbles across a volume of Shakespeare in some vine-grown ruins and squats on a potsherd to read it is in a fairer way of getting at a sonnet than the Harvard sophomore taking English Poetry II.

The educator whose business it is to teach students biology or poetry is unaware of a whole ensemble of relations which exist between the student and the dogfish and between the student and the Shakespeare sonnet. To put it bluntly: A student who has the desire to get at a dogfish or a Shakespeare sonnet may have the greatest difficulty in salvaging the creature itself from the educational package in which it is presented. The great difficulty is that he is not aware that there is a difficulty; surely, he thinks, in such a fine classroom, with such a fine textbook, the sonnet must come across! What's wrong with me?

The sonnet and the dogfish are obscured by two different processes. The sonnet is obscured by the symbolic package which is formulated not by the sonnet itself but by the *media* through which the sonnet is transmitted, the media which the educators believe for some reason to be transparent. The new textbook, the type, the smell of the page, the classroom, the aluminum windows and the winter sky, the personality of Miss Hawkins—these media which are supposed to transmit the sonnet may only succeed in transmitting themselves. It is only the hardiest and cleverest of students who can salvage the sonnet from this many-tissued package. It is only the rarest student who knows that the sonnet must be salvaged from the package. (The educator is well aware that there is something wrong, that there is a fatal gap between the student's learning and the student's life: The student reads the poem, appears to understand it, and gives all the answers. But what does he recall if he should happen to read a Shakespeare sonnet twenty years later? Does he recall the poem or does he recall the smell of the page and the smell of Miss Hawkins?)

One might object, pointing out that Huxley's citizen reading his sonnet in the ruins and the Falkland Islander looking at his dogfish on the beach also receive them in a certain package. Yes, but the difference lies in the fundamental placement of the student in the world, a placement which makes it possible to extract the thing from the package. The pupil at Scarsdale High sees himself placed as a consumer receiving an experience-package; but the Falkland Islander exploring his dogfish is a person exercising the sovereign right of a person in his lordship and mastery of creation. He too could use an instructor and a book and a technique, but he would use them as his subordinates, just as he uses his jackknife. The biology student does not use his scalpel as an instrument; he uses it as a magic wand! Since it is a "scientific instrument," it should do "scientific things."

The dogfish is concealed in the same symbolic package as the sonnet. But the dogfish suffers an additional loss. As a consequence of this double deprivation, the Sarah Lawrence student who scores A in zoology is apt to know very little about a dogfish. She is twice removed from the dogfish, once by the symbolic complex by which the dogfish is concealed, once again by the spoliation of the dogfish by theory which renders it invisible. Through no fault of zoology instructors, it is nevertheless a fact that the zoology laboratory at Sarah Lawrence College is one of the few places in the world where it is all but impossible to see a dogfish.

The dogfish, the tree, the seashell, the American Negro, the dream, are rendered invisible by a shift of reality from concrete thing to theory which Whitehead has called the fallacy of misplaced concreteness. It is the mistaking of an idea, a principle, an abstraction, for the real. As a consequence of the shift, the "specimen" is seen as less real than the theory of the specimen. As Kierkegaard said, once a person is seen as a specimen of race or a species, at that very moment he ceases to be an individual. Then there are no more individuals but only specimens.

To illustrate: A student enters a laboratory which, in the pragmatic view, offers the student the optimum conditions under which an educational experience may be had. In the existential view, however—that view of the student in which he is regarded not as a receptacle of experience but as a knowing being whose peculiar property it is to see himself as being in a certain situation—the modern laboratory could not have been more effectively designed to conceal the dogfish forever.

The student comes to his desk. On it, neatly arranged by his instructor, he finds his laboratory manual, a dissecting board, instruments, and a mimeographed list:

Exercise 22

Materials: 1 dissecting board

1 scalpel

1 forceps

1 probe

1 bottle india ink and syringe

1 specimen of *Squalus acanthias*

The clue to the situation in which the student finds himself is to be found in the last item: 1 specimen of *Squalus acanthias*.

The phrase *specimen of* expresses in the most succinct way imaginable the radical character of the loss of being which has occurred under his very nose. To refer to the dogfish, the unique concrete existent before him, as a "specimen of *Squalus acanthias*" reveals by its grammar the spoliation of the dogfish by the theoretical method. This phrase, *specimen of*, example of, instance of, indicates the ontological status of the individual creature in the eyes of the theorist. The dogfish itself is seen as a rather shabby expression of an ideal reality, the species *Squalus acanthias*. The result is the radical devaluation of the individual dogfish. (The *reductio ad absurdum* of Whitehead's shift is Toynbee's employment of it in his historical method. If a gram of NaCl is referred to by the chemist as a "sample of" NaCl, one may think of it as such and not much is missed by the oversight of the act of being of this particular pinch of salt, but when the Jews and the Jewish religion are understood as—in Toynbee's favorite phrase—a "classical example of" such and such a kind of *Voelkerwanderung*, we begin to suspect that something is being left out.)

If we look into the ways in which the student can recover the dogfish (or the sonnet), we will see that they have in common the stratagem of avoiding the educator's direct presentation of the object as a lesson to be learned and restoring access to sonnet and dogfish as beings to be known, reasserting the sovereignty of knower over known.

In truth, the biography of scientists and poets is usually the story of the discovery of the indirect approach, the circumvention of the educator's presentation—the young man who was sent to the *Technikum* and on his way fell into the habit of loitering in book stores and reading poetry; or the young man dutifully attending law school who on the way became curious about the comings and goings of ants. One remembers the scene in *The Heart Is a Lonely Hunter* where the girl hides in the bushes to hear the Capehart in the big house play Beethoven. Perhaps she was the lucky one after all. Think of the unhappy souls inside, who see the record, worry about scratches, and most of all worry about whether they are *getting it,* whether they are bona fide music lovers. What is the best way to hear Beethoven: sitting in a proper silence around the Capehart or eavesdropping from an azalea bush?

However it may come about, we notice two traits of the second situation: (1) an openness of the thing before one—instead of being an exercise to be learned according to an approved mode, it is a garden of delights which beckons to one; (2) a sovereignty of the knower—instead of being a consumer of a prepared experience, I am a sovereign wayfarer, a wanderer in the neighborhood of being who stumbles into the garden.

One can think of two sorts of circumstances through which the thing may be restored to the person. (There is always, of course, the direct recovery: A student may simply be strong enough, brave enough, clever enough to take the dogfish and the sonnet by storm, to wrest control of it from the educators and the educational package.) First by ordeal: The Bomb falls; when the young man recovers consciousness in the shambles of the biology laboratory, there not ten inches from his nose lies the dogfish. Now all at once he can see it, directly and without let, just as the exile or the prisoner or the sick man sees the sparrow at his window in all its inexhaustibility; just as the commuter who has had a heart attack sees his own hand for the first time. In these cases, the simulacrum of everydayness and of consumption has been destroyed by disaster; in the case of the bomb, literally destroyed. Secondly, by apprenticeship to a great man: One day a great biologist walks into the laboratory; he stops in front of our student's desk; he leans over, picks up the dogfish, and, ignoring instruments and procedure, probes with a broken fingernail into the little carcass. "Now here is a curious business," he says, ignoring also the proper jargon of the specialty. "Look here how this little duct reverses its direction and drops into the pelvis. Now if you would look into a coelacanth, you would see that it—" And all at once the student can see. The technician and the sophomore who loves his textbook are always offended by the genuine research man because the latter is usually a little vague and always humble before the thing; he doesn't have much use for the equipment or the jargon. Whereas the technician is never vague and never humble before the thing; he holds the thing disposed of by the principle, the formula, the textbook outline; and he thinks a great deal of equipment and jargon.

But since neither of these methods of recovering the dogfish is pedagogically feasible—perhaps the great man even less so than the Bomb—I wish to propose the following educational technique which should prove equally effective for Harvard and Shreveport High School. I propose that English poetry and biology should be taught as usual, but that at irregular intervals, poetry students should find dogfishes on their desks and biology students should find Shakespeare sonnets on their dissecting boards. I am serious in declaring that a Sarah Lawrence English major who began poking about in a dogfish with a bobby pin would learn more in thirty minutes than a biology major in a whole semester; and that the latter upon reading on her dissecting board

> That time of year Thou may'st in me behold
> When yellow leaves, or none, or few, do hang
> Upon those boughs which shake against the cold—
> Bare ruin'd choirs where late the sweet birds sang.

might catch fire at the beauty of it.

The situation of the tourist at the Grand Canyon and the biology student are special cases of a predicament in which everyone finds himself in a modern technical society—a society, that is, in which there is a division between expert and layman, planner and consumer, in which experts and planners take special measures to teach and edify the consumer. The measures taken are measures appropriate to the consumer: The expert and the planner *know* and *plan*, but the consumer *needs* and *experiences*.

There is a double deprivation. First, the thing is lost through its packaging. The very means by which the thing is presented for consumption, the very techniques by which the thing is made available as an item of need-satisfaction, these very means operate to remove the thing from the sovereignty of the knower. A loss of title occurs. The measures which the museum curator takes to present the thing to the public are self-liquidating. The upshot of the curator's efforts are not that everyone can see the exhibit but that no one can see it. The curator protests: Why are they so indifferent? Why do they even deface the exhibits? Don't they know it is theirs? But it is not theirs. It is his, the curator's. By the most exclusive sort of zoning, the museum exhibit, the park oak tree, is part of an ensemble, a package, which is almost impenetrable to them. The archaeologist who puts his find in a museum so that everyone can see it accomplishes the reverse of his expectation. The result of his action is that no one can see it now but the archaeologist. He would have done better to keep it in his pocket and show it now and then to strangers.

The tourist who carves his initials in a public place, which is theoretically "his" in the first place, has good reasons for doing so, reasons which the exhibitor and planner know nothing about. He does so because in his role of consumer of an experience (a "recreational experience" to satisfy a "recreational need") he knows that he is disinherited. He is deprived of his title over being. He knows very well that he is in a very special sort of zone in which his only rights are the rights of a consumer. He moves like a ghost through schoolroom, city streets, trains, parks, movies. He carves his initials as a last desperate measure to escape his ghostly role of consumer. He is saying in effect: I am not a ghost after all; I am a sovereign person. And he establishes title the only way remaining to him, by staking his claim over one square inch of wood or stone.

Does this mean that we should get rid of museums? No, but it means that the sightseer should be prepared to enter into a struggle to recover a sight from a museum.

The second loss is the spoliation of the thing, the tree, the rock, the swallow, by the layman's misunderstanding of scientific theory. He believes that the thing is *disposed of* by theory, that it stands in the Platonic relation of being a *specimen of* such and such an underlying principle. In the transmission of scientific theory from theorist to layman, the expectation of the theorist is reversed. Instead of the marvels of the universe being made available to the public, the universe is disposed of by theory. The loss of sovereignty takes this form: As a result of the science of botany, trees are not made available to every man. On the contrary. The tree loses its proper density and mystery as a concrete existent and, as merely another *specimen of* a species, becomes itself nugatory.

Does this mean that there is no use taking biology at Harvard and Shreveport High? No, but it means that the student should know what a fight he has on his hands to rescue the specimen from the educational package. The educator is only partly to blame. For there is nothing the educator can do to provide for this need of the student. Everything the educator does only succeeds in becoming, for the student, part of the educational package. The highest role of the educator is the maieutic role of Socrates: to help the student come to himself not as a consumer of experience but as a sovereign individual.

The thing is twice lost to the consumer. First, sovereignty is lost: It is theirs, not his. Second, it is radically devalued by theory. This is a loss which has been brought about by science but through no fault of the scientist and through no fault of scientific theory. The loss has come about as a consequence of the seduction of the layman by science. The layman will be seduced as long as he regards beings as consumer items to be experienced rather than prizes to be won, and as long as he waives his sovereign rights as a person and accepts his role of consumer as the highest estate to which the layman can aspire.

As Mounier said, the person is not something one can study and provide for; he is something one struggles for. But unless he also struggles for himself, unless he knows that there is a struggle, he is going to be just what the planners think he is.

1975

GETTING STARTED

1. What is the "creature" that Percy says is lost?

2. What does Percy want us to *do* with his essay? He seems to ask us to discover for ourselves how the world works, and yet he offers his own opinions. Is he just an expert who is guilty of trying to seduce us with his own "preformed" ideas?

3. What would a world full of "sovereign knowers" look like? Is such a place possible? What might be some of the (perhaps unforeseen) consequences of a world in which everybody was trying to seize experience in the ways Percy recommends? Does this thought experiment suggest any problems with Percy's argument?

WRITING

4. What is wrong with trying to get people to see things the way that we do? Doesn't community life depend on shared experiences? Write an essay in which you consider the place of sharing in Percy's argument. If you think he values freedom over connection with others, show where in his text he suggests this. Can one have "sovereignty" and still have relationships with others?

5. Consider Percy's idea of the "sovereign experience" and the examples he uses to explore it. Use one or two of Percy's suggestions to develop your own example of a sovereign experience. Describe the obstacles that arise when one tries to have what Percy refers to as an "authentic" encounter. Are we ever free of the "packaging" that surrounds experience?

USING THE LIBRARY AND THE INTERNET

6. Find a Web site for a popular tourist attraction and find places where it seems to present a "preformed symbolic complex." List several of the ways in which the Web site tries to predict and even script the experience of tourists, and consider the effects of these gestures. Does the site make any promises or guarantees about the tourist's encounter? What other strategies might it use to entice travelers? Can it avoid offering "preformed" ideas?

MAKING CONNECTIONS

7. How is the frustration that Coleman Hawkins exhibits about his fans (in Scott DeVeaux's "Progress and the Bean") emblematic of

the packaging that often "encrusts" our experience? What, in Percy's terms, prevents the listener from hearing the "true" Coleman Hawkins?

8. Why might Percy have difficulty having fun at Disney World? Look at Susan Willis's piece through Percy's eyes. Are Willis and Percy arguing the same point? Analyze at least one important difference between the two.

9. Use Percy's ideas about the "symbolic complexes" that can stand between us and real discovery to write a paper analyzing Scott McCloud's "Setting the Record Straight," Rebecca Solnit's "Aerobic Sisyphus and the Suburbanized Psyche," or Jane Tompkins's "At the Buffalo Bill Museum, June, 1988." To what extent does that essayist's analysis of the comics, walking, or the museum become a symbolic complex for you? To what extent do you gain something from that analysis that leads to real discovery or makes up for the loss of the "creature" in some way?

WITOLD RYBCZYNSKI

Witold Rybczynski (1943–) is the Martin and Margy Meyerson Professor of Urbanism and Director of the Urban Design Program at the University of Pennsylvania and Professor of Real Estate at the Wharton School of Business. Rybczynski is also a practicing architect and the author of eight books, including *Home: A Short History of an Idea* (1986) and *City Life: Urban Expectations in a New World* (1995). "Designs for Escape" was originally published in the *New Yorker.*

To learn more about Witold Rybczynski, read "Landscape Artist," an interview published in the *Atlantic Monthly* and available online at <http://www.theatlantic.com/unbound/interviews/ba990714.htm>.

Designs for Escape

Last summer, I was in Montreal on a brief visit from Philadelphia, where I now live. I had some small business to conduct there, but the visit was mainly an opportunity to look up old friends. I called Danièle, whom I hadn't seen in a couple of years, and we arranged to have dinner together that evening. She promised to take me to a new bistro, and I looked forward to it: Montreal is no longer the premier city of Canada—that role now belongs to Toronto—and it seemed a bit shabbier than I remembered, but it still has more than its share of exceptional restaurants.

"Shall we meet there?" I asked.

"No," she said, "you must come by the apartment first." She told me excitedly that she wanted to show me the plans of a weekend house that she and Luc were going to build. Danièle is not an architectural neophyte: she had been married to an architect for twenty years. True, the marriage had ended in divorce—Luc, her current beau, is in public relations—and I didn't remember her having expressed strong ideas about architecture in the past. But I knew her ex well; he had been a student of mine. You can't live with someone for twenty years and not be influenced by what that person does. At least, that's what my wife tells me. So I was curious to see what sort of house Danièle had come up with.

She and Luc and I sat around the kitchen table, and they showed me snapshots of the site, which was in the Laurentian Mountains, a popular recreation area north of Montreal. The Laurentians are an old volcanic range, and the worn, rounded mountains recall the Berkshires or the Catskills, but they're wilder, with fewer signs of human habitation. Though I prefer pastoral scenery—rolling fields and gentle hills—to mountains, I had to admit that Danièle and Luc's land was beautiful: a wooded hilltop with long views in several directions.

I sensed that Danièle was a bit nervous about showing me the drawings of the house. That was understandable. She knew that I taught architecture and wrote about domestic design. She and her husband had helped my wife and me when we built our own house in the country. Now it was her turn. Building a house for yourself is exciting, because of the feeling of possibility that a new house carries, and because creating shelter is a basic human urge, whether or not you are an architect. It is the same urge that makes children erect playhouses out of blankets and cardboard boxes, and build sandcastles at the beach. But building a house—a real house—is also scary, and not just because of the money involved or the fear of making mistakes. A new house is revealing. It tells you—and everyone else—"This is how I live. This is what's important to me. This is what I dream about." I think that's why home magazines—from *Ladies' Home Journal* to *Architectural Digest*—have always been popular. It's not just a matter of looking for decorating hints. Rather, houses intrigue us because they tell us so much about their owners.

Danièle spread out the sketches, which had been prepared by a local architect. Siting is always a crucial decision for a country house. I could see that the house would stand almost at the top of the hill, and so would be approached from below, as, ideally, it should be; walking down to a house is always unpleasant. The hilltop had obviously been chosen for the views it offered, but it also meant that the house would be some distance from the road, and would require a short walk through the trees to arrive at the front door.

The floor layout of the house was simple enough. Because of the sloping ground, the lower level, containing two bedrooms and a bathroom, would be dug partly into the ground. The floor above, which could be entered directly from the upper part of the slope, would hold the living areas, and there would be a sleeping loft in a sort of tower. Danièle explained that they wanted to be able to rent a room to skiers during the winter season, which was why the lower level would have its own front door and could be separated from the rest of the house. The exterior would be mainly wood, with several sloping roofs. It was hard to put your finger on the architectural style of the house. It wasn't going to have the curved eaves and dormer windows of the traditional Breton style, which is still popular with many Québécois. Although the functional-looking window frames and rather spare exterior couldn't be called old-fashioned, neither did they seem aggressively modern. I suppose most people would use the term "contemporary."

The three of us got into a long discussion about how best to rearrange one of the bathrooms. I pointed out that if they moved the door to the other side and changed the site of the toilet, they could gain space and improve the circulation in the kitchen area as well. Not very inspirational stuff. I could see that Luc and Danièle expected something more. I had unconsciously fallen into a bad habit of architecture teachers: if you really don't know what to say about a project, focus on some practical improvement, no matter how small. How often had I sat on design juries at the university, taking part in interminable discussions about fire exits or corridor widths, when the real problem was something else entirely.

It wasn't that Danièle and Luc's house looked boring—quite the opposite. "The architect told us that she worked hard to make each side of the house different," Danièle explained. Differences there certainly were, and, I thought, that was part of the problem. The little house was trying too hard to be unusual and interesting. The perimeter was animated by indentations and protrusions—architectural bumps and grinds. Instead of a single sheltering gable, the roof was broken up into several slopes. This is a favorite device of commercial homebuilders and is obviously a crowd pleaser, though the roof has always seemed to me an odd thing to spend your money on. The complexity of the roof was mirrored by the intricacy of the fenestration: there were half a dozen different window shapes and sizes. The modest house was hardly in league with Frank Gehry and Peter Eisenman, but it *was* busy.

I realized that I had to say something more substantive about the house, but I wasn't sure where to start. I think that small, inexpensive houses like Danièle and Luc's should be as simple as possible. This is partly a question of economics; complexity costs money, after all, and I would rather see a restricted budget devoted to better-quality materials than to architectural bravura. But it is also an aesthetic issue. I like plain farmhouses and straightforward country buildings. They usually look good in the landscape, and they have a kind of directness and honesty that appeals to me. True, they are often really just boxes, but boxes can be given charm through relatively inexpensive details of construction, such as bay windows, trellises, and even shutters.

A simple way to dress up a house is to add a porch. Porches, with their columns, balustrades, and ornamental fretwork, are pleasant to look at, and they are also pleasant places to sit. They are like rooms, but without walls, and they encourage the sort of lazy inactivity that has always seemed to me to be the essence of leisure. I noticed that Danièle's house didn't have any covered outdoor area, and I suggested that they might consider adding a screened porch. This would also be a useful feature, since the Laurentian summers are notorious for their mosquitoes and blackflies.

"No," Luc said, "A porch won't do at all. Porches and balconies are something for a city house. We want our house to look rustic."

That was interesting. I had always associated porches and verandas with country houses. Evidently, for Danièle and Luc they were an urban feature. (Indeed, Montreal row houses traditionally do have verandas.) A little later, they asked me what sort of material I thought should be used to finish the inside walls. I said that I liked plaster wallboard—that it was inexpensive, you could paint it whatever color you wanted, and, furthermore, it was fire-resistant—an important consideration when you're building miles from a fire station. They looked skeptical and said that they had been thinking, rather, of wood. "We want this to be a different sort of place, where we can get away from our city life," Luc said.

A lot of architecture has to do with images—and imaginings. For one person, getting away means a broad porch with a rocking chair and a slowly turning ceiling fan. The image may be the result of a remembered family photograph, or a painting, or even the experience of a real porch somewhere. That particular porch image has haunted me for years—I think I saw it first in a magazine ad for whiskey. And one of the side benefits of watching the film "Out of Africa" is the beautiful porch of Karen Blixen's plantation house in Kenya, with Mozart's Clarinet Concerto playing on a windup gramophone. Alas, for Luc a porch was just a utilitarian appendage. Moreover, the image it conjured up for him was not rural but urban. I also had the impression that he considered porches to be old-fashioned—or maybe just places for old people.

I have always liked farmhouse kitchens—large, comfortable rooms where you can cook and eat and socialize around the kitchen table. (That's probably a remembered image, too.) The plans of Danièle and Luc's house, on the other hand, showed a small efficiency kitchen, with a separate dining area. It was an arrangement that reminded me—but, obviously, not them—of a city apartment. I realized that their idea of getting away from it all was more dynamic than mine: not a cabin in the woods but a striking ski chalet on a hilltop, with different views from each room, beamed ceilings, knotty-pine walls, and a dramatic fireplace. I was starting to understand why the house looked the way it did. It was not a question of money—theirs was hardly an extravagant house. It reflected a different idea of rusticity.

Getting away from it all has a long history; almost as soon as people started living in towns, they felt the need to build country retreats. In ancient times, it was the common practice of wealthy Romans to decamp periodically to country estates. "You should take the first opportunity yourself to leave the din, the futile bustle, and the useless occupations of the city," Pliny the Younger wrote in a letter to a friend. Pliny owned two country retreats, one a large agricultural estate in present-day Umbria, the other his famous seaside villa in Latium, of which he wrote, "There I do most of my writing, and instead of the land I lack, I work to cultivate myself." The sentiment—re-creation—is recognizably modern. Modern-sounding, too, is the

Renaissance architect Leon Battista Alberti's advice that "if the villa is not distant, but close by a gate of the city, it will make it easier and more convenient to flit, with wife and children, between town and villa, whenever desirable."

In nineteenth-century America, such flitting usually meant taking a steamboat or a train. Summer houses sprang up along the Hudson River, in New York, and the Schuylkill, in Philadelphia, or in places like Newport, Rhode Island. In Newport you'll find many early examples of the Shingle Style, one of the high accomplishments of American architecture. The Watts Sherman house, designed by the great architect H. H. Richardson in 1874, is irregular in composition, and the granite, the half-timbering, and the wooden shingles on the exterior give it the picturesque appearance that is a trademark of the Shingle Style. Still, it is provided with a drawing room, a dining room, and a library, and so is not really a radical departure from a typical middle-class suburban or urban house of the period.

Although rich New Yorkers commuted to their villas in Newport, these were summer houses, not weekend houses. Indeed, the full weekend—a two-day holiday at the end of the workweek—didn't appear until the twentieth century. It arrived first in Britain, as a one-and-a-half-day holiday, and by the early nineteen-hundreds more and more Americans were also working "short Saturdays." Eventually, the five-day workweek became commonplace, and the combination of the two-day holiday and the automobile produced the vast proliferation of weekend retreats that we know today.

The weekend cottage continues the time-tested tradition of the summer get-away house, but with a crucial difference. Instead of being used for an entire season, it is chiefly a two-day retreat. Hence it is less a place of long and lazy summers than of sometimes frantic spurts of recreation. Perhaps that's why the architecture is often intentionally unusual, with dramatic fireplaces, tall spaces, and cantilevered decks. That was what Luc meant when he said he wanted "a different sort of place." It was probably the late architect Charles Moore who started the trend toward spatial excitement. In the mid-nineteen-sixties he designed a series of weekend houses, chiefly in Northern California, with deceptively simple exteriors and with interiors that were a cross between barns and jungle gyms. Although designed with considerable sophistication, these houses could also be described as the architectural equivalent of the then popular leisure suit. That is, they were intended to put people instantaneously in a different mood and also to tell the world that here the owner was off duty. Moore's approach was influential, and versions of his houses sprang up in vacation spots from Colorado to Vermont.

Like many people, I spend my weekends in a worn pair of shorts and an old polo shirt. Perhaps that's why my ideal of a weekend house is more like a farmhouse—commodious rather than exciting, a place to kick your shoes off and relax, a place that can get scuffed up and still feel comfortable. Sculptural staircases and eye-popping fireplaces are not a priority. Now, I don't want to give the impression that I think weekend houses should be Thoreau-style shacks, without conveniences, or even without luxuries. I would have no objection to a Miele range and a Sub-Zero refrigerator in my country kitchen. After all, that has always been the paradoxical thing about second homes: we want to feel that we're roughing it, but we want our comforts, too. Pliny schlepped around his villa in an old tunic, but he had a proper warmed swimming bath as well as a banqueting hall. When Richardson designed the Watts Sherman house in Newport, he made it look rustic, but he also incorporated a novel amenity. Central heating. Even Thoreau, whose cabin at Walden Pond didn't have a kitchen (in warm weather, he cooked outside over an open fire), regularly walked to nearby Concord to have dinner at friends' houses.

I remember once visiting an Adirondack camp on Lower Saranac Lake. It was one of many in the area that had been built by rich New Yorkers during the Gilded Age. The house itself was typical—a charming, rough-hewn log building with a massive granite fireplace, columns made of peeled and polished tree trunks, and spartan Art-and-Crafts-style furniture. Here was rusticity laid on with a trowel. When this particular camp, Knollwood, was built, in 1899, it consisted of six cottages, a so-called casino (a social gathering place, not a gambling hall), and a boathouse, all designed by William Coulter, the architect of some of the buildings at Sagamore, the Vanderbilts' famous camp. Although the ample cottages contained several bedrooms, there were only small service kitchens. That was because the six families and their guests had their meals prepared and served to them in the casino, which did have a large kitchen. You went boating on the lake and hiking in the forest, but that was no reason you couldn't have a proper dinner, prepared by your New York cook. The Knollwood boathouse contains canoes and handmade Adirondack guide boats but also, on the upper floor, a huge billiard table. I don't think I would require a billiard table in my ideal weekend house, but, on the other hand, I wouldn't do without a compact-disk player. Getting away from it all has always involved compromise as well as a certain degree of make-believe.

It's hard to comment on—let along judge—other people's fantasies. If Danièle and Luc wanted a house in the country, well, they would have to make their own compromises. I don't think I was really much help to my friends; our ideas of weekend houses were probably just too different. Anyway, we all went out to dinner, the atmosphere in the bistro was convivial, the food was excellent, and everyone had a good time. A week later, when I got home to Philadelphia, I just couldn't resist making some sketches of my own, trying to accommodate all their requirements. I drew a little cottage, twenty feet by thirty feet, clapboard above and with a stone base—for the two bedrooms—below. The house was sheltered by a broad gable roof (to accommodate the sleeping loft). The loft looked down on the main living space, a large family room with a kitchen at one end and a sitting area at the other. In the center of the room, a Franklin stove served for warming cold toes and cold plates. A pair of glazed doors opened onto a large screened porch. It was only a sketch, just to keep my hand in, I told myself. But if I shut my eyes I could almost hear the strains of the Clarinet Concerto in the woods.

1995

GETTING STARTED

1. Before reading the essay, write down as many possible definitions of "escape" as you can think of. After reading the essay, examine your list. Which of your definitions best describes the type of escape that Rybczynski has in mind in his essay?
2. Why is building one's own house exciting, according to Rybczynski? Do you know anyone who has built his or her own house or who has built a house for someone else? Would they agree with Rybczynski?
3. Reread the tenth paragraph and put into your own words what Rybczynski means when he says "it is also an aesthetic issue" (p. 427). (You may want to look up the definition of "aesthetic" in a dictionary.)
4. In a group, identify the rustic qualities that Rybczynski likes. Compare those with the qualities that Danièle and Luc prefer.

WRITING

5. Write a paragraph that summarizes the "problem" Rybczynski sees in the design of the house that Danièle and Luc plan to build.
6. Think about why Rybczynski prefers a plain style of architecture for a house like the one his friends plan to build. Write an essay that draws an analogy between the plain style of architecture that Rybczynski prefers and a plain writing style. What are the similarities? How is a writing style also an "aesthetic issue" (p. 427)? Is Rybczynski's writing style plain or fancy? Give examples to support why you think so.

7. Write an essay that analyzes Rybczynski's diction (his word choice) and his references to architects, movies, and literary figures. In what ways is his writing style not as plain as the well-worn shorts and polo shirt he likes to wear on weekends?

8. Write an essay in which you compare your ideal design for escape with Rybczynski's. In writing, summarize his ideal, quote from his essay, and discuss the significance of the quotations you choose.

USING THE LIBRARY AND THE INTERNET

9. Use a popular Internet search engine such as Excite or Ask Jeeves to find information about three of the architects that Rybczynski mentions in his essay. What kinds of houses or buildings do the architects design? Find photographs or sketches of their work to bring to class.

10. Use an encyclopedia or the Internet to learn more about Pliny the Younger. When did he live? What is he famous for? Was there a Pliny the Elder? If so, who was he?

11. Using a reference database such as MAS Full Text Ultra that includes general-interest and current-events magazines, try several searches using the terms "rustic" and "rustic and life." Scan the results for articles that show some of the differing ways in which people think about that concept.

MAKING CONNECTIONS

12. Write an essay that compares Rybczynski's use of the word "escape" with Yi-Fu Tuan's discussion of "escapism" in "Earth: Nature and Culture" (p. 535). Where do their conceptions of escape and escapism intersect? Where do they diverge? In your essay, you might explore how each writer links art or aesthetics to the idea of escape. What significant relationships do you see between art and escape as a result of reading, thinking, and writing about these two essays?

13. Write an essay that compares Rybczynski's aesthetic ideals to Jeanette Winterson's ideas about art in "Imagination and Reality" (p. 593). What relations do you see between the art of architectural design that Rybczynski describes and the powers of art and imagination that Winterson discusses? In your essay, be sure to incorporate key quotations from each text.

Rebecca Solnit

Rebecca Solnit is a writer, art critic, photographer, and antinuclear activist. She is the author of *Savage Dreams: A Journey into the Landscape Wars of the American West* (1994), *A Book of Migrations: Some Passages in Ireland* (1997), and the editor of several photography books. She has also curated exhibitions and has written museum catalog essays. "Aerobic Sisyphus and the Suburbanized Psyche" was taken from her most recent book, *Wanderlust: A History of Walking* (2000). Solnit's new book, *Hollow City: Gentrification and the Eviction of Urban Culture,* will be published in 2001.

For alternative views of walking, see *Walking Magazine* at <http://www.walkingmag.com/>.

Aerobic Sisyphus and the Suburbanized Psyche

Freedom to walk is not of much use without someplace to go. There is a sort of golden age of walking that began late in the eighteenth century and, I fear, expired some decades ago, a flawed age more golden for some than others, but still impressive for its creation of places in which to walk and its valuation of recreational walking. This age peaked around the turn of the twentieth century, when North Americans and Europeans were as likely to make a date for a walk as for a drink or meal, walking was often a sort of sacrament and a routine recreation, and walking clubs were flourishing. At that time, nineteenth-century urban innovations such as sidewalks and sewers were improving cities not yet menaced by twentieth-century speedups, and rural developments such as national parks and mountaineering were in first bloom. . . . [T]he history of walking is a history of cities and countryside, with a few towns and mountains thrown in for good measure. Perhaps 1970, when the U.S. Census showed that the majority of Americans were—for the first time in the history of any nation—suburban, is a good date for this golden age's tombstone. Suburbs are bereft of the natural glories and civic pleasures of those older spaces, and suburbanization has radically changed the scale and texture of everyday life, usually in ways inimical to getting about on foot. This transformation has happened in the mind as well as on the ground. Ordinary Americans now perceive, value, and use time, space, and their own bodies in radically different ways than they did before. Walking still covers the ground between cars and buildings and the short distances within the latter, but walking as a cultural activity, as a pleasure, as travel, as a way of getting around, is fading, and with it goes an ancient and profound relationship between body, world, and imagination. Perhaps walking is best imagined as an "indicator species," to use an ecologist's term. An indicator species signifies the health of an ecosystem, and its endangerment or diminishment can be an early warning sign of systemic trouble. Walking is an indicator species for various kinds of freedoms and pleasures: free time, free and alluring space, and unhindered bodies.

1. Suburbia

In *Crabgrass Frontier: The Suburbanization of the United States,* Kenneth Jackson outlines what he calls "the walking city" that preceded the development of middle-class suburbs: it was densely populated; it had "a clear distinction between city and country," often by means of walls or some other abrupt periphery; its economic and social functions were intermingled (and "factories were almost nonexistent" because "production took place at the small shops of artisans"); people rarely lived far from work; and the wealthy tended to live in the center of the city. His walking city and my golden age find their end in the suburbs, and the history of suburbia is the history of fragmentation.

Middle-class suburban homes were first built outside London in the late eighteenth century, writes Robert Fishman in another history of suburbs, *Bourgeois Utopias,* so that pious merchants could separate family life from work. Cities themselves were looked upon askance by these upper-middle-class evangelical Christians: cards, balls, theaters, street fairs, pleasure gardens, taverns were all condemned as immoral. At the same time the modern cult of the home as a consecrated space apart from the world began, with the wife-mother as a priestess who was, incidentally, confined to her temple. This first suburban community of wealthy merchant families who shared each other's values sounds, in Fishman's account, paradisiacal and, like most paradises, dull: a place of spacious freestanding houses, with little for their residents to do outside the home and garden. These villas were miniaturized English country estates, and like such estates they aspired to a kind of social self-sufficiency. However, a whole community of farmworkers, gamekeepers, servants, guests, and extended families had inhabited the estate, which usually encompassed working farms and had thus been a place of production, while the suburban home housed little more than the nuclear family and was to become more and more a site only of consumption. Too, the estate was on a scale that permitted walking without leaving the grounds; the suburban home was not, but suburbia would eat up the countryside and diffuse the urban anyway.

It was in Manchester, during the industrial revolution, that the suburb came into its own. The suburb is a product of that revolution, radiating outward from Manchester and the north Midlands, which has so thoroughly fragmented modern life. Work and home had never been very separate until the factory system came of age and the poor became wage-earning employees. Those jobs, of course, fragmented work itself as craftsmanship was broken down into unskilled repetitive gestures in attendance on machines. Early commentators deplored how factory work destroyed family life, taking individuals out of the home and making family members strangers to each other during their prodigiously long workdays. Home for factory workers was little more than a place to recuperate for the next day's work, and the industrial system made them far poorer and unhealthier than they had been as independent artisans. In the 1830s Manchester's manufacturers began to build the first large-scale suburbs to escape the city they had created and to enhance family life for their class. Unlike the London evangelicals, they were fleeing not temptation but ugliness and danger—industrial pollution, the bad air and sanitation of a poorly designed city, and the sight and threat of their miserable workforce.

"The decision to suburbanize had two great consequences," says Fishman. "First the core emptied of residents as the middle class left and workers were pushed out by the conversion of their rooms in the back streets to offices. . . . Visitors were surprised to find an urban core that was totally quiet and empty after business hours. The central business district was born. Meanwhile, the once peripheral factories were now enclosed by a suburban belt, which separated them from the now-distant rural fields. The grounds of the suburban villas were enclosed by walls, and even the tree-lined streets on which they stood were often forbidden except to the residents and their guests. One group of workers attempted to keep open a once-rural footpath that now ran through the grounds of a factory owner's suburban villa. . . . Mr. Jones responded with iron gates and ditches." Fishman's picture shows a world where the fertile mix of urban life in the "walking city" has been separated out into its sterile constituent elements.

The workers responded by fleeing to the fields on Sundays and, eventually, fighting for access to the remaining rural landscape in which to walk, climb, cycle, and breathe. . . . The middle class responded by continuing to develop and dwell in suburbs. Men commuted to work and women to shop by private carriages, then horse-drawn omnibuses (which, in Manchester, were priced too high to accommodate the poor), and eventually trains. In fleeing the poor and the city, they had left behind pedestrian scale. One could walk in the suburbs, but there was seldom anyplace to go on foot in these homogenous expanses of quiet residential streets behind whose walls dwelt families more or less like each other. The twentieth-century

American suburb reached a kind of apotheosis of fragmentation when proliferating cars made it possible to place people farther than ever from work, stores, public transit, schools, and social life. The modern suburb as described by Philip Langdon is antithetical to the walking city: "Offices are kept separate from retailing. The housing is frequently divided into mutually exclusive tracts . . . with further subdivision by economic status. Manufacturing, no matter how clean and quiet—today's industries are rarely the noisy, smoke-belching mills of urban memory—is kept away from residential areas or excluded from the community entirely. Street layouts in new developments enforce apartness. To unlock the rigid geographic segregation, an individual needs to obtain a key—which is a motor vehicle. For obvious reasons those keys are not issued to those under sixteen, the very population for whom the suburbs are supposedly most intended. These keys are also denied to some of the elderly who can no longer drive."

Getting a license and a car is a profound rite of passage for modern suburban teenagers; before the car, the child is either stranded at home or dependent upon chauffeuring parents. Jane Holtz Kay, in her book on the impact of cars, *Asphalt Nation,* writes of a study that compared the lives of ten-year-olds in a walkable Vermont small town and an unwalkable southern California suburb. The California children watched four times as much television, because the outdoor world offered them few adventures and destinations. And a recent study of the effects of television on Baltimore adults concluded that the more local news television, with its massive emphasis on sensational crime stories, locals watched, the more fearful they were. Staying home to watch TV discouraged them from going out. That *Los Angeles Times* advertisement for an electronic encyclopedia . . . —"You used to walk across town in the pouring rain to use our encyclopedias. We're pretty confident we can get your kid to click and drag"—may describe the options open to a child who no longer has a library within walking distance and may not be allowed to walk far alone anyway (walking to school, which was for generations the great formative first foray alone into the world, is likewise becoming a less common experience.) Television, telephones, home computers, and the Internet complete the privatization of everyday life that suburbs began and cars enhanced. They make it less necessary to go out into the world and thus accommodate retreat from rather than resistance to the deterioration of public space and social conditions.

These American suburbs are built car-scale, with a diffuseness the unenhanced human body is inadequate to cope with, and just as gardens, sidewalks, arcades, and wilderness trails are a kind of infrastructure for walking, so modern suburbs, highways, and parking lots are an infrastructure for driving. Cars made possible the development of the great Los Angelean sprawls of the American West, those places not exactly suburbs because there is no urbanity to which they are subsidiary. Cities like Albuquerque, Phoenix, Houston, and Denver may or may not have a dense urban core floating somewhere in their bellies like a half-digested snack, but most of their space is too diffuse to be well served by public transit (if it exists) or to be traversed on foot. In these sprawls, people are no longer expected to walk, and they seldom do. There are many reasons why. Suburban sprawls generally make dull places to walk, and a large subdivision can become numbingly repetitious at three miles an hour instead of thirty or sixty. Many suburbs were designed with curving streets and cul-de-sacs that vastly expand distances: Langdon gives an example of an Irvine, California, subdivision where in order to reach a destination a quarter mile away as the crow flies the traveler must walk or drive more than a mile. Too, when walking is not an ordinary activity, a lone walker may feel ill at ease about doing something unexpected and isolated.

Walking can become a sign of powerlessness or low status, and new urban and suburban design disdains walkers. Many places have replaced downtown with shopping malls inaccessible by any means but cars, or by building cities that never had downtowns, buildings meant to be entered through parking garages rather than front doors. In Yucca Valley, the town near Joshua Tree National Park, all the businesses are strung out along several miles of highway, and crosswalks and traffic lights are rare: though, for example, my bank and food store are only a few blocks apart, they are on opposite sides of the highway, and a car is the only safe, direct way to travel between them. Throughout California more than 1,000 crosswalks have been removed in recent years, more than 150 of them in traffic-clogged Silicon Valley, apparently in the spirit of the L.A. planners who proclaimed in the early 1960s, "The pedestrian remains the largest single obstacle to free traffic movement." Many parts of these western sprawl-cities were built without sidewalks altogether, in both rich and poor neighborhoods, further signaling that walking has come to an end by design. Lars Eigner, who during a homeless and largely penniless phase of his life in the 1980s hitchhiked with his dog Lizbeth between Texas and southern California, wrote eloquently about his experiences, and one of the worst came about when a driver dropped him off in the wrong part of town: "South Tucson simply has no sidewalks. I thought at first this was merely in keeping with the general wretchedness of the place, but eventually it seemed to me that the public policy in Tucson is to impede pedestrians as much as possible. In particular, I could find no way to walk to the main part of town in the north except in the traffic lanes of narrow highway ramps. I could not believe this at first, and Lizbeth and I spent several hours wandering on the south bank of the dry gash that divides Tucson as I looked for a walkway."

Even in the best places, pedestrian space is continually eroding: in the winter of 1997–98, New York mayor Rudolph Giuliani decided that pedestrians were interfering with traffic (one could just as well have said, in this city where so many still travel and take care of their business on foot, that cars interfere with traffic). The mayor ordered the police to start citing jaywalkers and fenced in the sidewalks of some of the busiest corners of the city. New Yorkers, to their eternal glory, rebelled by staging demonstrations at the barriers and jaywalking more. In San Francisco, faster and denser traffic, shorter walk lights, and more belligerent drivers intimidate and occasionally mangle pedestrians. Here 41 percent of all traffic fatalities are pedestrians killed by cars, and more than a thousand walkers are injured every year. In Atlanta, the figures are 80 pedestrians killed per year and more than 1,300 injured. In Giuliani's New York, almost twice as many people are killed by cars as are murdered by strangers—285 versus 150 in 1997. Walking the city is not now an attractive prospect for those unequipped to dodge and dash.

Geographer Richard Walker defines urbanity as "that elusive combination of density, public life, cosmopolitan mixing, and free expression." Urbanity and automobiles are antithetical in many ways, for a city of drivers is only a dysfunctional suburb of people shuttling from private interior to private interior. Cars have encouraged the diffusion and privatization of space, as shopping malls replace shopping streets, public buildings become islands in a sea of asphalt, civic design lapses into traffic engineering, and people mingle far less freely and frequently. The street is public space in which First Amendment rights of speech and assembly apply, while the mall is not. The democratic and liberatory possibilities of people gathered together in public don't exist in places where they don't have space in which to gather. Perhaps it was meant that way. As Fishman argues, the suburbs were a refuge—first from the sin and then from the ugliness and anger of the city and its poor. In postwar America "white flight" sent middle-class whites to the suburbs from multiracial cities, and in the new sprawl-cities of the West and suburbs around the country a fear of crime that often seems to be a broader fear of difference is further eliminating public space and pedestrian possibilities. Political engagement may be one of the things suburbs have zoned out.

Early on in the development of the American suburbs, the porch, an important feature for small-town social life, was replaced at the front of the home by the blind maw of the garage (and the sociologist Dean McCannell tells me some new homes have pseudo-porches that make them look sweetly old-fashioned but are actually too shallow to sit on). More recent developments have been more radical in their retreat from communal space: we are in a new era of walls, guards, and security systems, and of architecture, design, and technology intended to eliminate or nullify public space. This withdrawal from shared space seems, like that of the Manchester merchants a century and a half ago, intended to buffer the affluent from the consequences of economic inequity and resentment outside the gates; it is the alternative to social justice. The new architecture and urban design of segregation could be called Calvinist: they reflect a desire to live in a world of predestination rather than chance, to strip the world of its wide-open possibilities and replace them with freedom of choice in the marketplace. "Anyone who has tried to take a stroll at dusk through a neighborhood patrolled by armed security guards and signposted with death threats quickly realizes how merely notional, if not utterly obsolete, is the old idea of 'freedom of the city,'" writes Mike Davis of the nicer suburbs of Los Angeles. And Kierkegaard long ago exclaimed, "It is extremely regrettable and demoralizing that robbers and the elite agree on just one thing—living in hiding."

If there was a golden age of walking, it arose from a desire to travel through the open spaces of the world unarmored by vehicles, unafraid to mingle with different kinds of people. It emerged in a time when cities and countryside grew safer and desire to experience that world was high. Suburbia abandoned the space of the city without returning to the country, and in recent years a second wave of impulse has beefed up this segregation with neighborhoods of high-priced bunkers. But even more importantly, the disappearance of pedestrian space has transformed perception of the relationship between bodies and spaces. Something very odd has happened to the very state of embodiment, of being corporeal, in recent decades.

II. The Disembodiment of Everyday Life

The spaces in which people live have changed dramatically, but so have the ways they imagine and experience that space. I found a strange passage in a 1998 *Life* magazine celebrating momentous events over the past thousand years. Accompanying a picture of a train was this text: "For most of human history, all land transport depended on a single mode of propulsion—feet. Whether the traveler relied on his own extremities or those of another creature, the drawbacks were the same, low cruising speed, vulnerability to weather, the need to stop for food and rest. But on September 15, 1830, foot power began its long slide toward obsolescence. As brass bands played, a million Britons gathered between Liverpool and Manchester to witness the inauguration of the world's first fully steam-driven railway. . . . Despite the death of a member of Parliament who was run down by the train at the opening ceremony, the Liverpool and Manchester inspired a rash of track-laying round the world." The train was, like the factory and the suburb, part of the apparatus of the industrial revolution; just as factories mechanically sped up production, so trains sped up distribution of goods, and then of travelers.

Life magazine's assumptions are interesting; nature as biological and meteorological factors is a drawback rather than an occasional inconvenience; progress consists of the transcendence of time, space, and nature by the train and later the car, airplane, and electronic communications. Eating, resting, moving, experiencing the weather, are primary experiences of being embodied; to view them as negative is to condemn biology and the life of the senses, and the passage does exactly that in its most lurid statement, that "foot power began its long slide toward obsolescence." Perhaps this is why neither *Life* nor the crowd apparently mourned the squashed Parliamentarian. In a way, the train mangled not just that one man's body, but all bodies in the places it transformed, by severing human perception, expectation, and action from the organic world in which our bodies exist. Alienation from nature is usually depicted as estrangement from natural spaces. But the sensing, breathing, living, moving body can be a primary experience of nature too: new technologies and spaces can bring about alienation from both body and space.

In his brilliant *The Railway Journey: The Industrialization of Time and Space in the Nineteenth Century,* Wolfgang Schivelbusch explores the ways trains changed their passengers' perceptions. Early railroad travelers, he writes, characterized this new technology's effects as the elimination of time and space, and to transcend time and space is to begin to transcend the material world altogether—to become disembodied. Disembodiment, however convenient, has side effects. "The speed and mathematical directness with which the railroad proceeds through the terrain destroy the close relationship between the traveler and the traveled space," Schivelbusch writes. "The train was experienced as a projectile, and traveling on it as being shot through the landscape—thus losing control of one's senses. . . . The traveler who sat inside that projectile ceased to be a traveler and became, as noted in a popular metaphor of the century, a parcel." Our own perceptions have sped up since, but trains were then dizzyingly fast. Earlier forms of land travel had intimately engaged travelers with their surroundings, but the railroad moved too fast for nineteenth-century minds to relate visually to the trees, hills, and buildings whipping by. The spatial and sensual engagement with the terrain between here and there began to evaporate. Instead, the two places were separated only by an ever-shortening amount of time. Speed did not make travel more interesting, Schivelbusch writes, but duller; like the suburb, it puts its inhabitants in a kind of spatial limbo. People began to read on the train, to sleep, to knit, to complain of boredom. Cars and airplanes have vastly augmented this transformation, and watching a movie on a jetliner 35,000 feet above the earth may be the ultimate disconnection of space, time, and experience. "From the elimination of the physical effort of walking to the sensorimotor loss induced by the first fast transport, we have finally achieved states bordering on sensory deprivation," writes Paul Virilio. "The loss of the thrills of the old voyage is now compensated for by the showing of a film on a central screen."

The *Life* writers may be right. Bodies are not obsolete by any objective standard, but they increasingly are perceived as too slow, frail, and unreliable for our expectations and desires—as parcels to be transported by mechanical means (though of course many steep, rough, or narrow spaces can only be traversed on foot, and many remote parts of the world can't be reached by any other means; it takes a built environment, with tracks, graded roads, landing strips, and energy sources, to accommodate motor transport). A body regarded as adequate to cross continents, like John Muir's or William Wordsworth's or Peace Pilgrim's, is experienced very differently than a body inadequate to go out for the evening under its own power. In a sense the car has become a prosthetic, and though prosthetics are usually for injured or missing limbs, the auto-prosthetic is for a conceptually impaired body or a body impaired by the creation of a world that is no longer human in scale. In one of the *Alien* movies, the actress Sigourney Weaver lurches along in a sort of mechanized body armor that wraps around her limbs and magnifies her movements. It makes her bigger, fiercer, stronger, able to battle with monsters, and it seems strange and futuristic. But this is only because the relationship between the body and the prosthetic machine is so explicit here, the latter so obviously an extension of the former. In fact, from the first clasped stick and improvised carrier, tools have extended the body's strength, skill, and reach to a remarkable degree. We live in a world where our hands and feet can direct a ton of metal to go faster than the fastest land animal, where we can speak across thousand of miles, blow holes in things with no muscular exertion but the squeeze of a forefinger.

It is the unaugmented body that is rare now, and that body has begun to atrophy as both a muscular and a sensory organism. In the century and a half since the railroad seemed to go too fast to be interesting, perceptions and expectations have sped up, so that many now identify with the speed of the machine and look with frustration or alienation at the speed and ability of the body. The world is no longer on the scale of our bodies, but on that of our machines, and many need—or think they need—the machines to navigate that space quickly enough. Of course, like most "time-saving" technologies, mechanized transit more often produces changed expectations than free time; and modern Americans have significantly less time than they did three decades ago. To put it another way, just as the increased speed of factory production did not decrease working hours, so the increased speed of transportation binds people to more diffuse locales rather than liberating them from travel time (many Californians, for example, now spend three or four hours driving to and from work each day). The decline of walking is about the lack of space in which to walk, but it is also about the lack of time—the disappearance of that musing, unstructured space in which so much thinking, courting, daydreaming, and seeing has transpired. Machines have sped up, and lives have kept pace with them.

The suburbs made walking ineffective transportation within their expanses, but the suburbanization of the American mind has made walking increasingly rare even when it is effective. Walking is no longer, so to speak, how many people think. Even in San Francisco, very much a "walking city" by Jackson's criteria, people have brought this suburbanized consciousness to their local travel, or so my observations seem to indicate. I routinely see people drive and take the bus remarkably short distances, often distances that could be covered more quickly by foot. During one of my city's public transit crises, a commuter declared he could *walk* downtown in the time it took the streetcar, as though walking was some kind of damning comparison—but he had apparently been traveling from a destination so near downtown he could've walked every day in less than half an hour, and walking was one transit option the newspaper coverage never proposed (obvious things could be said about bicycling here, were this not a book about walking). Once I made my friend Maria—a surfer, biker, and world traveler—walk the half mile from her house to the bars on Sixteenth Street, and she was startlingly pleased to realize how close they were, for it had never occurred to her before that they were accessible by foot. Last Christmas season, the parking lot of the hip outdoor equipment store in Berkeley was full of drivers idling their engines and waiting for a parking space, while the streets around were full of such spaces. Shoppers weren't apparently willing to walk two blocks to buy their outdoor gear (and since then I have noticed that nowadays drivers often wait for a close parking spot rather than walk in from the farther reaches of the lot). People have a kind of mental radius of how far they are willing to go on foot that seems to be shrinking; in defining neighborhoods and shopping districts, planners say it is about a quarter mile, the distance that can be walked in five minutes, but sometimes it hardly seems to be fifty yards from car to building.

Of course the people idling their engines at the outdoor equipment store may have been there to buy hiking boots, workout clothes, climbing ropes—equipment for the special circumstances in which people will walk. The body has ceased to be a utilitarian entity for many Americans, but it is still a recreational one, and this means that people have abandoned the everyday spaces—the distance from home to work, stores, friends—but created new recreational sites that are most often reached by car: malls, parks, gyms. Parks, from pleasure gardens to wilderness preserves, have long accommodated bodily recreation, but the gyms that have proliferated wildly in the past couple of decades represent something radically new. If walking is an indicator species, the gym is a kind of wildlife preserve for bodily exertion. A preserve protects species whose habitat is vanishing elsewhere, and the gym (and home gym) accommodates the survival of bodies after the abandonment of the original sites of bodily exertion.

III. The Treadmill

The suburb rationalized and isolated family life as the factory did manufacturing work, and the gym rationalizes and isolates not merely exercise but nowadays even each muscle group, the heart rate, the

FIGURE 24 A typical power-producing treadmill as pictured in *The Operative Mechanic and British Machinist*, 1831. (Image courtesy of Larry Witte. Found at <www.uh.edu/engines/epi374.htm>.)

"burn zone" of most inefficient calorie use. Somehow all this history comes back to the era of the industrial revolution in England. "The Tread-Mill," writes James Hardie in his little book of 1823 on the subject, "was, in the year 1818, invented by Mr. William Cubitt, of Ipswich, and erected in the House of Correction at Brixton, near London." The original treadmill was a large wheel with sprockets that served as steps that several prisoners trod for set periods. It was meant to rationalize prisoners' psyches, but it was already an exercise machine. Their bodily exertion was sometimes used to power grain mills or other machinery, but it was the exertion, not the production, that was the point of the treadmill. "It is its monotonous steadiness and not its severity, which constitutes its terror, and frequently breaks down the obstinate spirit," Hardie wrote of the treadmill's effect in the American prison he oversaw. He added, however, that "the opinions of the medical officers in attendance at the various prisons, concur in declaring that the general health of the prisoners has, in no degree suffered injury, but that, on the contrary, the labor has, in this respect, been productive of considerable benefit." His own prison of Bellevue on New York's East River included 81 male and 101 female vagrants, as well as 109 male and 37 women convicts, and 14 female "maniacs." Vagrancy—wandering without apparent resources or purpose—was and sometimes still is a crime, and doing time on the treadmill was perfect punishment for it.

Repetitive labor has been punitive since the gods of Greek myth sentenced Sisyphus—who had, Robert Graves tells us, "always lived by robbery and often murdered unsuspecting travelers"—to his famous fate of pushing a boulder uphill. "As soon as he has almost reached the summit, he is forced back by the weight of the shameless stone, which bounces to the very bottom once more; where he wearily retrieves it and must begin all over again, though sweat bathes his limbs." It is hard to say if Sisyphus is the first weight lifter or the first treadmiller, but easy to recognize the ancient attitude to repetitive bodily exertion without practical results. Throughout most of human history and outside the first world nowadays, food has been relatively scarce and physical exertion abundant; only when the status of these two things is reversed does "exercise" make sense. Though physical training was part of ancient Greek citizens' education, it had social and cultural dimensions missing from modern workouts and Sisyphean punishments, and while walking as exercise had long been an aristocratic activity, industrial workers' enthusiasm for hiking, particularly in Britain, Austria, and Germany, suggests that it was far more than a way to make the blood circulate or calories burn. Under the heading "Alienation," Eduardo Galeano wrote a brief essay about fishermen in a remote village of the Dominican Republic puzzling over an advertisement for a rowing machine not very long ago. "Indoors? They use it indoors? Without water? They row without water? And without fish? And without the sun? And without the sky?" they exclaimed, telling the resident alien who has shown them the picture that they like everything about their work *but* the rowing. When he explained that the machine was for exercise, they said "Ah. And exercise—what's that?" Suntans famously became status symbols when most of the poor had moved indoors from the farm to the factory, so that browned skin indicated leisure time rather than work time. That muscles have become status symbols signifies that most jobs no longer call upon bodily strength; like tans, they are an aesthetic of the obsolete.

The gym is the interior space that compensates for the disappearance of outside and a stopgap measure in the erosion of bodies. The gym is a factory for the production of muscles or of fitness, and most of them look like factories: the stark industrial space, the gleam of metal machines, the isolated figures each absorbed in his or her own repetitive task (and like muscles, factory aesthetics may evoke nostalgia). The industrial revolution institutionalized and fragmented labor; the gym is now doing the same thing, often in the same place, for leisure. Some gyms actually are born-again industrial sites. The Chelsea Piers in Manhattan were built in the first decade of this century for ocean liners—for the work of longshoremen, stevedores, and clerks, and for the travel of emigrants and elites. They now house a sports center with indoor track, weight machines, pool, climbing gym, and most peculiarly, a four-story golf driving range, destinations in themselves rather than points of arrival and departure. An elevator takes golfers to their stalls, where all the gestures of golf—walking, carrying, gazing, situating, removing, communicating, retrieving or following the ball—have vanished with the landscape of the golf course. Nothing remains but the single arc of a drive: four tiers of solitary stationary figures making the same gesture, the sharp sound of balls being hit, the dull thud of their landing, and the miniaturized armored-car vehicles that go through the green artificial-grass war zone to scoop up the balls and feed them into the mechanism that automatically pops up another ball as each one is hit. Britain has specialized in the conversion of industrial sites into climbing gyms. Among them are a former electrical substation in London, the Warehouse on Gloucester's Severn River waterfront, the Forge in Sheffield on one side of the Peak District, an early factory in downtown Birmingham, and, according to a surveyor friend, a "six-story former cotton mill near Leeds" I couldn't locate (not to mention a desanctified church in Bristol). It was in some of these buildings that the industrial revolution was born, with the Manchester and Leeds textile mills, Sheffield's iron- and steelworks, the innumerable manufactories of "the workshop of the world" that Birmingham once was. Climbing gyms are likewise established in converted industrial buildings in the United States, or at least in those cities old enough to have once had industrial-revolution architecture. In those buildings abandoned because goods are now made elsewhere and First World work grows ever more cerebral, people now go for recreation, reversing the inclinations of their factory-worker predecessors to go out—to the outskirts of town or at least out-of-doors—in their free time. (In defense of climbing gyms, it should be said they allow people to polish skills and, during foul weather, to stay fit; for some the gym has only augmented the opportunities, not replaced the mountain, though for others the unpredictabilities and splendors of real rock have become dispensible, annoying—or unknown.)

And whereas the industrial revolution's bodies had to adapt to the machines, with terrible consequences of pain, injury, and deformity, exercise machines are adapted to the body. Marx said history happens the first time as tragedy, the second as farce; bodily labor here happens the first time around as productive labor and the second as leisuretime consumption. The deepest sign of transformation is not merely that this activity is no longer productive, that the straining of the arms no longer moves wood or pumps water. It is that the straining of the muscles can require a gym membership, workout gear, special equipment, trainers and instructors, a whole panoply of accompanying expenditures, in this industry of consumption, and the resulting muscles may not be useful or used for any practical purpose. "Efficiency" in exercise means that consumption of calories takes place at the maximum rate, exactly the opposite of what workers aim for, and while exertion for work is about how the body shapes the world, exertion for exercise is about how the body shapes the body. I do not mean to denigrate the users of gyms—I have sometimes been one myself—only to remark on their strangeness. In a world where manual labor has disappeared, the gym is among the most available and efficient compensations. Yet there is something perplexing about this semipublic performance. I used to try to imagine, as I worked out on one or another weight machine, that this motion was rowing, this one pumping water, this one lifting bales or sacks. The everyday acts of the farm had been reprised as empty gestures, for there was no water to pump, no buckets to lift. I am not nostalgic for peasant or farmworker life, but I cannot avoid being struck by how odd it is that we reprise those gestures for other reasons. What exactly is the nature of the transformation in which machines now pump our water but we go to other machines to engage in the act of pumping, not for the sake of water but for the sake of our bodies, bodies theoretically liberated by machine technology? Has something been lost when the relationship between our muscles and our world vanishes, when the water is managed by one machine and the muscles by another in two unconnected processes?

The body that used to have the status of a work animal now has the status of a pet: it does not provide real transport, as a horse might have; instead, the body is exercised as one might walk a dog. Thus the body, a recreational rather than utilitarian entity, doesn't work, but works out. The barbell is only abstracted and quantified materiality to shift around—what used to be a sack of onions or a barrel of beer is now a metal ingot—and the weight machine makes simpler the act of resisting gravity in various directions for the sake of health, beauty, and relaxation. The most perverse of all the devices in the gym is the treadmill (and its steeper cousin, the Stairmaster). Perverse, because I can understand simulating farm labor, since the activities of rural life are not often available—but simulating walking suggests that space itself has disappeared. That is, the weights simulate the objects of work, but the treadmill and Stairmaster simulate the surfaces on which walking takes place. That bodily labor, real or simulated, should be dull and repetitive is one thing; that the multifaceted experience of moving through the world should be made so is another. I remember evenings strolling by Manhattan's many glass-walled second-floor gyms full of rows of treadmillers looking as though they were trying to leap through the glass to their destruction, saved only by the Sisyphean contraption that keeps them from going anywhere at all—though probably they didn't see the plummet before them, only their own reflection in the glass.

I went out the other day, a gloriously sunny winter afternoon, to visit a home-exercise equipment store and en route walked by the University of San Francisco gym, where treadmillers were likewise at work in the plate-glass windows, most of them reading the newspaper (three blocks from Golden Gate Park, where other people were running and cycling, while tourists and Eastern European emigrés were walking). The muscular young man in the store told me that people buy home treadmills because they allow them to exercise after work when it might be too dark for them to go out safely, to exercise in private where the neighbors will not see them sweating, to keep an eye on the kids, and to use their scarce time most efficiently, and because it is a low-impact activity good for people with running injuries. I have a friend who uses a treadmill when it's painfully cold outside in Chicago, and another who uses a no-impact machine whose footpads rise and fall with her steps because she has an injured hamstring (injured by driving cars designed for larger people, not by running). But a third friend's father lives two miles from a very attractive Florida beach, she tells me, full of low-impact sand, but he will not walk there and uses a home treadmill instead.

The treadmill is a corollary to the suburb and the autotropolis: a device with which to go nowhere in places where there is now nowhere to go. Or no desire to go: the treadmill also accommodates the automobilized and suburbanized mind more comfortable in climate-controlled indoor space than outdoors, more comfortable with quantifiable and clearly defined activity than with the seamless engagement of mind, body, and terrain to be found walking out-of-doors. The treadmill seems to be one of many devices that accommodate a retreat from the world, and I fear that such accommodation disinclines people to participate in making that world habitable or to participate in it at all. It too could be called Calvinist technology, in that it provides accurate numerical assessments of the speed, "distance" covered, and even heart rate, and it eliminates the unpredictable and unforeseeable from the routine—no encounters with acquaintances or strangers, no sudden revelatory sights around a bend. On the treadmill, walking is no longer contemplating, courting, or exploring. Walking is the alternate movement of the lower limbs.

Unlike the prison treadmills, of the 1820s, the modern treadmill does not produce mechanical power but consumes it. The new treadmills have two-horsepower engines. Once, a person might have hitched two horses to a carriage to go out into the world without walking; now she might plug in a two-horsepower motor to walk without going out into the world. Somewhere unseen but wired to the home is a whole electrical infrastructure of power generation and distribution transforming the landscape and ecology of the world—a network of electrical cables, meters, workers, of coal mines or oil wells feeding power plants or of hydropower dams on rivers. Somewhere else is a factory making treadmills, though factory work is a minority experience in the United States nowadays. So the treadmill requires far more economic and ecological interconnection than does taking a walk, but it makes far fewer experiential connections. Most treadmillers read or otherwise distract themselves. *Prevention* magazine recommends watching TV while treadmilling and gives instructions on how treadmill users can adapt their routines to walking about outside when spring comes (with the implication that the treadmill, not the walk, is the primary experience). The *New York Times* reports that people have begun taking treadmill classes, like the stationary bicycling classes that have become so popular, to mitigate the loneliness of the long-distance treadmiller. For like factory labor, treadmill time is dull—it was the monotony that was supposed to reform prisoners. Among the features of the Precor Cardiologic Treadmill, says its glossy brochure, are "5 programmed courses" that "vary in distance, time and incline. . . . The Interactive Weight Loss course maintains your heart rate within your optimum weight loss zone by adjusting workload," while "custom courses allow you to easily create and store personalized programs of up to 8 miles, with variations as small as 1/10th mile increments." It's the custom courses that most amaze me; users can create an itinerary like a walking tour over varied terrain, only the terrain is a revolving rubber belt on a platform about six feet long. Long ago when railroads began to erode the experience of space, journeys began to be spoken of in terms of time rather than distance (and a modern Angeleno will say that Beverly Hills is twenty minutes from Hollywood rather than so many miles). The treadmill completes this transformation by allowing travel to be measured entirely by time, bodily exertion, and mechanical motion. Space—as landscape, terrain, spectacle, experience—has vanished.

2000

GETTING STARTED

1. Do you ever walk to places you usually travel to by car? Describe what you feel when you do this.

2. Does the place where you live allow you to go on long walks? List some of the places you can get to if you walk for more than thirty minutes. Do you agree with Solnit that walking is seen today as more of a nuisance than an activity to enjoy?

3. Why does Solnit believe that the "golden age" of walking has disappeared? Why, especially, does she equate the rise of the suburbs with the "golden age's tombstone"?

4. Solnit uses an example of a fisherman puzzling over a rowing machine. What does the example illustrate?

WRITING

5. Solnit has some very strong opinions about the history she describes. Write a short paper analyzing her point of view, looking closely at two or three places in the text where she reveals it. What do you think her goal is in writing this piece? To what extent do you find her argument persuasive?

6. Solnit poses this key question: "What exactly is the nature of the transformation in which machines now pump our water but we

go to other machines to engage in the act of pumping, not for the sake of water but for the sake of our bodies, bodies theoretically liberated by machine technology?" (p. 447). Write an essay explaining what Solnit suggests is the answer. How would you answer the question?

7. Solnit argues that because of our reliance on trains, cars, and airplanes we experience a disembodiment that greatly changes our sense of space and time. Write a paper in which you explore one part of our modern-day lives that this disembodiment affects. Develop an example that shows how lives in the twenty-first century have changed, and discuss the consequences of this change. (Note: Do not use either of Solnit's examples, walking or exercise, as your primary example.)

USING THE LIBRARY AND THE INTERNET

8. Find a Web site that focuses on the kind of exercise equipment that Solnit describes in her essay. (It could be a gym, fitness, or health Web site, for example.) Look at the language used to describe what the machines are designed to do. Make a list of the most vivid words, and write a paragraph in which you assess these descriptions in terms of Solnit's critique. Is there anything odd, funny, or even surprising about the language surrounding exercise?

MAKING CONNECTIONS

9. Does the present-day situation that Solnit describes constitute an example of what Walker Percy calls a "radical loss of sovereignty" (p. 397)? Discuss Solnit's essay using Percy's terms.

10. Using Jeanette Winterson's definition of an artist (p. 593), discuss walking as an art form. Use textual analysis to describe a connection you see between the two, and develop your own example of an everyday activity that might be raised to an art.

11. Both Solnit and Sherry Turkle describe ways in which technology can transform human behavior and habits of mind. Compare and contrast the processes of transformation that they describe to arrive at your own theory about the gains, or drawbacks, or both of a new technology you have experienced.

Nancy Sommers

Nancy Sommers (1951–) is the Sosland Director of Expository Writing at Harvard University. She is a well-known and often-quoted specialist in the teaching of writing. Sommers coedited *Student Writers at Work, the Bedford Prizes* (1989), *Writing with a Purpose* (1984), *The Harper-Collins Guide to Writing* (1993), and *Fields of Reading* (1986). She has written a number of important articles in the study of composition and rhetoric, including "Responding to Student Writing," "The Language of Coats," and "Revision in the Composing Process." Sommers is currently at work on a study of undergraduate writing at Harvard.

To learn more about Sommers's study of Harvard undergraduate writing, go to <http://www.fas.harvard.edu/~expos/study.html>.

I Stand Here Writing

I stand in my kitchen, wiping the cardamom, coriander, and cayenne off my fingers. My head is abuzz with words, with bits and pieces of conversation. I hear a phrase I have read recently, something about "a radical loss of certainty." But, I wonder, how did the sentence begin? I search the air for the rest of the sentence, can't find it, shake some more cardamom, and a bit of coriander. Then, by some play of mind, I am back home again in Indiana with my family, sitting around the kitchen table. Two people are talking, and there are three opinions; three people are talking, and there are six opinions. Opinions grow exponentially. I fight my way back to that sentence. Writing, that's how it begins: "Writing is a radical loss of certainty." (Or is it uncertainty?) It isn't so great for the chicken when all these voices start showing up, with all these sentences hanging in mid-air, but the voices keep me company. I am a writer, not a cook, and the truth is I don't care much about the chicken. Stories beget stories. Writing emerges from writing.

The truth. Has truth anything to do with the facts? All I know is that no matter how many facts I might clutter my life with, I am as bound to the primordial drama of my family as the earth is to the sun. This year my father, the son of a severe Prussian matriarch, watched me indulge my daughters, and announced to me that he wished I had been his mother. This year, my thirty-ninth, my last year to be thirty-something, my mother—who has a touch of magic, who can walk into the middle of a field of millions of clovers and find the *one* with four leaves—has begun to think I need help. She sends me cards monthly with four-leaf clovers taped inside. Two words neatly printed in capital letters—GOOD LUCK!! I look at these clovers and hear Reynolds Price's words: "Nobody under forty can believe how nearly everything's inherited." I wonder what my mother knows, what she is trying to tell me about the facts of my life.

When I was in high school studying French, laboring to conjugate verbs, the numerous four-leaf clovers my mother had carefully pressed inside her French dictionary made me imagine her in a field of clovers lyrically conjugating verbs of love. This is the only romantic image I have of my mother, a shy and conservative woman whose own mother died when she was five, whose grandparents were killed by the Nazis, who fled Germany at age thirteen with her father and sister. Despite the sheer facts of her life, despite the accumulation of grim knowable data, the truth is my mother is an optimistic person. She has the curious capacity always to be looking for luck, putting her faith in four-leaf clovers, ladybugs, pennies, and other amulets of fortune. She has a vision different from mine, one the facts alone can't explain. I, her daughter, was left, for a long time, seeing only the ironies; they were my defense against the facts of my life.

In this world of my inheritance in which daughters can become their fathers' mothers and mothers know their daughters are entering into a world where only sheer good luck will guide them, I hear from my own daughters that I am not in tune with their worlds, that I am just like a 50s mom, that they are 90s children, and I should stop acting so primitive. My children laugh uproariously at my autograph book, a 1959 artifact they unearthed in the basement of my parents' home. "Never kiss by the garden gate. Love is blind, but the neighbors ain't," wrote one friend. And my best friend, who introduced herself to me on the first day of first grade, looking me straight in the eye—and whispering through her crooked little teeth "the Jews killed Jesus"—wrote in this autograph book: "Mary had a little lamb. Her father shot it dead. Now she carries it to school between two slices of bread."

My ten-year-old daughter, Rachel, writes notes to me in hieroglyphics and tapes signs on the refrigerator in Urdu. "Salaam Namma Man Rachaal Ast" reads one sign. Simply translated it means "Hello, my name is Rachel." Alex, my seven-year-old daughter, writes me lists, new lists each month, visibly reminding me of the many things I need to buy or do for her. This month's list includes a little refrigerator filled with Coke and candy; ears pierced; a new toilet; neon nail polish and *real* adult make-up.

How do I look at these facts? How do I embrace these experiences, these texts of my life, and translate them into ideas? How do I make sense of them and the conversations they engender in my head? I look at Alex's list and wonder what kind of feminist daughter I am raising whose deepest desires include neon nail polish and *real* adult make-up. Looking at her lists a different way, I wonder if this second child of mine is asking me for something larger, something more permanent and real than adult make-up. Maybe I got that sentence wrong. Maybe it is that "Love (as well as writing) involves a radical loss of certainty."

Love is blind, but the neighbors ain't. Mary's father shot her little lamb dead, and now she carries it to school between two slices of bread. I hear these rhymes today, and they don't say to me what they say to my daughters. They don't seem so innocent. I hear them and think about the ways in which my neighbors in Indiana could only see my family as Jews from Germany, exotic strangers who ate tongue, outsiders who didn't celebrate Christmas. I wonder if my daughter Rachel needs to tell me her name in Urdu because she thinks we don't share a common language. These sources change meaning when I ask the questions in a different way. They introduce new ironies, new questions.

I want to understand these living, breathing, primary souces all around me. I want to be, in Henry James's words, "a person upon whom nothing is lost." These sources speak to me of love and loss, of memory and desire, of the ways in which we come to understand something through difference and opposition. Two years ago I heard the word *segue* from one of my students. At first the word seemed peculiar. Segue sounded like something you did only on the Los Angeles freeway. Now I hear that word everywhere, and I have begun using it. I want to know how to segue from one idea to the next, from one thought to the fragment lying beside it. But the connections don't always come with four-leaf clovers and the words GOOD LUCK neatly printed beside them.

My academic need to find connections sends me to the library. There are eleven million books in my University's libraries. Certainly these sanctioned voices, these authorities, these published sources can help me find the connections. Someone, probably some three thousand someones, has studied what it is like to be the child of survivors. Someone has written a manual on how the granddaughter of a severe Prussian matriarch and the daughter of a collector of amulets ought to raise feminist daughters. I want to walk into the fields of writing, into those eleven million books, and find the one book that will explain it all. But I've learned to expect less from such sources. They seldom have the answers. And the answers they do have reveal themselves to me at the most unexpected times. I have been led astray more than once while searching books for the truth.

Once I learned a lesson about borrowing someone else's words and losing my own.

I was fourteen, light years away from thirty-something. High school debate teams across the nation were arguing the pros and cons of the United States Military Aid Policy. It all came back to me as I listened to the news of the Persian Gulf War, as I listened to Stormin' Norman giving his morning briefings, an eerie resonance, all our arguments, the millions of combative words—sorties—fired back and forth. In my first practice debate, not having had enough time to assembly my own sources, I borrowed quote cards from my teammates. I attempted to bolster my position that the U.S. should limit its military aid by reading a quote in my best debate style: "W. W. Rostow says: 'We should not give military aid to India because it will exacerbate endemic rivalries.'"

Under cross-examination, my nemesis, Bobby Rosenfeld, the neighbor kid, who always knew the right answers, began firing a series of questions at me without stopping to let me answer:

"Nancy, can you tell me who W. W. Rostow is? And can you tell my why he might say this? Nancy, can you tell me what 'exacerbate' means? Can you tell me what 'endemic rivalries' are? And exactly what does it mean to exacerbate endemic rivalries'?"

I didn't know. I simply did not know who W. W. Rostow was, why he might have said that, what "exacerbate" meant, or what an "endemic rivalry" was. Millions of four-leaf clovers couldn't have helped me. I might as well have been speaking Urdu. I didn't know who my source was, the context of the source, nor the literal meaning of the words I had read. Borrowing words from authorities had left me without any words of my own.

My debate partner and I went on that year to win the Indiana state championship and to place third in the nationals. Bobby Rosenfeld never cross-examined me again, but for twenty years he has appeared in my dreams. I am not certain why I would dream so frequently about this scrawny kid whom I despised. I think, though, that he became for me what the Sea Dyak tribe of Borneo calls a *ngarong*, a dream guide, someone guiding me to understanding. In this case, Bobby guided me to understand the endemic rivalries within my self. The last time Bobby appeared in a dream he had become a woman.

I learned a more valuable lesson about sources as a college senior. I was the kind of student who loved words, words out of context, words that swirled around inside my mouth, words like *exacerbate, undulating, lugubrious,* and *zeugma.* "She stained her honour or her new brocade," wrote Alexander Pope. I would try to write zeugmas whenever I could, exacerbating my already lugubrious prose. Within the English department, I was known more for my long hair, untamed and untranslatable, and for my long distance bicycle rides than for my scholarship.

For my senior thesis, I picked Emerson's essay "Eloquence." Harrison Hayford, my advisor, suggested that I might just get off my bicycle, get lost in the library, and read all of Emerson's essays, journals, letters. I had picked one of Emerson's least distinguished essays, an essay that the critics mentioned only in passing, and if I were not entirely on my own, I had at least carved out new territory for myself.

I spent weeks in the library reading Emerson's journals, reading newspaper accounts from Rockford and Peoria, Illinois, where he had first delivered "Eloquence" as a speech. Emerson stood at the podium, the wind blowing his papers hither and yon, calmly picking them up, and proceeding to read page 8 followed by page 3, followed by page 6, followed by page 2. No one seemed to know the difference. Emerson's Midwestern audience was overwhelmed by this strange man from Concord, Massachusetts, this eloquent stranger whose unit of expression was the sentence.

As I sat in the library, wearing my QUESTION AUTHORITY T-shirt, I could admire this man who delivered his Divinity School Address in 1838, speaking words so repugnant to the genteel people of Cambridge that it was almost thirty years before Harvard felt safe having him around again. I could understand the Midwestern audience's awe and adulation as they listened but didn't quite comprehend Emerson's stunning oratory. I had joined the debate team not to argue the U.S. Military Aid Policy, but to learn how to be an orator who could stun audiences, to learn a personal eloquence I could never learn at home. Perhaps only children of immigrant parents can understand the embarrassing moments of inarticulateness, the missed connections that come from learning to speak a language from parents who claim a different mother tongue.

As an undergraduate, I wanted to free myself from that mother tongue. Four-leaf clovers and amulets of oppression weighed heavy on my mind, and I could see no connection whatsoever between those facts of my life and the untranslatable side of myself that set me in opposition to authority. And then along came Emerson. Like his Midwest audience, I didn't care about having him whole. I liked the promise and the rhapsodic freedom I found in his sentences, in his invitation to seize life as our dictionary, to believe that "Life was not something to be learned but to be lived." I loved his insistence that "the only thing of value is the active soul." I read that "Books are for the scholar's idle time," and I knew that he had given me permission to explore the world. Going into Emerson was like walking into a revelation; it was the first time I had gone into the texts not looking for a specific answer, and it was the first time the texts gave me the answers I needed. Never mind that I got only part of what Emerson was telling me. I got inspiration, I got insight, and I began to care deeply about my work.

Today I reread the man who set me off on a new road, and I find a different kind of wisdom. Today I reread "The American Scholar," and I don't underline the sentence "Books are for the scholar's idle time." I continue to the next paragraph, underlining the sentence "One must be an inventor to read well." The second sentence doesn't contradict the one I read twenty years ago, but it means more today. I bring more to it, and I know that I can walk into text after text, source after source, and they will give me insight, but not answers. I have learned too that my sources can surprise me. Like my mother, I find myself sometimes surrounded by a field of four-leaf clovers, there for the picking, waiting to see what I can make of them. But I must be an inventor if I am to read those sources well, if I am to imagine the connections.

As I stand in my kitchen, the voices that come to me come by way of a lifetime of reading, they come on the waves of life, and they seem to be helping me translate the untranslatable. They come, not at my bidding, but when I least expect them, when I am receptive enough to listen to their voices. They come when I am open.

If I could teach my students one lesson about writing it would be to see themselves as sources, as places from which ideas originate, to see themselves as Emerson's transparent eyeball, all that they have read and experienced—the dictionaries of their lives—circulating through them. I want them to learn how sources thicken, complicate, enlarge writing, but I want them to know too how it is always the writer's voice, vision, and argument that create the new source. I want my students to see that nothing reveals itself straight out, especially the sources all around them. But I know enough by now that this Emersonian ideal can't be passed on in one lesson or even a semester of lessons.

Many of the students who come to my classes have been trained to collect facts; they act as if their primary job is to accumulate enough authorities so that there is no doubt about the "truth" of their thesis. They most often disappear behind the weight and permanence of their borrowed words, moving their pens, mouthing the words of others, allowing sources to speak through them unquestioned, unexamined.

At the outset, many of my students think that personal writing is writing about the death of their grandmother. Academic writing is reporting what Elisabeth Kübler-Ross has written about death and dying. Being personal, I want to show my students, does not mean being autobiographical. Being academic does not mean being remote, distant, imponderable. Being personal means bringing their judgments and interpretation to bear on what they read and write, learning that they never leave themselves behind even when they write academic essays.

Last year, David Gray came into my essay class disappointed about everything. He didn't like the time of the class, didn't like the reading list, didn't seem to like me. Nothing pleased him. "If this is a class on the essay," he asked the first day, "why aren't we reading real essayists like Addison, Steele, and Lamb?" On the second day, after being asked to read Annie Dillard's "Living Like Weasels," David complained that a weasel wasn't a fit subject for an essay. "Writers need big subjects. Look at Melville. He needed a whale for *Moby-Dick*. A weasel—that's nothing but a rodent." And so it continued for a few weeks.

I kept my equanimity in class, but at home I'd tell my family about this kid who kept testing me, seizing me like Dillard's weasel, and not letting go. I secretly wanted him out of my class. But then again, I sensed in him a kindred spirit, someone else who needed to question authority.

I wanted my students to write exploratory essays about education, so I asked them to think of a time when they had learned something, and then a time when they had tried to learn something but couldn't. I wanted them to see what ideas and connections they could find between these two very different experiences and other essays they were reading for the class. I wanted the various sources to work as catalysts. I wanted my students to find a way to talk back to those other writers. The assigned texts were an odd assortment with few apparent connections. I hoped my students would find the common ground, but also the moments of tension, the contradictions, and the ambiguities in those sources.

David used the assigned texts as a catalyst for his thinking, but as was his way, he went beyond the texts I offered and chose his own. He begins his essay, "Dulcis Est Sapientia," with an account of his high school Latin class, suggesting that he once knew declensions, that he had a knack for conjugations, but has forgotten them. He tells us that if his teacher were to appear suddenly today and demand the perfect subjunctive of *venire*, he would stutter hopelessly.

About that Latin class, David asks, "What is going on here? Did I once know Latin and forget it through disuse? Perhaps I never learned Latin at all. What I learned was a bunch of words which, with the aid of various ending sounds, indicated that Gaius was either a good man delivering messages to the lieutenant or a general who struck camp at the seventh hour. I may have known it once, but I never learned it." The class never gave David the gift of language. There was something awry in the method.

What is learning? That's what David explores in his essay as he moves from his Latin lesson to thinking about surrealist paintings, to thinking about barriers we create, to Plato, to an airplane ride in which he observed a mother teaching her child concepts of color and number, all the time taking his readers along with him on his journey, questioning sources, reflecting, expanding, and enriching his growing sense that learning should stress ideas rather than merely accumulating facts and information.

David draws his essay to a close with an analysis of a joke: A man goes to a cocktail party and gets soused. He approaches his host and asks, "Pardon me, but do lemons whistle?"

The host looks at him oddly and answers, "No, lemons don't whistle."

"Oh dear," says the guest, "then I'm afraid I just squeezed your canary into my gin and tonic."

David reflects about the significance of this joke: "One need not be an ornithologist to get the joke, but one must know that canaries are yellow and that they whistle. . . . What constitutes the joke is a connection made between two things . . . which have absolutely nothing in common except for their yellowness. It would never occur to us to make a comparison between the two, let alone to confuse one with the other. But this is the value of the joke, to force into our consciousness the ideas which we held but never actively considered. . . . This knocking down of barriers between ideas is parallel to the process that occurs in all learning. The barriers that we set . . . suddenly crumble; the boundaries . . . are extended to include other modes of thought." Learning, like joking, David argues, gives us pleasure by satisfying our innate capacity to recognize coherence, to discern patterns and connections.

David's essay, like any essay, does not intend to offer the last word on its subject. The civilizing influence of an essay is that it keeps the conversation going, chronicling an intellectual journey, reflecting conversations with sources. I am confident that when David writes for his philosophy course he won't tell a joke anywhere in his essay. But if the joke—if any of his sources—serves him as a catalyst for his thinking, if he makes connections among the sources that circulate within him, between Plato and surrealism, between Latin lessons and mother-child lessons—the dictionaries of *his* life—then he has learned something valuable about writing.

I say to myself that I don't believe in luck. And yet. Not too long ago Rachel came home speaking with some anxiety about an achievement test that she had to take at school. Wanting to comfort her, I urged her to take my rabbit's foot to school the next day. Always alert to life's ironies, Rachel said, "Sure, Mom, a rabbit's foot will really help me find the answers. And even if it did, how would I know the answer the next time when I didn't have that furry little claw?" The next day, proud of her ease at taking the test, she remained perplexed by the one question that seized her and wouldn't let go. She tried it on me: "Here's the question," she said. "Can you figure out which of these sentences cannot be true?"

(a) We warmed our hands by the fire.
(b) The rain poured in and around the window.
(c) The wind beckoned us to open the door.

Only in the mind of someone who writes achievement tests, and wants to close the door on the imagination, could the one false sentence be "The wind beckoned us to open the door." Probably to this kind of mind, Emerson's sentence "Life is our dictionary" is also not a true sentence.

But life *is* our dictionary, and that's how we know that the wind can beckon us to open the door. Like Emerson, we let the wind blow our pages hither and yon, forcing us to start in the middle, moving from page 8 to page 2, forward to page 7, moving back and forth in time, losing our certainty.

Like Emerson, I love basic units, the words themselves, words like cardamom, coriander, words that play around in my head, swirl around in my mouth. The challenge, of course, is not to be a ventriloquist—not to be a mouther of words—but to be open to other voices, untranslatable as they might be. Being open to the unexpected, we can embrace complexities: canaries and lemons, amulets and autograph books, fathers who want their daughters to be their mothers, and daughters who write notes in Urdu—all those odd, unusual conjunctions can come together and speak through us.

The other day, I called my mother and told her about this essay, told her that I had been thinking about the gold bracelet she took with her as one of her few possessions from Germany—a thin gold chain with three amulets: a mushroom, a lady bug, and, of course, a four-leaf clover. Two other charms fell off years ago—she lost one, I the other. I used to worry over the missing links, thinking only of the loss, of what we could never retrieve. When I look at the bracelet now, I think about the Prussian matriarch, my grandmother, and my whole primordial family drama. I think too of Emerson and the pages that blew in the wind and the gaps that seemed not to matter. The bracelet is but one of many sources that intrigues me. Considering them in whatever order they appear, with whatever gaps, I want to see where they will lead me, what they tell me.

With writing and with teaching, as well as with love, we don't know how the sentence will begin and, rarely ever, how it will end. Having the courage to live with uncertainty, ambiguity, even doubt, we can walk into all of those fields of writing, knowing that we will find volumes bidding *us* enter. We need only be inventors, we need only give freely and abundantly to the texts, imagining even as we write that we too will be a source from which other readers can draw sustenance.

1993

GETTING STARTED

1. Find one or two examples in Sommers's essay that help you to explain or to challenge the idea that "writing is a radical loss of certainty" (p. 451). Write a paragraph summarizing the examples and using them to explain this phrase.

2. Choose one of the personal examples that Sommers uses such as her experience on the high school's debate team or her wearing of a "QUESTION AUTHORITY" T-shirt in college. Write a short paragraph summarizing the example and relating it to the larger purpose of the essay.

3. Choose one or two of the examples in which Sommers discusses her student, David Gray (the high school Latin story or the canary and lemons joke, for instance). What does Sommers learn from these examples? How does her reaction to Gray change over the course of the essay?

WRITING

4. Write a paragraph analyzing one of the examples Sommers uses involving her own children (for instance, her reactions to her youngest daughter's request for pierced ears, neon nail polish, and adult make-up). How does this example compare to the ones involving Sommers's students or her own past? How does this example relate to Sommers's larger purpose in the essay?

5. Sommers writes (p. 456):

> If I could teach my students one lesson about writing it would be to see themselves as sources, as places from which ideas originate, to see themselves as Emerson's transparent eyeball, all that they have read and experienced—the dictionaries of their lives—circulating through them. I want them to learn how sources thicken, complicate, enlarge writing, but I want them to know too how it is always the writer's voice, vision, and argument that create the new source.

   Write a two-page analysis of the quotation. How are you a source from Sommers's perspective?

6. Write at least two paragraphs that analyze Sommers's attitude toward the following quotations from Ralph Waldo Emerson: "Books are for the scholar's idle time" and "One must be an inventor to read well" (p. 455).

7. Sommers begins her essay by saying that she stands in her kitchen, wiping spices from her fingers. She goes on to weave comments about writing with comments about her family. Write a short essay that examines why you think Sommers begins on such a personal note. What is the effect on you? How is her approach different from other essays you have read in *Making Sense*?

USING THE LIBRARY AND THE INTERNET

8. Sommers's title echoes the title of writer Tillie Olsen's story, "I Stand Here Ironing." Go to your library and read Olsen's story. What relations do you see between the story and Sommers's essay? Find a Web site about Olsen. What does Sommers appear to have in common with Olsen?

9. Using a reference database that includes a range of scholarly sources such as Academic Search Elite or a similar database recommended by your reference librarian, try the combined search term "writing and invention" as well as related keywords from Sommers's essay. Scan the resulting articles to find one or two that relate to Sommers's ideas in an interesting or revealing way. Print the articles or their abstracts and bring the results to class.

MAKING CONNECTIONS

10. Compare Sommers's ideas about learning with Sven Birkerts's ideas about knowledge and wisdom in "The Owl Has Flown." If Birkerts and Sommers were to address your composition class, what kind of conversation or debate can you imagine them having? Would they be likely to agree or disagree with one another and why? Write an essay in which you create a conversation or debate between Sommers and Birkerts and include quotations from both of their essays.

11. Toward the end of her essay, Sommers writes: "The challenge, of course, is not to be a ventriloquist—not to be a mouther of words—but to be open to other voices, untranslatable as they might be. Being open to the unexpected, we can embrace complexities" (p. 459). Apply Sommers's quotation to one of the other essays you have read this semester. Do the authors meet Sommers's challenge?

Susan Sontag

Susan Sontag (1933–) is a novelist and essay writer whose work focuses on the multiple levels of modern culture. Sontag has written essays and reviews on topics related to art, photography, literature, plays, films, and politics. Other topics include the cultural impact of illnesses such as cancer and AIDS and the cultural phenomenon of "camp." Sontag has also written and directed several films. "In Plato's Cave" is the first chapter of her collection, *On Photography* (1977). The title refers to Plato's allegory of the cave in which cave dwellers accustomed to the dark mistake shadows for reality.

To learn more about photography, visit the American Museum of Photography at <http://www.photographymuseum.com/>.

In Plato's Cave

Humankind lingers unregenerately in Plato's cave, still reveling, its age-old habit, in mere images of the truth. But being educated by photographs is not like being educated by older, more artisanal images. For one thing, there are a great many more images around, claiming our attention. The inventory started in 1839 and since then just about everything has been photographed, or so it seems. This very insatiability of the photographing eye changes the terms of confinement in the cave, our world. In teaching us a new visual code, photographs alter and enlarge our notions of what is worth looking at and what we have a right to observe. They are a grammar and, even more importantly, an ethics of seeing. Finally, the most grandiose result of the photographic enterprise is to give us the sense that we can hold the whole world in our heads—as an anthology of images.

To collect photographs is to collect the world. Movies and television programs light up walls, flicker, and go out; but with still photographs the image is also an object, lightweight, cheap to produce, easy to carry about, accumulate, store. In Godard's *Les Carabiniers* (1963), two sluggish lumpen-peasants are lured into joining the King's Army by the promise that they will be able to loot, rape, kill, or do whatever else they please to the enemy, and get rich. But the suitcase of booty that Michel-Ange and Ulysse triumphantly bring home, years later, to their wives turns out to contain only picture postcards, hundreds of them, of Monuments, Department Stores,

Mammals, Wonders of Nature, Methods of Transport, Works of Art, and other classified treasures from around the globe. Godard's gag vividly parodies the equivocal magic of the photographic image. Photographs are perhaps the most mysterious of all the objects that make up, and thicken, the environment we recognize as modern. Photographs really are experience captured, and the camera is the ideal arm of consciousness in its acquisitive mood.

To photograph is to appropriate the thing photographed. It means putting oneself into a certain relation to the world that feels like knowledge—and, therefore, like power. A now notorious first fall into alienation, habituating people to abstract the world into printed words, is supposed to have engendered that surplus of Faustian energy and psychic damage needed to build modern, inorganic societies. But print seems a less treacherous form of leaching out the world, of turning it into a mental object, than photographic images, which now provide most of the knowledge people have about the look of the past and the reach of the present. What is written about a person or an event is frankly an interpretation, as are handmade visual statements, like paintings and drawings. Photographed images do not seem to be statements about the world so much as pieces of it, miniatures of reality that anyone can make or acquire.

Photographs, which fiddle with the scale of the world, themselves get reduced, blown up, cropped, retouched, doctored, tricked out. They age, plagued by the usual ills of paper objects; they disappear; they become valuable, and get bought and sold; they are reproduced. Photographs, which package the world, seem to invite packaging. They are stuck in albums, framed and set on tables, tacked on walls, projected as slides. Newspapers and magazines feature them; cops alphabetize them; museums exhibit them; publishers compile them.

For many decades the book has been the most influential way of arranging (and usually miniaturizing) photographs, thereby guaranteeing them longevity, if not immortality—photographs are fragile objects, easily torn or mislaid—and a wider public. The photograph in a book is, obviously, the image of an image. But since it is, to begin with, a printed, smooth object, a photograph loses much less of its essential quality when reproduced in a book than a painting does. Still, the book is not a wholly satisfactory scheme for putting groups of photographs into general circulation. The sequence in which the photographs are to be looked at is proposed by the order of pages, but nothing holds readers to the recommended order or indicates the amount of time to be spent on each photograph. Chris Markers's film, *Si j'avais quatre dromadaires* (1966), a brilliantly orchestrated meditation on photographs of all sorts and themes, suggests a subtler and more rigorous way of packaging (and enlarging) still photographs. Both the order and the exact time for looking at each photograph are imposed; and there is a gain in visual legibility and emotional impact. But photographs transcribed in a film cease to be collectable objects, as they still are when served up in books.

Photographs furnish evidence. Something we hear about, but doubt, seems proven when we're shown a photograph of it. In one version of its utility, the camera record incriminates. Starting with their use by the Paris police in the murderous roundup of Communards in June 1871, photographs became a useful tool of modern states in the surveillance and control of their increasingly mobile populations. In another version of its utility, the camera record justifies. A photograph passes for incontrovertible proof that a given thing happened. The picture may distort; but there is always a presumption that something exists, or did exist, which is like what's in the picture. Whatever the limitations (through amateurism) or pretensions (through artistry) of the individual photographer, a photograph—any photograph—seems to have a more innocent, and therefore more accurate, relation to visible reality than do other mimetic objects. Virtuosi of the noble image like Alfred Stieglitz and Paul Strand, composing mighty, unforgettable photographs decade after decade, still want, first of all, to show something "out there," just like the Polaroid owner for whom photographs are a handy, fast form of note-taking, or the shutterbug with a Brownie who takes snapshots as souvenirs of daily life.

While a painting or a prose description can never be other than a narrowly selective interpretation, a photograph can be treated as a narrowly selective transparency. But despite the presumption of veracity that gives all photographs authority, interest, seductiveness, the work that photographers do is no generic exception to the usually shady commerce between art and truth. Even when photographers are most concerned with mirroring reality, they are still haunted by tacit imperatives of taste and conscience. The immensely gifted members of the Farm Security Administration photographic project of the late 1930s (among them Walker Evans, Dorothea Lange, Ben Shahn, Russell Lee) would take dozens of frontal pictures of one of their sharecropper subjects until satisfied that they had gotten just the right look on film—the precise expression on the subject's face that supported their own notions about poverty, light, dignity, texture, exploitation, and geometry. In deciding how a picture should look, in preferring one exposure to another, photographers are always imposing standards on their subjects. Although there is a sense in which the camera does indeed capture reality, not just interpret it, photographs are as much an interpretation of the world as paintings and drawings are. Those occasions when the taking of photographs is relatively undiscriminating, promiscuous, or self-effacing do not lessen the didacticism of the whole enterprise. This very passivity—and ubiquity—of the photographic record is photography's "message," its aggression.

Images which idealize (like most fashion and animal photography) are no less aggressive than work which makes a virtue of plainness

FIGURE 25 Arthur "Weegee" Fellig, *Top Hats—In Trouble,* 1942. Charles Sodokoff and Arthur Webber Use Their Top Hats to Hide Their Faces, January 27, 1942. New York Daily News Photo. (Weegee/ICP/Liaison.)

(like class pictures, still lifes of the bleaker sort, and mug shots). There is an aggression implicit in every use of the camera. This is as evident in the 1840s and 1850s, photography's glorious first two decades, as in all the succeeding decades, during which technology made possible an ever increasing spread of that mentality which looks at the world as a set of potential photographs. Even for such early masters as David Octavius Hill and Julia Margaret Cameron who used the camera as a means of getting painterly images, the point of taking photographs was a vast departure from the aims of painters. From its start, photography implied the capture of the largest possible number of subjects. Painting never had so imperial a scope. The subsequent industrialization of camera technology only carried out a promise inherent in photography from its very beginning: to democratize all experiences by translating them into images.

That age when taking photographs required a cumbersome and expensive contraption—the toy of the clever, the wealthy, and the obsessed—seems remote indeed from the era of sleek pocket cameras that invite anyone to take pictures. The first cameras, made in France and England in the early 1840s, had only inventors and buffs to operate them. Since there were then no professional photographers, there could not be amateurs either, and taking photographs had no clear social use; it was a gratuitous, that is, an artistic activity, though with few pretensions to being an art. It was only with its industrialization that photography came into its own as art. As industrialization provided social uses for the operations of the photographer, so the reaction against these uses reinforced the self-consciousness of photography-as-art.

Recently, photography has become almost as widely practiced an amusement as sex and dancing—which means that, like every mass art form, photography is not practiced by most people as an art. It is mainly a social rite, a defense against anxiety, and a tool of power.

Memorializing the achievements of individuals considered as members of families (as well as of other groups) is the earliest popular use of photography. For at least a century, the wedding photograph has been as much a part of the ceremony as the prescribed verbal formulas. Cameras go with family life. According to a sociological study done in France, most households have a camera, but a household with children is twice as likely to have at least one camera as a household in which there are no children. Not to take pictures of one's children, particularly when they are small, is a sign of parental indifference, just as not turning up for one's graduation picture is a gesture of adolescent rebellion.

Through photographs, each family constructs a portrait-chronicle of itself—a portable kit of images that bears witness to its connectedness. It hardly matters what activities are photographed so long as photographs get taken and are cherished. Photography becomes a rite of family life just when, in the industrializing countries of Europe and America, the very institution of the family starts undergoing radical surgery. As that claustrophobic unit, the nuclear family, was being carved out of a much larger family aggregate, photography came along to memorialize, to restate symbolically, the imperiled continuity and vanishing extendedness of family life. Those ghostly traces, photographs, supply the token presence of the dispersed relatives. A family's photograph album is generally about the extended family—and, often, is all that remains of it.

As photographs give people an imaginary possession of a past that is unreal, they also help people to take possession of space in which they are insecure. Thus, photography develops in tandem with one of the most characteristic of modern activities: tourism. For the first time in history, large numbers of people regularly travel out of their habitual environments for short periods of time. It seems positively unnatural to travel for pleasure without taking a camera along. Photographs will offer indisputable evidence that the trip was made, that the program was carried out, that fun was had. Photographs document sequences of consumption carried on outside the view of family, friends, neighbors. But dependence on the camera, as the device that makes real what one is experiencing, doesn't fade when people travel more. Taking photographs fills the same need for the cosmopolitans accumulating photograph-trophies of their boat trip up the Albert Nile or their fourteen days in China as it does for lower-middle-class vacationers taking snapshots of the Eiffel Tower or Niagara Falls.

A way of certifying experience, taking photographs is also a way of refusing it—by limiting experience to a search for the photogenic, by converting experience into an image, a souvenir. Travel becomes a strategy for accumulating photographs. The very activity of taking pictures is soothing, and assuages general feelings of disorientation that are likely to be exacerbated by travel. Most tourists feel compelled to put the camera between themselves and whatever is remarkable that they encounter. Unsure of other responses, they take a picture. This gives shape to experience: stop, take a photograph, and move on. The method especially appeals to people handicapped by a ruthless work ethic—Germans, Japanese, and Americans. Using a camera appeases the anxiety which the work-driven feel about not working when they are on vacation and supposed to be having fun. They have something to do that is like a friendly imitation of work: they can take pictures.

People robbed of their past seem to make the most fervent picture takers, at home and abroad. Everyone who lives in an industrialized society is obliged gradually to give up the past, but in certain countries, such as the United States and Japan, the break with the past has been particularly traumatic. In the early 1970s, the fable of the brash American tourist of the 1950s and 1960s, rich with dollars and Babbittry, was replaced by the mystery of the group-minded Japanese tourist, newly released from his island prison by the miracle of overvalued yen, who is generally armed with two cameras, one on each hip.

Photography has become one of the principal devices for experiencing something, for giving an appearance of participation. One full-page ad shows a small group of people standing pressed together, peering out of the photograph, all but one looking stunned, excited, upset. The one who wears a different expression holds a camera to his eye; he seems self-possessed, is almost smiling. While the others are passive, clearly alarmed spectators, having a camera has transformed one person into something active, a voyeur: only he has mastered the situation. What do these people see? We don't know. And it doesn't matter. It is an Event: something worth seeing—and therefore worth photographing. The ad copy, white letters across the dark lower third of the photograph like news coming over a teletype machine, consists of just six words: ". . . Prague . . . Woodstock . . . Vietnam . . . Sapporo . . . Londonderry . . . LEICA." Crushed hopes, youth antics, colonial wars, and winter sports are alike—are equalized by the camera. Taking photographs has set up a chronic voyeuristic relation to the world which levels the meaning of all events.

A photograph is not just the result of an encounter between an event and a photographer; picture-taking is an event in itself, and one with ever more peremptory rights—to interfere with, to invade, or to ignore whatever is going on. Our very sense of situation is now articulated by the camera's interventions. The omnipresence of cameras persuasively suggests that time consists of interesting events, events worth photographing. This, in turn, makes it easy to feel that any event, once underway, and whatever its moral character, should be allowed to complete itself—so that something else can be brought into the world, the photograph. After the event has ended, the picture will still exist, conferring on the event a kind of immortality (and importance) it would never otherwise have enjoyed. While real people are out there killing themselves or other real people, the photographer stays behind his or her camera, creating a tiny element of another world: the image-world that bids to outlast us all.

Photographing is essentially an act of non-intervention. Part of the horror of such memorable coups of contemporary photojournalism as the pictures of a Vietnamese bonze reaching for the gasoline can, of a Bengali guerrilla in the act of bayoneting a trussed-up collaborator, comes from the awareness of how plausible it has become, in situations where the photographer has the choice between a photograph and a life, to choose the photograph. The person who intervenes cannot record; the person who is recording cannot intervene. Dziga Vertov's great film, *Man with a Movie Camera* (1929), gives the ideal image of the photographer as someone in perpetual movement, someone moving through a panorama of disparate events with such agility and speed that any intervention is out of the question. Hitchcock's *Rear Window* (1954) gives the complementary image: the photographer played by James Stewart has an intensified relation to one event, through his camera, precisely because he has a broken leg and is confined to a wheelchair; being temporarily immobilized prevents him from acting on what he sees, and makes it even more important to take pictures. Even if incompatible with intervention in a physical sense, using a camera is still a form of participation. Although the camera is an observation station, the act of photographing is more than passive observing. Like sexual voyeurism, it is a way of at least tacitly, often explicitly, encouraging whatever is going on to keep on happening. To take a picture is to have an interest in things as they are, in the status quo remaining unchanged (at least for as long as it takes to get a "good" picture), to be in complicity with whatever makes a subject interesting, worth photographing—including, when that is the interest, another person's pain or misfortune.

"I always thought of photography as a naughty thing to do—that was one of my favorite things about it," Diane Arbus wrote, "and when I first did it I felt very perverse." Being a professional

FIGURE 26 Jimmy Stewart as L. B. Jeffries in *Rear Window,* directed by Alfred Hitchcock. (© Bettmann/CORBIS.)

photographer can be thought of as naughty, to use Arbus's pop word, if the photographer seeks out subjects considered to be disreputable, taboo, marginal. But naughty subjects are harder to find these days. And what exactly is the perverse aspect of picture-taking? If professional photographers often have sexual fantasies when they are behind the camera, perhaps the perversion lies in the fact that these fantasies are both plausible and so inappropriate. In *Blowup* (1966), Antonioni has the fashion photographer hovering convulsively over Verushka's body with his camera clicking. Naughtiness, indeed! In fact, using a camera is not a very good way of getting at someone sexually. Between photographer and subject, there has to be distance. The camera doesn't rape, or even possess, though it may presume, intrude, trespass, distort, exploit, and, at the farthest reach of metaphor, assassinate—all activities that, unlike the sexual push and shove, can be conducted from a distance, and with some detachment.

There is a much stronger sexual fantasy in Michael Powell's extraordinary movie *Peeping Tom* (1960), which is not about a Peeping Tom but about a psychopath who kills women with a weapon concealed in his camera, while photographing them. Not once does he touch his subjects. He doesn't desire their bodies; he wants their presence in the form of filmed images—those showing them experiencing their own death—which he screens at home for his solitary pleasure. The movie assumes connections between impotence and aggression, professionalized looking and cruelty, which point to the central fantasy connected with the camera. The camera as phallus is, at most, a flimsy variant of the inescapable metaphor that everyone unselfconsciously employs. However hazy our awareness of this fantasy, it is named without subtlety whenever we talk about "loading" and "aiming" a camera, about "shooting" a film.

The old-fashioned camera was clumsier and harder to reload than a brown Bess musket. The modern camera is trying to be a ray gun. One ad reads:

> The Yashica Electro-35 GT is the spaceage camera your family will love. Take beautiful pictures day or night. Automatically. Without any nonsense. Just aim, focus and shoot. The GT's computer brain and electronic shutter will do the rest.

Like a car, a camera is sold as a predatory weapon—one that's as automated as possible, ready to spring. Popular taste expects an easy, an invisible technology. Manufacturers reassure their customers that taking pictures demands no skill or expert knowledge, that the machine is all-knowing, and responds to the slightest pressure of the will. It's as simple as turning the ignition key or pulling the trigger.

Like guns and cars, cameras are fantasy-machines whose use is addictive. However, despite the extravagances of ordinary language and advertising, they are not lethal. In the hyperbole that markets cars like guns, there is at least this much truth: except in wartime, cars kill more people than guns do. The camera/gun does not kill, so the ominous metaphor seems to be all bluff—like a man's fantasy of having a gun, knife, or tool between his legs. Still, there is something predatory in the act of taking a picture. To photograph people is to violate them, by seeing them as they never see themselves, by having knowledge of them they can never have; it turns people into objects that can be symbolically possessed. Just as the camera is a sublimation of the gun, to photograph someone is a sublimated murder—a soft murder, appropriate to a sad, frightened time.

Eventually, people might learn to act out more of their aggressions with cameras and fewer with guns, with the price being an even more image-choked world. One situation where people are switching from bullets to film is the photographic safari that is replacing the gun safari in East Africa. The hunters have Hasselblads instead of Winchesters; instead of looking through a telescopic sight to aim a rifle, they look through a viewfinder to frame a picture. In end-of-the century London, Samuel Butler complained that "there is a photographer in every bush, going about like a roaring lion seeking whom he may devour." The photographer is now charging real beasts, beleaguered and too rare to kill. Guns have metamorphosed into cameras in this earnest comedy, the ecology safari, because nature has ceased to be what it always had been—what people needed protection from. Now nature—tamed, endangered, mortal—needs to be protected from people. When we are afraid, we shoot. But when we are nostalgic, we take pictures.

It is a nostalgic time right now, and photographs actively promote nostalgia. Photography is an elegiac art, a twilight art. Most subjects photographed are, just by virtue of being photographed, touched with pathos. An ugly or grotesque subject may be moving because it has been dignified by the attention of the photographer. A beautiful subject can be the object of rueful feelings, because it has aged or decayed or no longer exists. All photographs are *memento mori.* To take a photograph is to participate in another person's (or thing's) mortality, vulnerability, mutability. Precisely by slicing out this moment and freezing it, all photographs testify to time's relentless melt.

Cameras began duplicating the world at that moment when the human landscape started to undergo a vertiginous rate of change: while an untold number of forms of biological and social life are being destroyed in a brief span of time, a device is available to record what is disappearing. The moody, intricately textured Paris of Atget and Brassaï is mostly gone. Like the dead relatives and friends preserved in the family album, whose presence in photographs exorcises some of the anxiety and remorse prompted by their disappearance, so the photographs of neighborhoods now torn down, rural places disfigured and made barren, supply our pocket relation to the past.

A photograph is both a pseudo-presence and a token of absence. Like a wood fire in a room, photographs—especially those of people, of distant landscapes and faraway cities, of the vanished past—are incitements to reverie. The sense of the unattainable that can be evoked by photographs feeds directly into the erotic feelings of those for whom desirability is enhanced by distance. The lover's photograph hidden in a married woman's wallet, the poster photograph of a rock star tacked up over an adolescent's bed, the campaign-button image of a politician's face pinned on a voter's coat, the snapshots of a cabdriver's children clipped to the visor—all such talismanic uses of photographs express a feeling both sentimental and implicitly magical: they are attempts to contact or lay claim to another reality.

Photographs can abet desire in the most direct, utilitarian way—as when someone collects photographs of anonymous examples of the desirable as an aid to masturbation. The matter is more complex when photographs are used to stimulate the moral impulse. Desire has no history—at least, it is experienced in each instance as all foreground, immediacy. It is aroused by archetypes and is, in that sense, abstract. But moral feelings are embedded in history, whose personae are concrete, whose situations are always specific. Thus, almost opposite rules hold true for the use of the photograph to awaken desire and to awaken conscience. The images that mobilize conscience are always linked to a given historical situation. The more general they are, the less likely they are to be effective.

A photograph that brings news of some unsuspected zone of misery cannot make a dent in public opinion unless there is an appropriate context of feeling and attitude. The photographs Mathew Brady and his colleagues took of the horrors of the battlefields did not make people any less keen to go on with the Civil War. The photographs of ill-clad, skeletal prisoners held at Andersonville inflamed Northern public opinion—against the South. (The effect of the Andersonville photographs must have been partly due to the very novelty, at that time, of seeing photographs.) The political understanding that many Americans came to in the 1960s would allow them, looking at the photographs Dorothea Lange took of Nisei on the West Coast being transported to internment camps in 1942, to recognize their subject for what it was—a crime committed by the government against a large group of American citizens. Few people who saw these photographs in the 1940s could have had so unequivocal a reaction; the grounds for such a judgment were covered over by the pro-war consensus. Photographs cannot create a moral position, but they can reinforce one—and can help build a nascent one.

Photographs may be more memorable than moving images, because they are a neat slice of time, not a flow. Television is a stream of underselected images, each of which cancels its predecessor. Each still photograph is a privileged moment, turned into a slim object that one can keep and look at again. Photographs like the one that made the front page of most newspapers in the world in 1972—a naked South Vietnamese child just sprayed by American napalm, running down a highway toward the camera, her arms open, screaming with pain—probably did more to increase the public revulsion against the war than a hundred hours of televised barbarities.

One would like to imagine that the American public would not have been so unanimous in its acquiescence to the Korean War if it had been confronted with photographic evidence of the devastation of Korea, an ecocide and genocide in some respects even more thorough than those inflicted on Vietnam a decade later. But the supposition is trivial. The public did not see such photographs because there was, ideologically, no space for them. No one brought back photographs of daily life in Pyongyang, to show that the enemy had a human face, as Felix Greene and Marc Riboud brought back photographs of Hanoi. Americans did have access to photographs of the suffering of the Vietnamese (many of which came from military sources and were taken with quite a different use in mind) because journalists felt backed in their efforts to obtain those photographs, the event having been defined by a significant number of people as a savage colonialist war. The Korean War was understood differently—

as part of the struggle of the Free World against the Soviet Union and China—and, given that characterization, photographs of the cruelty of unlimited American firepower would have been irrelevant.

Though an event has come to mean, precisely, something worth photographing, it is still ideology (in the broadest sense) that determines what constitutes an event. There can be no evidence, photographic or otherwise, of an event until the event itself has been named and characterized. And it is never photographic evidence which can construct—more properly, identify—events; the contribution of photography always follows the naming of the event. What determines the possibility of being affected morally by photographs is the existence of a relevant political consciousness. Without a politics, photographs of the slaughter-bench of history will most likely be experienced as, simply, unreal or as a demoralizing emotional blow.

The quality of feeling, including moral outrage, that people can muster in response to photographs of the oppressed, the exploited, the starving, and the massacred also depends on the degree of their familiarity with these images. Don McCullin's photographs of emaciated Biafrans in the early 1970s had less impact for some people than Werner Bischof's photographs of Indian famine victims in the early 1950s because those images had become banal, and the photographs of Tuareg families dying of starvation in the sub-Sahara that appeared in magazines everywhere in 1973 must have seemed to many like an unbearable replay of a now familiar atrocity exhibition.

Photographs shock insofar as they show something novel. Unfortunately, the ante keeps getting raised—partly through the very proliferation of such images of horror. One's first encounter with the photographic inventory of ultimate horror is a kind of revelation, the prototypically modern revelation: a negative epiphany. For me, it was photographs of Bergen-Belsen and Dachau which I came across by chance in a bookstore in Santa Monica in July 1945. Nothing I have seen—in photographs or in real life—ever cut me as sharply, deeply, instantaneously. Indeed, it seems plausible to me to divide my life into two parts, before I saw those photographs (I was twelve) and after, though it was several years before I understood fully what they were about. What good was served by seeing them? They were only photographs—of an event I had scarcely heard of and could do nothing to affect, of suffering I could hardly imagine and could do nothing to relieve. When I looked at those photographs, something broke. Some limit had been reached, and not only that of horror; I felt irrevocably grieved, wounded, but a part of my feelings started to tighten; something went dead; something is still crying.

To suffer is one thing; another thing is living with the photographed images of suffering, which does not necessarily strengthen conscience and the ability to be compassionate. It can also corrupt them. Once one has seen such images, one has started down the road of seeing more—and more. Images transfix. Images anesthetize. An event known through photographs certainly becomes more real than it would have been if one had never seen the photographs—think of the Vietnam War. (For a counter-example, think of the Gulag Archipelago, of which we have no photographs.) But after repeated exposure to images it also becomes less real.

The same law holds for evil as for pornography. The shock of photographed atrocities wears off with repeated viewings, just as the surprise and bemusement felt the first time one sees a pornographic movie wear off after one sees a few more. The sense of taboo which makes us indignant and sorrowful is not much sturdier than the sense of taboo that regulates the definition of what is obscene. And both have been sorely tried in recent years. The vast photographic catalogue of misery and injustice throughout the world has given everyone a certain familiarity with atrocity, making the horrible seem more ordinary—making it appear familiar, remote ("it's only a photograph"), inevitable. At the time of the first photographs of the Nazi camps, there was nothing banal about these images. After thirty years, a saturation point may have been reached. In these last decades, "concerned" photography has done at least as much to deaden conscience as to arouse it.

The ethical content of photographs is fragile. With the possible exception of photographs of those horrors, like the Nazi camps, that have gained the status of ethical reference points, most photographs do not keep their emotional charge. A photograph of 1900 that was affecting then because of its subject would, today, be more likely to move us because it is a photograph taken in 1900. The particular qualities and intentions of photographs tend to be swallowed up in the generalized pathos of time past. Aesthetic distance seems built into the very experience of looking at photographs, if not right away, then certainly with the passage of time. Time eventually positions most photographs, even the most amateurish, at the level of art.

The industrialization of photography permitted its rapid absorption into rational—that is, bureaucratic—ways of running society. No longer toy images, photographs became part of the general furniture of the environment—touchstones and confirmations of that reductive approach to reality which is considered realistic. Photographs were enrolled in the service of important institutions of control, notably the family and the police, as symbolic objects and as pieces of information. Thus, in the bureaucratic cataloguing of the world, many important documents are not valid unless they have, affixed to them, a photograph-token of the citizen's face.

The "realistic" view of the world compatible with bureaucracy redefines knowledge—as techniques and information. Photographs are valued because they give information. They tell one what there is;

they make an inventory. To spies, meteorologists, coroners, archaeologists, and other information professionals, their value is inestimable. But in the situations in which most people use photographs, their value as information is of the same order as fiction. The information that photographs can give starts to seem very important at that moment in cultural history when everyone is thought to have a right to something called news. Photographs were seen as a way of giving information to people who do not take easily to reading. The *Daily News* still calls itself "New York's Picture Newspaper," its bid for populist identity. At the opposite end of the scale, *Le Monde,* a newspaper designed for skilled, well-informed readers, runs no photographs at all. The presumption is that, for such readers, a photograph could only illustrate the analysis contained in an article.

A new sense of the notion of information has been constructed around the photographic image. The photograph is a thin slice of space as well as time. In a world ruled by photographic images, all borders ("framing") seem arbitrary. Anything can be separated, can be made discontinuous, from anything else: all that is necessary is to frame the subject differently. (Conversely, anything can be made adjacent to anything else.) Photography reinforces a nominalist view of social reality as consisting of small units of an apparently infinite number—as the number of photographs that could be taken of anything is unlimited. Through photographs, the world becomes a series of unrelated, freestanding particles; and history, past and present, a set of anecdotes and *faits divers.* The camera makes reality atomic, manageable, and opaque. It is a view of the world which denies interconnectedness, continuity, but which confers on each moment the character of a mystery. Any photograph has multiple meanings; indeed, to see something in the form of a photograph is to encounter a potential object of fascination. The ultimate wisdom of the photographic image is to say: "There is the surface. Now think—or rather feel, intuit—what is beyond it, what the reality must be like if it looks this way." Photographs, which cannot themselves explain anything, are inexhaustible invitations to deduction, speculation, and fantasy.

Photography implies that we know about the world if we accept it as the camera records it. But this is the opposite of understanding, which starts from *not* accepting the world as it looks. All possibility of understanding is rooted in the ability to say no. Strictly speaking, one never understands anything from a photograph. Of course, photographs fill in blanks in our mental pictures of the present and the past: for example, Jacob Riis's images of New York squalor in the 1880s are sharply instructive to those unaware that urban poverty in late-nineteenth-century America was really that Dickensian. Nevertheless, the camera's rendering of reality must always hide more than it discloses. As Brecht points out, a photograph of the Krupp works reveals virtually nothing about that organization. In contrast to the amorous relation,

FIGURE 27 Jacob A. Riis, "Room in tenement flat, 1910," from *How the Other Half Lives,* by Jacob A. Riis. (Jacob A. Riis Collection, Museum of the City of New York.)

which is based on how something looks, understanding is based on how it functions. And functioning takes place in time, and must be explained in time. Only that which narrates can make us understand.

The limit of photographic knowledge of the world is that, while it can goad conscience, it can, finally, never be ethical or political knowledge. The knowledge gained through still photographs will always be some kind of sentimentalism, whether cynical or humanist. It will be a knowledge at bargain prices—a semblance of knowledge, a semblance of wisdom; as the act of taking pictures is a semblance of appropriation, a semblance of rape. The very muteness of what is, hypothetically, comprehensible in photographs is what constitutes their attraction and provocativeness. The omnipresence of photographs has an incalculable effect on our ethical sensibility. By furnishing this already crowded world with a duplicate one of images, photography makes us feel that the world is more available than it really is.

Needing to have reality confirmed and experience enhanced by photographs is an aesthetic consumerism to which everyone is now addicted. Industrial societies turn their citizens into image-junkies; it is the most irresistible form of mental pollution. Poignant longings for beauty, for an end to probing below the surface, for a redemption and celebration of the body of the world—all these elements of erotic feeling are affirmed in the pleasure we take in photographs. But other, less liberating feelings are expressed as well. It would not be wrong to speak of people having a *compulsion* to photograph: to turn experience itself into a way of seeing. Ultimately, having an experience becomes identical with taking a photograph of it, and participating in a public event comes more and more to be equivalent to looking at it in photographed form. That most logical of nineteenth-century aesthetes, Mallarmé, said that everything in the world exists in order to end in a book. Today everything exists to end in a photograph.

1977

GETTING STARTED

1. Before reading the essay, list all the ways you can think of that we use photographs in our daily lives and in the culture at large.

2. Sontag's essay gives an account of many historical and current uses of photography. Choose two examples that interest or reveal something to you. Write a one-paragraph summary of each example in which you cite a key quote, explain the example, and note why you found it interesting or revealing.

3. Working in a group, list all the positive and negative implications of photography that you find in Sontag's essay. Add your own positives and negatives as they come up in discussion.

4. Sontag says that "photographing is essentially an act of non-intervention" (p. 468) but later argues that cameras are like guns. Write a paragraph exploring and explaining this seeming contradiction.

5. What is the relationship between the event and the photograph? Choose a passage from Sontag that helps you to explore this question.

WRITING

6. Write a paper based on your research and your resulting class presentation in response to question 8. Quote from and explain the claims you are using from Sontag's essay so that your readers will understand how your selection of photos supports or contradicts those claims. Attach copies of the photos you are using if possible, but also give a detailed description of the relevant portions of the photos in your paper.

7. Sontag concludes her essay by saying (p. 476):

   > The knowledge gained through still photographs will always be some kind of sentimentalism, whether cynical or humanist. It

> will be a knowledge at bargain prices—a semblance of knowledge, a semblance of wisdom; as the act of taking pictures is a semblance of appropriation, a semblance of rape.

Write an essay in which you use examples from "In Plato's Cave" and from outside photographs to explain why Sontag has this seemingly dark vision of photography's impact on our society. To what extent do you share that vision? To what extent do you disagree with some of Sontag's claims or see some alternative implications of photography as a technology?

USING THE LIBRARY AND THE INTERNET

8. Search for photographs by looking in the library, in newspapers, on the Internet, in museums, or in your family's album. Use a group of photographs to supply evidence for or against one of Sontag's claims in this essay. For instance, you could use three photos to support or counter one of the following arguments: "To take a photograph is to participate in another person's (or thing's) mortality, vulnerability, mutability" (p. 471); "What determines the possibility of being affected morally by photographs is the existence of a relevant political consciousness" (p. 473); or "Images transfix. Images anesthetize" (p. 474). Share your findings with your group, and create an individual presentation for the class.

MAKING CONNECTIONS

9. Use some of the ideas in Jeanette Winterson's essay, "Imagination and Reality," to reconsider Sontag's conclusions about the functions of photography. To what extent does photography fulfill the function of art and imagination that Winterson describes? To what extent does it participate in "money culture"? In what ways does photography blur the boundaries between the two? Do Winterson and Sontag envision very different roles for photography? Are there overlaps?

10. Compare and contrast Sontag's discussion of photography as a technology to Sherry Turkle's essay, "The Triumph of Tinkering," which focuses on the varying uses of Internet technology. In each case, do the expectations, assumptions, and perceptions of the users seem to determine the outcome and implications of the technology? To what extent does the technology itself seem to teach its users new uses for the Internet or for photography and new ways of perceiving the world? What are the long-range implications of each technology?

Warren I. Susman

Warren I. Susman (1927–1985) was a prominent cultural historian and a Professor of History at Rutgers University. Susman specialized in the history of popular culture and authored many books. His most important works were *Culture as History: The Transformation of American Society in the Twentieth Century* (1984) and *Culture and Commitment, 1929–1945* (1973). " 'Personality' and the Making of the Twentieth-Century Culture" is a chapter from *Culture as History.*

To investigate today's attitudes toward character and personality, go to the home page of the Character Education Partnership at <http://www.character.org/>.

"Personality" and the Making of Twentieth-Century Culture

Perhaps the greatest problem which any historian has to tackle is neither the cataclysm of revolution nor the decay of empire but the process by which ideas become social attitudes.

J. H. Plumb

I have always observed a singular accord between supercelestial ideas and subterranean behavior.

Montaigne

The whole history of ideas should be reviewed in the light of the power of social structures to generate symbols of their own.

Mary Douglas

No ideas but in things.

William Carlos Williams

One of the things that make the modern world "modern" is the development of consciousness of self. The European world that produced the Reformation, the new capitalist order, and the growing system of nation-states also gave us a new vocabulary that revealed a new vision of the self. "Consciousness" became a key word in the seventeenth century; the new language of self announced what

Owen Barfield has called "the shifting of the centre of gravity of consciousness from the cosmos around him into the personal human being himself."[1] The results of such a shift were significant. Impulses that control human behavior and destiny were felt to arise more and more *within* the individual at the very time that the laws governing the world were seen as more and more impersonal. Not only was it more difficult to feel spiritual life and activity immanent in the world outside the self; as the rituals of the external church grew feebler, the needs of inner self grew also stronger.

This story is familiar to the historian of modern thought. He has charted the way of this newly developed self in a stormy and changing world from its beginning in Luther and Calvin, Descartes and Locke. To insist that the history of thought in the modern era is the history of thinking about that self may be an exaggeration. But the consequences of this vision of a self set apart have surely been felt in every field of inquiry, whether it be psychology or political theory, epistemology or economics. Freud, in one of his rare moments of historical analysis, pointed in 1917 to a series of blows that had been administered by modern science to the fragile self. In the sixteenth century, Copernicus gave it a cosmological buffeting by removing man from the center of the universe and insisting that he dwelled on a smaller fragment of matter, only one of a countless number of them. In the nineteenth century, Darwin made a biological assault on the self when he argued man's essential affinity with all animals and brought into doubt the special role of reason and civilization. The final blow, Freud thought, was that delivered upon our own century, the psychological blow. This vision (his own) denied that the center of personality was the ego or the soul, and it further suggested, from its new view of the unconscious, that man in the traditional sense did not have full control over himself.[2] In Freud's vision, the history of science is especially important because of its effect on man's view of himself.

All of this has been the stuff of the intellectual historian. He has studied each "crisis" in thought—as he calls it—brought about by a newer vision of new knowledge. He has attempted to assess the "influence" of major and even minor "thinkers" and has examined new "patterns" of thought emerging from the reconsideration of old problems in new contexts or from new problems arising in changed circumstances. On occasion, he has made an effort to relate "ideas" to the particular social structure in which they appear to have been generated. We have "seen" ideas become social attitudes. We have been made aware of the "impact" of Locke, Darwin, and Freud. Seldom do we even ask the question whether social attitudes do indeed become "ideas." When the historian talks of "popular" ideas, he rarely sees them as part of the world in which "ideas" (*real* ideas?) are born.

Yet that world—that combination of new social, economic, political, and religious structures—in which the new idea of self-consciousness developed belonged to others than just Hobbes and Locke—and I do not mean Descartes and Pascal! The same problems of self so important in the systematic thinking of the modern era were already widely felt. The changes in language and usage, the new words and word forms we find in the seventeenth and eighteenth centuries, are at least suggestive. It is striking, for example, to see the interest as early as the seventeenth century in what was called "character"; and how significant a cultural form character study became. Surely by the nineteenth century *character* was a key word in the vocabulary of Englishmen and Americans.

Philip Reiff has pointed out that as cultures change so do the modal types of persons who are their bearers.[3] By 1800 the concept of character had come to define that particular modal type felt to be essential for the maintenance of the social order. The term itself came to mean a group of traits believed to have social significance and moral quality, "the *sine qua non* of all collective adjustment and social intercourse."[4] In the age of self-consciousness, a popular vision of the self defined by the word "character" became fundamental in sustaining and even in shaping the significant forms of the culture. Such a concept filled two important functions. It proposed a method for both mastery and development of the self. In fact, it argued that its kind of self-control was the way to fullest development of the moral significance of self. But it also provided a method of presenting the self to society, offering a standard of conduct that assured interrelationship between the "social" and the "moral." The importance of character can be most easily established by examination of the hundreds of books, pamphlets, and articles produced during the century, the character studies providing examples for emulation, and the manuals promising a way to character development and worldly success. These were clearly a popular and important cultural form, but further examination of other aspects of the culture—literature, the arts, popular music, and the like—helps reinforce the importance of the concept of character to the culture of the nineteenth century. It was a culture of character.

It is significant in this context to call attention to the other key words most often associated with the concept of character. A review of over two hundred such items reveals the words most frequently related to the notion of character: *citizenship, duty, democracy, work, building, golden deeds, outdoor life, conquest, honor, reputation, morals, manners, integrity,* and above all, *manhood.* The stress was clearly moral and the interest was almost always in some sort of higher moral law. The most popular quotation—it appeared in dozens of works—was Emerson's definition of character: "Moral order through the medium of individual nature."

The problem of self, even as vaguely as it is defined here, thus becomes a fundamental one for almost all modern cultural development. The effort to achieve both a moral and a social order and a freely developing self shapes the cultural products of the times—high, middle, and low culture. The very existence of manuals (obviously necessary among the middle class in terms of their numbers and sales) indicates the reality of the problem. Further investigation would establish, I think, that the patterns of behavior, the institutions developed, the persistence in nineteenth-century America of a predominantly Arminian vision, the insistence on the so-called Protestant ethic, with emphasis on work as essential in a society that was constantly stressing producer values—all these are part of what I have suggested is a culture of character.

These are assertions, not proofs; these are not established propositions. Yet they illustrate my conviction that we can best understand modern cultural developments in all forms if we see and define the particular vision of the self basic to each cultural order. But my fundamental interest in the culture of character lies in the signs of its disappearance and the resulting call for a new modal type best suited to carry out the mission of a newer cultural order. It was not that the culture of character died suddenly or that books and manuals stressing the "character" vision of the self disappeared. In fact they are still being published. But, starting somewhere in the middle of the first decade of the twentieth century, there rapidly developed another vision of self, another vision of self-development and mastery, another method of the presentation of self in society. First, there is clear and growing evidence of an awareness of significant change in the social order, especially after 1880. Symptoms are easily suggested: what was called "American nervousness" and the various efforts at its diagnosis; the rash of utopian writings; the development of systematic sociological and economic analysis in the academic world; the development in government and public journals of a view of the need for "objective" and "scientific" gathering of data and treatment of social ills; and, even more important, the development of psychological and psychiatric studies. This awareness of change also suggested the need for a new kind of man, a new modal type to meet the new conditions. Perhaps few were as specific as Simon Patten and *The New Basis of Civilization* (1909), in which he argued that a society moving from scarcity to abundance required a new self. But it is hard to read the social theorists of the period—Sumner, Ward, Veblen—without some sense of the keen interest in the relation between social orders and psychological types, the belief that a change in the social order almost demanded a change in the people in it.

Writing in the middle of the century about the Renaissance in Italy, Jacob Burckhardt, the greatest of cultural historians, suggested:

> In the Middle Ages both sides of human consciousness—that which was turned within as well as that which was turned without—lay dreaming or half awake beneath a common veil. The veil was woven of faith, illusion, and childish prepossession. . . .

> Man was conscious of himself only as a member of a race, people, party, family, or corporation—only through some general category. In Italy this veil was first melted into air; and *objective* treatment and consideration of the State and all of the things of this world became possible. The *subjective* side at the same time asserted itself with corresponding emphasis. Man became a spiritual *individual* and recognized himself as such. . . . It will not be difficult to show that this result was due above all to the political circumstances of Italy.[5]

This analysis is valuable to us as a model. There is general agreement among historians that some significant material change occurred in the period we are considering. Whether it is a change from a producer to a consumer society, an order of economic accumulation to one of disaccumulation, industrial capitalism to finance capitalism, scarcity to abundance, disorganization to high organization—however that change is defined, it is clear that a new social order was emerging. But even more important than this was the growing awareness on the part of those living through the change that it was in fact occurring and that it was fundamental. The ability to treat this change with increasing "objectivity" made it possible to face the subjective or psychological changes that seemed to be mandated.

All of this is preface to the discovery of the beginnings of a radical shift in the kinds of advice manuals that appeared after the turn of the century, and to new preoccupations, which strike at the heart of the basis of the culture of character. In an important sense, however, the transition began in the very bosom of the old culture. For it was what might be called the other side of Emerson—his vision of a transcendent self—that formed the heart of that New Thought or Mind Cure movement so important in the process from a culture of character to a culture of personality. The key figures—Ralph Waldo Trine, Ella Wheeler Wilcox, Annie Payson Call, Horatio Dresser, Orison Swett Marden—attempted to combine the qualities of the works on character with a religious and even mystical stress on a spiritual vision of the self; they insisted not only on a higher moral order but also on the fulfillment of self by striving to become one with a higher self. As New Thought work proceeded, it was possible to note an increasing interest in self-development along these lines, with somewhat less interest in moral imperatives.

Meanwhile, in the American heartland, a careful reader of Ralph Waldo Trine was developing a method of production along with a new philosophy of industry. The results in all areas were revolutionary. When he made his famous 1907 announcement promising a motor car for the great multitude, he was favoring production, mass consumption, mass society. But he also stressed both the family (it would be a family car) and the individual (the owner could run and care for it). Everyone could have one. It would be made of the best materials by the best men. It would be simple in design. And what was its purpose? To "enjoy . . . the blessings of hours of pleasure in God's open spaces." A machine for pleasure. How much of Ford's world sounds like that of Simon Patten. No more austerity and sacrifice but rather leisure and rational enjoyment for all.[6] The world of the man of Dearborn—with its new ideas of production, consumption, and use—is not part of the culture of character.

It is further a striking part of the turn-of-the-century decade that interest grew in personality, individual idiosyncrasies, personal needs and interests. The vision of self-sacrifice began to yield to that of self-realization. There was fascination with the peculiarities of the self, especially the sick self. Miss Beauchamp, in Dr. Morton Prince's 1905 study *The Dissociation of Personality,* became a figure of popular discussion. At least five major studies of Jesus appeared in the same decade. But in these works the Nazarene is not the healer, the social problem-solver, the achieving man of character and moral exemplar. Rather he is a sick personality, a miserably maladjusted fanatic. So serious was the debate on this analysis that Albert Schweitzer felt called upon to reply to these studies in 1913 with *The Psychiatric Study of Jesus.* And our literature produced the strange heroine of William Vaughan Moody's *The Great Divide* (1909), with her peculiar problems of personality (in its way a precursor of the drama of Eugene O'Neill), and Gertrude Stein's remarkable portraits in *Three Lives* (1906), perhaps in its way a model for Sherwood Anderson's *Winesburg, Ohio* (1919). Literature was interested increasingly in probing personality and less in studying moral or social achievement in the more traditional way of a culture of character.

But even without these hints the evidence is readily available in hundreds of manuals and guides for self-improvement published between 1900 and 1920. One of Raymond Williams' "keywords," *personality,* is a modern term.[7] It appears in the late eighteenth century, and there is some evidence of its modern usage in the nineteenth century. While there are examples of its use by Emerson and Henry Adams, Walt Whitman alone, to my knowledge, made frequent and consistent use of the word in its current sense in the last century. By the first decade of this century, it was an important part of the American vocabulary. It is in that decade as well that a series of volumes and articles began to appear addressed to the problem of helping people develop their personalities. From the start *personality* was distinguished from *character.* In 1915 Funk and Wagnalls published a series of self-help books, their *Mental Efficiency Series.* (*Efficiency* and *energy* are also important words with significantly increased usage in the new culture of personality.) The series contains volumes on both character (How to Strengthen It") and personality ("How to Build It"). From the beginning the adjectives most frequently associated with personality suggest a very different concept from that of character: *fascinating, stunning, attractive, magnetic, glowing, masterful, creative, dominant, forceful.* These words would seldom if ever be used to modify the word *character.* One writer makes the point: character, he insists, is either good or bad; personality, famous or infamous.[8]

"Personality is the quality of being Somebody."[9] This definition—repeated in various ways in almost all of the manuals I have analyzed—is also a major theme of this literature. The problem is clear. We live now constantly in a crowd; how can we distinguish ourselves from others in that crowd? While the term is never used, the question is clearly one of life in a mass society (*crowd* is the most commonly used word). Since we live in such a world it is important to develop one's self—that is, those traits, "moral, intellectual, physical, and practical," that will enable us to think of ourselves and have others think of us as "somebodies." "To create a personality is power," one manual writer insists.[10] One does this by being "conscious of yourself and of others," by being discerning and sincere, by showing energy, by paying attention to others so that they will pay attention to you.

To be somebody one must be oneself (whatever that means). It is an almost too perfect irony that most of the works published and sold in large numbers as self-help in developing an effective personality insist that individuals should be "themselves" and *not* follow the advice or direction of others. The importance of being different, special, unusual, or standing out in a crowd—all of this is emphasized at the same time that specific directions are provided for achieving just those ends. In virtually the same breath, the reader is also urged repeatedly to "express your individuality" and to "eliminate the little personal whims, habit, traits that make people dislike you. Try in every way to have a ready command of the niceties, the manners, the ways of speech, etc. which make people think 'he's a mighty likable fellow.' That is the beginning of a reputation for personality."[11] Thus "personality," like "character" is an effort to solve the problem of self in a changed social structure that imposes its own special demands on the self. Once again, such a popular view of self proposes a method of both self-mastery and self-development as well as a method of the presentation of that self in society. Both methods differed from those proposed in the culture of character and they underpin the development of a new culture, the culture of personality.

This was also, of course, the age of Freud and psychoanalysis. Philip Rieff has argued that "psychoanalysis defends the private man against the demands of both culture and instinct." He asserts that this era was one dominated by a new character type, "psychological man."

> We will recognize in the case history of psychological man the nervous habits of his father, economic man, he is anti-heroic, shrewd, carefully counting his satisfactions and dissatisfactions, studying unprofitable commitments as the sins most to be

> avoided. From this immediate ancestor, psychological man has constructed his own careful economy of the inner life . . . and lives by the mastery of his own personality.[12]

In a general sense, the popular personality manuals I have investigated establish essentially the same new character type Rieff sees as the consequence of Freud's influence. I do not mean to suggest that Freudian theory is implicit in these works (although in the 1920s Freud was often explicitly cited on occasion to support the general position advanced). I mean rather that a vision of the self and its problems generated in large part by an awareness of a significant change in the social structure contains certain basic attitudes comparable to those of Rieff's "psychological man." Freud, without doubt an intellectual genius, lived after all in the social world. What I am suggesting is that general social attitudes exist in popular thought before the formal "ideas" expressing them rise to the level of general understanding. This is perhaps why so many ideas of major thinkers do finally win popular acceptance.

In the particular case under study, there is a striking example. Even in the early personality manuals in the first decade of the century there is singular emphasis not only on the need for self-confidence but also on the importance of not feeling "inferior." Not only are there constant warnings against the dangers of feeling inferior (if one harbors such feelings, one can never impress others and will always exhibit, as a result, a weak personality), but there is a positive injunction to appear superior (but not overly or aggressively so). This attitude was important long before Alfred Adler explained to the world the significance of the "inferiority complex" late in the 1920s.

A brief examination of two works by one of the most popular writers of the period will serve to press home the importance of the change in emphasis from character to personality. In 1899 Orson Swett Marden published *Character: The Greatest Thing in the World.* Crowded with character studies of special historical heroes as exemplars, this book dwells most particularly on the "mental and moral traits," the "high ideals," the "balance" that make character and therefore bring success in the world. Being a true Christian gentleman, pure, upright, intelligent, strong, and brave, possessing a sense of duty, having benevolence, moral courage, personal integrity, and the "highest kinship of soul," devoting service to mankind, being attentive to the "highest and most harmonious development of one's powers" to achieve "a complete and consistent whole"—these are the key words and phrases used in support of the argument. In the course of the volume, Marden stresses the basic values necessary in a producer-oriented society, including hard work (the "sacredness of one's work") and thrift. He ends the book with a powerful appeal. Quoting President Garfield ("I must succeed in making myself a man"),

Marden insists that character above all means, for those interested in developing it, "Let him first be a Man."

In 1921 Marden published *Masterful Personality.* It suggests a remarkably different set of interests. In this book Marden addresses himself to "man's mysterious atmosphere," the aura and power of personality that can "sway great masses." Against the profound dangers of feeling inferior, he proposes a search for supremacy. Much attention is focused on "personal charm." He urges women not only to rely on physical beauty but also to develop "fascination." The ability to attract and hold friends is important. "You can," Marden insists, "compel people to like you." "So much of our success in life depends upon what others think of us." Manners, proper clothes, good conversation ("to know *what* to say and *how* to say it"), energy, "life efficiency," poise—these are the concerns of this volume. In the course of 20 years Marden had come to see the need for a different character type.[13]

The older vision of self expressed in the concept of character was founded in an inner contradiction. That vision argued that the highest development of self ended in a version of self-control or self-mastery, which often meant fulfillment through sacrifice in the name of a higher law, ideals of duty, honor, integrity. One came to selfhood through obedience to law and ideals. Brilliantly sustaining the human needs of a producer-oriented society, it urged in effect a sublimation of self-needs or their redefinition in Arminian terms. But the newer vision of personality also had its paradox. It stressed self-fulfillment, self-expression, self-gratification so persistently that almost all writers as an afterthought gave a warning against intolerable selfishness, extreme self-confidence, excessive assertions of personal superiority. But the essential antinomian vision of this, with its view not of a higher law but of a higher self, was tempered by the suggestion that the self ought to be presented to society in such a way as to make oneself "well liked." There is an obvious difficulty here. One is to be unique, be distinctive, follow one's own feelings, make oneself stand out from the crowd, and at the same time appeal—by fascination, magnetism, attractiveness—to it.

Both visions of self—visions I argue shaped the very nature of the culture—are assumed from the start not to be natural but to be things that can be learned and practiced, through exercise and by study of guidebooks to success. Both visions relate to the needs of a particular social structure and do not develop in an atmosphere of pure philosophical speculation. The older vision no longer suited personal or social needs; the newer vision seemed particularly suited for the problems of the self in a changed social order, the developing consumer mass society.

The new personality literature stressed items that could be best developed in leisure time and that represented in themselves an emphasis on consumption. The social role demanded of all in the new culture of personality was that of a performer. Every American was to become a performing self. Every work studied stressed the importance of the human voice in describing methods of voice control and proper methods of conversation or public speaking. Everyone was expected to impress and influence with trained and effective speech. Special books and courses were developed to meet demands in this area alone. In these books and articles exercise, proper breathing, sound eating habits, a good complexion, and grooming and beauty aids were all stressed. At the same time, clothing, personal appearance, and "good manners" were important, but there was little interest in morals. Poise and charm top the list of necessary traits and there was insistence that they could be learned and developed through careful practice. The new stress on the enjoyment of life implied that true pleasure could be attained by making oneself pleasing to others.

Often the books stressed the role of personality in business success. *Personality in Business,* a series of 50 articles on every aspect of business activity by some of the most distinguished businessmen and publicists of the period, was first issued in 1906 and then reprinted in 1910 and 1916. The new stress on personality in business, in fact, led to a reaction by some of the older character-based authors. George Horace Lorimer, in his 1902 best seller, *Letters from a Self-Made Merchant to His Son,* specifically warned against the attempt to be popular, suggesting that the effort took too much time and was not always successful in a business way. But in general the personality manuals move away from an interest in business or even financial success and provide a newer definition of what constitutes genuine success in life.[14]

The new interest in personality—both the unique qualities of an individual and the performing self that attracts others—was not limited to self-help authors in this period. It extended to participants in the high culture as well. In 1917 Ezra Pound pleaded for the struggle that would assure what he called "the rights of personality," and even earlier he had insisted to a friend that mass society created a world in which man was continually being used by others. For him, *the* issue of the modern world was "the survival of personality." Earlier, Herbert Croly explained in *The Promise of American Life* (1909) that "success in any . . . pursuit demands that an individual make some sort of personal impression." Painters, architects, politicians, all depend "upon a numerous and faithful body of admirers." Emancipation, self-expression, excellent work are all meaningless unless such gifted individuals have the support of a following. This is only one of many works in the period that stress the role of personal magnetism in leadership. And in 1913 Randolph Bourne pleaded with young radicals to understand the new order of things, which included the importance of personality, sincerity, and the like, and which is interpreted in terms of these attainments. In stressing the importance of influence Bourne proposed that nothing was so important as a "most glowing personality." Self-cultivation, he maintained, "becomes almost a duty, if one wants to be effective towards the great end (the regeneration of the social order). And not only personality, but prestige."[15]

At the outset of the century, Nathaniel Southgate Shaler wrote in *The Individual* (1900), which he insisted was a purely scientific analysis, a central chapter on "Expression of the Individuality." Here he demonstrated the importance of what he called "modes of externalization," the ways people gain the attention of others. He believed these things are done not simply for gain or esteem but because there is an instinctive need "to externalize the self." He saw this in dress and fashion, in song and speech, in the richness of language. Each culture, he suggested, has different "motives of self-presentation." The key to all expression of self, however, is the face. We are, in Shaler's view, all actors, and the face has the power of an instrument able to express intellect as well as emotion.

The test of the general approach proposed in this paper would be a more specific analysis of the cultural forms of our century to see whether in fact they share the characteristics of a culture of personality, whether they can be examined as manifestations of the working out of the basic ideas central to this vision of self. Investigations have convinced me that most cultural forms studied to date reveal a kinship to the culture of personality. Comic strips, radio programs, even beauty pageants have yielded evidence of significant dependence on these ideas. For purposes of this paper, however, I want to offer only one example. I am convinced that the nature and form of the modern motion picture as it developed as a middle-class popular art between 1910 and 1915 clearly show its participation in the culture of personality. Technically, the film, especially in the hands of its major developer as a middle-class art, D. W. Griffith, and those who followed him, depended on two major modes and used them dramatically in startling juxtaposition. The first was the handling of vast groups of people. Vachel Lindsay in his brilliant 1915 book on film speaks of the role of what he calls "crowd splendor" in motion pictures.[16] Films are not only a mass medium, they also represent one of the major ways in which a mass society can examine itself as mass. There was from the start of serious motion pictures an intimate relationship between it and the portraying of the role of crowds. To the depiction of the crowd, and often in striking contrast to it, Griffith added the extraordinary form of the closeup. Almost as if he were following the teachings of Shaler, the face, bigger than life and abstracted from it, provides a brilliant expression of self, of an individual. The importance of this contrast—the mass and the isolated individual apart from that mass—to the development of film, and thus of film's role in the culture of personality, cannot be exaggerated.

Up to 1910, motion picture studios generally concealed the identity of most screen players. In 1910, however, the idea of the movie star was born. The creation of the star changed the nature of the role of motion pictures in our society. It brought into even more prominent use the press agent and modern advertising. "Henceforth, a screen player was to be marketed for her admirers as a personality, an image and, to an increasingly sinister extent, an object," the historian of the star system suggests.[17] This immediately leads to fan magazines and to a new consciousness of the importance of personality. It leads, in fact, to a new profession—that of being a movie star or a celebrity. In the culture of character, the public had insisted on some obvious correlation between achievement and fame. Now that insistence is gone. The very definition of reality was altered, as Richard Schickel explains in his suggestive study of Douglas Fairbanks, Sr.: "Indeed, it is now essential that the politician, the man of ideas, and the non-performing artist become performers so that they may become celebrities so that in turn they may exert genuine influence on the general public."[18] Fairbanks himself was dedicated not to his art but to himself. As early as 1907 a famous actress said of him that he would be famous in films: "He's not good looking. But he has worlds of personality."

Fairbanks is important to us in this analysis. He becomes one of those symbols social structures generate—and in this case an active agent as well. Not only was he a star and a topnotch public relations man, but he also wrote his own kind of self-help books *(Make Life Worth-While, Laugh and Live)* and a column in one of the leading movie magazines. He provided a link between the pioneers for the new self-help literature and the new social world that Henry Ford was building. In 1928, Ralph Waldo Trine published *The Power That Wins,* the report of an intimate talk on life with Henry Ford. Trine begins his conversation with Ford by recalling a trip to Hollywood and a visit to Douglas Fairbanks. He assumes, of course, that Fairbanks doesn't know who he is.

> "Don't I?" he replied. "Just wait until I show you a specially inscribed copy of *In Tune with the Infinite* that Henry Ford sent me."
>
> MR. FORD. Yes, I remember sending that book to Mr. Fairbanks. Back in 1914, when my associates and I were working out some very difficult problems here, some of your books were of great help to me. I used to keep a stock of your books in my office, to give to friends or associates who, I thought would be benefited by them as the same as I.[19]

Trine, Ford, Fairbanks, three major figures in the transition from a culture of character to a culture of personality, are here neatly linked together.

If Fairbanks was at the beginning of this world of stars and press agents, we know that it was only the beginning. There *are* ideas in things (maybe *only* in things, as William Carlos Williams insists), but we are only beginning to understand our cultural developments in terms of the system of ideas on which they are in fact based, the system of ideas inherent in the cultural forms we study. Movies suggest many explorations not yet undertaken. For films have been an agency fundamental for the generation of the key symbols for our social structure. Complete with stars and even gods and goddesses, housed in places that (even down to the massive organ) resemble huge cathedrals, motion pictures became for thousands a new religion (perhaps a special religion for the antinomians of the twentieth century). No wonder some more fundamentalist Protestant religionists forbid movie-going to their congregants. They know a surrogate or competing religious order when they see one.

A Concluding, Most Unscientific, Postscript

Some unproven assertions about the emergence of a culture of personality in twentieth-century America lead me to attempt to confirm these speculations. Convinced that the nature of cultural development specifically depends for its forms on the existing vision of self—in terms of its definition of its problem in development and presentation in society—I am also anxious to press the analysis further and account for the significant changes clearly visible in our cultural history during the century. Thus within the culture of personality there are divisions based on special readings of the problem of personality at different times within the whole range and in response to shifts in social structure. In the period from 1910 through the late 1920s, the problem was most often defined in terms of guilt and the need to eliminate guilt. One might think of this period, at least metaphorically, as the age of Freud—not so much in terms of direct influence but rather in terms of the point of view from which the culture viewed its problem of self. I have already argued elsewhere that the period from 1929 to 1938 might be seen as one dominated by the problem of shame, and I have, again metaphorically, called this the age of Alfred Adler. From 1939 through the late 1940s we do not need to invent a name. The period self-consciously thought of itself as the age of anxiety. The major concern for moral, national identity and character led increasingly to an interest in myth, to a search for some collective unconscious brought to awareness. Let me call this the age of Jung. From the end of the 1940s to almost the end of the 1950s the problem was fundamentally redefined as that of personal identity. Who could object to seeing this as the age of Erik Erikson? The 1960s and the profound interest in liberation, especially sexual liberation, provided still another modification in the culture of personality. Perhaps this will be known as the age of Wilhelm Reich. I refuse to speculate on the immediate present for fear I will be regarded as irresponsible. Yet, wild as these speculations may seem, I remain convinced that the changes in culture do mean changes in modal types of character and that social structures do generate their own symbols. Intellectual historians would do well to begin to see ideas in things and to see that there is in fact some connection between the most ethereal of ideas and common, and even basic, human behavior.

1984

Notes

1. Owen Barfield, *History in English Words* (London, 1954), p. 166.
2. The essay "A Difficulty in the Path of Psycho-Analysis" is reprinted in *Standard Edition of the Collected Psychological Works of Sigmund Freud,* 23 vols. (London, 1955), XVII, 135–144.
3. Philip Rieff, *The Triumph of the Therapeutic Uses of Faith after Freud* (New York, 1966), p. 2.
4. A. A. Roback in the article "Character" in the *Encyclopaedia of the Social Sciences,* 14 vols. (New York, 1930), III, 335.
5. Jacob Burckhardt, *The Civilization of the Renaissance in Italy* (New York, 1954), pp. 100–101.
6. I have developed this analysis at greater length in a piece on Henry Ford, "Piety, Profits, and Play: The 1920s," in *Men, Women, and Issues in American History,* ed. A. Quint and M. Cantor, 2 vols. (Homewood, Ill., 1975), II, Chapter 10.
7. Raymond Williams, *Keywords: A Vocabulary of Culture and Society* (New York, 1976), pp. 194–197. The word "character" does not appear in Mr. Williams's study.
8. Henry Laurent, *Personality: How to Build It* (New York, 1915), p. iv. This volume was translated from the French by Richard Duff.
9. Ibid., p. 25.
10. Ibid., pp. iv, 29. I have used this manual as typical. Part 1 deals with the "building" of personality, and Part 2 with "how to impress." It stresses self-control as a way to control others. I find all of the themes of other manuals studied stated here more boldly and precisely.
11. B. C. Bean, *Power of Personality* (Meriden, Conn., 1920), p. 3. This is one of a series of pamphlets called The Science of Organizing Personal Powers for Success.
12. Philip Rieff, *Freud: The Mind of a Moralist* (New York, 1961), pp. 391–392. The whole of Chapter 10, "The Emergence of Psychological Man," makes an important statement.
13. Orison Swett Marden, *Character, The Greatest Thing in the World* (New York, 1899), pp. 7, 11, 16, 21, 25, 30, 37, 50; idem, *Masterful Personality* (New York, 1921), pp. 1, 3, 17, 23, 33, 68, 291.
14. George Horace Lorimer, *Letters from a Self-Made Merchant to His Son* (New York, 1902). See especially pp. 40, 88–89. This is striking in almost all the self-help manuals studied. There is clearly a relationship between this new definition of success and the contemporary religious interest in personality. I address this issue in another paper, "The Religion of Per-

sonality and Personality as a Religion." This issue is of considerable importance to the theme I am attempting to develop. In this context let me cite only one of many theologians and philosophers on the importance of personality, J. Herman Randall, in *The Culture of Personality* (New York, 1912), p. xiii: "[Personality] is by far the greatest work in the history of the human mind. [It is the key] that unlocks the deeper mysteries of Science and Philosophy, of History and Literature, of Art and Religion, of all of man's ethical and social relationships."

15. Ezra Pound, "Provincialism the Enemy," *The New Age,* XXI (July 19, 1917), 268–269. See also letter to Margaret Anderson, reprinted in her *My Thirty Years War* (New York, 1930), p. 171. Herbert Croly, *The Promise of American Life* (New York, 1909), p. 432. His whole analysis of individualism and leadership can be best understood in terms of the premises of this paper. In another paper, "Leadership and Public Opinion in a Culture of Personality," I deal with the implications in political theory and especially in political rhetoric in the period from 1890 to 1920. Randolph Bourne, *Youth and Life* (New York, 19813), p. 294.
16. Nathaniel Southgate Shaler, *The Individual: A study of Life and Death* (New York, 1900), Chapter 7. Vachel Lindsay, *The Art of the Moving Picture* (New York, 1915). There was a revised edition in 1922. It remains a classic work for all cultural historians.
17. Alexander Walker, *Stardom: The Hollywood Phenomenon* (New York, 1970), p. 36.
18. Richard Schickel, *His Picture in the Papers: A Speculation on Celebrity in America Based on the Life of Douglas Fairbanks, Sr.* (New York, 1974), p. 9.
19. Ralph Waldo Trine, *The Power That Wins* (Indianapolis, Ind., 1928), pp. 2–3.

GETTING STARTED

1. What are the defining aspects of a culture of "character" versus a culture of "personality"? Working individually or in groups, list terms associated with each concept. Choose one term from each column, and find one example in the essay that helps to explain the difference between them. Present your findings to the class.

2. Susman uses the changes he has observed in "personality manuals" to describe the inner contradictions or paradoxes that accompanied both the old and new visions of the self. Reread that section (pp. 484–488), discuss it in a group, and then write a one-paragraph summary of Susman's points.

3. Collect examples from current movies, comic strips, advertisements, magazines, and television shows that demonstrate how Americans view the "self" today. Working in groups, test Susman's definition of the culture of personality against your examples. Do

your examples confirm or refute Susman's theory? Focus on psychology, self-expression, and celebrity. What elements in the examples, if any, suggest the older model of character? Do some elements in the examples suggest a new model of the self that Susman does not foresee?

WRITING

4. Write a paper based on your findings from questions 3 and 7. Choose one or two of the examples that your group assembled from movies, self-help books, comic strips, advertisements, and television shows that best demonstrate how Americans currently view the self. Use those examples to test how well Susman's definition of the culture of personality continues to apply to our contemporary ways of viewing the self. To test Susman's theory, you will need to summarize and explain it. Use the list of characteristics and one or two examples from Susman's essay to show what he means by the "culture of personality."

5. Analyze the rhetorical features of Susman's essay. Who is his audience? What is his purpose in writing? Who is he as an author? What is his argument? Use quotations from the text as evidence to support your conclusions. Pay close attention to tone and style as well as to content.

6. Review your work from question 1. Write a one-page paper in which you contrast several crucial aspects of cultures of character and cultures of personality. Use one or two examples from Susman to help explain the difference.

USING THE LIBRARY AND THE INTERNET

7. Do an Internet search for contemporary self-help books, tapes, videos, and classes. How do the advice and approaches of these materials compare and contrast to the personality manuals that Susman describes? Print out your best examples. Working in small groups, discuss your findings. What promises do these contemporary self-help manuals make? What aspect of the individual do they focus on? Do they rely on the concept of character or of personality?

8. Using a reference database that includes a range of scholarly sources, such as Academic Search Elite or a similar database recommended by your reference librarian, try various search terms from Susman: "public debate," "public debate and democracy," "argument and democracy." For each search, scan the results for

articles that support, challenge, or extend Susman's ideas and note how the number and type of sources varies with each search. Bring some of your most interesting findings to class.

MAKING CONNECTIONS

9. Is the transition from a culture of character to one of personality an example of a paradigm shift? Review Thomas Kuhn's essay, "The Historical Structure of Scientific Discovery," and write your own working definition of "paradigm shift." Use that definition to help you write an essay that answers the question. Can Kuhn's descriptions of the scientific community apply to the general public as well?

10. How does Susman's concept of the culture of personality affect your understanding of the ethical debates over cloning as described by Michio Kaku and Richard C. Lewontin? If, as Susman argues, culture can change character, can genetics in turn change culture? Would a clone from one culture have a different character than a clone from another culture? Write a paper in which you explore these ideas.

Jane Tompkins

Jane Tompkins (1940–   ) is a professor in the School of Education at the University of Illinois, Chicago. Before moving to UIC, Tompkins was Professor of English at Duke University. She is the author of *Sensational Designs: The Cultural Work of American Fiction, 1790–1860* (1985), a book widely credited with renewing scholarly interest in the writing of nineteenth-century American women. Tompkins has also written *West of Everything: The Inner Life of Westerns* (1992), from which "At the Buffalo Bill Museum, June 1988" was taken, and *A Life in School: What the Teacher Learned* (1996).

To explore an alternate view of Plains Indian culture, visit the home page for the Plains Indians Cultural Survival School at <http://www.cbe.ab.ca/b864/default.htm>.

At the Buffalo Bill Museum, June 1988

The video at the entrance to the Buffalo Bill Historical Center says that Buffalo Bill was the most famous American of his time, that by 1900 more than a billion words had been written about him, and that he had a progressive vision of the West. Buffalo Bill had worked as a cattle driver, a wagoneer, a Pony Express rider, a buffalo hunter for the railroad, a hunting guide, an army scout and sometime Indian fighter; he wrote dime novels about himself and an autobiography by the age of thirty-four, by which time he was already famous; and then he began another set of careers, first as an actor, performing on the urban stage in wintertime melodramatic representations of what he actually earned a living at in the summer (scouting and leading hunting expeditions), and finally becoming the impresario of his great Wild West show, a form of entertainment he invented and carried on as actor, director, and all-around idea man for thirty years. Toward the end of his life he founded the town of Cody, Wyoming, to which he gave, among other things, two hundred thousand dollars. Strangely enough, it was as a progressive civic leader that Bill Cody wanted to be remembered. "I don't want to die," the video at the entrance quotes him as saying, "and have people say—oh, there goes another old showman. . . . I would like people to say—this is the man who opened Wyoming to the best of civilization."

FIGURE 28 Photograph of Buffalo Bill. (Courtesy of the Buffalo Bill Memorial Museum and the Denver Parks and Recreation Department, Denver, Colorado.)

"The best of civilization." This was the phrase that rang in my head as I moved through the museum, which is one of the most disturbing places I have ever visited. It is also a wonderful place. It is four museums in one: the Whitney Gallery of Western Art, which houses artworks on Western subjects; the Buffalo Bill Museum proper, which memorializes Cody's life; the Plains Indian Museum, which exhibits artifacts of American Indian civilization; and the Winchester Arms Museum, a collection of firearms historically considered.

The whole operation is extremely well designed and well run, from the video program at the entrance that gives an overview of all four museums, to the fresh-faced young attendants wearing badges that say "Ask Me," to the museum shop stacked with books on Western Americana, to the ladies room—a haven of satiny marble, shining mirrors, and flattering light. Among other things, the museum is admirable for its effort to combat prevailing stereotypes about the "winning of the West," a phrase it self-consciously places in quotation marks. There are placards declaring that all history is a matter of interpretation, and that the American West is a source of myth. Everywhere, except perhaps in the Winchester Arms Museum, where the rhetoric is different, you feel the effort of the museum staff to reach out to the public, to be clear, to be accurate, to be fair, not to condescend—in short, to educate in the best sense of the term.

On the day I went, the museum was featuring an exhibition of Frederic Remington's works. Two facts about Remington make his work different from that of artists usually encountered in museums. The first is that Remington's paintings and statues function as a historical record. Their chief attraction has always been that they transcribe scenes and events that have vanished from the earth. The second fact, related to this, is the brutality of their subject matter. Remington's work makes you pay attention to what is happening in the painting or the piece of statuary. When you look at his work you cannot escape from the subject.

Consequently, as I moved through the exhibit, the wild contortions of the bucking broncos, the sinister expression invariably worn by the Indians, and the killing of animals and men made the placards discussing Remington's use of the "lost wax" process seem strangely disconnected. In the face of unusual violence, or implied violence, their message was: what is important here is technique. Except in the case of paintings showing the battle of San Juan Hill, where white Americans were being killed, the material accompanying Remington's works did not refer to the subject matter of the paintings and statues themselves. Nevertheless, an undertone of disquiet ran beneath the explanations; at least I thought I detected one. Someone had taken the trouble to ferret out Remington's statement of horror at the slaughter on San Juan Hill; someone had also excerpted the judgment of art critics commending Remington for the lyricism, interiority, and mystery of his later canvasses—pointing obliquely to the fascination with bloodshed that preoccupied his earlier work.

The uneasiness of the commentary, and my uneasiness with it, were nothing compared to the blatant contradictions in the paintings themselves. A pastel palette, a sunlit stop-action haze, murderous movement arrested under a lazy sky, flattened onto canvas and fixed in azure and ochre—two opposed impulses nestle here momentarily. The tension that keeps them from splitting apart is what holds the viewer's gaze.

The most excruciating example of what I mean occurs in the first painting in the exhibit. Entitled *His First Lesson,* it shows a horse standing saddled but riderless, the white of the horse's eye signaling his fear. A man using an instrument to tighten the horse's girth, at arm's length, backs away from the reaction he clearly anticipates, while the man who holds the horse's halter is doing the same. But what can they be afraid of? For the horse's right rear leg is tied a foot off the ground by a rope that is also tied around his neck. He can't move. That is the whole point.

His First Lesson. Whose? And what lesson, exactly? How to stand still when terrified? How not to break away when they come at you with strange instruments? How to be obedient? How to behave? It is impossible not to imagine that Remington's obsession with physical cruelty had roots somewhere in his own experience. Why else, in statue after statue, is the horse rebelling? The bucking bronco, symbol

FIGURE 29 *His First Lesson,* by Frederic Remington, 1903. Oil on canvas. (Courtesy of the Amon Carter Museum, Fort Worth, Texas. Accession no. 1961.231.)

of the state of Wyoming, on every license plate, on every sign for every bar, on every belt buckle, mug, and decal—this image Remington cast in bronze over and over again. There is a wild diabolism in the bronzes; the horse and rider seem one thing, not so much rider and ridden as a single bolt of energy gone crazy and caught somehow, complicatedly, in a piece of metal.

In the paintings, it is different—more subtle and bizarre. The cavalry on its way to a massacre, sweetly limned, softly tinted, poetically seized in mid-career, and gently laid on the two-dimensional surface. There is about these paintings of military men in the course of performing their deadly duty an almost maternal tenderness. The idealization of the cavalrymen in their dusty uniforms on their gallant horses has nothing to do with patriotism; it is pure love.

Remington's paintings and statues, as shown in this exhibition, embody everything that was objectionable about his era in American history. They are imperialist and racist; they glorify war and the torture and killing of animals; there are no women in them anywhere. Never the West as garden, never as pastoral, never as home. But in their aestheticization of violent life, Remington's pictures speak (to me, at least) of some other desire. The maternal tenderness is not an accident, nor is the beauty of the afternoons or the warmth of the desert sun. In them Remington plays the part of the preserver, as if by catching the figures in color and line he could save their lives and absorb some of that life into himself.

FIGURE 30 Frederic Remington, *Coming to the Call.* (Courtesy of Frederic Remington Art Museum, Ogdensburg, N.Y.)

In one painting that particularly repulsed and drew me, a moose is outlined against the evening sky at the brink of a lake. He looks expectantly into the distance. Behind him and to one side, hidden from his view and only just revealed to ours, for it is dark there, is a hunter poised in the back of a canoe, rifle perfectly aimed. We look closer; the title of the picture is *Coming to the Call.* Ah, now we see. This is a sadistic scene. The hunter has lured the moose to his death. But wait a moment. Isn't the sadism really directed at us? First we see the glory of the animal; Remington has made it as noble as he knows how. Then we see what is going to happen. The hunter is one up on the moose, but Remington is one up on us. He makes us feel the pain of the anticipated killing, and makes us want to hold it off, to preserve the moose, just as he has done. Which way does the painting cut? Does it go against the hunter—who represents us, after all—or does it go against the moose who came to the call? Who came, to what call? Did Remington come to the West in response to it—to whatever the moose represents or to whatever the desire to kill the moose represents? But he hasn't killed it; he has only preserved an image of a white man about to kill it. And what call do we answer when we look at this painting? Who is calling whom? What is being preserved here?

The last question is the one that for me hung over the whole museum.

The Whitney Gallery is an art museum proper. Its allegiance is to art as academic tradition has defined it. In this tradition, we come to understand a painting by having in our possession various bits of information. Something about the technical process used to produce it (pastels, watercolors, woodblock prints, etc.); something about the elements of composition (line and color and movement); something about the artist's life (where born, how educated, by whom influenced, which school belonged to or revolted against); something about the artist's relation to this particular subject, such as how many times the artist painted it or whether it contains a favorite model. Occasionally there will be some philosophizing about the themes or ideas the paintings are said to represent.

The problem is, when you're faced with a painter like Remington, these bits of information, while nice to have, don't explain what is there in front of you. They don't begin to give you an account of why a person would have depicted such things. The experience of a lack of fit between the explanatory material and what is there on the wall is one I've had before in museums, when, standing in front of a painting or a piece of statuary, I've felt a huge gap between the information on the little placard and what it is I'm seeing. I realize that works of art, so-called, all have a subject matter, are all engaged with life, with some piece of life no less significant, no less compelling than Remington's subjects are, if we could only see its force. The idea that art is somehow separate from history, that it somehow occupies a space that is not the same as the space of life, seems out of whack here.

I wandered through the gallery thinking these things because right next to it, indeed all around it, in the Buffalo Bill Museum proper and in the Plains Indian Museum, are artifacts that stand not for someone's expertise or skill in manipulating the elements of an artistic medium, but for life itself; they are the residue of life.

The Buffalo Bill Museum is a wonderful array of textures, colors, shapes, sizes, forms. The fuzzy brown bulk of a buffalo's hump, the sparkling diamonds in a stickpin, the brilliant colors of the posters—the mixture makes you want to walk in and be surrounded by it, as if you were going into a child's adventure story. For a moment you can pretend you're a cowboy too; it's a museum where fantasy can take over. For a while.

As I moved through the exhibition, with the phrase "the best of civilization" ringing in my head, I came upon certain objects displayed in a section that recreates rooms from Cody's house. Ostrich feather fans, peacock feather fans, antler furniture—a chair and a table made entirely of antlers—a bearskin rug. And then I saw the heads on the wall: Alaska Yukon Moose, Wapiti American Elk, Muskox (the "Whitney," the "DeRham"), Mountain Caribou (the "Hyland"), Quebec Labrador Caribou (the "Elbow"), Rocky Mountain Goat (the "Haase," the "Kilto"), Woodland Caribou (world's record, "DeRham"), the "Rogers" freak Wapiti, the "Whitney" bison, the "Lord Rundlesham" bison. The names that appear after the animals are the names of the men who killed them. Each of the animals is scored according to measurements devised by the Boone and Crockett Club, a big-game hunters' organization. The Lord Rundlesham bison, for example, scores $124\frac{6}{8}$, making it number 25 in the world for bison trophies. The "Reed" Alaska Yukon Moose scores 247. The "Witherbee" Canada moose holds the world's record.

Next to the wall of trophies is a small enclosure where jewelry is displayed. A buffalo head stickpin and two buffalo head rings, the heads made entirely of diamonds, with ruby eyes, the gifts of the Russian crown prince. A gold and diamond stickpin from Edward VII; a gold, diamond, and garnet locket from Queen Victoria. The two kinds of trophies—animals and jewels—form an incongruous set; the relationship between them compelling but obscure.

If the rest of the items in the museum—the dime novels with their outrageous covers, the marvelous posters, the furniture, his wife's dress, his daughter's oil painting—have faded from my mind it is because I cannot forget the heads of the animals as they stared down, each with an individual expression on its face. When I think about it I realize that I don't know why these animal heads are there. Buffalo Bill didn't kill them; perhaps they were gifts from the famous people he took on hunts. A different kind of jewelry.

After the heads, I began to notice something about the whole exhibition. In one display, doghide chaps, calfskin chaps, angora goathide chaps, and horsehide chaps. Next to these a rawhide lariat and a horsehair quirt. Behind me, boots and saddles, all of leather. Everywhere I looked there was tooth or bone, skin or fur, hide or hair, or the animal itself entire—two full-size buffalo (a main feature of the exhibition) and a magnificent stone sheep (a mountain sheep with beautiful curving horns). This one was another world's record. The best of civilization.

In the literature about Buffalo Bill you read that he was a conservationist, that if it were not for the buffalo in his Wild West shows the species would probably have become extinct. (In the seventeenth century 40 million buffalo roamed North America; by 1900 all the wild buffalo had been killed except for one herd in northern Alberta.) That the man who gained fame first as a buffalo hunter should have been an advocate for conservation of the buffalo is not an anomaly but typical of the period. The men who did the most to preserve America's natural wilderness and its wildlife were big-game hunters. The Boone and Crockett Club, founded by Theodore Roosevelt, George Bird Grinnell, and Owen Wister, turns out to have been one of the earliest organizations to devote itself to environmental protection in the United States. *The Reader's Encyclopedia of the American West* says that the club "supported the national park and forest reserve movement, helped create a system of national wildlife refuges, and lobbied for the protection of threatened species, such as the buffalo and antelope." At the same time, the prerequisites for membership in the club were "the highest caliber of sportsmanship and the achievement of killing 'in fair chase' trophy specimens [which had to be adult males] from several species of North American big game."

The combination big-game hunter and conservationist suggests that these men had no interest in preserving the animals for the animals' sake but simply wanted to ensure the chance to exercise their sporting pleasure. But I think this view is too simple; something further is involved here. The men who hunted game animals had a kind of love for them and a kind of love for nature that led them to want to preserve the animals they also desired to kill. That is, the desire to kill the animals was in some way related to a desire to see them live. It is not an accident, in this connection, that Roosevelt, Wister, and Remington all went west originally for their health. Their devotion to the West, their connection to it, their love for it are rooted in their need to reanimate their own lives. The preservation of nature, in other words, becomes for them symbolic of their own survival.

In a sense, then, there is a relationship between the Remington exhibition in the Whitney Gallery and the animal memorabilia in the Buffalo Bill Museum. The moose in *Coming to the Call* and the mooseheads on the wall are not so different as they might appear. The heads on the wall serve an aesthetic purpose; they are decorative objects, pleasing to the eye, which call forth certain associations. In this sense they are like visual works of art. The painting, on the other hand, has something of the trophy about it. The moose as Remington painted it is about to become a trophy, yet in another sense it already is one. Remington has simply captured the moose in another form. In both cases the subject matter, the life of a wild animal, symbolizes the life of the observer. It is the preservation of that life that both the painting and the taxidermy serve.

What are museums keeping safe for us, after all? What is it that we wish so much to preserve? The things we put in safekeeping, in our safe-deposit boxes under lock and key, are always in some way intended finally as safeguards of our own existence. The money and jewelry and stock certificates are meant for a time when we can no longer earn a living by the sweat of our brows. Similarly, the objects in museums preserve for us a source of life from which we need to nourish ourselves when the resources that would normally supply us have run dry.

The Buffalo Bill Historical Center, full as it is of dead bones, lets us see more clearly than we normally can what it is that museums are for. It is a kind of charnel house that houses images of living things that have passed away but whose life force still lingers around their remains and so passes itself on to us. We go and look at the objects in the glass cases and at the paintings on the wall, as if by standing there we could absorb into ourselves some of the energy that flowed once through the bodies of the live things represented. A museum, rather than being, as we normally think of it, the most civilized of places, a place most distant from our savage selves, actually caters to the urge to absorb the life of another into one's own life.

If we see the Buffalo Bill Museum in this way, it is no longer possible to separate ourselves from the hunters responsible for the trophies with their wondering eyes or from the curators who put them there. We are not, in essence, different from Roosevelt or Remington or Buffalo Bill, who killed animals when they were abundant in the Wild West of the 1880s. If in doing so those men were practicing the ancient art of absorbing the life of an animal into their own through the act of killing it, realizing themselves through the destruction of another life, then we are not so different from them; as visitors to the museum, we stand beside the bones and skins and nails of beings that were once alive, or stare fixedly at their painted images. Indeed our visit is only a safer form of the same enterprise as theirs.

So I did not get out of the Buffalo Bill Museum unscathed, unimplicated in the acts of rapine and carnage that these remains represent. And I did not get out without having had a good time, either, because however many dire thoughts I may have had, the exhibits were interesting and fun to see. I was even able to touch a piece of buffalo hide displayed especially for that purpose (it was coarse and springy). Everyone else had touched it too. The hair was worn down, where people's hands had been, to a fraction of its original length.

After this, the Plains Indian Museum was a terrible letdown. I went from one exhibit to another expecting to become absorbed, but nothing worked. What was the matter? I was interested in Indians, had read about them, taught some Indian literature, felt drawn by accounts of native religions. I had been prepared to enter this museum as if I were going into another children's story, only this time I would be an Indian instead of a cowboy or a cowgirl. But the objects on display, most of them behind glass, seemed paltry and insignificant. They lacked visual presence. The bits of leather and sticks of wood triggered no fantasies in me.

At the same time, I noticed with some discomfort that almost everything in those glass cases was made of feathers and claws and hide, just like the men's chaps and ladies' fans in the Buffalo Bill Museum, only there was no luxury here. Plains Indian culture, it seemed, was made entirely from animals. Their mode of life had been even more completely dedicated to carnage than Buffalo Bill's, dependent as it was on animals for food, clothing, shelter, equipment, everything. In the Buffalo Bill Museum I was able to say to myself, well, if these men had been more sensitive, if they had had a right relation to their environment and to life itself, the atrocities that produced these trophies would never have occurred. They never would have exterminated the Indians and killed off the buffalo. But the spectacle before me made it impossible to say that. I had expected that the Plains Indian Museum would show me how life in nature ought to be lived: not the mindless destruction of nineteenth-century America but an ideal form of communion with animals and the land. What the museum seemed to say instead was that cannibalism was universal. Both colonizer and colonized had had their hands imbrued with blood. The Indians had lived off animals and had made war against one another. Violence was simply a necessary and inevitable part of life. And a person who, like me, was horrified at the extent of the destruction was just the kind of romantic idealist my husband sometimes accused me of being. There was no such thing as the life lived in harmony with nature. It was all bloodshed and killing, an unending cycle, over and over again, and no one could escape.

But perhaps there was a way to understand the violence that made it less terrible. Perhaps if violence was necessary, a part of nature, intended by the universe, then it could be seen as sacramental. Perhaps it was true, what Calvin Martin had said in *Keepers of the Game:* that the Indians had a sacred contract with the animals they killed, that they respected them as equals and treated their remains with honor and punctilio. If so, the remains of animals in the Plains Indian Museum weren't the same as those left by Buffalo Bill and his friends. They certainly didn't look the same. Perhaps. All I knew for certain was that these artifacts, lifeless and shrunken, spoke to me of nothing I could understand. No more did the life-size models of Indians, with strange featureless faces, draped in costumes that didn't look like clothing. The figures, posed awkwardly in front of tepees too white to seem real, carried no sense of a life actually lived, any more than the objects in the glass cases had.

The more I read the placards on the wall, the more disaffected I became. Plains Indian life apparently had been not only bloody but exceedingly tedious. All those porcupine quills painstakingly softened, flattened, dyed, then appliqued through even more laborious methods of stitching or weaving. Four methods of attaching porcupine quills, six design groups, population statistics, patterns of migration. There wasn't any glamour here at all. No glamour in the lives the placards told about, no glamour in the objects themselves, no glamour in the experience of looking at them. Just a lot of shriveled things accompanied by some even drier information.

Could it be, then, that the problem with the exhibitions was that Plains Indian culture, if representable at all, was simply not readable by someone like me? Their stick figures and abstract designs could convey very little to an untrained Euro-American eye. One display in particular illustrated this. It was a piece of cloth, behind glass, depicting a buffalo skin with some marks on it. The placard read: "Winter Count, Sioux ca. 1910, after Lone Dog's, Fort Peck, Montana, 1877." The hide with its markings had been a calendar, each year represented by one image, which showed the most significant event in the life of the tribe. A thick pamphlet to one side of the glass case explained each image year by year: 1800–1801, the attack of the Uncapoo on a Crow Indian Fort; 1802–1803, a total eclipse of the sun. The images, once you knew what they represented, made sense, and seemed poetic interpretations of the experiences they stood for. But without explanation they were incomprehensible.

The Plains Indian Museum stopped me in my tracks. It was written in a language I had never learned. I didn't have the key. Maybe someone did, but I wasn't too sure. For it may not have been just cultural difference that made the text unreadable. I began to suspect that the text itself was corrupt, that the architects of this museum were going through motions whose purpose was, even to themselves, obscure. Knowing what event a figure stands for in the calendar doesn't mean you understand an Indian year. The deeper purpose of the museum began to puzzle me. Wasn't there an air of bad faith about preserving the vestiges of a culture one had effectively extinguished? Did the museum exist to assuage our guilt and not for any real educational reason? I do not have an answer to these questions. All I know is that I felt I was in the presence of something pious and a little insincere. It had the aura of a failed attempt at virtue, as though the curators were trying to present as interesting objects whose purpose and meaning even they could not fully imagine.

In a last-ditch attempt to salvage something, I went up to one of the guards and asked where the movie was showing which the video had advertised, the movie about Plains Indian life. "Oh, the slide show, you mean," he said. "It's been discontinued." When I asked why, he said he didn't know. It occurred to me then that that was the message the museum was sending, if I could read it, that that was the bottom line. Discontinued, no reason given.

The movie in the Winchester Arms Museum, *Lock, Stock, and Barrel,* was going strong. The film began with the introduction of cannon into European warfare in the middle Ages, and was working its way slowly toward the nineteenth century when I left. I was in a hurry. Soon my husband would be waiting for me in the lobby. I went from room to room, trying to get a quick sense impression of the objects on display. They were all the same: guns. Some large drawings and photographs on the walls tried to give a sense of the context in which the arms had been used, but the effect was nil. It was case after case of rifles and pistols, repeating themselves over and over, and even when some slight variation caught my eye the differences meant nothing to me.

But the statistics did. In a large case of commemorative rifles, I saw the Antlered Game Commemorative Carbine. Date of manufacture: 1978. Number produced: 19,999. I wondered how many antlered animals each carbine had killed. I saw the Canadian Centennial (1962): 90,000; the Legendary Lawman (1978): 19,999; the John Wayne (1980–81): 51,600. Like the titles of the various sections of the museum, these names had a message. The message was: guns are patriotic. Associated with national celebrations, law enforcement, and cultural heroes. The idea that firearms were inseparable from the march of American history came through even more strongly in the titles given to the various exhibits: Firearms in Colonial America; Born in America: The Kentucky Rifle; The Era of Expansion and Invention; The Civil War: Firearms of the Conflict; The Golden Age of Hunting; Winning the West. The guns embodied phases of the history they had helped to make. There were no quotation marks here to indicate that expansion and conquest might not have been all they were cracked up to be. The fact that firearms had had a history seemed to consecrate them; the fact that they had existed at the time when certain famous events had occurred seemed to make them not only worth preserving but worth studying and revering. In addition to the exhibition rooms, the museum housed three "study galleries": one for hand arms, one for shoulder arms, one for U.S. military firearms.

As I think back on the rows and rows of guns, I wonder if I should have looked at them more closely, tried harder to appreciate the workmanship that went into them, the ingenuity, the attention. Awe and admiration are the attitudes the museum invites. You hear the ghostly march of military music in the background; you imagine flags waving and sense the implicit reference to feats of courage in battle and glorious death. The place had the air of an expensive and well-kept reliquary, or of the room off the transept of a cathedral where the vestments are stored. These guns were not there merely to be seen or even studied; they were there to be venerated.

But I did not try to appreciate the guns. They were too technical, too foreign. I didn't have their language, and, besides, I didn't want to learn. I rejoined my husband in the lobby. The Plains Indian Museum had been incomprehensible, but in the Winchester Arms Museum I could hardly see the objects at all, for I did not see the point. Or, rather, I did see it and rejected it. Here in the basement the instruments that had turned live animals into hides and horns, had massacred the Indians and the buffalo, were being lovingly displayed. And we were still making them: 51,600 John Waynes in 1980–81. Arms were going strong.

As I bought my books and postcards in the gift shop, I noticed a sign that read "Rodeo Tickets Sold Here," and something clicked into place. So that was it. *Everything* was still going strong. The whole museum was just another rodeo, only with the riders and their props stuffed, painted, sculpted, immobilized and put under glass. Like the rodeo, the entire museum witnessed a desire to bring back the United States of the 1880s and 1890s. The American people did not want to let go of the winning of the West. They wanted to win it all over again, in imagination. It was the ecstasy of the kill, as much as the life of the hunted, that we fed off here. The Buffalo Bill Historical Center did not repudiate the carnage that had taken place in the nineteenth century. It celebrated it. With its gleaming rest rooms, cute snack bar, opulent museum shop, wooden Indians, thousand rifles, and scores of animal trophies, it helped us all reenact the dream of excitement, adventure, and conquest that was what the Wild West meant to most people in this country.

This is where my visit ended, but it had a sequel. When I left the Buffalo Bill Historical Center, I was full of moral outrage, an indignation so intense it made me almost sick, though it was pleasurable too, as such emotions usually are. But the outrage was undermined by the knowledge that I knew nothing about Buffalo Bill, nothing of his life, nothing of the circumstances that led him to be involved in such violent events. And I began to wonder if my reaction wasn't in some way an image, however small, of the violence I had been objecting to. So when I got home I began to read about Buffalo Bill, and a whole new world opened up. I came to love Buffalo Bill.

"I have seen him the very personification of grace and beauty . . . dashing over the free wild prairie and riding his horse as though he and the noble animal were bounding with one life and one motion." That is the sort of thing people wrote about Buffalo Bill. They said "he was the handsomest man I ever saw." They said "there was never another man lived as popular as he was." They said "there wasn't a man woman or child that he knew or ever met that he didn't speak to." They said "he was handsome as a god, a good rider and a crack shot." They said "he gave lots of money away. Nobody ever went hungry around him." They said "he was way above the average, physically and every other way."

These are quotes from people who knew Cody, collected by one of his two most responsible biographers, Nellie Snyder Yost. She puts them in the last chapter, and by the time you get there they all ring true. Buffalo Bill was incredibly handsome. He was extremely brave and did things no other scout would do. He would carry messages over rugged territory swarming with hostile Indians, riding all night in bad weather and get through, and then take off again the next day to ride sixty miles through a blizzard. He was not a proud man. He didn't boast of his exploits. But he did do incredible things, not just once in a while but on a fairly regular basis. He had a great deal of courage; he believed in himself, in his abilities, in his strength and endurance and knowledge. He was very skilled at what he did—hunting and scouting—but he wasn't afraid to try other things. He wrote some dime novels, he wrote his autobiography by age thirty-four, without very much schooling; he wasn't afraid to try acting, even though the stage terrified him and he knew so little about it that, according to his wife, he didn't even know you had to memorize lines.

Maybe it was because he grew up on the frontier, maybe it was just the kind of person he was, but he was constantly finding himself in situations that required resourcefulness and courage, quick decisions and decisive action and rising to the occasion. He wasn't afraid to improvise.

He liked people, drank a lot, gave big parties, gave lots of presents, and is reputed to have been a womanizer (Cody, 16). When people came to see him in his office tent on the show grounds, to shake his hand or have their pictures taken with him, he never turned anyone away. "He kept a uniformed doorman at the tent opening to announce visitors," writes a biographer. "No matter who was outside, from a mayor to a shabby woman with a baby, the Colonel would smooth his mustache, stand tall and straight, and tell the doorman to 'show 'em in.' He greeted everyone the same" (Yost, 436).

As a showman, he was a genius. People don't say much about *why* he was so successful; mostly they describe the wonderful goings-on. But I get the feeling that Cody was one of those people who was connected to his time in an uncanny way. He knew what people wanted, he knew how to entertain them, because he *liked* them, was open to them, felt his kinship with them, or was so much in touch with himself at some level that he was thereby in touch with almost everybody else.

He liked to dress up and had a great sense of costume (of humor, too, they say). Once he came to a fancy dress ball, his first, in New York, wearing white tie and tails and a large Stetson. He knew what people wanted. He let his hair grow long and wore a mustache and beard, because, he said, he wouldn't be believable as a scout otherwise. Hence his Indian name, Pahaska, meaning "long hair," which people loved to use. Another kind of costume. He invented the ten-gallon hat, which the Stetson company made to his specifications. Afterward, they made a fortune from it. In the scores of pictures reproduced in the many books about him, he most often wears scout's clothes—usually generously fringed buckskin, sometimes a modified cavalryman's outfit—though often he's impeccably turned out in a natty-looking three-piece business suit (sometimes with overcoat, sometimes not). The photographs show him in a tuxedo, in something called a "Mexican suit" which looks like a cowboy outfit, and once he appears in Indian dress. In almost every case he is wearing some kind of hat, usually the Stetson, at exactly the right angle. He poses deliberately, and with dignity, for the picture. Cody didn't take himself so seriously that he had to pretend to be less than he was.

What made Buffalo Bill so irresistible? Why is he still so appealing, even now, when we've lost, supposedly, all the illusions that once supported his popularity? There's a poster for one of his shows when he was traveling in France that gives a clue to what it is that makes him so profoundly attractive a figure. The poster consists of a huge buffalo galloping across the plains, and against the buffalo's hump, in the center of his hump, is a cutout circle that shows the head of Buffalo Bill, white-mustachioed and bearded now, in his famous hat, and beneath, in large red letters, are the words "Je viens."

Je viens ("I am coming") are the words of a savior. The announcement is an annunciation. Buffalo Bill is a religious figure of a kind who makes sense within a specifically Christian tradition. That is, he comes in the guise of a redeemer, of someone who will save us, who will through his own actions do something for us that we ourselves cannot do. He will lift us above our lives, out of the daily grind, into something larger than we are.

His appeal on the surface is to childish desires, the desire for glamour, fame, bigness, adventure, romance. But these desires are also the sign of something more profound, and it is to something more profound in us that he also appeals. Buffalo Bill comes to the child in us, understood not as that part of ourselves that we have outgrown but as the part that got left behind, of necessity, a long time ago, having been starved, bound, punished, disciplined out of existence. He promises that that part of the self can live again. He has the power to promise these things because he represents the West, that geographical space of the globe that was still the realm of exploration and discovery, that was still open, that had not yet quite been tamed, when he began to play himself on the stage. He not only represented it, he *was* it. He brought the West itself with him when he came. The very Indians, the very buffalo, the very cowboys, the very cattle, the very stagecoach itself which had been memorialized in story. He performed in front of the audience the feats that had made him famous. He shot

FIGURE 31 *Je Viens*, c. 1900. Color lithograph. (Courtesy of the Buffalo Bill Historical Center, Cody, Wyoming.)

glass balls and clay pigeons out of the air with amazing rapidity. He rode his watersmooth silver stallion at full gallop. "Jesus he was a handsome man," wrote e. e. cummings in "Buffalo Bill's Defunct."

"I am coming." This appearance of Buffalo Bill, in the flesh, was akin to the apparition of a saint or of the Virgin Mary to believers. He was the incarnation of an ideal. He came to show people that what they had only imagined was really true. The West really did exist. There really were heroes who rode white horses and performed amazing feats. E. e. cummings was right to invoke the name of Jesus in his poem. Buffalo Bill was a secular messiah.

He was a messiah because people believed in him. When he died, he is reputed to have said, "Let my show go on." But he had no show at the time, so he probably didn't say that. Still, the words are prophetic because the desire for what Buffalo Bill had done had not only not died but would call forth the countless reenactments of the Wild West, from the rodeo—a direct descendant of his show—to the thousands of Western novels, movies, and television programs that comprise the Western genre in the twentieth century, a genre that came into existence as a separate category right about the time that Cody died. Don Russell maintains that the way the West exists in our minds today is largely the result of the way Cody presented it in his show. That was where people got their ideas of what the characters looked like. Though many Indian tribes wore no feathers and fought on foot, you will never see a featherless, horseless Indian warrior in the movies, because Bill employed only Sioux and other Plains tribes which had horses and traditionally wore feathered headdresses. "Similarly," he adds, "cowboys wear ten-gallon Stetsons, not because such a hat was worn in early range days, but because it was part of the costume adopted by Buffalo Bill for his show" (Russell, 470).

But the deeper legacy is elsewhere. Buffalo Bill was a person who inspired other people. What they saw in him was an aspect of themselves. It really doesn't matter whether Cody was as great as people thought him or not, because what they were responding to when he rode into the arena, erect and resplendent on his charger, was something intangible, not the man himself, but a possible way of being. William F. Cody and the Wild West triggered the emotions that had fueled the imaginative lives of people who flocked to see him, especially men and boys, who made up the larger portion of the audience. He and his cowboys played to an inward territory; a Wild West of the psyche that hungered for exercise sprang into activity when the show appeared. *Je viens* was a promise to redeem that territory, momentarily at least, from exile and oblivion. The lost parts of the self symbolized by buffalo and horses and wild men would live again for an hour while the show went on.

People adored it. Queen Victoria, who broke her custom by going to see it at all (she never went to the theater, and on the rare occasions when she wanted to see a play she had it brought to her), is supposed to have been lifted out of a twenty-five-year depression caused by the death of her husband after she saw Buffalo Bill. She liked the show so much that she saw it again, arranging for a command performance to be given at Windsor Castle the day before her Diamond Jubilee. This was the occasion when four kings rode in the Deadwood stagecoach with the Prince of Wales on top next to Buffalo Bill, who drove. No one was proof against the appeal. Ralph Blumenfeld, the London Correspondent for the New York *Herald,* wrote in his diary while the show was in London that he'd had two boyhood heroes, Robin Hood and Buffalo Bill, and had delighted in Cody's stories of the Pony Express and Yellow Hand:

> Everything was done to make Cody conceited and unbearable, but he remained the simple, unassuming child of the plains who thought lords and ladies belonged in the picture books and that the story of Little Red Riding Hood was true. I rode in the Deadwood coach. It was a great evening in which I realized a good many of my boyhood dreams, for there was Buffalo Bill on his white rocking horse charger, and Annie Oakley behind him. (Weybright, 172)

Victor Weybright and Henry Blackman Sell, from whose book on the Wild West some of the foregoing information has come, dedicated their book to Buffalo Bill. It was published in 1955. Nellie Snyder Yost, whose 1979 biography is one of the two scholarly accounts of Cody's life, dedicates her book "to all those good people, living or dead, who knew and liked Buffalo Bill." Don Russell's *The Lives and Legends of Buffalo Bill* (1960), the most fact-filled scholarly biography, does not have a dedication, but in the final chapter, where he steps back to assess Cody and his influence, Russell ends by exclaiming, "What more could possibly asked of a hero? If he was not one, who was?" (Russell, 480).

Let me now pose a few questions of my own. Must we throw out all the wonderful qualities that Cody had, the spirit of hope and emulation that he aroused in millions of people, because of the terrible judgment history has passed on the epoch of which he was part? The kinds of things he stands for—courage, daring, strength, endurance, generosity, openness to other people, love of drama, love of life, the possibility of living a life that does not deny the body and the desires of the body—are these to be declared dangerous and delusional although he manifested some of them while fighting Indians and others while representing his victories to the world? And the feelings he aroused in his audiences, the idealism, the enthusiasm, the excitement, the belief that dreams could become real—must these be declared misguided or a sham because they are associated with the imperialistic conquest of a continent, with the wholesale extermination of animals and men?

It is not so much that we cannot learn from history as that we cannot teach history how things should have been. When I set out to discover how Cody had become involved in the killing of Indians and the slaughter of buffalo, I found myself unable to sustain the outrage I had felt on leaving the museum. From his first job as an eleven-year-old herder for an army supply outfit, sole wage earner for his ailing widowed mother who had a new baby and other children to support, to his death in Colorado at the age of seventy-one, there was never a time when it was possible to say, there, there you went wrong, Buffalo Bill, you should not have killed that Indian. You should have held your fire and made your living some other way and quit the army and gone to work in the nineteenth-century equivalent of the Peace Corps. You should have known how it would end. My reading made me see that you cannot prescribe for someone in Buffalo Bill's position what he should have done, and it made me reflect on how eager I had been to get off on being angry at the museum. The thirst for moral outrage, for self-vindication, lay pretty close to the surface.

I cannot resolve the contradiction between my experience at the Buffalo Bill Historical Center with its celebration of violent conquest and my response to the shining figure of Buffalo Bill as it emerged from the pages of books—on the one hand, a history of shame; on the other, an image of the heart's desire. But I have reached one conclusion that for a while will have to serve.

Major historical events like genocide and major acts of destruction are not simply produced by impersonal historical processes or economic imperatives or ecological blunders; human intentionality is involved and human knowledge of the self. Therefore, if you're really, truly interested in not having any more genocide or killing of animals, no matter what else you might do, if you don't first, or also, come to recognize the violence in yourself and your own anger and your own destructiveness, whatever else you do won't work. It isn't that genocide doesn't matter. Genocide matters, and it starts at home.

1992

Works Cited

Cody, Iron Eyes. *Iron Eyes: My Life as a Hollywood Indian,* as told to Collin Perry. New York: Everest House, 1982.

Russell, Donald B. *The Lives and Legends of Buffalo Bill.* Norman, Okla.: University of Oklahoma Press, 1960.

Weybright, Victor, and Henry Blackman Sell. *Buffalo Bill and the Wild West.* New York: Oxford University Press, 1955.

Yost, Nellie Snyder. *Buffalo Bill, His Family, Friends, Fame, Failure, and Fortunes.* Chicago: Sage Books, 1979.

GETTING STARTED

1. Before reading the essay, list the images that come to mind when you think about the Wild West. After reading the essay, compare your list with the images that Tompkins focuses on.
2. Why does Tompkins label Remington's paintings and statues "imperialist and racist" (p. 499)? Do you agree with her?
3. In a group, list the different kinds of museums you can think of. Use your list to help you answer Tompkins's question, "What are museums keeping safe for us, after all?"
4. Why does Tompkins find the Plains Indian Museum "a terrible letdown" (p. 504)? What was she expecting to see?
5. How and why does Tompkins come to "love Buffalo Bill" (p. 504)? How does her love of Buffalo Bill affect her understanding of her experience at the Buffalo Bill Museum?

WRITING

6. Write two paragraphs that summarize why Tompkins finds the Buffalo Bill Museum "disturbing" and "wonderful."
7. Write a letter to Tompkins offering possible answers or explanations for her questions about the Remington painting *Coming to the Call.* Particularly, respond to her question, "And what call do we answer when we look at this painting? Who is calling whom? What is being preserved here?" (p. 507).
8. Tompkins keeps referring to the phrase "the best of civilization," which she hears on a videotape at the entrance to the Buffalo Bill Museum. What does the phrase mean to you? What does Tompkins think about that phrase and why? Write a short essay that links your own understanding of "the best of civilization" with what you believe to be Tompkins's attitude toward the phrase. Does her attitude change over the course of her essay? If so, how and why? If not, why not?

USING THE LIBRARY AND THE INTERNET

9. Find a book of Remington's paintings and statues in your library and find a Web site that features Remington's work. (Hint: Use a popular Internet search engine such as AltaVista, search in the "Arts" category, and limit the search to "Images.") Take some notes about your reactions to a Remington painting and a Rem-

ington statue. Compare your impressions of Remington's work with Tompkins's impressions of his artistry.

10. Search for a Web site for the Buffalo Bill Museum. Compare the impressions the Web site gives you of the museum to the impressions of the museum you get from reading Tompkins's essay.

MAKING CONNECTIONS

11. Write an essay that compares Tompkins's experience in the Plains Indian Museum with Gloria Anzaldúa's experience in the Denver Museum of Natural History. What do these writers see that motivates them to write? What do their experiences have in common?

12. In "I Stand Here Writing," Nancy Sommers quotes Ralph Waldo Emerson's remark that "One must be an inventor to read well" (p. 501). In her essay, Tompkins presents readings of artwork and artifacts. Use Sommers's sense of the Emerson quotation to help you analyze Tompkins's acts of reading art and artifacts. How is Tompkins an "inventor" as she interprets museum displays?

13. Jeanette Winterson claims, "Art is not documentary. It may incidentally serve that function in its own way but its true effort is to open to us dimensions of the spirit and of the self that normally lie smothered under the weight of living" (p. 595). Compare Winterson's claim with Tompkins's comments about the function of art. Based on your reading of both essays, would Tompkins likely agree or disagree with Winterson's claim? Why? Find a couple of other key quotations about art in Winterson's essay, and compare them to Tompkins's attitude. Where do you see the two writers agreeing and why? Where do you see possible differences of opinion and why?

Christopher P. Toumey

Christopher P. Toumey (1949–   ) is an Associate Professor of Anthropology at the University of Kentucky, where he teaches the anthropology of science, the anthropology of religion, and the history of anthropological theory. Toumey is the author of *God's Own Scientists: Creationists in a Secular World* (1994) and *Conjuring Science: Scientific Symbols and Cultural Meanings in American Life* (1996), from which "Science in an Old Testament Style" is excerpted.

To learn more about social studies of science, explore the *Techno-science* Web site at <http://www.cis.vt.edu/technoscience/technohome.html>.

Science in an Old Testament Style

In 1988, a television commercial for a common drugstore product made an uncommon claim about the endorsement of medical science. An actor from a daytime soap opera appeared on-screen in a white lab coat and declared, "I'm not a doctor, but I play one on TV." Then with those credentials he endorsed the product, recommending it in the authoritative voice of a medical doctor.

Such a commercial would be preposterous if it were generally recognized that there is a real difference between a doctor with genuine credentials and an actor who plays a doctor on TV. After all, the actor who played a doctor was not a doctor, and he candidly declared that he was not.

If a real physician is a symbol of medical science once removed from that kind of abstract institutional authority, and if an actor who pretends to be a doctor, like Robert Young as Marcus Welby, M.D., is a symbol twice removed, then the actor who did not even pretend to be a doctor was thrice removed from medical science. Nevertheless, for the purpose of pitching the product, he was an effective simulacrum of the authority of medical science.

The town of New Madrid, Missouri, devoted itself single-mindedly to emergency preparations for an earthquake in November and December 1990. The city council stockpiled drinking water, the mayor positioned his fire trucks in open fields far from buildings that might collapse, the local elementary school canceled classes for the day the earthquake was expected to hit, and the local insurance business sold many earthquake policies. At nearby St. John Missionary Baptist Church, Sunday school on December 2 began with the invocation to "Bless all of us, oh Father, that are upset about the earthquake."

The reason? Iben Browning, Ph.D., had predicted that a massive earthquake of at least 6.5 Richter had a 50 percent chance of striking New Madrid on December 3, 1990. It was said that Browning had predicted California's 1989 Loma Prieta earthquake. Surely an earthquake warning from someone with credentials and experience like Browning's was serious scientific advice, not to be taken lightly. Indeed, David Stewart, Ph.D., a geophysicist at nearby Southeast Missouri State University, endorsed Dr. Browning's prediction for 1990 in Missouri.

In truth, Iben Browning's Ph.D. was in zoology, not seismology. He had not predicted the Loma Prieta event. His supporter, David Stewart, had previously employed paranormal methods, including the services of psychic Clarissa Bernhard from the *National Enquirer,* to anticipate an earthquake in North Carolina that never happened. The National Earthquake Prediction Evaluation Council, under the auspices of the U.S. Geological Survey, adamantly denounced the faulty logic of Browning's seismological theories.

No matter. Tens of thousands of people in the region around New Madrid changed their plans and their behavior in anticipation of Iben Browning's earthquake. And never mind the skeptical bureaucrats of the U.S. Geological Survey, who seemed indifferent to the worries of the people of New Madrid. Was it not better to choose concerned scientists like Iben Browning and David Stewart as one's friends and advisers?

Tension was as bad as it could be when December 1990 came around. But the earth did not shake.

For many years, the tobacco lobby challenged the conclusion that smoking causes cancer, by drawing a hard distinction between the kind of scientific proof that comes from replicable demonstrations of cause and effect, and the epidemiological conclusions that are drawn from statistical correlations: the absolute proof of test-tube science, so to speak, versus the uncertainty of statistical probability. Then with scientific proof defined in terms of test-tube science, the tobacco advocates argued that scientists have not proven that smoking causes cancer since they have not elucidated the biochemical pathways by which the cause (smoking) leads to the effect (cancer). True, scientists have not, so the tobacco advocates are correct, provided that scientific proof is defined this way.

This logic implicitly compares the value of one form of scientific reasoning with that of another: a statistical conclusion is always inferior to a replicable demonstration of causation since the former is always less than 100 percent certain. More to the point, one can then say that the smoking and cancer connection is *possible* but far from certain, which is enormously useful to smokers who want a reason for not giving up smoking and to those who want to sell them tobacco products.

In June 1993, attorneys for the tobacco industry initiated a lawsuit to reverse the decision of the Environmental Protection Agency (EPA) designating secondhand smoke as a carcinogen. Their legal reasoning centered on the issue of statistical significance. Six of the thirty studies cited by the EPA had confidence levels of 95 percent ($p < .05$) for the conclusion that secondhand smoke causes cancer, but the other twenty-four studies had lower levels, for example, 80 or 85 percent.

Was this really a change in the standards of scientific proof? It seems to have been since the attorneys for the tobacco interests implicitly conceded that epidemiological-statistical methods *might* have scientific merit, provided that they met confidence levels of 95 percent or above (which is entirely reasonable for epidemiological research that has real policy implications). But the weaker studies had an equally important role in this argument. Every scientific study with a confidence level less than 95 percent could be interpreted to impeach all the studies with a level greater than 95 percent. So epidemiological-statistical studies of carcinogenicity can now be legally credible, but only in the sense that weaker studies have the effect of impeaching stronger studies, which is to say that weaker ones are more credible than stronger ones.

This medley of incidents reflects two aspects of the peculiar role of science in American culture. On the one hand, the institutional endorsement of the scientific authority is so greatly respected that the TV doctor, the credentials of Iben Browning, and the august weight of test-tube scientific proof are believed to enhance the worth of drugstore products, disaster preparations, and health regulations. On the other hand, the public understanding of the scientific knowledge and scientific reasoning in which that respect is grounded is so shallow that an *appearance* of scientific authority can be easily conjured from cheap symbols and ersatz images like an actor's white lab coat, a zoologist's credentials in a controversy about seismology, and a definition of scientific proof that makes epidemiological evidence irrelevant to an epidemiological question of carcinogenicity.

In other instances, the raw material for conjuring a semblance of science might be the solemn sounds of Greek or Latin terminology, visual images of shiny laboratory paraphernalia, or graphs and charts that pop up on the monitors of humming computers. Rich and deep is the supply of scientific iconography that can be borrowed for the purpose of cobbling together an image of science.

To understand the strength of popular respect for scientific authority, consider that certain theologians speak of the plenary authority of scripture, meaning that the written word of revelation embodies all the wisdom one needs to answer any of life's questions, big or small, spiritual or secular. We can borrow the term "plenary" to describe the way many citizens feel about science. The prestige of science is so great that it, too, is believed to possess such authority and be able to answer any of life's questions. This is so because science is widely believed to transcend the social forces that obviously shape other human institutions, such as politics or religion. Science is believed to be, in a word, "objective."

Science does not really deserve such awe, nor do most scientists believe such things about it. But many nonscientists do. Thus, to invoke the symbols of science is to make policies sound, commodities desirable, and behavior legitimate. By definition, these things are meritorious when they have the appearance of being scientific.

And yet surrounding the plenary authority of science is a great vacuum of understanding about scientific knowledge and reasoning. Studies of science education and scientific literacy reveal that large portions of the American public do not know such essential scientific concepts as "molecule" or "radiation," cannot comprehend the methods of scientific reasoning, and could not apply either to public issues. Historical surveys of science in America demonstrate that the intangible meanings cherished within the institutional culture of science—the pleasures that make science rewarding to scientists—are alien to most of the American public.

The religion of the Old Testament could be the pattern for this combination of respect without comprehension. The chosen people believed in God, feared Him, and doubted His power only at great risk to themselves; yet they understood God very imperfectly since this being was a distant mystery who made himself known by awesome signs: burning bushes, pillars of fire, dreadful plagues. So it is with science in America today. Instead of comprehending scientific knowledge, scientific methods, or scientific standards, much of the adult population knows science only in terms of certain symbols that stand for science and that stand between people and scientific understanding. An actor who stands for medical science, for example, because he plays a doctor and wears a white lab coat, or a courtroom definition of scientific standards, or a zoologist's credentials in an argument about earthquakes.

This paradox of respect without comprehension can be broken down into three questions. First, what are the historical conditions that have caused the culture of science to be so estranged from other parts of American culture? This is a question of how science is perceived by nonscientists such that the values and meanings of science, as understood by scientists, are not well integrated into the values and meanings of American life. Scientific judgment is one thing, but nonscientists' everyday thinking about science is something else.

Second, how does science fit into American democratic culture today? Even though the values and standards of science are somewhat alien to the rest of American culture, and even though much of the American public is ill-equipped to make informed decisions about scientific issues, decisions affecting science (appropriations, legislation, policy, and the curriculum of public school science education, to name a few) are nevertheless made according to democratic processes. Science in America is strongly affected by extrascientific factors. One consequence of this effect is that various parties can invoke the symbols of science to claim that science endorses their own respective positions and can do so with little or no regard for scientific standards. Because there is too little public understanding of scientific knowledge or reasoning, it is possible to borrow, steal, distort, or manipulate these symbols for causes and ideologies that do not necessarily have anything to do with science.

That, in turn, begs the third question: if the symbols of science are being used to endorse or legitimize certain values and meanings but not the values and meanings of science, then to what exactly do these symbols refer? What do the symbols of science convey, if not the content of science? What are the nonscientific ideas that are being expressed by means of scientific symbols?

. . . By tracing a series of changing notions about science across the last two hundred years, I suggest that science, loosely defined, fit quite comfortably into American democratic culture in the early nineteenth century. Both the empirical content and the intellectual structure of science were relatively simple, so it was easy for the average person to understand science and appreciate it. After the arrival in the United States of modern scientific thinking and methods, however, beginning around the middle of the nineteenth century, a great divergence appeared between science as understood by scientists and science as understood by other Americans.

In the gap between those two ways of understanding science, there arose a certain kind of mischief, namely, the conjuring of science. One could use the common symbols and images of science, as understood by nonscientists, to make it seem that scientists were bestowing the plenary authority of science on various causes and ideologies that had nothing to do with science. By placing this mischief in American history, we can see how and when it arose and how it has been maintained throughout the twentieth century. . . .

. . . Undoubtedly, science occupies an important place in American life by virtue of its authority to bless or curse one commodity or another, one cause or another. But it cannot be taken for granted that the internal values and standards of science will have much effect in a public dispute about science, let alone that they will govern such a dispute. The critical question is not how science influences American culture but rather how American culture treats science. . . . The heart of my anthropological approach is an argument about the cultural conditions that enable various parties to separate the symbols of science from the substantive content of science so as to invoke and deploy those symbols to bestow the plenary authority of science on almost any commodity, ideology, or behavior. . . .

[M]y argument is as follows: In American culture, science is widely believed to possess a plenary authority. But this authority is not really grounded in the values and standards of science because they are estranged from the main themes of American life. Nevertheless, symbols of science are frequently invoked to support claims that science has endorsed a given commodity or cause, which is to say that semblance of scientific authority can be conjured. In which case, it is worth discovering what nonscientific values and meanings do the symbols of science stand for, which is a question of *why* science is conjured, and how it is that those symbols of science serve those nonscientific meanings, which is to ask *how* science is conjured.

I confess that my anthropology of science has very little to do with the methods, the knowledge, or the theories that we point to as the intellectual content of science. Instead, this anthropology is a story about how we borrow bits and pieces of science, loose and jagged, to aid our existential efforts to make sense of our lives. We think we know something about reality or about human existence or about right and wrong, and maybe we do. But our confidence is much enhanced when we think that science endorses or corroborates the things we think we know.

Why do we think so? How do we conclude that science takes sides in moral or existential questions? Why do we believe that a policy is better if it seems that science has blessed it? Why does it appear that one person's behavior is more righteous, or another's less, when a claim is made that science recommends this habit or that? . . .

My argument is that, regardless of the metaphysical status of science, its value in American life is contingent on the cultural values and meanings that frame science. And so I offer a story not about science but about the moralities, the philosophies, the ideologies, and the beliefs that surround science. I ask how the American people attribute the plenary authority of science to those values and meanings by disconnecting the popular symbols of science from its intellectual substance and attaching those symbols to other matters instead. In other words, I ask how we conjure a semblance of science.

1996

GETTING STARTED

1. Look up the word "plenary" in a college edition dictionary, and compare this definition with the way in which Toumey uses the term. Why does he describe science in America as having "plenary" authority? Think of at least three different words or phrases that might also describe the attitude Americans have about science.

2. Think of the last newspaper story, movie, or book you encountered that referred to or used a difficult scientific concept. How was science represented? Is the authority of science questioned in any way? In a short paragraph, summarize this use of science describing the way in which the nonspecialist writer or director handles the scientific material. Does this example qualify as an example of Toumey's idea of science "in the Old Testament style": that is, does the example convey what Toumey describes as "respect without comprehension" (p. 519)?

WRITING

3. Generate an example of a scientist or a doctor as represented by popular culture. You might think of a movie, a television ad, or a video game. What powers are granted to the scientist or doctor because of his or her knowledge? Does the scientist have powers over others or over nature? What does your example suggest about the way we tend to view scientists?

4. Toumey suggests that we allow representations of science to go unquestioned at our peril. "Because there is too little public understanding of scientific knowledge or reasoning, it is possible to borrow, steal, distort, or manipulate these symbols for causes and ideologies that do not necessarily have anything to do with science" (p. 520). But if we are not scientists ourselves, what are we to do about this problem? What strategies or attitudes might help us overcome this so-called manipulation? Write an essay in which you explain what a healthier approach to scientific iconography might look like, being sure to refer to Toumey's argument.

USING THE LIBRARY AND THE INTERNET

5. Explore some of Toumey's concepts by looking up some questionable "scientific" practices in books, in magazines, or on Web sites. (Hint: Try the combined search term "science and magic" in a reference database that includes general interest and current events related magazines, such as MAS Full Text Ultra or a similar database recommended by your reference librarian.) Find examples that show how scientific materials are sometimes used to promote ideas that actually seem to run counter to the ideals or objectives of science. In a group, share and analyze your findings: Where do you see science invoked in ways that seem suspicious or misleading to you? Is there reference to reputable or legitimate science in each example? Do you think scientists "conjure science" as much as nonscientists do?

MAKING CONNECTIONS

6. In Julie English Early's account of Mary Kingsley, Early tells us that Kingsley courted popularity and created a stir with her unorthodox presentations of scientific materials. Was Kingsley guilty of what Toumey calls "conjuring science," or rather was she *de*-conjuring science with her self-conscious, idiosyncratic style? How did she use, appeal to, and sometimes thwart so-called legitimate scientific authority? Would Toumey say that Kingsley was dangerous?

7. In "The Loss of the Creature," Walker Percy argues that very often experts have assumed too much power over ordinary folk. Percy focuses on how to "recover sovereignty" in a world overrun by such experts. Would Percy's strategies work to dispel "conjured science"? Write an essay in which you test Percy's ideas by applying them to one of Toumey's examples.

HAUNANI-KAY TRASK

Haunani-Kay Trask is a Hawaiian nationalist, political organizer, poet, and Professor of Hawaiian Studies at the University of Hawaii. She is the coproducer of the award-winning documentary *Act of War: The Overthrow of the Hawaiian Nation* and the author of three books, including *From a Native Daughter: Colonialism and Sovereignty in Hawaii* (1993), in which she offers some political readings of Hawaiian history and, especially, the place of white colonialism in that history. "From a Native Daughter" was published in *The American Indian and the Problem of History* (1987), a collection of essays edited by Calvin Martin.

To learn more about Hawaiian claims to sovereignty, visit the Hawaii Nation's home page at <http://www.hawaii-nation.org/>.

From a Native Daughter

E noi'i wale mai no ka haole, a,
'a'ole e pau na hana a Hawai'i 'imi loa
Let the haole *freely research us in detail*
But the doings of deep delving Hawai'i
will not be exhausted.

KEPELINO
19th-century Hawaiian historian

Aloha kākou. Let us greet each other in friendship and love. My given name is Haunaniokawēkiu o Haleakalā, native of *Hawai'i Nei.* My father's family is from the *'āina* (land) of *Kaua'i,* my mother's family from the *'āina* of Maui. I reside today among my native people in the community of *Waimānalo.*

I have lived all my life under the power of America. My native country, Hawai'i, is owned by the United States. I attended missionary schools, both Catholic and Protestant, in my youth, and I was sent away to the American mainland to receive a "higher" education at the University of Wisconsin. Now I teach the history and culture of my people at the University of Hawai'i.

When I was young the story of my people was told twice: once by my parents, then again by my school teachers. From my *'ohana* (family), I learned about the life of the old ones: how they fished and planted by the moon; shared all the fruits of their labors, especially their children; danced in great numbers for long hours; and honored the unity of their world in intricate genealogical chants. My mother said Hawaiians had sailed over thousands of miles to make their home in these sacred islands. And they had flourished, until the coming of the *haole* (whites).

At school, I learned that the "pagan Hawaiians" did not read or write, were lustful cannibals, traded in slaves, and could not sing. Captain Cook had "discovered" Hawai'i and the ungrateful Hawaiians had killed him. In revenge, the Christian god had cursed the Hawaiians with disease and death.

I learned the first of these stories from speaking with my mother and father. I learned the second from books. By the time I left for college, the books had won out over my parents, especially since I spent four long years in a missionary boarding school for Hawaiian children.

When I went away I understood the world as a place and a feeling divided in two: one *haole* (white), and the other *kānaka* (native). When I returned ten years later with a Ph.D., the division was sharper, the lack of connection more painful. There was the world that we lived in—my ancestors, my family, and my people—and then there was the world historians described. This world, they had written, was the truth. A primitive group, Hawaiians had been ruled by bloodthirsty priests and despotic kings who owned all the land and kept our people in feudal subjugation. The chiefs were cruel, the people poor.

But this was not the story my mother told me. No one had owned the land before the *haole* came; everyone could fish and plant, except during sacred periods. And the chiefs were good and loved their people.

Was my mother confused? What did our *kūpuna* (elders) say? They replied: Did these historians (all *haole*) know the language? Did they understand the chants? How long had they lived among our people? Whose stories had they heard?

None of the historians had ever learned our mother tongue. They had all been content to read what Europeans and Americans had written. But why did scholars, presumably well-trained and thoughtful, neglect our language? Not merely a passageway to knowledge, language is a form of knowing by itself; a people's way of thinking and feeling is revealed through its music.

I sensed the answer without needing to answer. From years of living in a divided world, I knew the historian's judgment: *There is no value in things Hawaiian; all value comes from things haole.*

Historians, I realized, were very like missionaries. They were a part of the colonizing horde. One group colonized the spirit; the other, the mind. Frantz Fanon had been right, but not just about Africans. He had been right about the bondage of my own people: "By a kind of perverted logic, [colonialism] turns to the past of the oppressed people, and distorts, disfigures, and destroys it" (1968:210). The first step in the colonizing process, Fanon had written, was the deculturation of a people. What better way to take our culture than to remake our image? A rich historical past became small and ignorant in the hands of Westerners. And we suffered a damaged sense of people and culture because of this distortion.

Burdened by a linear, progressive conception of history and by an assumption that Euro-American culture flourishes at the upper end of that progression, Westerners have told the history of Hawai'i as an inevitable if occasionally bitter-sweet triumph of Western ways over "primitive" Hawaiian ways. A few authors—the most sympathetic—have recorded with deep-felt sorrow the passing of our people. But in the end, we are repeatedly told, such an eclipse was for the best.

Obviously it was best for Westerners, not for our dying multitudes. This is why the historian's mission has been to justify our passing by celebrating Western dominance. Fanon would have called this missionizing, intellectual colonization. And it is clearest in the historian's insistence that pre-*haole* Hawaiian land tenure was "feudal"—a term that is now applied, without question, in every monograph, in every schoolbook, and in every tour guide description of my people's history.

From the earliest days of Western contact my people told their guests that *no one* owned the land. The land—like the air and the sea—was for all to use and share as their birthright. Our chiefs were *stewards* of the land; they could not own or privately possess the land any more than they could sell it.

But the *haole* insisted on characterizing our chiefs as feudal landlords and our people as serfs. Thus, a European term which described a European practice founded on the European concept of private property—feudalism—was imposed upon a people halfway around the world from Europe and vastly different from her in every conceivable way. More than betraying an ignorance of Hawaiian culture and history, however, this misrepresentation was malevolent in design.

By inventing feudalism in ancient Hawai'i, Western scholars quickly transformed a spiritually-based, self-sufficient economic system of land use and occupancy into an oppressive, medievel European practice of divine right ownership, with the common people tied like serfs to the land. By claiming that a Pacific people lived under a European system—that the Hawaiians lived under feudalism—Westerners could then degrade a successful system of shared land use with a pejorative and inaccurate Western term. Land tenure changes instituted by Americans and in line with current Western notions of private property were then made to appear beneficial to the Hawaiians. But in practice, such changes benefited the *haole,* who alienated the people from the land, taking it for themselves.

The prelude to this land alienation was the great dying of the people. Barely half a century after contact with the West our people had declined in number by eighty percent. Disease and death were rampant. The sandalwood forests had been stripped bare for international commerce between England and China. The missionaries had insinuated themselves everywhere. And a debt-ridden Hawaiian king (there had been no king before Western contact) succumbed to enormous pressure from the Americans and followed their schemes for dividing up the land.

This is how private property land tenure entered Hawai'i. The common people, driven from their birthright, received less than one percent of the land. They starved while huge *haole*-owned sugar plantations thrived.

And what had the historians said? They had said that the Americans "liberated" the Hawaiians from an oppressive "feudal" system. By inventing a false feudal past, the historians justify—and become complicitous in—massive American theft.

Is there "evidence"—as historians call it—for traditional Hawaiian concepts of land use? The evidence is in the sayings of my people and in the words they wrote more than a century ago, much of which has been translated. However, historians have chosen to ignore any references here to shared land use. But there *is* incontrovertible evidence in the very structure of the Hawaiian language. If the historians had bothered to learn our language (as any American historian of France would learn French) they would have discovered that we show possession in two ways: through the use of an "a" possessive, which reveals acquired status, and through the use of an "o" possessive, which denotes inherent status. My body (*ko 'u kino*) and my parents (*ko 'u mākua*), for example, take the "o" form; most material objects, such as food (*ka'u mea'ai*) take the "a" form. But land, like one's body and one's parents, takes the "o" possessive (*ko'u 'āina*). Thus, in our way of speaking, land is inherent to the people; it is like our bodies and our parents. The people cannot exist without the land, and the land cannot exist without the people.

Every major historian of Hawai'i has been mistaken about Hawaiian land tenure. The chiefs did not own the land: they *could not* own the land. My mother was right and the *haole* historians were wrong. If they had studied our language they would have known that no one owned the land. But was their failing merely ignorance, or simple ethnocentric bias?

No, I did not believe them to be so benign. As I read on, a pattern emerged in their writing. Our ways were inferior to those of the West, to those of the historians' own culture. We were "less developed," or "immature," or "authoritarian." In some tellings we were much worse. Thus, Gavan Daws (1968), the most famed modern historian of Hawai'i, had continued a tradition established earlier by missionaries Hiram Bingham (1848) and Sheldon Dibble (1909), by referring to the old ones as "thieves" and "savages" who regularly practiced infanticide and who, in contrast to "civilized" whites, preferred "lewd dancing" to work. Ralph Kuykendall (1938), long considered the most thorough if also the most boring of historians of Hawai'i, sustained another fiction—that my ancestors owned slaves, the outcast *Kauwā*. This opinion, as well was the description of Hawaiian land tenure as feudal, had been supported by respected sociologist Andrew Lind (1938).[1] Finally, nearly all historians had refused to accept our genealogical dating of A.D. 400 or earlier for our arrival from the South Pacific. They had, instead, claimed that our earliest appearance in Hawai'i could only be traced to A.D. 1100. Thus at least seven hundred years of our history were repudiated by "superior" Western scholarship. Only recently have archeological data confirmed what Hawaiians had said these many centuries (Tuggle 1979).

Suddenly the entire sweep of our written history was clear to me. I was reading the West's view of itself through the degradation of my own past. When historians wrote that the king owned the land and the common people were bound to it, they were saying that ownership was the only way human beings in their world could relate to the land, and in that relationship, some one person had to control both the land and the interaction between humans.

And when they said that our chiefs were despotic, they were telling of their own society, where hierarchy always results in domination. Thus any authority or elder is automatically suspected of tyranny.

And when they wrote that Hawaiians were lazy, they meant that work must be continuous and ever a burden.

And when they wrote that we were promiscuous, they meant that love-making in the Christian West is a sin.

And when they wrote that we were racist because we preferred our own ways to theirs, they meant that their culture needed to dominate other cultures.

And when they wrote that we were superstitious, believing in the *mana* of nature and people, they meant that the West has long since lost a deep spiritual and cultural relationship to the earth.

And when they wrote that Hawaiians were "primitive" in their grief over the passing of loved ones, they meant that the West grieves for the living who do not walk among their ancestors.

For so long, more than half my life, I had misunderstood this written record, thinking it described my own people. But my history was nowhere present. For we had not written. We had chanted and sailed and fished and built and prayed. And we had told stories through the great blood lines of memory: genealogy.

To know my history, I had to put away my books and return to the land. I had to plant taro in the earth before I could understand the inseparable bond between people and *'āina*. I had to feel again the spirits of nature and take gifts of plants and fish to the ancient altars. I had to begin to speak my language with our elders and leave long silences for wisdom to grow. But before anything else, I had to learn the language like a lover so that I could rock within her and lay at night in her dreaming arms.

There was nothing in my schooling that had told me of this, or hinted that somewhere there was a longer, older story of origins, of the flowing of songs out to a great but distant sea. Only my parents' voices, over and over, spoke to me of a Hawaiian world. While the books spoke from a different world, a Western world.

And yet, Hawaiians are not of the West. We are of *Hawai'i Nei,* this world where I live, this place, this culture, this *'aina.*

What can I say, then, to Western historians of my place and people? Let me answer with a story.

A while ago I was asked to share a panel on the American overthrow of our government in 1893. The other panelists were all *haole.* But one was a *haole* historian from the mainland who had just published a book on what he called the American anti-imperialists. He and I met briefly in preparation for the panel. I asked him if he knew the language. He said no. I asked him if he knew the record of opposition to our annexation to America. He said there was no real evidence for it, just comments here and there. I told him that he didn't understand and that at the panel I would share the evidence. When we met in public and spoke, I said this:

There is a song much loved by our people. It was sung when Hawaiians were forbidden from congregating in groups of more than three. Addressed to our imprisoned Queen, it was written in 1893, and tells of Hawaiian feelings for our land and against annexation. Listen to our lament:

Kaulana na pua a'o Hawai'i	Famous are the children of Hawai'i
Kūpa'a mahope o ka 'āina	Who cling steadfastly to the land
Hiki mai ka 'elele o ka loko 'ino	Comes the evil-hearted with
Palapala 'ānunu me ka pākaha	A document greedy for plunder
Pane mai Hawai'i moku o Keawe	Hawai'i, island of Keawe, answers
Kokua na hono a'o Pi'ilani	The bays of Pi'ilani [of Maui, Moloka'i, and Lana'i] help
Kāko'o mai Kaua'i o Mano	Kaua'i of Mano assists
Pau pu me ke one o Kakuhihewa	Firmly together with the sands of Kakuhihewa
'A'ole a'e kau i ka pūlima	Do not put the signature
Maluna o ka pepa o ka 'enemi	On the paper of the enemy
Ho'ohui 'āina kū'ai hewa	Annexation is wicked sale
I ka pono sīvila a'o ke kānaka	Of the civil rights of the Hawaiian people
Mahope mākou o Lili'ulani	We support Lili'uokalani
A loa'a 'e ka pono o ka 'āina	Who has earned the right to the land
Ha'ina 'ia mai ana ka puana	The story is told
'O ka po'e i aloha i ka 'āina	Of the people who love the land

This song, I said, continues to be sung with great dignity at Hawaiian political gatherings. For our people still share the feelings of anger and protest that it conveys.

But our guest, the *haole* historian, answered that this song, although beautiful, was not evidence of either opposition or of imperialism from the Hawaiian perspective.

Many Hawaiians in the audience were shocked at his remarks, but, in hindsight, I think they were predictable. They are the standard response of the historian who does not know the language and has no respect for its memory.

Finally, I proceeded to relate a personal story, thinking that surely such a tale could not want for authenticity since I myself was relating it. My *tūtū* (grandmother) had told my mother who had told me that at the time of the overthrow a great wailing went up throughout the islands, a wailing of weeks, a wailing of impenetrable grief, a wailing of death. But he remarked again, this too is not evidence.

And so, history goes on, written in long volumes by foreign people. Whole libraries begin to form, book upon book, shelf upon shelf.

At the same time, the stories go on, generation to generation, family to family.

Which history do Western historians desire to know? Is it to be a tale of writings by their own countrymen, individuals convinced of their "unique" capacity for analysis, looking at us with Western eyes, thinking about us within Western philosophical contexts, categorizing us by Western indices, judging us by Judeo-Christian morals, exhorting us to capitalist achievements, and finally, leaving us an authoritative-because-Western record of their complete misunderstanding?

All this has been done already. Not merely a few times, but many times. And still, every year, there appear new and eager faces to take up the same telling, as if the West must continue, implacably, with the din of its own disbelief.

But there is, as there has been always, another possibility. If it is truly our history Western historians desire to know, they must put down their books, and take up our practices. First, of course, the language. But later, the people, the *'āina,* the stories. Above all, in the end, the stories. Historians must listen, they must hear the generational connections, the reservoir of sounds and meanings.

They must come, as American Indians suggested long ago, to understand the land. Not in the Western way, but in the indigenous way, the way of living within and protecting the bond between people and *'āina.*

This bond is cultural, and it can be understood only culturally. But because the West has lost any cultural understanding of the bond between people and land, it is not possible to know this connection through Western culture. This means that the history of indigenous people cannot be written from within Western culture. Such a story is merely the West's story of itself.

Our story remains unwritten. It rests within the culture, which is inseparable from the land. To know this is to know our history. To write this is to write of the land and the people who are born from her.

1987

Notes

1. See also Fornander (1878–85). Lest one think these sources antiquated, it should be noted that there exist only a handful of modern scholarly works on the history of Hawai'i. The most respected are those by Kuykendall (1938) and Daws (1968), and a social history of the twentieth century by Lawrence Fuchs (1961). Of these, only Kuykendall and Daws claim any knowledge of pre-*haole* history, while concentrating on the nineteenth century. However, countless popular works have relied on these two studies which, in turn, are themselves based on primary sources written in English extremely by biased, anti-Hawaiian Westerners such as explorers, traders, missionaries (e.g., Bingham [1848] and Dibble [1909]), and sugar planters. Indeed, a favorite technique of Daws's—whose *Shoal of Time* is the most acclaimed and recent general history—is the lengthy quotation without comment of the most racist remarks by missionaries and planters. Thus, at one point, half a page is consumed with a "white man's burden" quotation from an 1886 *Planter's Monthly* article ("It is better for the colored man of India and Australia that the white man rules, and it is better here that the white man should rule. . . ," etc., p. 213). Daws's only comment is, "The conclusion was inescapable." To get a sense of such characteristic contempt for Hawaiians, one has but to read the first few pages, where Daws refers several times to the Hawaiians as "savages" and "thieves" and where he approvingly has Captain Cook thinking, "It was a sensible primitive who bowed before a superior civilization" (p. 2). See also—among examples too numerous to cite—his glib description of sacred *hula* as a "frivolous diversion," which, instead of work, the Hawaiians "would practice energetically in the hot sun for days on end . . . their bare brown flesh glistening with sweat" (pp. 65–66). Daws, who repeatedly displays an affection for descriptions of Hawaiian skin color, taught Hawaiian history for some years at the University of Hawai'i; he now holds the Chair of Pacific History at the Australian National University's Institute of Advanced Studies.

Works Cited

Bingham, Hiram. *A Residence of Twenty-one Years in the Sandwich Islands.* 2nd ed. New York: Converse, 1848.

Daws, Gavan. *Shoal of Time: A History of the Hawaiian Islands.* Toronto and New York: Macmillan, 1968.

Dibble, Sheldon. *History of the Sandwich Islands.* Honolulu: Thrum, 1909.

Fanon, Frantz. *The Wretched of the Earth.* New York: Grove, Evergreen Edition, 1968.

Kuykendall, Ralph S. *The Hawaiian Kingdom, 1778–1854.* Honolulu: University of Hawaii Press, 1938.

Lind, Andrew. *An Island Community: Ecological Succession in Hawaii.* New York: Greenwood, 1938.

Tuggle, H. David. "Hawaii." In *The Prehistory of Polynesia,* ed. Jesse D. Jennings, pp. 167–199. Cambridge, Mass.: Harvard Univ. Press, 1979.

GETTING STARTED

1. Working individually or in a group, look at the places where Trask describes the difference between the stories her family told her and the stories she learned in school. Have you or the other members of your group experienced similar contradictions between the information, messages, and values you learned at home and what you learned in school? Present one or two of your group's examples to the class and explain how they connect to Trask's experience.

2. In a small group, discuss Trask's attitude toward historians of Hawai'i who do not know the Hawaiian language. Why does she place so much emphasis on the Hawaiian language? Organize and present at least one example from her text. Summarize the example in your own words, cite a key sentence or passage, and explain how Trask uses the example to build her argument.

3. Why might historians not have accepted Hawaiian songs and oral tradition as valid historical evidence? What is the difference between, on the one hand, the songs and oral histories and, on the other hand, the written records? Why have written records traditionally been accorded greater historical weight?

4. What effect does Trask hope to produce with her epigraph from Kepelino (p. 524)? Why does Trask include language that is unfamiliar to most of her readers?

WRITING

5. Use the results of your research in response to question 7 to write a longer paper in which you agree or disagree with Trask's assessment of mainstream Western histories. In the materials you found, is historic Hawai'i presented as it was in Trask's experience—as a barbarian, feudal society that was civilized by its colonizers? What differences do you see? What kinds of evi-

dence do the histories you found use to back up their claims? To what extent do any of the histories support Trask's claim that Hawai'i was a peaceful, egalitarian culture with a stewardship relationship to the land that prevented private ownership? Is Trask making too strong a distinction between Western historians and her own approach, or is her condemnation of Western historians justified? Explain your answer citing specific examples from the materials you found.

6. Use examples from Trask and from your own experience to make a case for what constitutes "good" evidence. What evidence do Western historians rely on, according to Trask? What kinds of evidence does she accumulate to rebut their claims?

USING THE LIBRARY AND THE INTERNET

7. Trask writes, "Historians, I realized, were very like missionaries" (p. 525). How can historians, who rely on historical, objective facts and arguments, be compared to missionaries, who preach subservience to a religious order? How can Trask argue that the two world-views, history and religion, work together? Use library or Internet resources to look up some histories of Hawai'i. These can include everything from encyclopedia entries to old and current histories and textbook accounts. Print the results of your search and share your findings in a group. To what extent do these accounts resemble the faulty histories that Trask deplores? To what extent do they resemble Trask's own view of Hawaiian history? Write a one-page paper summarizing your findings.

8. Use a scholarly database such as Academic Search Elite that includes sources from scholarly journals or one such as MAS Full Text Ultra that includes general-interest and current-events related magazines, to search for some key concepts from Trask. Try search terms such as "language and exclusion" or "language and racism." List some of the important issues and debates that occur, and print out several articles or abstracts that relate to Trask's ideas in interesting ways.

MAKING CONNECTIONS

9. Compare Trask's argument about the importance of oral history with Patricia J. Williams's arguments in "The Ethnic Scarring of American Whiteness." How can language be used to discriminate against or erase a group of people (Williams) or to prevent

discrimination by rewriting history (Trask)? How does what you say about a situation—your language—influence others' responses to that situation? Can there be any history or past without the shaping influence of language? How do we protect ourselves from the bias and discrimination of language?

10. In "Chicana Artists: Exploring *Nepantla, el Lugar de la Frontera,*" Gloria Anzaldúa argues that "border art challenges and subverts the imperialism of the United States, and combats assimilation by either the United States or Mexico, yet it acknowledges its affinities to both cultures" (p. 52). Do you think that Trask's brand of history is a kind of border art? Can a historian be a border artist? How should a historian truthfully relate extreme differences of opinion?

Yi-Fu Tuan

Yi-Fu Tuan (1930–) is Professor Emeritus of Geography at the University of Wisconsin, Madison, and the author of *Space and Place: The Perspective of Experience* (1977), *Landscapes of Fear* (1979), and *Escapism* (1998). Tuan is known as a pioneer of interdisciplinary scholarship, bringing elements of philosophy, psychology, urban planning, anthropology, and landscape architecture into conversation with a geography that incorporates the study of morals. The son of a Chinese diplomat, Tuan attended schools in China, Australia, and the Philippines before landing at Oxford University. He earned his Ph.D. from the University of California, Berkeley, and spent his scholarly career teaching in the United States. "Earth: Nature and Culture" is a chapter from Tuan's book *Escapism.*

For photographs of Yi-Fu Tuan and more information about his life and work, see <http://www.cwu.edu/~geograph/yi_fu.html>.

Earth

Nature and Culture

"Escapism" has a somewhat negative meaning in our society and perhaps in all societies. It suggests an inability to face facts—the real world. We speak of escapist literature, for instance, and we tend to judge as escapist places such as mega-shopping malls, fancy resorts, theme parks, or even picture-perfect suburbs. They all lack—in a single word—weight.

Suspicion of escapism has many causes. The most obvious is that no animal can survive unless it perceives its environment as it really is. Daydreaming or wishful thinking would not answer. The hard facts cannot be made to go away by shutting one's eyes. But so far as we know, only humans may withdraw, eyes shut, to ponder the nature of a threat rather than confront it directly, muscles tense, eyes open; only they daydream and engage in wishful thinking. Significantly, only humans have culture. By culture I mean not just certain acquired habits, the manufacture and use of certain tools, but a whole world of thought and belief, habits and customs, skills and artifacts. Culture is more closely linked to the human tendency not to face facts, our ability to escape by one means or another, than we are accustomed to believe. Indeed, I should like to add another definition of what it is to be human to the many that already exist: A human being is an animal who is congenitally indisposed to accept reality as it is. Humans not only submit and adapt, as all animals do; they transform in accordance with a preconceived plan. That is, before transforming, they do something extraordinary, namely, "see" what is not there. Seeing what is not there lies at the foundation of all human culture.

Reality and the Real

What do the words "reality" and "real" mean? Although philosophers do not find it easy to agree on an answer, ordinary thinking people have little difficulty using these words in everyday talk, often in conjunction with their opposites, "fantasy" and "unreal." Such talk, when looked at closely, shows how the meaning of "real" shifts, even radically, as the context changes. A common meaning draws on the model of animal life. The idea is that animals live in the real world, respond as best they can to outside forces and their own nature, free of unsettling images and aspirations. Humans can approach that state of existence by also living close to nature, curbing the imagination and jettisoning excess cultural baggage. Nature itself is real. It is indubitably real to humans when they feel it as a blast of cold wind, a sudden shower, or the skin rash caused by contact with poison ivy. So another meaning of "real" emerges: the real as impact. It is not just nature; it is whatever in nature or in society imposes itself on a human being or group, doing so either suddenly or as a consistently felt pressure. "Reality" in this sense is intractable, and it is indifferent to the needs and desires of particular individuals and groups. Facing reality, then, implies accepting one's essential powerlessness, yielding or adjusting to circumambient forces, taking solace in some local pattern or order that one has created and to which one has become habituated. This "local pattern or order" points to another sense of the real: a small and thoroughly humanized world. Far from being shock or impact, the real is the familiar, the predictable, the nurturing and all-enveloping. Home is the prime example. Home is a place to which one is attached by myriad habits of thought and behavior—culturally acquired, of course, yet in time they become so intimately woven into everyday existence that they seem primordial and the essence of one's being. Moving out of home and the familiar, even when this is voluntary and of short duration, can feel like escapism, sojourn in a fantasy world, less real because less dense and all-encompassing.

Does this conclude the list of commonly accepted meanings of "real"? No. For completion, at least one more sense of the word demands to be added. Disconcertingly, it is the opposite of the one I have just given. In this usage, it is daily life, with its messy details and frustrating lack of definition and completion—its many inconclusive moves and projects twisting and turning as in a fitful dream—that is unreal. Real, by contrast, is the well-told story, the clear image, the well-defined architectural space, the sacred ritual, all of which give a heightened sense of self—a feeling of aliveness.

The Earth

The earth is our home. Trips to the moon, another planet, a distant star, have haunted the human imagination and may even become a commonplace reality one day. But they nevertheless have an aura of fantasy about them. Real life is life on earth; it is here that we have our roots and our being. Geographers study the earth as human habitat or home. Interestingly, they discover that the earth is never quite the home humans want it to be; hence the dreams of flying and of a paradise located elsewhere that are common to many cultures. Most people, when they think of the earth, think not of the entire planet but of a part of it—the part they live in. Wherever they happen to be, provided they have been settled there for some time, they consider home. Yet this is not quite the case either, if only because if it were, there would be no story, no *human* story, to tell; people, like other animals, will be "immersed in nature," as G. W. F. Hegel put it. It is the restless activity that produces the story line. Human beings have been and continue to be profoundly restless. For one reason or another, they are not content with being where they are. They move, or if they stay in place, they seek to rearrange that place. Migration and the in situ transformation of the environment are two major themes—*the* two major themes—in human geography. They both reveal a discontent with the status quo, a desire to escape. Geographers have written voluminously on these themes without using "escape" or "escapism" as a guiding concept. What is to be gained by using it now? The gain is that it forces us to reconsider nature and culture, and thereby who we are and what we aspire to, in productive tandem with "real and imagined," "reality and fantasy"—ideas that traditionally are at the core of humanist scholarship and thinking.

Migration

Migration is clearly a type of escape. Animals move out when their home ground starts to deteriorate. Humans have done so since the earliest times; and it now appears that as they acquired certain critical marks of culture—outstandingly, language around sixty thousand years ago—they became better able to organize themselves in complex ways and meet the challenges of the environment by migrating, sometimes over great distances. To overcome great distance, our remote ancestors must have had not only organizational ability, enormously enhanced by language, but also new technical means at their disposal—seaworthy craft, for example. Such people must have been of lively mind and were, I will assume, quite capable of envisaging "greener pastures" elsewhere and making plans as to how best to reach their destination. By the end of the Ice Age, some twelve thousand years ago, human beings had spread into every kind of natural environment, from the Tropics to the Arctic, the major exceptions being ice sheets and the highest mountains.

Much of the human story can be told as one of migration. People move a short distance to a better hunting ground, richer soil, better economic opportunity, greater cultural stimulus. Short-distance movements are likely to be periodic, their paths winding back on themselves with changing circumstance. Over the years such movements become habit, their circuits habitat. Long-distance migrations, by contrast, are likely to be in one direction and permanent. A certain epic grandeur attaches to them, for migrants must be willing to take steps that make life even more difficult than it already is in the hope of future felicity. Before people make a risky move, they must have information about their destination point. What kinds of information are available? To what extent does the need to believe in a better world at the horizon overrule or distort the "hard facts" that people know? Is reality so constraining and unbearable at home that it becomes the seedbed for wild longings and images? And do these images, by virtue of their simplicity and vividness, seem not a dream but more "real" than the familiar world? A great modern epic of migration is the spread of Europeans to the New World. The United States of America proclaims itself a land of immigrants. It would not want to be known as a "land of escapists," yet many did just that: escape from the intolerable conditions of the Old World for the promises of the New.

Nature and Society

Human restlessness finds release in geographical mobility. It also finds release (and relief) in bringing about local change. The circumstances one wishes to change—to escape from—can be social, political, or economic; it can be a run-down urban neighborhood or a ravaged countryside. And it can be nature. In telling a human story, we may start at any point in time, but if we go back far enough we necessarily have nature, untouched nature, as stage: first the swamp, forest, bush, or desert, then . . . then what? Then humans enter, and our story begins.

In the long run, humans everywhere experience, if not forthrightly recognize, nature as home and tomb, Eden and jungle, mother and ogre, a responsive "thou" and an indifferent "it." Our attitude to nature was and is understandably ambivalent. Culture reflects this ambivalence; it compensates for nature's defects yet fears the consequences of overcompensation. A major defect is nature's undependability and violence. The familiar story of people altering nature can thus be understood as their effort to distance themselves from it by establishing a mediating, more constant world of their own making. The story has many versions. Almost all are anguish-ridden, especially early on, when pioneers had to battle nature for a precarious toehold.

A natural environment can itself seem both nourishing and stable to its human habitants. A tropical forest, for example, provides for the modest needs for hunter-gatherers throughout the year, year after year. However, once a people start to change the forest, even if it is only the making of a modest clearing for crops and a village, the forest can seem to turn into a malevolent force that relentlessly threatens to move in and take over the cleared space. Some such experience of harassment is known to villagers all over the world, though perhaps not to the same degree as in the humid Tropics. Villagers are therefore inclined to see nature in a suspicious light. Of course they know that it provides for their needs and are grateful—a gratitude expressed by gestures and stories of respect. But they also know from hard experience that nature provides grudgingly, and that from time to time it acts with the utmost indifference to human works and lives.

Carving a space out of nature, then, does not ensure stability and ease. To the contrary, it can make people feel more than ever vulnerable. What to do? Lacking physical power, the most basic step they can take is to rope nature into the human world so that it will be responsive—as difficult people are—to social pressures and sanctions. If these don't work, they try placatory ritual, and if this in turn fails, they appeal to the higher authority of heaven or its human regents on earth. By one means or another they seek control, with at best only tenuous success. What appears stable to the visiting ecologist, whose discipline predisposes him to focus on long-range people-environment interactions, may be not stable at all but rather full of uncertainty to the local inhabitants struggling to survive from day to day, week to week, one season to another.

Aztec and Chinese

Now, suppose we turn to a more advanced society, one in which the people, unlike isolated and poorly equipped villagers, have the technical and organizational means to make extensive permanent clearings, raise crops, and build monuments, including cities. Won't the exercising of that power and the looming presence of large human works impress on them a sense of their own efficacy and the world's permanence?

The answer is, Not always. The Aztecs of Mexico are a case in point. Here is a people who continued to feel insecure despite the scope and sophistication of their material attainments. Nature's instabilities, made evident by the ominous presence of volcanoes and experienced repeatedly in the wayward behavior of weather, stream flow, and lake level, more than overruled whatever reassurance human artifacts could give. Moreover, in the Aztec civilization the architectural monuments of temple and altar themselves attested more to fear and anxiety than to confidence, for they were built to conduct human sacrifice, with the end in view of sustaining and regulating the enfeebled forces of the cosmos.

Consider another, more confident civilization, the Chinese. The Chinese struggled to regulate nature through physical intervention and by such institutional means as the establishment of public granaries. In these respects the two civilizations, Aztec and Chinese, had something in common. However, unlike the Aztecs, the Chinese managed to sustain over the course of millennia, and in the teeth of abundant contrary evidence, a magnificent model of cosmic harmony. This ability to overlook evidence may earn the Chinese the label of escapists, but without it—without their tenacious hold on the dream of harmony—they would have deprived themselves of optimism and fortitude, psychological advantages that helped them to create an enduring culture. To the Chinese architect-engineer, barriers such as swamp, forest, and hillock could be overcome; they did not have to be accepted as embossed in the eternal order of things. And to the Chinese philosopher—indeed, to the philosopher in any culture—wayward facts and contingencies were not just there to be noted and accepted; rather, they were puzzling pieces of reality that could stimulate one to search for a more comprehensive world-view.

Chinese composure has its source in a number of factors. Tangible architectural and engineering achievements no doubt promoted confidence, as did the memory of extended periods of peace and prosperity during a great dynasty such as the Han, T'ang, or Sung. The Chinese inclination to see the universe as orderly and hence accessible to reason surely also promoted composure. Even more reassuring—more wishful and escapist, from our secularist-modern perspective—is the idea that the universe is moral and hence responsive to moral suasion. China has had its share of natural disasters; these might well have been more devastating and frequent than those that afflicted the Aztec empire. When disasters visited China and could not be alleviated by ordinary means, the emperor took responsibility, for he considered them to be a consequence of his own moral failing. To reestablish order, he "memorialized heaven," imposing a penance on himself on his own and humankind's behalf. As exemplary man, the emperor was the ultimate mediator between heaven and earth; and for this reason he could by his own conduct and sacrifice right wrong, restore harmony throughout the worlds of nature and of people. The emperor was called Son of Heaven rather than Son of Earth. There is no doubt a heavenward tilt in Chinese high culture, as there is in all high cultures. What high culture offers is escape from bondage to earth.

Premodern and Early Modern Europe

Escape from nature's vagaries and violence—except during a blizzard or hurricane—may seem a strange idea to modern Westerners, for whom society rather than nature is unpredictable and violent. How short is their memory! Any full account of life and livelihood in the West from the Middle Ages to the eighteenth century must give a prominent role to weather—that is, if we are more interested in ordinary people than in potentates and their political high jinks. So much misery had its immediate cause in meteorological freakishness. Too much rain or too little, prolonged cold or withering heat, led to crop failure and, all too often—at least locally—to famine and starvation.

Records from the early modern period show how frequently people even in the richest parts of Europe suffered and died from lack of food. In 1597 a citizen of Newcastle wrote of "sundry starving and dying in our streets and in the fields for lack of bread." And this despite importation of foreign grain into the port city. In France, rather than the sort of cosmic stability to be expected from a Sun King, wild swings of lean and fat years seemed more the rule. In 1661–62 much of France was afflicted by bad weather, poor harvests, and famine. Beggars from the countryside flocked to the towns, where citizens formed militias to drive them back. Good weather produced good harvests in 1663; there followed a decade of prosperity. From 1674 onward, however, the times were once more "out of joint." A wet summer curtailed the harvests of 1674; those of 1677, 1678, and 1679 were worse. Yields were again poor in 1681 and catastrophic in some regions in 1684. Between 1679 and 1684 the death toll rose throughout much of France. Good weather prevailed from 1684 to 1689; magnificent harvests made for cheap grain, and the people were, for a change, more than adequately fed. Then came the great famine of 1693–94, the culmination of a succession of cold and wet years. A majority of people in France suffered, though in varying degree. Poor folks resorted to eating "such unclean things as cats and the flesh of horses flayed and cast on to dung heaps," and some starved to death.

In premodern and early modern Europe, uncertainty in both nature and society put a heavy burden on the poor. That hardly surprises us. More difficult for us to imagine now is how uncertainty could haunt the well-to-do, even the rich and the powerful. When uncertainty is so much a fact of life, escape into a make-believe world of perfect order may be excused. Make-believe was one way—an important way—that Renaissance princes coped. They produced elaborate masques in which they themselves sometimes played the roles of gods and goddesses reigning in a pastoral heaven of abundance and peace. If ordinary people sought to exclude unruly weather by putting a roof over their heads, Renaissance rulers did that and far more. By means of the art at their command they produced an alternative heaven: the palace itself and, even more overtly, the theatrical stage of floating clouds, flying chariots, pastures and billowing fields of surpassing fertility.

What was the nature of this art? Shakespeare hinted at it in the magic powers of Prospero. A Renaissance prince was a Prospero—a magician. A magician was not the marginal entertainer we now see him to be. Rather, he was considered a person of deep knowledge—someone who knew how things worked below the surface and so could do wonders. Whereas a prince only purchased such power, a genius like Leonardo da Vinci possessed it in his own person to a remarkable degree. It doesn't seem to me far-fetched to call Leonardo a magician. Indeed, a much later figure, Isaac Newton, has been called a magician, the last one. An important difference, however, separates a Renaissance figure like Leonardo and the outstanding genius of a later time, Newton: Leonardo approached knowledge through art, technique, and technology, skills that would have been necessary to the making of the sort of surrogate heaven that Renaissance princes yearned for. By contrast, Newton showed little interest in the earthbound phenomena such as anatomy and geology that fascinated Leonardo. Nor was he concerned with building a surrogate heaven on earth in the manner of an artist-architect. Rather, his gaze was directed to heaven itself, and his singular contribution to knowledge was through the abstractions of mathematics.

Physical vs. Biological Science: Heaven vs. Earth

Alfred North Whitehead, an outstanding mathematician-philosopher of our time, famously designated the seventeenth century the Century of Genius. He gave twelve names: Bacon, Harvey, Kepler, Galileo, Descartes, Pascal, Huyghens, Boyle, Newton, Locke, Spinoza, and Leibniz. He apologized for the predominance of Englishmen, then noted without apology that he had only one biologist on the list: Harvey. Genius in that century showed itself in celestial mechanics and physics rather than in biology or organic nature, to which humans belong and upon which they depend. At the threshold of the modern age, human helplessness—the recurrent famines and starvation I mentioned earlier—continued to exist even in the developed parts of Europe; on the other hand, the laws of celestial nature were being mapped with unprecedented accuracy. On earth, both nature and human affairs often seemed to verge on chaos; heaven, by contrast, exhibited perfect order. Cosmic order gave the natural philosophers of the seventeenth century confidence, as it has given confidence to priest-kings throughout human history. In premodern times, rulers believed that the regularities discernible above could somehow be brought down below. In early modern Europe, natural philosophers had grounds for hoping that the rigorous method that opened the secrets of heaven could work similar wonders on earth. For two centuries, however, there was hardly any link between the splendid theoretical reaches of the new science and applications that catered to ordinary human needs. Agricultural advances during the eighteenth century had more to do with changes in practice (crop rotation, for example), in a more systematic use of knowledge gained through centuries of trial and error, in changes of land tenure and ownership, and suchlike than with the bright discoveries of an abstract, mechanistic, heaven-inspired science.

To this observation a critic may say, "Well, what do you expect? The challenges of agriculture can be met only by close attention to the intricacies and interdependencies of land and life, to what is happening at our feet and before our eyes rather than in a scientist's playpen (the laboratory), or by seeking models of analysis and conceptualization suited to the world of astronomy and physics. In short, to live well, one needs more down-to-earth realism, not escapism."

This sensible answer has its own difficulties. As we now know, what may be deemed escapism turns out to be a circuitous route to unprecedented manipulative power over organic life, and not just predictive power over the stars. One branch of the route took the scientific and entrepreneurial spirits of the West from the study of general chemistry to the study of soil chemistry, and from there to the manufacture of chemical fertilizers, the use of which led to impressively higher crop yields; another branch took them from the study of genetics to the scientific breeding of plants and animals, which became more and more ingenious, reaching a high peak in the Green Revolution, and onward to genetic engineering. While all this was taking place, the same theoretic-analytic bent of mind produced agricultural machines of increasing power and flexibility, and, one might add, the complex organizational and marketing strategies of advanced farming. Countries that embraced these discoveries and inventions prospered. In the second half of the twentieth century, cornucopia no longer seems just a dream, as it has been for the vast majority of people throughout human time. A substantial number of people in the developed parts of the world encounter it day after day. They have learned to take the supermarket's dazzling pyramids of fruits and vegetables, its esplanades of meat, for granted. And yet a doubt lingers as to whether such abundance is real and can last, whether it is not just an effect of Prospero's magic wand. The upward curve of success in the West has not altogether removed the feeling that technological society must, sooner or later, pay for its arrogation of powers that rightly belong only to nature and nature's God.

Escape to Nature

I have given a brief and sweeping account of "escape from nature," which has taken us from uncertain yields in village clearings to supermarket cornucopia. The escape is made possible by different kinds of power: the power of humans working cooperatively and, deliberatively together, the power of technology, and underlying them, the power of images and ideas. The realities thus created do not, however, necessarily produce contentment. They may, on the contrary, generate frustration and restlessness. Again people seek to escape—this time "back to nature."

Escaping or returning to nature is a well-worn theme. I mention it to provide a counterpoint to the story of escaping *from* nature, but also to draw attention to certain facets of the "back to nature" sentiment that have not yet entered the common lore. One is the antiquity of this sentiment. A yearning for the natural and the wild goes back almost to the beginning of city building in ancient Sumer. A hint of it can already be found in the epic of Gilgamesh, which tells of the natural man Enkidu, who was seduced by gradual steps to embrace the refinements of civilization, only to regret on his deathbed what he had left behind: a free life cavorting with gazelles.

The second point I wish to underline is this: Although a warm sentiment for nature is common among urban sophisticates, as we know from well-documented European and East Asian history, it is not confined to them. The extreme artificiality of a built environment is not itself an essential cause or inducement. Consider the Lele of Kasai in tropical Africa. They do not have cities, yet they know what it is like to yearn for nature. What they wish to escape from is the modestly humanized landscape they have made from the savanna next to the Kasai River, for to keep everything there in good order—from social relations to huts and groundnut plots—they must be constantly vigilant, and that proves burdensome. To find relief, the Lele men periodically leave behind the glare and heat of the savanna, with its interminable chores and obligations, to plunge into the dark, cool, and nurturing rain forest on the other side of the river, which to them is the source of all good things, a gift of God.

The third point is that "back to nature" varies enormously in scale. At one end of the scale are such familiar and minor undertakings as the weekend camping trip to the forest and, more permanently, the return to a rural commune way of life. At the other end of the scale is the European settlement of North America itself. It too might be considered a type of "escape to nature." Old Europe was the city; the New World was nature. True, many settlers came from Europe's rural towns and villages rather than from its large cities. Nevertheless, they were escaping from a reality that seemed too firmly set and densely packed to the spaces and simpler ways of life in the New World.

My final point is this: Back-to-nature movements at all scales, including the epic scale of transatlantic migration, have seldom resulted in the abandonment, or even serious depletion, of populations in the home bases—the major cities and metropolitan fields, which over time have continued to gain inhabitants and to further distance themselves from nature.

This last point serves to remind us that "escape to nature" is dependent on "escape *from* nature." The latter is primary and inexorable. It is so because pressures of population and social constraint must build up first before the desire to escape from them can arise; and I have already urged that these pressures are themselves a consequence of culture—of our desire and ability to escape from nature. "Escape from nature" is primary for another reason, namely, that the nature one escapes to, because it is the target of desire rather than a vague "out there" to which one is unhappily thrust, must have been culturally delineated and endowed with value. What we wish to escape to is not "nature" but an alluring conception of it, and this conception is necessarily a product of a people's experience and history—their culture. Paradoxical as it may sound, "escape to nature" is a cultural undertaking, a covered-up attempt to "escape from nature."

Nature and Culture

Nature is culturally defined, a point of view that is by now widely accepted among environmental theorists. Culturally defined? Humanly constituted? Is this the latest eruption of hubris in the Western world? Not necessarily, for the idea can reasonably be coupled with another one, inspired by Wittgenstein, namely this: That which is defined and definable, that which can be encompassed by language or image, may be just a small part of all there is—Nature with a capital *N*. Now, in this chapter I myself have been using the word "nature" in a restricted sense—nature with a small *n*. What do I mean by it? What is the culture that has influenced me? It is the culture of academic geography. The meaning that I give the word is traditional among geographers: Nature is that layer of the earth's surface and the air above it that have been unaffected, or minimally affected, by humans; hence, the farther back we reach in time, the greater will be the extent of nature. Another way of putting it is this: Nature is what remains or what can recuperate over time when all humans and their works are removed.

These ideas of nature are a commonplace in today's world, thanks in part to their popularization in the environmental movement. They seem nonarbitrary, an accurate reflection of a common type of human experience and not just the fantasy of a particular people and time. But is this true? I believe it is. The nature/culture distinction, far from being an academic artifact, is recognized, though in variant forms, in all civilized societies—"civilized" itself being a self-conscious self-designation that postulates an opposite that is either raw and crude or pure and blissful. More generally, the distinction is present—in the subtext, if not the text—whenever and wherever humans have managed to create a material world of their own, even if this be no more than a rough clearing in which are located a few untidy fields and huts. I have already referred to the Lele in Africa. Their appreciation for a pure nature away from womenfolk, society, and culture is as romantic (and sexist) as that of modern American males. Thousands of miles away live the Gimi of New Guinea, another people of simple material means, whose bipolar *kore/dusa* is roughly equivalent to our "nature/culture." *Dusa* is the cultural and social world, opposed to *kore,* which means "wild"—the rain forest with forms of life, plant and animal, that occur spontaneously and hence are "pure."

What about hunter-gatherers, who live off nature and have not carved a permanent cultural space from it? "Nature/culture" is unlikely to be a part of their vocabulary; they don't need it in their intimate, personal, and constant involvement with the individualized, all-encompassing natural elements. But since they undoubtedly feel at home in the midst of these elements, what an outsider calls wild and natural is to them not that at all; rather, it is a world acculturated by naming, storytelling, rituals, personal experience. This familiar world is bounded. Hunter-gatherers are aware that it ends somewhere—at this cliff or that river. Beyond is the Unknown, which, however, is not "nature" as understood by other peoples. It is too underdefined, too far beyond language and experience, to be that.

A current trend in anthropological thinking is to wonder whether the nature/culture dichotomy is not more an eighteenth-century European invention than anything fundamental to human experience. The binary in Western usage has fallen into disfavor because it is considered too categorical or abstract, and because it almost invariably sets up a rank order with women somehow ending at the bottom, whether they be identified with nature or with culture. One may also raise the linguistic conundrum of how far meanings must overlap to justify the use of European-language terms for non-European ones. I now offer one more reason for the declining popularity of the nature/culture binary. It is that one of the two terms has come to be dominant. In our time, culture seems to have taken over nature. Hardly any place on earth is without some human imprint. True, nature in the large sense includes the molten interior of the earth and the distant stars, and these we have not touched. But even they bear our mental imprint. Our minds have played over them; they are, as it were, our mental/cultural constructs. The ubiquity of culture in the life experience of modern people is surprisingly like that of hunter-gatherers, who, as I have indicated, live almost wholly in a cultural world with no nature, separate and equal, to act as a counterweight. There remains what I have called Nature with the capital *N*. But it, like the Unknown of hunter-gatherers, is beyond thought, words, and pictures. Whatever we touch and modify, whatever we see or even think about, falls into the cultural side of the ledger, leaving the other side devoid of content. Culture is, in this sense, everywhere. But far from feeling triumphant, modern men and women feel "orphaned." A reality that is merely a world ("world" derives from *wer* = man) can seem curiously unreal, even if that world is functional and harmonious, which is far from being always the case. The possibility that everywhere we look we see only our own faces is not reassuring; indeed, it is a symptom of madness. In order to feel real, sane, and anchored, we need nature as impact—the "bites and blows [of wind] upon my body . . . that feelingly persuade me what I am" (Shakespeare, *As You Like It* 2.I.8, II); and we may even need nature as that which forever eludes the human mind.

But this hardly exhausts the twists and turns in meaning of nature/culture, real/imaginary. So the real is impact—the unassimilable and natural. But, as I have noted earlier, the opposite can seem more true. The real is the cultural. The cultural trumps the natural by appearing not so much humanmade as spiritual or divine. Thus, the cosmic city is more real than wilderness. The poem is more real than vague feeling. The ritual is more real than everyday life. In all of them there is a psychological factor that enhances the sense of the real and couples it with the divine, namely, lucidity. My own exposition of nature and culture, to the extent that it seems to me lucidly revelatory, is more real to me than whatever confused experiences I have of both. When I am thinking and writing well, I feel I have escaped to the real.

Escape to the Real and the Lucid

I began this chapter by noting that escapism has a somewhat negative meaning because of the common notion that what one escapes from is reality and what one escapes to is fantasy. People say, "I am fed up with snow and slush and the hassles of my job, so I am going to Hawaii." Hawaii here stands for paradise and hence the unreal. In place of Hawaii, one can substitute any number of other things: from a good book and the movies to a tastefully decorated shopping mall and Disneyland, from a spell in the suburbs or the countryside to a weekend at a first-rate hotel in Manhattan or Paris. In other societies and times, the escape might be to a storyteller's world, a communal feast, a village fair, a ritual. What one escapes to is culture—not culture that has become daily life, not culture as a dense and inchoate environment and way of coping, but culture that exhibits lucidity, a quality that often comes out of a process of simplification. Lucidity, I maintain, is almost always desirable. About simplification, however, one can feel ambivalent. If, for example, a people's experience of a place or event is one of simplification, they may soon feel bored and dismiss it—in retrospect, if not at that time—as a thinly constructed fantasy of no lasting significance. Escape into it from time to time, though understandable, is suspect. If, however, their experience has more the feel of clarity than of simplification, they may well regard it as an encounter with the real. Escape into a good book is escape into the real, as the late French president François Mitterrand insisted. Participation in a ritual is participation in something serious and real; it is escape from the banality and opaqueness of life into an event that clarifies life and yet preserves a sense of mystery.

To illustrate the wide acceptance of the idea that whatever is lucid feels real, consider two worlds of experience that superficially have nothing in common: academia and wild nature. Society at large has often called academia "an ivory tower," implying that life there is not quite real. Academics themselves see otherwise; it is their view that if they escape from certain entanglements of "real life," it is only so that they may better engage with the real, and it is this engagement with the real that makes what they do so deeply rewarding. And how do they engage with the real? The short answer is, Through processes and procedures of simplification that produce clarity and a quasi-aesthetic sense of having got the matter under study right. Now, consider wild nature. A sojourn in its midst may well be regarded as an escape into fantasy, far from the frustrations and shocks of social life. Yet nature lovers see otherwise. For them, the escape into nature is an escape into the real. One reason for this feeling certainly does not apply to academia. It is that the real *is* the natural, the fundament that has not been disturbed or covered up by human excrescences. What academia and nature share—perhaps the only outstanding characteristic that they share—is simplicity. Academic life is self-evidently a simpler organization than the greater society in which it is embedded. As for nature, in what sense is it simple or simpler—and simpler than what? However the answer is given, one thing is certain: People of urban background—and increasingly people are of such background—know little about plants and animals, soils and rock, even if they now live in exurbia or have a home in rural Idaho. Other than the few trained naturalists among them, their images of nature tend to be highly selective and schematic; indeed, for lack of both knowledge and experience, they may well carry reductionism further in the imaging of nature than in the imaging of social life, with the result that nature becomes the more clearly delineated of the two, more comprehensible, and therefore more real.

Middle Landscapes As Ideal and Real

Between the big artificial city at one extreme and wild nature at the other, humans have created "middle landscapes" that, at various times and in different parts of the world, have been acclaimed the model human habitat. They are, of course, all works of culture, but not conspicuously or arrogantly so. They show how humans can escape nature's rawness without moving so far from it as to appear to deny roots in the organic world. The middle landscape also earns laurels because it can seem more real—more what life is or ought to be like—compared with the extremes of nature and city, both of which can seem unreal for contradictory reasons of thinness and inchoateness. Thinness occurs when nature is reduced to pretty image and city is reduced to geometric streets and high-rises; inchoateness occurs when nature and city have become a jungle, confused and disorienting. Historically, however, the middle landscape has its problems serving as ideal habitat. One problem is that it is not one, but many. Many kinds of landscape qualify as "middle"—for example, farmland, suburbia, garden city and garden, model town, and theme parks that emphasize the good life. They all distance themselves from wild nature and the big city but otherwise have different values. The second problem is that the middle landscape, whatever the kind, proves unstable. It reverts to nature, or, more often, it moves step by step toward the artifices of the city even as it strives to maintain its position in the middle.

Of the different kinds of middle landscape, the most important by far, economically, is the land given over to agriculture. People who live on and off the land are rooted in place. Peasant farmers all over the world—the mass of human population until well into the twentieth century—live, work, and die in the confines of their village and its adjoining fields. So the label "escapist" has the least application to them. Indeed, they and their way of life can so blend into nature that to visitors from the city they are nature—elements of a natural scene. That merging into nature is enhanced by another common perception of peasant life: its quality of "timelessness." Culture there is visibly a conservative force. To locals and outsiders alike, its past as a succession of goals, repeatedly met or—for lack of power—renounced, is lost to consciousness. Yet farmers, like everybody else, make improvements whenever they can and with whatever means they have. Their culture has taken cumulative steps forward, though these are normally too gradual to be noticed. Of course, one can find exceptions in the better endowed and politically more sophisticated parts of the world—Western Europe in the eighteenth century, for example. There, science in the broad sense of the systematic application of useful knowledge enabled agriculture to move from triumph to triumph in the next two hundred years, with far-ranging consequences, including one of psychological unease. An "unbearable lightness of being" was eventually to insinuate itself into the one area of human activity where people have felt—and many still feel—that they ought to be more bound than free. Nostalgia for traditional ways of making a living on the family farm is at least in part a wish to regain a sense of weight and necessity, of being subjected to demands of nature that allow little or no room for fanciful choice.

The garden is another middle landscape between wild nature and the city. Although the word evokes the natural, the garden itself is manifestly an artifact. In China one speaks of "building" a garden, whereas in Europe one may speak of "planting" a garden. The difference suggests that the Chinese, unlike Europeans, are more ready to admit the garden's artifactual character. Because artifice connotes civilization to the Chinese elite, it doesn't have quite the negative meaning it has for Europeans brought up on stories of prelapsarian Eden and on Romantic conceptions of nature. European gardens were originally planted to meet certain basic needs around the house: food, medicinal herbs, and suchlike. In early medieval times they were an indiscriminate mixture of the useful and the beautiful, as much horticulture as art. Progressively, however, the gardens of the potentates moved in the direction of aesthetics and architecture. From the sixteenth century onward, first in Renaissance Italy, then in Baroque France, gardens were proudly built to project an air of power and artifice. The technical prowess that made playful foundations and mechanical animals possible, together with the garden's traditional link to the phantasms of theater, resulted in the creation of an illusionary world remote indeed from its humble beginnings close to the soil and livelihood.

A striking example of the pleasure garden in our century is the Disney theme park—a unique American creation that, thanks to modern technology, is able to produce wonder and illusion far beyond that which could be achieved in earlier times. Unique too is the theme park's erasure of the present in favor of not only a mythic past but also a starry future—in favor, moreover, of a frankly designed Fantasyland peopled by characters from fairy tales and from Disney's own fertile imagination. What is more escapist than that? In the spectrum of middle landscapes, a countryside of villages and fields stands at the opposite pole to a Disney park. The one lies closest to nature; the other is as far removed from it as possible without becoming "city." Disney's carefully designed and controlled world has often been criticized for encouraging a childish and irresponsible frame of mind. But again my question is, What if culture *is,* in a fundamental sense, a mechanism of escape? To see culture as escape or escapism is to share a disposition common to all who have had some experience in exercising power—a disposition that is unwilling to accept "what is the case" (reality) when it seems to them unjust or too severely constraining. Of course, their efforts at escaping, whether purely in imagination or by taking tangible steps, may fail—may end in disaster for themselves, for other people, for nature. The human species uniquely confronts the dilemma of a powerful imagination that, while it makes escape to a better life possible, also makes possible lies and deception, solipsistic fantasy, madness, unspeakable cruelty, violence, and destructiveness—evil.

1998

GETTING STARTED

1. Tuan says that "'escapism' has a somewhat negative meaning in our society and perhaps in all societies" (p. 535). How does he defend that claim? Use the dictionary and the thesaurus to find and write down synonyms for "escapism." Do they have positive

or negative connotations? What does "escapism" mean to you? Is there a difference between "escape" and "escapism"?

2. "Seeing what is not there lies at the foundation of all human culture," according to Tuan (p. 536). Do you agree? Spend twenty minutes free writing on the topic. Analyze the statement. What oppositions is Tuan assuming? Does he see this ability as positive or negative? How do you see it?

3. Consider Tuan's distinctions between "nature" and "Nature" and between nature and culture. How do these oppositions operate? In a group, make a list of the other oppositions Tuan names. From your reading for this class and others and from your own experience, make a list of other pairs of terms that operate in similar ways. Compare your list with lists generated by the other members of your working group and with Tuan's list. Which pairs of terms appear on more than one list? What makes these common pairs different?

WRITING

4. Write a short essay in which you demonstrate through examples from your own experience the difference between "escape from" and "escape to." When you think about escaping, where do you imagine yourself going? How would it be different from where you are? You might use examples from Tuan's essay as a way of explaining your own.

5. Write a short essay that summarizes and then responds to the following quotation from Tuan's essay: "What one escapes to is culture—not culture that has become daily life, not culture as a dense and inchoate environment and way of coping, but culture that exhibits lucidity, a quality that often comes out of a process of simplification" (p. 547). Look at the oppositions presented in the quotation. How do they operate? Give examples of the different types of culture he is referring to. How does Tuan define "lucidity"? Why does he value it?

USING THE LIBRARY AND THE INTERNET

6. Look up brochures or Web sites for travel destinations while considering Tuan's ideas about escape. Are the places you see advertised using "escape" as a selling point? Look carefully at your examples, and take notes on how vacations are represented. Find a place in Tuan's text where he provides an idea or statement that applies to your example.

7. Search for the term "escapism" using a database of scholarly articles such as Academic Search Elite or a database such as MAS Full Text Ultra that includes general-interest and current-events related magazines. Try related searches such as "nature and escapism" or "environment and escape." Scan your findings and print out one or two articles that seem to relate to Tuan's ideas in interesting ways.

MAKING CONNECTIONS

8. Compare Tuan's idea of "the real" on page 536 with Jeanette Winterson's discussion of "reality" in "Imagination and Reality" (p. 593). Why do both writers seize on "reality" as an idea to be challenged? Do these writers share common ground on this issue? To what extent are they making similar arguments? Would either Winterson or Tuan see art as an escape?

9. Examine Tuan's concept of the "middle landscape," and use it to analyze other potential middle landscapes in the essays you have read. For example, does Susan Willis's discussion of Disney World support Tuan's analysis? Is Gloria Anzaldúa's borderland, in "Chicana Artists: Exploring *Nepantla, el Lugar de la Frontera,*" a middle landscape? What can we learn by applying Tuan's term in these examples?

10. In "Designs for Escape," Witold Rybczynski explores one couple's attempt to construct their dream house. Discuss Rybczynski's account of this process in terms of Tuan's ideas of escape. Why do both writers spend so much time examining imagination? What is the relationship between imagination and escape?

Sherry Turkle

Sherry Turkle (1948–) is a licensed clinical psychologist and the Abby Rockefeller Mauze Professor of the Sociology of Science in the Program in Science, Technology, and Society at the Massachusetts Institute of Technology. Her work in psychology increasingly concerns the impact of technology on the human mind. In addition to three books, Turkle has written numerous articles, book reviews, and commentaries for scholarly and popular audiences. She frequently lectures and appears regularly on both television and radio. "The Triumph of Tinkering" is a section from *Life on the Screen: Identity in the Age of the Internet* (1995).

To learn more about Turkle and her current research, visit her home page at <http://www.mit.edu:8001/people/sturkle/>.

The Triumph of Tinkering

In the late 1960s, I studied history and political theory in Paris. In my academic program, all foreigners had to take a French composition class. Over the year, the format of this class never varied. A subject was set, everyone had one week to turn in an outline and two more to write the composition. Then the three-week cycle would begin again with the assignment of a new topic. The format of the composition never varied. Each one had to be written in three parts, with each of these parts further divided into three parts. Although I knew many of my classmates took to this style easily, for me this was a completely alien way of writing. My way had been to read, think, and make notes on little pieces of paper. I would spread these notes out in my room, across my bed, desk, and floor. Then I would immerse myself in their contents, move them around into patterns, scribble in their margins, associate to new patterns, write small bits of text, and frequently rewrite sections. Now, under pressure from the new rules, I developed a technique for getting by. I did my reading and thinking, wrote my notes and bits of text, spread them out in my room, and let my composition emerge—but I did all this in the first week, periodically adjusting the emerging composition so that it would grow with the right number of divisions and subdivisions. After a week of hectic activity, I extracted an outline in three parts. I turned in that outline and put the completed composition in my desk drawer, where it waited two weeks for its turn to be handed in to the instructor.

I am tempted to tell this story in a way that makes it sound like a triumph of my creativity over Gallic rigidity. But that would miss an important aspect of what these French lessons meant to me. Far from increasing my confidence, they undermined it. I wrote my composition before my outline in order to survive, but in the process I came to think of my kind of writing as wrong. My kind of writing was, after all, cheating. The instructor in my 1978 programming class at Harvard—the one who called the computer a giant calculator—described programming methods in universal terms, which he said were justified by the computer's essential nature. But from the very beginning of my inquiries into the computer culture, it became clear that different people approach programming in very different ways. Where my professor saw the necessary hegemony of a single correct style, I found a range of effective yet diverse styles among both novices and experts.

The "universal" method recommended by my Harvard instructor is known as structured programming. A model of the modernist style, it is rule-driven and relies on top-down planning. First you sketch out a master plan in which you make very explicit what your program must do. Then you break the task into manageable subprograms or subprocedures, which you work on separately. After you create each piece, you name it according to its function and close it off, a procedure known as black boxing. You need not bother with its details again. By the 1970s, this structured, planner's method was widely accepted as the canonical style in computing. Indeed, many engineers and computer scientists still see it as the definitive procedure, as simply the way things must be done. They have a powerful, practical rationale for this method. In real organizations, many people have to be able to understand and use any particular piece of software. That means it has to be understandable and fixable (debuggable) long after its programmer has left the research team or business setting.

Others, however, had a style of programming that bore a family resemblance to my associative style of writing, a "soft" style as opposed to a "hard" one. It was bottom-up rather than top-down. It was built up by playing with the elements of a program, the bits of code, much as I played with the elements of my essay, the bits of paper strewn across my room. It is best captured by a word, bricolage, that Claude Lévi-Strauss has used to contrast the analytic methodology of Western science with an associative science of the concrete practiced in many non-Western societies. The tribal herbalist, for example, does not proceed by abstraction but by thinking through problems using the materials at hand. By analogy, problem-solvers who do not proceed from top-down design but by arranging and rearranging a set of well-known materials can be said to be practicing bricolage. They tend to try one thing, step back, reconsider, and try another. For planners, mistakes are steps in the wrong direction; bricoleurs navigate through midcourse corrections. Bricoleurs approach problem-solving by entering into a relationship with their work materials that has more the flavor of a conversation than a monologue. In the context of programming, the bricoleur's work is marked by a desire to play with lines of computer code, to move them around almost as though they were material things—notes on a score, elements of a collage, words on a page.

Through the mid-1980s, soft-style programmers, programming's bricoleurs, received their own discouraging "French lessons" from a mainstream computer culture deeply committed to structured programming. People who did not program according to the canon were usually told that their way was wrong. They were forced to comply with the officially sanctioned method of doing things. Today, however, there has been a significant change. As the computer culture's center of gravity has shifted from programming to dealing with screen simulations, the intellectual values of bricolage have become far more important. In the 1970s and 1980s, computing served as an initiation into the formal values of hard mastery. Now, playing with simulation encourages people to develop the skills of the more informal soft mastery because it is so easy to run "What if?" scenarios and tinker with the outcome.

The revaluation of bricolage in the culture of simulation includes a new emphasis on visualization and the development of intuition through the manipulation of virtual objects. Instead of having to follow a set of rules laid down in advance, computer users are encouraged to tinker in simulated microworlds. There, they learn about how things work by interacting with them. One can see evidence of this change in the way businesses do their financial planning, architects design buildings, and teenagers play with simulation games.

There is something ironic about the computer presence playing a role in nurturing such "informalist" ways of knowing, since for so long, the computer was seen as the ultimate embodiment of the abstract and formal. But the computer's intellectual personality has always had another side. Computational objects—whether lines of codes or icons on a screen—are like abstract and mathematical objects, defined by the most formal of rules. But at the same time, they are like physical objects—like dabs of paint or cardboard cutouts. You can see them and move them, and in some cases you can place one on top of another. Computational objects have always offered an almost-physical access to the world of formal systems. There have always been people whose way of interacting with them had more in common with the style of the painter than with that of the logician.

Consider Lisa, an eighteen-year-old freshman in my Harvard programming course. Lisa's first experiences in the course were very positive. She wrote poetry and found that she was able to approach programming with ways of thinking that she had previously found useful in working with words. But as the term progressed, she came under increasing pressure from her instructors to think in ways that were not her own. Her alienation did not stem from an inability to cope with programming but rather from her preference to do it in a way that came into conflict with the structured and rule-driven style of the computer culture she had entered.

In high school, Lisa had turned away from her own natural abilities in mathematics. "I didn't care if I was good at it. I wanted to work in worlds where languages had moods and connected you with people." She was equally irritated when her teachers tried to get her interested in mathematics by calling it a language. As a senior in high school, she wrote a poem that expressed her sentiments.

If you could say in numbers what I say now in words,
If theorems could, like sentences, describe the flight of birds,
If PPL [a computer language] had meter and parabolas had rhyme,
Perhaps I'd understand you then,
Perhaps I'd change my mind. . . .

But all this wishful thinking only serves to make things worse,
When I compare my dearest love with your numeric verse.
For if mathematics were a language, I'd succeed, I'd scale the hill,
I know I'd understand, but since it's not, I never will.

When she wrote poetry, Lisa knew where all the elements were at every point in the development of her ideas. "I feel my way from one word to another," she said. She wanted her relationship to computer language to be the same. She wanted to tinker, to work as close to the programming code as she did to the words in her poems. When she spoke about the lines of code in her programs, she gestured with her hands and body in a way that showed her moving them and among them. She talked about the elements of her programs as if they were physically graspable.

When Lisa worked on large programs she preferred to write her own smaller subprograms even though she was encouraged to use prepackaged ones available in a program library. She resented that she couldn't tinker with the prepackaged routines. Her teachers chided her, insisting that her demand for hands-on contact was making her work more difficult. They told her that the right way to do things was to control a program by planning. Lisa recognized the value of these techniques for someone else. She herself was reluctant to use them as starting points for her learning. Although her teachers tried to convert her to what they considered proper style, Lisa insisted that she had to work her way if she were ever going to feel comfortable with computers. But two months into the programming course, Lisa abandoned the fight to do things her way and decided to do things their way. She called it her "not-me strategy" and began to insist that it didn't matter because "the computer was just a tool."

Lisa's classmate, Robin, was a pianist with a similar learning style. She wanted to play with computational elements, to manipulate the bits of code, as though they were musical notes or phrases. She, too, was told her way was wrong. Her instructor told her it was "a waste of time."

Lisa and Robin came to the programming course with anxieties about not belonging because they did not see themselves as "computer people." Although both could master the class material intellectually, the course exacerbated their anxieties about not belonging because it insisted on a style of work so different from their own. Both received top grades, but each had to deny who she was in order to succeed. Lisa said that she turned herself "into a different kind of person," and Robin described what she had to do as "faking it."

In the 1970s and 1980s, soft mastery was computing's "different voice." Different and in no way equal. The authorities (teachers and other experts) actively discouraged it, deeming it incorrect or improper. But I found many Lisas and many Robins in schools, universities, and local computer clubs. These were boys and girls, men and women, novices and experts, who reported that they had changed their styles to suit the fashion when they had started to interact with the official computer world. "I got my wrists slapped enough times and I changed my ways," says a college student for whom soft style programming was a passion until he entered MIT and was instructed in the canonical programming style. The cost of such wrist slapping was high. On an individual level, talent was wasted, self-image eroded. On the social level, the computer culture was narrowed.

With the rise of a personal computer culture in the 1980s, more people owned their own machines and could do what they pleased with them. This meant that more people began to experience the computer as an expressive medium that they could use in their own ways. Yet for most, the notion that the computer was a calculator died hard. The idea that the computer was a new medium of expression would not make sense until the 1990s, when large numbers of people owned personal computers with color screens, powerful graphics, and CD-ROMs. In the 1970s through the mid-1980s, the ideology that there was only one right way to "do" computers nearly masked the diversity of styles in the computer culture. In those days top-down thinkers didn't simply share a style; they constituted an epistemological elite.

Discoveries and Denigrations of the Concrete

The elite status of abstract thinking in Western thought can be traced back at least to Plato. Western scientific culture has traditionally drawn a firm line between the abstract and the concrete. The tools of abstraction are propositions; the tools of concrete thinking are objects, and there has always been a right and wrong side of the tracks.

The terms "pure science" and "pure mathematics" made clear the superiority of selecting for the pristine propositions and filtering out the messy objects. In the twentieth century, the role of things-in-thinking has had powerful intellectual champions. But, even among these champions there has been resistance to the importance of the bottom-up style of thought preferred by Lisa and Robin. For example, Lévi-Strauss and the noted Swiss psychologist Jean Piaget both discovered ways of reasoning that began with objects and moved to theory, but then they found ways to marginalize them.

In the 1920s and 1930s, Piaget first noticed concrete modes of reasoning among children. Children thought that when you spread three marbles apart there were more marbles than when you moved three marbles close together. Through such observations, Piaget was able to see what others had not: Concrete mapping and manipulation of objects enable children to develop the concept of number, a concept that only gradually becomes a formal sense of quantity. The construction of number, in other words, is born through bricolage.

Piaget fought for the recognition of this kind of concrete thinking, but at the same time he saw it as something to be outgrown. The adult was "beyond" the concrete. For Piaget there was a progression in modes of reasoning that culminates in a final, formal stage when propositional logic liberates intelligence from the need to think with things. So Piaget both discovered the power of the concrete in the construction of the fundamental categories of number, space, time, and causality, and denigrated what he had found by relegating concrete ways of knowing to an early childhood stage of development.

Piaget's discoveries about the processes of children's thinking challenged a kind of cultural amnesia. Adults forget the way they reasoned as children. And we forget very quickly. While Freud discovered the forgetting of infantile sexuality, Piaget identified a second amnesia: the forgetting of concrete styles of thinking. In both, our stake in forgetting is highly charged. In our culture, the divide between abstract and concrete is not simply a boundary between propositions and objects but a way of separating the clean from the messy, virtue from taboo.

Lévi-Strauss, too, both discovered and denied the concrete. He described bricoleur scientists who do not move abstractly and hierarchically from axiom to theorem to corollary but construct theories by arranging and rearranging a set of well-known materials. But the bricoleur scientists he described all operated in non-Western societies. As Piaget had relegated the concrete to childhood, Lévi-Strauss relegated it to the so-called "primitive" and to modern Western humanists. What Lévi-Strauss had a hard time seeing were the significant elements of bricolage in the practice of Western science.

Am I practicing a similar devaluation of the concrete when I characterize the rule-based planner's programming style as hard mastery and Lisa and Robin's style as soft? Our culture tends to equate the word "soft" with unscientific and undisciplined as well as with the feminine and with a lack of power. Why use a term like "soft" when it could turn difference into devaluation? What interests me here is the transvaluation of values. "Soft" is a good word for a flexible, nonhierarchical style, one that allows a close connection with one's objects of study. Using the term "soft Mastery" goes along with seeing negotiation, relationship, and attachment as cognitive virtues. And this is precisely what the culture of simulation encourages us to do.

The soft approach is not a style unique to either men or women. However, in our culture it is a style to which many women are drawn. Among other reasons, we train girls in the component skills of a soft approach—negotiation, compromise, give and take—as psychological virtues, while dominant models of desirable male behavior stress decisiveness and the imposition of will. Boys and girls are encouraged to adopt different relational stances in the world of people. It is not surprising that these differences show up when men and women deal with the world of things.

Through the mid-1980s, a male-dominated computer culture that took one style as the right and only way to program discriminated against soft approaches. Although this bias hurt both male and female computer users, it fell disproportionately on women because they were disproportionately represented in the ranks of the soft masters. But even when women felt free to experiment with soft mastery, they faced a special conflict. Tinkering required a close encounter with the computer. But this violated a cultural taboo about being involved with "machines" that fell particularly harshly on women. When I was a young girl, I assembled the materials to build a crystal radio. My mother, usually encouraging, said, "Don't touch it, you'll get a shock." Her tone, however, did not communicate fear for my safety, but distaste. A generation later, many women were learning to identify being a woman with all that a computer is not, and computers with all that a woman is not. In this cultural construction, computers could be very threatening. In recent years, things have started to change. As the emerging culture of simulation becomes increasingly associated with negotiational and nonhierarchical ways of thinking, it has made a place for people with a wider range of cognitive and emotional styles. In particular, women have come to feel that computers are more culturally acceptable.

The Revaluation of the Concrete

Soft mastery is not a stage, it is a style. Bricolage is a way to organize work. It is not a stage in a progression to a superior form. Richard Greenblatt is a renowned first-generation MIT hacker, a computer culture legend whose virtuoso style of work incorporates a strong dose of bricolage. He has made significant contributions to the development of chess programs as well as systems programming. In the spirit of the painter who steps back to look at the canvas before proceeding to the next step, Greenblatt developed software that put him in a conversation, a negotiation with his materials. He used bricolage at a high level of artistry.

Yet even internationally recognized bricoleur virtuosos such as Richard Greenblatt lived within a dominant computer culture that was scornful of their approach. One of that culture's heroes was the mathematician Edsger W. Dijkstra. Dijkstra, the leading theorist of hard, structured programming, emphasized analytical methods and scientific rigor in the development of programs. In Dijkstra's view, a rigorous planning coupled with mathematical analysis should produce a computer program with mathematically guaranteed success. In this model, there is no room for bricolage. When Dijkstra gave a lecture at MIT in the late 1970s, he demonstrated his points by taking his audience step by step through the development of a short program. Richard Greenblatt was in the audience, and the two men had an exchange that has entered into computer culture mythology. It was a classic confrontation between two opposing aesthetics. Greenblatt asked Dijkstra how he could apply his mathematical methods to something as complicated as a chess program. "I wouldn't write a chess program," Dijkstra replied, dismissing the issue.

In the field of computing, the existence of the bricolage style at virtuoso levels challenged the idea of there being only one correct, mature approach to problem-solving. In the 1980s, this challenge was supported by several currents of research on concrete styles of problem-solving in other domains. Each in its own way called into question the hegemony of the abstract, formal, and rule-driven. Each contributed to a revaluation of the contextual and concrete, in which computers were now playing an unexpected role.

First, psychologists showed the way ordinary people in their kitchens and workplaces make effective use of a down-to-earth mathematical thinking very different from the abstract, formal mathematics they were often so unsuccessfully taught at school. Kitchen mathematics relies on the familiar feel and touch of everyday activities. Second, sociologists and anthropologists demonstrated that in scientific laboratories, there is a time-honored tradition of tinkering first and creating formal rationalizations later. Ethnographers of science showed that bench science often depends on a long, messy process of trial and error followed by the final, frantic scramble to rationalize the results. Similarly, close studies of the way scientific papers are written indicated that successive drafts cover the tracks of messy bricoleurs. Finally, feminist scholars gave evidence for the power of contextual reasoning.

The psychologist Carol Gilligan discerned two voices in the development of moral reasoning. We can hear both in the stories she told about children's responses to moral dilemmas. One well-known story involves a man named Heinz. His wife is dying. He needs a drug to save her. He has no money. What should he do? Gilligan reports that when confronted with Heinz's dilemma, (Should Heinz steal a drug to save a life?), eleven-year-old Jake saw it "sort of like a math problem with humans." Jake set it up as an equation and arrived at what he believed was the correct response: Heinz should steal the drug because a human life is worth much more than money. While Jake accepted the problem as a quantitative comparison of two evils, eleven-year-old Amy looked at it in concrete terms, breaking down the problem's restrictive formal frame, and introducing a set of new elements. In particular, she brought the druggist, who probably had a wife of his own, into the story. Amy proposed that Heinz should talk things over with the druggist, who surely would not want anyone to die.

For Jake, justice was like a mathematical principle. To solve a problem, you set up the right algorithm, put it in the right box, crank the handle, and the answer comes out. In contrast, Amy's style of reasoning required her to stay in touch with the inner workings of her arguments, with the relationships and possibly shifting alliances of a group of actors. In other words, Amy was the bricoleur. Her resemblance to Lisa and Robin is striking. They were all very bright. They were all tinkerers who preferred to stay close to their materials as they arranged and rearranged them. And they were all open to the same kind of criticism. Theorists of structured programming would criticize Lisa and Robin's style for the same kind of reasons that "orthodox" academic psychology would classify Amy at a lower intellectual level than Jake. In both cases, criticism would center on the fact that the bricoleurs were unprepared to take a final step in the direction of abstraction. For orthodox psychology, mature thinking is abstract thinking.

Gilligan argued for equal respect for a line of development that uses concrete, increasingly sophisticated ways of thinking about morality. Some people solved problems contextually, through examples, while others relied on rules and abstractions. Gilligan's work supported the idea that abstract reasoning is not a stage but a style. And contextual, situated reasoning is another. Instead of consigning concrete methods to children, "primitives," and humanists, Gilligan validated bricolage as mature, widespread, and useful.

Bricolage is one aspect of soft mastery. Lisa and Robin showed us a second: a desire to work "close to the object." In a biography of the Nobel Prize-winning geneticist Barbara McClintock, Evelyn Fox Keller wrote about this second aspect of soft mastery. McClintock spoke of her work as a conversation with her materials, a conversation that would have to be held in intimate whispers. "Over and over again," says Keller, McClintock "tells us one must have the time to look, the patience to 'hear what the material has to say to you,' the openness to 'let it come to you.' Above all, one must have a 'feeling for the organism.' "

McClintock related to chromosomes much as Lisa and Robin related to computational objects. The neurospora chromosomes McClintock worked with were so small that others had been unable to identify them, yet the more she worked with them, she said, "the bigger [they] got, and when I was really working with them I wasn't outside, I was down there. I was part of the system. I actually felt as if I were right down there and these were my friends. . . . As you look at these things, they become part of you and you forget yourself."

In the course of her career, McClintock's style of work came into conflict with the formal, hard methods of molecular biology. She was recognized and rewarded by the scientific establishment only when others using the formal approach came independently, and much later, to conclusions that she had derived from her investigations. Many of the things that bricoleur programmers have said to me recalled McClintock's creative aesthetic as well as the resistance to it that she encountered. Lorraine, a computer science graduate student, told me that she used "thinking about what the program feels like inside to break through difficult problems." She added, "For appearances' sake I want to look like I'm doing what everyone else is doing, but I'm doing that with only a small part of my mind. The rest of me is imagining what the components feel like. It's like doing my pottery. . . . Keep this anonymous. It makes me sound crazy." This young woman wanted to downplay her style for the same reasons that McClintock had found hers burdensome. People didn't expect it, they didn't understand it, and they didn't see it as scientific.

In her work on McClintock, Keller remarked on the difficulty people face when they try to understand what it might mean to do science in anything other than the formal and abstract canonical style. In the 1980s, personal computers provided a cultural medium in which ideas about noncanonical styles of science could blossom. Many more people could understand the kind of closeness to a scientific object that McClintock was talking about, because they saw themselves relating to icons or lines of computer code in that very way.

Then and Now

In her late-1970s introduction of the computer culture, Lisa saw computers encouraging social isolation and intellectual regimentation. Not only did she complain that the canonical style constrained her to one way of doing things, but she had contempt for "computer people" who were "always working with their machines. . . . They turn to computers as imaginary friends."

Today, significant changes in the computer culture are responding to both of Lisa's objections. Today's high school students are more likely to think of computers as fluid simulation surfaces for writing and game playing than as rigid machines to program. Or they are likely to think of computers as gateways to communication. When fourteen-year-old Steven describes the importance of his personal computer he says, "It has all the programs that make my modem work." Steven uses his family's account on a commercial online service to chat with net-friends. He borrows his mother's university account to join Internet discussion groups and mailing lists on topics ranging from satanism to *Forrest Gump,* and he participates in Multi-User-Domains, or MUDs, in which he plays a character who inhabits the science fiction world of *Dune.* In MUDs, Steven interacts with other real people, although all of them have created imaginary characters. So the social image of the computer is far more complex than before. It now evokes both physical isolation and intense interaction with other people.

On the issue of intellectual regimentation, there has been an equally dramatic change. In essence, software designers have come to agree with Lisa's concern about computers offering only one way. Instead of rules to learn, they want to create environments to explore. These new interfaces project the message, "Play with me, experiment with me, there is no one correct path." The new software design aesthetic effectively says that computer users shouldn't have to work with syntax; they should be able to play with shape, form, color, and sound. Computer users shouldn't have to concern themselves with the complexity of a programming language; they should be given virtual objects that can be manipulated in as direct a way as possible. Whether for serious or recreational purposes, simulations should be placed to try out alternatives, to escape from planning into the world of "What if?" In the 1990s, as computing shifts away from a culture of calculation, bricolage has been given more room to flourish.

Today's software programs typically take the form of a simulation of some reality—playing chess or golf, analyzing a spreadsheet, writing, painting, or making an architectural drawing—and try to place the user within it. Children don't learn natural language by learning its rules, but through immersion in its cadences. Similarly, today's most popular software is designed for immersion. One writer described her relationship with wordprocessing software this way: "At first I felt awkward. I was telling the computer what I wanted to write. Now, I think in Microsoft Word." An architect uses similar language to describe his computer design tools: "At first I was not comfortable with the program. There was just so much I had to tell it. . . . But once I got comfortable designing inside of it, I felt so much freer."

People look at a technology and see beyond it to a constellation of cultural associations. When they saw the early computer enthusiasts take the machine and make a world apart, many people felt they did not belong and did not want to belong. Now, the machine no longer has to be perceived as putting you in a world apart. Indeed, it can put you in the center of things and people—in the center of literature, politics, art, music, communication, and the stock market. The hacker is no longer necessarily or only a "nerd"; he or she can be a cultural icon. The hacker can be Bill Gates.

In the emerging culture of simulation, the computer is still a tool but less like a hammer and more like a harpsichord. You don't learn how to play a harpsichord primarily by learning a set of rules, just as you don't learn about a simulated microworld, whether a Macintosh-like graphical interface or a video game, by delving into an instruction manual. In general, you learn by playful exploration. An architect describes how computer tools help him to design housing units: "I randomly . . . digitize, move, copy, erase the elements—columns, walls, and levels—without thinking of it as a building but rather a sculpture . . . and then take a fragment of it and work on it in more detail." In computer-assisted design environments, those who take most advantage of soft-approach skills are often taking most advantage of computing. In the culture of simulation, bricolage can provide a competitive edge.

The computer culture is close to the point where full membership does not require programming skills, but is accorded to people who use software out of a box. Bricoleurs function well here. Recall that they like to get to know a new environment by interacting with it. When all the computer culture offered were programming environments, the bricoleur wanted to get close to the code. Now when dealing with simulation software, the bricoleur can create the feeling of closeness to the object by manipulating virtual objects on the screen. And bricoleurs are comfortable with exploring the Internet through the World Wide Web. Exploring the Web is a process of trying one thing, then another, of making connections, of bringing disparate elements together. It is an exercise in bricolage.

Gender and Computing: Some Special Lessons

From its very foundations, the notion of scientific objectivity has been inseparable from the image of the scientist's aggressive relationship to nature. And from its very foundations, the quest for scientific objectivity was metaphorically engaged with the language of male domination and female submission. Francis Bacon used the image of the male scientist putting female nature on the rack.

Given this, it is not surprising that many women have felt uncomfortable with the language and ways of thinking traditionally associated with science. And computer science has not been exempt. Programs and operating systems are "crashed" and "killed." For years I wrote on a computer whose operating system asked me if it should "abort" an instruction it could not "execute." This is a language that few women fail to note. Women have too often been faced with the choice—not necessarily conscious—of putting themselves at odds either with the cultural meaning of being a scientist or with the cultural construction of being a woman.

For example, when Lisa minimized the importance the computer had for her by insisting that it was "just a tool," it was more than a way of withdrawing because her programming course had forced her into an uncomfortable approach. It was also a way of insisting that what was most important about being a person (and a woman) was incompatible with close relationships to the technology as it had been presented to her.

Lisa was not alone. Through the 1980s, I found many women who vehemently insisted on the computer's neutrality. There was a clear disparity between their message ("It means nothing to me") and their strong emotion. These women were fighting their own experience of the computer as psychologically gripping. I have noted that they were fighting against an element of their own soft approach. Their style of thinking would have them get close to computational objects, but the closer they got, the more anxious they felt. The more they became involved with the computer in the culture of calculation, the more they insisted that it was only a neutral tool and tried to keep their distance from it.

But women do not insist on distance from all tools. Music students live in a culture that, over time, has slowly grown a language for appreciating close relationships with musical instruments. The harpsichord is just a tool. And yet we understand that artists' encounters with their tools will most probably be close, sensuous, and relational. We assume that artists will develop highly personal styles of working with them.

In the mid-1990s, in the culture of simulation, a new "musical" culture of computing is developing. To get to this point has required technical progress that has permitted new cultural associations to grow. Now that computers are the tools we use to write, to design, to play with ideas and shapes and images, to create video sequences and musical effects, to create interactive novels and graphic images, they are developing a new set of intellectual and emotional associations, more like those we apply to harpsichords than to hammers. The culture of personal computing now makes room for ways of knowing that depend on the "concrete" manipulation of virtual paintbrushes and paints, virtual pens and paper. And we shall see that intellectual disciplines such as cognitive science and artificial intelligence, which previously supported hard mastery, are themselves undergoing changes that make it possible for them to support a somewhat more "informalist" intellectual climate.

A classical modernist vision of computer intelligence has made room for a romantic postmodern one. At this juncture, there is potential for a more welcoming environment for women, humanists, and artists in the technical culture. . . .

1995

GETTING STARTED

1. Working in a group, explore Turkle's idea of "bricolage." Give an example of bricolage from the text. Give a few examples of your own. What does Turkle contrast with bricolage?

2. Choose one of Turkle's examples—the story of Lisa, Robin, Carol Gilligan, or Barbara McClintock—and summarize the example in your own words. Then explain the point that Turkle is making in using that example.

3. Working in a group, list the advantages and disadvantages of the planned or structured style of programming versus the bricolage style. In what ways is each style effective? What are the limitations of each? Apply these terms to other activities, such as writing. What does this awareness of style help you see?

4. Working in a group, track down two or three places in the essay where Turkle discusses gender-related language, such as the use of "abort" or the implications of "soft mastery." Prepare a presentation for the class in which you start with a quote, discuss the gender implications, and add an example from your own experience where an approach, an activity, a word or a phrase has similar gendered implications.

5. Paraphrase the final paragraph of the piece. What does Turkle mean by a "romantic postmodern" vision of computer intelligence?

WRITING

6. Use examples from your own experience and from Turkle's essay to show the differences between planned and structured approaches (to programming, writing, or any other activity) and the bricolage approach. What are the effects and limitations of each? Choose one example of your own to discuss in detail. Does your approach to the activity you have chosen to write about depend strongly on one of these styles or does it mix aspects of each? How does your writing for this class fit into these categories? Why?

7. Turkle favors a problem-solving style "that has more the flavor of a conversation than a monologue" (p. 555). How does tinkering (or bricolage) partake of the conversation model? Why is it like a conversion?

USING THE LIBRARY AND THE INTERNET

8. Use the Internet to test some of Turkle's claims. Choose a topic that you want to learn about and perform two separate Internet searches using a popular search engine. For the first search, follow the planned style by devising a very specific set of goals for

your search. Do not follow links or revise your search unless it is part of the original plan. For the second search, become a bricoleur, improvising and following leads wherever and however you can. Take notes on what you see in both searches and on the advantages and disadvantages of each approach.

9. Using a database such as Academic Search Elite that includes a range of scholarly articles, or one such as MAS Full Text Ultra that includes general-interest and current-events related magazines, try various searches for "computer and gender," "computer and women," or "technology and gender."

MAKING CONNECTIONS

10. Turkle celebrates the "art" of tinkering by comparing creative computer use with the methods of an artist. Comparing the computer to the harpsichord, she argues that "a new 'musical' culture of computing is developing" (p. 565). In "Progress and the Bean," Scott DeVeaux introduces us to Coleman Hawkins, a renowned jazz musician who thinks of himself as a doctor or a scientist of music, working to solve each musical problem as it comes along. Discuss this "cross-pollination" of the arts and the sciences. What are some of the reasons that people who work in one field use analogies from another?

11. Turkle dislikes top-down authority: what she calls the "hegemony" of universal rules (p. 554). Examine the consequence of rules in this essay and in either Susan Willis's analysis of play at Disney World or Gloria Anzaldúa's description of border art. Is bricolage always the better approach? Are there other ways to deal with the hegemony of rules?

Patricia J. Williams

Patricia J. Williams (1951–) is a Professor of Law at Columbia University. She began her legal career as a city attorney in Los Angeles. She has worked for the Western Center on Law and Poverty and taught at a number of law schools across the country. She writes for both scholarly and general audiences on topics relating to race, gender and the law, legal theory, and legal writing. Williams is the author of six books, including *The Rooster's Egg* (1995) and *The Alchemy of Race and Rights* (1991). She also writes a news column, "Diary of a Mad Law Professor." "The Ethnic Scarring of American Whiteness" comes from the essay collection *The House That Race Built: Black Americans, U.S. Terrain* (1997), edited by Wahneema Lubiano.

To learn more about how researchers have begun to think about the topic of American whiteness, go to <http://www.uwm.edu/People/gjay/Whiteness/>.

The Ethnic Scarring of American Whiteness

Representations of race and gender inequality in the United States are endlessly complicated. While I have spent most of my career thinking and writing about the social history packed into being "black" and "female," I am increasingly absorbed by the extent to which Europeans and European-Americans consider and battle among themselves as "minorities." It has been too easy, perhaps, to allow the relative freedoms found by some European immigrants in the "New World" of the United States to obscure the experiences of terrible discrimination in the "Old World," against women, Jews, gays, and certain ethnic groups. And in a time of reawakened national and ethnic warring abroad, it is easy to over-generalize from the privileges of the United States's great wealth, by making money or its lack, the explanation for all divisions here. In doing so, however, one underestimates the extent to which markets themselves may be deeply distorted by racial and gender prejudice; one loses sight of the fact that some "successfully assimilated" ethnics in the United States have become so only by paying the high cost of burying forever languages, customs, and cultures.

Sometimes I wonder how many of our present American cultural clashes are the leftover traces of the immigrant wars of the last century and the beginning of the twentieth, how much of our reemerging jingoism is the scar that marks the place where Italian kids were mocked for being too dark-skinned, where Jewish kids were taunted for being Jewish, where poor Irish rushed to place lace curtains at the window as the first act of climbing the ladder up from social scorn, where Chinese kids were tortured for not speaking good English.

I think of some Russian neighbors of ours when I was growing up (most of the whites in that section of Boston at that time were first-generation immigrant working-class). There were two girls in the family, the older of whom was an excellent student and who went on to attend college. Her accomplishment, however, was met with great ambivalence within her family—much of which was no doubt provoked by the elder sister's affecting a bourgeois snobbishness that cast continual aspersion upon the traditions and education of her family for what she perceived as their provincialism. She found embarrassing their conformity to old ways (cast paradoxically as nonconformity to "the mainstream"—her term for a naturalized, universalized, upwardly mobile middle class). While this young woman's accomplishments were indeed the source of much pride in her family, they were also the source of at least as much anxiety. As her younger sister once expressed it to me, she became a kind of "chafing agent" in the family's already insecure and somewhat self-effacing sense of how it fit into the social order of the United States. The elder sister, who lost her rich Russian-inflected Boston Irish accent for a tersely monitored version of Boston Brahmin the first semester of college, was pretty hard to take, I do remember. She was endlessly promoting herself as a citizen of the world, able to wade in all waters, tasting widely, knowing all, possessing everything. She became suffused in a passion for openness, a compulsion for boundlessness that is all to the good, but compulsive because so tied to fear of being bounded, so linked to fear of being made fun of for being "too ethnic," too closed, too ignorant of "the larger society." While this should in no way be taken as a necessarily bad thing, it can also signal a lost balance, a sacrifice of appreciation for the bonds, the links, the ties that bind, that make family, connection, identity.

I wonder, in these times of heated put-down, about the genealogy of so much of what sometimes leaps out as quite irrational fears of what has been dismissively labeled "identity politics." Some identity politics are genuinely fearsome, genuinely rooted in the neofascist tendencies—but the larger measure of concern strikes me as a not-yet-resolved peculiarly American anxiety about our immigrant, peasant, sharecropper roots. Some of it strikes me as being a demand for conformity to what keeps being called the "larger" American way, a tyrannical rather than a willing assimilation in which there is little room for accounts of the Ellis Island variety of the past as contiguous with the present. Rather all such accounts are thought to be in tension with some static image of a monolithic, preexisting rather than vividly evolving, American culture.

This genealogy of status regard might be suggested more easily by the following example: I was purchasing rugs in a store in New York City. The rug salesman was an amiable young man, whose ethnicity I couldn't begin to guess, but who in the assimilative order of most parts of the United States generally would be identified as "white." The rugs I was considering were in a huge heavy heap in the middle of the floor, and the store had positioned two men on either side of the pile to peel the layers of rugs back for customer viewing. The two rug turners were handsome brown men, perhaps East Indian, but, again, I'm a bad guesser. They spoke very halting English, although with a very distinct British rather than American inflection. At one point they apparently misunderstood which rug I had wanted to see; the salesman curtly corrected them, and then turned to me, rolled his eyes, and sighed in all apparent seriousness: "It's *so* hard to find good help these days."

Now I am definitely the wrong person with whom to lodge such a complaint, but before I could start in with what he would have undoubtedly found to be a very annoying little disquisition, the salesman reached over and carelessly, messily, flipped back the edge of the top rug. One of the rug turners, who was clearly seething, snapped at him to "take his hands off" that rug, that that was their job; and then said, very carefully, but with great passion: "What's the matter, don't you understand English?!"

I was struck by how quickly and completely, in the context of this apparent employment hierarchy, the lower-status person had learned the lesson of stealing the power and thunder of the high-status person's insult by turning it back on itself. There was something about this exchange that marked a ritual of assimilative initiation: Did someone hurl those words to the salesman's great grandmother as she scrubbed floors, or did he just see it in a movie? Will the high sarcasm of the rug turner's remark lose its irony and retain only its demand as the rug turners or their children lose their accents but keep the gesture of power?

The ability to see the commonalities of a hand-me-down heritage of devalued humanity, even as our specific experiences with that devaluation may differ widely with time and place, is in need of serious cultivation. The ability to fully understand the desperate socioeconomic circumstances of blacks in the United States is, I think, intricately linked with the tangled and evolving histories of oppression throughout the world, and the analytical conundrums that they present for us all.

Against this backdrop, and in view of the relatively advantaged situation of whites and particularly white men in the United States, the constantly bunkered sense of transgressed rights that appears to be the chief theme of much of today's right-leaning radio and television probably needs more excavation to be understood as the powerfully appealing narrative of "white" (versus ethnic) neonationalism that it appears to have become. I think that the appeal is attributable to at least two factors: (1) the persuasive form of the narrative itself, and (2) the ennobling romantic vision of its content in which tropes of local inclusion or representation are played out against the backdrop of intense global debates about democracy, citizenship, and community.

There are any number of junctures in history where a shift in the boundaries of law or some political movement has been signaled by very particular uses of rhetoric, peculiar twists of the popular imagination. American presidents, for example, routinely attempt to harness the irresistible rhetorical movement of the Puritan jeremiad as a persuasive form by intertwining the language of divine proclamation and political mission. At the same time, the appeal for equality, of African Americans and many others, has always been boosted by the power of great rhetorical moments. During the entire civil rights movement social activists were at their most effective when they were able to capture certain material events within the metaphoric unfolding of destiny, or of apocalypse, or of nature and "the natural." Martin Luther King's heart-wrenching vision of the mountaintop owes many a tip of the hat, of course, to the oral traditions of Africa, but also to the forms of political discourse that influenced the Boston missionaries and New England abolitionists whose words have so necessarily infiltrated the expression of black aspiration.

But is it also true that the deepest of our social divisions have been powerfully perpetuated by precisely such devices. From the earliest Supreme Court cases, the authority of the law was hitched to a myth of compelling mission and sacred vision, an endowment emanating from God but ultimately speaking through the naturalized logic of positivism. The dispossession of aboriginal people from their land was accomplished by legal opinions that figured the land in question as "virgin," a holy female, a queen whose honor is upheld in the very fact of conquest. The legal awards of "charter," "title," "fee" and "possession" wrested land not from Native American people but from "idleness," "wilderness" and "emptiness."[1]

This particular way of imagining is not just "how the west was won," but has characterized much of the "impersonal" discourse of conquest and exclusion throughout our jurisprudence. If "the wilderness" was a term whose use effectively obliterated the existence of the humans who lived there, "the underclass" is a contemporary device to achieve very much the same end. This issue of class is underscored by the vocabulary of the so-called taxpayer revolt, which, while rooted in the sober reality of a stunning national deficit, has found unfortunate expression in a bitter discourse of deservedness in which the deserving are those whose material accumulation identifies them as those who "can't" "keep on" paying taxes, while the undeserving are figured as those who supposedly "don't" pay taxes. Making the streets "safe for taxpaying citizens," for example, has become a rallying point for the criminalization or institutionalization of the homeless in cities as supposedly "liberal" as San Francisco and New York. Author Mike Davis observes that "restaurants and markets have responded to the homeless by building ornate enclosures to protect their refuse. Although no one in Los Angeles has yet proposed adding cyanide to the garbage, as happened in Phoenix a few years back, one popular seafood restaurant has spent $12,000 to build the ultimate bag-lady-proof trash cage: made of three-quarter-inch steel rods with alloy locks and vicious out-turned spikes to safeguard priceless moldering fishheads and stale french fries."[2]

A friend tells the story of her young niece, who is growing up in New York City. The little girl and a friend were walking into their apartment building when they saw an old man who lived on the street. "Hi, Sam," said my friend's niece, for she and her parents saw him every day and had grown to know him. The other little girl ran at once to her parents and said, very distressed, "You can't call a homeless a name! Mommy, she called a homeless a name!"[3] It is telling, this story, the blanket anonym of "a homeless" revealing the extent to which a whole generation of children are being cultured not to see those who live all around us. The very simplest of social exchanges struck this little girl as something like a blasphemous epithet against the safe borders of what exists, of what *can* be known and named.

Similarly, if the "underclass" is a way of unnaming the poor, "whiteness" is a way of not naming ethnicity. And "blackness," of course, has been used as a most effective way of marking the African-American quest for either citizenship or market participation as the very antithesis: blacks are defined as those whose expressed humanity is too often perceived as "taking" liberties, whose submission is seen as a generous and proper "gift" to others rather than as involving personal cost.

The fraternal bliss of romanticized racism, in which professions of liberty and inseparable union could simultaneously signify and even reinforce an "American" national identity premised on deep social division is, again, the central paradox of our times. D. W. Griffith's filmic paean to the founding of the Ku Klux Klan, *The Birth of a Nation,* ends with all the features of a classic jeremiad, imploring the Invisible Empire of decent white people who care about their daughters to dare "dream of a Golden Day when the Bestial War shall rule no more. But instead the gentle Prince in the Hall of Brotherly Love in the City of Peace." The last scene of that movie shows a hall full of industrious white citizens attired in togas, in an apparent state of fraternal bliss, a giant, ghostly figure of Jesus Christ hovering above them all. "Liberty and Union, One and Inseparable, Now and Forever!" reads the very last subtitle.

I would like to explore simultaneously the suggestion that at least part of the sense of victimization coalescing a class of "oppressed" or "trumped" white men is primed by a certain class coding in the appeals of many right-wing political and media commentators. I began to take this possibility seriously during the media blare about the attack on figure skater Nancy Kerrigan, allegedly engineered by the shady retinue of her rival, Tonya Harding. I was startled by mainstream "respectable" print and television media's repeated characterization of Harding and company as "poor white" or even "white trash." Then, weeks in to the debacle, I heard an interview with residents of East Portland, the Oregon neighborhood in which Harding grew up. In the eyes of these people, Tonya Harding was a heroine—and for precisely all the reasons the dominant media opinion attacked her. She was tough, she was crafty, she had muscles, she could throw back a few beers with the boys, wasn't too fanatic to have a cigarette every once and again; she was *not* America's sweetheart, *not* Cinderella, *not* Pollyanna, this little girl who knew trucks and could handle a chain saw. What could be better than that?

Indeed, I thought. Might really be handy to be able to overhaul an engine.

And with that interview I began to listen much more closely for the ways in which poor whites are depicted in insulting and dehumanized ways by mainstream media, even when it's too "respectable" to use overt markers like "white trash." The *New Yorker* magazine, for example, ran a piece about the community of Clackamas County, where Harding lives, where her fan club is based, where the rink at which she learned to skate is located. Even as the piece purports to air the felt sense of class division (" 'Trailer trash is what they call people out here,' [said a member of Harding's fan club]"), it exudes a profoundly insulting barrier of voyeuristic condescension. The author lingers on the physical attributes of everyone she meets: the bodies of the natives range from "meaty" to "fleshy." "Ruddy faces" are set with "pinkish eyelids" that are, in the case of the girls, "rimmed in black liner." Their dispositions run from "weary" to "jittery." Their children are "restless," "shrill-voiced," and "strange." Their hair is "greased-back" or "frosted" or "fading" or "stringy blond." They wear "inexpensive-looking clothing" like "worn-out chambray work shirt[s]" and "plastic windbreaker[s]." Even as the natives insist that Clackamas is a "good neighborhood" and "a very warmy place," the author warns the gentle reader that while such words may "make it sound soothing and regular," it's really "more haphazard and disjointed." In fact, every evidence of habitation and community is read right out of existence in this piece: the author finds only a wilderness of "drab rooms," floors that "felt hollow," houses that "look as though they had been built for dolls or chickens," "tumbledown farmhouses," "idle pastures" and "weedy tracts waiting to be seized and subdivided." "There really isn't a town of Clackamas . . . ," opines the New Yorker-on-safari; ". . . there are pockets of businesses having to do with toys and mufflers and furniture, but there really isn't any town to speak of, or even a village to drive through."[4]

Once I developed an eye and an ear for it, I began to see the vast body of sitcoms, talk shows, editorials, and magazines as not just "mainstream," but class-biased and deeply hypocritical. The most interesting aspect of this hypocrisy rests, I think, in the wholesale depiction of "poor whites" as bigoted, versus the enlightened, ever-so-*liberal* middle and upper classes who enjoy the privilege of thinking of themselves as "classless." I can well imagine that this might encourage residents of white poor and working-class communities from East Portland, Oregon, to Charlestown, Massachusetts, to hear the word "liberal" as just another synonym for hypocrite.

If I hold in my mind this particular construction of a "powerful liberal media," then I begin to understand how poor whites could feel victimized in very much the same way—if to varying degree—that blacks do by their image in the media. But blacks, by and large, tend to call the identical phenomenon the product of "conservative" or "right-wing" rather than liberal media, perhaps because no one has ever tried to market bigotry against blacks (as conceivably they have in the case of bigotry against poor whites) as "liberalism." It is instructive to see how the experience of race puts enough of a spin on just this much of the vocabulary that without any other experience than an arguably shared one, blacks and poor whites end up on opposite sides of a right-left divide. And looking at it this way gives me some insight into the way in which those who are in one sense aligned with a powerful majority could feel so paradoxically threatened, *as* a "minority' in a world overrun *by* "minorities."

If this much has any validity, then the complex ideological overlays of everyday racial dramas can only confound the picture more. In one direction it might be argued that many African Americans identify with and understand the ways in which aspects of white blue-collar life are shared lifestyles. As media expert John Fiske observes, the cartoon character Bart Simpson's "defiance, his street smarts, his oral skills, together with his rejection, appeared to resonate closely with many African Americans. The Simpsons are a blue-collar family whose class difference from mainstream America is frequently emphasized, and as race is often encoded into class, so class difference can be decoded as racial. Bart's double disempowerment, by class and age, made him readily decodable as socially 'black.'"[5]

But from the other direction I think it is very hard for lower-class whites to decode *themselves* as socially black—there is simply too much representational force militating against it. I keep thinking back to the paradigm of *The Birth of a Nation,* in which upper-class whites were depicted not merely as suffering at the hands of out-of-control blacks, but also as suffering lowered status at the hands of northern "radicals"—a misfortune that eventually brought ladies to the point of having to trim their frocks with unprocessed cotton, or "poor man's lace." By the same token, in Margaret Mitchell's *Gone with the Wind,* Scarlett O'Hara is a woman of great "breeding" unjustly reduced by crazed Yankee social engineering, a point made most memorable by her having to tear down the velvet curtains in order to clothe herself according to her lost station. These images tap into powerful myths that invite the average American working-class dreamer—who is, after all, the intended consumer of such romantic pulp—to imagine a great and primeval fall from Edenic upper-class status, *and to do so in racial terms.*

The rhetoric of such southern Gothic dramas bears the earmarks of a poor man's jeremiad—the mythic sense of banishment from the classier classes, the pathetic grace of struggle against the odds, the conjunction of just deserts and a clever needle (or a shiny pair of ice skates) saving the day for a brighter tomorrow when North and South, rich and poor shall sit down at the same table and be properly waited on by you-know-who. But it is also a jeremiad in which the borders of the lower-class wilderness are guarded by federally funded "outsiders" who "don't understand" and who block exodus to the promised land by unleashing upon them running-dog hordes of black heathens and criminal "elements" who *belong* in a wilderness.

It is not surprising that empirical information has such a hard time standing up to the passionate desire to don crinoline; and it is not surprising, I suppose, that if a badly written rip-off sequel to the badly written original of *Gone with the Wind* can just about outstrip the Bible in worldwide sales, then some savvy disc jockeys spinning the same yarn could capture quite a lot of market share.

Let me end with a story about how I think the imaginary line drawing of national identity operates on the very local level, indeed, at home.

Some months ago I was riding on a train. In between napping and reading the newspaper, I languidly fell into overhearing the conversation of a very well-dressed, well-educated family seated across the aisle from me. Here was a family with traditional values *and* Ralph Lauren looks—mother, father, bright little girl, and a big, bearded friend of the family who looked like that seafaring guy on the clam chowder label. It was a fascinatingly upper-class conversation, about investments, photography, and Japanese wood-joinery. It was also a soothingly pleasant conversation, full of affection, humor, and great politeness. I enjoyed listening to them, and allowed myself the pleasure of my secret participation in their companionability. Then they started telling redneck jokes.

There was no shift in their voices to warn me of it; they spoke in the same soft, smiling voices as before, with those deliciously crisp *t*'s and delicately rounded *r*'s.

The little girl, who was probably around seven or eight years old, asked, "What's a redneck?" (No longer napping, I leaned closer, titillated and intrigued by what this moment of sharp but innocent intervention promised in terms of drawing these otherwise thoughtful adults up short in a lifeboat of glorious contrition and renewed sense of social awareness.)

"Drinks beer, drives a pickup, low-class, talks bad," came the unselfconscious reply. Then the three adults told more jokes to illustrate. Being very bright, the little girl dumped innocence by the wayside, and responded promptly by telling a bunch of blond jokes and then one involving "black"—but I couldn't hear if she were talking about hair or skin.

The father told another joke—what's got ten teeth and something I couldn't hear. The answer was the front row of a Willie Nelson concert.

They were so pleasant and happy. Their conversation was random, wandering. They showed pictures of each other's kids, they played word games, they shared hot dogs. And yet they were transporting a virus.

This process of marking. No wonder it is so hard to get out of our race and class binds. It occurred to me, as I watched this family in all its remarkable typicality, that that little girl will have to leave the warmth of the embracing, completely relaxed circle of those happy people before she can ever appreciate the humanity of someone who drives a pickup, who can't afford a dentist. "Rednecks" were lovingly situated, by that long afternoon of gentle joking, in the terrible vise of the comic, defined by the butt of a joke.

The prevalence of how *givingly* social divisions are transmitted was brought home to me in an essay written by one of my former students: She described her father as a loving family man, who worked six and a half days a week to provide for his wife and children. He always took Sunday afternoons off; that was sacred time, reserved for a "family drive." Yet the family's favorite pastime, as they meandered in Norman Rockwell contentment, was, according to this student, "trying to pick the homosexuals out of the crowd." ("Bill Clinton would have *homosexuals* in his administration!" railed Pat Robertson in his speech to the 1992 Republican National Convention, during which convention homophobic violence reportedly rose 8 percent in the city of Houston.)

Hate learned in a context of love is a complicated phenomenon. And love learned in a context of hate endangers all our family.

1998

Notes

1. *Johnson and Graham's Lessee v. William M'Intosh,* 21 U.S. 543 (1823).
2. Mike Davis, *City of Quartz* (New York: Vintage Books, 1992), 233.
3. Ariella Gross, letter of March 14, 1994, on file with author.
4. Susan Orlean, "Figures in a Mall," *New Yorker,* February 21, 1994, 48ff.
5. John Fiske, *Media Matters: Everyday Culture and Political Change* (Minneapolis: University of Minnesota Press, 1994), 123.

GETTING STARTED

1. Williams uses a number of stories as extended examples of ideas, assumptions, and ways of living that are encoded into the everyday language that individuals use. Working in groups, list each of these stories. What words or phrases does each example focus on? What points does each example allow Williams to raise and to underscore? Are her examples effective?

2. Williams uses the term "jeremiad" several times in her essay. Use your dictionary to define it. Working in a group, find those places in the essay where she uses the term. How does using this term rather than a synonym help Williams to make her argument?

3. Reread the essay's conclusion and compare it to the title. What is this essay about? What is Williams's purpose in writing it? What is her attitude toward the stories she tells? Why does she tell stories instead of just telling us what she thinks?

WRITING

4. Review the list of examples your group compiled in response to question 1. Are any of these examples familiar to you? Have you had a similar experience? Write a paper in which you describe your experience and compare it to an example from the essay. How do you think Williams would interpret your experience? Would you agree with her?

5. Write a paper in which you analyze Williams's language just as she analyzes the language used by the people in her examples. What does her language tell you about her persona as a writer? What does it tell you about her intended audience? Is this article an example of a jeremiad?

6. Write a paper in which you analyze the language used in the news story you find in response to question 7. Identify the publication from which you have drawn the account of your story. Does the account of the story have an "angle" or an attitude it expresses about the conflict? What is the intended audience of this account? What might Williams say about your example?

USING THE LIBRARY AND THE INTERNET

7. Williams uses the news stories surrounding Tonya Harding's competition with Nancy Kerrigan in 1994 as examples of the ways in which "the mainstream media" depict minority communities. Go

to the library or use the Internet to scan current newspapers and news magazines for another story of conflict between individuals or groups from different racial, ethnic, or class backgrounds. (Hint: Try a reference database that includes newspaper sources, like Lexis/Nexis or Newspaper Source, or ask your reference librarian for a recommendation. Try search terms such as "ethnicity and conflict" or "class and conflict.")

MAKING CONNECTIONS

8. Williams describes the family on the train as "transporting a virus" (p. 576). Write a paper in which you analyze her use of this metaphor and relate it to the metaphors used by the individuals cited in Emily Martin et al.'s article on scientific literacy. How do the metaphors used in both articles help the authors to make sense of their examples? How do the metaphors help the authors to make their points?

9. Both Williams and Gloria Anzaldúa are concerned with problems relating to assimilation. Look at Anzaldúa's essay, "Chicana Artists: Exploring *Nepantla, el Lugar de la Frontera,*" and pay particular attention to the way she describes a kind of "scarring." To what extent would Anzaldúa agree with Williams's argument? Would she find similarities between the experiences that she and Williams describe? Do you? What important differences remain?

Susan Willis

Susan Willis is an Associate Professor at Duke University, where she teaches courses in minority writing and popular culture. Her research focuses on exposing both the contradictions of capitalism in everyday life and the utopian content in culture. She is the author of *Specifying: Black Women Writing the American Experience* (1987) and *A Primer for Daily Life* (1991). Willis is coauthor of *Inside the Mouse: Work and Play at Disney World* (1995), from which "Disney World: Public Use/Private State" was excerpted.

To get the Walt Disney Company's side of the story, visit their corporate Web site at <http://www.disney.go.com>.

Disney World
Public Use/Private State

At Disney World, the erasure of spontaneity is so great that spontaneity itself has been programmed. On the "Jungle Cruise" khaki-clad tour guides teasingly engage the visitors with their banter, whose apparent spontaneity has been carefully scripted and painstakingly rehearsed. Nothing is left to the imagination or the unforeseen. Even the paths and walkways represent the programmed assimilation of the spontaneous. According to published reports, there were no established walkways laid down for the opening-day crowds at Disneyland.[1] Rather, the Disney Imagineers waited to see where people would walk, then paved over their spontaneous footpaths to make prescribed routes.

The erasure of spontaneity has largely to do with the totality of the built and themed environment. Visitors are inducted into the park's program, their every need predefined and presented to them as a packaged routine and set of choices. "I'm not used to having everything done for me." This is how my companion at Disney World reacted when she checked into a Disney resort hotel and found that she, her suitcase, and her credit card had been turned into the scripted

1. Scott Bukatman, "There's Always Tomorrowland: Disney and the Hypercinematic Experience," *October* 57 (Summer 1991), pp. 55–78.

components of a highly orchestrated program. My companion later remarked that while she found it odd not to have to take care of everything herself (as she normally does in order to accomplish her daily tasks), she found it "liberating" to just fall into the proper pattern, knowing that nothing could arise that hadn't already been factored into the system. I have heard my companion's remarks reiterated by many visitors to the park with whom I've talked. Most describe feeling "freed up" ("I didn't have to worry about my kids," "I didn't have to think about anything") by the experience of relinquishing control over the complex problem-solving thoughts and operations that otherwise define their lives. Many visitors suspend daily perceptions and judgments altogether, and treat the wonderland environment as more real than real. I saw this happen one morning when walking to breakfast at my Disney resort hotel. Two small children were stooped over a small snake that had crawled out onto the sun-warmed path. "Don't worry, it's rubber," remarked their mother. Clearly only Audio-Animatronic simulacra of the real world can inhabit Disney World. A real snake is an impossibility.

In fact, the entire natural world is subsumed by the primacy of the artificial. The next morning I stepped outside at the end of an early morning shower. The humid atmosphere held the combination of sun and rain. "Oh! Did they turn the sprinklers on?" This is the way my next-door neighbor greeted the day as she emerged from her hotel room. The Disney environment puts visitors inside the world that Philip K. Dick depicted in *Do Androids Dream of Electric Sleep?*—where all animal life has been exterminated, but replaced by the production of simulacra, so real in appearance that people have difficulty recalling that real animals no longer exist. The marvelous effect of science fiction is produced out of a dislocation between two worlds, which the reader apprehends as an estrangement, but the characters inside the novel cannot grasp because they have only the one world: the world of simulacra. The effect of the marvelous cannot be achieved unless the artificial environment is perceived through the retained memory of everyday reality. Total absorption into the Disney environment cancels the possibility for the marvelous and leaves the visitor with the banality of a park-wide sprinkler system. No muggers, no rain, no ants, and no snakes.

Amusement is the commodified negation of play. What is play but the spontaneous coming together of activity and imagination, rendered more pleasurable by the addition of friends? At Disney World, the world's most highly developed private property "state" devoted to amusement, play is all but eliminated by the absolute domination of program over spontaneity. Every ride runs to computerized schedule. There is no possibility of an awful thrill, like being stuck at the top of a ferris wheel. Order prevails particularly in the queues for the rides that zigzag dutifully on a prescribed path created out of stanchions and ropes; and the visitor's assimilation into the queue does not catapult him or her into another universe, as it would if Jorge Luis Borges fabricated the program. The Disney labyrinth is a banal extension of the ride's point of embarkation, which extends into the ride as a hyper-themed continuation of the queue. The "Backstage Movie Tour" has done away with the distinction between the ride and its queue by condemning the visitor to a two-and-a-half-hour-long pedagogical queue that preaches the process of movie production. Guests are mercilessly herded through sound stages and conveyed across endless back lots where one sees the ranch-style houses used in TV commercials and a few wrecked cars from movie chase scenes. Happily, there are a few discreet exit doors, bail-out points for parents with bored children. Even Main Street dictates programmed amusement because it is not a street but a conduit, albeit laden with commodity distractions, that conveys the visitor to the Magic Kingdom's other zones where more queues, rides, and commodities distinguish themselves on the basis of their themes. All historical and cultural references are merely ingredients for decor. Every expectation is met programmatically and in conformity with theme. Mickey as Sorcerer's Apprentice does not appear in the Wild West or the exotic worlds of Jungle and Adventure, the niches for Davey Crockett and Indiana Jones. Just imagine the chaos, a park-wide short circuit, that the mixing of themed ingredients might produce. Amusement areas are identified by a "look," by characters in costume, by the goods on sale: What place—i.e., product—is Snow White promoting if she's arm in arm with an astronaut? The utopian intermingling of thematic opportunities such as occurred at the finale of the movie *Who Framed Roger Rabbit?,* with Warner and Disney "toons" breaking their copyrighted species separation to cavort with each other and the human actors, will not happen at Disney World.

However, now that the costumed embodiment of Roger Rabbit has taken up residence at Disney World, he, too, can expect to have a properly assigned niche in the spectacular Disney parade of characters. These have been augmented with a host of other Disney/Lucas/Spielberg creations, including Michael Jackson of "Captain EO" and C_3PO and R2D2 of *Star Wars* , as well as Disney buyouts such as Jim Henson's Muppets and the Saturday morning cartoon heroes, the Teenage Mutant Ninja Turtles. The Disney Corporation's acquisition of the stock-in-trade of popular culture icons facilitates a belief commonly held by young children that every popular childhood figure "lives" at Disney World. In the utopian imagination of children, Disney World may well be a never-ending version of the finale to *Roger Rabbit* where every product of the imagination lives in community. In reality, the products (of adult imaginations) live to sell, to be consumed, to multiply.

What's most interesting about Disney World is what's not there. Intimacy is not in the program even though the architecture includes several secluded nooks, gazebos, and patios. During my five-day stay, I saw only one kiss—and this a husbandly peck on the cheek. Eruptions of imaginative play are just as rare. During the same five-day visit, I observed only one such incident even though there were probably fifty thousand children in the park. What's curious about what's not at Disney is that there is no way of knowing what's not there until an aberrant event occurs and provokes the remembrance of the social forms and behaviors that have been left out. This was the case with the episode of spontaneous play. Until I saw real play, I didn't realize that it was missing. The incident stood out against a humdrum background of uniform amusement: hundreds of kids being pushed from attraction to attraction in their strollers, hundreds more waiting dutifully in the queues or marching about in family groups—all of them abstaining from the loud, jostling, teasing, and rivalrous behaviors that would otherwise characterize many of their activities. Out of this homogenous "amused" mass, two kids snagged a huge sombrero each from an open-air stall at the foot of the Mexico Pavilion's Aztec temple stairway and began their impromptu version of the Mexican hat dance up and down the steps. Their play was clearly counterproductive as it took up most of the stairway, making it difficult for visitors to enter the pavilion. Play negated the function of the stairs as conduit into the attraction. The kids abandoned themselves to their fun, while all around them, the great mass of visitors purposefully kept their activities in line with Disney World's prescribed functions. Everyone but the dancers seemed to have accepted the park's unwritten motto: "If you pay, you shouldn't play." To get your money's worth, you have to do everything and do it in the prescribed manner. Free play is gratuitous and therefore a waste of the family's leisure time expenditure.

Conformity with the park's program upholds the Disney value system. Purposeful consumption—while it costs the consumer a great deal—affirms the value of the consumer. "Don't forget, we drove twenty hours to get here." This is how one father admonished his young son who was squirming about on the floor of EPCOT's Independence Hall, waiting for the amusement to begin. The child's wanton and impatient waste of time was seen as a waste of the family's investment in its amusement. If a family is to realize the value of its leisure time consumptions, then every member must function as a proper consumer.

The success of Disney World as an amusement park has largely to do with the way its use of programming meshes with the economics of consumption as a value system. In a world wholly predicated on consumption, the dominant order need not proscribe those activities that run counter to consumption, such as free play and squirming, because the consuming public largely polices itself against gratuitous acts which would interfere with the production of consumption as a value. Conformity with the practice of consumption is so widespread and deep at Disney World that occasional manifestations of boredom or spontaneity do not influence the compulsively correct behavior of others. Independence Hall did not give way to a seething mass of squirming youngsters even though all had to sit through a twenty-minute wait. Nor did other children on the margins of the hat dance fling themselves into the fun. Such infectious behavior would have indicated communally defined social relations or the desire for such social relations. Outside of Disney World in places of public use, infectious behavior is common. One child squirming about on the library floor breeds others; siblings chasing each other around in a supermarket draw others; one child mischievously poking at a public fountain attracts others; kids freeloading rides on a department store escalator can draw a crowd. These playful, impertinent acts indicate an imperfect mesh between programmed environment and the value system of consumption. Consumers may occasionally reclaim the social, particularly the child consumer who has not yet been fully and properly socialized to accept individuation as the bottom line in the consumer system of value. As an economic factor, the individual exists to maximize consumption—and therefore profits—across the broad mass of consumers. This is the economic maxim most cherished by the fast-food industry, where every burger and order of fries is individually packaged and consumed to preclude consumer pooling and sharing.

At Disney World the basic social unit is the family. This was made particularly clear to me because as a single visitor conducting research, I presented a problem at the point of embarkation for each of the rides. "How many in your group?" "One." The lone occupant of a conveyance invariably constructed to hold the various numerical breakdowns of the nuclear family (two, three, or four) is an anomaly. Perhaps the most family-affirming aspect of Disney World is the way the queues serve as a place where family members negotiate who will ride with whom. Will Mom and Dad separate themselves so as to accompany their two kids on a two-person ride? Will an older sibling assume the responsibility for a younger brother or sister? Every ride asks the family to evaluate each of its member's needs for security and independence. This is probably the only situation in a family's visit to Disney World where the social relations of family materialize as practice. Otherwise and throughout a family's stay, the family as nexus for social relations is subsumed by the primary definition of family as the basic unit of consumption. In consumer society at large, each of us is an atomized consumer. Families are composed of autonomous, individuated consumers, each satisfying his or her age- and gender-differentiated taste in the music, video, food, and pleasure marketplace. In contrast, Disney World puts the family back together. Even teens are integrated in their families and are seldom seen roaming the park in teen groups as they might in shopping malls.

Families at Disney World present themselves as families, like the one I saw one morning on my way to breakfast at a Disney resort hotel: father, mother, and three children small to large, each wearing identical blue Mickey Mouse T-shirts and shorts. As I walked past them, I overheard the middle child say, "We looked better yesterday—in white." Immediately, I envisioned the family in yesterday's matching outfits, and wondered if they had bought identical ensembles for every day of their stay.

All expressions of mass culture include contradictory utopian impulses, which may be buried or depicted in distorted form, but nevertheless generate much of the satisfaction of mass cultural commodities (whether the consumer recognizes them as utopian or not). While the ideology of the family has long functioned to promote conservative—even reactionary—political and social agendas, the structure of the family as a social unit signifies communality rather than individuality and can give impetus to utopian longings for communally defined relations in society at large. However, when the family buys into the look of a family, and appraises itself on the basis of its look ("We looked better yesterday"), it becomes a walking, talking commodity, a packaged unit of consumption stamped with the Mickey logo of approval. The theoretical question that this family poses for me is not whether its representation of itself as family includes utopian possibilities (because it does), but whether such impulses can be expressed and communicated in ways not accessible to commodification.

In its identical dress, the family represents itself as capitalism's version of a democratized unit of consumption. Differences and inequalities among family members are reduced to distinctions in age and size. We have all had occasion to experience the doppelgänger effect in the presence of identical twins who choose (or whose families enforce) identical dress. Whether chosen or imposed, identical twins who practice the art of same dress have the possibility of confounding or subverting social order. In contrast, the heterogeneous family whose members choose to dress identically affirms conformity with social order. The family has cloned itself as a multiple, but identical consumer, thus enabling the maximization of consumption. It is a microcosmic representation of free market democracy where the range of choices is restricted to the series of objects already on the shelf. In this system there is no radical choice. Even the minority of visitors who choose to wear their Rolling Stones and Grateful Dead T-shirts give the impression of having felt constrained not to wear a Disney logo.

Actually, Disney has invented a category of negative consumer choices for those individuals who wish to express nonconformity. This I discovered as I prepared to depart for my Disney research trip, when my daughter Cassie (fifteen years old and "cool" to the max) warned me, "Don't buy me any of that Disney paraphernalia." As it turned out, she was happy to get a pair of boxer shorts emblazoned with the leering images of Disney's villains: two evil queens, the Big Bad Wolf, and Captain Hook. Every area of Disney World includes a Disney Villains Shop, a chain store for bad-guy merchandise. Visitors who harbor anti-Disney sentiments can express their cultural politics by consuming the negative Disney line. There is no possibility of an anticonsumption at Disney World. All visitors are, by definition, consumers, their status conferred with the price of admission.

At Disney World even memories are commodities. How the visitor will remember his or her experience of the park has been programmed and indicated by the thousands of "Kodak Picture Spot" signposts. These position the photographer so as to capture the best views of each and every attraction, so that even the most inept family members can bring home perfect postcard-like photos. To return home from a trip to Disney World with a collection of haphazardly photographed environments or idiosyncratic family shots is tantamount to collecting bad memories. A family album comprised of picture-perfect photo-site images, on the other hand, constitutes the grand narrative of the family's trip to Disney World, the one that can be offered as testimony to money well spent. Meanwhile, all those embarrassing photos, the ones not programmed by the "Picture Spots," that depict babies with ice cream all over their faces or toddlers who burst into tears rather than smiles at the sight of those big-headed costumed characters that crop up all over the park—these are the images that are best left forgotten.

The other commodified form of memory is the souvenir. As long as there has been tourism there have also been souvenirs: objects marketed to concretize the visitor's experience of another place. From a certain point of view, religious pilgrimage includes aspects of tourism, particularly when the culmination of pilgrimage is the acquisition of a transportable relic. Indeed, secular mass culture often imitates the forms and practices of popular religious culture. For many Americans today who make pilgrimages to Graceland and bring home a mass-produced piece of Presley memorabilia, culture and religion collide and mesh.

Of course, the desire to translate meaningful moments into concrete objects need not take commodified form. In Toni Morrison's *Song of Solomon,* Pilate, a larger-than-life earth mother if there ever was one, spent her early vagabondage gathering a stone from every place she visited. Similarly, I know of mountain climbers who mark their ascents by bringing a rock back from each peak they climb. Like Pilate's stones, these tend to be nondescript and embody personal remembrances available only to the collector. In contrast, the commodity souvenir enunciates a single meaning to everyone: "I was there. I bought something." Unlike the souvenirs I remember having seen as a child, seashells painted with seascapes and the name of some picturesque resort town, most souvenirs today are printed with logos (like the Hard Rock Cafe T-shirt), or renderings of copyrighted material (all the Disney merchandise). The purchase of such a souvenir allows the consumer the illusion of participating in the enterprise as a whole, attaining a piece of the action. This is the consumerist version of small-time buying on the stock exchange. We all trade in logos—buy them, wear them, eat them, and make them the containers of our dreams and memories. Similarly, we may all buy into capital with the purchase of public stock. These consumerist activities give the illusion of democratic participation while denying access to real corporate control which remains intact and autonomous, notwithstanding the mass diffusion of its logos and stock on the public market. Indeed the manipulation of public stock initiated during the Reagan administration, which has facilitated one leveraged buyout after another, gives the lie to whatever wistful remnants of democratic ownership one might once have attached to the notion of "public" stocks.

Disney World is logoland. The merchandise, the costumes, the scenery—all is either stamped with the Disney logo or covered by copyright legislation. In fact, it is impossible to photograph at Disney World without running the risk of infringing a Disney copyright. A family photo in front of Sleeping Beauty's Castle is apt to include dozens of infringements: the castle itself, Uncle Harry's "Goofy" T-shirt, the kids' Donald and Mickey hats, maybe a costumed Chip 'n Dale in the background. The only thing that saves the average family from a lawsuit is that most don't use their vacation photos as a means for making profit. I suspect the staff of "America's Funniest Home Videos" systematically eliminates all family videos shot at Disney World; otherwise prize winners might find themselves having to negotiate the legal difference between prize and profit, and in a larger sense, public use versus private property. As an interesting note, Michael Sorkin, in a recent essay on Disneyland, chose a photo of "[t]he sky above Disney World [as a] substitute for an image of the place itself." Calling Disney World "the first copyrighted urban environment," Sorkin goes on to stress the "litigiousness" of the Disney Corporation.[2] It may be that *Design Quarterly*, where Sorkin published his essay, pays its contributors, thus disqualifying them from "fair use" interpretations of copyright policy.

Logos have become so much a part of our cultural baggage that we hardly notice them. Actually they are the cultural capital of corporations. Pierre Bourdieu invented the notion of cultural capital with reference to individuals. In a nutshell, cultural capital represents the sum total of a person's ability to buy into and trade in the culture. This is circumscribed by the economics of class and, in turn, functions as a means for designating an individual's social standing. Hence people with higher levels of education who distinguish themselves with upscale or trendy consumptions have more cultural capital and can command greater privilege and authority than those who, as Bourdieu put it, are stuck defining themselves by the consumption of necessity.

---

2. Michael Sorkin, "See You in Disneyland," *Design Quarterly* (Winter 1992), pp. 5–13.

There are no cultural objects or practices that do not constitute capital, no reserves of culture that escape value. Everything that constitutes one's cultural life is a commodity and can be reckoned in terms of capital logic.

In the United States today there is little difference between persons and corporations. Indeed, corporations enjoy many of the legal rights extended to individuals. The market system and its private property state are "peopled" by corporations, which trade in, accumulate, and hoard up logos. These are the cultural signifiers produced by corporations, the impoverished imagery of a wholly rationalized entity. Logos are commodities in the abstract, but they are not so abstracted as to have transcended value. Corporations with lots of logos, particularly upscale, high-tech logos, command more cultural capital than corporations with fewer, more humble logos.

In late twentieth-century America, the cultural capital of corporations has replaced many of the human forms of cultural capital. As we buy, wear, and eat logos, we become the henchmen and admen of the corporations, defining ourselves with respect to the social standing of the various corporations. Some would say that this is a new form of tribalism, that in sporting corporate logos we ritualize and humanize them, we redefine the cultural capital of the corporations in human social terms. I would say that a state where culture is indistinguishable from logo and where the practice of culture risks infringement of private property is a state that values the corporate over the human.

While at Disney World, I managed to stow away on the behind-the-scenes tour reserved for groups of corporate conventioneers. I had heard about this tour from a friend who is also researching Disney and whose account of underground passageways, conduits for armies of workers and all the necessary materials and services that enable the park to function, had elevated the tour to mythic proportions in my imagination.

But very little of the behind-the-scenes tour was surprising. There was no magic, just a highly rational system built on the compartmentalization of all productive functions and its ensuing division of labor, both aimed at the creation of maximum efficiency. However, instances do arise when the rational infrastructure comes into contradiction with the onstage (parkwide) theatricalized image that the visitor expects to consume. Such is the case with the system that sucks trash collected at street level through unseen pneumatic tubes that transect the backstage area, fully depositing the trash in Disney's own giant compactor site. To the consumer's eye, trash is never a problem at Disney World. After all, everyone dutifully uses the containers marked "trash," and what little manages to fall to the ground (generally popcorn) is immediately swept up by the French Foreign Legion trash brigade. For the consumer, there is no trash beyond its onstage collection. But there will soon be a problem as environmental pressure groups press Disney to recycle. As my companion on the backstage tour put it, "Why is there no recycling at Disney World—after all, many of the middle-class visitors to the park are already sorting and recycling trash in their homes?" To this the Disney guide pointed out that there is recycling, backstage: bins for workers to toss their Coke cans and other bins for office workers to deposit papers. But recycling onstage would break the magic of themed authenticity. After all, the "real" Cinderella's Castle was not equipped with recycling bins, nor did the denizens of Main Street, U.S.A., circa 1910, foresee the problem of trash. To maintain the image, Disney problem solvers are discussing hiring a minimum-wage workforce to rake, sort, and recycle the trash on back lots that the environmentally aware visitor will never see.

While I have been describing the backstage area as banal, the tour through it was not uneventful. Indeed there was one incident that underscored for me the dramatic collision between people's expectations of public use and the highly controlled nature of Disney's private domain. As I mentioned, the backstage tour took us to the behind-the-scenes staging area for the minute-by-minute servicing of the park and hoopla of its mass spectacles such as firework displays, light shows, and parades. We happened to be in the backstage area just as the parade down Main Street was coming to an end. Elaborate floats and costumed characters descended a ramp behind Cinderella's Castle and began to disassemble before our eyes. The floats were alive with big-headed characters, clambering off the superstructures and out of their heavy, perspiration drenched costumes. Several "beheaded" characters revealed stocky young men gulping down Gatorade. They walked toward our tour group, bloated Donald and bandy-legged Chip from the neck down, carrying their huge costume heads, while their real heads emerged pea-sized and aberrantly human.

We had been warned *not* to take pictures during the backstage tour, but one of our group, apparently carried away by the spectacle, could not resist. She managed to shoot a couple of photos of the disassembled characters before being approached by one of the tour guides. As if caught in a spy movie, the would-be photographer pried open her camera and ripped out the whole roll of film. The entire tour group stood in stunned amazement; not, I think, at the immediate presence of surveillance, but at the woman's dramatic response. In a situation where control is so omnipresent and conformity with control is taken for granted, any sudden gesture or dramatic response is a surprise.

At the close of the tour, my companion and I lingered behind the rest of the group to talk with our tour guides. As a professional photographer, my companion wanted to know if there is a "normal" procedure for disarming behind-the-scenes photographic spies. The guide explained that the prescribed practice is to impound the cameras, process the film, remove the illicit photos, and return the camera, remaining photos, and complimentary film to the perpetrator. When questioned further, the guide went on to elaborate the Disney rationale for control over the image: the "magic" would be broken if photos of disassembled characters circulated in the public sphere; children might suffer irreparable psychic trauma at the sight of a "beheaded" Mickey; Disney exercises control over the image to safeguard childhood fantasies.

What Disney employees refer to as the "magic" of Disney World has actually to do with the ability to produce fetishized consumptions. The unbroken seamlessness of Disney World, its totality as a consumable artifact, cannot tolerate the revelation of the real work that produces the commodity. There would be no magic if the public should see the entire cast of magicians in various stages of disassembly and fatigue. That selected individuals are permitted to witness the backstage labor facilitates the word-of-mouth affirmation of the tremendous organizational feat that produces Disney World. The interdiction against photography eliminates the possibility of discontinuity at the level of image. There are no images to compete with the copyright-perfect onstage images displayed for public consumption. It's not accidental that our tour guide underscored the fact that Disney costumes are tightly controlled. The character costumes are made at only one production site and this site supplies the costumes used at Tokyo's Disneyland and EuroDisney. There can be no culturally influenced variations on the Disney models. Control over the image ensures the replication of Disney worldwide. The prohibition against photographing disassembled characters is motivated by the same phobia of industrial espionage that runs rampant throughout the high-tech information industry. The woman in our tour group who ripped open her camera and destroyed her film may not have been wrong in acting out a spy melodrama. Her photos of the disassembled costumes might have revealed the manner of their production—rendering them accessible to non-Disney replication. At Disney World, the magic that resides in the integrity of childhood fantasy is inextricably linked to the fetishism of the commodity and the absolute control over private property as it is registered in the copyrighted image.

As I see it, the individual's right to imagine and to give expression to unique ways of seeing is at stake in struggles against private property. Mickey Mouse, notwithstanding his corporate copyright, exists in our common culture. He is the site for the enactment of childhood wishes and fantasies. for early conceptualizations and renderings of the body, a being who can be imagined as both self and other. If culture is held as private property, then there can be only one correct version of Mickey Mouse, whose logo-like image is the cancellation of creativity. But the multiplicity of quirky versions of Mickey Mouse that children draw can stand as a graphic question to us as adults: Who, indeed, owns Mickey Mouse?

What most distinguishes Disney World from any other amusement park is the way its spatial organization, defined by autonomous "worlds" and wholly themed environments, combines with the homogeneity of its visitors (predominantly white, middle-class families) to produce a sense of community. While Disney World includes an underlying utopian impulse, this is articulated with nostalgia for a small-town, small-business America (Main Street, U.S.A.), and the fantasy of a controllable corporatist world (EPCOT). The illusion of community is enhanced by the longing for community that many visitors bring to the park, which they may feel is unavailable to them in their own careers, daily lives, and neighborhoods, thanks in large part to the systematic erosion of the public sector throughout the Reagan and Bush administrations. In the last decade the inroads of private, for-profit enterprise in areas previously defined by public control, and the hostile aggression of tax backlash coupled with "me first" attitudes have largely defeated the possibility of community in our homes and cities.

Whenever I visit Disney World, I invariably overhear other visitors making comparisons between Disney World and their home towns. They stare out over EPCOT's lake and wonder why developers back home don't produce similar aesthetic spectacles. They talk about botched, abandoned, and misconceived development projects that have wrecked their local landscapes. Others see Disney World as an oasis of social tranquility and security in comparison to their patrolled, but nonetheless deteriorating, maybe even perilous neighborhoods. A recent essay in *Time* captured some of these sentiments: "Do you see anybody [at Disney World] lying on the street or begging for money? Do you see anyone jumping on your car and wanting to clean your windshield—and when you say no, they get abusive?"[3]

Comments such as these do more than betray the class anxiety of the middle strata. They poignantly express the inability of this group to make distinctions between what necessarily constitutes the public and the private sectors. Do visitors forget that they pay a daily use fee (upwards of $150 for a four-day stay) just to be a citizen of Disney World (not to mention the $100 per night hotel bill)? Maybe so—and maybe it's precisely *forgetting* that visitors pay for.

If there is any distinction to be made between Disney World and our local shopping malls, it would have to do with Disney's successful exclusion of all factors that might put the lie to its uniform social fabric. The occasional Hispanic mother who arrives with extended family and illegal bologna sandwiches is an anomaly. So too is the first-generation Cubana who buys a year-round pass to Disney's nightspot, Pleasure Island, in hopes of meeting a rich and marriageable British tourist. These women testify to the presence of Orlando, Disney World's marginalized "Sister City," whose overflowing cheap labor force and overcrowded and under-funded public institutions are the unseen real world upon which Disney's world depends.

1995

---

3. "Fantasy's Reality," *Time*, 27 May 1991, p. 54.

GETTING STARTED

1. What is the true subject of Willis's essay? What is Disney World an example of? What other examples might Willis have used?

2. Throughout this essay, Willis describes Disney's programmed amusement as the opposite of spontaneity and play. As you read, look for clues in the essay that show how she is defining those terms. When you have read through the essay once, go back and find two examples that show the difference between programmed amusement and spontaneous play. Note page numbers for those examples and write a paragraph describing the difference.

3. Working in groups, list everything that gets "commodified" by Disney World, according to Willis. Then go back through your list and choose two examples that show how commodification works. Present your examples to the class. What does Willis want us to think about commodification?

4. Analyze the title of this essay. How is Willis using the term "state"? Identify other terms in the essay that are unfamiliar to you or are used in unfamiliar ways. How do "state" and the other terms used in the title help to categorize the type of language Willis uses in the essay? What does this language tell us about Willis's opinion of Disney World?

WRITING

5. Write a paper based on your computer game or Web site analysis in response to question 8. Use definitions and examples from Willis's essay to explain her terms as you apply them to aspects of your example. Are there ways to subvert the goals and rules of the program? Are there features of the site that do not fit Willis's terms or that go beyond them? What happens when you think of the rules that order your example as restrictive or limiting? Is there a place for spontaneity within the rules? Explain.

6. Use Willis's essay as a model for creating your own analysis of a commodifying place, such as a chain store, a tourist spot, or a shopping mall. What are the possibilities for planned amusement versus spontaneous play in your example? What is being commodified as compared to Disney World, where Willis argues that the family, memory, and attempted subversion all get commodified? Are there ways to imagine similar spaces but ones that have more room for play? In your writing, design some improvements that would lessen the commodifying effect in the example you've chosen.

7. Write an essay in response to Willis's claim that "what's most interesting about Disney World is what's not there" (p. 581). Read the quotation closely. What does Willis believe is missing? Why does she think its absence is interesting and to whom? Do you agree with her assessment?

USING THE LIBRARY AND THE INTERNET

8. Because computer games and Internet Web sites are able to create virtual realities, they may be even more capable than Disney of creating seamless, imaginary worlds. Explore a video game or an appropriate Web site, and analyze what you see using Willis's terms. How much of the site is structured around amusement? How much spontaneous play is possible? What is being commodified? Are there ways to subvert the commodification? Is the site preserving a "magic" that could be spoiled by knowing its "backstage" programs?

MAKING CONNECTIONS

9. Use Jeanette Winterson's essay, "Imagination and Reality," to test Willis's argument. Is Disney World just an outgrowth of "money culture," of commodification taken to the extreme? Or does Disney World embody some of the aspects of art and imagination that Winterson values? Can money culture and the function of imagination be kept as separate as Winterson implies?

10. Willis claims that "many visitors . . . treat the wonderland environment as more real than real" (p. 580). What does she mean? How does her use of the word "real" compare and contrast to Yi-Fu Tuan's use of it (p. 536)?

11. Look back at Stuart Ewen's essay, "The Marriage Between Art and Commerce." Is Disney World as Willis describes it an example of "consumer engineering"? How do Disney's images relate to Ewen's discussion of style? Ewen claims that style is always being used up. Will Disney's images also be used up? Explain.

Jeanette Winterson

Jeanette Winterson (1959–   ) is an acclaimed writer of creative fiction whose novels include *The Passion* (1988), *Sexing the Cherry* (1990), and *Written on the Body* (1993). Her most recent work is a collection of short stories entitled *The World and Other Places* (1999). Among her many jobs, Winterson includes work as a makeup artist at a funeral parlor, an assistant at a mental hospital, and a publisher. She became a full-time writer in 1987. "Imagination and Reality" is a selection from her essay collection, *Art Objects: Essays on Ecstasy and Effrontery* (1996).

To learn more about Winterson and her loyal fans, visit the Jeannette Winterson Reader's Page at <http://home.swipnet.se/~w-83331/>.

Imagination and Reality

The reality of art is the reality of the imagination.

What do I mean by reality of art?

What do I mean by reality of imagination?

My statement, and the questions it suggests, are worth considering now that the fashionable approach to the arts is once again through the narrow gate of subjective experience. The charge laid on the artist, and in particular on the writer, is not to bring back visions but to play the Court photographer.

Is this anathema to art? Is it anti-art? I think so. What art presents is much more than the daily life of you and me, and the original role of the artist as visionary is the correct one.

'Real' is an old word, is an odd word. It used to mean a Spanish sixpence; a small silver coin, money of account in the days when the value of a coin was the value of its metal. We are used to notional money but 'real' is an honest currency.

The honest currency of art is the honest currency of the imagination.

The small silver coin of art cannot be spent; that is, it cannot be exchanged or exhausted. What is lost, what is destroyed, what is tarnished, what is misappropriated, is ceaselessly renewed by the mining, shaping, forging imagination that exists beyond the conjectures of the everyday. Imagination's coin, the infinitely flexible metal of the Muse, metal of the moon, in rounded structure offers new universes, primary worlds, that substantially confront the pretences of notional life.

Notional life is the life encouraged by governments, mass education and the mass media. Each of those powerful agencies couples an assumption of its own importance with a disregard for individuality. Freedom of choice is the catch phrase but streamlined homogeneity is the objective. A people who think for themselves are hard to control and what is worse, in a money culture, they may be sceptical of product advertising. Since our economy is now a consumer economy, we must be credulous and passive. We must believe that we want to earn money to buy things we don't need. The education system is not designed to turn out thoughtful individualists, it is there to get us to work. When we come home exhausted from the inanities of our jobs we can relax in front of the inanities of the TV screen. This pattern, punctuated by birth, death and marriage and a new car, is offered to us as real life.

Children who are born into a tired world as batteries of new energy are plugged into the system as soon as possible and gradually drained away. At the time when they become adult and conscious they are already depleted and prepared to accept a world of shadows. Those who have kept their spirit find it hard to nourish it and between the ages of twenty and thirty, many are successfully emptied of all resistance. I do not think it an exaggeration to say that most of the energy of most of the people is being diverted into a system which destroys them. Money is no antidote. If the imaginative life is to be renewed it needs its own coin.

We have to admit that the arts stimulate and satisfy a part of our nature that would otherwise be left untouched and that the emotions art arouses in us are of a different order to those aroused by experience of any other kind.

We think we live in a world of sense-experience and what we can touch and feel, see and hear, is the sum of our reality. Although neither physics nor philosophy accepts this, neither physics nor philosophy has been as successful as religion used to be at persuading us of the doubtfulness of the seeming-solid world. This is a pity if only because while religion was a matter of course, the awareness of other realities was also a matter of course. To accept God was to accept Otherness, and while this did not make the life of the artist any easier (the life of the artist is never easy,) a general agreement that there is more around us than the mundane allows the artist a greater licence and a greater authority than he or she can expect in a society that recognises nothing but itself.

An example of this is the development of the visual arts under Church patronage during the late medieval and Renaissance periods in Europe. This was much more than a patronage of money, it was a warrant to bring back visions. Far from being restricted by Church rhetoric, the artist knew that he and his audience were in tacit agreement; each went in search of the Sublime.

Art is visionary; it sees beyond the view from the window, even though the window is its frame. This is why the arts fare much better alongside religion than alongside either capitalism or communism. The god-instinct and the art-instinct both apprehend more than the physical biological material world. The artist need not believe in God, but the artist does consider reality as multiple and complex. If the audience accepts this premise it is then possible to think about the work itself. As things stand now, too much criticism of the arts concerns itself with attacking any suggestion of art as Other, as a bringer of realities beyond the commonplace. Dimly, we know we need those other realities and we think we can get them by ransacking different cultures and rhapsodising work by foreign writers simply because they are foreign writers. We are still back with art as the mirror of life, only it is a more exotic or less democratic life than our own. No doubt this has its interests but if we are honest, they are documentary. Art is not documentary. It may incidentally serve that function in its own way but its true effort is to open to us dimensions of the spirit and of the self that normally lie smothered under the weight of living.

It is in Victorian England that the artist first becomes a rather suspect type who does not bring visions but narcotics and whose relationship to different levels of reality is not authoritative but hallucinatory. In Britain, the nineteenth century recovered from the shock of Romanticism by adopting either a manly Hellenism, with an interest in all things virile and Greek, or a manly philistinism, which had done with sweet Jonney Keats and his band and demanded of the poet, if he must be a poet, that he be either declamatory or decorative. Art could be rousing or it could be entertaining. If it hinted at deeper mysteries it was effeminate and absurd. The shift in sensibility from early to late Wordsworth is the shift of the age. For Tennyson, who published his first collection in 1830, the shift was a painful one and the compromises he made to his own work are clear to anyone who flicks through the collected poems and finds a visionary poet trying to hide himself in legend in order to hint at sublimities not allowed to his own time. Like Wordsworth before him, Tennyson fails whenever he collapses into the single obsessive reality of the world about him. As a laureate we know he is lying. As a visionary we read him now and find him true.

And what are we but our fathers' sons and daughters? We are the Victorian legacy. Our materialism, our lack of spirituality, our grossness, our mockery of art, our utilitarian attitude to education, even the dull grey suits wrapped around the dull grey lives of our eminent City men, are Victorian hand-me-downs. Many of our ideas of history and society go back no further than Victorian England. We live in a money culture because they did. Control by plutocracy is a nineteenth-century phenomenon that has been sold to us as a blueprint for reality. But what is real about the values of a money culture?

Money culture recognizes no currency but its own. Whatever is not money, whatever is not making money, is useless to it. The entire efforts of our government as directed through our society are efforts towards making more and more money. This favours the survival of the dullest. This favours those who prefer to live in a notional reality where goods are worth more than time and where things are more important than ideas.

For the artist, any artist, poet, painter, musician, time in plenty and an abundance of ideas are the necessary basics of creativity. By dreaming and idleness and then by intense self-discipline does the artist live. The artist cannot perform between 9 and 6, five days a week, or if she sometimes does, she cannot guarantee to do so. Money culture hates that. It must know what it is getting, when it is getting it, and how much it will cost. The most tyrannical of patrons never demanded from their protegées what the market now demands of artists; if you can't sell your work regularly and quickly, you can either starve or do something else. The time that art needs, which may not be a long time, but which has to be its own time, is anathema to a money culture. Money confuses time with itself. That is part of its unreality.

Against this golden calf in the wilderness where all come to buy and sell, the honest currency of art offers quite a different rate of exchange. The artist does not turn time into money, the artist turns time into energy, time into intensity, time into vision. The exchange that art offers is an exchange in kind; energy for energy, intensity for intensity, vision for vision. This is seductive and threatening. Can we make the return? Do we want to? Our increasingly passive diversions do not equip us, mentally, emotionally, for the demands that art makes. We know we are dissatisfied, but the satisfactions that we seek come at a price beyond the resources of a money culture. Can we afford to live imaginatively, contemplatively? Why have we submitted to a society that tries to make imagination a privilege when to each of us it comes as a birthright?

It is not a question of the money in your pocket. Money can buy you the painting or the book or the opera seat but it cannot expose you to the vast energies you will find there. Often it will shield you from them, just as a rich man can buy himself a woman but not her love. Love is reciprocity and so is art. Either you abandon yourself to another world that you say you seek or you find ways to resist it.

Most of us are art-resisters because art is a challenge to the notional life. In a money culture, art, by its nature, objects. It fields its own realities, lives by its own currency, aloof to riches and want. Art is dangerous.

For Sale: My Life. Highest Bidder Collects.

The honest currency of art is the honest currency of the imagination.

In Middle English, 'real' was a variant of 'royal'.

Can we set aside images of our own dishonoured monarchy and think instead about the ancientness and complexity of the word 'royal'?

To be royal was to be distinguished in the proper sense; to be singled out, by one's fellows and by God or the gods. In both the Greek and the Hebraic traditions, the one who is royal is the one who has special access to the invisible world. Ulysses can talk to Hera, King David can talk to God. Royalty on earth is expected to take its duties on earth seriously but the King should also be a bridge between the terrestrial and the supernatural.

Perhaps it seems strange to us that in the ancient world the King was more accessible to his people than were the priests. Although King and priest worked together, priesthood, still allied to magic, even by the Hebrews, was fully mysterious. The set-apartness of the priest is one surrounded by ritual and taboo. The priest did not fight in battle, take concubines, hoard treasure, feast and riot, sin out of humanness, or if he did, there were severe penalties. The morality of the priesthood was not the morality of Kingship and whether you read *The Odyssey* or The Bible, the difference is striking. The King is not better behaved than his subjects, essentially he was (or should have been) the nobler man.

In Britain, royalty was not allied to morality until the reign of Queen Victoria. Historically, the role of the King or Queen had been to lead and inspire, this is an imaginative role, and it was most perfectly fulfilled by Elizabeth the First, Gloriana, the approachable face of Godhead. Gloriana is the Queen whose otherness is for the sake of her people, and it is important to remember that the disciplines she laid upon her own life, in particular her chastity, were not for the sake of example but for the sake of expediency. The Divine Right of Kings was not a good conduct award it was a mark of favour. God's regent upon earth was expected to behave like God and anyone who studies Greek or Hebrew literature will find that God does not behave like a Christian schoolmistress. God is glorious, terrifying, inscrutable, often capricious to human eyes, extravagant, victorious, legislative but not law-abiding, and, the supreme imagination. 'In the beginning was the Word.'

At its simplest and at its best, royalty is an imaginative function; it must embody in its own person, subtle and difficult concepts of Otherness. The priest does not embody these concepts, the priest serves them. The priest is a functionary, the King is a function.

Shakespeare is preoccupied with Kingship as a metaphor for the imaginative life. Leontes and Lear, Macbeth and Richard II, are studies in the failure of the imagination. In *The Winter's Tale,* the redemption of Leontes is made possible through a new capacity in him; the capacity to see outside of his own dead vision into a chance as vibrant as it is unlikely. When Paulina says to him, 'It is required you do awake your faith' she does not mean religious faith. If the statue of Hermione is to come to life, Leontes must believe it *can* come to life. This is not common sense. It is imagination.

In the earliest Hebrew creation stories Yahweh makes himself a clay model of a man and breathes on it to give it life. It is this supreme confidence, this translation of forms, the capacity to recognise in one thing the potential of another, and the willingness to let that potential realise itself, that is the stamp of creativity and the birthright that Yahweh gives to humans. Leontes' failure to acknowledge any reality other than his own is a repudiation of that birthright, a neglect of humanness that outworks itself into the fixed immobility of his queen. When Hermione steps down and embraces Leontes it is an imaginative reconciliation.

I hope it is clear that as I talk about King and priest I am dealing in abstracts and not actualities. I do not wish to upset republicans anywhere. What I do want to do is to move the pieces across the chessboard to see if that gives us a different view.

By unraveling the word 'real' I hope to show that it contains in itself, and without any wishful thinking on my part, those densities of imaginative experience that belong to us all and that are best communicated through art. I see no conflict between reality and imagination. They are not in fact separate. Our real lives hold within them our royal lives; the inspiration to be more than we are, to find new solutions, to live beyond the moment. Art helps us to do this because it fuses together temporal and perpetual realities.

To see outside of a dead vision is not an optical illusion.

The realist (from the Latin *res* = thing) who thinks he deals in things and not images and who is suspicious of the abstract and of art, is not the practical man but a man caught in a fantasy of his own unmaking.

The realist unmakes the coherent multiple world into a collection of random objects. He thinks of reality as that which has an objective existence, but understands no more about objective existence than that which he can touch and feel, sell and buy. A lover of objects and of objectivity, he is a fact caught in a world of symbols and symbolism, where he is unable to see the thing in itself, as it really is, he sees it only in relation to his own story of the world.

The habit of human beings is to see things subjectively or not to see them at all. The more familiar a thing becomes the less it is seen. In the home, nobody looks at the furniture, they sit on it, eat off it, sleep on it and forget it until they buy something new. When we do look at other people's things, we are usually thinking about the cachet, their value, what they say about their owner. Our minds work to continually label and absorb what we see and to fit it neatly into our own pattern. That done, we turn away. This is a sound survival skill but it makes it very difficult to let anything have an existence independent of ourselves, whether furniture or people. It makes it easier to buy symbols, things that have a particular value to us, than it does to buy objects.

My mother, who was poor, never bought objects, she bought symbols. She used to save up to buy something hideous to put in the best parlour. What she bought was factory made and beyond her purse. If she had ever been able to see it in its own right, she could never have spent money on it. She couldn't see it, and nor could any of the neighbours dragged in to admire it. They admired the effort it had taken to save for it. They admired how much it cost. Above all, they admired my mother; the purchase was a success.

I know that when my mother sat in her kitchen that had only a few pieces of handmade furniture, she felt depressed and conscious of her lowly social status. When she sat in her dreadful parlour with a china cup and a bought biscuit, she felt like a lady. The parlour, full of objects unseen but hard won, was a fantasy chamber, a reflecting mirror. Like Mrs. Joe, in *Great Expectations,* she finally took her apron off.

Money culture depends on symbolic reality. It depends on a confusion between the object and what the object represents. To keep you and me buying and upgrading an overstock of meaningless things depends on those things having an acquisitional value. It is the act of buying that is important. In our society, people who cannot buy things are the underclass.

Symbolic man surrounds himself with objects as tyrants surround themselves with subjects: 'These will obey me. Through them I am worshipped. Through them I exercise control.' These fraudulent kingdoms, hard-headed and practical, are really the soft-centre of fantasy. They are wish fulfillment nightmares where more is piled on more to manufacture the illusion of abundance. They are lands of emptiness and want. Things do not satisfy. In part they fail to satisfy because their symbolic value changes so regularly and what brought whistles of admiration one year is next year's car boot sale bargain. In part they fail to satisfy because much of what we buy is gadgetry and fashion, which makes objects temporary and the need to be able to purchase them, permanent. In part they fail to satisfy because we do not actually want the things we buy. They are illusion, narcotic, hallucination.

To suggest that the writer, the painter, the musician, is the one out of touch with the real world is a doubtful proposition. It is the artist who must apprehend things fully, in their own right, communicating them not as symbols but as living realities with the power to move.

To see outside of a dead vision is not an optical illusion.

According to the science of optics, if an image consists of points through which light actually passes, it is called real. Otherwise it is called virtual.

The work of the artist is to see into the life of things; to discriminate between superficialities and realities; to know what is genuine and what is a make-believe. The artist through the disciplines of her work, is one of the few people who does see things as they really are, stripped of associative value. I do not mean that artists of whatever sort have perfect taste or perfect private lives, I mean that when the imaginative capacity is highly developed, it is made up of invention and discernment. Invention is the shaping spirit that re-forms fragments into new wholes, so that even what has been familiar can be seen fresh. Discernment is to know how to test the true and the false and to reveal objects, emotions, ideas in their own coherence. The artist is a translator; one who has learned how to pass into her own language the languages gathered from stones, from birds, from dreams, from the body, from the material world, from the invisible world, from sex, from death, from love. A different language is a different reality; what is the language, the world, of stones? What is the language, the world, of birds? Of atoms? Of microbes? Of colours? Of air? The material world is closed to those who think of it only as a commodity market.

> How do you know but every bird that cuts the airy way
> Is an immense world of delight closed by your senses five?
>
> William Blake,
> *The Marriage of Heaven and Hell* (*c.* 1790)

To those people every object is inanimate. In fact they are the ones who remain unmoved, fixed rigidly within their own reality.

The artist is moved.

The artist is moved through multiple realities. The artist is moved by empty space and points of light. The artist tests the image. Does light pass through it? Is it illuminated? It is sharp, clear, its own edges, its own form?

The artist is looking for real presences. I suppose what the scientist Rupert Sheldrake would call 'morphic resonance'; the inner life of the thing that cannot be explained away biologically, chemically, physically. In the Catholic Church 'real presence' is the bread and wine that through transubstantiation becomes the living eucharist; the body and blood of Christ. In the Protestant Church the bread and wine are symbols only, one of the few places where we recognise that we are asking one thing to substitute for another. For the average person, this substitution is happening all the time.

The real presence, the image transformed by light, is not rare but it is easily lost or mistaken under clouds of subjectivity. People who claim to like pictures and books will often only respond to those pictures and books in which they can clearly find themselves. This is ego masquerading as taste. To recognise the worth of a thing is more than recognising its worth to you. Our responses to art are conditioned by our insistence that it present to us realities we can readily accept, however virtual those realities might be. Nevertheless art has a stubborn way of cutting through the subjective world of symbols and money and offering itself as a steady alternative to the quick change act of daily life.

We are naturally suspicious of faculties that we do not ourselves possess and we do not quite believe that the poet can read the sermons in stones or the painter know the purple that bees love. Still we are drawn to books and pictures and music, finding in ourselves an echo of their song, finding in ourselves an echo of their sensibility, an answering voice through the racket of the day.

Art is for us a reality beyond now. An imaginative reality that we need. The reality of art is the reality of the imagination.

The reality of art is not the reality of experience.

The charge laid on the artist is to bring back visions.

In Shakespeare's *Othello,* we find that the Moor wins Desdemona's heart by first winning her imagination. He tells her tales of cannibals and of the Anthropophagi whose heads grow beneath their shoulders. What he calls his 'round unvarnished tale' is a subtle mixture of art and artfulness. When a Shakespearean hero apologises for his lack of wit we should be on our guard. Shakespeare always gives his heroes the best lines, even when the hero is Richard II.

Othello's untutored language is in fact powerful and wrought. He is more than a master of arms, he is a master of art. It is his words that win Desdemona. She says 'I saw Othello's visage in his mind.' His face, like his deeds, belongs to the world of sense-experience, but it is his wit that makes both dear to her. For Desdemona, the reality of Othello is his imaginative reality.

OTHELLO she thank'd me,
And bade me, if I had a friend that lov'd her,
I should but teach him how to tell my story,
And that would woo her.

The clue here is not the story but the telling of it. It is not Othello the action man who has taught Desdemona to love him, it is Othello the poet.

We know that Shakespeare never bothered to think of a plot. As a good dramatist and one who earned his whole living by his work, he had to take care to make his historical ransackings stage-satisfactory. The engineering of the plays gives pleasure even to those who are not interested in the words. But the words are the thing. The words are what interested Shakespeare and what should closely interest us. Shakespeare is a dramatic poet. He is not a chronicler of experience.

I have to say something so obvious because of the multitude of so called realists, many making money out of print, who want art to be as small as they are. For them, art is a copying machine busily copying themselves. They like the documentary version, the 'life as it is lived'. To support their opinions they will either point to Dickens or Shakespeare. I have never understood why anyone calls Dickens a realist, but I have dealt with that myth elsewhere. . . . As for Shakespeare, they will happily disregard the pervading spirit behind the later plays, and quote *Hamlet* Act III, Scene II 'the purpose of playing . . . is, to hold, as 'twere, the mirror up to nature.'

But what is nature?

From the Latin *Natura,* it is my birth, my characteristics, my condition. It is my nativity, my astrology, my biology, my physiognomy, my geography, my cartography, my spirituality, my sexuality, my mentality, my corporeal, intellectual, emotional, imaginative self. And not just my self, every self and the Self of the world. There is no mirror I know that can show me all of these singularities, unless it is the strange distorting looking-glass of art where I will not find my reflection nor my representation but a nearer truth than I prefer. *Natura* is the whole that I am. The multiple reality of my existence.

The reality of the imagination leaves out nothing. It is the most complete reality that we can know. Imagination takes in the world of sense experience, and rather than trading it for a world of symbols, delights in it for what it is. The artist is physical and it is in the work of true artists in any medium, that we find the most moving and the most poignant studies of the world that we can touch and feel. It is the writer, the painter, and not the realist, who is intimate with the material world, who knows its smells and tastes because they are fresh in her nostrils, full in her mouth. What her hand touches, she feels. R. A. Collingwood said that Cézanne painted like a blind man (critics at the time agreed though for different reasons). He meant that the two-dimensional flimsy world of what is overlooked by most of us, suddenly reared out of the canvas, massy and tough. Cézanne seems to have hands in his eyes and eyes in his hands. When Cézanne paints a tree or an apple, he does not paint a copy of a tree or an apple, he paints its nature. He paints the whole that it is, the whole that is lost to us as we pass it, eat it, chop it down. It is through the painter, writer, composer, who lives more intensely than the rest of us, that we can rediscover the intensity of the physical world.

And not only the physical world. There is no limit to new territory. The gate is open. Whether or not we go through is up to us, but to stand mockingly on the threshold, claiming that nothing lies beyond, is something of a flat earth theory.

The earth is not flat and neither is reality. Reality is continuous, multiple, simultaneous, complex, abundant and partly invisible. The imagination alone can fathom this and it reveals its fathomings through art.

The reality of art is the reality of the imagination.

1996

GETTING STARTED

1. According to Winterson, what is "the charge laid on the artist" (p. 593)?

2. Look up the words "reality" and "imagination" in the dictionary. Does Winterson's use of these words follow these definitions? What new or unexpected elements does she add to these terms?

3. Winterson gives an example of her mother's perception of and relationship to her furniture. Working in a group, explain the author's example. Then read the paragraphs before and after the example to look for clues about Winterson's larger point. What is Winterson trying to explain about our subjective relationship to the things around us?

4. In the paragraph beginning "The work of the artist . . ." (p. 600), Winterson tries to describe the artist's relationship to things. How is that relationship different from the relationship of her mother to her furniture?

WRITING

5. In two paragraphs, discuss whether Winterson's essay fulfills her definition of "art." Respond not only to specific passages from Winterson's essay but also to the form of it. How and why does Winterson attempt to connect the content of the essay—her ideas—with the form of the essay—its appearance and style?

6. Assume that you read Winterson's essay in your campus newspaper. Write a letter to the editor that responds to Winterson's discussion of "money culture" and her provocative claim that "the education system is not designed to turn out thoughtful individualists, it is there to get us to work" (p. 594).

7. Write an essay describing your sense of who "uses" art and who does not. Connect quotations from Winterson's essay with examples from your own experience. Your essay should include your response to some of the following questions. Which of Winterson's details, examples, or references suggest that she imagines her readers to be well educated? Where does art fit into Winterson's understanding of what it means to be well educated? What have been your experiences with art? Where do you see art fitting into your college education? If your campus has an art museum, have you been to it? If you have, what did you see? Did you like what you saw? If you have not visited, why not?

USING THE LIBRARY AND THE INTERNET

8. Find a painting or visual image in a book or on the Internet that you consider to be art (Hint: Try a popular search engine such as AltaVista, limit your search to images, and search in the "Arts" category.) You could even choose a work by Cézanne, an artist Winterson clearly admires. Copy or print out this image, and bring it to class to discuss in the context of Winterson's claims about art. Begin thinking about this by asking yourself what your example suggests about two of Winterson's key terms, "imagination" and "reality." What makes this image "art"?

9. Search for the combined term "art and money" using a database of scholarly articles, such as Academic Search Elite, or a database that includes general-interest and current-events related magazines such as MAS Full Text Ultra. Scan the resulting articles for overlaps between the worlds of "money culture" and "art and imagination" that might help you to question or challenge Winterson's ideas about the split between these worlds.

MAKING CONNECTIONS

10. Use Winterson's ideas about the imagination to analyze an example from Stuart Ewen's "The Marriage Between Art and Commerce." Ewen discusses how styles impact on marketing and sales. How does his argument fit into Winterson's ideas about the link between imagination and money? You might consider the following quotation from Ewen as a point of entry: "Styling, it was increasingly argued, must speak to the unconscious, to those primal urges and sensations that are repressed in the everyday confines of civilization."

11. Use Wanda M. Corn's description and analysis of *American Gothic* and its artist, Grant Wood, to test Winterson's vision of the role of the artist. What role is Wood's painting playing? Is the painting visionary? Is it dangerous? Does it challenge notional life or money culture? To what extent does it provide an imaginative reality? Does it suggest a function or a role for the artist other than the one Winterson describes?

12. Use Winterson's idea about the artist as visionary to test Ralph Ellison's definition of the particular requirements of an American art as outlined in "The Little Man at Chehaw Station." Does Winterson's idea of the artist's role support or resist Ellison's sense of how American artists are always up against "the little man behind the stove"? Does the United States as Ellison imagines it present an artistic environment that is impoverished by the money culture that Winterson decries? What do you think Winterson, who is British, would say about Ellison's idea of America?

Part III

Assignment Sequences

SEQUENCE 1: The Arts and Sciences

Readings: Frye, Kuhn, Winterson, Ellison

ASSIGNMENT 1

Compare Northrop Frye's general discussion of science in "The Motive for Metaphor" with Thomas Kuhn's more specific discussion of the processes of scientific discovery in "The Historical Structure of Scientific Discovery." What parallels do you see between Frye and Kuhn? Does Kuhn's argument complicate or call into question Frye's general assumptions about science?

ASSIGNMENT 2

In "Imagination and Reality," Jeanette Winterson identifies the artist as a "visionary." Write an essay that explores some of the significant intersections you see between Winterson's view of the artist and Northrop Frye's more general discussion of art and science. Would Frye likely agree or disagree with Winterson's claim that the work of the artist is to be a visionary? Are scientists, as Thomas Kuhn describes them in "The Historical Structure of Scientific Discovery," visionaries as well? In your essay, be sure to define "visionary."

ASSIGNMENT 3

Select a key moment in Ralph Ellison's account of his developing understanding of art and identity in America in "The Little Man at Chehaw Station." Use Jeanette Winterson's discussion of "the charge laid on the artist" in "Imagination and Reality" and Thomas Kuhn's discussion of "anomaly" in "The Historical Structure of Scientific Discovery" to help you analyze the Ellison moment that you selected for analysis. In what ways does Ellison's discovery involve an intellectual paradigm shift? In what ways does it exemplify the visionary qualities that Winterson ascribes to the artist? Be specific about the connections you find.

ASSIGNMENT 4

Write an essay that applies Ellison's ideas to Northrop Frye's and Jeanette Winterson's views of art. Would Ellison likely applaud their views? Or would he protest like the "little man" he describes in his essay? Would Ellison be more receptive to the views of one author over the other? As you write, consider the consequences of the position you take. What does Ellison enable you to see about Frye and Winterson?

SEQUENCE 2: Reading Art and Culture

Readings: Tompkins, Anzaldúa, Birkerts, Ewen

Assignment 1

Jane Tompkins's essay "At the Buffalo Bill Museum" recounts her experience of the four museums in the Buffalo Bill Historical Center. Gloria Anzaldúa, in "Chicana Artists: Exploring *Nepantla, el Lugar de la Frontera,*" writes of a similar experience at the Denver Museum of Natural History. Write an essay in which you consider the reactions that both authors have to the exhibits they encounter. What pieces do they respond to and why? How, in each case, does the exhibit lead the author to wider reflections? What topics do they proceed to consider?

Assignment 2

Use Sven Birkerts's discussion of vertical and horizontal consciousness in "The Owl Has Flown" to analyze Gloria Anzaldúa's "reading" of the "Aztec: The World of Moctezuma" exhibition in the Denver Museum of Natural History. In what ways are Birkerts's discussions of reading and wisdom similar to Anzaldúa's experience of attending the exhibition? Why might Anzaldúa object to your use of Birkerts's terminology as a framework for interpreting her arguments? Do you find Birkerts's discussions helpful or unhelpful in analyzing Anzaldúa's text?

Assignment 3

Imagine a conversation between Gloria Anzaldúa and Stuart Ewen about art in America. What does "border art" mean to Anzaldúa? What are the key features in the "marriage between art and commerce" according to Ewen? How might Anzaldúa respond to the "marriage between art and commerce"? How has this marriage impacted border art? Consider Anzaldúa's argument that

> the dominant culture consumes, swallows whole the ethnic artist, sucks out her vitality, and then spits out the hollow husk along with its labels (such as Hispanic). The dominant culture shapes the ethnic artist's identity if she does not scream loud enough to name herself. Until we live in a society where all people are more or less equal, we need these labels to resist the pressure to assimilate. (p. 52)

How might Ewen respond to these assertions by Anzaldúa? Quote from both texts to present your interpretation of how Ewen and Anzaldúa might interpret and respond to each other's work. Provide a shaping idea for your essay that tells your reader how *you* see this conversation.

ASSIGNMENT 4

In "Chicana Artists: Exploring *Neplantla, el Lugar de la Frontera,*" Gloria Anzaldúa laments that "border art" is "becoming trendy" and that it is being "misappropriated by pop culture" (p. 52). What danger does Anzaldúa see? Is her anxiety justified, or is she overreacting? Analyze this question of the appropriation of border art by popular culture in terms of Stuart Ewen's discussion of "the style market" in "The Marriage Between Art and Commerce" and in terms of Sven Birkerts's argument about losing touch with depth and wisdom in our culture of superabundance.

SEQUENCE 3: Technology and Understanding

Readings: Sontag, Lasch, Turkle

ASSIGNMENT 1

Although Susan Sontag writes of the "promise" of photography "to democratize all experiences by translating them into images" (p. 465), she soon seems suspicious of that promise. She writes, "Taking photographs has set up a chronic voyeuristic relation to the world which levels the meaning of all events" (p. 467). What is the difference between democratizing and leveling? What does photography do to experience to make Sontag suspicious? If a photograph can be said to establish authority (as in photographic evidence), can this authority be abused? How? What is the place of power or control in photography? Why might this work against the goals of democracy?

Write an essay that uses Sontag's text as a point of departure for discussing the differences between the democratizing and leveling consequences of technology. How does technology transform the world or at least our understanding of it? Consider at least one of her examples in some detail. You might find it useful to discuss a photographic object, such as a family photo, a newspaper photo, or an ad. Discuss the "way of seeing" the object seeks to promote. You might consider using or analyzing some of the following concepts to help you make your argument: objectivity, voyeurism, surveillance, evidence, cataloguing, compulsion, or art.

ASSIGNMENT 2

In "The Lost Art of Argument," Christopher Lasch argues that the art of argument has suffered in the information age as scientific observation and objective press coverage "provide us with a copy of reality that we can all recognize" (p. 321). He believes that only real, sustained public debate can help us to synthesize and make productive use of the information that bombards us daily.

Test Lasch's claims by examining them in the terms of Susan Sontag's example of photography. Look closely at Lasch's contrasting of the two possible roles for the press—"to circulate information" or "to encourage debate." Use his analysis of this distinction to formulate a response to Sontag that addresses her claim that "in these last decades, 'concerned' photography has done at least as much to deaden conscience as to arouse it" (p. 474).

ASSIGNMENT 3

Sherry Turkle's "The Triumph of Tinkering" describes a technologically driven shift similar to the histories of change narrated by Susan Sontag and Christopher Lasch. Turkle's tone, however, is almost completely different. Where Sontag and Lasch see manipulation and abuse, Turkle sees progress and opportunity. She writes to persuade us to take advantage of these positive events: "A classical modernist vision of computer intelligence has made room for a romantic postmodern one. At this juncture, there is potential for a more welcoming environment for women, humanists, and artists in the technical culture" (p. 565). Turkle speaks here of "room" being "made" to allow for voices and ideas that had been traditionally silenced. She is specifically interested in opportunities for women. How does Turkle's more specific audience and more detailed example allow her to emphasize potential over abuse? What is it about Turkle's approach that differs from Sontag's and Lasch's?

Write an essay that treats Turkle's text as an extended example for your analysis of the possibilities and problems that come with technological expansion. How does what Turkle describes as a change in the "center of gravity" of computer programming—a change in which the experimental methods of bricolage and simulation helped undermine the authority of traditional formal methods—relate to changes outside the immediate sphere of the computer field? How does this example extend or complicate your previous discussion of democracy and its values? What other examples can you think of?

SEQUENCE 4: Status, Self, and Authority

Readings: Anzaldúa, Trask, Early

ASSIGNMENT 1

In gaining experience in a particular field, one often learns to recognize one's own personal experience within the accepted categories of the world of experts. That is, as we learn to associate ourselves with specific groups (in terms of national origin, gender, race, political affiliation), we see our experience as linked in some way to that of others. Academic disciplines such as history, sociology, and linguistics exist, in part, to categorize and place behavior into specific groupings. Gloria Anzaldúa and Haunani-Kay Trask are troubled by the boundaries they see drawn up by the world of experts; they do not recognize themselves in the histories they read. For them, the authorities that speak and write about the Chicana and the Hawaiian experience do not make sense. As a result, both Anzaldúa and Trask write in order to force scholars and others to reexamine the ways in which Chicana and Hawaiian experience have been categorized.

In her essay, Anzaldúa introduces a word to help define the place where personal identity meets these established social categories: "*Nepantla* is the Nahuatl word for an in-between state, that uncertain terrain one crosses when moving from one place to another, when changing from one class, race, or gender position to another, when traveling from the present identity into a new identity" (p. 50). Anzaldúa wants us to see how uncertainty about labels and categories can be productive and can foster new ways of seeing.

In an essay of at least three pages, use Anzaldúa's word "*Nepantla*" to explain Trask's argument. How does border art help us to make sense of the world in a way that differs from the traditional history that Trask describes? You might choose to look closely at how both writers use language to express identity or to examine one or more of the examples from the essays. In any case, look carefully at the ways these writers use their own experience as evidence.

Assignment 2

Build on the paper that you wrote for your first assignment by selecting and analyzing an example from your own personal history. Are Anzaldúa's and Trask's arguments valid only because they are writing from historically marginalized points of view, or is there a way in which *anyone* can use personal experience to problematize or refine established categories? Become a historian of your own life for this assignment and describe an in-between state that you have passed through or are currently in. How does your experience contribute to your understanding of *Nepantla*? Does your argument from your first paper apply to the example you choose? What aspects of your own example cannot be neatly compared to Anzaldúa and Trask? Why? Finally, what does your comparison to Anzaldúa and Trask tell you about the importance of documenting and examining personal history?

Assignment 3

Because of her status as a woman in the nineteenth century, Mary Kingsley could not gain full admittance to the scientific community of her time. She wrote popular treatments of scientific phenomena and gave lectures valued as much for their entertainment value as for their scientific information. And yet, Julie English Early wants us to consider Kingsley as a legitimate, if unorthodox, voice of nineteenth-century science. What makes Kingsley's contributions to scientific discourse especially worthy to Early? Drawing on your previous two essays in this sequence, use Kingsley as an example of a border artist whose commitment to her own personal style makes her an interesting case today. What factors might explain the renewed interest in Kingsley's writings? Kingsley lived a privileged life among some of the wealthiest people in the world. Can we equate her situation with the violent struggles that Anzaldúa and Trask describe?

SEQUENCE 5: Imagination, Possibility, and Control

Readings: Winterson, Mosley, Willis, Toumey

Assignment 1

In "Imagination and Reality," Jeanette Winterson concludes with the following statement: "The earth is not flat and neither is reality. Reality is continuous, multiple, simultaneous, complex, abundant and partly invisible. The imagination alone can fathom this and it reveals its fathomings through art. The reality of art is the reality of the imagination" (p. 603). Winterson's conclusion requires interpretation; it is not immediately clear what she means. In fact, Winterson's entire essay develops an idea of imagination that is slippery and diffuse and that seems designed to be itself "continuous, multiple, simultaneous," and so on.

Consider the implications of imaginative and artful writing. How does Winterson's essay differ from other, more conventional essays you have read or written? List some of these differences; then describe Winterson's writing strategy. Why is she writing in this way? How does her writing enact the qualities of imagination that she admires?

Assignment 2

Novelist Walter Mosley advises fellow writers to be wary of surrendering to what he calls "reality": "Reality fights against your dreams, it tries to deny creation and change. The world wants you to be someone known, someone with solid ideas, not blowing smoke. Given a day, reality will begin to scatter your notions; given two days, it will drive them off" (p. 407). What does Mosley mean by "reality"? How or why should we escape it? What other words might be used to label what Mosley is describing? Why is Mosley suspicious of "solid ideas"?

Write an essay that compares Mosley's sense of reality with Jeanette Winterson's. Pay close attention to the things they associate with reality. What forces or attitudes are they struggling against?

How do both authors believe writing offers a challenge to reality? Are there dangers in resisting reality?

ASSIGNMENT 3

In "Disney World: Public Use / Private State," Susan Willis complains about the "erasure of spontaneity" at Disney World and argues that Disney functions by limiting the possibilities of "play." Apply your understanding of Jeanette Winterson's "Imagination and Reality" to Willis's example of Disney World. How, in your estimation, does Disney sell amusement to consumers? Why might Disney seek to control the experiences of those who come to Disney World? Does this controlling of possibilities eliminate or smother imagination? Explore at least one example in detail. You might consider the role of what Winterson calls "money culture" in the realm of entertainment. Does what we call the "entertainment industry" promote or curb imagination?

ASSIGNMENT 4

In "Science in an Old Testament Style," Christopher P. Toumey argues that science has "plenary authority" in American society. That is, Toumey argues that most Americans assume an attitude Toumey describes as "respect without comprehension" when viewing anything associated with science. In an essay that draws on your ideas from Jeanette Winterson, Walter Mosley, and Susan Willis, discuss the problems with allowing anything to have unquestioned authority. How do the examples Toumey uses demonstrate the dangers of unimaginative obedience? What can happen if authority remains unquestioned?

SEQUENCE 6: "Progress" in Art and Technology

Readings: DeVeaux, Ewen, Birkerts

ASSIGNMENT 1

In "Progress and the Bean," Scott DeVeaux shows that one of the "sense-making" concepts of the sciences, the idea of progress, does not fully explain the process of innovation and change in an artistic field such as music.

> In particular, it is grating to find notions of progress applied to the arts. To claim progress in the fields of science and technology is one thing. Some may argue whether such "advances" actually improve life, but few disagree that new solutions to old problems have rendered previous efforts obsolete. . . . In the arts, however, such wholesale dismissal of the past seems unthinkable. As museums attest, the old retains its power and actively shapes the sensibilities of the present. (p. 108)

Unlike technological progress, artistic "advances" do not make past achievements obsolete. We do not hand crank our car's engine anymore, nor do we travel across the ocean by boat, but we may still be deeply interested in the Impressionists' paintings or Shakespeare's plays. Why do artistic creations sometimes become classics while scientific or technological precedents are discarded or described as just plain wrong?

In an essay, develop your own ideas about the place of progress and obsolescence in the arts and sciences. Consider why DeVeaux thinks that speaking of progress in the arts is "grating." Do you think that artistic creations such as books, movies, and music should be thought of as part of a progression? (Keep in mind that Coleman Hawkins thought that his music was progressive.) Conversely, why do you suppose science and technology so readily scrap the achievements of the past? Is there a danger of losing track of what has come before?

Assignment 2

In his history of the development of style in industry, "The Marriage Between Art and Commerce," Stuart Ewen speaks in many ways to the concerns of your first essay by showing a marriage of technological and artistic goals in the form of advertising and marketing. Ewen refers to this as "the instrumental use of style as a business device" (p. 205). In your second essay, apply your ideas about progress and obsolescence to the historical narrative that Ewen provides. What factors allowed the marriage to occur? What unsatisfying effects came out of this transformation? Does the market provide a suitable arena for the cooperation of art and technology, or are the sacrifices that must be made too great?

Assignment 3

In "The Owl Has Flown," Sven Birkerts laments the destructive consequences of the information age and argues that technological development—the profound increase in the availability of information—has affected the ways in which our minds work. Birkerts describes how a broader and more superficial "extensive reading" has replaced "intensive reading." How does this categorization of a dramatic cultural shift affect our modern-day lives? Do you agree with Birkerts that this period in history is marked by a profound "loss of depth"? Are there advantages to having extensive knowledge? In an essay that incorporates your ideas from the previous two assignments in this sequence, respond to Birkerts's claim that we have almost wholly forsaken "wisdom." Why do you suppose he locates art as the place where depth survives?

SEQUENCE 7: Technology and Change
Readings: Sontag, Turkle, Kuhn

ASSIGNMENT 1

Susan Sontag concludes her essay by saying:

> The knowledge gained through still photographs will always be some kind of sentimentalism, whether cynical or humanist. It will be a knowledge at bargain prices—a semblance of knowledge, a semblance of wisdom; as the act of taking pictures is a semblance of appropriation, a semblance of rape. . . . The omnipresence of photographs has an incalculable effect on our ethical sensibility. By furnishing this already crowded world with a duplicate one of images, photography makes us feel that the world is more available than it really is. (p. 476)

Look at photographs displayed in library books, in newspapers, on the Internet, in museums, or in your family albums. Use a group of photographs to supply evidence for or against Sontag's seemingly dark vision of photography's impact on our society. To what extent do you share her vision? To what extent do you disagree with some of Sontag's claims, or see some alternative implications of photography as a technology? Be specific and direct about the connections you see between your ideas and Sontag's.

ASSIGNMENT 2

Compare and contrast Sontag's discussion of photography as a technology to Sherry Turkle's essay on the varying uses of computer technology. In each case, do the expectations, assumptions, and perceptions of the users seem to determine the outcome and implications of the technology? In other words, how does the "tool" of technology affect the outlook of those who use it? To what extent does the technology itself seem to teach its users both new ways of using it and new ways of perceiving the world? What are the long-range implications of each technology?

ASSIGNMENT 3

Use Thomas Kuhn's discussion of scientific change to analyze Sherry Turkle's description of developments in the field of computer programming. What were the reigning ideas in the field and to what extent have newer ideas successfully challenged or replaced them? Which "anomalies" have become the new laws in the field? How did these new "discoveries" alter the direction of computer science?

SEQUENCE 8: What Is Scientific Literacy?

Readings: Martin et al., Frye, Lewontin

ASSIGNMENT 1

Write a paper in which you explore the relationship between "facts" and "local knowledge" that Emily Martin et al. use in "Scientific Literacy, What It Is, Why It's Important, and Why Scientists Think We Don't Have It: The Case of Immunology and the Immune System." What does it mean to "know" something? Is knowledge the same for everyone? Use examples from Martin et al. to help you illustrate the ways that individuals or small "local" environments sometimes invent new ways to represent facts.

ASSIGNMENT 2

Paraphrasing the poet Wallace Stevens, Northrop Frye writes that "the motive for metaphor . . . is a desire to associate, and finally to identify, the human mind with what goes on outside it, because the only genuine joy you can have is in those rare moments when you feel that although we may know in part, as Paul says, we are also a part of what we know" (p. 224). How do the metaphors employed by Mike, Elizabeth, and the others whose stories are presented in Emily Martin et al.'s piece help them to become a part of what they know? Write a paper in which you analyze the metaphors used by Mike, Elizabeth, and the others in Frye's terms. Do they represent a scientific or an artistic approach to the problem of making sense of the immune system? Is one way of knowing better than the other?

ASSIGNMENT 3

Richard C. Lewontin in "Science as Social Action" writes to oppose something he calls "reductionism," a theory that argues that "we are totally at the mercy of internal forces present within ourselves from birth" (p. 326). Lewontin sees such a view as ideological. That is, he thinks reductionism is a story told about how the world works, a story that does not make sense to him. Using Emily Martin et al.'s ideas about scientific literacy, examine Lewontin's essay as an attempt to tell a new story about genetics. How do the examples and the language he uses shed new light on genetic phenomena and their consequences for our lives?

ASSIGNMENT 4

If we reread "Scientific Literacy" as representative of its authors' work, what can we say about them and about their approach to knowledge? What is their purpose in writing the article? How do they compare to Northrop Frye's poet? Martin and her coauthors are sometimes called "social scientists." Write a paper in which you construct a preliminary definition of a social scientist based on your analysis of Martin et al.'s work. (Keep in mind that we are looking at only a small sample of their work.)

SEQUENCE 9: The Art of "Reality"

Readings: Winterson, Corn, Kaku, Gould

ASSIGNMENT 1

In "Imagination and Reality," Jeanette Winterson begins her essay with the question, "What do I mean by reality of art?" Write an essay that explores your interpretations of Winterson's answer to her question. Trace how she defines and redefines "reality" and "the real." Piece together the examples and definitions from her essay that best explain what she means. You might choose to bring in a photograph, painting, poem, or other art object that helps you exemplify or interpret Winterson's point. (If you do so, attach a photocopy of the art object to the paper.)

Thinking about and writing preliminary responses to one or more of the following questions can help you to construct a rough draft. How is "the real" related to the goal of art and the imagination? How is it related to the goal of science? How is it opposed to the pressure of "money culture"?

ASSIGNMENT 2

Wanda M. Corn, in "The Birth of a National Icon: *American Gothic,*" claims that Grant Wood's painting has become a "national icon" not because it depicts a "real" rural couple, but because it successfully renders qualities that many see as uniquely American. Use Corn's analysis of *American Gothic* to help you explain Jeanette Winterson's comment that "art is not documentary. . . . [I]ts true effort is to open to us dimensions of the spirit and of the self that normally lie smothered under the weight of living" (p. 595). Why does Corn believe *American Gothic* symbolizes American life? How does Wood go beyond the "documentary"? In what ways has Wood used imagination to comment on reality?

ASSIGNMENT 3

In "Second Thoughts: The Genetics of a Brave New World," Michio Kaku explores some of the positive and negative possibilities of scientific research, saying that "the awesome scientific knowledge that will be unveiled early in the next century must be tempered by the enormous ethical, social, and political questions that it raises" (p. 281). Use two key ideas from Jeanette Winterson's "Imagination and Reality" to help you write an essay that analyzes two scientific goals Kaku presents that you think will require the public to ask serious "ethical, social, and political questions."

In planning your argument, you might consider the following questions. What is the role of imagination in Kaku's essay? Is the pressure of "money culture" operating in the debates over cloning? To what extent are the goals of science "fus[ing] together temporal and perpetual realities" in the future that Kaku envisions, and to what extent are they constrained by "money culture"?

Assignment 4

In "The Smoking Gun of Eugenics," Stephen Jay Gould argues that "bad and biased arguments can have serious, even deadly, consequences" (p. 256). His example is Sir Ronald Aylmer Fisher, an influential genetics theorist who also argued that smoking does not cause cancer. Gould explains that Fisher, who was hired by the Tobacco Manufacturers' Standing Committee, sacrificed his impartiality by constructing arguments that would please the committee.

Looking closely at your earlier essays, write a new essay that explores Fisher's theorizing as an attempt to "imaginatively" revise reality. What methods does Fisher use in his attempt to prove that smoking does not lead to cancer? What does Gould want us to learn from Fisher's example? How does your understanding of Jeanette Winterson, Wanda M. Corn, and Michio Kaku shed light on Fisher?

SEQUENCE 10: Democracy and Debate

Readings: Lasch, Ingham, Williams

Assignment 1

In "The Lost Art of Argument," Christopher Lasch claims that there has been a decline in the kind of public debate that forms the basis for a working democracy. Test Lasch's argument by choosing a newspaper article from the press coverage of a current political issue. Does the article have an "aura of objectivity," does it present information, or does it openly argue an opinion? Are you getting a "painstaking analysis of complex issues"? Are you getting more than one side to the issue? Do you see evidence of a public debate or a way in which public debate might reshape this political issue? Which of the historical factors that Lasch mentions best explain the way the article is written? Even if you end up disagreeing with Lasch, demonstrate an understanding of his examples and point of view.

ASSIGNMENT 2

Your first paper reflects on whether public debate can help to build a working democracy. Zita Ingham's "Landscape, Drama, Dissensus" gives us a test case for analyzing how the people of Red Lodge, Montana, used public debate to try to change their community. Would Lasch see this community as a working democracy? Do the strategies of "dissensus" or "deferred consensus" used by the people of Red Lodge have any connection to the historical uses of public debate that Lasch describes? Does the role of the Sonoran Institute, the "outsiders" who in some ways prompted the debate, affect the democratic significance of this community? Use this second paper to illustrate the connections you see between Lasch and Ingham.

ASSIGNMENT 3

In "The Ethnic Scarring of American Whiteness," Patricia J. Williams provides examples of the way race and class prejudices continue to function in American life and continue to be transferred from one generation to the next. To what extent can argument, consensus, or "dissensus" begin to heal these scars? Use Williams's examples to test some of Christopher Lasch's and Zita Ingham's conclusions about the ways communities and democracies can and should function. Do Lasch and Ingham offer proposals that might resolve some of the problems that Williams describes? Does Williams identify aspects of community interaction that Lasch and Ingham fail to consider? Be specific and detailed about the examples you use to illustrate your points.

SEQUENCE 11: *Seeing and Knowing*

Readings: Percy, Winterson, Dillard

ASSIGNMENT 1

Write an essay in which you use Walker Percy's ideas of "sovereignty" and "preformed symbolic complex" to analyze the link Percy makes between "experts" and "theory" in the second half of "The Loss of the Creature." What is Percy trying to say about experts and what they know? Develop an example of your own to explore Percy's claims. Does Percy think we should avoid experts?

ASSIGNMENT 2

This new assignment allows you to extend and revise your understanding of Walker Percy's essay, "The Loss of the Creature." What relationships do you see between Walker Percy's idea of "sovereignty" and Jeanette Winterson's understanding of the artist in her essay "Imagination and Reality"? Write an essay that examines whether Percy's sovereign person is a type of artist, a "visionary" in Winterson's terms. As you begin to draft your essay, you might think about some of the following questions: What are Winterson's and Percy's attitudes toward imagination? What would Percy likely say in response to Winterson's claim that "the more familiar a thing becomes the less it is seen" (p. 599)? How does Percy define or characterize artists in his essay? Your essay should develop an idea about the consequences of the connections you see. Can we think of travel, schoolwork, or conversation as an "art"?

ASSIGNMENT 3

In "Seeing," Annie Dillard discusses Marius von Senden's book *Space and Sight,* which analyzes the spatial perception of the "newly sighted." The newly sighted are blind people who are given sight after successful cataract operations. "In general," Dillard writes, "the newly sighted see the world as a dazzle of color-patches," and "many newly sighted people . . . teach us how dull is our own vision" (p. 148). Use Dillard's discussion of the newly sighted to assess the most significant arguments about "vision" in Walker Percy's "The Loss of the Creature" and Jeanette Winterson's "Imagination and Reality." Does Dillard's discussion of the newly sighted help you produce a re-vision of your previous understanding of Percy's or Winterson's main arguments about sight and insight? What does the comparison reveal?

SEQUENCE 12: Writing on Writing

Readings: Sommers, Mellix, Williams

ASSIGNMENT 1

Write a short paper comparing and contrasting some of Nancy Sommers's ideas and examples about writing in "I Stand Here Writing" to your own observations and experiences involving writing. For instance, what does Sommers mean when she says that writing involves "a radical loss of certainty" (p. 451), and to what extent has that been your experience? What does Sommers learn from Ralph Waldo Emerson's sentence, "One must be an inventor to read well," and to what extent does that apply to your experience? What have you learned about writing that you would want to communicate to a classmate or student?

ASSIGNMENT 2

Write a longer paper assessing how well Nancy Sommers's ideas about writing apply to Barbara Mellix's experiences in "From Outside, In" and to your own experiences as a writer. To what extent does Mellix experience a "radical loss of certainty" or learn to "be an inventor"? Does Mellix learn things that challenge, contradict, or go beyond Sommers's ideas about writing? What is your sense of identity as a writer in relation to the ideas and experiences of these two writers?

ASSIGNMENT 3

In "The Ethnic Scarring of American Whiteness," Patricia J. Williams examines intersections of class and ethnicity. Think about how these intersections are also tied to relationships of language and power, relationships that you have been exploring in the first two paper assignments in this sequence. For your third assignment, write a paper that uses ideas and examples from the readings by Williams, Barbara Mellix, and Nancy Sommers to explain some key relationships you see between either class or ethnicity and styles of reading, speaking, and writing. The topic is large, so you will need to be selective about what you present in your final draft. Be sure to avoid unnecessary summary as you synthesize your analyses of Williams's, Mellix's, and Sommers's ideas.

SEQUENCE 13: Visual Literacy

Readings: Sontag, Berger, McGraw, McCloud

ASSIGNMENT 1

Collect your own "anthology of images," including several photographs that interest you, and use them to write an essay explaining and testing some of Susan Sontag's claims in "In Plato's Cave." What are some of the problems that Sontag sees with photography? Do the images you have chosen support, contradict, or go beyond her arguments? Be specific about which passages in Sontag you are responding to.

ASSIGNMENT 2

In "The Changing View of Man in the Portrait," John Berger argues that the invention of photography changed the way people see paintings. Use Berger's ideas about photography to return to Susan Sontag's essay with fresh eyes. For instance, Berger argues that photographs are superior to painted portraits in that they are "more informative, more psychologically revealing, and in general more accurate" (p. 60). But he also says that they are much less able to persuade or be conclusive about their effect on the viewer. How does Berger's vision of the role of photography challenge or extend your understanding of Sontag?

ASSIGNMENT 3

In "Bad Eyes," Erin McGraw describes some of ways in which her vision affected how she behaved and how she thought about herself. To what extent are John Berger and Susan Sontag making similar arguments that because photographs have changed the way our culture as a whole sees, they have also changed the way we behave and think about ourselves? Write an essay using ideas and examples from Sontag, Berger, and McGraw to develop your own theory about the connection between vision and identity, between how we see and how we think about ourselves.

ASSIGNMENT 4

John Berger tracks some of the historical changes in the ways that painted portraits and photographs have related to individual identity. Use ideas and examples from Berger and from Scott McCloud's "Setting the Record Straight" to discuss where comics would fit into this history. What role do comics play in characterizing individual identity? Is it closer to the role played by painted portraits or the role played by photographs? Feel free to draw on examples from comics other than those used by McCloud and to use examples from Susan Sontag or Erin McGraw if you find them useful.

SEQUENCE 14: Escapes

Readings: Tuan, Rybczynski, Solnit

ASSIGNMENT 1

Geographer Yi-Fu Tuan suggests in "Earth" that "escapism" is a uniquely human response to uncertainty. Tuan writes that "by one means or another [humans] seek control, with at best only tenuous success" (p. 539). Looking closely at Tuan's argument, develop your own idea about why people spend so much time and energy thinking about escaping from their lives. Does any good come of imagining that life could be better, smoother, or less uncertain?

ASSIGNMENT 2

Witold Rybczynski's "Designs for Escape" tells the story of a couple who are building a weekend house. Use the couple as a test case for the ideas you pursued in this sequence's first essay. What are Danielle and Luc trying to ensure or confirm with their new house, and why does Rybczynski have different ideas? What does he want us to see about the relationship between fantasy and architecture? Why is Danielle so interested in getting Rybczynski's approval? Use a passage from Yi-Fu Tuan's essay to highlight your sense of Danielle and Luc.

ASSIGNMENT 3

Rebecca Solnit, in "Aerobic Sisyphus and the Suburbanized Psyche," explains that much of the contemporary fascination with physical fitness is a perverse response to the fact that modern living no longer requires much physical strength. "That muscles have become status symbols signifies that most jobs no longer call upon bodily strength: like tans, they are an aesthetic of the obsolete" (p. 445). Compare this idea with Yi-Fu Tuan's notion that "nostalgia for traditional ways of making a living on the family farm is at least in part a wish to regain a sense of weight and necessity, of being subjected to demands of nature that allow little or no room for fanciful choice" (p. 549). Write an essay that considers the place of nostalgia in the mindset of one who exercises. Why do so many modern exercise machines replicate the work activities of an earlier period—lifting, rowing, climbing, and walking? What might Tuan say about the desires of the people who engage in these activities? What role does discipline have in this phenomenon?

SEQUENCE 15: Making Common Sense

Readings: Geertz, Diamond, Susman, Percy

Assignment 1

Can common sense be analyzed? Clifford Geertz, in "Common Sense as a Cultural System," argues that it is the resistance of common sense to analysis that makes it so powerful. "Religion rests its case on revelation, science on method, ideology on moral passion; but common sense rests its on the assertion that it is not a case at all, just life in a nutshell" (p. 228). What happens, then, if we challenge common sense and, with Geertz, view it as a "cultural system"? Write an essay in which you use Geertz's idea to analyze an example you have of a commonsense belief that ought to be tested. How does viewing this idea as part of a system change your sense of it? Why did this idea become commonsensical in the first place, and why has it persisted?

Assignment 2

In "Necessity's Mother," Jared Diamond confronts the commonsense idea that "necessity is the mother of invention." What problems does he see with this notion, and how do the examples he uses serve to illustrate these problems? Specifically, how does Diamond shed light on the issues you raised in Assignment 1? In this essay, include at least one paragraph in which you use Clifford Geertz's language to comment on an example from Diamond. In using Geertz and Diamond together, what are you seeing about how change occurs? Is common sense an obstacle to change?

Assignment 3

In "'Personality' and the Making of Twentieth-Century Culture," Warren I. Susman argues that a new style of imagining one's self emerged gradually but powerfully throughout the twentieth century. Look carefully at some of the specific transformations that he describes, and write an essay in which you explore these changing attitudes as manifestations of a changing common sense. Why does a culture imagine itself differently in different eras? How is "personality" a "cultural system"?

ASSIGNMENT 4

Can we view Walker Percy's struggles for sovereignty in "The Loss of the Creature" as struggles against common sense? Apply Clifford Geertz's idea that common sense is "what the mind filled with presuppositions . . . concludes" (p. 235) to Percy's attack on "preformed" ideas and the "packaging" of experience. You might also wish to consider Jared Diamond's examination of the impulse for invention. What do you think keeps many people from seeing things through new perspectives? Why are some people more inclined to challenge old and accepted ideas?

Part IV

Writing in the Disciplines

Writing in the Disciplines

Your first-year composition course is preparing you and the other students in your classroom for any number of majors or professions. The skills you learn in the writing classroom must be adaptable to the differing demands of the other courses you go on to take, whether they are in sociology, history, accounting, political science, biology, English, or a foreign language. To better address what those differing demands might be, we asked people in a range of disciplines to consider the role of writing in their fields, the kinds of writing assignments you might expect in their classes, and the ways those assignments function as preparation for further work in that field.

As you read these essays, you will notice that different disciplines have different expectations. In biology, for example, you probably will not be asked to work with direct quotation, but you probably will be asked to summarize your data in a table, graph, or picture; to explain that graphic clearly; and to show logically how it supports your conclusions. An assignment in political science might require you to interpret a political speech by using quotations as evidence and including explanations and interpretations of the quotations to support your thesis statement and argument. In foreign language classes you might be asked to fill out government or other forms in the language you are learning. In accounting, you might need to summarize "a page of numbers in a sentence or two" (Scofield p. 632), while in sociology you might be asked to go beyond "a bland summary of the text" when writing about your reaction to an assigned reading (McClelland p. 640). One assignment might ask for your perspective on the material, while another might ask you to synthesize literature in the field without giving your own opinion.

The commonalities are more important than the differences, however, when it comes to the varied expectations about writing among disciplines, instructors, and assignments. One commonality that becomes apparent is this: Assignments in college courses almost always depend on the ability to *respond to material in that field, whether that material involves readings or numerical or statistical data.* College writing is almost never done in isolation from the materials in that field. Thus, for example, you probably will be asked to write personal narratives or creative pieces only in creative writing courses, where personal expression is part of the subject matter, or in foreign language courses, where personal or creative writing can help you to gain fluency in another language (Lomangino, p. 643). Other commonalities include:

- clarity of presentation, including grammar and mechanics, and correct citation form;
- logical organization and progression of ideas;
- accurate paraphrase, summary, and analysis of evidence;
- interpretation of evidence or data to demonstrate how it supports arguments or conclusions; and
- adaptation of ideas or information for a particular audience.

The greatest commonality, however, is the importance all professionals place on writing. Accounting professor Barbara Scofield notes that "Big 5 accounting firms require interviewees to complete written questions *during the interview* to evaluate applicants' skills" (p. 632). Or, as German Professor Heide R. Lomangino puts it, writing "consolidates and reinforces grammar and vocabulary learning and promotes the development of listening, speaking, and reading skills" (p. 642). This is true of all classroom and learning situations. Writing helps you to make sense of unfamiliar arenas of knowledge, to develop your own ideas and abilities in relation to that knowledge, and to communicate those ideas to others.

BARBARA SCOFIELD
University of Texas at the Permian Basin

Writing in Accounting

As technology takes on more and more of the work of gathering, recording, and summarizing information, an accountant's competitive advantage is the ability to analyze and communicate financial information. Consider the following scenario.

The printout for the profit for this year states:

	2001	*2002*
Sales	$40,000,000	$60,000,000
Net Income	$4,000,000	$5,000,000

Based on the figures alone, management is in a quandary. Then the accountant's report arrives:

> Although sales increased 50%, net income only increased 25%, suggesting that there is a steep cost to expanding sales internationally. As the company moves into markets even further from its base customers, the company must increase the efficiency of its selling costs or profit growth will continue to lag.

Or perhaps . . .

> The company achieved its target 25% growth in profit by broad market expansion internationally that saw sales increase 50%. Much of the initial advertising expenses in entering new markets will pay off next year when the company expands in each of these new markets, boosting profit margins.

The accountant decided whether the numbers were good news or bad news and turned these numbers into information that could be used in making business decisions.

In creating information from data, accountants need to summarize information succinctly. Two years of data is communicated by the percentage change. Numbers that are accurate to the penny appear to the nearest million. Sales from the best and worst districts merit a line in reports, but the normal and the routine do not appear. The precision required in preparation of the financial information can obscure the point in narrative form. Beginning accounting students are asked to explain why a company is profitable or unprofitable based on their own computations of net income, an assignment that requires them to summarize a page of numbers in a sentence or two.

Accountants connect evidence with conclusions. Typically accountants have supporting charts or tables for assertions they make. But every chart and table must have written titles, legends, and footnotes that allow the graphic to communicate without an accompanying narrative, and the narrative must provide a clear enough verbal picture so that the graphic is optional. The first step for accounting students is writing footnote disclosures that provide the context for the specific debits and credits used in journal entries.

Accountants organize logically but in a manner that sometimes seems upside down to nontechnical writers. Building suspense is anathema. The best report provides its conclusion in the first paragraph and uses the body of the report to persuade the audience. No one wants to know how the author developed his or her own opinion. Explanations of the process of gathering evidence are placed in appendices, if included at all. A typical research assignment for a new accounting student teaches this organizational skill by having the student gather financial information about a consumer-oriented company and providing a "Buy," "Sell," or "Hold" recommendation on its stock.

Accountants match vocabulary to the expertise of the audience. Some accounting writings are workpapers that are used only by successor accountants. A common, technical vocabulary (e.g., "accruals") and routine abbreviations (AJE) are appropriate. Some accounting writings communicate within a company. No business executive mistakes the meaning of "net income" and "revenues." Some accounting writing communicates with suppliers and clients outside of a company. "The value of all goods delivered to customers during the year" distinguishes what is meant by "revenues" from cash received from customers or value of goods available for sale. Reports are customized to the needs of the audience. A typical audience for an entering student is fellow students. Can you explain accounting terminology so that another freshman can understand it?

How important is writing in the field of accounting? Big 5 accounting firms require interviewees to complete written questions *during the interview* to evaluate applicants' skills. The Certified Public Accounting examination grade is based on writing skills as well as technical skills. The Securities and Exchange Commission identifies good writing as an essential part of its investor protection program (see *A Plain English Handbook* at <http://www.sec.gov/pdf/handbook.pdf>). So you want to be an accountant? Start writing!

STEVEN GERENCSER
Indiana University, South Bend

Writing in Political Science

Writing for a course in political science offers many opportunities and, of course, many challenges. The student of political science might need to write an interpretation of the classical philosopher Plato's conception of the ideal political regime for one class and an analysis of statistical polling data for another. Some assignments will ask students to write about their response to an argument they have read or a film they have seen; others will ask them to avoid putting their personal opinions into their analyses. Some instructors will ask a student to write about an assignment that all students have read for class; others will require a student to do individual research about anything from the various electoral systems of countries around the world to how congressional subcommittees develop policies. Given this range of writing, what, if anything, ties together writing for political science?

Good writing in political science shares with good writing in all disciplines an attention to the mechanics of good grammar and syntax. Accurate spelling, correct punctuation, proper sentence structure, and good paragraph organization are not only important for English composition courses, but also for clear writing in political science. But the variety of writing assignments mentioned above means that more than attention to good mechanics is important.

Most important is to convey immediately and directly to the reader what the writer is attempting to accomplish in the piece. What is the thesis of the argument, the significance of the explanation, or the point of the interpretation? What is the purpose of the writing? Is it to persuade? To interpret? To inform? To argue? Who is the audience for this writing? Should the writer assume the reader knows as much as the political science instructor? Another student in the class? Someone with no knowledge of the subject matter? Of course, to convey his or her intentions to the reader, the writer must know what he or she is trying to accomplish. Is he, for example, trying to argue that Plato's ideal city is fundamentally problematic? If so, the writer might start by declaring, "In this paper I will argue that Plato's favorite political regime is flawed because it makes accidental differences between people the basis of political inequality." Is the writer instead trying to interpret and explain a feature of Plato's discussion? In that case, the writer might state her thesis as "Plato's suggestion that the best city would be ruled by a philosopher might sound odd, but I will show how it is based upon his theory of knowledge." These two sentences indicate quite different papers, but each thesis statement makes it clear what the writer is attempting. Each statement assumes that the reader is aware of Plato's conception of the ideal city and knows some of its features.

A student could also be asked to provide a narative that makes sense of the numbers in a statistical survey or to construct an argument that uses those numbers to persuade the reader to pursue a particular course of action. Again, the thesis statement makes the paper's direction clear to the reader. In the first case, the writer might begin by informing the reader, "This paper will attempt to explain the complex responses to a recent healthcare survey by discussing how the survey was taken, what questions were asked, and how the answers changed depending on the order in which those questions were asked." The writer of the second paper might announce, "I will contend in this paper that the results of a recent healthcare survey clearly show this country is ready to extend healthcare to all its citizens." Each of these thesis statements indicates that the reader is not required to know anything about the healthcare survey; the writer will explain what is necessary. Before beginning any writing assignment, of course, it is important to ask for clear directions from the instructor. The student can then use the instructor's guidelines to consider the topic of the assignment before developing an approach to writing it.

One of the most important and difficult aspects of learning to write in political science is knowing how to use evidence to support the argument, explanation, or interpretation. Whether it is the text of a philosophical treatise or a political speech, the data from a statistical survey or the Gross National Product of a Third World country, the evidence never speaks for itself. The writer needs to use the data or text to support his or her argument, explanation, or interpretation, but he cannot simply assemble a puzzle of pieces of data or quotes. This is a tricky task. The writer must be able to point to specific data or quotations from a text and explain or interpret what she thinks they mean. Again, it is important to ask the instructor assigning a paper how she expects the writer to refer to the evidence. Does she want direct quotations? Should statistical figures be brought into the text directly or left for footnotes?

Asking how best to use quotations or data raises the question of how to cite the sources the writer uses. As a general recommendation, it is a good idea to write down the bibliographic information for any source used at any stage of writing, even if it is unclear if it will make it into a final draft; this way, a writer does not have to scurry back to the library to find that information, risking the possibility that the source is being used by someone else. There are many different styles used in many different political science publications, so again, consult with the instructor to determine which style he or she prefers.

ANN GRENS, DEBORAH MARR, AND
ANDREW SCHNABEL
Indiana University, South Bend

Writing in the Sciences

Writing is a central part of being a professional scientist. Scientists write the results of their research for publication, write proposals to obtain funding for research, and write reviews to present new ideas that are emerging from the results of many experiments. One of the major goals of writing in undergraduate science classes is to develop skills in two major categories: research papers and literature reviews.

Both research papers and literature reviews are structured in a fundamentally similar way, which reflects the scientific process. In all cases, a scientific paper begins with an introduction to the hypothesis to be tested and a brief review of relevant background information. In research papers, but typically not in literature reviews, the introduction is followed by a detailed description of the methods and materials used to conduct the study. The true heart of any scientific paper, however, is the presentation of observations or experimental results, which are often in the form of quantitative data. In a research paper, the author reports the results he or she generated, while in a review the author summarizes results from previously published work. Finally, the author presents his or her conclusions and explains how the experimental evidence supports those conclusions.

Because the primary purpose of writing in the sciences is to convey factual information, the key skills for success are clear presentation and the ability to develop a logical argument. Conveying accurate meaning to the reader requires correct spelling, punctuation, and grammar. Sloppiness, in the form of imprecise wording or inaccurate phrasing, can lead a reader to misunderstand how or why an experiment was performed or what results were obtained. If the reader is unable to determine precisely what was done, he or she is unlikely to accept the results as reliable. Thus, accuracy is of greater importance than originality; it is far preferable to use a term repeatedly that conveys the precise meaning intended than to lose clarity or accuracy by substituting nearly synonymous terms for the sake of variety. Accuracy in wording also requires clearly distinguishing between fact and possibility. For example, compare these two statements:

1. Species A cannot tolerate temperatures above 30°C.
2. Our data suggest that species A cannot tolerate temperatures above 30°C.

The first statement is factual, whereas the second is an interpretation of the data.

The logic by which the author has drawn conclusions from experimental results must also be clearly presented and supported both with examples from previously published work and by reference to the data contained in earlier portions of the paper. The author must explain his or her conclusions, discuss how those conclusions were reached, and convincingly demonstrate that alternative explanations are unlikely to explain the observed results. Finally, the author should resist overinterpretation and should limit conclusions to those that can be logically supported by the available data. Consider the conclusions a student could make from an experiment that involved measuring light absorption for various plant pigments. The first student states that the plant pigments absorbed primarily blue and red wavelengths, and predicts that blue and red wavelengths promote the greatest amount of plant growth because capturing light is critical for plant growth. The second student makes the same statement, but then predicts that blue and red wavelengths are best for promoting growth of all photosynthetic organisms. The first statement is a logical extension of the results, whereas the second conclusion overinterprets the results because many photosynthetic organisms are not plants and have different pigments.

Most writing in the sciences is related to qualitative or quantitative results generated by testing hypotheses. Students therefore also must develop the ability to present such information accurately and clearly. Little scientific information lends itself well to narrative description. Instead, most research results are best summarized in a figure, such as a table, graph, or picture. This is especially true for numerical data, which is the most common type of information presented in scientific studies. The author must construct appropriate figures that present the relevant information and must explain the figures in such a manner that the reader can easily extract that information. The reader should be led through a figure, with specific results of interest clearly indicated. The author should not simply include the figure and trust that the reader will interpret it correctly.

Figure 1, for example, shows data on human survivorship that were collected by students in an introductory biology class. A student writing a lab report about human survivorship based on these data would need to refer to the figure in the results section of the paper and explain the main points of the graph. Suppose the explanatory text accompanying the figure states, "Figure 1 shows that females had high survival through the early and middle years and began to suffer high mortality rates only in older age classes." This text helps ensure that the reader understands the information that is being presented. It also makes it easier for the author to refer to the figure in support of his or her conclusions. In the discussion section of the report, for example, the student might argue, "The high survivorship of each individual offspring, as shown in Figure 1, reflects important aspects of human life history that are similar to those of many other mammals, such as large energetic investment in producing offspring, having small numbers of offspring per reproductive episode, and investing heavily in parental care of the young."

The final part of the scientific paper presents complete bibliographic information for each source used to support statements in the text. The precise format for presenting bibliographic information varies depending on the scientific discipline and journal, but there are two general rules that apply across virtually all forms of scientific writing. First, and most importantly, an accurate citation must be given for any results or ideas that are not the author's original work. Second, direct quotes are extremely rare; the author generally paraphrases hypotheses, experimental results, and interpretations that originated elsewhere. A citation in the format required by the journal (or the instructor, in the case of class assignments) should immediately follow the paraphrase and should refer the reader to a complete reference for the original source in the "Works Cited" or "References" section of the paper.

In summary, the general rules of basic composition apply in scientific writing as much as in any other discipline. Writing in the sciences is somewhat different from writing in many other fields, however, because of a difference in emphasis and intention. Scientific writing aims to convey factual information accurately and precisely,

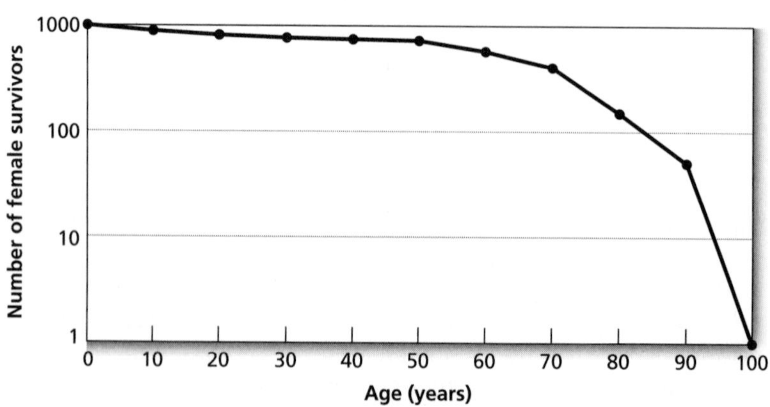

FIGURE 1 Survivorship curve for females born between 1850 and 1869

whether communicating novel results of new experiments performed by the author or a summary of previously published results in a literature review. In either case, clarity of presentation is considered to be of far greater importance than literary style. As discussed here, most scientific writing follows a basic structure that mirrors the scientific process of observation, hypothesis testing, and analysis and interpretation of quantitative data. Students who become skilled at the clear presentation and explanation of scientific methods and results will have a distinct advantage in their science courses.

KENT McCLELLAND

Grinnell College

Writing in Sociology

As a sociology student, you are likely to get paper assignments asking for your reactions to assigned readings. For example, you might be asked to write an essay discussing the "sociological imagination" (Mills 1959:3–24). Such papers too often end up as little more than a bland summary of the text. To avoid this pitfall and to make your paper more interesting, imagine your essay as a three-way conversation among the author of the text, your readers, and you. If you hope to write a really good essay, you cannot hide behind the author whose work you are analyzing. Instead you must stake out your own position in the conversation.

The first side of the three-way conversation in a good essay links the author of the text with the readers of the paper, whom you should think of as intelligent students who have not yet read the text. In this part of the conversation, you convey to your readers what this author is saying. The second conversation connects you personally with these readers, as you tell them what interests you most about these ideas. The third and most important conversation requires you to confront the author directly by engaging in a critical analysis and appreciation of the text. Since these conversations cannot all occur at once, knowing when to hold each can help you to structure your paper.

A well-written introduction gets all three of the conversations under way. You start the first conversation by introducing your readers to the author and the central ideas under discussion. In almost the same breath, you can begin the second conversation, the one between you and your readers, by finding a way to catch your readers' interest. You might hook your readers, for example, by showing how the chosen text creates an apparent contradiction or a problem to be solved. Your introduction must also initiate the crucial third conversation by stating your thesis, the main point of your critical comments on the author's ideas. Many introductions end by quickly returning to the conversation between you and your readers, as you forecast the direction the paper will take.

In the middle paragraphs, or body of the essay, you focus on the two conversations involving the author of the text. While it is tempting to devote most sentences in these paragraphs to the first conversation—the one conveying the author's ideas to your readers—you should not neglect the even more important exchange—the one between you and the author. Which of the author's ideas do you believe are on the right track and which off course? Which ideas can be extended or applied? This critical commentary constitutes your essay's *argument,* and readers expect to find it in the transitional sentences at the beginnings and ends of these paragraphs.

Your essay's concluding paragraph ordinarily sums up the highlights of your argument, but the conclusion also offers you a chance to turn to your readers and renew your conversation with them by putting things in perspective. Where should we go with the new insights developed here? What might it all mean in the scheme of things?

With all these conversations going on, readers may need help in keeping them straight. Thus, careful citation is crucial. Citations enable you to separate your own voice from the voice of the author. You can also clarify the separation of voices by not trying to sound like the original author. As a college student, you need not pretend that you have already earned a Ph.D., and, in fact, such pretension risks making you sound foolish. Readers want to hear your perspective on the material in your own words as you add your voice to the ongoing discourse of academic scholarship.

References

Mills, C. Wright. 1959. *The Sociological Imagination.* New York: Grove Press.

HEIDE R. LOMANGINO

University of South Alabama

Writing in Foreign Languages

Students write a lot in foreign language classes. Some assignments are similar to those required in other disciplines, but others are quite different and unique to foreign language learning. Unless students advance to the third and fourth year of college-level study, they generally are not required, nor able, to produce research papers or other formal writing in the target language. Writing in another language is a complex skill that must be developed and practiced thoroughly. The overall objective of writing instruction is to enable students to express their ideas in written form and produce messages that are comprehensible and acceptable to native speakers. This, however, does not imply native speaker proficiency, because it is rare that nonnative speakers, even after many years of language study, are able to write as well as educated native speakers.

Writing fulfills two basic roles in foreign language acquisition. First, it consolidates and reinforces grammar and vocabulary learning and promotes the development of listening, speaking, and reading skills. In this case, writing functions as a support skill. Second, writing is an important mode of communication as, for example, in correspondence of all kinds: notes, forms, reports, essays, and creative writing.

The writing activities in foreign language courses reflect the many skills that are involved in the writing process. If the writing system is different from English as, for example, in Russian, Arabic, or Japanese, students initially may spend considerable time practicing how to write the new symbols.

To help students learn the spelling rules of the new language, early writing activities may consist of copying written texts or writing down words and phrases that students have heard or spoken. These exercises involve noting and remembering the choice of letters and their sequence. It also means associating speech sounds with graphic symbols and recognizing instances of unsounded letters. Students must also learn to use grammar according to target language norms.

In addition, they must acquire skill in selecting and using words and phrases that convey the meanings they wish to express.

Other writing activities on the beginning level are listing, labeling, matching, filling out forms, and answering questions on simple readings. In addition, students begin to create their own texts by writing brief descriptions of people and places, short messages for postcards and letters, and dialogue journals.

On the intermediate level, roughly the second year of language study in college, students are able to produce longer sentences and short connected texts. Writing is still used to consolidate the learning of vocabulary and grammar, but also to promote personal expression that includes the composing of notes, letters, descriptions, guided and free compositions, advertisements, daily journals, and simple poems.

On the advanced level, students generally are required to take several specialized courses in literature, language, and culture. There they engage in a variety of demanding writing tasks. The content of these courses is drawn from a number of diverse disciplines and fields of inquiry, such as literary criticism, history, politics, art, music, and business. Consequently, students must not only develop skill in organizing their ideas effectively and creating texts coherently, they also must learn how to use subject-specific language appropriately.

In some upper-level composition courses, students are systematically introduced to the composing process. The different steps, from prewriting to revising, are practiced in a variety of formats. Writing projects may include research papers and reports, letters, essays, compositions, journals, poetry, and translation. Expressive writing usually is graded holistically or analytically. Holistic evaluation is done quickly and impressionistically, and a single grade is assigned based on the overall impression of the clarity and effectiveness of the work and its linguistic and organizational quality. In analytical evaluation, significant elements of a composition are separated into components for scoring purposes, for example, grammar, vocabulary, spelling, stylistic technique, organization, and content. Based on the nature of the writing activity, each component is assigned a certain weight and value, and thus students are given an accurate diagnosis of the strengths and weaknesses of their written work.

Foreign language learners have access to many tools and resources to assist them with their writing. Dictionaries are available in book form, on CD-ROMs, and on the Internet. Most writing instructors have definite preferences in respect to dictionaries and other reference works. Bilingual or learners' dictionaries generally are not recommended because the excessive use of bilingual dictionaries tends to encourage translation from the native to the target language, a practice that can be detrimental to the development of natural and fluent expression.

Computer-assisted instruction is now popular in foreign language education, and word processing programs, electronic mail, and computer conferencing systems are being used to promote writing skills. In addition, special writing assistant programs have been designed to facilitate the writing process. These contain guided composing activities as well as bilingual dictionaries, verb conjugators, and vocabulary, grammar, and phrase indexes.

Learning to write in a second language is a demanding but rewarding process. It requires continuous practice. Extensive reading in the target language is one of the best ways to maintain and expand this skill. Fortunately, traditional and modern media offer an abundance of suitable reading material to the foreign language learner.

Appendix

Alternate Tables of Contents

Alternate Table of Contents I

Thematic Table of Contents

Arts

Art, Science, Industry, and Commerce

Communication and Critical Thinking

Culture

Democracy

History

Nature and Environments

Scientific Literacy and Technology

Visual Literacy

Alternate Table of Contents II

Disciplinary Table of Contents

African-American Studies

Anthropology

Architecture

Art History

Biology

Composition and Rhetoric

Computer Science

Creative Writing—Nonfiction

Education

English Studies

Geography

History

Author and Title Index

Acknowledgments

GLORIA ANZALDÚA Gloria Anzaldúa, "Chicana Artists: Exploring *Nepantla, el Lugar de la Frontera,*" *NACLA Report on the Americas.* 27/1 (July/August 1993). Reprinted by permission of the North American Congress on Latin America.

JOHN BERGER From *The Moment of Cubism and Other Essays* by John Berger, Copyright © 1969 by John Berger. Used by permission of Pantheon Books, a division of Random House, Inc.

SVEN BIRKERTS "The Owl Has Flown," from *The Gutenberg Elegies: The Fate of Reading in an Electronic Age* by Sven Birkerts. Copyright © 1994 by Sven Birkerts. Reprinted by permission of Faber and Faber, Inc., an affiliate of Farrar, Straus and Giroux, LLC.

WANDA M. CORN Wanda M. Corn, "The Birth of a National Icon: Grant Wood's *American Gothic,*" originally published in full in Mosche Barasch and H. N. Abrams, *Art, the Ape of Nature: Studies in Honor of H. W. Janson.* Englewood Cliffs: Prentice-Hall, 1981. Used by permission of the author.

SCOTT DEVEAUX Scott DeVeaux, "Progress and the Bean," in *The Birth of Bebop: A Social and Musical History.* Berkeley, CA: University of California Press. Used by permission of the University of California Press.

JARED DIAMOND Jared Diamond, "Necessity's Mother," from *Guns, Germs, and Steel: The Fates of Human Societies* by Jared Diamond. Copyright © 1997 by Jared Diamond. Used by permission of W. W. Norton & Company, Inc.

ANNIE DILLARD "Seeing" from *Pilgrim at Tinker Creek* by Annie Dillard. Copyright © 1974 by Annie Dillard. Reprinted by permission of HarperCollins Publishers, Inc.

JULIE ENGLISH EARLY Julie English Early, "The Spectacle of Science and Self: Mary Kingsley," in Barbara T. Gates and Ann B. Shteir, *Natural Eloquence.* © 1997. Reprinted by permission of The University of Wisconsin Press.

RALPH ELLISON From *Going to the Territory* by Ralph Ellison, copyright © 1986 by Ralph Ellison. Used by permission of Random House, Inc.

STUART EWEN From *All Consuming Images* by Stuart Ewen. Copyright © 1988 by Basic Books, Inc. Reprinted by permission of Basic Books, a member of Perseus Books, L.L.C.

NORTHROP FRYE Northrop Frye, "The Motive for Metaphor," in *The Educated Imagination.* Bloomington, Indiana: Indiana University Press, 1964. Reprinted by permission of the publisher.

CLIFFORD GEERTZ Clifford Geertz, "Common Sense as a Cultural System." Copyright © 1975 by The Antioch Review, Inc. First appeared in the *Antioch Review*, Vol. 33, No. 1. Reprinted by permission of the Editors.

Stephen Jay Gould From *Dinosaur in a Haystack* by Stephen Jay Gould. Copyright 1995 by Stephen Jay Gould. Used by permission of Harmony Books, a division of Random House, Inc.

Zita Ingham Zita Ingham, "Landscape, Drama, and Dissensus: The Rhetorical Education of Red Lodge, Montana," in Carl G. Herndl and Stuart C. Brown, *Green Culture.* © 1996. Reprinted by permission of The University of Wisconsin Press.

Michio Kaku From *Visions: How Science Will Revolutionize the 21st Century* by Michio Kaku, copyright © 1997 by Michio Kaku. Used by permission of Doubleday, a division of Random House, Inc.

Thomas Kuhn Reprinted with permission from Thomas Kuhn, "The Historical Structure of Scientific Discovery." *Science,* Vol. 136 (June 1, 1962). Copyright © 1988 by American Association for the Advancement of Science.

Christopher Lasch Christopher Lasch, "The Lost Art of Argument," in *The Revolt of the Elites and the Betrayal of Democracy.* New York: W.W. Norton, 1996. This essay was originally published as "Journalism, Publicity, and the Lost Art of Argument" in the Spring 1990 issue of *Media Studies Journal* and is reprinted by permission of the Freedom Forum.

Richard C. Lewontin "Science as Social Action" from *Biology as Ideology* by R. C. Lewontin. Copyright © 1991 by R. C. Lewontin and the Canadian Broadcasting Corporation. Reprinted by permission of HarperCollins Publishers, Inc.

Emily Martin, Bjorn Claeson, Wendy Richardson, Monica Schoch-Spana, and Karen-Sue Taussig Emily Martin, Bjorn Claeson, Wendy Richardson, Monica Schoch-Spana, and Karen-Sue Taussig, " Scientific Literacy, What It Is, Why It's Important, and Why Scientists Think We Don't Have It: The Case of Immunology and the Immune System." Copyright 1996. From *Naked Science: Anthropological Inquiry into Boundaries, Power, and Knowledge,* edited by Laura Nader. Reproduced by permission of Emily Martin and Taylor & Francis, Inc. <http://www.routledge-ny.com>

Scott McCloud Chapter One, "Setting the Record Straight," from *Understanding Comics* by Scott McCloud. Copyright © 1993, 1994 by Scott McCloud. Reprinted by permission of HarperCollins Publishers, Inc.

Erin McGraw Erin McGraw, "Bad Eyes," *The Gettysburg Review.* Copyright © 1998 by Erin McGraw. Reprinted by permission of the author.

Barbara Mellix "From Outside, In" originally appeared in *The Georgia Review,* Volume XLI, No. 2 (Summer 1987), © 1987 by The University of Georgia / © 1987 by Barbara Mellix. Reprinted by permission of Barbara Mellix and *The Georgia Review.*

Walter Mosley Walter Mosley, "For Authors, Fragile Ideas Need Loving Every Day," *The New York Times,* July 3, 2000. Reprinted by permission of Walter Mosley and the Watkins/Loomis Agency.

Walker Percy "The Loss of the Creature," from *The Message in the Bottle* by Walker Percy. Copyright © 1975 by Walker Percy. Reprinted by permission of Farrar, Straus and Giroux, LLC.

Witold Rybczynski Witold Rybczynski, "Designs for Escape." Originally published in *The New Yorker,* October 16, 1995. Copyright © by Witold Rybczynski. Reprinted by permission of the author.

Rebecca Solnit "Aerobic Sisyphus and the Suburbanized Psyche," from *Wanderlust: A History of Walking* by Rebecca Solnit. Copyright © 2000 by Rebecca Solnit. Used by permission of Viking Penguin, a division of Penguin Putnam, Inc.

Nancy Sommers Nancy Sommers, "I Stand Here Writing," *College English* 55.4, April 1993. Copyright 1993 by the National Council of Teachers of English. Reprinted with permission.

SUSAN SONTAG "In Plato's Cave," from *On Photography* by Susan Sontag. Copyright © 1977 by Susan Sontag. Reprinted by permission of Farrar, Straus and Giroux, LLC.

WALLACE STEVENS (Quoted in Northrop Frye selection, "The Motive for Metaphor.") From *The Collected Poems of Wallace Stevens* by Wallace Stevens, copyright 1954 by Wallace Stevens. Used by permission of Alfred A. Knopf, a division of Random House, Inc.

WARREN I. SUSMAN Warren I. Susman, " 'Personality' and the Making of Twentieth-Century Culture," from Higham, John and Paul K. Conkin, eds. *New Directions in American Intellectual History,* pp. 212–226. © 1979 by The Johns Hopkins University Press. Reprinted with permission of The Johns Hopkins University Press.

JANE TOMPKINS "At the Buffalo Bill Museum," from *West of Everything* by Jane Tompkins, copyright 1992 by Jane Tompkins. Used by permission of Oxford University Press, Inc.

CHRISTOPHER P. TOUMEY Toumey, Christopher P., "Science in an Old Testament Style" in *Conjuring Science: Scientific Symbols and Cultural Meanings in American Life,* copyright © 1996 by Christopher P. Toumey. Reprinted by permission of Rutgers University Press, 1996.

HAUNANI-KAY TRASK Haunani-Kay Trask, "From a Native Daughter," in *The American Indian and the Problem of History* edited by Calvin Martin. New York: Oxford University Press, 1987. Haunani-Kay Trask is Professor of Hawaiian Studies, University of Hawaii. Used by permission of the author.

YI-FU TUAN Tuan, Yi-Fu. "Earth: Nature and Culture" in *Escapism*, pp. 5–17. © 1998 by Yi-Fu Tuan. Reprinted with permission of The Johns Hopkins University Press.

SHERRY TURKLE Reprinted with the permission of Simon & Schuster from *Life on the Screen: Identity in the Age of the Internet* by Sherry Turkle. Copyright © 1995 by Sherry Turkle.

PATRICIA J. WILLIAMS From *The House That Race Built* by Wahneema Lubiano, Copyright Introduction and compilation copyright © 1997 by Wahneema Lubiano. " The Ethnic Scarring of American Whiteness," copyright © 1997 by Patricia J. Williams. Used by permission of Pantheon Books, a division of Random House, Inc.

SUSAN WILLIS Susan Willis, "Disney World: Public Use/ Private State," *South Atlantic Quarterly*, 92:1 (Winter 1993). Copyright 1993, Duke University Press. All rights reserved. Reprinted with permission.

JEANETTE WINTERSON Jeanette Winterson, "Imagination and Reality," in *Art Objects: Essays on Ecstasy and Effrontery.* New York: Vintage Books, 1995. Reprinted by permission of International Creative Management. Copyright © 1995 by Jeanette Winterson.